Linux® Programming Bible

Linux® Programming Bible

Bible

John Goerzen

IDG Books Worldwide, Inc.
An International Data Group Company

Foster City, CA ✦ Chicago, IL ✦ Indianapolis, IN ✦ New York, NY

Linux® Programming Bible

Published by
IDG Books Worldwide, Inc.
An International Data Group Company
919 E. Hillsdale Blvd., Suite 400
Foster City, CA 94404
www.idgbooks.com (IDG Books Worldwide Web site)

Library of Congress Catalog Card Number: 00-100275

ISBN: 0-7645-4657-0

Printed in the United States of America

10 9 8 7 6 5 4 3 2 1

1B/SY/QS/QQ/FC

Distributed in the United States by IDG Books Worldwide, Inc.

Distributed by CDG Books Canada Inc. for Canada; by Transworld Publishers Limited in the United Kingdom; by IDG Norge Books for Norway; by IDG Sweden Books for Sweden; by IDG Books Australia Publishing Corporation Pty. Ltd. for Australia and New Zealand; by TransQuest Publishers Pte Ltd. for Singapore, Malaysia, Thailand, Indonesia, and Hong Kong; by Gotop Information Inc. for Taiwan; by ICG Muse, Inc. for Japan; by Intersoft for South Africa; by Eyrolles for France; by International Thomson Publishing for Germany, Austria and Switzerland; by Distribuidora Cuspide for Argentina; by LR International for Brazil; by Galileo Libros for Chile; by Ediciones ZETA S.C.R. Ltda. for Peru; by WS Computer Publishing Corporation, Inc., for the Philippines; by Contemporanea de Ediciones for Venezuela; by Express Computer Distributors for the Caribbean and West Indies; by Micronesia Media Distributor, Inc. for Micronesia; by Chips Computadoras S.A. de C.V. for Mexico; by Editorial Norma de Panama S.A. for Panama; by American Bookshops for Finland.

For general information on IDG Books Worldwide's books in the U.S., please call our Consumer Customer Service department at 800-762-2974. For reseller information, including discounts and premium sales, please call our Reseller Customer Service department at 800-434-3422.

For information on where to purchase IDG Books Worldwide's books outside the U.S., please contact our International Sales department at 317-596-5530 or fax 317-572-4002.

For consumer information on foreign language translations, please contact our Customer Service department at 800-434-3422, fax 317-572-4002, or e-mail rights@idgbooks.com.

For information on licensing foreign or domestic rights, please phone +1-650-653-7098.

For sales inquiries and special prices for bulk quantities, please contact our Order Services department at 800-434-3422 or write to the address above.

For information on using IDG Books Worldwide's books in the classroom or for ordering examination copies, please contact our Educational Sales department at 800-434-2086 or fax 317-572-4005.

For press review copies, author interviews, or other publicity information, please contact our Public Relations department at 650-653-7000 or fax 650-655-3299.

For authorization to photocopy items for corporate, personal, or educational use, please contact Copyright Clearance Center, 222 Rosewood Drive, Danvers, MA 01923, or fax 978-750-4470.

ABOUT IDG BOOKS WORLDWIDE

Welcome to the world of IDG Books Worldwide.

IDG Books Worldwide, Inc., is a subsidiary of International Data Group, the world's largest publisher of computer-related information and the leading global provider of information services on information technology. IDG was founded more than 30 years ago by Patrick J. McGovern and now employs more than 9,000 people worldwide. IDG publishes more than 290 computer publications in over 75 countries. More than 90 million people read one or more IDG publications each month.

Launched in 1990, IDG Books Worldwide is today the #1 publisher of best-selling computer books in the United States. We are proud to have received eight awards from the Computer Press Association in recognition of editorial excellence and three from Computer Currents' First Annual Readers' Choice Awards. Our best-selling ...*For Dummies*® series has more than 50 million copies in print with translations in 31 languages. IDG Books Worldwide, through a joint venture with IDG's Hi-Tech Beijing, became the first U.S. publisher to publish a computer book in the People's Republic of China. In record time, IDG Books Worldwide has become the first choice for millions of readers around the world who want to learn how to better manage their businesses.

Our mission is simple: Every one of our books is designed to bring extra value and skill-building instructions to the reader. Our books are written by experts who understand and care about our readers. The knowledge base of our editorial staff comes from years of experience in publishing, education, and journalism — experience we use to produce books to carry us into the new millennium. In short, we care about books, so we attract the best people. We devote special attention to details such as audience, interior design, use of icons, and illustrations. And because we use an efficient process of authoring, editing, and desktop publishing our books electronically, we can spend more time ensuring superior content and less time on the technicalities of making books.

You can count on our commitment to deliver high-quality books at competitive prices on topics you want to read about. At IDG Books Worldwide, we continue in the IDG tradition of delivering quality for more than 30 years. You'll find no better book on a subject than one from IDG Books Worldwide.

John Kilcullen
Chairman and CEO
IDG Books Worldwide, Inc.

Eighth Annual
Computer Press
Awards ≥1992

Ninth Annual
Computer Press
Awards ≥1993

Tenth Annual
Computer Press
Awards ≥1994

Eleventh Annual
Computer Press
Awards ≥1995

IDG is the world's leading IT media, research and exposition company. Founded in 1964, IDG had 1997 revenues of $2.05 billion and has more than 9,000 employees worldwide. IDG offers the widest range of media options that reach IT buyers in 75 countries representing 95% of worldwide IT spending. IDG's diverse product and services portfolio spans six key areas including print publishing, online publishing, expositions and conferences, market research, education and training, and global marketing services. More than 90 million people read one or more of IDG's 290 magazines and newspapers, including IDG's leading global brands — Computerworld, PC World, Network World, Macworld and the Channel World family of publications. IDG Books Worldwide is one of the fastest-growing computer book publishers in the world, with more than 700 titles in 36 languages. The "...For Dummies®" series alone has more than 50 million copies in print. IDG offers online users the largest network of technology-specific Web sites around the world through IDG.net (http://www.idg.net), which comprises more than 225 targeted Web sites in 55 countries worldwide. International Data Corporation (IDC) is the world's largest provider of information technology data, analysis and consulting, with research centers in over 41 countries and more than 400 research analysts worldwide. IDG World Expo is a leading producer of more than 168 globally branded conferences and expositions in 35 countries including E3 (Electronic Entertainment Expo), Macworld Expo, ComNet, Windows World Expo, ICE (Internet Commerce Expo), Agenda, DEMO, and Spotlight. IDG's training subsidiary, ExecuTrain, is the world's largest computer training company, with more than 230 locations worldwide and 785 training courses. IDG Marketing Services helps industry-leading IT companies build international brand recognition by developing global integrated marketing programs via IDG's print, online and exposition products worldwide. Further information about the company can be found at www.idg.com.   1/26/00

Credits

Acquisitions Editor
Debra Williams Cauley

Project Editors
Michael Koch
Terri Varveris

Technical Editors
Douglas T. Hayden
Joseph Traub
Eric Foster-Johnson

Copy Editors
Mildred Sanchez
Robert Campbell

Project Coordinators
Linda Marousek
Joe Shines

Cover Design
Larry S. Wilson

Graphics and Production Specialists
Jude Levinson
Michael Lewis
Ramses Ramirez
Victor Pérez-Varela
Dina Quan

Quality Control Specialists
Chris Weisbart
Laura Taflinger

Book Designer
Kurt Krames

Proofreading and Indexing
York Production Services

Illustrator
Mary Jo Richards

About the Author

John Goerzen is a developer for the Debian GNU/Linux operating system since 1996. Currently, he is involved with porting Debian to 64-bit architectures. John works as a Linux consultant in Dallas, TX.

To my parents, whose support makes anything possible

Preface

The secret is out—there's something special about Linux. The operating system that began life as a way for then-student Linus Torvalds to do his homework has evolved into a powerful force in the marketplace, literally earning money overnight.

What is so special about Linux? And why should you, a programmer, care? You'll find the answers in the pages of this book. Linux is more than just a new operating system. It represents the very best of what developers all over the world over like to see. Its rich multitasking capabilities and powerful communication features enable you to write powerful and fast applications quickly. Linux supports literally dozens of languages, including C, C++, Perl, Java, LISP, Prolog, Scheme, Pascal, BASIC, two shell flavors, assembler, Ada, Smalltalk, and FORTRAN. The programming environment in Linux is first-rate; many tools have had a chance to be refined since before Linux even existed, thanks to its UNIX heritage.

As Linux is a fairly new system, I discovered that there is a lack of information for the Linux programmer. That is where this book comes in. By reading this book, you not only get to learn what Linux is doing under the hood, but also how to take advantage of that knowledge in your own applications. Most of the extensive code examples in this book are complete programs, ready to run, and some of which are also available online.

Why You Need This Book

Part of the power of Linux is its versatility. For example, you can pick any of five different ways to communicate between programs. Or, you can pick from various different languages to implement your code. With this flexibility comes decisions. Don't get me wrong, I love choices—having many options when solving a problem makes it easier to solve. But you need information—which communica-tion methods are right for you, for instance. There is little existing documentation that gives you a big picture like this. Furthermore, when you are ready to imple-ment your program, you need to know not only why to use a certain feature, but *how* to use it. Through the use of examples and commentary in this book, you will see the ideas and concepts put into action, and use the code as a basis for your own programs.

Linux is also helping to break new ground in computing. It has one of the best shared library systems available anywhere, but again the system is new enough that barely any documentation exists for it at all. Before this book, programmers had to stumble their way through the system before being able to use shared libraries effectively. The *Linux Programming Bible* shows you exactly how shared libraries work and how you can use them.

In addition to its use as a tutorial, the *Linux Programming Bible* can help you as a reference book as well. Because of its in-depth coverage of so many different aspects of Linux, you're sure to find the information you need here.

With the huge installed base of Linux, most rapid growth in the industry, and rich development environment, companies are realizing that they lose customers and money by not supporting Linux. It is my hope that this book will be able to help you develop programs on Linux, and I want to welcome you to the Linux revolution!

Prerequisites

Before you begin programming in Linux with this book as your guide, I need to make sure that you have a few things ready to go. Ideally, you should meet the following requirements before you start to work with this book:

- ✦ You should have a working knowledge of a programming language, preferably C, C++, or Perl. This knowledge does not have to come from Linux. You will be introduced to Linux-specific features in C and C++ throughout this book.

- ✦ You should have Linux installed on your computer.

- ✦ You should have a basic understanding of how to get around in Linux: files, directories, and a few command-line basics. For the chapters on GUI programming (Chapters 24 and 25), you also should be able to navigate the X Window System interface.

If you meet these three simple prerequisites, this book is for you. Anyone from someone just making the switch to Linux to someone that has been programming on Linux for years will benefit from the information presented in these pages.

How This Book Is Organized

You can read this book either as a reference or as a tutorial. If you want to read the book as a tutorial, you might find it most useful to read it in the order presented more or less.

Because of the huge volume of information, I have split the book into seven main parts. Here is a summary of each of the seven parts and what you can find in each.

Part I: Shell and Basic Tools

The first part of the book introduces you to some basics that will form an undercurrent through the entire remaining part of the book. In Chapter 1, for instance, you will learn about the design of the Linux development environment, as well as how to find reference material online and navigate through the different material available to you.

The remaining chapters in Part I cover some other basics. Chapter 2 introduces shell programming. Many people like to use a good editor and development environment; Chapter 4 introduces you to Emacs, which is both. For parsing tasks, regular expressions can be found in many areas, and you will learn about them in Chapter 3. The first part concludes with Chapter 5, which takes a look at data files and scripts in Linux.

Part II: The C Environment

The C environment in Linux is not only the largest, but also of the most immediate interest to programmers. Because Linux itself is written in C, you'll find that function calls in other languages, such as Perl, are implemented in terms of the underlying C version. The chapters in Part II cover C (and C++) programming, starting with the C compiler in Chapters 6 and 7, moving through memory management and libraries in Chapters 8 and 9, and ending with the debugger in Chapter 10.

Part III: The Linux Model

Before we can talk about more advanced topics such as multitasking, you need to have some knowledge of what is going on inside Linux. That is the focus of this part of the book. In Chapter 11, you will learn how data is stored on Linux — a key to being able to take advantage of some of the more advanced features of the Linux file system. You'll also learn about the process model, which is an undercurrent of most of the rest of the topics that will be presented in Chapter 12. Chapters 13 through 15 finish up with discussions on signals, Linux I/O, and terminals.

Part IV: Talking to the World

Now we come to one of the most exciting aspects of Linux — talking to everyone. Linux literally makes this possible. Support for communication in Linux has been there since day one — not just an afterthought. You can see this for yourself in the rich array of communication tools that are available for your use.

The discussion of communication begins with coverage of shared memory and semaphores in Chapter 16. Though other models, such as pipes, are now preferred over shared memory for some things for which it was once popular, still shared memory is a unique way of approaching communication. Some people, especially those doing real-time projects, find shared memory to be the fastest method of communication available.

After shared memory, I turn to the more standardized methods of communication in Linux. These include pipes and FIFOs, which are discussed in Chapter 17. Chapters 18 and 19 are devoted to the topic of sockets, which are used for communication across the Internet. With the knowledge you get from this part of the book, you will be able to write your own Internet client or server software, and you will literally be able to talk to the world!

Part V: The Glue: Perl

No book on Linux programming would be complete without devoting some space to Perl. Perl is a language that is rapidly gaining favor as one used for all the odd jobs that face a programmer. It is especially agile in bringing together data from many different sources, processing it, and generating output suitable for further analysis or import into other systems. With its integrated support for CGI, SQL databases, and powerful parsing capabilities, it's a natural fit for Linux.

Chapters 20 and 21 cover general Perl topics, introducing you to Perl and then teaching you how to use it to manipulate your data. Chapters 22 and 23 conclude with coverage of CGI programming with Perl, and SQL database access from Perl.

Part VI: Graphical Interfaces With X

The X Window System, the dominant GUI in Linux, is a powerful and exciting environment for writing GUI programs. In this section, you will learn two different ways of doing so: Perl/Tk and Gnome. Chapter 24 covers perl/TK and Chapter 25 covers Gnome.

Part VII: Putting It All Together

There are some concepts that I want to present to you that do not fit neatly into any other part because they are applicable to everything you have done. These topics are presented in Part VII. The part begins with Chapter 26, which covers CVS — a powerful tool for managing your projects and aiding collaboration on them. Chapter 27 covers security, which is one of the most important topics that any Linux programmer must face. Finally, you will learn about some ways to improve the performance of your code on Linux in Chapter 28.

Online Companion

You may find information about the Linux Programming Bible online at `http://www.complete.org/lpb/`. This website contains a downloadable version of all of the longer code examples in the book to save you retyping. Various links are mentioned throughout the text; you may find some of them conveniently online at that page. Also, any errata or corrections will be announced there, should this be necessary. Throughout the text, if there is online information relating to a topic being discussed, you will see the Note icon referring you to this website.

Conventions

Throughout this book, I will use numerous examples of interaction with the computer. In these examples, you will see the text that you should type at the keyboard in **boldface** print. Throughout the text itself, references to language syntax or parts of code will appear in monospace font. Any new terms that are introduced in the book are *italicized*.

Also, you will find that the following icons are used throughout the Linux Programming Bible:

The note icon indicates something that may be an important exception to normal rules, or anything that you ought to pay particular attention to. This icon also indicates accompanying material on the book's website, http://www.complete. org/lpb/.

This icon indicates a unique way of doing a particular task.

This icon alerts you if you need to take special care during a procedure or of potential problems that may occur.

The cross-reference icon indicates a reference to a different section in the book that might go into additional detail on a particular aspect of a topic.

Feedback

I would appreciate hearing your comments about the *Linux Programming Bible*! Even if it is a simple a line or two to let me know whether or not you liked the book, I'd like to hear about it. You can do this by registering on the http://my2cents. idgbooks.com Web site. (Details are listed on the my2cents page in the back of the book.) You also can send me an e-mail personally at lpb@complete.org.

Acknowledgments

I'd like to thank everyone that has helped to make this book become a reality. The people at IDG Books were great to work with and were a big help with making this book the best it can possibly be. They are Robert Campbell, Michael Koch, Mildred Sanchez, Terri Varveris, and Debra Williams Cauley. I'd also like to thank the technical editors for this book, Joseph Traub, Eric Foster-Johnson, and Douglas T. Hayden. Thanks also to the thousands of developers worldwide who have made the GPL-based GNU/Linux platform a reality — and thus given us something to write about. It's impossible to mention them all, but I'd like to especially thank Richard M. Stallman and the Free Software Foundation.

Contents at a Glance

Contents

· ·

Part III: The Linux Model   311

Shell and Basic Tools

Introducing the Linux Programming Environment

Welcome to the Linux programming environment! This chapter introduces you to some of the basic concepts of programming in Linux—how Linux thinks about the world. These are concepts that you will read about in more detail later in the book. This chapter also shows you how to find help when you need it. You'll find information about online manual pages, info pages, Perl program documentation, and Internet resources here.

Basic Linux Programming Concepts

The programming environment in Linux is one that follows one of the design philosophies of Linux itself. That is, you are given many small components that you can assemble in any way you wish to solve your task.

As an example, you have a C preprocessor, a linker, an assembler, and a compiler. If you want, you can call these all manually to build your program. Many people, however, prefer to just let the gcc front-end automatically handle those details.

You may observe, as you start programming in Linux, that a number of the tools are command-line based. This is correct, but there is a reason for it: It is much easier to reuse and automate command line tools than GUI tools. In fact, there are several GUI environments that provide you with a graphical interface to these command line tools.

The C-development environment on Linux consists of the C-development tools (compiler, linker, etc.), an optional project management utility (make), an editor or IDE (Emacs), and analysis tools (gdb). People who work in large groups or require archiving may also use a source code control system (CVS).

There are also a few other pieces of the puzzle. These are actually present on every platform, but you may not be aware of them. One is the C library. On Linux, the C library provides everything from basic string functions, such as strcpy(), to functions to access the system's database of users. The C library system consists of both a library to be linked into your programs and a set of header files.

Development with Perl is similar, although Perl programs require no compilation. Therefore, there is no compiler, and little need for a project management utility in Perl.

Next we will look at the Linux design and how it differs from Programming in the Windows 95 and 98 environments.

Linux Design

If you are new to the Linux platform, there are several important distinctions that I would like to mention in regard to its design. Some other operating systems, particularly other POSIX systems, might have many of these in common. However, if you are accustomed to programming in Windows 95 or 98 environments, you might find significant differences here:

✦ Linux is multitasking. You can create multiple threads and processes at once. You can never assume that yours is the only instance of the program running; both the same user and other users may be running other copies of it. Therefore, you have to be careful to synchronize access in some situations.

✦ Linux is a true multi-user system. This means that there are security measures involved to isolate one user's files from another. Your programs will not be able to modify or replace any file on the system as they can on some other platforms, unless they are running as the superuser (root).

✦ Linux has timesharing. Timesharing means that there can be several users logged in to the system at once, or that a single user may be logged in more than once. People may use technologies such as telnet or X to log on to the system remotely. Thus your programs need to be aware that they may be executed by several users simultaneously.

For simple programs, these differences are irrelevant. If you are writing an editor, for instance, you most likely don't care about timesharing or multitasking, since the system is handling all these details for you. But what if you are working with a database or some other shared resource? In this case, you have to synchronize with other processes to make sure that no two processes try to write to the file or database at once. This might mean synchronizing with other copies of your own program or with other programs.

Linux has a rich history. Linux is designed to work like UNIX, an operating system that's been around since approximately 1970. Over the years, UNIX has evolved significantly. It turns out that one key aspect of the design on UNIX—giving the user small components and then assembling them as desired—is one of the most useful aspects of Linux. It underlies not just shell scripting, but also shared library systems and widget libraries for the X Window System.

Linux Documentation

One of the most important things about being a programmer in any environment is to know where to turn when you need information. This book can be the first place to look for many questions. If you can't find the answer you need within these pages, you can look in the array of online documentation that comes with any Linux system.

Back in the early days of UNIX, the system shipped with volumes upon volumes of bound documentation—dry reference material, with few examples, filling up entire bookshelves. The modern descendents of these books are called *manpages* (short for "manual pages" from the defunct paper editions). In this chapter, you'll learn about these and other forms of documentation on your Linux system.

If you get stuck and need to ask someone for help, you can check out various Internet resources. Some common ones include Usenet newsgroups, Web sites, online chat areas, and more. The Internet is the primary vehicle for communication for development on Linux itself, and you can find archives of discussions on everything from kernel design to selections of standard pathnames, because most development work is done openly.

In some cases, people use the phrase, "the source is the documentation." Because Linux comes with complete source code, if you ever have a question that no documentation can answer for you, you can go directly to the source code for the operating system to find out. While preparing material for this book, for instance, I referred to the source code many times to find out specific details of behavior in Linux.

Manpages

In Linux and UNIX systems, manpages are the mainstay of reference information. These pages are primarily reference material, and one manpage exists for virtually every shell command, system call, library function, configuration file, and daemon on the system. The entries in manpages often presuppose knowledge about the topic they're documenting and contain few examples, so you'll need some other material—such as this book—to help you with the information that you won't find in the manpages.

Manpages in Linux are separated into eight sections, each with a specific general topic:

✦ Section 1 covers shell commands and user-level programs.

✦ Section 2 documents system calls.

✦ Section 3 documents C and C++ library calls and macros.

✦ Section 4 documents special files and devices that you might find as kernel modules, /dev entries, or /proc entries.

✦ Section 5 documents the format of various files on the system; mostly configuration files.

✦ Section 6 historically covers games, but these are increasingly covered under section 1.

✦ Section 7 describes languages (such as SQL) or mini-languages.

✦ Section 8 describes daemons or other sysadmin-only commands.

To look up a manpage, use the command man `topic`, where topic is the name of the command, program, function, macro, or file about which you want information. For instance, to find information on `ls`, you can type man `ls` at the prompt. The man browser searches for `ls` in each section, beginning with section 1 and progressing to section 8, and then displays the first page that it finds. In this case, there is only one entry in section 1. (Notice that *page* is somewhat misleading; the man page for `ls` is really four pages long!)

In most situations, man invokes either more or less to display the page. You can press spacebar to advance a page, Enter to advance a line, b to go back a page, and / to search. When done, you can press q to quit.

The front page looks something like Figure 1-1.

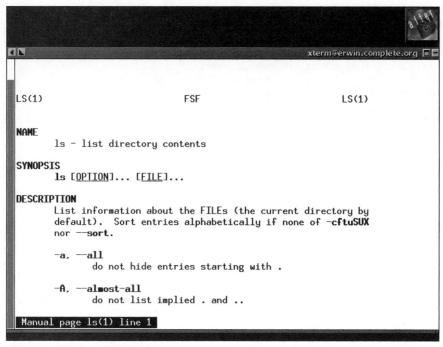

```
LS(1)                          FSF                          LS(1)


NAME
       ls - list directory contents

SYNOPSIS
       ls [OPTION]... [FILE]...

DESCRIPTION
       List information about the FILEs (the current directory by
       default).  Sort entries alphabetically if none of -cftuSUX
       nor --sort.

       -a, --all
              do not hide entries starting with .

       -A, --almost-all
              do not list implied . and ..

Manual page ls(1) line 1
```

Figure 1-1: Manual page of ls

Sometimes, you'll find that a given entry may occur in multiple sections. For instance, the kill entry is both a command (in section 1) and a system call (in section 2). If you are trying to find documentation on the system call, typing **man kill** will get you documentation on the shell command. What you need to do is explicitly specify the manual section by typing man *section topic* (e.g., **man 2 kill**). You'll be taken directly to the entry in that particular section of the manual. While you're programming, you'll probably use entries in sections 2 and 3 the most. If you have a configured printer in Linux, you can also get a typeset hardcopy of any manpage on the system. To do so, you can use a command such as:

```
$ man -t 2 kill | lpr
```

The -t instructs the system to generate PostScript output, which is then piped to the printer spooler. You can also omit the section number if it's unambiguous, as before with the ls example.

If you are unsure of where the information about a particular topic is located, you can perform a keyword search with -k. Consider this example:

```
$ man -k syslog
syslog (2) - read and/or clear kernel message ring buffer; set console_loglevel
syslog (3)          - send messages to the system logger
Sys::Syslog (3pm)   - Perl interface to the UNIX syslog(3) calls
syslog (2)          - read and/or clear kernel message ring buffer; set
console_loglevel
syslog (3)          - send messages to the system logger
syslog (3pm) [Sys::Syslog] - Perl interface to the UNIX syslog(3) calls
syslog-facility (8)  - Setup and remove LOCALx facility for sysklogd
syslog.conf (5)      - syslogd(8) configuration file
syslogd (8)          - Linux system logging utilities.
syslogd-listfiles (8) - list system logfiles
```

This causes the manual browser to display a list of all the manpages whose name or topic contains the string "syslog."

As with other Linux commands, the manpage browser comes with its own manpage, which you can view with by typing **man man** at the command prompt. It gives you a summary of the command-line arguments available for the browser.

When referring to manpages, or even to specific functions, it is customary to include the section number. For instance, if I mention printf(3), this is a reference to the `printf` function, as documented in section 3 of the manual. Such usage is common not only in this book but in other literature, both online and off, as well.

Info Pages

Although manpages are the backbone for reference information in Linux for some time, some information is being presented increasingly in *GNU info* format. GNU info is a hypertext format that is used to present information. It can be viewed in several viewers including a standalone viewer named info, a special mode in Emacs or XEmacs, a CGI script to present info pages as HTML, and various X-based interfaces. In this section, I'll discuss the standalone browser first, and then I will cover the mode as it is seen in XEmacs; these are the two most popular methods of reading info pages.

If you run info with no arguments, by default it displays a main menu of available topics, as shown in Figure 1-2. You can also invoke info on a particular manual; for instance, info libc displays the documentation for the C library.

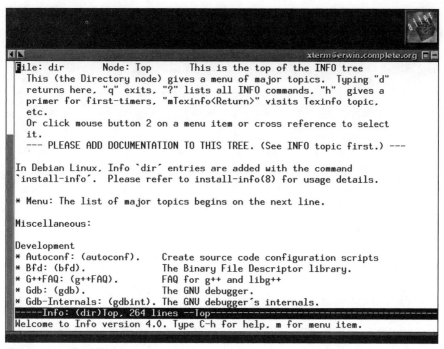

Figure 1-2: The info browser

When an info page is displayed, you'll need to know how to navigate it. Table 1-1 lists the keys that you can use to navigate info pages.

Table 1-1
Info Page Navigation Keys

Key	Function
N	Takes you to the next page in sequence after the present one, as displayed at the top of the screen.
P	Takes you to the previous page in sequence after the present one, as displayed at the top of the screen.
U	Takes you up one level in the page hierarchy, as displayed at the top of the screen.

Continued

Table 1-1 (continued)	
Key	**Function**
Enter	Displays whatever link is under the cursor at the time.
M	Follows a link from a menu, and asks you which entry to use.
F	Follows a standard cross-reference, which usually has "Note" listed close to it.
L	Displays the last page shown. This is similar to clicking a Back button in a web browser.
Spacebar	Scroll forward by one page.
Backspace	Scroll backward by one page.

Navigation in the XEmacs version of the info browser is somewhat easier. You enter the info browser by pressing Ctrl+H, then i or by clicking the Info icon on the tool bar. XEmacs's info browser is mouse-aware and presents an interface not unlike that of a web browser. Figure 1-3 shows the index page of XEmacs's info browser.

You can use all of the same keystrokes in the XEmacs info browser as you can in the standalone version. To follow a link, simply middle-click it.

Tip   If your mouse has only two buttons, you may simulate a middle-click by pressing both buttons at once.

Perl Documentation

The documentation for Perl is unique among that on Linux in that Perl is the only language that provides its own documentation system. You may find some information through the regular manpages. The perl(1) manpage contains a listing of all the other Perl pages. Of these, perlfunc(1) will probably be of the most practical use.

In addition to these pages, many Perl modules provide their own documentation in the form of a POD. You can view these modules' manuals by typing `perldoc modulename`, which displays them in a format similar to a manual page. Some Linux distributions pre-format module POD documentation into manual pages for you, so you can access it via the standard manual page interface as well.

You can also look up information on a specific part of Perl. For example, you can type `perldoc -f split` to find documentation on the built-in split function. You can also type `perldoc Data::Dumper` to find information on the module by that name.

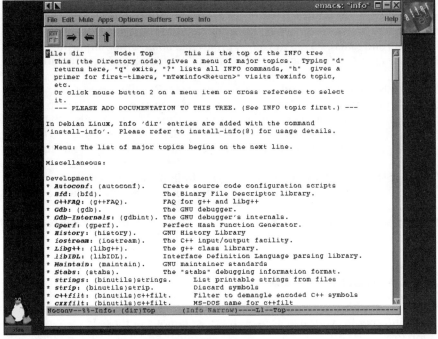

Figure 1-3: Index page of XEmacs's info browser

Program Documentation

Many programs also come with text files or HTML files that describe their operation. These files may contain anything from a few brief usage hints to a complete overview of the principles behind the algorithms used inside the program. For programs you install, these files are usually in the distribution source tarball. For distributions, you can generally find these files in /usr/doc/programname or /usr/share/doc/programname. Some distributions also include the program version in the doc path. You may sometimes need to use zless to view this documentation, especially if it's compressed.

If applicable, you also might check to see if a webpage exists for your program, and if so, check it for the documentation. Some programmers prefer to keep some documentation there.

Sometimes, this documentation might come in PostScript format, indicated by a .ps extension. To view such documents, you'll need, at minimum, the GhostScript interpreter or a PostScript printer. Many people prefer to use gv to display those files; it is a nice front-end to the GhostScript interpreter.

I mentioned at the start of this chapter that you can sometimes treat source code as documentation. In such a case, you might want to look at the files and directories inside /usr/include, which includes the prototypes and definitions of the functions and macros used in your C programs. Some other important directories in the area include /usr/include/sys, /usr/include/linux, and /usr/include/asm.

You can also find source code for your programs. Exactly where this is stored depends on your distribution; some may have it on a separate CD with separate packages; others, with the same CD as the binaries. You might also check inside /usr/src to see if you can find source code there. In particular, this is a traditional place to put the sources to the Linux kernel, which can be a useful resource.

One trick that is useful when you are trying to find a certain entry in either the header files or the kernel source is to change into either /usr/include or /usr/src/linux and issue a command line such as `grep sigaction ` `find . -type f`` that will search for the specified string in all files underneath the current directory.

Internet Resources

As you work with programming on Linux, you'll find a lot of resources are available on the Internet for your use. One of the most famous of these is the Linux Documentation Project (LDP), at `http://www.linuxdoc.org/`. The LDP contains a lot of documentation on Linux, most of which is geared at system administrators or end users instead of developers. However, several of their HOWTOs and mini-HOWTOs do contain information that useful to programmers. Some distributions also contain this information in either /usr/doc/HOWTO or /usr/share/doc/HOWTO.

Several websites provide information on Linux and links to other information. Among the most well-known are `http://linux.com/` and `http://linuxlinks.com/`. You also can use a search engine such as `http://www.google.com/` to find information about Linux from the various corners of the Internet.

Additionally, you can find a number of newsgroups in the `comp` hierarchy relating to UNIX and Linux programming. Here is a list of some of these newsgroups that are relevant to some of the topics covered in this book:

   ✦ comp.os.linux.development.apps

   ✦ comp.os.linux.development.system

   ✦ comp.os.linux.x

   ✦ comp.security.unix

   ✦ comp.unix.internals

   ✦ comp.unix.programmer

   ✦ comp.unix.shell

If your news server carries it, you can find a number of newsgroups in the linux hierarchy that could be helpful as well.

If you want to participate in real-time chat with other Linux programmers and users, point your IRC client (such as xchat or ircII if you're using Linux) to the server `irc.us.openprojects.net` (for American servers; use `irc.eu.openprojects.net` for European servers, or `irc.openprojects.net` for a random server). Channels you may be interested in include #linpeople and #linuxhelp. There are also distribution-specific channels such as #debian and #redhat.

Summary

In this chapter, you learned about the various sources of documentation in Linux. Specifically, you learned:

✦ Linux is based on a system of using small components that can be assembled in different ways to solve a given problem.

✦ Linux's programming environment fits this model by giving you many tools that you can use to write programs.

✦ Linux is multitasking, multi-user, and timesharing. Some programs may not care; other programs may take advantage of these specific features.

✦ You can find reference information online on your Linux system.

✦ Manpages contain reference information and are separated into eight sections.

✦ A reference, such as printf(3), means to look up the `printf` function in section 3 of the manual.

✦ GNU info documentation is a hypertext format. Many different viewers exist, including a mode for Emacs and XEmacs.

✦ Perl contains its own set of manpages, as well as a `perldoc` tool for looking up information on Perl or its modules.

✦ Many programs ship with some documentation files, which distributions often package and place in /usr/doc or /usr/share/doc.

✦ Several resources are available on the Internet if you need additional information.

✦   ✦   ✦

Introducing Shell Programming

Welcome to the exciting world of programming under Linux! Throughout this book, I'll cover topics that range from Perl to C++ — languages you probably have heard of, if not used, even if your programming experience hasn't been under the Linux or UNIX platforms. However, a place to start is certainly with shell programming.

Shell programming often can be the easiest way to accomplish some simple tasks, such as finding data, some simple data manipulations, file management, and so on. Furthermore, as you learn about programming with the shell, you also learn about many of the commands that are available in Linux. These commands can be used with equal ease at both the interactive command line and a shell script.

In this chapter, you'll be introduced to Bash, the most popular shell in Linux. Then I discuss redirection and piping, two powerful ways to combine Linux utilities to achieve powerful solutions. Next, I'll cover variables, useful both for saving keystrokes and storing data for later usage, and functions, which enable you to combine commands in more powerful ways. Finally, I go into loops, conditionals, and shell utilities, which document ways to use flow control in your programs and other common utilities in your scripts.

Quick Introduction to Bash

When you log on to your Linux machine or open an xterm, chances are that your default shell is Bash. Bash is the GNU Project's shell. The GNU Project is a part of the Free Software Foundation that is responsible for many of the programming tools you'll be using on Linux. If you have experience with other shells, you may be interested to know that Bash is a derivative of the Bourne shell but adds many features from Korn, and even a few from csh. If you are unsure whether or not your shell is Bash, you can type at the shell prompt:

```
$ echo $BASH_VERSION
2.02.1(1)-release
```

If you get a version number displayed on your screen, such as 2.02.1(1)-release in this example, you know that you are running Bash. If instead you get an error message or no version number, you probably are running a different shell. To invoke Bash, you can generally type:

```
$ exec /bin/bash
```

As you know by now, you can type commands at a Bash command line and the shell will execute them for you. This is only a small part of Bash's functionality, however. In addition to this, Bash provides functionality for shell scripts. These scripts are, in their simplest form, just collections of commands that are run one after another — a way to automate repetitious tasks. However, the capabilities of scripts don't end there. Shell scripting is a simplistic programming language in itself, and combined with the shell utilities in Linux, can enable you to craft solutions to some problems in a remarkably short amount of time.

Creating a script

This is a good time to learn how to create a shell script. The first step is to open a script file in your favorite editor. If you have experience with Linux, you already may have an editor with which you're familiar; feel free to use it. If you're new to Linux editors, you can try the Emacs editor; a little experience with it now could come in handy when you get to the Chapter 4, "Introducing Emacs."

Suppose you want to name your file myscript. To edit the file with Emacs, type this at the shell prompt:

```
$ emacs myscript
```

Depending on which version of Emacs you have, and whether or not you are running in X (the graphical interface system used in Linux), Emacs will either start in your terminal or bring up another window in X. Either way, you're ready to begin typing in the script. Type the following:

```
#!/bin/bash

echo Hello!
echo This is my first script with Bash.
echo Press Enter to exit.
read
```

Now, you're ready to save. To do this, press C-x C-s, that is, hold down the Ctrl key and press X, and then do the same for S. (You can actually hold down the Ctrl key and press the other two in that order.) Emacs will save the file. Now, exit Emacs with C-x C-c.

When you're back at the prompt, you can now test your script:

```
$ source myscript
Hello!
This is my first script with Bash.
Press Enter to exit.
```

If all is well, the above should appear on your screen. After you press Enter, the script will exit. If you get an error message, double-check that you typed in the script exactly as shown here.

Generally, you don't use the source command to execute a script but it can be useful in some situations. Usually, you will want to mark your script executable. This sets a flag telling the operating system that the script can be executed as a program.

If you don't mark it executable, but try to run it, you get the following error:

```
$ ./myscript
bash: ./myscript: Permission denied
```

To mark the script executable, use the chmod command:

```
$ chmod a+x myscript
```

Now, you can try executing the script:

```
$ ./myscript
Hello!
This is my first script with Bash.
Press Enter to exit.
```

This time, the script works!

To summarize, here are the steps for creating a Bash script:

1. Load the file into your favorite editor.

2. Make sure that the first line of the script is: `#!/bin/bash`.

3. Save the script and exit the editor.

4. Mark the script executable with `chmod a+x scriptname`.

5. You can now run the script with `./scriptname`.

Tip   When you want to run an executable or script stored in your current directory (as opposed to one that comes with the system), you will want to use `./` in front of the name. The reason is that the current directory (signified by the period) is generally not in the list of directories searched for when running a program (specified in the PATH variable). This is because explicitly including the current directory in PATH can be a security risk. Therefore, you need to specify the directory when running these programs. As a shortcut, you can simply use the period to specify the current directory instead of having to type out the entire path to the executable.

Bash startup

When a Bash session is invoked, the shell can execute a shell script for you automatically. Many programmers use these to set some options such as, what the shell prompt should be, how frequently new e-mail should be checked, or even how many programs should run when logging in. A whole system of scripts can be executed with Bash at startup. The primary one is named `.profile`.

If you create a shell script and save it with the name `.profile`, it will be executed every time you log in. Sometimes this script may not be executed when you want it to, such as when you run Bash in an xterm. In that case, you can set a symbolic link to point .bashrc sto .profile with this command:

```
$ ln -s .profile .bashrc
```

Return values

Whenever you run a command at the Bash command prompt or in a script, this program has a return value (also known as an exit code). Thus far, you probably have not had a need for examining this return value. However, many constructs in Bash take advantage of it. The return value is used in `if` statements, for instance, to determine whether a certain action should be taken. It can also be used to determine when to run other commands.

You may use `echo $?` to display the exit code from the last command to run. Table 2-1 shows how the codes can be interpreted.

Table 2-1 Exit Codes and Their Meanings	
Exit Code	*Meaning*
0	The program terminated successfully.
1 – 127	The program terminated with an error condition. Some programs assign a specific meaning to their return codes, so you may be able to find more information by looking up the specific return code in the documentation for the program.
128 or above	The program was terminated by a signal. The exit code, minus 128, indicates the signal number that terminated the program.

Let's look at some examples. When a program finishes successfully, it should return a successful value (zero) to the shell as in the following example:

```
$ ls /proc
1        2      4      529    9222         ksyms        slabinfo
12011    2066   4685   544    976          loadavg      sound
13192    2067   4686   551    bus          locks        stat
1372     2108   4687   556    cmdline      meminfo      swaps
1452     2111   482    5812   cpuinfo      misc         sys
1453     2177   499    615    devices      modules      tty
15       2220   501    618    dma          mounts       uptime
1622     24293  506    640    filesystems  net          version
1623     25497  509    650    fs           parport
16231    25499  513    651    ide          partitions
16234    25561  517    652    interrupts   pci
16285    26000  518    653    ioports      rtc
17008    26004  519    817    kcore        scsi
17010    3      520    818    kmsg         self
$ echo $?
0
```

In this example, you can see that `ls` performed its task normally; that is, it displayed a list of files as is customary. No errors occurred, so running `echo $?` caused a zero to be displayed, indicating successful execution.

However, sometimes things can go wrong. For example, you might specify an invalid filename or directory after typing `ls`. When this happens, `ls` can't find the information to display, and thus returns an error code. Here's an example of what happens when `ls` encounters an error.

```
$ ls /proc/some-nonexistant-filename
ls: /proc/some-nonexistant-filename: No such file or directory
$ echo $?
1
```

This time, the exit code was 1, indicating an error. At this point, your script might take some special action because of the problem. Depending on the script, this action might include aborting the script, calling some special subroutine to clean up after the error, displaying a special message, or even simply ignoring the error.

Simple command combinations

When you want to run a series of commands, you give them to Bash one per line either at the prompt or in a script. As you get into more complex shell scripting, however, you'll find that more powerful ways of chaining commands together become useful.

Chaining with the Semicolon

The simplest way to chain two commands together is with the semicolon. When you combine two commands with the semicolon, Bash acts as if you typed them at the prompt, or in a script, one per line.

As an example, first try two separate commands at the prompt:

```
$ ls /dev/hda*
/dev/hda      /dev/hda13   /dev/hda18   /dev/hda4   /dev/hda9
/dev/hda1     /dev/hda14   /dev/hda19   /dev/hda5
/dev/hda10    /dev/hda15   /dev/hda2    /dev/hda6
/dev/hda11    /dev/hda16   /dev/hda20   /dev/hda7
/dev/hda12    /dev/hda17   /dev/hda3    /dev/hda8
$ echo Done.
Done.
```

As expected, Bash executes your first command, and then your second. If you know that you will want to execute the second right after the first, you can combine them with a semicolon as follows:

```
$ ls /dev/hda*; echo Done.
/dev/hda      /dev/hda13   /dev/hda18   /dev/hda4   /dev/hda9
/dev/hda1     /dev/hda14   /dev/hda19   /dev/hda5
/dev/hda10    /dev/hda15   /dev/hda2    /dev/hda6
/dev/hda11    /dev/hda16   /dev/hda20   /dev/hda7
/dev/hda12    /dev/hda17   /dev/hda3    /dev/hda8
Done.
```

When you press Enter to send the command to the shell, Bash runs both commands, one after the other, before returning to the prompt.

More than two commands can also be used in this fashion. In fact, there is no fixed limit on the number of commands that can be chained together with the semicolon. You might choose to use three commands on one line, as in following example:

```
$ echo Starting.; ls /dev/hda*; echo Finishing.
Starting.
/dev/hda      /dev/hda13  /dev/hda18  /dev/hda4   /dev/hda9
/dev/hda1     /dev/hda14  /dev/hda19  /dev/hda5
/dev/hda10    /dev/hda15  /dev/hda2   /dev/hda6
/dev/hda11    /dev/hda16  /dev/hda20  /dev/hda7
/dev/hda12    /dev/hda17  /dev/hda3   /dev/hda8
Finishing.
```

As discussed earlier, Bash executes each command, one at a time.

Conditional Chaining

Although combining commands with a semicolon can be useful at the shell prompt, it simply provides another option for something already present in the shell script language. There are more options for combining commands. The first one is a Boolean OR operation, which means that the second (and subsequent) command should be executed only if the prior one fails. If you have multiple commands, the effect is to continue until one command succeeds or the end of the commands is reached.

The second option is a Boolean AND operation, which means that the second (and subsequent) command should be executed only if the prior one is a success. In this case, the effect is to continue until one command fails or the end of the command is reached.

You must use the double-pipe symbol to execute the Boolean OR. This command is frequently used to emit an error message when something fails, as in the following example:

```
$ ls -l /proc/foo || echo The ls failed.
ls: /proc/foo: No such file or directory
The ls failed.
$ echo $?
0
```

In this case, the ls command returned an error. Therefore, Bash proceeds to the next command, the echo. Incidentally, this one returns true. The entire statement takes on the return value of the last command, so echo $? displays the return value from the previous echo command.

Recall that the || will continue executing commands until one of them is successful. In the next example, the final command is not executed because of this behavior:

```
$ ls -l /proc/foo || echo The ls failed. || echo Bye
ls: /proc/foo: No such file or directory
The ls failed.
```

This time, the ls returns failure, as before. The first echo invocation is then called to display its message. The echo command, of course, has no trouble doing that, so it returns a success code. Because success is reached, there is no need to execute the final echo command.

If ls succeeds, none of the following commands are executed. In the following example, because ls is a success, it is the last command run:

```
$ ls -l /proc/tty || echo The ls failed. || echo Bye
total 0
dr-xr-xr-x   2 root       root            0 Jul 24 20:13 driver
-r--r--r--   1 root       root            0 Jul 24 20:13 drivers
dr-xr-xr-x   2 root       root            0 Jul 24 20:13 ldisc
-r--r--r--   1 root       root            0 Jul 24 20:13 ldiscs
```

Essentially, Bash will continue executing commands with the OR operator, trying to find one that works, and when such a command is found, it doesn't execute any more commands until the next line.

In contrast, the AND operator will continue executing commands but will stop after one fails as in the following example:

```
$ ls -d /* && ls -d /usr/* && ls /usr/foo/* && echo done
/bin      /etc       /initrd        /mnt    /tmp        /vmlinuz.old
/boot .   /floppy    /lib           /proc   /usr
/cdrom    /ftp       /lost+found    /root   /var
/dev      /home      /mass1         /sbin   /vmlinuz
/usr/A3        /usr/games           /usr/local         /usr/share
/usr/X11R6     /usr/i486-linuxlibc1 /usr/lost+found    /usr/src
/usr/bin       /usr/include         /usr/man
/usr/dict      /usr/info            /usr/openwin
/usr/doc       /usr/lib             /usr/sbin
ls: /usr/foo/*: No such file or directory
```

This time, the first two ls commands were a success. If you use the || operator, execution will stop after the first ls command returns a successful result. However, with the && operator, execution proceeds on to the third ls command. This one looks for a nonexistent file, and returns an error code. Because of that, the echo command is never executed.

You might also consider combining the two operators. The rules for doing so can be a bit confusing at first, but a quick example shows the most popular usage for doing so:

```
$ ls /proc/foo && echo It Worked || echo Failure
ls: /proc/foo: No such file or directory
Failure
```

In this example, you are executing a command (ls). If this command is successful, one action is taken; if it's unsuccessful, another action is taken.

To ensure that you get the expected results you should try using both operators with a valid ls command. In the following example, the ls is successful, so the first echo is executed; because it is successful, the second is skipped:

```
$ ls /proc && echo It Worked || echo Failure
1     182   204   236   bus            kmsg        pci
103   185   205   237   cmdline        ksyms       scsi
105   192   206   238   cpuinfo        loadavg     self
113   195   207   239   devices        locks       slabinfo
118   196   208   240   dma            meminfo     stat
121   197   214   241   fb             misc        swaps
13    198   215   280   filesystems    modules     sys
144   199   216   281   fs             mounts      tty
149   2     217   3     ide            mtrr        uptime
162   200   218   4     interrupts     net         version
172   202   219   557   ioports        parport
176   203   226   apm   kcore          partitions
It Worked
```

Yes, the command did work as expected. However, you might note that the above command works exactly the same as:

```
$ if ls /proc; then echo It Worked; else echo Failure; fi
1     182   204   236   bus            kmsg        pci
103   185   205   237   cmdline        ksyms       scsi
105   192   206   238   cpuinfo        loadavg     self
113   195   207   239   devices        locks       slabinfo
118   196   208   240   dma            meminfo     stat
121   197   214   241   fb             misc        swaps
13    198   215   280   filesystems    modules     sys
144   199   216   281   fs             mounts      tty
149   2     217   3     ide            mtrr        uptime
162   200   218   4     interrupts     net         version
172   202   219   563   ioports        parport
176   203   226   apm   kcore          partitions
It Worked
```

Many programmers will readily identify this form as being more similar to other structured programming languages, and rightly so. Perl (and to a lesser extent, C) supports something resembling the syntax of the first form.

Caution Although these two commands work the same in the preceding examples, they do not in some cases. In particular, if the first echo were replaced by a command that failed, both the echo and the final command would be executed. Therefore, in non-trivial situations, the if syntax is generally preferable because it avoids this problem.

The following two commands are not identical. The first will proceed to announce failure; the second will remain quiet after displaying the output:

```
$ ls /proc && false || echo Failure
1    182  204  236  bus           kmsg        pci
103  185  205  237  cmdline       ksyms       scsi
105  192  206  238  cpuinfo       loadavg     self
113  195  207  239  devices       locks       slabinfo
118  196  208  240  dma           meminfo     stat
121  197  214  241  fb            misc        swaps
13   198  215  280  filesystems   modules     sys
144  199  216  281  fs            mounts      tty
149  2    217  3    ide           mtrr        uptime
162  200  218  4    interrupts    net         version
172  202  219  564  ioports       parport
176  203  226  apm  kcore         partitions
Failure
$ if ls /proc; then false; else echo Failure; fi
1    182  204  236  bus           kmsg        pci
103  185  205  237  cmdline       ksyms       scsi
105  192  206  238  cpuinfo       loadavg     self
113  195  207  239  devices       locks       slabinfo
118  196  208  240  dma           meminfo     stat
121  197  214  241  fb            misc        swaps
13   198  215  280  filesystems   modules     sys
144  199  216  281  fs            mounts      tty
149  2    217  3    ide           mtrr        uptime
162  200  218  4    interrupts    net         version
172  202  219  565  ioports       parport
176  203  226  apm  kcore         partitions
```

Both commands successfully executed ls. The first command then executed the false command, which is a simple program that always returns an unsuccessful return value. Instead of ending there, this command went on to display Failure even though the ls was a success. This behavior is probably a bug. The second command executed the same ls, and the same false command. However, it skips the echo if the ls is successful, regardless of the result of the false command. This is probably the desired behavior.

Wildcards

Shell scripts frequently need to be capable of processing groups of files at once. Linux shells provide a capability of specifying multiple files at once by giving a particular pattern. These files that match the pattern are then specified as if they had been typed on the command line. Wildcards are the special characters used to form these patterns. The entire operation of specifying groups of files in this way is often referred to as *globbing*.

Each wildcard has a special meaning; that is, it can represent certain characters. Table 2-2 lists the most common wildcards and explains their meaning and usage.

	Table 2-2	
	Common Wildcards	
Character	*Meaning*	*Example*
*	Matches zero or more characters.	*.c matches the a.c, asdf. c, and even .c files.
?	Matches exactly one character.	`Letter9?.txt` matches `Letter90.txt`, `Letter95. txt`, `Letter9A.txt`, and `Letter9..txt`, but not `Letter95A.txt`.
`[...]` (character class)	Matches exactly one character from the characters specified between the brackets.	`Letter9[A13].txt` matches only `Letter9A.txt`, `Letter91.txt`, and `Letter93.txt`. No other files match.
`[...]` (character range)	Matches exactly one character from the range (or ranges) of characters specified between the brackets.	`Letter9[a-c1-3].txt` matches `Letter9a.txt`, `Letter9b.txt`, `Letter9c.txt`, `Letter91.txt`, `Letter92.txt`, and `Letter93. txt`. No other files match.
`[^...]` (Negated character class or range)	Matches exactly one character that does not occur in the specified ranges or characters listed.	`Letter9[^9a-c1-2].txt` matches any files that would normally match the `Letter9?. txt` pattern *except* for the files `Letter99.txt`, `Letter9a. txt`, `Letter9b.txt`, `Letter9c. txt`, `Letter91.txt`, and `Letter92.txt`.
`{..., ...}`	Alternation; matches exactly one of the given substrings.	`Letter{90,92,ABC}.txt` matches only the files `Letter90. txt`, `Letter92.txt`, and `LetterABC.txt`.

Quoting and escaping

In some situations, you may prefer to avoid having the shell interpret the wildcards, variables, or other special characters that may occur on your command lines. Bash provides you with ways to indicate that these items should not be treated as normal characters, without special meaning.

There are two methods for doing this. The first method, *quoting*, enables you to enclose whatever items you want to be taken literally inside either single or double quotes. The second method, *escaping*, enables you to place a backslash immediately before the character that you wish to be taken literally.

You use two characters for quoting: " and '. The double-quote character is a bit weaker than the single-quote character; the double-quote permits some special characters to function as they normally do. The single quote is stronger and prevents nearly everything from functioning. Let's examine a situation in which the single quote is more useful than the double quote, which is shown in the following example:

```
$ echo hi > "Test File"
$ ls -l Test File
ls: Test: No such file or directory
ls: File: No such file or directory
$ ls -l "Test File"
-rw-rw-r--   1 username username     3 Jul 23 09:08 Test File
$ rm "Test File"
```

The first line generates a file named Test File (note the space) and places the word "hi" into it. The second line is an attempt to display information about the file. However, it doesn't work. In this situation, the space character is special! It acts as a separator between files, so Bash tells ls that it should act upon two separate files: Test and File. Obviously, this isn't quite going to work right.

Next, the third command places the filename inside double quotes. This time, Bash does not split the name into two files, so ls looks for information on only one file. Similarly, with the rm command, the file must be placed in quotes in order for it to function properly.

A key difference between " and ' lies with variable interpolation, which will be discussed in the Variables section later in this chapter. The ' character prohibits variable interpolation, while the " character does not. This means that the dollar sign is not safe inside strings quoted with the double quote. Here's an example of that behavior:

```
$ echo "Path: $PATH"
Path: /usr/local/bin:/usr/bin:/bin:/usr/bin/X11:/usr/games
$ echo 'Path: $PATH'
Path: $PATH
```

Because of this, many Bash programmers prefer to use single quotes for safety unless they have a specific reason to use double quotes.

An alternative to quoting is escaping. Escaping can provide some benefits; when you use escaping for a particular character, you always know that it is effective. A problem occurs when a string being quoted must contain the quote character itself; in such a situation, escaping must be used.

Escaping is done in Bash by inserting a backslash before the special character. You don't need to enclose the entire string in quotes. However, every special character must be escaped. Here is an example:

```
$ echo hello > "Another Test File"
$ ls -l Another Test\ File
ls: Another: No such file or directory
ls: Test File: No such file or directory
$ ls -l Another\ Test\ File
-rw-rw-r--   1 user user 6 Jul 23 09:25 Another Test File
$ rm Another\ Test\ File
```

The first line uses quoting as before. In the second line, one of the space characters is escaped. Because of this, ls looks for two instead of three files; however, this is still not the desired behavior. When both spaces are escaped, the entire name is passed to ls intact just as with the quotes. Similarly, the filename is passed intact with rm.

Unlike quotes, you should not escape things that are not special characters. Some sequences, such as \n, have special meanings and generate other characters in some situations.

Sometimes you may need to combine escapes with quotes. A typical example occurs when the string that is quoted contains an example of the quote character itself. This situation can be extremely confusing at a shell prompt, so create the following script and name it quotetest.sh:

```
#!/bin/bash

echo 'Mary said, "I don't use DOS."'
```

After you have saved the file, you need to mark it executable, and then run it:

```
$ chmod a+x quotetest.sh
$ ./quotetest.sh
./quotetest.sh: line 3: unexpected EOF while looking for matching `"'
./quotetest.sh: line 4: syntax error: unexpected end of file
```

Bash obviously had some terrible trouble trying to deal with that statement. What happened is that the apostrophe in "don't" was treated as the end of the quoted string. When Bash encountered the quote after the word DOS, it considered it to be the start of a new quoted string. However, this new string was never terminated.

The solution to this mess is to use escaping. Should you stay with single quotes and escape the apostrophe, or should you use double quotes and escape them inside the string as necessary? Well, recall earlier that the single quotes are stronger than the double quotes. One of the things that this applies to is escaping; escaping the apostrophe isn't going to help. You can try this at the prompt:

```
$ echo 'Test \' Test2
Test \ Test2
```

The backslash was taken literally, and did not cause Bash to actually print the embedded quote. The solution is to use double-quote characters. Modify the script so it looks like this:

```
#!/bin/bash

echo "Mary said, \"I don't use DOS.\""
```

This time, the string is set off by double quotes. When you try running that script, you finally get the desired result:

```
$ ./quotetest.sh
Mary said, "I don't use DOS."
```

The script looks a bit complicated, but really it's not tricky once you understand what's going on. Everything is as we've seen before, prior to the first backslash. The \" sequence tells Bash to print a quote character rather than use that character to indicate the end of the string. Because the string is delimited by double quotes in this situation, the embedded apostrophe doesn't pose any challenge. Towards the end of the string, there is another \" sequence. Once again, this informs Bash to print the character instead of interpreting it as the end of the string. Finally, the last character on the line is the character that closes the string.

Another option for all of this is to use escaping. You could use it like this:

```
$ echo Mary\ said,\ \"I\ don\'t\ use\ DOS.\"
Mary said, "I don't use DOS."
```

This option is somewhat less intuitive; you must escape every space and quote character. However, the effect is the same as with the double quotes used above.

You should be familiar with two more special cases. First, if you want to send a backslash itself to a program, you need to escape it. This is done as follows:

```
$ echo Good \\ Morning
Good \ Morning
$ echo Good \ Morning
Good  Morning
```

Notice that the backslash didn't appear in the output from the second command. The reason is that Bash interpreted it as escaping the following space. In the first command, however, it did appear.

One other reason you might want to use the backslash is to enable you to split l ong lines into pieces. If you choose to do that, the backslash must be the very last character on the line preceding the one with which it should be combined. Here's an example script.

```
#!/bin/bash

ls -l /dev/hda1 /dev/hda2 /dev/hda3 \
/dev/hda4 /dev/hda5 /dev/hda6 \
/dev/hda7
```

In this script, the long `ls` command line was split into three parts to make editing and manipulation easier. When the script is run, Bash will combine the three parts back into a single line before executing the command.

Comments

You can insert comments into your Bash script. Like Perl, comments begin with a # symbol. Any text from that symbol until the end of the line is ignored by Bash. Here are some examples of using comments in a script.

```
#!/bin/bash
# This is a Bash script.

ls /proc                # Display a list of files in /proc
cat /proc/devices       # Display the devices on the system
cat /proc/interrupts    # Display a list of IRQs
```

Commenting is a very important part of writing programs. As you move into writing larger and larger ones, comments will play an increasingly important role in maintainability and documentation. This idea applies to shell scripts as well.

Note   The line beginning with #! at the start of each shell script has special meaning for the operating system. It indicates the name of the interpreter used to execute the script. However, because # is the Bash comment character, Bash ignores the line when the file is processed as a script. Therefore, it does not bother Bash when your script is executed.

Redirection and Piping

One of the most powerful features of the Linux shell is being able to combine programs in unique, arbitrary ways to form solutions to new problems. The primary ways of doing this are with redirection and piping.

Redirection enables you to take that which would normally be displayed on the terminal and save it into a file. Also, input redirection enables you to substitute the contents of a file for what would normally be typed on the keyboard.

Piping enables you to chain commands together, sending the output from one command into the input of the next. All the commands run simultaneously, processing the data at once, as parts of a pipe.

These different capabilities are made possible by the Linux notion of the standard input and output for programs. By default, each program has three standard file handles: standard input, standard output, and standard error. Standard input is used for reading data, and reads data from the terminal's keyboard by default. Standard output is used for displaying normal data, and is connected to the terminal's screen by default. Standard error is used for displaying error messages, and is also connected to the terminal's screen by default.

Table 2-3 contains a summary of these three Input/Output (I/O) channels.

Table 2-3
Standard Input/Output Channels

Name	Shorthand	Number	Purpose	Default Connection
Standard Input	Stdin	0	Reading input for a program	The terminal's keyboard
Standard Output	stdout	1	Displaying normal output from a program	The terminal's display
Standard Error	stderr	2	Displaying error messages or warnings of unusual situations	The terminal's display

Output redirection

The most straightforward way to use redirection is to use output redirection. In its simplest form, the messages that normally go to the screen instead are placed into a file.

```
$ ls -l /dev/hda*
brw-rw----  1 root     disk      3,  0 Feb 22 21:41 /dev/hda
brw-rw----  1 root     disk      3,  1 Feb 22 21:41 /dev/hda1
brw-rw----  1 root     disk      3, 10 Feb 22 21:41 /dev/hda10
brw-rw----  1 root     disk      3, 11 Feb 22 21:41 /dev/hda11
brw-rw----  1 root     disk      3, 12 Feb 22 21:41 /dev/hda12
brw-rw----  1 root     disk      3, 13 Feb 22 21:41 /dev/hda13
brw-rw----  1 root     disk      3, 14 Feb 22 21:41 /dev/hda14
brw-rw----  1 root     disk      3, 15 Feb 22 21:41 /dev/hda15
brw-rw----  1 root     disk      3, 16 Feb 22 21:41 /dev/hda16
brw-rw----  1 root     disk      3, 17 Feb 22 21:41 /dev/hda17
brw-rw----  1 root     disk      3, 18 Feb 22 21:41 /dev/hda18
brw-rw----  1 root     disk      3, 19 Feb 22 21:41 /dev/hda19
```

```
brw-rw----   1 root    disk     3,   2 Feb 22 21:41 /dev/hda2
brw-rw----   1 root    disk     3,  20 Feb 22 21:41 /dev/hda20
brw-rw----   1 root    disk     3,   3 Feb 22 21:41 /dev/hda3
brw-rw----   1 root    disk     3,   4 Feb 22 21:41 /dev/hda4
brw-rw----   1 root    disk     3,   5 Feb 22 21:41 /dev/hda5
brw-rw----   1 root    disk     3,   6 Feb 22 21:41 /dev/hda6
brw-rw----   1 root    disk     3,   7 Feb 22 21:41 /dev/hda7
brw-rw----   1 root    disk     3,   8 Feb 22 21:41 /dev/hda8
brw-rw----   1 root    disk     3,   9 Feb 22 21:41 /dev/hda9
$ ls -l /dev/hda* > listing
```

The first `ls` command displays a long listing of the files in `/dev` beginning
with hda. As is customary, this listing is displayed on the screen. The second
command requests the same listing, this time redirecting the output into the file
named `listing`. The greater-than symbol (>) is the output redirection operator;
it requests that the items that would normally go to standard output be sent to
the specified file. To be specific, it is changing what standard output is connected
to; normally, it's connected to the terminal's display. Here, standard output is
connected to the file named `listing`. You can verify that this file actually
contains the data that normally would have been sent to the screen by
using the `cat` command:

```
$ cat listing
brw-rw----   1 root    disk     3,   0 Feb 22 21:41 /dev/hda
brw-rw----   1 root    disk     3,   1 Feb 22 21:41 /dev/hda1
brw-rw----   1 root    disk     3,  10 Feb 22 21:41 /dev/hda10
brw-rw----   1 root    disk     3,  11 Feb 22 21:41 /dev/hda11
brw-rw----   1 root    disk     3,  12 Feb 22 21:41 /dev/hda12
brw-rw----   1 root    disk     3,  13 Feb 22 21:41 /dev/hda13
brw-rw----   1 root    disk     3,  14 Feb 22 21:41 /dev/hda14
brw-rw----   1 root    disk     3,  15 Feb 22 21:41 /dev/hda15
brw-rw----   1 root    disk     3,  16 Feb 22 21:41 /dev/hda16
brw-rw----   1 root    disk     3,  17 Feb 22 21:41 /dev/hda17
brw-rw----   1 root    disk     3,  18 Feb 22 21:41 /dev/hda18
brw-rw----   1 root    disk     3,  19 Feb 22 21:41 /dev/hda19
brw-rw----   1 root    disk     3,   2 Feb 22 21:41 /dev/hda2
brw-rw----   1 root    disk     3,  20 Feb 22 21:41 /dev/hda20
brw-rw----   1 root    disk     3,   3 Feb 22 21:41 /dev/hda3
brw-rw----   1 root    disk     3,   4 Feb 22 21:41 /dev/hda4
brw-rw----   1 root    disk     3,   5 Feb 22 21:41 /dev/hda5
brw-rw----   1 root    disk     3,   6 Feb 22 21:41 /dev/hda6
brw-rw----   1 root    disk     3,   7 Feb 22 21:41 /dev/hda7
brw-rw----   1 root    disk     3,   8 Feb 22 21:41 /dev/hda8
brw-rw----   1 root    disk     3,   9 Feb 22 21:41 /dev/hda9
```

And, indeed, the contents is as expected. Now, let's move on to something a bit
stranger — standard error redirection. Notice that, in the preceding table, standard
output and standard error are sent to your screen by default. However, when
dealing with redirection, they are not treated the same:

```
$ ls -l /dev/hda* /dev/nonexistant
ls: /dev/nonexistant: No such file or directory
brw-rw----   1 root     disk       3,    0 Feb 22 21:41 /dev/hda
brw-rw----   1 root     disk       3,    1 Feb 22 21:41 /dev/hda1
brw-rw----   1 root     disk       3,   10 Feb 22 21:41 /dev/hda10
brw-rw----   1 root     disk       3,   11 Feb 22 21:41 /dev/hda11
brw-rw----   1 root     disk       3,   12 Feb 22 21:41 /dev/hda12
brw-rw----   1 root     disk       3,   13 Feb 22 21:41 /dev/hda13
brw-rw----   1 root     disk       3,   14 Feb 22 21:41 /dev/hda14
brw-rw----   1 root     disk       3,   15 Feb 22 21:41 /dev/hda15
brw-rw----   1 root     disk       3,   16 Feb 22 21:41 /dev/hda16
brw-rw----   1 root     disk       3,   17 Feb 22 21:41 /dev/hda17
brw-rw----   1 root     disk       3,   18 Feb 22 21:41 /dev/hda18
brw-rw----   1 root     disk       3,   19 Feb 22 21:41 /dev/hda19
brw-rw----   1 root     disk       3,    2 Feb 22 21:41 /dev/hda2
brw-rw----   1 root     disk       3,   20 Feb 22 21:41 /dev/hda20
brw-rw----   1 root     disk       3,    3 Feb 22 21:41 /dev/hda3
brw-rw----   1 root     disk       3,    4 Feb 22 21:41 /dev/hda4
brw-rw----   1 root     disk       3,    5 Feb 22 21:41 /dev/hda5
brw-rw----   1 root     disk       3,    6 Feb 22 21:41 /dev/hda6
brw-rw----   1 root     disk       3,    7 Feb 22 21:41 /dev/hda7
brw-rw----   1 root     disk       3,    8 Feb 22 21:41 /dev/hda8
brw-rw----   1 root     disk       3,    9 Feb 22 21:41 /dev/hda9
$ ls -l /dev/hda* /dev/nonexistant > listing
ls: /dev/nonexistant: No such file or directory
```

Notice how everything except the error message was redirected this time. This is because ls sent the error message to standard error instead of standard output. The message is still displayed on the screen because you did not redirect standard error.

Recall from Table 2-3 that standard output is file descriptor number 1 and standard error is number 2. With this knowledge, you can tell Bash what to do with each specific file descriptor.

```
$ ls -l /dev/hda* /dev/foo > listing 2> listing.err
$ cat listing.err
ls: /dev/foo: No such file or directory
```

In this example, the standard output is sent to the file listing. If you don't specify a particular file descriptor with the > operator, file descriptor 1 (standard output) is assumed. However, you also sent standard error (file descriptor 2) to the file listing.err. Now, displaying listing.err shows the message that before managed to escape to the screen. If you were to run cat listing, you would see the same file listing as you have seen before.

In this particular case, you ended up with separate files for standard output and standard error. Sometimes it's preferable to have both standard output and standard error sent to a single file. You can do this by redirecting standard output, and then telling Bash to send standard error to standard output.

```
$ ls -l /dev/hda* /dev/foo > listing 2>&1
$ cat listing
ls: /dev/foo: No such file or directory
brw-rw----   1 root    disk      3,    0 Feb 22 21:41 /dev/hda
brw-rw----   1 root    disk      3,    1 Feb 22 21:41 /dev/hda1
brw-rw----   1 root    disk      3,   10 Feb 22 21:41 /dev/hda10
brw-rw----   1 root    disk      3,   11 Feb 22 21:41 /dev/hda11
brw-rw----   1 root    disk      3,   12 Feb 22 21:41 /dev/hda12
brw-rw----   1 root    disk      3,   13 Feb 22 21:41 /dev/hda13
brw-rw----   1 root    disk      3,   14 Feb 22 21:41 /dev/hda14
brw-rw----   1 root    disk      3,   15 Feb 22 21:41 /dev/hda15
brw-rw----   1 root    disk      3,   16 Feb 22 21:41 /dev/hda16
brw-rw----   1 root    disk      3,   17 Feb 22 21:41 /dev/hda17
brw-rw----   1 root    disk      3,   18 Feb 22 21:41 /dev/hda18
brw-rw----   1 root    disk      3,   19 Feb 22 21:41 /dev/hda19
brw-rw----   1 root    disk      3,    2 Feb 22 21:41 /dev/hda2
brw-rw----   1 root    disk      3,   20 Feb 22 21:41 /dev/hda20
brw-rw----   1 root    disk      3,    3 Feb 22 21:41 /dev/hda3
brw-rw----   1 root    disk      3,    4 Feb 22 21:41 /dev/hda4
brw-rw----   1 root    disk      3,    5 Feb 22 21:41 /dev/hda5
brw-rw----   1 root    disk      3,    6 Feb 22 21:41 /dev/hda6
brw-rw----   1 root    disk      3,    7 Feb 22 21:41 /dev/hda7
brw-rw----   1 root    disk      3,    8 Feb 22 21:41 /dev/hda8
brw-rw----   1 root    disk      3,    9 Feb 22 21:41 /dev/hda9
```

In this case, you capture the output from ls exactly as it appeared on the screen previously. The 2>&1 syntax tells Bash to send that which would normally go to file descriptor 2 (standard error) to file descriptor 1 (standard output). Because file descriptor 1 already was redirected to a file, standard error will be sent to that file as well.

This operation is so common that Bash has a special shortcut for it. This command is the same as the one you just ran:

```
$ ls -l /dev/hda* /dev/foo &> listing
```

That is, &> filename is equivalent to > filename 2>&1.

All of the commands you have been dealing with are destructive to the output file. That is, if the output file (listing or listing.err in these examples) already exists, the existing contents will be erased and replaced by the new contents. That is the desired behavior but sometimes it is preferable to leave the existing contents intact and simply append data to the end of a file. Bash provides a special redirection operator that opens the files in append mode. That is, if there is data in the file, the new data that is entered will be added to the end of the file, after any data already there.

The basic operator for an append is >. In many situations, you will find that shell scripts start with the > operator to ensure that any existing data in a file is cleared. Then, the > operator is used to add data after that. Of course, if your script is writing to a file that already exists and you want to preserve that data, you should not use the > operator:

```
$ ls -l /dev/hda1 > listing
$ ls -l /dev/hda[2-9] > listing
$ cat listing
brw-rw----  1 root      disk       3,  1 Jul  4  1998 /dev/hda1
brw-rw----  1 root      disk       3,  2 Jul  4  1998 /dev/hda2
brw-rw----  1 root      disk       3,  3 Jul  4  1998 /dev/hda3
brw-rw----  1 root      disk       3,  4 Jul  4  1998 /dev/hda4
brw-rw----  1 root      disk       3,  5 Jul  4  1998 /dev/hda5
brw-rw----  1 root      disk       3,  6 Jul  4  1998 /dev/hda6
brw-rw----  1 root      disk       3,  7 Jul  4  1998 /dev/hda7
brw-rw----  1 root      disk       3,  8 Jul  4  1998 /dev/hda8
brw-rw----  1 root      disk       3,  9 Jul  4  1998 /dev/hda9
```

In this example, you can tell what is going on. The first ls command wrote its one line of output to the file. Then, the second command wrote its eight lines of output to the same file, appending them after the first. Thus, the data from the second command is appended to the file that already existed.

You can also use appending with redirection. For example, you can use 2>filename to send standard error to a file. You may also use a command such as this:

```
$ ls -l /dev/hda10 /dev/foo > listing 2>&1
$ cat listing
brw-rw----  1 root      disk       3,  1 Jul  4  1998 /dev/hda1
brw-rw----  1 root      disk       3,  2 Jul  4  1998 /dev/hda2
brw-rw----  1 root      disk       3,  3 Jul  4  1998 /dev/hda3
brw-rw----  1 root      disk       3,  4 Jul  4  1998 /dev/hda4
brw-rw----  1 root      disk       3,  5 Jul  4  1998 /dev/hda5
brw-rw----  1 root      disk       3,  6 Jul  4  1998 /dev/hda6
brw-rw----  1 root      disk       3,  7 Jul  4  1998 /dev/hda7
brw-rw----  1 root      disk       3,  8 Jul  4  1998 /dev/hda8
brw-rw----  1 root      disk       3,  9 Jul  4  1998 /dev/hda9
ls: /dev/foo: No such file or directory
brw-rw----  1 root      disk       3, 10 Jul  4  1998 /dev/hda10
```

Thus, you may redirect both standard output and standard error to be appended to a file.

Input redirection

So far, we have been dealing with the data that programs generate. You can also control the data that is fed into programs with Bash. Consider the simple program called rev. The task of rev is to take whatever you type at the keyboard, reverse it, and then display it on-screen. When you are done with rev, press Ctrl+D to exit. A sample session with rev might go like this:

```
$ rev
Hello.
.olleH
Linux is great!
!taerg si xuniL
1234 one two three four
ruof eerht owt eno 4321
Ctrl+D
```

So, rev looks like a somewhat boring little program. After all, if you can type
something forwards, you can probably type it backwards.

But imagine that you have three megabytes of text that you need to reverse for
some odd reason. Perhaps it would be easier to redirect the input for rev than
to type it in. As an example, we'll look at the /proc/devices file. This file may
be quite different on your system but should have essentially the same form.

```
$ cat /proc/devices
Character devices:
  1 mem
  2 pty
  3 ttyp
  4 ttyS
  5 cua
  6 lp
  7 vcs
 10 misc
 14 sound
128 ptm
136 pts


Block devices:
  1 ramdisk
  2 fd
  3 ide0
  8 sd
 22 ide1
$ rev < /proc/devices
:secived retcarahC
mem 1
ytp 2
pytt 3
Sytt 4
auc 5
pl 6
scv 7
csim 01
dnuos 41

mtp 821stp 631

:secived kcolB
```

```
ksidmar 1
df 2
0edi 3
ds 8
1edi 22
```

You may also note at this point that instead of running `cat /proc/devices`, you can use `cat < /proc/devices`. The cat program happens to accept filenames on its command line; not all do.

It is also possible to redirect the input and output from a program at the same time as in following example:

```
$ grep -v devices: < /proc/devices > file1
$ rev < file1 > file2
$ cat file2
mem 1
ytp 2
pytt 3
Sytt 4
auc 5
pl 6
scv 7
csim 01 dnuos 41

mtp 821stp 631

ksidmar 1
df 2
0edi 3
ds 8
1edi 22
```

In this example, the `grep -v` statement removes two lines: those containing the word "devices:". The result is then saved into a file. This file is sent through `rev` and saved in another file, which is finally displayed by `cat`. When you send data from one program to another like this, pipes are generally a better solution than redirection; they completely avoid the need to have temporary files to hold the output of one program before sending it to the input of the next.

Pipes

Pipes enable you to take the output from one program and send it directly to the input of another. No temporary files are created with pipes. Rather, both programs are invoked and run at the same time. When the first generates some output, it is fed directly into the second as input. No files are created by the process because the data is sent directly from one process to the next.

Pipes are used with the vertical bar character (which may appear as either a broken or solid vertical bar on your keyboard). To redo the previous example with pipes, it would look like this:

```
$ grep -v devices: < /proc/devices | rev | cat
mem 1
ytp 2
pytt 3
Sytt 4
auc 5
pl 6
scv 7
csim 01
dnuos 41

mtp 821stp 631

ksidmar 1
df 2
0edi 3
ds 8
1edi 22
```

Note that the call to `cat` is actually unnecessary; unless you redirect or pipe it away, the output from `rev` will go to standard output. Here are some more practical uses of piping:

```
$ ls /dev/hd* | wc -l
    168
```

This command counts the number of files in /dev that begin with the letters hd. When ls is run in this fashion, it generates a list of the matching files, one per line. This is then fed to wc -l, which displays a count of the lines of output — 168 in this case. Therefore, 168 files match /dev/hd*.

You can also use this to replace text. In the following example, the device filename is capitalized:

```
$ ls -l /dev/hda* | sed s/hda/HDA/
brwxrwx--x  1 root      disk      3,   0 Jul  4  1998 /dev/HDA
brw-rw----  1 root      disk      3,   1 Jul  4  1998 /dev/HDA1
brw-rw----  1 root      disk      3,  10 Jul  4  1998 /dev/HDA10
brw-rw----  1 root      disk      3,  11 Jul  4  1998 /dev/HDA11
brw-rw----  1 root      disk      3,  12 Jul  4  1998 /dev/HDA12
brw-rw----  1 root      disk      3,  13 Jul  4  1998 /dev/HDA13
brw-rw----  1 root      disk      3,  14 Jul  4  1998 /dev/HDA14
brw-rw----  1 root      disk      3,  15 Jul  4  1998 /dev/HDA15
brw-rw----  1 root      disk      3,  16 Jul  4  1998 /dev/HDA16
brw-rw----  1 root      disk      3,  17 Jul  4  1998 /dev/HDA17
```

```
brw-rw----   1 root     disk     3,  18 Jul  4  1998 /dev/HDA18
brw-rw----   1 root     disk     3,  19 Jul  4  1998 /dev/HDA19
brw-rw----   1 root     disk     3,   2 Jul  4  1998 /dev/HDA2
brw-rw----   1 root     disk     3,  20 Jul  4  1998 /dev/HDA20
brw-rw----   1 root     disk     3,   3 Jul  4  1998 /dev/HDA3
brw-rw----   1 root     disk     3,   4 Jul  4  1998 /dev/HDA4
brw-rw----   1 root     disk     3,   5 Jul  4  1998 /dev/HDA5
brw-rw----   1 root     disk     3,   6 Jul  4  1998 /dev/HDA6
brw-rw----   1 root     disk     3,   7 Jul  4  1998 /dev/HDA7
brw-rw----   1 root     disk     3,   8 Jul  4  1998 /dev/HDA8
brw-rw----   1 root     disk     3,   9 Jul  4  1998 /dev/HDA9
```

The sed command here is used to match a particular pattern in text, and replace it with something else. In this case, hda is replaced with HDA. Much more powerful patterns are also possible with grep and sed by using regular expressions, which are discussed in detail in Chapter 3, "Working with Regular Expressions." As a quick introduction, the following command removes much of the display:

```
$ ls -l /dev/hda* | sed 's/^.*,[^A-Z]*//'
Jul  4  1998 /dev/hda
Jul  4  1998 /dev/hda1
Jul  4  1998 /dev/hda10
Jul  4  1998 /dev/hda11
Jul  4  1998 /dev/hda12
Jul  4  1998 /dev/hda13
Jul  4  1998 /dev/hda14
Jul  4  1998 /dev/hda15
Jul  4  1998 /dev/hda16
Jul  4  1998 /dev/hda17
Jul  4  1998 /dev/hda18
Jul  4  1998 /dev/hda19
Jul  4  1998 /dev/hda2
Jul  4  1998 /dev/hda20
Jul  4  1998 /dev/hda3
Jul  4  1998 /dev/hda4
Jul  4  1998 /dev/hda5
Jul  4  1998 /dev/hda6
Jul  4  1998 /dev/hda7
Jul  4  1998 /dev/hda8
Jul  4  1998 /dev/hda9
```

In this particular case, sed was used to trim much of the output of ls -l, leaving only the date. Don't worry about the particular sed command for now; you'll understand how to use regular expressions when you read Chapter 3.

Here's one more example of piping before moving on. This example takes four commands in a pipeline:

```
$ ls /dev/hda[1-9] | sed s./dev/.. | tac | rev
9adh
8adh
```

```
7adh
6adh
5adh
4adh
3adh
2adh
1adh
```

Examining this command, first you see an ls command that displays the first nine hda files. Next, the leading /dev/ from each filename is stripped off by the sed command. Then, the lines (not their contents) are reversed by tac; that is, instead of going from 1 to 9, the order of the lines now goes from 9 to 1. Finally, the rev command reverses the contents of each line.

Command substitution

Another powerful feature of Bash is its capability of transforming the output from commands into arguments for others. One usage of this is to operate on a selected set of files. Consider this example:

```
$ less `grep -l Linux *.txt`
```

The text between the backticks is treated as a command to execute. In this case, grep -l is used to display a list of all .txt files containing the word Linux. Because it occurs inside the backticks, each name is then converted to be an argument to less, which is used to display the files. You might prefer to use cat instead of less to generate a display of the contents of all the matching files combined.

In Bash, you can also use a $(command) syntax to take the place of the `command` syntax. This method enables *nesting*; that is, you can use command substitution inside another command substitution. For instance, it might be used like this:

```
$ cat $(grep -l Linux $(find . -name "*.txt"))
```

In this case, the find program is used to find all of the .sh files in or beneath the current directory. Then, grep searches through them and generates a list as before, and finally, the content in all the files are displayed.

You'll learn more uses for loops when they are introduced later in this chapter, but for now, here's an example:

```
for FILE in *.txt; do mv $FILE `echo $FILE | sed 's/txt$/html/'`; done
```

In this case, for any files with an extension of .txt, this extension is changed to .html.

Variables

Now that you have learned many of the basic elements of the Bash syntax, it's time to move on to data storage. Of course, data can often be stored in files. However, this is inconvenient. Like any programming language you'll find on Linux, variables are necessary in order to accomplish more complex tasks.

Assigning values to a variable is quite simple. The following example stores the word listing in the variable FILENAME.

```
$ FILENAME=listing
```

By convention, all caps are used for variable names, but this is not a requirement that is imposed on you by Bash. To access the contents of a variable, you simply add a dollar sign to the front of it. You can then use this virtually anywhere — on command lines, in strings, and even in the middle of some filenames.

```
$ FILENAME=listing
$ echo $FILENAME
listing
$ DEVICEDIR=/dev
$ ls $DEVICEDIR/hda* > $FILENAME
$ cat $FILENAME
/dev/hda
/dev/hda1
/dev/hda10
/dev/hda11
/dev/hda12
/dev/hda13
/dev/hda14
/dev/hda15
/dev/hda16
/dev/hda17
/dev/hda18
/dev/hda19
/dev/hda2
/dev/hda20
/dev/hda3
/dev/hda4
/dev/hda5
/dev/hda6
/dev/hda7
/dev/hda8
/dev/hda9
$ rm $FILENAME
```

In this example, the value listing is assigned to the variable FILENAME. Then, DEVICEDIR is set to hold the value /dev. Now, there is a command that says this:

```
ls $DEVICEDIR/hda* > $FILENAME
```

When Bash encounters this line, it first replaces $DEVICEDIR with /dev and $FILENAME with listing. The command is then executed as is customary.

If you ever wish to remove a variable, you can use the unset command. This command will delete the variable and the memory holding its contents.

```
$ MYVAR=myvalue
$ echo $MYVAR
myvalue
$ unset MYVAR
$ echo $MYVAR
```

Another interesting effect of variables is delayed expansion of wildcards. Consider the following example, which illustrates this behavior.

```
$ MYVAR=/dev/hda*
$ echo "$MYVAR"
/dev/hda*
$ echo $MYVAR
/dev/hda /dev/hda1 /dev/hda10 /dev/hda11 /dev/hda12 /dev/hda13
/dev/hda14 /dev/hda15 /dev/hda16 /dev/hda17 /dev/hda18
/dev/hda19 /dev/hda2 /dev/hda20 /dev/hda3 /dev/hda4 /dev/hda5
/dev/hda6 /dev/hda7 /dev/hda8 /dev/hda9
```

When you use a variable inside double quotes, as is done with the first echo command in this example, the variable is inserted verbatim; its contents are not examined further by the shell. However, when it is used outside of the quotes, the shell is free to examine its contents. In this case, the shell expands the wildcard to a file list. If you prefer to store the names in the variable right from the start, you can use command substitution to your advantage. For example:

```
$ MYVAR=`echo /dev/hda*`
$ echo "$MYVAR"
/dev/hda /dev/hda1 /dev/hda10 /dev/hda11 /dev/hda12 /dev/hda13
/dev/hda14 /dev/hda15 /dev/hda16 /dev/hda17 /dev/hda18
/dev/hda19 /dev/hda2 /dev/hda20 /dev/hda3 /dev/hda4 /dev/hda5
/dev/hda6 /dev/hda7 /dev/hda8 /dev/hda9
$ echo $MYVAR
/dev/hda /dev/hda1 /dev/hda10 /dev/hda11 /dev/hda12 /dev/hda13
/dev/hda14 /dev/hda15 /dev/hda16 /dev/hda17 /dev/hda18
/dev/hda19 /dev/hda2 /dev/hda20 /dev/hda3 /dev/hda4 /dev/hda5
/dev/hda6 /dev/hda7 /dev/hda8 /dev/hda9
```

This time, both expressions display the same text. This is because MYVAR held the list of filenames from the start. This behavior can be useful if, for instance, the set of files that might match a given pattern could change during the execution of a script.

Environment variables

There is a special type of variable known as an environment variable. These variables are special in two ways: 1) they can be passed to your script by other programs, and 2) any programs that are invoked from your script inherit the environment variables.

Identifying an environment variable in Bash is not always easy. You can set a variable as is done normally. If you want it to be flagged as an environment variable, you then need to use the export command:

```
$ LESS=-i
$ export LESS
$ echo $LESS
-i
```

In this example, you can tell that even after a variable has been exported, it can still be accessed as any other variable in Bash. The less file viewer will look for an environment variable named LESS. If it can find one, it will process the options contained in it. Here, the -i option tells less to treat all searches as case-insensitive ones.

You can get a list of all variables in the current context, whether or not they are marked as environment variables, by running set. This list will contain a number of variables that you did not set explicitly. Some are set for you by Bash itself; others, by various initialization scripts. Your own list may differ significantly from the one shown here:

```
$ set
BASH=/bin/bash
BASH_VERSINFO=([0]="2" [1]="02" [2]="1" [3]="1" [4]="release" [5]="alpha-unknown
-linux-gnu")
BASH_VERSION='2.02.1(1)-release'
BIBINPUTS='~/bibtex'
CVSROOT=/home/username/cvsroot
DIRSTACK=()
DISPLAY=:0.0
EDITOR=/usr/bin/emacs
EUID=1000
GROUPS=()
HISTFILE=/home/username/.bash_history
HISTFILESIZE=500
HISTSIZE=500
HOME=/home/username
HOSTNAME=myhost
```

```
HOSTTYPE=alpha
LESS=-i
LOGNAME=username
MACHTYPE=alpha-unknown-linux-gnu
MAILCHECK=60
MINICOM='-l -c on'
MPAGE=-bLetter
OPTERR=1
OPTIND=1
OSTYPE=linux-gnu
PAGER=less
PATH=/home/username/bin:/usr/local/bin:/usr/bin:/bin:/usr/bin/X11:/usr/games:
PILOTRATE=115200
PIPESTATUS=([0]="0")
PPID=32533
PS1='\h \w\$ '
PS2='> '
PS4='+ '
PWD=/home/username
SHELL=/bin/bash
SHELLOPTS=braceexpand:hashall:histexpand:monitor:history:interactive-comments:
    emacs
SHLVL=1
TERM=xterm-debian
UID=1000
USER=username
WINDOWID=67108878
WMAKER_BIN_NAME=/usr/bin/X11/WindowMaker
WRASTER_COLOR_RESOLUTION0=4
_=cd
```

This list can serve as an excellent reference as you read through the next section on special variables; it presents some examples of the contents of those variables.

Special variables

Bash defines numerous special variables. These variables are initialized to special values by Bash; the values can then be used in your script. Alternatively, some of them are set by you and cause Bash to act in special ways. Some of these variables do not necessarily have special meaning to Bash but rather to other programs on the system. Finally, some do not act as true variables at all, but they are still accessed with the traditional interface. Remember that to read the current value of any of these items, you need to use the dollar sign in front of them. This is true even for strange looking ones; for instance, echo $$ is valid to display the pid of the current shell. Table 2-4 lists these variables.

Table 2-4
Bash Special Variables

Variable Name	Primary Access Method	Description
!	Read	Use this variable to get the Linux process ID of the most recent process set to background.
@	read	Contains all parameters to the current context. When used in double quotes, evaluates to separate quoted values, one for each parameter passed to the current context.
#	read	Contains the number of parameters to the current context.
*	read	Contains all parameters to the current context. If used within double quotes, the result is a single parameter containing all passed parameters, separated by spaces.
$	read	Contains the Linux process ID of the current Bash process.
-	read	Contains a list of the current option flags (from the set command), one letter each, with no separation.
_	read	Contains the full path name of the current process during initialization. When looking for mail, contains the name of the current mail file. At all other times, contains the final argument to the previous command.
0	read	Holds the name of the current process or script.
From 1 to 9	read	Contains the first nine parameters to the current script or function.
BASH	read	Contains the full path name of the current shell.
BASH_VERSION	read	A printable string that contains the version number of your Bash version.

Variable Name	Primary Access Method	Description
BASH_VERSINFO	read	Contains an array of information about the current version of Bash.
DISPLAY	write	Contains the name of and display number on the machine on which X-based GUI clients should display their interfaces.
EUID	read	Contains the numeric effective user ID of the current shell process.
HISTCMD	read	Contains the numeric index of the current command in the command history.
HISTFILE	write	Contains the location of the file to hold the Bash history; defaults to $HOME/.bash_history.
HISTSIZE	write	Specifies the maximum size of the command history.
HOME	read	Contains the full path name of the home directory for the current user.
HOSTNAME	read	Contains the short name of the current machine.
HOSTTYPE	read	Contains the short name of the current machine's architecture.
IFS	write	Holds the value of the Internal Field Separator. This value is used for splitting up commands into their component parts.
LANG	write	Indicates the current (or preferred) locale to programs that support Linux internationalization. As such, it is frequently used as an environment variable.
LD_LIBRARY_PATH	write	Specifies additional (colon-separated) locations in which to search when loading the shared libraries for dynamically-linked executables.

Continued

Table 2-4 *(continued)*

Variable Name	Primary Access Method	Description
LD_PRELOAD	write	Specifies a list (space-separated) of specific libraries to be loaded into dynamically linked programs before any others, including those specified by the program itself. For security reasons, this specification can be incompatible with setuid and setgid features.
LINENO	read	When used within a shell or function, contains the offset in lines from the start of that shell or function.
MACHTYPE	read	Contains the GNU machine type identifier for this machine
MAIL	write	Informs you when new mail arrives in a UNIX mbox-style mailbox. If you want Bash to automatically inform you, set this variable to point to the location of that mailbox.
MAILCHECK	write	Contains the interval, in seconds, which indicates how frequently the specified mailbox should be checked for new mail.
OLDPWD	read	Holds the name of the previous working directory.
OSTYPE	read	Holds the name of the current operating system.
PATH	write	This variable holds a colon-separated list of directories that should be searched for binaries when executing Linux programs. This is generally an environment variable.
PPID	read	The process ID of the current process's parent process.
PS1	write	This variable holds a string describing how to generate the main prompt in Bash.
PWD	read	Contains the name of the current working directory.

Variable Name	Primary Access Method	Description
RANDOM	read	Returns a different random value each time the contents of this variable is accessed. The exact range of the values returned is implementation-dependant, so its usefulness can be limited.
REPLY	read	Contains the value of the data read from standard input when accessed after the read command, unless a different variable is specified to read.
SECONDS	read	Contains the number of seconds that elapsed since the current shell process was invoked.
SHELLOPTS	read	Contains a list of the current shell options.
UID	read	Contains the numeric real user ID of the owner of the current shell process.

Functions

In addition to creating separate scripts to perform repetitive tasks, you can use functions within scripts (or even at the command line) to minimize the need to retype code multiple times. You must define Bash functions before you can use them.

These functions can take parameters just as shell scripts can. A key difference between the two is that the shell script generally requires the invocation of a separate process to handle the script. Thus, the script cannot modify variables in the current shell's context. Furthermore, there is overhead with starting another shell process.

On the other hand, sometimes it is good to have a script that cannot modify variables in the current shell. For instance, if the script is acting almost as a complete program with its own internal variables, it's generally a good idea to keep it isolated from the current shell.

A function is defined in a script as follows:

```
function MyFunc {
   command1
```

```
    command2
    command3
}
```

You can use this function later as you would use any other command. You can also call it with arguments. The following examples are valid ways to call the function:

```
MyFunc
MyFunc *.c
MyFunc /dev/hda*
```

Let's create a sample function and corresponding script. Type the following code into your favorite editor, and save it as func.sh:

```
#!/bin/bash

function CountMatches {
  echo -n "Number of matches for $1: "
  ls $1 2>/dev/null | wc -l
}

CountMatches /dev/hda*
CountMatches /proc/*
CountMatches /foo/*
```

This particular script will execute, but it will not display the intended results — the number of files that match the given pattern. Mark the script executable and run it:

```
$ chmod a+x func.sh
$ ./func.sh
Number of matches for /dev/hda:      1
Number of matches for /proc/1:      11
Number of matches for /foo/*:       0
```

Notice how the number of matches are not correct; you already know that there is more than one match for /dev/hda*. Also, the text reported by the function does not match the pattern sent to it. Further investigation reveals the reason: the text passed to the function is not quoted. Because the function looks at $1 (the first parameter) only, it should display one result.

Why then the count of 11 for /proc/1? The reason is that /proc/1 is a directory. Try looking at it yourself at a prompt:

```
$ ls -l /proc/1
ls: /proc/1/exe: Permission denied
ls: /proc/1/root: Permission denied
ls: /proc/1/cwd: Permission denied
```

```
total 0
-r--r--r--   1 root       root            0 Jul 26 05:47 cmdline
lrwx------   1 root       root            0 Jul 26 05:47 cwd
-r--------   1 root       root            0 Jul 26 05:47 environ
lrwx------   1 root       root            0 Jul 26 05:47 exe
dr-x------   2 root       root            0 Jul 26 05:47 fd
pr--r--r--   1 root       root            0 Jul 26 05:47 maps
-rw-------   1 root       root            0 Jul 26 05:47 mem
lrwx------   1 root       root            0 Jul 26 05:47 root
-r--r--r--   1 root       root            0 Jul 26 05:47 stat
-r--r--r--   1 root       root            0 Jul 26 05:47 statm
-r--r--r--   1 root       root            0 Jul 26 05:47 status
```

You can expect permission denied errors in this listing when running this particular command. In this listing, if ls is given the name of a directory, by default, it displays the contents of the directory instead of the directory itself.

Now, perhaps you would like to fix the problems with the script. One way to go about that is to quote the pattern. Change your script so it matches the following code:

```
#!/bin/bash

function CountMatches {
  echo -n "Number of matches for $1: "
  ls $1 2>/dev/null | wc -l
}

CountMatches '/dev/hda*'
CountMatches '/proc/*'
CountMatches '/foo/*'
```

Because the patterns are now quoted, they won't be expanded until asked for with $1 in the function itself. Try running this new script:

```
$ ./func.sh
Number of matches for /dev/hda*:       21
Number of matches for /proc/*:      724
Number of matches for /foo/*:        0
```

The value for /dev/hda* now appears correct. However, there is still something strange going on with /proc/*. A quick examination shows that there are not really as many files in /proc as indicated:

```
$ ls /proc
1     173  196  233  bus        kmsg       pci
103   176  197  237  cmdline    ksyms      scsi
105   183  198  247  cpuinfo    loadavg    self
```

```
113   186   199   248   devices        locks        slabinfo
118   187   2     249   dma            meminfo      stat
121   188   205   250   fb             misc         swaps
13    189   206   251   filesystems    modules      sys
134   190   207   252   fs             mounts       tty
136   191   208   3     ide            mtrr         uptime
146   193   209   4     interrupts     net          version
156   194   210   400   ioports        parport
160   195   232   apm   kcore          partitions
```

If you run ls /proc/*, you will see the difference; when you use /proc/*, the shell explicitly mentions every entry in /proc, including the directories. When a directory is explicitly given to ls, ls displays its contents. So, the result is that ls is displaying much more than is being asked for.

To avoid this, use ls -d, which tells ls to display only the directory names. When you make this change, your func.sh should look like this:

```
#!/bin/bash

function CountMatches {
   echo -n "Number of matches for $1: "
   ls -d $1 2>/dev/null | wc -l
}
CountMatches '/dev/hda*'
CountMatches '/proc/*'
CountMatches '/foo/*'
```

Now, try running this modified script. This time, you should be getting correct results for each item as in the following example.

```
$ ./func.sh
Number of matches for /dev/hda*:      21
Number of matches for /proc/*:        84
Number of matches for /foo/*:         0
```

The results are now correct. However, note that there is no way to determine that an error occurred with the /foo/* pattern. You can detect errors by making several modifications:

```
#!/bin/bash

function CountMatches {
   MATCHES=`ls -d $1 2>/dev/null | wc -l`
   echo "$MATCHES"
   if [ $MATCHES != 0 ] ; then return 0 ; else return 1; fi
}
```

```
function DispMatches {
  if MATCHES=`CountMatches "$1"` ; then
    echo -n "Number of matches for $1: "
    echo $MATCHES
  else
    echo "$1 is not a valid pattern."
  fi
}

DispMatches '/dev/hda*'
DispMatches '/proc/*'
DispMatches '/foo/*'
```

There are several constructs in this script that you have not yet been introduced to. Several things about this new version of the script should be noted. First, the backtick operator is used twice to capture the output from a command: once in CountMatches to capture the output of wc -l, and once in DispMatches to actually capture the output of the CountMatches function. Also, the functionality to count the number of matches has been separated from the code to display this number in a pleasant way. The reason for this is that some other function or code in the script might want to get a count of the matches without actually getting a message to go along with it. With the separate functions, doing this becomes easy. Also, take special note of this line:

```
if MATCHES=`CountMatches "$1"` ; then
```

There is a reason that $1 is enclosed in double quotes. If it were not in quotes, it would be expanded right there — in DispMatches — before being passed to CountMatches. If this premature evaluation would occur, the result would be the same as with the earlier bug; that is, CountMatches would generally report only one match.

Now, try running this script. Notice how it is able to detect the error with /foo/* this time:

```
$ ./func.sh
Number of matches for /dev/hda*: 21
Number of matches for /proc/*: 86
/foo/* is not a valid pattern.
```

Now that the script works, you may be wondering why things are done in certain ways. For instance, why bother with capturing the output from the CountMatches function when CountMatches could simply return the number of matches to the caller? The reason is that the return call can return only an exit code that is in the range of 0 to 255 in Bash. If a pattern matches more than 255 files, this method yields incorrect results.

What about using some global variable for holding the number of matches? Perhaps CountMatches could set this variable and DispMatches could read it. Although this option would work in this particular case, it is not a good idea in general. The reason is that things can become tricky if global variables are used for communication, especially in larger scripts or programs. You must always remember to retrieve the value from the variable immediately, or it may be clobbered. Furthermore, if you wish to write a recursive function for some reason, using globals for communication will probably not be an option.

Conditionals and Loops

There are many uses for various conditional expressions in Bash. A conditional is simply a language construct that enables your program to do one thing if a given expression is true, and a different thing if the expression is false.

In Bash, you were introduced to a sort of lazy conditional: the && and || operators. Although these can result in conditional execution of commands, the operators in Bash specifically designed for the purpose are more powerful.

if

The cornerstone of the Bash conditionals is the if ... fi clause. The Bash documentation provides a formal definition of it:

```
if  list; then list; [ elif list; then list; ] ... [ else list; ] fi
```

This definition, unfortunately, makes the statement look more difficult than it really is. An if statement can be very simple:

```
$ if ls /foo; then echo Success.; else echo Failure.; fi
ls: /foo: No such file or directory
Failure.
```

In this example, if the call to ls is a success, then one message is printed. Otherwise, a different message is displayed. This simple example shows all that there is to the basic usage of the if statement in Bash. Essentially, the return value of the test expression (ls /foo in this case) is checked. If it indicates a successful completion, then the "then" clause is executed. Otherwise, the optional "else" clause is executed.

Using conditionals can get more complex if you need to nest your conditionals. Here's one example script:

```
#!/bin/bash

if [ -x /bin/foo ]; then
  echo "/bin/foo exists and is executable. Exiting."
elif [ -x /bin/bash ]; then
  echo "/bin/bash exists and is executable.  Exiting."
elif [ -x /bin/sh ]; then
  echo "/bin/sh exists and is executable.  Exiting."
else
  echo "Found no executable program."
fi
```

In this script, the elif defines an "else if" condition. That is, in this situation, Bash keeps trying each condition until it finds one that is true. If none of them are true, the final else clause is executed. Running this script produces the following output:

```
/bin/bash exists and is executable.  Exiting.
```

Testing with [...]

In Bash, you typically need to test various items. In the previous example, the script tests to see whether certain files exist and are executable. Sometimes, you may need to test for the existence of files. In other situations, you may want to compare two strings to see if they are equal.

There are two equivalent ways to perform this testing. One is to put the test expression inside [ ] characters. The other is to use the test command. Both use the same syntax. As an illustration, the example in the previous section also works with test

```
#!/bin/bash

if test -x /bin/foo ; then
  echo "/bin/foo exists and is executable. Exiting."
elif test -x /bin/bash ; then
  echo "/bin/bash exists and is executable.  Exiting."
elif test -x /bin/sh ; then
  echo "/bin/sh exists and is executable.  Exiting."
else
  echo "Found no executable program."
fi
```

The syntax of test is simple; it takes some options indicating what it should check, and returns an exit code indicating whether or not the expression turns out to be true.

Table 2-5 shows the operators in test and [...].

Table 2-5
Test and [ ] Operators

Syntax	Description
! expression	Evaluates to true if the specified expression is false. This can be used to negate any of the other tests.
-b filename	Evaluates to true if the specified filename is a block special device.
-c filename	Evaluates to true if the specified filename is a character special device.
-d filename	Evaluates to true if the specified filename is a directory.
-e filename	Evaluates to true if the specified filename exists, regardless of its type.
-f filename	Evaluates to true if the specified filename is a normal file.
-g filename	Evaluates to true if the specified filename has the setgid bit set.
-G filename	Evaluates to true if the specified filename is owned by the same group as the effective GID of the current process.
-k filename	Evaluates to true if the specified filename has the sticky bit set.
-L filename	Evaluates to true if the specified filename is a symbolic link.
-n string	Evaluates to true if the specified string has a nonzero length.
-O filename	Evaluates to true if the specified filename is owned by the same person as the effective UID of the current process.
-p filename	Evaluates to true if the specified filename is a FIFO (named pipe).
-r filename	Evaluates to true if the current user's permissions are sufficient to read data from the specified file.
-S filename	Evaluates to true if the specified filename corresponds to a UNIX domain socket.
-t [fd]	Evaluates to true if the specified file descriptor corresponds to a real terminal. The default for fd is 1 – standard output.

Syntax	Description
`-u filename`	Evaluates to true if the specified filename has the setuid bit set.
`-w filename`	Evaluates to true if the current user's permissions are sufficient to write data to the specified file.
`-x filename`	Evaluates to true if the current user's permissions are sufficient to execute the specified file.
`-z string`	Evaluates to true if the specified string is zero-length.
`Expression1 -a expression2`	Evaluates to true if both specified expressions are also true.
`Expression1 -o expression2`	Evaluates to true if at least one specified expression is true; a binary or operation.
`filename1 -ef filename2`	Evaluates to true if both specified file names correspond to the same inode number on the same device.
`filename1 -nt filename2`	Evaluates to true if the first file's last modified date is newer than that of the second.
`filename1 -ot filename2`	Evaluates to true if the first file's last modified date is older than that of the second.
`number1 -eq number2`	Evaluates to true if number1 is numerically equal to number2.
`number1 -ne number2`	Evaluates to true if number1 is numerically different (not equal) than number 2.
`number1 -le number2`	Evaluates to true if number1 is numerically less than or equal to number2.
`number1 -lt number2`	Evaluates to true if number1 is numerically strictly less than number2.
`number1 -ge number2`	Evaluates to true if number1 is numerically greater than or equal to number2.
`number1 -gt number2`	Evaluates to true if number1 is numerically strictly greater than number2.
`String`	Evaluates to true if the specified string has a nonzero length.
`string1 = string2`	Evaluates to true if both strings are equal.
`string1 != string2`	Evaluates to true if the strings specified are not equal.

case

The case command is used to select one option out of a list of alternatives based on the value of something. It can be thought of as a more elegant replacement for some long lists of if ... elif statements. The basic syntax as defined in the Bash documentation is:

```
case word in [ ( pattern [ | pattern ] ... ) list ;; ] ... esac
```

This definition looks somewhat confusing. Instead of worrying about it, here's an example script that you can type and save as case.sh:

```
#!/bin/bash

echo -n "Enter your favorite Linux command: "

read

case "$REPLY" in
  sed)
    echo "sed is used for stream editing."
    echo "You can try this:  echo Hi | sed s/i/j/"
  ;;

  grep | egrep)
    echo "grep and egrep are used for pattern matching."
    echo "You can also use regular expressions with egrep."
  ;;

  bash)
    echo "Bash is a popular shell under Linux."
  ;;

  *awk)
    echo "These tools are interpreters for the awk language."
  ;;

  *)
    echo "I'm not familiar with the $REPLY command "
    echo "but here's what Bash knows about it: "
    type $REPLY
  ;;
esac
```

This script begins by prompting the user for a favorite Linux command. This command is read and stored in REPLY. Then, depending on the command that is supplied, a special message is displayed. This is where the case comes in; it provides a set of patterns (that use the same rules as wildcards) for checking the data.

For instance, if the supplied string matches sed, then the commands for sed (up until the double semicolon) are executed. If the string matches either grep or egrep, then those commands are executed.

If the command matches the wildcard pattern *awk, then information about the awk interpreters is displayed. Finally, if nothing else matches, the * pattern is found. Because * matches anything, and occurs last, it effectively acts as a default case if nothing else matches. If this occurs, a message is displayed indicating that the script isn't familiar with the particular command. It then uses a Bash built-in command, type, to get some information about it.

Try the script a few times to see how it works. Here are some sample sessions:

```
$ ./case.sh
Enter your favorite Linux command: gawk
These tools are interpreters for the awk language.
$ ./case.sh
Enter your favorite Linux command: egrep
grep and egrep are used for pattern matching.
You can also use regular expressions with egrep.
$ ./case.sh
Enter your favorite Linux command: less
I'm not familiar with the less command
but here's what Bash knows about it:
less is /usr/bin/less
$ ./case.sh
Enter your favorite Linux command: nawk
These tools are interpreters for the awk language.
```

Apparently, the case statement worked as desired in this example. It enabled the script to identify particular input options, and to take appropriate action based on what was supplied.

while

The first looping construct to examine in Bash is called while. Like its counterparts, which go by the same name in other languages, while will continue executing a piece of code until the exit condition turns false. In Bash, the syntax is defined as:

```
while list; do list; done
```

A simple example is reading input and acting upon it. Here is a sample session. Like before, you can use Ctrl+D to indicate that you are done supplying input:

```
$ while read; do echo "You typed: $REPLY"; done
I'm experimenting with while!
```

```
You typed: I'm experimenting with while!
qwerty
You typed: qwerty
Ctrl+D
```

You could also do something more complex with a `while` loop. Here is a script, based on the previous concept:

```
#!/bin/bash

echo "Type some text; press Ctrl+D when done."

echo -n "Your input: "
while read; do
  TEXT=`echo "$REPLY" | rev`
  echo "Reversed, your message is: $TEXT"
  echo -n "Your input: "
done
```

The indentation used in this script is strictly optional. However, it is quite useful for larger scripts, as it makes the structure of the script visually discernible. Running this script produces the following:

```
$ ./while.sh
Type some text; press Ctrl+D when done.
Your input: Good morning!
Reversed, your message is: !gninrom dooG
Your input: Linux is great!
Reversed, your message is: !taerg si xuniL
Your input: While is interesting.
Reversed, your message is: .gnitseretni si elihW
Your input: Ctrl+D
```

You might notice that when you exit this program, the prompt appears directly after the "Your input" message instead of on its own line. This is because you used `echo -n`, which suppresses the automatic use of the newline character. The solution to the problem is to print a newline after exiting the loop. This simple script modification will make the script look like this:

```
#!/bin/bash

echo "Type some text; press Ctrl+D when done."

echo -n "Your input: "
while read; do
  TEXT=`echo "$REPLY" | rev`
  echo "Reversed, your message is: $TEXT"
  echo -n "Your input: "
done

echo
```

If you choose to run the script again, you will see that the prompt occurs at the normal position after exiting the script.

for

The `for` syntax is used to iterate over a predetermined list of items, executing specific commands for each one. The Bash documentation defines the syntax as follows:

```
for name [ in word; ] do list ; done
```

This is similar to the `foreach` syntax in some other languages. In Bash, the name refers to the name of a variable. For each item in the list, the specified variable will be set to hold that item. Then the given commands will be executed as illustrated by the following example:

```
#!/bin/bash

for FILENAME in /dev/hda*; do
  echo "I found the file $FILENAME"
done
```

When Bash evaluates this statement, it first expands /dev/hda* to the list of matching files. Then, for each file, `FILENAME` is set to its name and the `echo` command is executed for the file. Running the script produces the following output:

```
$ ./for.sh
I found the file /dev/hda
I found the file /dev/hda1
I found the file /dev/hda10
I found the file /dev/hda11
I found the file /dev/hda12
I found the file /dev/hda13
I found the file /dev/hda14
I found the file /dev/hda15
I found the file /dev/hda16
I found the file /dev/hda17
I found the file /dev/hda18
I found the file /dev/hda19
I found the file /dev/hda2
I found the file /dev/hda20
I found the file /dev/hda3
I found the file /dev/hda4
I found the file /dev/hda5
I found the file /dev/hda6
I found the file /dev/hda7
I found the file /dev/hda8
I found the file /dev/hda9
```

You can also use `for` to iterate over lists of arbitrary items. You don't have to restrict yourself to using only filenames:

```
$ for NAME in Jill Richard Sam Jane; do echo "Hello, $NAME."; done
Hello, Jill.
Hello, Richard.
Hello, Sam.
Hello, Jane.
```

You can also use the `for` command to perform several operations on a single set of files. See if you can determine what the following script does:

```
#!/bin/bash

for FILENAME in `grep -l Linux Report-199[7-9].txt`; do
  echo "Processing $FILENAME..."
  a2ps -2 $FILENAME
  mail -s "Contents of file $FILENAME" friend@example.com < $FILENAME
  fax send 555-1234 $FILENAME
done
```

This short shell script is quite powerful. First, it selects those text reports from 1997 to 1999 that contain the word Linux in them. Then, for all those files, it does the following:

✦ Displays a message on the user's screen indicating the current status of the script.

✦ Processes the file with a2ps, which adds page borders, a filename, and reformats the text so that it prints on half as much paper. Then this file is sent to the printer. (Note that a2ps is an optional utility that you may have to install if it isn't available by default on your system.)

✦ Sends an e-mail to friend@example.com, the body of which is the contents of the file. The subject of this message is set to "Contents of file," followed by the name of the file.

✦ Sends a FAX of the document to somebody at 555-1234.

So, by combining `for` with a few other shell constructs already covered, as well as a few basic Linux utilities, you have a solution for some specialized document processing. Other optimizations and enhancements are possible as well. For instance, if you have a more advanced FAX suite installed, the FAX could be queued for background delivery. Also, you could opt to rename or move the files after they have been dealt with. You could use the output of `find` to search documents that are deep in the directory tree. All of this can take place without any user interaction; it's fully automated.

Shell Utilities

You will find a number of useful shell utilities that you can use in your scripts or while programming. All of these have manpages available on-line in your Linux system; to view the manpage, simply use man command, where command is the name of the program for which you are looking for information. Some of these are implemented as shell built-ins; that is, the shell handles the command for you, rather than a separate program to do so.

Many of them read from standard input and write to standard output. This means that they are ideal for being combined with others in a pipeline. For instance, you could use:

```
cat somefile.txt | sort | uniq | tac
```

This will read data from somefile.txt, sort it, remove the duplicates, and then invert the order of its lines. There are several other useful tools for the shell; they are summarized in Table 2-6.

Table 2-6 Useful Tools for Shell Scripts	
Command	**Purpose**
awk	This is an interpreter for the awk programming language.
Bash	Starts up another shell process beneath the current one.
cat [file ...]	Reads from each specified file in order, displaying its entire contents to standard output. The effect of this is to concatenate the files together, hence the name. If no names are specified, cat copies from standard input to standard output.
exec command [arguments ....]	Executes the specified program, with the given optional arguments. This program replaces the current shell. That is, the current shell ceases to exist once the program begins. When the program exits, you will probably be logged off or your xterm closed.
find	Selects files based on a search through directories for files with matching name, modification dates, permissions, or other attributes. The manpage for find contains an exhaustive description of its syntax.

Continued

Table 2-6 *(continued)*

Command	Purpose
grep / egrep	Search inside of files for specific text or patterns. The egrep tool uses regular expressions for searches, and on Linux, grep can use regular expressions as well.
gunzip	Sends uncompressed data to standard output when compressed data is piped to gunzip.
gzip	Reads data on standard input, and writes a compressed version to standard output. This command can be used in a pipe. Normally, after the data is compressed, the pipeline ends; the data will be saved to a file. This program can also work on separate files.
perl	Invokes the interpreter for the Perl programming language.
rev	Copies from standard input to standard output, reversing the order of the characters in each line of the file.
sed	Reads from standard input, makes some modifications to the data, and writes the result to standard output; that is it's a stream editor. Today, the most frequent use of sed is its pattern replacement operator, s///.
tac	Copies from standard input to standard output, reversing the order in which the lines appear (but not the order of characters in those lines).
tee	Reads from standard input, and copies the data to multiple sources. It can write the data to several files as well as to standard output, for instance.
tr	Performs basic transformations on data. For instance, the command tr A-Z a-z will convert all capital letters to lowercase in its input. This command reads from standard input, makes the modifications, and writes the result to standard output.
sort	Reads from standard input, sorts the lines in the file, and writes the ordered data to standard output.
uniq	Removes duplicate lines from input. You usually have to send the input through sort before you can send it through uniq. The output from uniq is the same as the input, with duplicate lines removed.

Summary

In this chapter, you learned about shell scripting with Bash. Shell scripts can be created with any text editor and contain commands like those you could type at a shell prompt.

✦ Executable Bash scripts should start with `#!/bin/bash` and must be marked executable with `chmod a+x`. Programs and commands indicate success or failure with a return value: 0 for success, or any nonzero value for failure. This value can be used with conditionals to determine what to do next. Wildcards are used to select a group of filenames based on a pattern. Quoting and escaping are used to prevent the normal interpretation of special characters in Bash.

✦ There are three standard file descriptors for each Linux process: standard input, standard output, and standard error. Bash enables you to redirect any of those to or from a file. Furthermore, you can use a pipe to send the output from one program directly into the input of another. Another option is command substitution, which converts the output of one program into arguments for another.

✦ Variables are used to store small amounts of data for later access. They can be set with the equals sign (=), or by Bash in a situation such as a `for` loop. The contents of variables are accessed with the dollar sign ($). Variables may be exported to the environment, which enables programs invoked by the shell to see their values. There are also many special variables, which enable your scripts to find out information about the shell and the machine it's running on, and to control some aspects of shell behavior.

✦ Functions are used to store frequently used code in only one place. Unlike shell scripts, functions modify variables in the current shell, so they must be used with care. Functions, once defined, can behave like any other shell command when called.

✦ Conditionals are used to make execution of some code dependent upon the success or failure of some earlier command or expression. Loops are used either to iterate over a list of items, or to continue executing a block of code until some condition becomes false. The `test`, or `[ ... ]`, operator can be used to perform some simple tests that are useful with conditionals and loops.

✦ Linux comes with a rich variety of shell utilities that make excellent additions to your scripts. Many of these utilities are specifically designed for use in a pipeline, so they can be easily combined in powerful ways. Utilities exist to do everything from searching files, to finding files, and sorting them.

✦   ✦   ✦

Working with Regular Expressions

Reading and processing data is one of the most frequent tasks that programmers face, and programming under Linux is no exception. Many Linux languages offer a standardized parsing mechanism known as regular expressions. In this chapter, you will learn all about this mechanism and how to use it. The chapter begins with an introduction to regular expressions. It continues with coverage of three major areas of regular expressions: character classes, quantifiers, and alternation and grouping. Finally, you will learn how to use regular expressions in various languages.

Introducing Regular Expressions

Many times, when writing programs, you need to parse data — separate input into its component bits. Sometimes, this parsing is easy — maybe your input data is separated by commas. Sometimes, the task is much more difficult, especially if your input is more free-form. You may even have to pick out the values you want from within free-form text. This type of task can be very tricky.

No matter what language you use, even if you don't use regular expressions, your parsing algorithms, no doubt, will be focused around recognizing patterns. You might notice that certain text is always ignored, such as column headings. Or, the values that you want might be separated by commas. Maybe you notice that there is one record per line, or one record per page. All of these are patterns that you can use to pick out the pieces of useful data from your input.

In some languages, such as C, you write code to explicitly search through your input. Even with functions such as strtok() and strsep(), this process can be difficult and bug-prone.

Regular expressions provide an alternative to writing search algorithms. With regular expressions (also known as *regexps*), you define the pattern that you are looking for, and let the regular expression engine do the searching for you. The regular expression pattern that you give to the engine defines which parts of the text are interesting, and can return those bits only. Alternatively, it can return all text that matches your pattern — presumably for later processing or display.

Regular expressions are not tied to any particular language, although Perl makes particularly heavy use of them. You can find regular expression support in grep (searches through files), sed (edits files based on regular expressions), several libraries for C, and several other languages and utilities as well.

In this chapter, you will learn how to form basic regular expression patterns, how to fit regular expressions to patterns in data, and then more advanced regular expression syntax such as quantifiers, character classes, grouping, and alternation. Finally, you'll learn about some particular features or limitations of the regular expression support in some of the different languages that support them.

To the greatest extent possible, the examples in this chapter are designed to work with regular expressions in any language that uses them. However, some languages have a more powerful implementation than others, and so some of these examples may only work in a language with such an implementation, such as Perl.

Patterns

The first step to writing a useful regular expression is to figure out what sort of patterns are present in your data. In some situations, this is trivial. For instance, here are a few lines from the /etc/passwd file on my Linux machine:

```
root:x:0:0:root:/root:/bin/bash
daemon:x:1:1:daemon:/usr/sbin:/bin/sh
bin:x:2:2:bin:/bin:/bin/sh
sys:x:3:3:sys:/dev:/bin/sh
sync:x:4:100:sync:/bin:/bin/sync
games:x:5:100:games:/usr/games:/bin/sh
man:x:6:100:man:/var/catman:/bin/sh
lp:x:7:7:lp:/var/spool/lpd:/bin/sh
mail:x:8:8:mail:/var/spool/mail:/bin/sh
news:x:9:9:news:/var/spool/news:/bin/sh
uucp:x:10:10:uucp:/var/spool/uucp:/bin/sh
proxy:x:13:13:proxy:/bin:/bin/sh
postgres:x:31:32:postgres:/var/postgres:/bin/sh
```

From this example, you can already note several features about the data. For one, there is one record per line, and the fields in the record are separated by colons. With a bit more knowledge of the format, you know that there are fields for user-name, password, uid (numeric user ID), gid (numeric group ID), real name, home directory, and default shell.

This is a format that is very easy to parse with a regular expression. Most languages are well suited towards regular expression parsing with the one record per line format.

A format that is more difficult to parse is the output from an `ls -l` command. For instance, consider these lines from such a command:

```
drwxr-xr-x    3 root      root        1024 Feb  7 16:42 CORBA
-rw-r--r--    1 root      root        6350 Jun  9 16:01 Muttrc
-rw-r--r--    1 root      root        1646 Jan 11  1998 adduser.conf
drwxr-xr-x    2 root      root        1024 May 24 19:01 ae
-rw-r--r--    1 root      root         233 Oct 26  1998 aliases.safe
lrwxrwxrwx    1 root      root          27 Jul 12 07:23 localtime ->
        /usr/share/zoneinfo/CST6CDT
drwxr-xr-x    5 root      root        1024 Jul 18 10:19 texmf
-rw-r--r--    1 root      root         373 Feb 16 11:03 updatedb.conf
-rw-r--r--    1 root      root         222 Sep 30  1998 upload.sites
drwxr-xr-x    4 uucp      uucp        1024 Apr 30 20:31 uucp
-rw-r--r--    1 root      root        4623 Feb 10 15:18 vnc.conf
-rw-r--r--    1 root      root        3293 Sep 28  1998 wgetrc
drwxr-xr-x    3 root      root        1024 Oct 30  1998 xemacs
-rw-r--r--    1 root      root          56 Feb 17 22:18 ytalkrc
```

From this listing, you can tell that there is a pattern. Each line starts out with some permissions, a count of the hard links, the user and group that own the file, and its size. After that, there is a date. But this date is not always in the same format. Sometimes, it lists the month, day, and time; other times, it lists the month, day, and year. After that, there's a filename. But, if the file is a symbolic link, the name of the linked-to file will follow.

So, even though the format is not hard to understand when you look at the display onscreen, it can be difficult to parse for a program.

Regular expression syntax

Table 3-1 summarizes the syntax in regular expressions. This table is designed to be your map through the vast terrain of regular expressions. You can use it to find the operator you need, to discover what an operator used by someone else does, or simply to browse and see what you can do with regular expressions. If you use regular expressions frequently in your programming, and you probably will if you do a lot of parsing, this table will no doubt become a valuable reference.

Note

Don't worry if you don't understand the meaning of most of the items here yet; they will be explained in detail in the remainder of this chapter. Some of these items apply only to certain languages, and some languages define more special operators than are listed here. Some of these differences will be highlighted at the end of the chapter, but if you are having difficulties with a given regular expression in a particular language, consult the documentation for that language. Of the items listed here, the most likely to cause trouble are the various backslash operators.

Table 3-1
Regular Expression Syntax Elements

Syntax	Description	Example
\	Escape operator; the next character (if special) has its literal meaning. Some languages may ascribe special meanings to sequences with normal characters, such as \n.	Foo.*\.txt matches any string beginning with Foo and ending with .txt.
\0xx	Matches the octal character indicated by the xx digits.	Bell\007Beep matches a string that begins with Bell, and then has the ASCII bell character, and ends with Beep.
\a	Matches the ASCII bell character. This is the same as \x07 and \007.	Bell\aBeep matches a string that begins with Bell, and then has the ASCII bell character, and ends with Beep.
\A	Matches the beginning of the string. This is a Perl-ism; it acts exactly like the caret character (^) except it does not match multiple times when the m option is used.	\AHello matches only a string whose first five letters are Hello.
\b	Matches the boundary between two words. This does not actually match any particular character, but rather a specific location.	1234\b.+9 matches 1234 2359 and 1234 a9 but not 1234a9.
\B	The opposite of \b, matches any location that is not a word boundary.	1234\B.+9 matches 1234689 and 1234asdf9 but not 1234 589.

Syntax	Description	Example
\d	Matches any digit character. The definition of this varies between implementation and locale, but you can generally consider it to be the same as [0-9].	Report\d+ matches Report12, Report1351134, and Report0, but not ReportA.
\D	The opposite of \d, matches any character that is not a digit. and even Report___.txt.	Report\D+ matches ReportA, ReportForBob,
\f	Matches the ASCII form-feed character.	Form\fFeed matches a string containing the words Form and Feed, separated only by the ASCII form-feed character.
\n	Matches the ASCII newline character. With some implementations, this may match the carriage return character also. Some implementations strip off the final newline before passing the string to the regular expression parser, so if you are looking for the end of the line, you may want to use $ instead.	ine1\nLine2 matches a Lstring containing two lines, with the first ending with Line1 and the second beginning with Line2.
\r	Matches the ASCII carriage return character.	Word1\rWord2 matches a string containing Word1 and Word2, separated only by the carriage return character.
\s	Matches any white space character. The exact definition of this can vary potentially between locales, but generally include spaces, tabs, carriage returns, and linefeeds.	Foo\s+Bar matches a string ontaining Foo and Bar, cseparated by at least one white space character.

Continued

Table 3-1 *(continued)*

Syntax	Description	Example
\S	The opposite of \s, matches any character that is not a white space character.	Foo\S+Bar matches a string containing Foo and Bar, with at least one non-white space character between them. For instance, Foo1234Bar, Foo_Bar, FooqwertyBar, and FooBazBar
\t	Matches the ASCII horizontal tab character.	Tab\tHere matches text with an embedded horizontal tab character.
\w	Matches a word character. This will vary between locales, as the alphabet in some areas includes characters not present in others. In English, this is generally the same as [0-9a-zA-Z_].	The pattern \w+ matches any word without embedded white space. Examples include Linux4You, RegexpsAreFun, and so on.
\W	The opposite of \w, matches any character that would not be matched by \w.	The pattern \W+ matches any string without word characters in it. Examples include !<>, \~`, and ";".
\xyy	Matches the character specified by the two-digit hexadecimal number yy.	The pattern \x07 matches the ASCII bell character.
\Z	This is a Perl-ism. This acts like $, but doesn't match multiple times when the m option is in effect.	The pattern .*end\Z matches such strings as end, This Is The end, I'm at the string's end, and so on.
.	Matches any single character. Depending on the implementation and options given to the regular expression engine, this may or may not match a newline character.	Hello.txt matches Hello4txt, Helloqtxt, Hello!txt, and even Hello.txt.

Syntax	Description	Example
`[ ... ]` (character class)	Denotes a character class. This usage gives a listing of characters, any of which may be matched once. Ranges may also be specified. Negation may be specified by using a leading ^ after the opening bracket.	`Letter199[14-79]` matches only `Letter1991`, `Letter1994`, `Letter1995`, `Letter1996`, `Letter1997`, and `Letter1999`. `Letter199[^14-79]` matches many items, such as `Letter199Q`, `Letter1992`, `Letter199!`, and many more.
`[[:alnum:]]`	Matches alphabetic and numeric characters; the same as `[[:alpha:][:digit:]]`	The pattern `Word1[[:alnum:]]+Word2` matches patterns such as `Word1HelloWord2`, `Word1123456789Word2`, and any others with at least one alphanumeric character between `Word1` and `Word2`.
`[[:alpha:]]`	Matches alphabetic characters. The definition of this may vary between locales, but in English, it generally means `[A-Za-z]`.	The pattern `Word1[[:alpha:]]Word2` matches patterns such as `Word1HelloWord2` and `Word1GoodbyeWord2`, and any others with at least one alphabetic character between the first and second words. Numeric characters do not match this pattern.
`[[:blank:]]`	Matches horizontal white space characters. Currently, this matches only space and tab.	The pattern `Lots[[:blank:]]+Of[[:blank:]]Spaces` matches patterns such as `Lots Of Spaces`, `Lots    Of Spaces`, and `Lots Of    Spaces`.
`[[:cntrl:]]`	Matches the ASCII control characters, which are generally characters 1 through 31 in ASCII.	The pattern `Strange[[:cntrl:]]Characters` matches two words separated by one control character.

Continued

Table 3-1 *(continued)*

Syntax	Description	Example
`[[:digit:]]`	Matches any numeric character. This is the same as writing [0-9].	`Hi [[:digit:]]+` matches such strings as `Hi 123456789`, `Hi 12`, and `Hi 99`.
`[[:graph:]]`	Matches non-white space characters that are printable. This includes, for instance, alphabetic characters, numbers, and so on.	The pattern `To:[[:graph]]` matches a string such as `To:q`, `To:5`, and so on.
`[[:lower:]]`	Matches lower-case alphabetic characters. In English locales, this is the same as [a-z].	The pattern `[[:lower:]]` matches such strings as `linuxprogrammingisfun`, `regularexpressionsare useful`, and so on.
`[[:print:]]`	Matches printable characters. This is the opposite of `[[:cntrl:]]`	`[[:print:]]+` matches almost any string that contains plain text characters.
`[[:punct:]]`	Matches punctuation characters. This can vary significantly between locale, but for English locations, consider it to be essentially any nonalphanumeric keys in the main area of your keyboard.	The pattern `[[:punct:]]` matches such characters as %, (, and $.
`[[:space:]]`	Matches white space characters. These might include space, tab, carriage return, linefeed, form feed, vertical tab, and so on.	`Word1[[:space:]]+ Word2` matches two words separated by at least one white space character. They could perhaps be on different lines or even different pages, depending on your language and options.
`[[:upper:]]`	Matches uppercase letters. The precise listing of the letters that match can vary between locale.	The pattern `[[:upper:]]+` matches any string consisting solely of uppercase characters. Examples include `WOW`, `HELLO`, `LINUX`, and `GNU`.

Syntax	Description	Example
`[[:xdigit:]]`	Matches characters that are valid hexadecimal digits.	The pattern `[[:xdigit:]]` will match strings containing solely hexadecimal characters. Examples of these can include `01234ABCD`, `F00F`, `AA55`, and `FFEF`.
`{x}`	Matches the preceding character or operator exactly x times.	`Q{5}` matches only the string `QQQQQ`.
`{x,}`	Matches the preceding character or operator at least x times.	`Q{5,}` matches strings such as `QQQQQ`, `QQQQQQQ`, and `QQQQQQQQQ`.
`{x,y}`	Matches the preceding character or operator no less than x times and no more than y times.	`Q{3,5}` matches only the strings `QQQ`, `QQQQ`, and `QQQQQ`.
`|`	Denotes alternation in a pattern, used to specify multiple options for matches at a particular point. Unless used inside the grouping operator, (...), the entire regular expression is split into pieces, any of which will be considered a successful match.	`Report.|Memo199.` matches such strings as `ReportA`, `Memo1999`, `Report2`, and `Memo199a`.
`?`	Indicates that the preceding operator should match as few times as possible while still allowing the regular expression to find a match. This is valid in Perl only.	The pattern `.+?(Q+)` ensures that the trailing Q characters in the string are returned. With this question-mark operator, a string such as `LinuxQQQQ` returns the `QQQQ` string. Without it, the same string returns only a single `Q` because the `.+` before matches the remaining ones.
`$`	Matches the end of the current line. This does not correspond directly to any particular character; it is simply used to match the end of the line. Language options and implementation details may modify the notion of *line*.	`Linux.$` matches only the strings that end with the word Linux and then one other character.

Continued

	Table 3-1 *(continued)*	
Syntax	**Description**	**Example**
^	Matches the beginning of the current line. This does not directly correspond to any particular character; it is simply used to match the beginning of a line. Language options and implementation details may modify the notion of *line*.	`^Hello` matches only those lines whose first five characters spell `Hello`.
*	Modifies the behavior of the immediate preceding character or operator to match 0 or more times. (The standard behavior is to match exactly 1 time.)	`Document.*html` matches any string beginning with `Document` and ending with `html`, including such examples as `Document.html`, `Document12.html`, `Document135html`, and even `Documenthtml`.
(...)	This operator serves two functions: 1) it acts as a grouping operator, restricting the boundaries of the alternation operator; and 2) it is used to denote interesting segments of the regular expression, which are then processed in an implementation-specific way such as setting special variables or returning arrays.	`(Memo|Report)20.\.txt` matches `Memo201.txt`, `Report20a.txt`, and `Report209.txt`. Furthermore, the matching text for the alternation (either `Memo` or `Report`) will be returned or assigned to a variable, depending on the language or implementation in use.
+	Matches the immediate preceding character or operator 1 or more times.	`7+` matches strings such as `7`, `77`, `77777`, and `7777777`.

An introduction to egrep

One of the most basic, and most useful, tools that you will find for doing simple pattern matching is grep. There is an extension to grep, named egrep that supports more powerful pattern matching like the regular expressions in other languages such as Perl. On many Linux systems, grep is actually the same as egrep. However, in order to maintain portability, it's a good idea to get into the habit of using egrep when you want to use sophisticated regular expressions.

The egrep tool is fundamentally simple. You give it a pattern (regexp) to look for and some data in which to look. It then displays all lines in the file that the pattern is capable of matching. For such a simple concept, it's amazing the power that is behind egrep.

As an example, I'll look at some ways to manipulate the /etc/passwd file. For this book, I have selected a few lines from a real passwd file that I can use as examples. If you want to follow along and get the same results, you should type the following data to your favorite editor:

```
root:x:0:0:root:/root:/bin/bash
daemon:x:1:1:daemon:/usr/sbin:/bin/sh
bin:x:2:2:bin:/bin:/bin/sh
sys:x:3:3:sys:/dev:/bin/sh
sync:x:4:100:sync:/bin:/bin/sync
games:x:5:100:games:/usr/games:/bin/csh
man:x:6:100:man:/var/catman:/bin/sh
lp:x:7:7:lp:/var/spool/lpd:/usr/bin/tcsh
www-data:x:33:33:www-data:/var/www:/bin/sh
pilot:x:1002:1002:Pilot Guy,.,:/home/pilot:/bin/bash
```

You can save the file with the name passwd in your home directory, for example, and it will work fine for you with these examples. If you prefer to use your own passwd file, note that it may not have some of the particular situations that will arise in these examples. However, you can still try to follow along; however, cd to /etc first.

Given the preceding snippet, some of these examples may seem a bit trivial. However, when you realize that some passwd files can contain thousands of entries, searching them like this is a powerful capability indeed.

When you invoke egrep, it expects at least one parameter: the pattern to look for. If you run it like this, you will need to pipe the data into it, or redirect its standard input. Alternatively, you may specify one or more filenames on its command line, and it will read directly from those files.

For the first egrep example, start by finding a way to get a list of all the people that use the csh shell. A first try might look like this:

```
$ egrep csh passwd
games:x:5:100:games:/usr/games:/bin/csh
lp:x:7:7:lp:/var/spool/lpd:/usr/bin/tcsh
```

Close, but not quite right. Notice how it found the string csh in the second displayed line, so it was displayed as well. You need to find a way to narrow it down to find only the csh users. By using regular expressions, you can do that. The key is to match the string :/bin/csh when it occurs at the end of the line. For example:

```
$ egrep ':/bin/csh$' passwd
games:x:5:100:games:/usr/games:/bin/csh
```

That's better! I need to explain a few details about this example, though. First, note the usage of the dollar sign at the end of the pattern. If you look up that character in Table 3-1, you'll notice that it is used to match the end of the line. In this case, you need to be sure that the text being matched is at the end of the line. The colon before the pattern is not a special regular expression character; it simply matches the colon in the passwd file. If you didn't explicitly match the colon, then paths such as /usr/local/bin/csh could match as well. Finally, note that the pattern is in single quotes. This is because the dollar sign is also a shell special character. To prevent the shell from trying to interpret the dollar sign as a shell character, it's a good idea to place any pattern containing such characters in single quotes.

An introduction to sed

Sed is so named because it is a Stream Editor. That is, sed is used to perform automated edits on a data stream, and write the results to standard output. Sed is, actually, a simplistic programming language. In this chapter, I'll use only one or two of these features. The features I'll explore, however, do not require you to learn the programming language, and in fact, map directly into Perl statements. Therefore, you'll have some knowledge for dealing with Perl regular expressions later.

Instead of giving sed a pattern, like you do with egrep, you give it a command. This command could be anything ranging from deleting a line to a search and replace request. I will use this search and replace feature, affectionately known to sed aficionados as s///.

The syntax of s/// is this:

```
s/search-pattern/replacement-pattern/[options]
```

For the time being, the options will not be important. Here's a look at a simple example:

```
$ sed s/csh/CSH/ passwd
root:x:0:0:root:/root:/bin/bash
daemon:x:1:1:daemon:/usr/sbin:/bin/sh
bin:x:2:2:bin:/bin:/bin/sh
sys:x:3:3:sys:/dev:/bin/sh
sync:x:4:100:sync:/bin:/bin/sync
games:x:5:100:games:/usr/games:/bin/CSH
man:x:6:100:man:/var/catman:/bin/sh
lp:x:7:7:lp:/var/spool/lpd:/usr/bin/tCSH
www-data:x:33:33:www-data:/var/www:/bin/sh
pilot:x:1002:1002:Pilot Guy,,,:/home/pilot:/bin/bash
```

This command went through the input, searching for the csh text on each input line. When the text was found, it was changed to CSH and then displayed. You can also do more interesting things. For instance, if you want to delete everything from the input except the shell, you can run this:

```
$ sed s/^.*:// passwd
/bin/bash
/bin/sh
/bin/sh
/bin/sh
/bin/sync
/bin/csh
/bin/sh
/usr/bin/tcsh
/bin/sh
/bin/bash
```

What happened here? Well, first, sed is given a pattern to match. In this case, that pattern indicated to start matching with the beginning of the line, and continue up until and including the last colon on the line. This leaves only the shell that is not matched. Then, sed is told to replace the matched portion with an empty string — which has the effect of deleting that part of the line.

You could achieve the opposite effect by matching only the text after the final colon. Because of this, you need to match all text that is not a colon and occurs only prior to the end of the line. Here's one way to do that:

```
$ sed 's/[^:]*$//' passwd
root:x:0:0:root:/root:
daemon:x:1:1:daemon:/usr/sbin:
bin:x:2:2:bin:/bin:
sys:x:3:3:sys:/dev:
sync:x:4:100:sync:/bin:
games:x:5:100:games:/usr/games:
man:x:6:100:man:/var/catman:
lp:x:7:7:lp:/var/spool/lpd:
www-data:x:33:33:www-data:/var/www:
pilot:x:1002:1002:Pilot Guy,,,:/home/pilot:
```

In this case, a particular feature of the character class is used to match everything except the colon. The asterisk indicates that this character class should match zero or more times, up until the end of the line. Then, the matched part is deleted.

Regular expressions in Perl

Perl is a full-fledged modern programming language. One of its most useful features is its integrated regular expression support, which is quite powerful. Perl's regular expression support enables you to generate an array full of values based on picking apart data with a regular expression, all in one single command. This functionality, as well as many more advanced uses for it, makes a very powerful solution in Perl.

Cross-Reference   Perl programming will be discussed in more detail in Chapter 20, "Introducing Perl."

For now, I am going to introduce to you a Perl program that enables you to see how Perl evaluates your regular expressions. Don't worry if you don't understand the code in this program now; I'll analyze it (and make some improvements) later in Chapter 21, "Manipulating Data with Perl." Type the following text using your favorite editor, and save the result as pattest:

```perl
#!/usr/bin/perl

while (1) {
  print "Enter pattern";
  print ", or . to re-use previous," if ($LASTREGEXP);
  print " or leave empty to exit:\n";
  print "> ";
  $REGEXP = <STDIN>;
  chomp $REGEXP;
  if ($REGEXP eq '.') {
    $REGEXP = $LASTREGEXP;
  }
  exit (0) unless ($REGEXP);
  print "Enter string to match";
  print " or . to re-use previous" if ($LASTSTRING);
  print ":\n";
  print "> ";
  $STRING = <STDIN>;
  chomp $STRING;
  if ($STRING eq '.') {
    $STRING = $LASTSTRING;
  }

  $LASTREGEXP = $REGEXP;
  $LASTSTRING = $STRING;

  @MATCHES = $STRING =~ /$REGEXP/;
  if ($#MATCHES > -1) {
    print "Successful match!\n";
    print "There were " . ($#MATCHES) + 1 .
" strings returned: \n";
    $counter = 0;
    foreach $MATCH (@MATCHES) {
      $counter++;
      print "String $counter: $MATCH\n";
    }
  } else {
    print "There was not a successful match.\n";
  }
  print "\n\n";
}
```

Now, as with shell scripts, you need to mark the program executable. Do so by typing the following shell command:

```
$ chmod a+x pattest
```

Now, it's time to give our pattern-testing program a try. Here's a sample session with it:

```
$ ./pattest
Enter pattern or leave empty to exit:
> ^Linux Is.*Great$
Enter string to match:
> Linux IsGreat
Successful match!
There were 1 strings returned:
String 1: 1


Enter pattern, or . to re-use previous, or leave empty to exit:
> .
Enter string to match or . to re-use previous:
> Linux Is Really Great
Successful match!
There were 1 strings returned:
String 1: 1


Enter pattern, or . to re-use previous, or leave empty to exit:
> .
Enter string to match or . to re-use previous:
> Linux Is Really Great!
There was not a successful match.


Enter pattern, or . to re-use previous, or leave empty to exit:
>
```

Here, I supplied one pattern for testing; as a shortcut, you can simply use a period in place of the pattern thereafter—this can really save some tedious typing. Then, I tried three strings with that pattern. Each time, pattest displayed a correct result; the third string will not match because of the trailing exclamation point; the pattern indicated that Great must be the last word on the line.

When you place items inside the grouping operator, Perl returns them in array form. Here is one example:

```
$ ./pattest
Enter pattern or leave empty to exit:
> ^Linux(.*)Great$
```

```
Enter string to match:
> Linux Is Great
Successful match!
There were 1 strings returned:
String 1:  Is
```

Because I placed the match inside of parentheses this time, the effect is that any text that I insert between the two words will be returned in array form. The pattest program then displays each item in the array, so you can see exactly what Perl is returning.

You can use pattest to confirm the validity of the rest of the regular expression examples in this chapter. Better yet, you can use it to experiment with regular expressions on your own.

Understanding Character Classes

Character classes are devices used in regular expressions for specifying which characters are acceptable at a particular point, or which are not. With character classes, you can specify characters individually or give a range of allowable characters. Furthermore, you can negate the meaning of your character class, indicating which characters are not acceptable instead of indicating which characters are acceptable.

A simple usage might be to specify a range of allowable numbers. This might occur, for instance, when you are looking for data with a specific date. Here's an example:

```
Letters from 199[0-246-9]
```

This regular expression indicates that and of the characters between 0 and 2, 6, and 9, or the number 4 will be acceptable at that position. Thus, the strings that this regular expression will match include:

```
Letters from 1990
Letters from 1991
Letters from 1992
Letters from 1994
Letters from 1996
Letters from 1997
Letters from 1998
Letters from 1999
```

This type of usage is fairly straightforward. You can, however, combine character classes to form new types of patterns. For instance, consider the following regular expression:

```
Letters from 19[89][2-5]
```

With this pattern, any year whose third digit is an 8 or 9 and final digit falls between 2 and 5, inclusive, will be matched. Thus, these are the potential matches for the previous pattern:

```
Letters from 1982
Letters from 1983
Letters from 1984
Letters from 1985
Letters from 1992
Letters from 1993
Letters from 1994
Letters from 1995
```

So, for each option in the first character class, each option in the second is valid. You can think of it in terms of the regular expression engine evaluating each option in the second for each option in the first, although generally this would not be the algorithm used internally by the engine.

Another feature presented by the character class is negation. That is, you can specify which characters should not occur at a particular location. Negation is indicated by a leading caret (^) in the character class. Here's an example:

```
Letters from 199[^0-246-9]
```

This particular regular expression matches so many strings that it's not practical to list all of the possibilities here, but here are some of the strings that match:

```
Letters from 1995
Letters from 199!
Letters from 199z
Letters from 199=
Letters from 1993
Letters from 199\
```

So, you can see that everything except those particular characters listed are valid. This may not be the desired effect in this situation, but it can be helpful often with parsing. For instance, earlier I used such a syntax to match everything except for a colon. You can use that kind of syntax to your benefit, often combined with quantifiers. For instance, you may want to match a number of characters that are not spaces. You can simply use negation with a character class along with a quantifier indicating how many characters to match, as discussed in the next section.

As a final note, if you want to include a dash (–) in your character class, you can make it either the first or the last character in the class. If you want to include the caret in your class, you can make it the last character in the class — or any position other than the first character.

For instance, the following character class allows both to match:

```
[A-Za-z^-]
```

If you try it out with pattest, you can see the result:

```
$ ./pattest
Enter pattern or leave empty to exit:
> [A-Za-z^-]
Enter string to match:
> A
Successful match!
There were 1 strings returned:
String 1: 1


Enter pattern, or . to re-use previous, or leave empty to exit:
> .
Enter string to match or . to re-use previous:
> -
Successful match!
There were 1 strings returned:
String 1: 1


Enter pattern, or . to re-use previous, or leave empty to exit:
> .
Enter string to match or . to re-use previous:
> ^
Successful match!
There were 1 strings returned:
String 1: 1


Enter pattern, or . to re-use previous, or leave empty to exit:
> .
Enter string to match or . to re-use previous:
> 5
There was not a successful match.


Enter pattern, or . to re-use previous, or leave empty to exit:
>
```

From these results, you can verify that indeed the dash and the caret are allowed to match this particular character class, and those characters not specified are correctly prevented from matching.

Using Quantifiers

When you are looking for data in a regular expression, you frequently need to specify how many times certain characters may appear. For instance, you might want to indicate that the pattern matcher should skip over any number of spaces when searching for data.

Quantifiers provide a way to do this. They work by specifying how many times the immediately preceding character or operator is supposed to match. One of the most frequently used quantifiers is the asterisk (*). This indicates that the preceding item should match zero or more times. Here are some examples.

```
Hi*
```

This regular expression matches strings such as Hi, H, Hii, Hiiiiiii, and so on. Notice that because the asterisk allows the i to match zero times, the H all by itself matches.

Whereas this may be useful in some cases, quantifiers frequently are combined with other items to achieve more powerful results. For instance, the period means that the regular expression should match any single character at that position. So, adding an asterisk after it means that the regular expression matches any number of characters. As an example, consider this:

```
Linux Is.*Great
```

This regular expression will match many various strings. Some of them are:

```
Linux IsGreat
Linux Is Really Great
Linux Is123456789Great
```

Basically, this regular expression allows anything (including nothing) to be inserted between Is and Great.

Sometimes, matching zero or more times is not appropriate. In many cases when parsing text files, you face a situation in which you know white space will separate different values, but you don't know how much white space there will be. In this case, you have to match at least one character of white space, so the asterisk isn't appropriate. Instead, you can use the plus character (+). For instance:

```
Linux Is.+Great
```

This regular expression will match the following:

```
Linux Is Really Great
Linux Is123456789Great
```

And, of course, there are many other strings that can match. Note, though, that `Linux IsGreat` will no longer match this regular expression. The reason is that, unlike the asterisk, the plus character must have something in its place.

Another example of quantifiers are the braces. These enable you to specify precisely how many times the preceding item can match. You can specify either one or two numbers inside the braces. If you specify one number only, then you ask that the previous item be matched exactly that many times. If you add a comma after that number, you ask that the previous item be matched no less than the number of times indicated. Finally, if you provide two numbers, you ask that the previous item be matched no less than the first number or no greater than the second. You may also want to note that the asterisk and the plus characters are equivalent to `{0,}` and `{1,}`, respectively.

Here are some examples of the braces in action:

```
Report-.{3,}-finished
Report-.{3,9}-finished
Report-.{9}-finished
```

The first line of text there matches anything with at least three characters in the middle. Some matches include the following:

```
Report-Nov-finished
Report-November-1999-finished
Report-+=?-finished
```

The second line matches anything that has at least three characters but no more than nine in the center. The final line matches anything that has exactly nine characters in the center.

Another powerful feature of quantifiers is that they can be combined with other operators to greatly extend their capabilities. For instance, you could use the following to pick apart a passwd file line in Perl:

```
^([^:]*):([^:]*):([^:]*):([^:]*):([^:]*):([^:]*):([^:]*)$
```

This looks like a strange, convoluted mess, but taken one piece at a time, it makes sense. First, be aware that the pattern needs to match the entire line, so the start-of-line (^) and end-of-line ($) operators are used. Next, you need to match seven different sections of data for which any character except the colon is valid. Some of these sections could be empty; for simplicity's sake, we assume that all of them could be here. So, to match everything except the colon, you use the character class `[^:]`. Then, to indicate that character class applies to zero or more characters, the asterisk follows. These things are enclosed in parentheses, which indicate to Perl that they should be set in the resulting array. Finally, between each parenthesis group, there is a colon, which matches the separator. Let's see if pattest is capable of correctly understanding this pattern:

```
$ ./pattest
Enter pattern or leave empty to exit:
> ^([^:]*):([^:]*):([^:]*):([^:]*):([^:]*):([^:]*):([^:]*)$
Enter string to match:
> pilot:x:1002:1002:Pilot Guy,,,:/home/pilot:/bin/bash
Successful match!
There were 7 strings returned:
String 1: pilot
String 2: x
String 3: 1002
String 4: 1002
String 5: Pilot Guy,,,
String 6: /home/pilot
String 7: /bin/bash
```

Indeed, the match was successful! Notice how each of the seven components of the string is separated into its own element in the array.

Note   Perl also provides a `split` operator that can accomplish this same task with less effort. For details, see the Perl language notes later in this chapter.

Now that you managed to dissect a passwd file line, I'll move on to something more complex: `ls -l` output. First, I'll analyze the output in terms of `ls -l`. For your convenience, here's a reproduction of the data set that was printed from `ls -l` earlier in this chapter:

```
drwxr-xr-x   3 root     root     1024 Feb  7 16:42 CORBA
-rw-r--r--   1 root     root     6350 Jun  9 16:01 Muttrc
-rw-r--r--   1 root     root     1646 Jan 11  1998 adduser.conf
drwxr-xr-x   2 root     root     1024 May 24 19:01 ae
-rw-r--r--   1 root     root      233 Oct 26  1998 aliases.safe
lrwxrwxrwx   1 root     root       27 Jul 12 07:23 localtime -> /usr/share/z
drwxr-xr-x   5 root     root     1024 Jul 18 10:19 texmf
-rw-r--r--   1 root     root      373 Feb 16 11:03 updatedb.conf
-rw-r--r--   1 root     root      222 Sep 30  1998 upload.sites
drwxr-xr-x   4 uucp     uucp     1024 Apr 30 20:31 uucp
-rw-r--r--   1 root     root     4623 Feb 10 15:18 vnc.conf
-rw-r--r--   1 root     root     3293 Sep 28  1998 wgetrc
drwxr-xr-x   3 root     root     1024 Oct 30  1998 xemacs
-rw-r--r--   1 root     root       56 Feb 17 22:18 ytalkrc
```

Our analysis can begin with the basics. The file contains various columns, separated by white space—either spaces or tabs. In Perl, the \s operator represents white space, so this is convenient. In other languages, you'll have to use a character class for that instead. Now then, looking at the first five fields on each line, you can tell that they come in a regular order: permissions, number of hard links, name of the user owning the file, name of the group owning the file, and the file size. The next part is trickier: the date. However, as long as you don't care about exactly what the date is, you will note that with either date format, there are three separate items. The line is then terminated by the filename—usually. If there's a symbolic link, that accounts for one more element.

Because it took a whole paragraph to describe the format, you might imagine that the corresponding regular expression would be somewhat complex. That is, in fact, correct. Here it is:

```
^(\S+)\s+(\S+)\s+(\S+)\s+(\S+)\s+(\S+)\s+(\S+\s+\S+\s+\S+)
\s+([^>]+)( -> .+){0,1}$
```

That's a monster of a regular expression! Even though it appears as two lines here, it is all a single expression. I'll look through each part:

✦ The leading ^ matches the start of the line.

✦ Now, you need to match the mode and permissions area. You can do this by matching everything that is not white space. In Perl, there is a \S operator for this purpose. This is then enclosed in parentheses to indicate that it ought to be returned to Perl for later usage. After all of the permissions data is matched, you have to match the white space separating it from the next entry, which accounts for the \s+. In Perl, \s is used to match white space.

✦ A similar (\S+)\s+ pattern is used to match the hard link count, and return the count (without the trailing white space) into an array.

✦ The same (\S+)\s+ pattern is also used for the name of the owner, the group, and the file size.

✦ When you arrive at the date, the following is used to match it: (\S+\s+\S+\s+\S+) This part of the expression matches three separate fields, separated by at least one character of white space. Because all of these are inside of parentheses, the three fields are returned into one position in the array.

✦ Then, a \s+ matches the space between the date and the filename.

✦ ([^>]+) is the pattern that matches the filename. You may be wondering why I didn't simply use (.+) here instead of the character class. The reason is that the symbolic link is optional. Normally, regular expression operators are greedy; because the symbolic link is optional, the .+ would have slurped up all the remaining text (including any symbolic link, if any) up until the end of the line. By excluding the greater-than sign, through the use of the [^>] character class, you can force the engine to stop matching when it gets to that spot. Because text remains after it, the engine backtracks to the point where the optional symbolic link pattern can take effect.

◆ The optional symbolic link is matched with (-> .+){0,1}. Because the symbolic link is optional, the {0,1} quantifier follows the parentheses indicating this. Inside the parentheses, there is the simple matter of matching the -> symbol and any text that follows it.

◆ Finally, a dollar sign concludes the line.

Try some examples of this in the pattest program. That program shows you exactly what is returned into the array by the parentheses:

```
$ ./pattest
Enter pattern or leave empty to exit:
> ^(\S+)\s+(\S+)\s+(\S+)\s+(\S+)\s+(\S+)\s+(\S+\s+\S+\s+\S+)
\s+([^>]+)( -> .+){0,1}$
Enter string to match:
> drwxr-xr-x   3 root      root           1024 Feb  7 16:42 CORBA
Successful match!
There were 8 strings returned:
String 1: drwxr-xr-x
String 2: 3
String 3: root
String 4: root
String 5: 1024
String 6: Feb  7 16:42
String 7: CORBA
String 8:
```

The pattern worked! All of the components of the listing were separated into separate parts. For the next test, try a line with a date in the other format.

```
Enter pattern, or . to re-use previous, or leave empty to exit:
> .
Enter string to match or . to re-use previous:
> -rw-r--r--   1 root      root           3293 Sep 28  1998 wgetrc
Successful match!
There were 8 strings returned:
String 1: -rw-r--r--
String 2: 1
String 3: root
String 4: root
String 5: 3293
String 6: Sep 28  1998
String 7: wgetrc
String 8:
```

Once again, everything parsed correctly. Notice how string 8 is always empty; this is where the symbolic link will go if it is present. Try a sample that has a symbolic link in it:

```
Enter pattern, or . to re-use previous, or leave empty to exit:
> .
Enter string to match or . to re-use previous:
> lrwxrwxrwx   1 root       root            27 Jul 12 07:23 localtime ->
/usr/share/zoneinfo/CST6CDT
Successful match!
There were 8 strings returned:
String 1: lrwxrwxrwx
String 2: 1
String 3: root
String 4: root
String 5: 27
String 6: Jul 12 07:23
String 7: localtime
String 8:  -> /usr/share/zoneinfo/CST6CDT
```

Success again! This time, the string 8 is filled in with the appropriate data from the symbolic link. Notice, though, that the -> symbol was included here. With the knowledge of regular expressions presented thus far, it's nontrivial to rid yourself of it. However, one option you do have in these situations is to use alternation (discussed later in this chapter) and actually provide two separate options for evaluation in a single regular expression.

From this experience, you can see how simply combining quantifiers with other syntactic elements can provide you with much power. You successfully parsed, with one regular expression, the text from a listing containing either nine or ten fields (depending on whether or not a symbolic link is present) and a total of four different variations. All of this was parsed with a piece of code that occupies slightly more than one line. Parsing the same text requires many more lines, and most likely even greater complexity, in a language that does not have a pattern-matching capability such as regular expressions.

Introducing Alternation and Grouping

You have already seen how character classes work and how extremely powerful then can be. This is great for many types of matching. However, there is an additional situation not covered well by character classes. If you have a set of different options for strings, instead of single characters, that you need matched, character classes do not really help you. This is where alternation comes in. With this capability, you can specify several different options for a match. These options can be as long as you wish, and represent different options the engine can use when trying to find a match for your pattern.

What's more, though, is that these options can use all the standard regular expression operators you've already learned about. That is, you can effectively get a regular expression inside of a regular expression!

The most basic usage of alternation is to provide several separate complete regular expressions. This is done by using the pipe symbol, |, to separate the various options from each other. For instance:

```
Letters from 199[0-246-9]|Doc-.{3}-finished
```

This generates matches such as the following:

```
Letters from 1990
Doc-123-finished
Letters from 1992
Letters from 1994
Doc-GCC-finished
Letters from 1995
Letters from 1996
Letters from 1999
Doc-----finished
```

Notice how extremely different these things are, and how you could match such drastically different strings with a single regular expression. If your data is highly variable, or if it arrives in an unknown order, you can use alternation to help sort it out. This particular usage of alternation is fairly straightforward.

However, alternation is rarely used to split an entire regular expression into pieces. Rather, it is more commonly used to split up pieces inside of a larger expression. To do this, you have to define boundaries of what should be split. These are defined when you use grouping. Grouping separates part of the regular expression to which you want to apply alternation. You can think of it as a similar, but much more powerful, equivalent to Bash's { . . . } operator. Here's an example:

```
(Letter|Report)s (to|from) 199[0-246-9]
```

This regular expression can match a total of 32 (2 letter or report times 2 to or from times 8 digits) different strings. Some of the matching ones include:

```
Letters from 1990
Reports from 1992
Letters to 1999
Reports to 1996
Letters from 1992
Reports from 1994
```

This is a fairly basic usage of grouping compared to some of the more advanced things that are possible, when data arrives in different formats.

Supporting Regular Expressions in Linux

Many different Linux languages have support for regular expressions. This wide support is part of their appeal. However, there are differences between the support in these various languages. Some add their own special extensions that they support. A few of these differences are noted here.

Perl

Of late, Perl has been pushing the envelope with regular expressions, often introducing new features before they appear in other regular expression systems. For details on Perl regular expressions, see the perlre(1) manpageperlre. Many of the Perl syntax options have been mentioned in this chapter, but there are some additional things to mention as well.

$1 Variables

Perl not only returns an array of matching values when you use the parentheses; it sets special variables as well. These variables have names such as $1, $2, $3, and so on, each corresponding to the appropriate match in the string. For instance, consider this code:

```
#!/usr/bin/perl

$val = <STDIN>;
chomp $val;
@VALUES = $val =~ /^Perl is (\S+)\s(.+)$/;
print "Values, first: $VALUES[0]; second: $VALUES[1]\n";
print "Variables, first: $1; second: $2\n";
```

When run, it produces a result like this:

```
$ ./specialvar.pl
Perl is very nice!
Values, first: very; second: nice!
Variables, first: very; second: nice!
```

So you can see that the variables and the array hold the same thing. There are some things to watch out for with the variables, however. The first is that they are overwritten automatically with the next regular expression. Because regular expressions are used quite frequently in many Perl programs, you may be in for a surprise if you try to access a variable, but it has been replaced with data from a different regular expression. The second is that, if you want to pass along a group of matches to somewhere else, an array is better for the task anyway.

The array does have its downsides. For one, if you are simply looking for a quick match that you'll use immediately afterwards, it's an extra hassle to create an array when $1 will do. There can also be a slight performance hit if you do this when the $1 variables will be sufficient.

Regular Expression Operators

In Perl, there are two main regular expression operators: m// and s///. In this chapter, we have been using the m// operator. The leading m is implicit if it is not specified and you are using slashes to delimit the regular expression. The m// is the matching operator, and s/// is the replacement operator, which works like the one in sed.

Each of these can take options, which are specified immediately following the closing slash. You may specify as many as you want; simply put the corresponding character after the slash with no spaces or other separation between them. Table 3-2 lists the options available to you in Perl.

Table 3-2
Perl Regular Expression Options

Option	Behavior
C	The current position within the search is no longer rewound when the g option is specified. Valid for m// only.
E	Indicates to Perl that the replacement part of the operator should also be treated as a regular expression. Valid for s/// only.
G	Causes Perl to use a global search (or replace for s///). Normally, only the first match is found. With this option, Perl continues searching the string for additional possible matches.
I	Causes the regular expression to match strings without regard to case. That is, suspend the normal case-sensitive behavior of regular expressions.
M	Modifies the behavior of ^ and $ such that they match the beginning and end of lines inside the string, instead of the beginning and end of the entire string.
O	Tells Perl that your regular expression should be compiled only one time. This is of primary concern within a loop. If your expression remains constant; that is, any interpolated variables do not change during the course of the loop, you can tell Perl to only compile the expression once. This gives your program a performance benefit.
S	Causes the string to be treated as a single line. Operators such as . will now match the newline character.
X	Allow comments and white space inside the regular expression; see the perlre manpage for more details.

In addition to these options, you have even more. You can use characters other than slashes for your regular expression delimiters. The valid ones are generally the punctuation keys on your keyboard. This is of primary importance when you want to use slashes in your pattern (and thus want to avoid having to escape them inside the pattern, which can make the pattern less readable). As an example, the following code snippets all match the same thing:

```
/usr\/local\/bin\/.*/
m/usr\/local\/bin\/.*/
m'usr/local/bin/.*'
```

The split Operator

One frequently occurring situation in data parsing is that you need to split data based upon a certain separator. This separator could be a single character, as in the colon for the passwd file. Or, it could be a longer string or pattern. With Perl's split operator, you specify the pattern that is used to delimit the different parts. For the passwd file, for instance, this would simply be a colon. This pattern is not included in any of the resulting strings themselves; it's only used to determine where to break them apart.

Recall the pattest program from earlier. With a few simple modifications, it can become a splittest program. Here is the code for splittest:

```
#!/usr/bin/perl

while (1) {
  print "Enter split pattern";
  print ", or . to re-use previous," if ($LASTREGEXP);
  print " or leave empty to exit:\n";
  print "> ";
  $REGEXP = <STDIN>;
  chomp $REGEXP;
  if ($REGEXP eq '.') {
    $REGEXP = $LASTREGEXP;
  }
  exit (0) unless ($REGEXP);
  print "Enter string to match";
  print " or . to re-use previous" if ($LASTSTRING);
  print ":\n";
  print "> ";
  $STRING = <STDIN>;
  chomp $STRING;
  if ($STRING eq '.') {
    $STRING = $LASTSTRING;
  }

  $LASTREGEXP = $REGEXP;
  $LASTSTRING = $STRING;
```

```
  @MATCHES = split(/$REGEXP/, $STRING);
  print "There were " . ($#MATCHES + 1) . " strings returned:
\n";
  $counter = 0;
  foreach $MATCH (@MATCHES) {
    $counter++;
    print "String $counter: $MATCH\n";
  }
  print "\n\n";
}
```

You can test the `split` operator by using a simple regular expression suitable for splitting apart passwd file lines. Remember that the regular expression for the `split` operator is one that matches the delimiter:

```
$ ./splittest
Enter split pattern or leave empty to exit:
> :
Enter string to match:
> pilot:x:1002:1002:Pilot Guy,,,:/home/pilot:/bin/bash
There were 7 strings returned:
String 1: pilot
String 2: x
String 3: 1002
String 4: 1002
String 5: Pilot Guy,,,
String 6: /home/pilot
String 7: /bin/bash
```

In this case, a single-character regular expression is able to pick apart the passwd file entries — much simpler than the previous one. You can try it again on another line, just to make sure it isn't a fluke:

```
Enter split pattern, or . to re-use previous, or leave empty to
exit:
> :
Enter string to match or . to re-use previous:
> www-data:x:33:33:www-data:/var/www:/bin/sh
There were 7 strings returned:
String 1: www-data
String 2: x
String 3: 33
String 4: 33
String 5: www-data
String 6: /var/www
String 7: /bin/sh
```

Again, the match is successful. Now, try something more complicated. You can give pattest a regular expression to match, and then modify passwd file lines a bit to see what happens:

```
$ ./splittest
Enter split pattern or leave empty to exit:
> [:|]
Enter string to match:
> pilot:x:1002:1002|Pilot Guy|/home/pilot|/bin/bash
There were 7 strings returned:
String 1: pilot
String 2: x
String 3: 1002
String 4: 1002
String 5: Pilot Guy
String 6: /home/pilot
String 7: /bin/bash
```

This time, Perl is told to match either the colon or the pipe as a separator. As you can see, when some of the colons are changed to pipe symbols in the passwd file line, Perl is still able to split the line apart.

sed and awk

These two languages use essentially the same regular expression support, which is fairly standard regular expression syntax. Some important additions to these languages are the character class operators such as [[:alpha:]]. These are useful not only as shortcuts, but also because the notion of what constitutes an alphanumeric character varies between locales. For instance, some languages contain characters with umlauts, while English does not. Using simply [A-Za-z] can mean that your programs will parse data incorrectly when used outside of English-speaking areas.

The info page for gawk (GNU awk) describes regular expressions as used in both sed and gawk.

C/C++

Neither C nor C++ has built-in support for regular expressions. However, several libraries are available to add such support. One that is recommended these days is Philip Hazel's Perl-Compatible Regular Expression (pcre) library. It comes with some distributions. If yours doesn't have it, you may find it via anonymous FTP to cus.cam.ac.uk in the directory /pub/software/programs/pcre.

Summary

This chapter discussed the usage of regular expressions. Specifically, you learned:

✦ Parsing jobs find patterns in data.

✦ Regular expressions are used to indicate what these patterns are.

✦ Many different languages have regular expression support, and there are some differences between their implementations.

✦ A tool called egrep enables you to search through a file for lines matching a certain regular expression.

✦ The sed command enables you to use regular expressions to make modifications to data as it passes through.

✦ Perl has support for regular expressions as an integral part of the language.

✦ You use character classes to specify which characters can match at a given point. You also can negate them by using the ^ symbol.

✦ Quantifiers are used to indicate how many times the preceding item can match. When combined with character classes, they form a powerful way of matching text.

✦ Parentheses can be used both to indicate items to be returned (or placed in a variable) and to indicate grouping. When using grouping combined with alternation, you achieve the powerful capability of using a regular expression nested inside another.

✦ Perl also provides a `split` command, which is useful when you break apart data that is separated by a certain pattern.

✦ The sed and gawk systems add some unique options that act like a character class.

✦ You can also find regular expression libraries for C.

✦   ✦   ✦

Introducing Emacs

As you program in Linux, no doubt you will run into the two editors that form the mainstay in the arsenal of Linux and UNIX programmers: *vi* and *Emacs*, and their derivatives. These two editors have been around for years and predate Linux itself. In this chapter, I cover the Emacs editor, which is an IDE (Integrated Development Environment) as well as an editor. You'll learn about the different flavors of Emacs, how to use the different modes in Emacs, the IDE features of Emacs, and getting help from Emacs.

Emacs 101

Emacs comes in several flavors. Your first task in using the system is going to be picking which flavor to use. The standard version is GNU Emacs from the FSF (Free Software Foundation). There are also several derivatives of GNU Emacs that you can use. Among them, the most popular is *XEmacs*. XEmacs is, in large part, compatible with GNU Emacs but adds a much better graphical interface to the system. Both XEmacs and GNU Emacs are powerful, full-featured editors with interfaces for both X and the console. You may use GNU Emacs instead of XEmacs for the examples in this chapter; the screenshots and the menus will look a bit different, but other than that, all will be the same. The two editors are sometimes collectively referred to as *Emacsen*.

Figure 4-1 shows the startup screen of XEmacs. As soon as you press any key, you will be taken to the `*scratch*` buffer, which you can use as a temporary scratchpad.

From here on, the screenshots and examples in this chapter will focus in XEmacs.

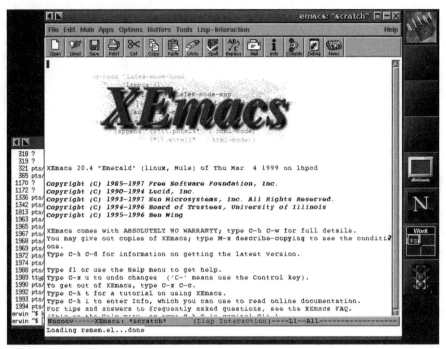

Figure 4-1: The XEmacs startup screen

Emacs key notation

The first thing you will learn about is the key notation in Emacs. The Emacs key sequence notation is used to specify keyboard combinations that are used to invoke commands. They are shown to you by the XEmacs menus, by online help, and by other documentation. For the purposes of consistency in this chapter, I will refer to key notation as is done in Emacs and XEmacs.

Emacs and XEmacs were both designed to be completely operable without any sort of GUI or pointing device (such as a mouse). As such, you can operate the system completely by using the keyboard. Many programmers prefer to do this, even when running the system in a graphical environment, because it is faster than moving the hands from the keyboard to the mouse. Others prefer to use the mouse extensively. Either approach is possible; you'll learn which you prefer after working with the system for some time.

Because of the tremendous number of features available in the XEmacs system, some have multi-key combinations to access. Even if you don't like to use these key combinations, you can still use the mouse; or completely reconfigure the keyboard in XEmacs.

The key notation used in Emacsen is as follows:

✦ Keys that should be pressed simultaneously are separated by dashes.

✦ Keys that should be pressed and then released in a series are separated by spaces.

✦ C is used to represent the Control key.

✦ M is used to represent the Meta key. On PC keyboards, this will be one of the Alt keys, or perhaps a Windows key, depending on how your distribution configures the keyboard. If you can't find the key, you can press and release Esc to function as the Meta key — in fact, in some terminal situations, this is the only way to do so.

✦ RET is used to represent your Return or Enter key.

For instance, this is how you save the current file in Emacs:

```
C-x C-s
```

Press Ctrl, and then press X. Do the same for S. Note that it is not necessary to release Ctrl between the two keys; you can simply hold it down. Some other applications might describe the same action as Ctrl+X+S.

Sometimes, you are asked to type a word. For instance, you might see the following:

```
M-x query-replace RET
```

This means to press M-x (probably Alt+X, or Esc X), and then type the word **query-replace**, and then press Return (Enter).

As an alternative to these key combinations, you can use the menus. For instance, you may navigate to the File menu and select Save. The XEmacs menus conveniently list the keyboard shortcuts, so you can pick them up as you go.

Now I will show you how to load a file into XEmacs and edit it. I will use the second example file from Chapter 10, "Debugging with gdb;" if you want to work with the same file on your system, you may find it printed at the end of Chapter 10.

To load the file, you may use C-x C-f from the keyboard. You may also choose Open from the File menu. If you use the former, you will be given an area in which to type the filename at the bottom of your XEmacs window; this area is called the *minibuffer*. If you choose to use the menus, and are using X, you will be given a navigation box. You may type the filename or use the mouse to find one; highlight and middle-click on your choice. The file will now load into the editor.

Tip   If your mouse has two buttons instead of three, you will not have a middle mouse button. In most cases, you can simulate the middle button by pressing the left and right buttons simultaneously.

At this point, you should be aware of the following important key combinations:

✦ C-g is a cancel key, which generally exits any special mode you may be in or cancels any current command.

✦ C-x C-c is used to exit Emacs.

✦ C-h enters the help area. C-h i brings up the GNU info browser; C-h a brings up apropos, which you can use to search for information on a topic.

✦ C-x C-f is used to load a new file into Emacs.

✦ C-x C-s is used to save the current file.

✦ C-x k is used to tell Emacs to close the current buffer.

Navigation

When you run Emacs or XEmacs under X, many of the keys you may be accustomed to already will work. These include the arrow keys, Page Up, Page Down, Backspace, Home, End, Insert, Ctrl+Home, and Ctrl+End. Although this is great when you run Emacs or XEmacs under X, it is not so great when you run these editors in a terminal. Many terminal emulation programs do not have the correct implementation of these keys, or the keys are simply not defined for a given terminal. In those cases, you can use the following keys as a substitute:

✦ M-< (same as Esc+Shift+comma) positions the cursor at the top of the document. C-Home may also do the same thing.

✦ M-> positions the cursor at the bottom of the document. C-End may also do the same thing.

✦ C-a positions the cursor at the start of the current line. You can think of this as going to the start of the line, just as the letter a is at the start of the alphabet. Home may also do the same thing for you.

✦ C-e positions the cursor at the end of the current line. The End key may also do the same thing for you.

Finally, you will often need to go to a specific line number within a file. To do this, press M-g, and then the number, and then RET. If you are using a very old version of Emacs, you may need to type M-x goto-line RET instead of M-g.

Tip   You can ask Emacs to display the line number of your current line on the status bar. To enable this, type M-x line-number-mode RET.

Searching

Emacs has a unique interactive search feature. With this feature, the system starts the search immediately as you begin typing. You can see how each additional letter affects the result right as you type it; often, you don't even need to finish typing the search word or phrase you were looking for.

To start a search, press C-s. You will be prompted for the search phrase. You may type it at this point. If you find your match, press Enter and you'll be returned to the document. If you want to search with the same term again, simply press C-s again; do not press Enter until you have completely finished your search. Figure 4-2 shows what your screen will look like when you are partially done typing in the search word, **getinput**.

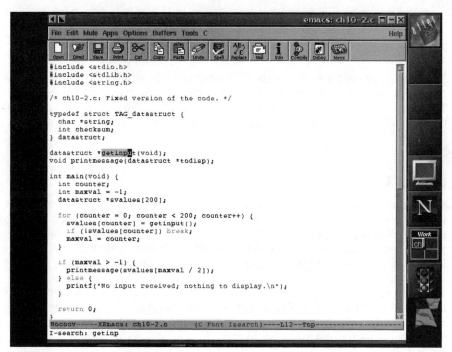

Figure 4-2: Search in progress

You can also recall a previous search term by pressing C-s C-s when starting a new search. Just remember to press Enter when you have found the item you were looking for.

You may also press C-g to cancel a search; this returns your cursor to the location prior to beginning the search.

The Emacs region

When you wish to perform a particular operation on a certain part of text in Emacs, you activate the region. You can do this by simply highlighting the block with the mouse. Alternatively, you may do the same with the keyboard after enabling the region. When using the keyboard, first move to one end of the region — either the start or the end — and then press C-@ (Ctrl+Shift+2). Now, position the cursor to the other end of the region. At this point, you are ready to do something with the region.

You could use it in a manner akin to the clipboard in other applications. Here are the commonly used commands for such a usage:

✦ You can cut the text with C-w.

✦ You can copy the text with M-w.

✦ You can paste a copy of previously cut or copied text with C-y (the "y" stands for "yank").

You can use any of these commands either after highlighting text with the mouse or with the keyboard. There are many more commands that operate on a region. These commands can do things as varied as indenting the whole region, wrapping the text in it, or turning it into a large comment in your current programming language.

Buffers

Emacs allows you to open many files at once. When you do this, you are working with several *buffers* in Emacs. A buffer in Emacs is simply an area that you use to edit files. When you open a file with C-x C-f, Emacs creates a buffer in which you edit the file. You can open other files in additional buffers with the same command. If you want, you can load up another file. Now, both files are present in your editor.

There are several ways to switch between buffers in your current window. The first is to use the Buffers menu. The contents of that menu are set to include all the different buffers that are open at the moment. You can switch between them by selecting the buffer that you wish to edit.

You can also switch buffers by using the keyboard. The command for this is C-x b. If you press RET at this point, you'll be switched immediately to the buffer that you were editing prior to this one. Otherwise, you may type the name of the buffer to which you will switch. Finally, you may simply press Tab to display a list of buffers available as shown in Figure 4-3. You may then type the name of the buffer you wish to use, or middle-click it.

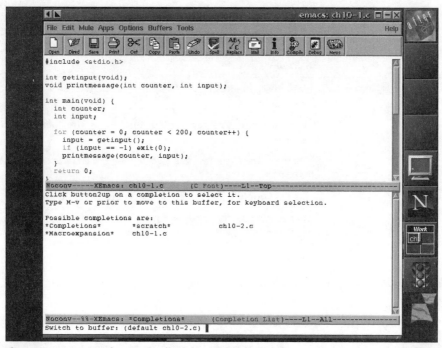

Figure 4-3: Press Tab to see a list of available buffers

Windows

Switching buffers is a powerful way to work with multiple files, but another powerful option is windows. These are separate areas on the screen. You can work on different sections of the same buffer in these separate windows, or you can work on separate buffers. The windows can be tiled horizontally or vertically.

When you create or remove a window, the buffers being edited are not modified. When a window is closed, the buffer in which you are editing the file is not closed; you can still switch to all your buffers as described in the previous Buffers section.

Table 4-1 lists the key commands that you can use to work with multiple windows. You can find equivalent options for most of these key commands under the File menu.

When you first use a command such as C-x 2 to split a window, you may want to load separate files into each one. If you already have multiple buffers going, you may use C-x b or the Buffers menu in one. Alternatively, you may open new files in each window. You can even have two windows working on different parts of the same file.

Table 4-1
Window-Related Key Sequences

Key Command	Function
C-x 0	Deletes the current window. The buffer is unaffected. Note that this is the number zero.
C-x 1	Deletes all windows except for the current one. The buffers are unaffected.
C-x 2	Splits the current window into two separate ones, one on top of the other.
C-x 3	Splits the current window into two separate ones, side-by-side.
C-x o	Switches to the other window. You can also do this by clicking in it. Note that this is a letter O, not a number zero.

It's even possible to split windows several ways as shown in Figure 4-4.

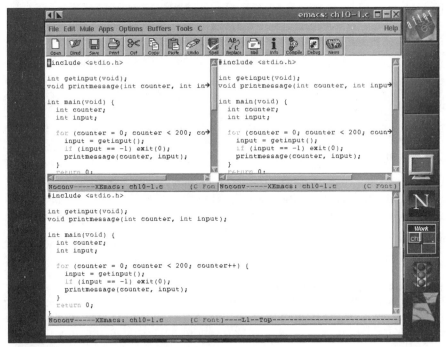

Figure 4-4: An example of split windows

To create the display as shown in Figure 4-4, start by splitting the current screen with C-x 2. Then, select the top window and press C-x 3. Thus, you can split windows multiple times.

When you're done with windows, you can press C-x 0 and C-x 1 to get rid of them. Pressing C-x 0 removes only the current window; pressing C-x 1 removes all windows except the current one.

Frames

When you are running Emacs in X, you have access to another powerful feature: separate frames. Frames act as windows, except they are created in a separate top-level window on your X display. Because of this, you cannot use frames in a terminal.

A new frame is created with C-x 5 2 and the current frame is deleted with C-x 5 0. It is important to remember that even when you have several frames, they all belong to a single editor. Thus, you can switch between your various buffers in each of them.

Additionally, inside each separate frame, you can create multiple windows (as shown in Figure 4-5).

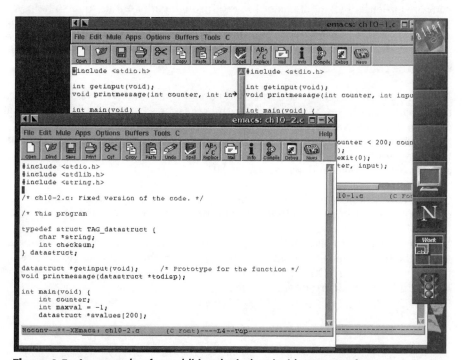

Figure 4-5: An example of an additional window inside separate frames

You can use your window manager's standard controls for moving and resizing your frames because they act as normal X windows.

Because all these frames correspond to a single Emacs process, when you exit Emacs with C-x C-c, all will be closed. The same applies to saving files; because the buffers are the same, but displayed in different frames, saving a buffer one place effects the buffer in every frame.

Syntax and paren highlighting

For this section, you might want to open up a C file for editing in XEmacs. Start the session by turning on syntax and paren highlighting. Go to the Options menu, select Syntax Highlighting, and then Colors. Go back to Options ⇨ Syntax Highlighting and choose Most. From the Paren Highlighting menu in Options, select Expression. Notice how XEmacs has highlighted the syntax for you. Strings are green; C keywords are highlighted in yellow, comments are red, variables and preprocessor directives are blue, and data types are purple. XEmacs understands the syntax of dozens of languages, including all of the ones covered here. To the greatest extent possible, XEmacs uses the same colors for syntax highlighting between all the different supported languages. If you now select Save Options from the Options menu, XEmacs automatically enables syntax highlighting for you each time you use it.

Syntax highlighting is a tremendous benefit to programmers. Not only does it make your life easier by making it easier to read through code, but it can also help you write good code. Consider, for instance, if you mistakenly forget to close a string with a quotation mark. The code that you type after that will remain green, instead of its proper color. You can immediately notice that there was a problem while writing the code.

Another powerful feature is the so-called *paren highlighting*. This feature highlights more than parentheses; it also works with braces, brackets, and other items that occur in pairs. As you write code, or even as you move through it, the system highlights the expression matched by your delimiters. This is great for ensuring that all your parentheses and braces are lined up properly—failure to do this is a major cause of bugs and syntax errors later.

Consider the example from this screenshot. XEmacs highlighted a portion of the code, starting at the opening brace that corresponds to the closing brace.

Your entire expression is highlighted; you can see instantly which statements fall within the boundaries of the block. If you make a mistake and your delimiters no longer match properly, XEmacs can sometimes detect this even as you write code, and highlights the incorrect area in pink.

Major Modes

In Emacs, whenever you edit a file, you do so in a particular mode. This mode enables Emacs to provide additional or specialized capabilities, depending on the specific type of file you are editing. Programmers appreciate capabilities such as syntax highlighting, commenting assistance, automatic indentation, controlled reindentation, and several other features.

C

The C mode is one of the most well-known and full-featured modes in XEmacs. As you've already seen, it has syntax and paren highlighting features. However, the features go much farther than that.

Indentation

One of the most powerful features in the C mode is the indentation support. This feature enables you to get proper indentation for your code, and also to re-indent code should the need arise. The primary key to do this is the Tab key. When you edit code in Emacs, the Tab key does not insert a tab character as it does in other editors. Instead, it automatically indents your current line to the proper position. As an example, consider what happens if the code is not properly indented, as shown in Figure 4-6.

Figure 4-6: An example of bad indentation

If you want to fix this problem, you can move your cursor to each line and press Tab, once per line. You don't even have to put the cursor at the start of the line; anywhere on the line will do. In this case, it's generally best to start with indenting from the top of the code sample as opposed to the end. This way, Emacs can learn the proper indentation from your code as an example.

Another powerful feature enables you to define for XEmacs which style of indentation you prefer. This is used when the system does automatic indentation for you. The command to do this is `M-x c-set-style RET` or simply `C-c`. XEmacs prompts you for your selection. Select `bsd` for these examples.

You can now re-indent the entire document according to the BSD style. To do this, highlight the entire document, and then run `M-x indent-region`. You can also do this entirely from the keyboard by specifically using the following key sequence:

```
M-< C-@ M-> M-x indent-region RET
```

Emacs then re-indents your file. In this case, the primary difference you'll notice is that more space is being used for indentation. However, even if you don't use indentation, the result will be the same; Emacs will indent the entire file as appropriate.

Comments

One of the most important aspects of writing maintainable code is good documentation. You often do this in the form of comments. The C mode in Emacs contains a good deal of support for helping you write comments.

One useful command is `M-;` — so named because the semicolon is the comment character in *LISP*, the language from which the internal programming language of Emacs is derived.

When you press `M-;` the editor set up a comment, indented to the right. Now you can type your comment in the area as if you had set up your own.

Emacs can do more than create placeholders for comments. It also can comment or uncomment large sections of code. Although this definitely is not good practice in production-quality code, you sometimes need to do this for debugging or tracking purposes while developing.

If you highlight some text, you can see how this works. After highlighting the text, press `C-c C-c` or choose Comment Out Region from the C menu.

Figure 4-7 shows a screenshot of the result.

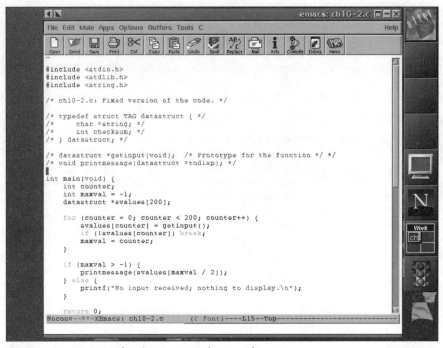

Figure 4-7: An example of commented-out code

Notice how Emacs automatically commented out the lines in the area. However, on line 12, there is an issue. A comment was already on that line, and C is not a language that permits embedded comments. So, at this point, compilation will fail because of the problem on line 12.

You also can remove the comments; highlight the same region and select Uncomment Region from the C menu. Emacs removes all the comments that it added.

Preprocessor Expansion

Emacs can run a portion of your code through the C preprocessor so that you can see the effect of macros, conditional compilation, and include statements on your code. For instance, consider the effect of the following screenshot:

To achieve this effect for yourself, follow these steps:

1. Type the code as you see it in the top window.

2. Highlight it as a region.

3. Press C-c C-e to invoke the macro expansion. You also can select Macro Expand Region from the C menu to do this.

Emacs then creates a second window and displays the result of the macro expansion there — you can see that the CALCULATE macro was expanded in this case. If you have any #include lines, and you expand that region, the entire included file will appear in the result. Therefore, you may wish to be cautious when expanding those lines, lest you have a huge amount of output to wade through to find something useful.

Auto State

The C environment in Emacs also has more features to help speed the development process. When running in auto mode, the C environment automatically takes care of inserting new lines, dealing with indentation, and other related tasks while you type. In many cases, this means you don't need to press Enter while you are coding; the system takes care of that automatically.

To engage auto mode, press C-c C-a or run M-x c-toggle-auto-state RET. As you type while in this mode, you'll notice that whenever you press the semicolon, the editor automatically positions your cursor on the next line, properly indented. Your code can end up looking exactly the same as if you had not used auto mode; it simply takes you fewer keystrokes to create.

If at some time you wish to turn the auto mode off again, simply press C-c C-a or run M-x c-toggle-auto-state. The system will return to normal behavior.

Perl mode

Emacs editors typically also have very strong support for Perl programming. The Perl mode found in modern flavors of Emacs is very powerful indeed. You should be aware that there are several different implementations of a Perl mode floating around, and several different versions of each of these. Therefore, you may have a different implementation than the one shown in this section. However, many things are quite similar between the different implementations of a Perl mode in Emacs in general. Current versions of Emacs generally come with a mode named CPerl, which is a powerful Perl mode with a number of advanced features.

Note

One of the challenges of writing an Emacs mode for Perl is that the Perl syntax can be difficult to parse because of its many features and different ways of doing things. You may find that, if you take frequent advantage of the more esoteric features of Perl, occasionally your syntax highlighting may be off; however, usually you won't see any problems other than those.

Several modes in Emacs are based on the C mode; you'll find that the Perl mode is no exception. Many of the keystrokes for doing various commands related to comments and indentations are the same. For instance, to insert a comment to the right on the current line, C-; is still the correct key.

There are some unique features of the CPerl mode in Emacs. One is that it can display the syntax for various functions directly within Emacs. To do this, move your cursor over the item on which you want help, and press C-c C-h v. The status line in Perl displays a syntax summary of the option.

Some versions of the CPerl mode also have extra support for dealing with POD (Plain Old Documentation) documentation in your Perl files. You can investigate these options under the Perl menu. Some options under Perl docs in the menu include a way to view the result of the POD in the file being edited, and other options include rescanning for PODs and here-documents.

Other modes

Emacs comes with editing modes for virtually every language you might work with. Some of the other modes that you may find useful in Linux include shell scripts, Makefiles, LISP, Prolog, LaTeX, plain text, and many more. Most of them try to use the same keystrokes that were popularized with the C or LISP modes. Therefore, you won't have to re-learn your commands when editing different types of files.

Occasionally, Emacs may not be able to determine automatically which mode to use for a specific file. This could happen, for instance, when you edit a file with no extension. You can switch modes manually with a command such as M-x c-mode, but you can tell Emacs to use a different mode automatically.

You can do this by adding a line near the top of your file to specify the mode. The following example has one in its second line. You will want to comment it out by using whatever syntax is appropriate for the language you're editing. For instance, if you're editing a Perl script, you might start it out like this:

```
#!/usr/bin/perl
# -*- Mode: Perl; -*-
```

When you load a file that contains this comment into your editor, Emacs automatically switches to the appropriate Perl mode.

Emacs as an IDE

Emacs is more than a basic programmer's editor. The Emacs system includes support for integrated compilation and debugging of your programs. This support enables you to work with building, running, and debugging programs from numerous languages — all without leaving the Emacs environment.

In Emacs, there is an emphasis on *integrated*. Other IDEs offer you an editor, an interface to a build system, and a debugger from a single interface. Compared to

Emacs, these systems look positively outdated. Emacs offers those basic features. In addition, it enables you to run your programs within the system, and even multitask with them, to examine their output with features such as the built-in web browser to read your e-mail with one of the several built-in mail readers. With Emacs, you can also cut and paste directly with your code or debugger to telnet elsewhere, and even play some games after a long day of programming—all without ever leaving the Emacs environment.

Every one of these features is completely customizable. Thanks to the ELISP programming language that is behind much of Emacs, if the built-in ways to exchange data between these different components aren't sufficient for you, you can script and automate the coordination completely to your every whim.

So are all these things really useful for development? Absolutely; although perhaps we should exclude the games from this list. When you are sitting comfortably at your own Linux machine, you can run all the various separate programs in X that you want. You can have your own web browser, your own debugger, your own shell windows, and so on. However, you are not always so lucky. Many programmers need to work through a text-only terminal, where the integration in Emacs is very important.

Even if you are working solely in X, the benefits of having components in Emacs fully integrated and scriptable can be a tremendous asset to your development process. For instance, you can press a single hotkey while reading your e-mail that can cause the contents of your message to be piped to your newly compiled program, and display the output in a web browser as HTML.

Compiling programs

Emacs enables you to compile your software while in the Emacs environment. When you do this, the editor can tie together the output from the compilers with the code of your program. This means that you can jump instantly to the location of an error or warning by simply middle-clicking it.

You can find such options under the Tools menu. When you select Compile from that menu, Emacs asks you for a compile command. If you have a Makefile, you can accept the default. Otherwise, you will want to supply the compilation command line appropriate for your program.

If your compilation has any errors or warnings, Emacs shows them in a separate window as shown in Figure 4-8.

Now, if you middle-click (or move the cursor to the location and press Enter) the error message, you will be taken to the location of the error in your source. In this case, the problem is simple: a capitalization error. Sometimes, your output may contain hundreds of warnings; being able to skip directly to each one can be a huge time saver.

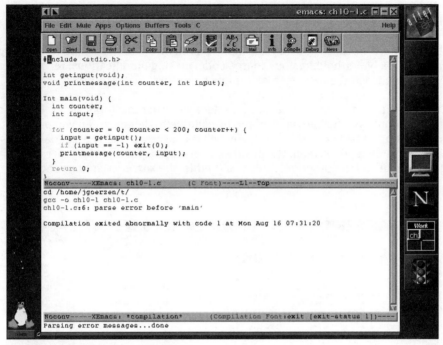

Figure 4-8: Error Display in XEmacs

As you may have noticed, the default for the compile command is an invocation of make. Emacs is perfectly capable of working with make and dealing with multiple files; there is no need to worry about Emacs support for large projects.

Debugging

Many integrated development environments provide a debugger. Although many provide a limited debugger, XEmacs provides a full-fledged interface to the powerful gdb debugger.

Cross-Reference For more details on using gdb, see Chapter 5, "Understanding Linux Data Files and Scripts."

When you use gdb in XEmacs, you get all the standard gdb features that you get when it is run any other way. However, some additional features are included as well, mostly by way of interface improvements.

To start with, when you debug a program using gdb in XEmacs, you can watch your own code file as execution proceeds through the program. This option is much easier to use than the default gdb operation, which displays only the current instruction.

Furthermore, because you can recompile directly from XEmacs, and the debugger runs with a buffer holding your source code, making modifications, recompiling, and rerunning in the debugger is a simple operation.

To invoke the debugger inside Emacs, select gdb from the Tools menu. The system then prompts you for the name of the executable to debug. When you provide the name, gdb will be invoked. At first, you will see a screen that is essentially the same as the standard gdb screen. Go ahead and set a breakpoint at the program entry point and begin the program. After you do this, the screen is split as shown in Figure 4-9.

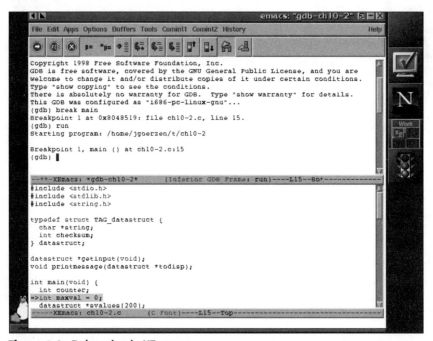

Figure 4-9: Debugging in XEmacs

The editor now highlights your current point of execution in the source for your program. There is no longer any need for gdb to display the code because it is now available directly from your Emacs window; therefore, the code output is omitted in the gdb window.

In the gdb window, you can use all of your traditional gdb commands; you don't need to learn any new commands when you use gdb in Emacs. For instance, if you decide to watch how variables change over time, you can use the display command in the gdb window exactly as you would in standard gdb. The lower window continues to trace through your code as it executes, regardless of the variables you are watching in the upper window.

You also may use gdb with a corefile in Emacs. To do so, invoke it with `M-x gdb-with-core`. This time, Emacs prompts you for the program and the name of the core file.

Using tags

Another powerful feature of Emacs is the capability of using tags. With these tags, the editor can identify which files belong to a single project. More importantly, the tags indicate exactly what is in each of these files. For instance, with C programs, the tags can indicate which file contains a given function. When editing your files, then, you can skip directly to any function — regardless of the file in which it is located. Moreover, you can apply various commands to the entire group of files instead of your current file only. For instance, a search operation could affect all files in the group.

To provide you with this functionality, Emacs needs to analyze your files and store information about the tags to be used with them. Traditionally, you do this by using a file named TAGS. You generate this file by running the etags program at the command line, giving it the names of the files you wish to index. For instance:

```
$ etags *.c
```

The etags program analyzes your source code and produces a TAGS file for use inside Emacs.

Now, you can use the Tags options in the Tools menu to navigate through your files. You might want to start with Find Tag (`M-.`) to see what happens. For example, type a function name. Emacs skips directly to the file containing that function, opening it if necessary, and positions your cursor on the line of its start. If the function appears in more than one file, you can continue to search for additional instances of it by using `M-` (that's ESC+comma).

Shells in Emacs

Emacs is much more than a run-of-the-mill editor. In fact, it is often billed as the editor that includes everything *and* the kitchen sink! One unique feature of Emacs is the capability of running a shell inside the editor — and using commands more reminiscent of a text editor to manipulate your command line. Some users absolutely love this feature; others really dislike it. You may or may not like to use it for yourself, but you can at least give it a try.

You can fire up a shell by typing M-x shell RET. You will receive a screen that looks like an ordinary shell window, albeit with various Emacs decorations around it. But do not be fooled; this window is anything but ordinary.

Try typing a command such as an ls command. If you're running in XEmacs and have color highlighting turned on, you'll notice immediately that your commands are highlighted for you.

When you enter your ls command, you see a directory output as is usual. Now press the up arrow. Instead of accessing a command history, you are moving about within the shell area—both with the program output and with your commands. You can even edit this output from other programs on-screen. After doing that, you can use the output as a command, or even save the buffer containing your interactions to a disk file as a transcript of your session.

Experiment a bit. For instance, after running an ls command, you can move the cursor back up to some output and press Enter. Emacs instantly copies the entire line of output underneath your cursor to the shell command prompt, as shown in Figure 4-10.

Figure 4-10: Running a shell in Emacs

At this point, if you press Enter, Emacs sends the command to the shell. Otherwise, you can make modifications to it before you send it to the shell and then press Enter. Either way, you have a new capability: directly moving the cursor through output and easily using it on the command line.

Another interesting capability of the shell is that, in some situations, Emacs can become aware of your command history with the shell. This extends beyond the involvement of Emacs all the way to the shell itself as shown in Figure 4-11.

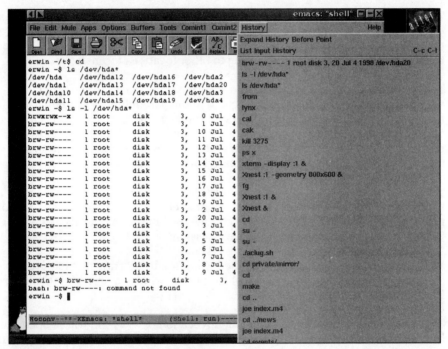

Figure 4-11: Using the Shell with Emacs

Even though most of the commands that Emacs lists are not issues from inside XEmacs but from a separate shell, they are still recognized by the editor.

Also note that certain functions in Emacs use the shell mode for interaction. The gdb interaction is one such situation. The features of the shell environment are thus available there as well.

The shell environment does have some drawbacks. Because it takes control of the terminal under which the shell is running, full-screen terminal-based programs such as Elm will not function properly. If you still need those features, you can use the term feature found in newer Emacsen.

The term mode

Current versions of Emacs ship with a term mode. This is a full-fledged terminal emulator in which you can run any full-screen applications such as Elm, ircII, or various other applications that use the terminal. The advantages of running programs inside Emacs like this include the capability of running multiple commands at once, even with a single terminal. With the capability of opening several windows in your Emacs session, you can view multiple programs at once — without needing to resort to a graphical system such as X.

This convenience comes as a cost, however. Because Emacs essentially must pass through commands verbatim and receive data in the same manner, you don't get the fancy editing support of the shell mode. Nevertheless, the term mode can be useful — especially if you are telnetting to other locations for instance.

You may also wonder: if all the data must be passed through to the terminal verbatim, how can commands be executed in the parent Emacs system? You have two options: you can use a mouse if you're running Emacs in X, or you can use the escape character. The escape character is C-c by default. When you press C-c, the characters you type after that are interpreted by Emacs instead of sent to the terminal. If you need to send ato the underlying terminal, you can press C-c twice.

You invoke term mode by typing M-x term RET. After you type this, Emacs prompts you for the command to run — your shell by default. Accept the default and use your shell. In Figure 4-12, you can see the full-screen interface of Midnight Commander running inside your XEmacs session!

You can run multiple programs with tiled windows, by starting up multiple instances of a term. It is generally best to split the windows first, and then invoke the term.

There is a trick here. Normally, a second invocation of M-x term will re-open the first buffer. In order to prevent this, you need to rename the first buffer. To do this, you need to issue a command to Emacs; the escape character doesn't provide this by default, so you need to switch the terminal into line mode, issue the command, and then switch it back. You can do so with the following command:

```
C-c C-j M-x rename-uniquely RET C-c C-k
```

Now, you get to invoke another terminal. Figure 4-13 shows XEmacs running with two terminal windows. The top window is actually running its own copy of XEmacs inside the parent copy of XEmacs; the bottom window is running the ircII chat program.

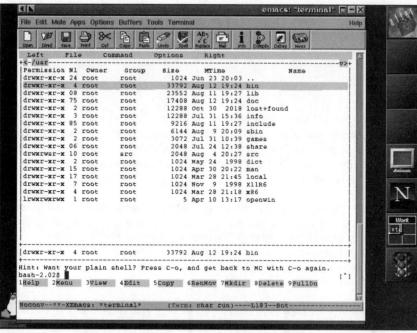

Figure 4-12: Midnight Commander inside a term window

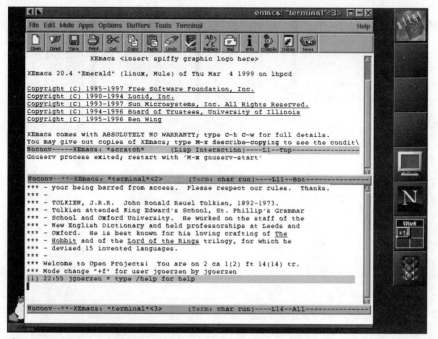

Figure 4-13: Two terms in XEmacs

Using this windowing capability is not limited to the X interface. You can also do this when running Emacs in a simple terminal—this is probably the most powerful application of the term because normally, you do not have windowing capabilities with a simple terminal.

Dired

Thus far, you've seen that the IDE that is Emacs includes support for compiling, debugging, running, and multitasking with your programs. You also get support for managing your files through a mode called Dired. Dired can be used as a simple file picker, or as a file manager. It runs inside of Emacs, and thus is integrated completely with the system.

You invoke Dired by specifying a directory instead of a filename when opening a file. For instance, you might specify C-c C-f /usr to open Dired on the /usr directory. When Dired starts, you get output resembling that from the ls -l command. From here, you can move the cursor to a line and press Enter to edit the file—or display the directory. As usual, if you are using the mouse, you may middle-click the appropriate area to do the same.

The XEmacs menus for Dired are excellent because you have many options from the menus. The character commands for Dired can be difficult to remember, especially if you don't use them frequently, so consider the menus your friends. Figure 4-14 shows Dired operating on the /usr directory, with the Do menu pulled down.

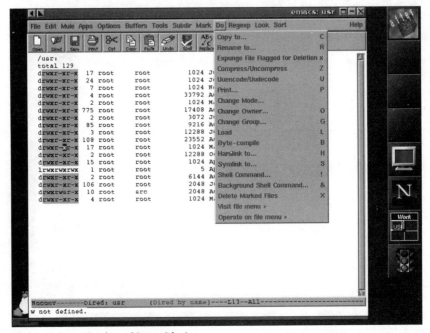

Figure 4-14: Dired working with /usr

w3

The built-in web browser available for Emacs is w3. This is a web browser that, when run under a system such as XEmacs, features full support for graphics, tables, and several other modern niceties. Although you may find better rendering with a program such as Netscape, you'll probably find that it's very convenient to have a browser integrated into Emacs. To invoke the w3 browser, run M-x w3 RET, or select it from the Apps menu in XEmacs.

When it opens, you see an introduction screen such as that shown in Figure 4-15. The operation of this browser is similar to that of others with which you may be familiar; the button bar and the menu bar both are modified to have web-specific items in them. The primary difference to be aware of from the start is that the middle button is used to follow links instead of the left button as is customary with other browsers.

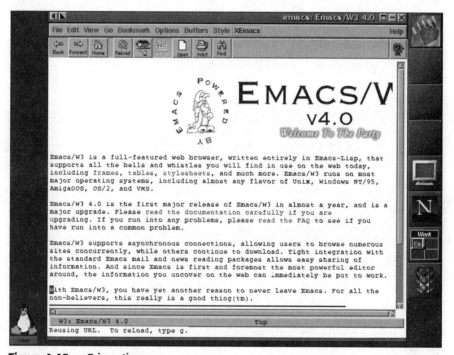

Figure 4-15: w3 in action

Gnus

Not satisfied with only being able to read mail, telnet, surf the web, write programs, run debuggers, and play Tetris from within an editor, the Emacs programmers set out to write Gnus — a mail and Usenet news reader written solely in ELISP and integrated into Emacs.

Gnus is invoked by either running M-x gnus RET or by selecting the appropriate option from the Apps menu. The Gnus system presents, in traditional Emacs fashion, an integrated interface for reading mail and news, along with message filtering, pre- and post-processing, scoring, and many more options that can be applied to both. Again as with Emacs itself, Gnus is completely scriptable and, with ELISP, can be customized in virtually infinite ways.

Gnus is configured through a .gnus file. This file defines where mail and news come from, how they are split, and also any additional customizations. For details on this file, you may consult the online info documentation for Gnus or the information on the website at www.gnus.org.

Figure 4-16 shows a system that uses Gnus to read a multitude of e-mail. The listing on the screen is a summary of the folders on the system with the amount of mail in each.

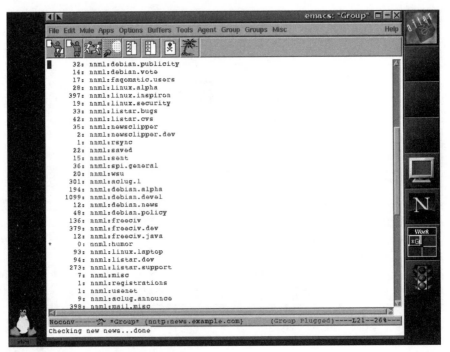

Figure 4-16: Summary screen in Gnus

For some users who are looking for a simpler but somewhat less powerful mail reader, the VM reader (also built into XEmacs) may prove a more viable option; it can also be found in the Apps menu.

Version control

As I'll discuss in detail in Chapter 26, "Archiving and Collaboration with CVS," version control systems such as CVS (Concurrent Version System) can be extremely beneficial for the development process, especially if multiple users are involved. Emacs, of course, has (surprise) integrated support for CVS. The module that provides this support is called `vc`.

Note   If the examples in this chapter do not work for you, you may need to load the `vc` module into Emacs manually. You can do that by running `M-x load-library RET vc RET`.

The command of primary use is `C-x v v`, which checks in your current file to the repository. The system asks for a changelog entry, which you can supply. When you are finished with the change comments, press `C-c C-c` and the file will be checked in with your comments.

The version control support in `vc` is not limited to CVS; it will also work with RCS. This can be convenient as you get a single interface to different version control systems available for Linux.

Getting Help

Emacs is a large and extremely versatile system. There is a large amount of documentation available with Emacs, and it comes in several forms.

You can access all of the help in Emacs by using `C-h`. Ironically enough, the Backspace key on some keyboards and with some systems will transmit that keystroke as well. From the initial `C-h` keypress, you select a command that will select the particular type of help to display. If you press two question marks at this point, you receive a summary of all the `C-h` commands, as shown in Figure 4-17.

Some of the most useful commands from this list include `C-c`, d, `C-f`, i, and t. Take a look by finding information about the command that opens files, `C-x C-f`. First thing you should do is find the appropriate function name. To do that, you use `C-h c`. The full key sequence is:

```
C-h c C-x C-f
```

The system responds with the name of the corresponding function. In this case, it displays:

```
C-x C-f runs the command find-file
```

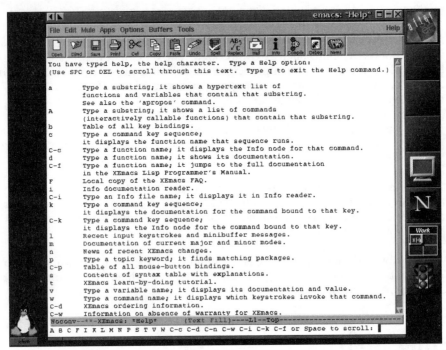

Figure 4-17: Summary of C-h commands

Armed with this information, you can go forth and look up more information about the specific function. You can use C-h d to bring up a summary of the command's usage. Running C-h d find-file RET displays a summary of the command:

```
`find-file' is an interactive compiled Lisp function
  -- loaded from "files.elc"
(find-file FILENAME &optional CODESYS)

Edit file FILENAME.
Switch to a buffer visiting file FILENAME,
creating one if none already exists.
Under XEmacs/Mule, optional second argument specifies the
coding system to use when decoding the file.  Interactively,
with a prefix argument, you will be prompted for the coding system.
```

Thus, you get a basic summary. However, you may want to get some more detailed information about the command. In this case, you can try C-h C-f to bring up the info page for the specific command you are curious about. In this case, the system brings up a good deal of information about find-file, including an ELISP scripting example.

Now, you can view the info documentation covering that specific command with C-h C-c. Info documentation is a hypertext documentation format used extensively by Emacsen and by various GNU software programs. Emacs contains an integrated browser for info documentation. You can invoke it on a specific part of the documentation with C-h C-c, or you can invoke it on the top of the Info tree with C-h i. Each documentation page in Info documents have specified ways of navigating. You can select options from a menu, navigate up, forwards, or backwards by using buttons on the tollbar or by using links inside the document itself.

When you first open the info browser, you see the master index. The actual contents varies depending on exactly which Linux distribution you have, which Emacs version you have, and what software you have.

Summary

In this chapter, you were introduced to the Emacs text editing and development system. You learned that:

✦ Emacs comes in different flavors, with different interfaces, but with much of the same technology under the hood.

✦ Emacs has its own special key notation for use in documentation and in scripts.

✦ Emacs has basic editing features.

✦ Emacs has different editing modes available, depending on the specific type of file you are working with.

✦ These modes define features syntax highlighting, extra commands and keystrokes, and so on.

✦ C and Perl modes are two examples of editing modes. Both provide a full suite of useful tools.

✦ Emacs can also be used as an IDE.

✦ Emacs is big on integration, with many components integrated into the system and written in ELISP.

✦ You can perform tasks such as compilation, debugging, and running your software all from within Emacs.

✦ The C-h keystroke is the first step towards finding help. Additional information can be found beneath that menu.

✦   ✦   ✦

Understanding Linux Data Files and Scripts

In this chapter, you'll learn about some of the system files on a Linux system. Although some of your programs may not need to deal with these files, others may need to know this information. For instance, you might want an e-mail program to be capable of finding out the real name that corresponds to a given username. A web server would want to be started at system boot time. An FTP server would want to be started when connections to the proper port arrive.

If you are writing a program that needs to interact well with the system — particularly one that you distribute — you need to make sure you interact with system files properly. You must use proper locations for your configuration files, and read existing configuration files properly.

General Concepts

In Linux, most configuration information is stored in plain text files. Many programs have both system-wide and user-specific configuration systems. The system-wide configuration generally is stored in /etc or a subdirectory thereof. User-specific configuration information generally is stored in the user's home directory, with a filename beginning with a period. The ls program avoids displaying such files, and wildcards avoid matching them by default. For instance, a shell might look first in /etc/profile and then augment (or override) those settings with a .profile file in the user's home directory.

With this approach, configuration files can be edited with any text editor; no special binary editor is required. Furthermore, each application is free to use a configuration file format that best suits its needs. For instance, the format necessary to describe printers is far different from that necessary to describe mail routing and rewriting tables. This approach works well for almost every part of the system.

The downside is that this system can be somewhat inefficient. For instance, if a given file is accessed frequently, there can be a performance hit. For this reason, a few files such as the passwd file are stored in a database format, generated from the plain text version. Because most configuration files are processed infrequently and are small, this particular problem does not apply to a majority of programs.

Because standard files are used to store configuration information, the existing Linux permissions mechanism is used to control who can read or write to the configuration of a given program. These permissions are used to prevent non-root users from writing to the configuration files in /etc and to prevent other users from modifying their own configuration files.

You'll also find that Linux's capability of mounting directories and files in any place in the file system hierarchy enables you to create a high level of organization and structure in the file system — a level unattainable by other operating systems that do not have such a system.

File system Layout

The file system layout in Linux can vary between distributions. Each distribution seeks to integrate hundreds or even thousands of packages and may settle on different standard locations for files.

In an attempt to rectify these problems, programmers got together and created the Linux Filsystem Standard (FSSTND). Many Linux distributions settled on this standard. Because of the expanding nature of Linux, particularly the proliferation of the system on non-Intel platforms, a newer version called the Filesystem Hierarchy Standard (FHS) appeared. Distributions are moving in the direction of this new standard. Some names or locations are presently in a state of flux because of this change but the differences are not significant relative to the overall picture. For details on these standards, see the web site at `http://www.pathname.com/fhs/`.

/: The root of everything

The root of the directory tree in Linux is /. This directory should contain either no files (only directories) or only very few files, such as a kernel image. The root directory is the first mounted by the kernel; it is, in fact, necessary to do so in order to boot the system. The scripts and programs contained in this file system are then responsible for starting up the remainder of the system.

Here's a sample listing on one system, which should look similar to yours.

```
drwxr-xr-x   2 root      root          2048 Jul 20 15:18 bin
drwxr-xr-x   2 root      root          1024 Jun 25 23:10 boot
drwxrwxr-x   2 root      cdrom         1024 Jun  2 19:22 cdrom
drwxr-xr-x   3 root      root         19456 Aug  7 09:48 dev
drwxr-xr-x  67 root      root          5120 Aug  7 09:48 etc
drwxrwxr-x   2 root      floppy        1024 Jun  2 19:22 floppy
drwxr-xr-x   2 root      root          1024 Jun  2 18:43 ftp
drwxrwsr-x   7 root      staff         1024 Jul 20 15:28 home
drwxr-xr-x   2 root      root          1024 Jun  2 19:22 initrd
drwxr-xr-x   5 root      root          4096 Jul 20 15:17 lib
drwxr-xr-x   2 root      root         12288 Jun  2 13:33 lost+found
drwxr-xr-x   2 root      root          1024 Feb  1  1999 mnt
dr-xr-xr-x  58 root      root             0 Aug  7 04:48 proc
drwx------   6 root      root          1024 Jul 20 19:02 root
drwxr-xr-x   2 root      root          3072 Jul 20 15:20 sbin
drwxrwxrwt   3 root      root          2048 Aug  7 19:18 tmp
drwxr-xr-x  18 root      root          1024 Jul 20 15:21 usr
drwxr-xr-x  14 root      root          1024 Jul 20 15:15 var
```

Each of these directories has specific purposes. Many users partition some directory trees for special use, in which case the rename() call cannot be used to move files from one tree to another. Table 5-1 lists the purposes of these directories.

Table 5-1
Standard Directories and Typical Functions

Directory	Function
/bin	Holds basic system binaries such as ls and cat. This directory must not be moved off the root partition.
/boot	Contains files required to boot the system. Examples of files included here are the kernel image itself, a map file, and perhaps some data for the architecture-specific boot loader. This directory must not be moved off the root partition.
/cdrom	Is a ready-made mount point for accessing CD-ROM disks. Some distributions instead place this in /mnt/cdrom.
/dev	Holds the entries for the various devices present on a Linux system. This directory must be present on the root partition.
/etc	Holds configuration files and initialization scripts for the system. This directory must be present on the root partition.

Continued

Table 5-1 *(continued)*

Directory	Function
/home	Typically holds home directories for each user, except root, with an account on the system. There is no reason that this must be the path; the path for each user's home directory is specified in the passwd file entry.
/lib	Contains the basic dynamic libraries necessary to run the programs required to start up and boot a basic system. It should not be moved off the root partition.
/lost+found	Is an entry found on every file system. This directory should not be deleted. If a file system ever develops a corruption, the file system repair tool (fsck) can sometimes place whatever data it can recover in this directory.
/mnt	Is a directory created for you by many distributions. Some distributions include additional directories beneath it; others have the directory without any subdirectories. In either case, the directory (or tree) is there for you to mount things temporarily. You are, of course, not required to use it; it's there as a convenience.
/proc	Is a virtual area. The files and directories in /proc are not real and do not exist on any disk on the system. Rather, they are generated by the system to communicate system information to (and from) various programs. For instance, the process display utility ps can use /proc to get information about the processes running on the system. Your programs can get all sorts of information about the system by examining the various files and information in this directory.
/root	Is the home directory for the root user. It must always remain on the root partition.
/sbin	Contains the programs and binaries necessary to boot the system. It must not be moved off the root partition. Unlike /bin, the files in /sbin are generally not designed to be run by ordinary users of the system.
/tmp	Is the canonical repository for temporary files and data. Because of security concerns, it is advised that this directory not be used. It still may be used, but must be done with extreme care.
/usr	Is the location for static files and data to be used by users in the normal course of running the system. This is often the largest, or nearly the largest, partition on a workstation. This tree should be considered read-only except during program installation or removal.
/var	Contains varying data. This could include cache data, persistent state information, or even a high-score file for games.

/dev: device files

When hardware devices are accessed on Linux systems by application programs, they are accessed through a specific entry customarily located in the /dev tree. These files have tuned permissions carefully. For instance, the device files for fixed disks are kept carefully guarded; any unauthorized access could permit security breaches.

There are a huge number of files in this directory; my systems have anywhere from 900 to 1200 files in this directory. Here is a summary of some of the files and their purposes:

✦ The `apm_bios` file interacts with the Advanced Power Management system found in many laptops and even some desktops.

✦ The `audio` files interact with the audio system — namely, digital waveform audio on a sound card.

✦ The `cdrom` entry is a symbolic link to the device used for the CD-ROM on your machine.

✦ The `dsp` entries also are used to interact with digital audio.

✦ The `fd` entry is a symbolic link into the appropriate area in `/proc` corresponding to the file descriptors held by the current process.

✦ The `fd*` devices (followed by at least one numeric digit) correspond to the floppy drives on the system.

✦ The `hd` devices correspond to IDE devices on your system. There are additional devices that correspond to the multiple partitions that some devices have.

✦ The `initrd` device holds the initial RAM disk for the system, and is used frequently on Linux boot floppies or rescue disks.

✦ The `lp` devices communicate with the computer's parallel port.

✦ The `midi` devices communicate with the sound card's synthesizer.

✦ The `mixer` device controls the amplitude of the various sound outputs from your sound card.

✦ The null device accepts anything sent to it and simply discards it. Any attempt to read from this device yields an immediate end-of-file result with no data.

✦ The `psaux` device communicates with the PS/2 mouse port on your system.

✦ The `pty` devices are pseudo-terminals that you can use in your programs. For details on pseudo-terminals, see Chapter 15, "Looking at Terminals."

✦ The `random` and `urandom` devices give you a stream of random characters. Some C library calls may use these devices to give you random numbers when asked for.

✦ The scd devices correspond to the SCSI CD-ROM devices that may be present on your system.

✦ The sd devices correspond to the SCSI disks that may be present on your system. Like their IDE versions, there are corresponding device entries for devices that support partitions.

✦ The tty device corresponds to the controlling terminal of the current process, regardless of which file that really is.

✦ The tty* devices, followed by numbers, correspond to the virtual consoles present on your system.

✦ The ttyS* devices communicate with the serial ports on your system. Some older programs may use cua devices; these devices are deprecated. Only the ttyS devices should be used for serial communication.

✦ The zero device, like the null device, accepts anything sent to it and discards it. When read from, the device gives you an endless stream of null characters.

With a few exceptions, your programs rarely will interact directly with these files, but you will sometimes encounter them through library calls.

/etc: configuration and startup files

Virtually all of the system-wide configuration files on any given Linux system reside in the /etc directory. These files hold per-application configuration information, system information such as which partitions are mounted in the file system, and initialization scripts.

If your application is installed as part of the default installation of an operating system, most likely it places one or more configuration files under /etc — assuming configuration files are necessary. There is no set format for these files; you are free to use whatever format suits your application best. However, Linux administrators are accustomed to several "familiar" formats: the printcap format, a shell format (key/value pairs separated by an equals sign), a colon-separated data file (such as passwd), and a newer C-style format like that which is used in BIND 8. Unless there is a special reason not to use these forms, it is best to stick to them so that the administrator doesn't have to learn a new configuration file format.

The other key feature of the files present in /etc is that the system startup files reside here. These files vary between distributions; consult your distribution's documentation or the init(1) manpage for more details. In general, though, the initialization scripts reside in /etc/init.d or /etc/rc.d/init.d and are shell scripts. If your program is started at boot, it needs to register itself with the system's startup system by providing a script that is placed in these locations, and setting some symbolic links.

/usr: standard system programs

The /usr tree contains programs installed as part of the operating system for the general use by users on the system. Many system binaries reside in /usr/bin. Binaries for the X11 system typically are stored in /usr/X11R6/bin. Many system-shared libraries reside in /usr/lib, and X11 libraries in /usr/X11R6/lib/X11.

Linux application developers should note the /usr/local directory, which stores applications not shipped with an operating system. This includes any application distributed by any third party. The /usr/local/bin, /usr/local/lib, and other directories in the hierarchy are used by these applications.

The /usr tree is considered one that can be mounted read-only except during software installation and deinstallation. Keep this in mind when you install your software; do not try to write anything here after the initial installation.

Furthermore, the /usr/share hierarchy is becoming more prominent. This directory contains non-executable read-only data in the /usr hierarchy. Examples include documentation, manpages, and info documents. These files are platform-independent, so they are prime candidates for NFS mounting in some situations — even if the Linux systems in question are not using the same system architecture.

/var: variable data

Data that is variable — that is, changing — should be stored in /var. Typical examples of this sort of data include spool files, queue files, cache data, state information, and data files or databases storing varying information.

Some prominent examples include /var/mail (or /var/spool/mail), which is the default primary mail repository for users of the system; /var/state/sendmail, which holds persistent state information for the sendmail server; and /var/cache/man, which holds preformatted manpages.

passwd and shadow Files

Two files in /etc are so important that they need some extra explanation. The /etc/passwd file holds information about each user account on the system. The format of the file is one record per line, with the fields separated by olons. The fields in the traditional passwd file format are:

✦ Username on the system.

✦ Hashed version of the login password. This may be set to a special value if shadow passwords are in use on the system.

✦ Numeric UID for this account.

✦ Numeric GID for the default group for this account.

✦ GECOS field, typically containing a real name, phone number, address, or some other related personal information.

✦ The full path to the home directory for the person.

✦ The full path to the default shell for the person. This entry must be present in /etc/shells.

Many of these fields are self-explanatory. However, the hashed password field deserves some additional attention. With a traditional passwd file, the value is generated by the C library's `crypt()` call. This is a one-way hash algorithm, meaning that it is not possible to decrypt the password after it is encrypted. To authenticate users, the password supplied is encrypted, and if this encrypted result is the same as the one listed for the correct password, the supplied password is considered a match.

Here are a few sample lines from a `passwd` file. Because the system from which this example comes is using shadow passwords, the real passwords are not shown in this file:

```
root:x:0:0:root:/root:/bin/bash
daemon:x:1:1:daemon:/usr/sbin:/bin/sh
bin:x:2:2:bin:/bin:/bin/sh
sys:x:3:3:sys:/dev:/bin/sh
sync:x:4:100:sync:/bin:/bin/sync
games:x:5:100:games:/usr/games:/bin/sh
man:x:6:100:man:/var/catman:/bin/sh
lp:x:7:7:lp:/var/spool/lpd:/bin/sh
alias:x:70:65534:qmail alias:/var/qmail/alias:/bin/sh
qmaild:x:71:65534:qmail daemon:/var/qmail:/bin/sh
qmails:x:72:70:qmail send:/var/qmail:/bin/sh
```

This scheme is technically secure. However, there are problems with password compromises. The reason is that many users choose insecure passwords for their accounts, sometimes as insecure as their login name or a name from the GECOS field. Crackers have written tools to try various permutations of these words, adding some from a dictionary, and resulting in various guesses. With these sorts of tools, up to a third of the passwords on some systems are guessed. Keep in mind that this problem only applies to passwords that are guessable.

In an effort to prevent these tools from functioning, the encrypted passwords need to be hidden. The remainder of the account information still needs to be available to programs — everything from `ls` to e-mail tools need it. The solution is to move the password data into a separate file. This file has restricted read permissions, keeping crackers at bay.

The problem remains — how are legitimate programs to be granted access to the data in that file? In many modern systems, the password is group-readable by a special system group. Programs needing to read it are setgid to that group, but good design dictates that they maintain this setgid permission only when actually needing to read from the file. Some older systems may have these programs setuid to root, which is somewhat more dangerous.

The shadow file, which holds this data, is a superb place to introduce newer features into the authentication mechanism. Some of these features include password and account expiration information. The specification for the shadow file on Linux is:

✦ The username of the account.

✦ The hashed password for the account.

✦ The date the password was last changed, recorded in days since January 1, 1970.

✦ A count of the number of days before the password must be changed. If this value is zero, no password change is mandated by the system.

✦ Number of days prior to password change that a warning should be given to the user whose account this belongs to.

✦ The date the account should be disabled because of an expired password, measured in the number of days after password expiry that the password has not been changed.

✦ The expiration date of the account, measured in the number of days since January 1, 1970.

✦ A reserved, and currently unused, field.

Here are a few sample lines from this file; note that at least one account here (root's) has an actual encrypted password listed:

```
root:TPwk6TEMDd3Ng:10618:0:99999:7:::
daemon:*:10529:0:99999:7:::
bin:*:10529:0:99999:7:::
sys:*:10529:0:99999:7:::
sync:*:10529:0:99999:7:::
games:*:10529:0:99999:7:::
man:*:10529:0:99999:7:::
lp:*:10529:0:99999:7:::
mail:*:10529:0:99999:7:::
news:*:10529:0:99999:7:::
uucp:*:10529:0:99999:7:::
proxy:*:10529:0:99999:7:::
majordom:*:10529:0:99999:7:::
```

Accessing account information from a shell

Several utilities are available on a Linux system for the purpose of modifying the passwd and/or shadow files.

For system administrators, a key tool is adduser. This program adds a new account to the system. The syntax of the adduser command varies between distributions but takes at least a username as a command-line parameter. Some versions of adduser may then prompt you for additional information, or ask for it on the command line. Some systems also provide a deluser command that removes a user from the system.

The vipw command is recommended for editing the passwd or shadow password files by hand. You should never edit these files by hand without using vipw. If you don't use vipw, you can corrupt the files unless your system is in single-user mode because other processes may try to write to the files at the same time you do.

When run without arguments, vipw loads the passwd file into your favorite editor for modifications. If you run vipw -s, the shadow file opens for you to edit. Additionally, the vigr utility can do the same with the group file.

The chfn and chsh utilities modify the "finger name" (GECOS field) and default shell of a given account, respectively. When run as root, they enable you to make these modifications for any account. When run as a regular user, that user is permitted to change the values on the user's own account only.

The passwd utility allows the same type of capability for the password of a given account. The root user can also modify the password expiration date, the account status, whether or not the account is considered locked, and so on. For more details on this utility, see the passwd(1) manpage; the capabilities vary from system to system and depend on whether or not shadow passwords are in use.

Bash defines some variables that can provide some quick information about the user who is running a script. For instance, $UID expands to the numeric user ID of the person running the script; $HOME to that person's home directory; and $USER to the text username of the person. Note that these variables should not be relied upon as absolutely secure, as they can be modified by the user.

Accessing account information from C

C on Linux provides numerous functions for getting information about the current process and the passwd file. You should never read the file directly; always use the C functions. Some systems use a network system such as NIS to provide a shared passwd file across machines; simply reading the file does not provide correct results in these cases. Furthermore, the system can use a database version of these files to improve performance; the C functions utilize this but a manual search most likely does not.

C provides several functions to get this data. One is `getpwnam()`, which returns a pointer to a static variable of type `struct passwd`. This structure is defined in `pwd.h` as follows:

```
struct passwd
{
  char *pw_name;              /* Username.  */
  char *pw_passwd;            /* Password.  */
  uid_t pw_uid;               /* User ID.  */
  gid_t pw_gid;               /* Group ID.  */
  char *pw_gecos;             /* Real name.  */
  char *pw_dir;               /* Home directory.  */
  char *pw_shell;             /* Shell program.  */
};
```

The argument to `getpwnam()` is a string—the person's username. The `getpwnam()` function will search for this username, returning the appropriate record if it is found. If not, `NULL` is returned.

The following C function returns a user's home directory:

```
char * getuserhomedir(char *user)
{
  static char homedir[_POSIX_PATH_MAX];
  struct passwd *pws;

  pws = getpwnam(user);
  if (!pws)
    return NULL;

  strcpy(homedir, pws->pw_dir);
  return homedir;
}
```

This function simply asks `getpwnam()` for the information on the specified user, saves it off, and returns the value. You'll want to include `string.h`, `pwd.h`, and `limits.h` for this code.

You can perform a similar operation with a person's numeric UID. The following code can do that for you:

```
char * gethomedir(int uidtofind)
{
  static char homedir[_POSIX_PATH_MAX];
  struct passwd *pws;

  pws = getpwuid(uidtofind);
  if (!pws)
    return NULL;

  strcpy(homedir, pws->pw_dir);
  return homedir;
}
```

In this example, you can see that the only difference lies in the call to getpwuid() instead of getpwnam(). The getpwuid() call yields the same result as getpwnam(), except that instead of searching for a username, it searches for a numeric UID. When combined with the getuid() call, which returns the numeric uid of the owner of the current process, you can get information about the person running your program by using this code:

```
getpwuid(getuid())
```

There is also a getpwent() function that enables you to step through the passwd file, reading in each line. If you are doing a search, you should use a different function if possible. Otherwise, if you need to look at each record, then this is the function you should use. When you're done with getpwent(), you should call endpwent() to close out the file. The following code uses getpwent():

```
/* Finds the highest uid in passwd file and sets the nextuid global
   variable to the next number. */
void inituid(void)
{
struct passwd *entry;
  uid_t nextuid = 0;                      /* uid_t is defined in sys/types.h */
  printf("Scanning for next available uid...\r"); fflush(stdout);
  while ((entry = getpwent()))
    if ((entry->pw_uid > nextuid) &&
        (entry->pw_uid < 32767))          /* Compensate for broken systems */
          nextuid = entry->pw_uid;
  endpwent();
  nextuid++;
  printf("The next uid will be %d%-20c\n", nextuid, '.');
}
```

In this example, you can see that getpwent() returns NULL when it encountered the end of the file. Therefore, using it in a while loop like this one is a common.

These functions are also available in Perl, and they function in the same way. A crypt() function is also used for generating the string for the passwd file. This too is used in Perl; see the next example for a sample usage.

Accessing from Perl

Perl provides access to the same functions as C for getting information from the passwd file. The examples in the C section above work almost the same way in Perl. In Perl, instead of returning a struct, the functions return an array with the elements in the order of the elements in the struct.

Both Perl and C also provide the crypt() function, and they work the same way. Take a look at this simple Perl script:

```
#!/usr/bin/perl

print "Enter a two-character salt: ";
chomp($salt = <STDIN>);
print "Enter the desired password: ";
chomp($plain = <STDIN>);
print "\n\nThe crypt string is:        " . crypt($plain, $salt) . "\n\n";
```

The two-character salt is chosen randomly. You can run the program and watch the results:

```
$ chmod a+x gencrypt.pl
$ ./gencrypt.pl
Enter a two-character salt: LI
Enter the desired password: Hey!


The crypt string is:        LIKJfmvCV1/QA

$ ./gencrypt.pl
Enter a two-character salt: NU
Enter the desired password: Hey!


The crypt string is:        NUH1u/11m77j2

$ ./gencrypt.pl
Enter a two-character salt: LI
Enter the desired password: Hello!


The crypt string is:        LI86QkktO1hho

$ ./gencrypt.pl
Enter a two-character salt: LI
Enter the desired password: Hey!


The crypt string is:        LIKJfmvCV1/QA
```

In this example, you can see that:

✦ Two different passwords hashed with the same salt produce different results.

✦ The same password hashed with different salts produce different results.

✦ A single password hashed with the same salt produces the same result.

This last behavior is relied upon for password authentication in the system. When a user tries to log in, his or her password is run through crypt() using the same salt as before (notice that the salt forms the first two characters of the crypt() output). If the result matches the one on record, the password is considered a match.

group File

The group file defines the group on the system and which users are in them. This file is a simple colon-delimited format akin to the passwd file. The format of the group file is:

✦ The name of the group.

✦ A group password.

✦ The numeric gid of the group.

✦ The comma-separated listing of members of the group. This optional listing does not include users that list this group as their default.

Your Linux distribution defines a number of groups that have predetermined functions on your systems. Some of these groups are intended for you to add users to; others, for specific programs on your system. If your application requires access to files by some users on the system, you (or the administrator) must add a custom entry to this group file.

Here are some sample lines from a group file:

```
root:x:0:
daemon:x:1:majordom
bin:x:2:
sys:x:3:
adm:x:4:
tty:x:5:
disk:x:6:
lp:x:7:lp
mail:x:8:
news:x:9:
```

Most of these group files simply define the name of a group. The daemon group, however, indicates that the majordom user is a member of the group. Because he or she is a member, that user can read any files that are group-readable by daemon, and can write to any files that are group-writable by daemon.

init Files

When the system boots, the /sbin/init program takes control of initializing the system and the user-land software. This task includes mounting and checking drives, initializing the network, and starting software and servers. The process of starting and stopping these servers is regulated by runlevels, the precise meaning of which can vary from distribution to distribution.

The init scripts reside in either /etc/init.d or /etc/rc.d/init.d, depending on your distribution. The scripts are invoked by init and are shell scripts used to start up particular system services.

The init scripts take a particular argument. The start and stop arguments are used by init itself. For the convenience of the system administrator, many distributions define additional arguments as well, such as restart or reload. The init scripts on your system vary from the mundane to the extraordinarily complex.

You may want to examine some of the scripts in your system for ideas. Some distributions add commands or have typical ways of accomplishing things; again, consult your distribution's documentation for specific details.

Listing 5-1 shows an example script from the Debian GNU/Linux operating system.

Note   Listing 5-1 is available online.

Listing 5-1: **Debian's /etc/init.d/sendmail script**

```sh
#!/bin/sh

# Start or stop sendmail
#
# Robert Leslie <rob@mars.org>
# Johnie Ingram <johnie@netgod.net>
# David Rocher <rocher@mail.dotcom.fr>
# Richard Nelson <cowboy@debain.org>

# How often to run the queue
Q="10m"

PATH=/bin:/usr/bin:/sbin:/usr/sbin
DAEMON=/usr/sbin/sendmail
COMMAND=/usr/sbin/sendmail
PIDFILE=/var/run/sendmail.pid
NAME=sendmail
FLAGS="defaults 50"

test -x $DAEMON -a -d /usr/doc/sendmail || exit 0

case "$1" in
    start)
        ( cd /var/spool/mqueue && rm -f [lnx]f* )
        echo -n "Starting mail transport agent: sendmail"
        start-stop-daemon --start --quiet --pidfile $PIDFILE -
-exec $DAEMON --startas $COMMAND -- -bd -q"$Q"
        echo "."
```

Continued

Listing 5-1 *(continued)*

```
        ;;

    stop)
        echo -n "Stopping mail transport agent: sendmail"
        start-stop-daemon --stop --quiet --pidfile $PIDFILE --
exec $DAEMON
        echo "."
        ;;

    restart)
        $0 stop
        sleep 2
        $0 start
        ;;

    reload)
        echo -n "Reloading sendmail configuration..."
        start-stop-daemon --stop --signal 1 --quiet  \
            --pidfile $PIDFILE --exec $DAEMON
        echo "done."
        ;;

    force-reload)
        $0 reload
        ;;

    debug)
        start-stop-daemon --stop --signal 10 --verbose  \
            --pidfile $PIDFILE --exec $DAEMON
        ;;

    *)
        echo "Usage: /etc/init.d/sendmail
{start|stop|restart|reload|force-reload|debug}"
        exit 1
        ;;
esac

exit 0
```

In this script, you can see that the system implements the standard commands. The script is recording the PID of the process when it is started so the PID can be reused when shutting down to properly stop the server.

When the init process starts, it must be told exactly what to do. It must know which runlevel to bring up, which terminals should have a getty process, and what to do when certain special events occur. This information is defined in inittab file.

The format of the inittab file is a colon-delimited file akin to the passwd file. However, inittab doesn't have such rigid format controls and allows comments. Listing 5-2 shows a sample file that we can analyze.

Note Listing 5-2 is available online.

Listing 5-2: **Sample /etc/inittab file**

```
# /etc/inittab: init(8) configuration.
# $Id: inittab,v 1.8 1998/05/10 10:37:50 miquels Exp $

# The default runlevel.
id:2:initdefault:

# Boot-time system configuration/initialization script.
# This is run first except when booting in emergency (-b) mode.
si::sysinit:/etc/init.d/rcS

# What to do in single-user mode.
~~:S:wait:/sbin/sulogin

# /etc/init.d executes the S and K scripts upon change
# of runlevel.
#
# Runlevel 0 is halt.
# Runlevel 1 is single-user.
# Runlevels 2-5 are multi-user.
# Runlevel 6 is reboot.

l0:0:wait:/etc/init.d/rc 0
l1:1:wait:/etc/init.d/rc 1
l2:2:wait:/etc/init.d/rc 2
l3:3:wait:/etc/init.d/rc 3
l4:4:wait:/etc/init.d/rc 4
l5:5:wait:/etc/init.d/rc 5
l6:6:wait:/etc/init.d/rc 6
# Normally not reached, but fallthrough in case of emergency.
z6:6:respawn:/sbin/sulogin

# What to do when CTRL+ALT+DEL is pressed.
ca:12345:ctrlaltdel:/sbin/shutdown -t1 -a -r now

# Action on special keypress (ALT-UpArrow).
```

Continued

Listing 5-2 *(continued)*

```
kb::kbrequest:/bin/echo "Keyboard Request--edit /etc/inittab to let this work."

# What to do when the power fails/returns.
pf::powerwait:/etc/init.d/powerfail start
pn::powerfailnow:/etc/init.d/powerfail now
po::powerokwait:/etc/init.d/powerfail stop

# /sbin/getty invocations for the runlevels.
#
# The "id" field MUST be the same as the last
# characters of the device (after "tty").
#
# Format:
#   <id>:<runlevels>:<action>:<process>
1:2345:respawn:/sbin/getty 38400 tty1
2:23:respawn:/sbin/getty 38400 tty2
3:23:respawn:/sbin/getty 38400 tty3
4:23:respawn:/sbin/getty 38400 tty4
5:23:respawn:/sbin/getty 38400 tty5
6:23:respawn:/sbin/getty 38400 tty6

# Example how to put a getty on a serial line (for a terminal)
#
#T0:23:respawn:/sbin/getty -L ttyS0 9600 vt100
#T1:23:respawn:/sbin/getty -L ttyS1 9600 vt100

# Example how to put a getty on a modem line.
#
#T3:23:respawn:/sbin/mgetty -x0 -s 57600 ttyS3
```

Reading this file from the top to the bottom, the first noncomment line you see is the initdefault line. This line defines the runlevel that the system enters into by default during boot. The next line with content is the sysinit line. This is the script that is used to initialize vital parts of the system. Typical duties for the script include mounting file systems, checking filsystems, and configuring the networking support on your machine.

The next line defines what program to use when the system is brought down into single-user mode. In this case, the sulogin program is run. This program requires the operator to enter the root password. Some older distributions do not have this; it is wise to add it in if multiple users have physical access to the console of your system.

Next, you see the definitions for the actions to take when being brought up into each specific runlevel. These scripts are responsible for making sure that the appropriate processes are running (or not running) for that particular runlevel.

Following those lines, there are definitions of what occurs when special events occur. These events include a Ctrl+Alt+Delete request, a special keyboard request, and situations in which a UPS (Uninterruptible Power Supply) unit indicates when main power is lost — or restored.

After these definitions, there are definitions of the terminals that are used on the system. Most Linux distributions default to starting up six virtual terminals. The `getty` program handles the initial login process; in this case, accepting username and password information. Finally, there are examples of how you can set up a serial terminal (as with a null-modem cable) and a dial-in modem terminal.

Network Files

Besides the configuration and initialization files on your system, you should be aware of a few others. These fall into the network file category, and are particularly relevant when you are writing network server programs.

DNS files

The Domain Name System (DNS) is the distributed database responsible for converting from the domain names used by humans to access Internet servers and the numeric addresses used internally by the TCP/IP protocol. When your programs call functions that perform DNS lookups, such as `gethostbyname()`, the standard implementation of these functions causes the system configuration files to be consulted.

The most well-known of these configuration files is resolv.conf (located in the /etc directory), which defines the location of your system's DNS servers and how to query them. Its entries specify the IP addresses of the servers used by your system. It can also specify a domain search order for resolving names that are not fully qualified.

An example file might be:

```
nameserver 10.0.0.1
nameserver 127.0.0.1
nameserver 10.11.12.13
search example.com
```

This states that the nameservers residing at $10.0.0.1$, $127.0.0.1$, and $10.11.12.13$ should be queried, in that order, when the system needs to access a nameserver. Additionally, if a fully-qualified domain is not specified, the example.com domain will be implicitly searched for a match.

Another relevant file is the /etc/hosts file, which holds local definitions of hostnames. The hosts defined in this file do not require a DNS lookup. Your own machine and `localhost` are always listed in here. Other machines that you may need to contact even in lieu of a working DNS system (such as NFS or NIS servers) should also be listed here. This way, your machine can continue to function even if the DNS server is down for some reason—an important step in network stability.

The /etc/nsswitch.conf file defines the order in which these files are checked. Here's a sample file:

```
passwd:         compat
group:          compat
shadow:         compat

hosts:          files dns
networks:       files

protocols:      db files
services:       db files
ethers:         db files
rpc:            db files

netgroup:       nis
```

In this way, the methods of accessing various types of information are clearly defined. For instance, to look up the IP address of a given host, first the file is checked and then, if no satisfactory result was obtained from the file, DNS is queried. This is defined on the `hosts` line in the file.

Security files

Also important are the network security files on your system. The most prominent of these are the files for TCP wrappers that define which machines are allowed to connect and access a given service, and which are not. These capabilities are defined in two files: /etc/hosts.allow and /etc/hosts.deny. Documentation for these files can be found in the `hosts_access(5)` manpage. These files work together to specify which hosts may connnect to which services. If there is no line matching a given connection request, access is granted by default. If a line in hosts.deny matches a connection request, access is denied unless there is a line in hosts.allow that matches the same connection request. This TCP wrapper mechanism only controls who may connect to your servers, not what they may do when connected.

Both files have the same syntax: a service name, a colon, and then a definition of which hosts may connect. Here's a sample hosts.deny file to analyze:

```
# /etc/hosts.deny: list of hosts that are _not_ allowed to access the system.
#                  See hosts_access(5) and /usr/doc/net/portmapper.txt
#
# Example:    ALL: some.host.name, .some.domain
#             ALL EXCEPT in.fingerd: other.host.name
#
# The PARANOID wildcard matches any host whose name does not match its
# address.
# ALL: PARANOID
ALL: PARANOID, ALL@ALL EXCEPT .example.com, localhost
imapd: PARANOID, ALL@ALL

uucp: ALL@ALL
telnetd, telnet, ssh, rlogin, rexec, rsh: ALL@ALL
```

In this file, access is denied by default to all users on all hosts (ALL@ALL) and to hosts that have suspicious DNS (PARANOID) to all services on the system. Note that you could use ALL instead of ALL@ALL; the latter simply does ident lookups where possible, and can log more information to your log files. Any hosts in the example.com domain, or the local machine, are exempted from this blanket deny rule already.

Next, the imap service denies connects from everywhere, including the local machine. The same occurs with UUCP. Finally, several remote access services declare the same thing.

Recalling that a hosts.allow file takes precedence over a hosts.deny file, take a look at this hosts.allow file:

```
sendmail: ALL
in.talkd: ALL@ALL EXCEPT PARANOID
in.ntalkd: ALL@ALL EXCEPT PARANOID
cvs: ALL@ALL EXCEPT PARANOID
```

According to this file, any machine is allowed to connect to the sendmail service on your local machine. Also, any machine with working DNS is permitted to connect to the talk and CVS services on your machine. These rules override the blanket deny in the hosts.deny file.

At this point, it should be noted that not all services honor the hosts.deny and hosts.allow files. Web servers, for instance, typically do not because of speed considerations. However, because Web documents are essentially public anyway, there's no particular need for this type of mechanism for Web servers.

Most servers that are started from the `inetd` super-server use TCP wrappers. Several other programs link in the library; examples include sendmail and ssh.

Super-server file

One significant piece of the networking puzzle remains: `inetd`, the Internet super-server. This program listens for connections to some of the simpler services on the system. Some of these are handled internally by `inetd`; most are passed on to individual programs that handle them. These items are defined in `/etc/inetd.conf`.

This file defines services for which the super-server listens (the details are covered later in Chapter 18, "Introducing TCP/IP Sockets"). Here are a few lines from a sample file:

```
discard         stream  tcp     nowait  root    internal
discard         dgram   udp     wait    root    internal
daytime         stream  tcp     nowait  root    internal
daytime         dgram   udp     wait    root    internal
time            stream  tcp     nowait  root    internal
time            dgram   udp     wait    root    internal

#:STANDARD: These are standard services.
telnet          stream  tcp     nowait  root    /usr/sbin/tcpd
/usr/sbin/in.telnetd
#<ftp-off>#ftp              stream  tcp     nowait  root    /usr/sbin/tcpd
/usr/sbin/in.ftpd
ftp             stream  tcp     nowait  root    /usr/sbin/tcpd  /usr/sbin/ftpd
```

The non-internal services in this example each have `/usr/sbin/tcpd` in them. This is the call to the TCP wrappers. If the TCP wrappers confirm that the connection is to be accepted, then `tcpd` invokes the actual server process.

Summary

In this chapter, you learned about the various files and scripts that are part of the initialization and configuration of Linux and its components. Specifically, you learned:

✦ Linux programs typically use plain text files for configuration. Many store the configuration files in the /etc directory and the per-user information in each user's home directory.

✦ Linux has a structured file system. The root file system holds files and directories necessary for the initial startup of the system. As part of this file system, /etc contains configuration and initialization files and /dev holds entries for system devices. The /usr tree has standard files for use during normal system operations. The /var tree contains data that may be variable. A virtual file system can be found in /proc, which provides information about the system.

✦ The passwd file is used to store information about the users with accounts on the system.

✦ Many modern distributions use a shadow password system, which stores the actual hashed password data in the /etc/shadow file, which is not readable by all users for security reasons.

✦ The group file defines which groups are present on the system, and which users are members of them.

✦ The init program is responsible for many aspects of system initialization. It uses initialization scripts from /etc/init.d or /etc/rc.d/init.d and has a configuration file in /etc/inittab.

✦ The nameservers to use for DNS lookups are defined in /etc/resolv.conf and the order to use when performing lookups is defined in /etc/nsswitch.conf.

✦ You may block access to certain services or hosts by using /etc/hosts.allow and /etc/hosts.deny.

✦ The inetd.conf file is used to configure the `inetd` super-server, which listens for requests on the behalf of many smaller servers on the system.

✦   ✦   ✦

The C
Environment

Welcome to gcc

As you work with your Linux development environment, much of your work will revolve around the centerpiece of the C development environment, gcc. gcc, short for the GNU C Compiler, is the standard C compiler on GNU/Linux systems.

This chapter will introduce you to and get you up to speed with gcc. You'll first learn the basic usage of gcc to compile single-module programs. Then, I will cover topics such as compiler warnings, debug symbols, and optimizations. In the next section, you'll learn about the big picture of the compilation process on Linux, including all of the tools and programs that gcc uses to generate your executables.

After discussing what the tools are and what they do, you'll be introduced to the ways in which you work with larger (multi-module) projects. Finally, some more advanced gcc options, such as linking with libraries and compilation with pipes, are discussed.

Compiling Programs with gcc

Now, I'll go through some sample usage of gcc together. First, I present for you a sample program to try compiling with gcc. You can use your favorite editor to type it in. For the purposes of this example, save it as test1.c. Here's the code:

```
#include <stdio.h>

void main(void) {
  printf("Hello World!\n");
}
```

This program looks — rightly so — fairly simple. Later, gcc will point out a few things that ought to be fixed, but for now, compile the program. To compile the program, type:

```
gcc test1.c
```

Tip If you are using Emacs or XEmacs, you may press M-x and then type `compile` RET `gcc test1.c` RET to compile the program from within Emacs. Later, for simple programs such as this one, you can run them in an Emacs shell as well: M-x `shell` RET.

Depending on your specific version of gcc, you may get a warning at this point. Ignore it for now; I'll talk about warnings later in the chapter. When gcc runs with the above usage, it generates a file named a.out that contains your program. You can run the program, as follows:

```
$ ./a.out
Hello World!
```

You've just compiled your first C program on Linux!

That was fairly trivial. However, unless you like naming every one of your programs a.out, you'll enjoy using the `-o` option of gcc, which enables you to change the names of your program. To use this option, type the following command:

```
gcc -o test1 test1.c
```

This is much better! You now have a file named test1 instead of a.out. As with the a.out program, you can run your newly named program:

```
$ ./test1
Hello World!
```

So, you can see that `-o` sets the output filename for gcc.

Warnings

Now, on to another important topic: warnings. Warnings are controlled by the `-W` switch to gcc. You can enable all of the most common warnings with the `-Wall` command like so:

```
$ gcc -Wall -o test1 test1.c
test1.c:3: warning: return type of `main' is not `int'
```

Note If you use a different version of gcc than that used for this book's examples, your warning messages may differ; this is normal.

The gcc compiler smartly pointed out that my `main()` function isn't exactly standard—excellent. Notice that even though there was a warning, gcc still compiled your program; it only aborts compilation on errors.

Now, perhaps, someone decides to fix the program like so:

```
#include <stdio.h>

int main(void) {
  printf("Hello World!\n");
}
```

Now, try to compile this:

```
$ gcc -Wall -o test1 test1.c
test1.c:5: warning: control reaches end of non-void function
```

Another good catch on gcc's part; because the main() function is declared to return an integer, and yet it doesn't, the return value is undefined. A proper fix here is fairly trivial. Change your test1.c to the following:

```
#include <stdio.h>
#include <stdlib.h>    /* for EXIT_SUCCESS */

int main(void) {
  printf("Hello World!\n");
  return EXIT_SUCCESS;
}
```

Now try compiling this one. You will get no warnings!

Another useful option is the −Werror switch, which causes gcc to treat all warnings as errors. This is particularly useful when using automated compilation, such as with the GNU make tool. When -Werror is used, gcc will not finish the compilation if any warning is detected.Therefore, you don't want to include this in release versions of software because other users' compilers may generate warnings on different things. However, when working with large projects with which gcc or make may generate several thousand lines of output, having the compilation aborted in this manner can be beneficial. You can use -Werror as follows:

```
$ gcc -Wall -Werror -o test1 test1.c
```

While gcc's warnings in this case were not really earth-shattering matters, you'll find that, as you write more complex programs, the -Wall switch can be an extremely valuable tool for tracking down and preventing bugs. I recommend that you use -Wall whenever you compile programs as a matter of habit; it's hard to go wrong with something that can often catch errors before you realize they're present!

Optimizations with gcc

One of the most exciting features of modern C compilers is the optimizer. The optimizer is a part of the compiler that is capable of examining your code (or the assembler code generated by the compiler), identifying those areas that are suboptimal, and rewriting them using code that does the same thing in less space or with better performance. gcc is no exception; it has a powerful and highly configurable optimizer that can be applied to your programs.

Optimization Options

In gcc, you can enable optimizations by using one of the -O options. You can specify several different levels of optimization for gcc. If you simply use -O, this is taken as level one (or -O1); -O is the same as -O1. In general, you can go up to level three (or -O3).

So, to use basic optimizations, you might use a command line such as the following:

```
$ gcc -Wall -O1 -o myprogram myprogram.c
```

You can, of course, also use -O2, -O3, or -O in place of -O1 above on your command line. These options control how aggressive gcc's optimizer is; the higher the number, the more aggressive gcc becomes with optimizations. More aggressive optimizations mean that your code runs faster.

Optimization Pitfalls

Optimization sometimes means tremendous gains for your program's performance. However, you should be aware of some potential pitfalls.

First, the more aggressive gcc becomes with optimizations, the longer it takes your program to compile. Therefore, some prefer to compile without optimizations during day-to-day development, but enable optimizations when the time to release and finish the program nears.

Second, some options—most notably, -O3—can increase the size of the generated program. Usually this difference is insignificant, but sometimes it can be important. If a program uses more RAM, then swapping may occur on the machines on which it runs, which can hurt performance more than the gain from the more efficient (but larger) code.

Finally, as mentioned earlier, debugging can be difficult when optimization is enabled. Because the optimizer can eliminate code that does not have a use in the final program, or re-arrange some statements for better performance, tracing the execution of the program can be difficult at best. Therefore, I recommend that you avoid optimizations as much as possible when debugging your programs.

Many people prefer to compile their programs with -O2 This option often provides the best compromise between optimization strength, compile time, and code size.

Optimizations: A Sample Session

In this section, we will take a look at some sample code to demonstrate optimization. The following code is the sample code for the test2.c program. This code is written inefficiently on purpose; you'll see how dramatic a difference gcc's optimizer can make with the execution time of the program. Note that the results you'll see here are more significant than those provided by the optimizer in a typical real-life situation, but nonetheless, you can sometimes see these results.

Here is the code for test2.c:

```c
#include <stdio.h>

int main(void) {
    int counter;
    int ending;
    int temp;
    int five;
    for (counter = 0; counter < 2 * 100000000 * 9 / 18 + 5131;
            counter += (5 - 3) / 2) {
        temp = counter / 15302;
        ending = counter;
        five = 5;
    }
    printf("five = %d; ending = %d\n", five, ending);
    return 0;
}
```

First, compile the program without optimizations, by typing the following:

```
$ gcc -Wall -o test2 test2.c
```

Normally, you would run the program by simply using ./test2. However, this time, you need to get some statistics. In order for the information to be useful, you need to time the execution on a machine that is not doing anything else, although you can still get some useful information even from a loaded system. You can do this with the time command, which reports information on resource utilization of your program when it finishes. Here is the command:

```
$ time ./test2
five = 5; ending = 100005130

real    0m15.146s
user    0m14.960s
sys     0m0.000s
```

These results almost certainly will be different on your system unless you have the same speed machine as the one on which this program was run. If the program takes an extremely long time to run, you may want to change the 100000000 number in the code to something smaller.

The time command is indicating that the program took a little more than 15 seconds to execute. Of this time, about 14.9 seconds were spent by the CPU with this program. If you are running the program on a heavily loaded machine, you might notice a larger difference between these two values.

 Tip   You can see this for yourself by opening two windows or terminals, and starting the program simultaneously in each.

Finally, the sys value indicates that a negligible amount of time is spent handling system calls, which is to be expected; almost all of the time in this program is for computation, and the only output occurs inside the printf() function.

Now, try gcc on the program again, this time with basic optimizations enabled:

```
$ gcc -Wall -O1 -o test2 test2.c
```

And examine the results of execution this time:

```
$ time ./test2
five = 5; ending = 100005130

real    0m2.220s
user    0m2.200s
sys     0m0.000s
```

A significant improvement; the execution time went from 15 seconds to about 2 seconds. In other words, the program took about 7 times longer to execute without optimizations as it takes now.

For comparison, one might want to use the -O2 level of optimization:

```
$ gcc -Wall -O2 -o test2 test2.c
$ time ./test2
five = 5; ending = 100005130

real    0m1.444s
user    0m1.420s
sys     0m0.000s
```

In round numbers, the program takes only about 75 percent as long to run with -O2 as it did with -O1. This is not as large as the previous difference, but still significant.

You might also want to try with `-O3`:

```
$ gcc -Wall -O3 -o test2 test2.c
$ time ./test2
five = 5; ending = 100005130

real    0m1.421s
user    0m1.400s
sys     0m0.000s
```

Here, there is still an improvement, but it's smaller this time—only about two hundredths of a second. Still, the improvement may be meaningful. For instance, if your program performs computations that take hours to complete, that which is a small difference here may become a large difference later.

As I mentioned previously, this is a contrived example; the code in this program was designed specifically such that the optimizer has a lot of improvements to make. Although gcc's optimizer is powerful, you can help by writing good code to start with. If you write code that is concise and has a good flow of logic, the optimizer may be able to do even more for you—or you may not even need optimizations at all.

If you analyze the code used in the preceding examples, you will see that there are many apparent problems. Here they are:

✦ First, the ending value of the counter is calculated every time through the loop as `2 * 100000000 * 9 / 18 + 5131`. If the code is modified such that it simply ends at `100005131`, the computer no longer has to calculate the value each time through the loop. Note that in this case, the optimizer simply performs that calculation beforehand. If you, for instance, have a variable `myvar` and use `2 * myvar` as the ending value, this has to be recalculated each time through the loop; the optimizer can't help in this case. You may want to use a temporary variable to hold the value instead.

✦ The increment is defined as `(5 - 3) / 2`—that is, 1. Again, the computer has to make a calculation here, defining what the end value is. Simply using `counter++` would save some time.

✦ The temporary variable `temp` itself is never used; it is wasteful to assign something to it each time through the loop.

✦ Even though the `five` variable is used, still it is inefficient to assign the same value to it each time through the loop. It's better to do that only once, either before or after the loop.

✦ The same concept applies with the ending variable. Because we know where the loop ends, it is possible to compute this as one less than the ending value—that is, `100005130`. Therefore, assigning this every time through the loop is also unnecessary.

✦ After you make the changes noted previously, the loop is empty; it only modifies `counter`. Because `counter` is used nowhere else, it can be removed as well.

Here's a revised version of the code, which incorporates the changes previously mentioned:

```c
#include <stdio.h>

int main(void) {
    int ending = 100005130;
    int five = 5;
    printf("five = %d; ending = %d\n", five, ending);
    return 0;
}
```

Even before running the code, you can tell that it's more straightforward and easier to follow. Now, try compiling and running it:

```
$ gcc -Wall -o test2 test2.c
$ time ./test2
five = 5; ending = 100005130

real    0m0.004s
user    0m0.000s
sys     0m0.000s
```

That's an incredible difference over even -O3. The original program took over 350 times longer, even with full optimizations.

Thus, there are two important points here: one, that the gcc optimizer can dramatically improve the performance of programs; and two, that you often can do more to increase the program speed than the optimizer can, if you write good code. Yes, gcc is smart, but a good programmer can still be more effective with speed optimizations.

Generating debug symbols

Another powerful feature of modern development systems is the availability of powerful debugging tools. These tools provide you, the programmer, with powerful ways to trace the execution of a program and to isolate problems. The GNU Debugger (gdb), is an example of such a tool. Here, you will learn how to compile your programs such that gdb can work with them.

Cross-Reference
The GNU Debugger (gdb), is discussed in detail in Chapter 10, "Debugging with gdb."

Before you can use gdb properly with your programs, you need to compile them with debugging symbols. When you do this, gcc inserts extra information into the object files (.o) and executable files that it generates. This extra information enables gdb to determine the relationship between the compiled code and the lines in your source file. Without that information, gdb would not be able to determine which line of code your program is executing at any given time.

These debug symbols are not compiled into your programs by default because of one important side effect: they increase the size of the executable, sometimes significantly. It is possible, however, to remove debug symbols from an already compiled program by using the strip(1) utility. This means that it's not necessary to recompile your programs after you're done debugging them.

There is a caveat with the powerful debug symbols mechanism, though. The uses of these symbols can be incompatible with optimizations. Because gcc can sometimes modify the order in which instructions are performed to gain speed benefits, the flow of control used by the final program may differ from that which you wrote, which can make debugging confusing or even practically impossible. For this reason, it is best to avoid using the -O or optimization-enabling -f options when you intend to debug a given piece of code eventually.

To generate debugging symbols, you use the -g option to gcc. In its basic form, it generates a default set of debugging options, which are usually sufficient. You might use a command such as:

```
$ gcc -g -Wall -o test1 test1.c
```

You can also enable more debugging information, which can be useful in some cases. If you will be using the gdb debugger (or one of its derivatives) later, you will want to use a command like this:

```
$ gcc -ggdb3 -Wall -o test1 test1.c
```

The gdb part of the preceding line instructs gcc to generate debugging symbols with the gdb extensions. The 3 means that it ought to use level-3 debugging information, the highest level possible. Thus, you get the maximum possible debugging information with -ggdb3. Level 3 adds information such as macro definitions to the debugging information, which can be valuable in certain situations.

We will look at an example of using debugging symbols to analyze a crash. Consider the following code:

```
#include <stdio.h>

int main(void) {
    int input = 0;
    printf("Enter an integer: ");
    scanf("%d", input);
    printf("Twice the number you supplied is %d.\n", 2 * input);
    return 0;
}
```

This simple program will crash with a core dump when run. For the sake of this example, assume that you don't know this beforehand. You might compile the program like this:

```
$ gcc -Wall -o crash crash.c
```

Some newer versions of the compiler will issue a warning about line 6 in the preceding example, which is a hint of trouble yet to come. Ignore that for now and try running the program:

```
$ ./crash
Enter an integer: 5
Segmentation fault
```

What a surprise—the program crashed! The next step is to compile with debugging symbols:

```
$ gcc -ggdb3 -Wall -o crash crash.c
```

Now, you need to enable core dumps. Under the Bash shell (the default with most Linux systems), you can do so by running:

```
$ ulimit -c unlimited
```

Next, run the program again:

```
$ ./crash
Enter an integer: 5
Segmentation fault (core dumped)
```

Excellent—it crashed again! Yes, this may sound ironic, but notice that you now have a file named core. This file can unlock the secret of why the program crashed.

The next step is to load the program and core file into gdb for analysis:

```
$ gdb crash core
GNU gdb 4.18
Copyright 1998 Free Software Foundation, Inc.
GDB is free software, covered by the GNU General Public License, and you are
welcome to change it and/or distribute copies of it under certain conditions.
Type "show copying" to see the conditions.
There is absolutely no warranty for GDB.  Type "show warranty" for details.
This GDB was configured as "i686-pc-linux-gnu"...
Core was generated by `./crash'.
Program terminated with signal 11, Segmentation fault.
Reading symbols from /lib/libc.so.6...done.
Reading symbols from /lib/ld-linux.so.2...done.
#0  0x400686fb in _IO_vfscanf () from /lib/libc.so.6
```

The last several lines are the ones that are interesting. First, the fact that the program crashed because of a segmentation fault indicates that some memory issue was probably at hand. Then, the fact that the crash occurred in a function containing the word scanf (_IO_vscanf ()) is a hint. You can, however, get more detailed information:

```
(gdb) bt
#0  0x400686fb in _IO_vfscanf () from /lib/libc.so.6
#1  0x4006a048 in scanf () from /lib/libc.so.6
#2  0x8048448 in main () at crash.c:6
```

Skipping past the first two lines, which occur inside of the C library, you see something that occurred on line 6 of crash.c. Now, one more check:

```
(gdb) frame 2
#2  0x8048448 in main () at crash.c:6
6               scanf("%d", input);
(gdb) print input
$1 = 0
```

First, you switch to frame 2 (the value on the appropriate line of the bt output). Then, you ask gdb to display the value of the variable input just before the crash. It is still zero—the value 5 was not stored into it, confirming the suspicion that the call to the scanf() function caused the crash.

Now that the problem is isolated, you may exit gdb by typing the following:

```
(gdb) q
```

Don't worry if you didn't understand all of the commands sent to gdb. These topics will be covered in more detail in Chapter 10, "Debugging with gdb."

Now that you know where the problem is, you can modify crash.c and insert an ampersand before input on line 6. Your program will now look like this:

```
#include <stdio.h>

int main(void) {
    int input = 0;
    printf("Enter an integer: ");
    scanf("%d", &input);
    printf("Twice the number you supplied is %d.\n", 2 * input);
    return 0;
}
```

Compiling and running this code results in a working program:

```
$ gcc -Wall -o crash crash.c
$ ./crash
Enter an integer: 5
Twice the number you supplied is 10.
```

This gives you only a quick glance at gdb and what it can do when you add debugging symbols to your program. The debugger also can run through your program step by step, and can enable you to examine it while it is running instead of after it has crashed. All these details will be covered in Chapter 10.

Taking a Look at the Big Picture of gcc

Thus far, you have learned how to use basic gcc options to generate a program, control optimization levels, enable debugging symbols, and so on. However, a lot of detail has been hidden from your view. This is done intentionally, so that using and learning the system is simplified. When you want to work with more advanced situations, though, it is important to understand the pieces of the puzzle and how they fit together. After you understand this, you can better understand various error or warning messages that might be produced at different times during the build process, or be able to control more precisely how your programs get compiled and linked.

In traditional UNIX fashion, the build system contains a number of components that you can assemble together to form a comprehensive solution to a problem. Even though you may have not noticed, running gcc does much more than run the compiler. A compiler simply translates source code to assembly code. After that, an assembler must be run to generate object code. Finally, a linker must be run to bind the object code together with all the things necessary for it to run.

As you have used it thus far, gcc has taken care of these extra details for you automatically. Even though you didn't explicitly request it, gcc has used several programs to generate your final output. I'm going to lead you through a small tour of the components, and, like a museum tour, I'll finish up with a look at the Linux developer's gift shop, filled with useful knick-knacks and small tools.

The C compiler: gcc

Thus far, this entire chapter covered gcc. At this point you should note that many of the programs discussed in the next section can be invoked by gcc, and in fact are invoked by gcc if you use it as the examples in this chapter have. Thus, gcc is more than a compiler; it's also a front-end that can be used to take care of the details of the build process for you.

The C++ compiler: g++

The GNU C++ compiler, g++, performs the same function for C++ programs as gcc does for C programs. Strictly speaking, gcc can compile C++ code, as well, given the proper circumstances. However, the result will not always be correct without manually specifying additional options. Therefore, when compiling C++ programs, g++ is generally the proper route to take. The options accepted by g++ are the same as those accepted for gcc, so there is no need to relearn commands.

When dealing with C++ code, you (generally) should give it a .C or .cxx extension (as opposed to .c) such that both the C++ compiler and other programmers can properly identify the code as C++ code. Then, you use g++ to compile in the same fashion as you would use gcc. For instance, consider this C++ program:

```
#include <iostream.h>

int main(void) {
  int input;

  cout << "Enter a number: ";
  cin > input;
  cout << "Twice the number you supplied is " << 2 * input << endl;
  return 0;
}
```

Assuming you save it as test3.C, you may compile this code by using the following command:

```
$ g++ -Wall -o test3 test3.C
```

Executing the program is done in the same fashion as with C programs:

```
$ ./test3
Enter a number: 21
Twice the number you supplied is 42
```

The C preprocessor: cpp

The cpp (C Preprocessor) command is responsible for the evaluation of macros, conditional compilation, and other tasks that need to take place before the code is passed through the compiler properly. In general, any of the # syntax items, and the code that they act upon, is preprocessed by cpp. For instance, consider the following code snippet:

```
#define FOO (5 * 2)
printf("%d\n", FOO * 2);   /* Display the number */
```

After running through cpp, the code will be modified to read:

```
printf("%d\n", (5 * 2) * 2);
```

So, cpp removes comments, interprets macros, handles include files, handles #if and #ifdef statements, and almost anything else that starts with a # sign. The gcc compiler normally calls cpp automatically; you also can call it with gcc -E or by using cpp on the command line.

Note   Some Linux distributions do not place cpp on your default path. You might need to find it for yourself if you get an error when you try to use it; look under /usr/lib/gcc-lib and its subdirectories.

One interesting thing to note is that cpp is not restricted to use with C programs. Because cpp does not deal in any way with the code it generates, one can use it to generate non-C code. Some people use it to automate the generation of HTML code for web pages; others, to process configuration files for networked computers.

Tip   If you want to try cpp in such a situation, you will probably want to use the -P option (which inhibits generation of line number information) on its command line, which prevents the output of line number information.

The GNU Linker: ld

With virtually every program you write, there are multiple parts that have to be brought together to form the final executable. Even if your program contains only one module that you've written, as is the case with the samples encountered thus far, still you must use the linker (ld). Items such as the C library, program initialization code, and so on, must be included. Without the C library, for instance, you wouldn't have such library function calls as strcpy() or getpwnam() available. Without these calls, you lose the capability of doing even some simple tasks unless you write your own replacements.

If larger programs are in your future, most likely you'll want to split them into separate modules. When this is done, the linker combines all the modules together, brings in the C library and startup code, and generates the finished product. Again, the linker plays a vital part in the generation of your executables.

Normally, ld is invoked by the compiler to generate the final executable. You can use ld manually, however, if you want more fine-grained control over the linking process.

The GNU Assembler: as

When gcc compiles your code, it generates assembly code. The job of as (GNU Assembler) is to take this assembly code and generate the object (binary) code that is used to form the .o files, libraries, or the final executable. The as program is rarely called independently; rather, it is almost always invoked by gcc. However, if you have a desire to program with assembly language — perhaps for fine-grained performance optimization or kernel modifications — you can invoke as manually also.

Note that because assembly is a low-level type of code, it varies between different platforms, even with the same operating system. For instance, the assembly code used to perform computations on a 32-bit x86 platform can vary significantly from that used to do the same computations on a 64-bit Alpha platform.

The Archiver: ar

To build static libraries, you need to use the ar (the archiver) program. This program is used for combining several small files into one large file. In the case of static libraries, this is precisely what must be done: you combine multiple .o files into a single .a file.

The Makefile Interpreter: make

Large programs can often contain dozens or even hundreds of separate modules. If compiling the program meant manually invoking gcc for each of these modules, the build procedure would be long, tedious, and error-prone. You might have to remember exactly which files have been modified, which files might depend on code elsewhere, and the proper gcc options for each of these items. Hopefully, as you are thinking about how tedious it would be to invoke gcc several hundred times, you're thinking, what a nightmare! Well, the make program is designed to automate this entire process.

With make, a file called Makefile is created. This file describes how to build each component of the system by using a set of rules. These rules define the commands necessary to build a component (such as a call to gcc or ar) as well as dependencies. For instance, if you modify a header file that several C source files include, you will want to rebuild these files to use the modifications to the header file. However, to save time, you probably don't want to rebuild all the other modules. GNU make is capable of figuring out such situations based on the rules in the Makefile, and thus can compile only the minimum set of files necessary to bring the final product up-to-date relative to the source.

Like cpp, make is not restricted to working only with C source code. Some use it to generate code for languages such as Pascal or Fortran, or even for other tasks such as automating web sites or the building of packages for a Linux distribution.

Unlike many of the programs covered to this point, make is not invoked by gcc. Rather, make invokes gcc.

The GNU Debugger: gdb

While not strictly part of the build process, gdb (GNU debugger) most certainly is part of the development process. As previously discussed, with gdb, you can track down any bugs that may be present in your software. Features of gdb include postcrash analysis, step-by-step execution, conditional breakpoints, and other modern debugger features.

Library Dependency Display: ldd

The ldd (Library Dependency Display) tool shows you which shared libraries a given executable (or library) requires in order to run. For a simple C program, the display often contains only two items: the C library, libc, and the dynamic loader, ld-linux. For instance:

```
$ ldd ./myprogram
        libc.so.6 => /lib/libc.so.6 (0x40004000)
        /lib/ld-linux.so.2 => /lib/ld-linux.so.2 (0x2aaaa000)
```

For C++ programs, you'll often see these, plus the C++ library (something like libg++, libstdc++, libc++, libg++272, and so on, depending on your distribution, library, and compiler versions). Here is a simple example:

```
$ ldd ./test3
        libstdc++-libc6.1-1.so.2 => /usr/lib/libstdc++-libc6.1-1.so.2
(0x40004000)
        libm.so.6 => /lib/libm.so.6 (0x40049000)
        libc.so.6 => /lib/libc.so.6 (0x40067000)
        /lib/ld-linux.so.2 => /lib/ld-linux.so.2 (0x2aaaa000)
```

This sample shows the usage of three libraries. The first line, mentioning libstdC++-libc6.1-1.so.2, indicates that the C++ library is linked into the program. The second line, with libm.so.6, tells you that the math library is used. The third line, libc.so.6, indicates that the standard C library is also used. The final line, /lib/ld-linux.so.2, is the standard inclusion of the dynamic loader.

For more complex programs, many libraries may be included:

```
        libgnorba.so.27 => /usr/lib/libgnorba.so.27 (0x40004000)
        libgnomeui.so.32 => /usr/lib/libgnomeui.so.32 (0x40010000)
        libart_lgpl.so.2 => /usr/lib/libart_lgpl.so.2 (0x400cf000)
        libgdk_imlib.so.1 => /usr/lib/libgdk_imlib.so.1 (0x400dd000)
        libSM.so.6 => /usr/X11R6/lib/libSM.so.6 (0x4010b000)
        libICE.so.6 => /usr/X11R6/lib/libICE.so.6 (0x40114000)
        libgtk-1.2.so.0 => /usr/lib/libgtk-1.2.so.0 (0x4012b000)
        libgdk-1.2.so.0 => /usr/lib/libgdk-1.2.so.0 (0x4024c000)
        libgmodule-1.2.so.0 => /usr/lib/libgmodule-1.2.so.0 (0x40282000)
        libXi.so.6 => /usr/X11R6/lib/libXi.so.6 (0x40285000)
        libXext.so.6 => /usr/X11R6/lib/libXext.so.6 (0x4028d000)
        libX11.so.6 => /usr/X11R6/lib/libX11.so.6 (0x40299000)
        libgnome.so.32 => /usr/lib/libgnome.so.32 (0x4033f000)
        libgnomesupport.so.0 => /usr/lib/libgnomesupport.so.0 (0x40353000)
        libesd.so.0 => /usr/lib/libesd.so.0 (0x4035a000)
        libaudiofile.so.0 => /usr/lib/libaudiofile.so.0 (0x40361000)
        libm.so.6 => /lib/libm.so.6 (0x4036f000)
        libdb.so.3 => /lib/libdb.so.3 (0x4038c000)
        libglib-1.2.so.0 => /usr/lib/libglib-1.2.so.0 (0x403c8000)
```

```
libdl.so.2 => /lib/libdl.so.2 (0x403ea000)
libORBitCosNaming.so.0 => /usr/lib/libORBitCosNaming.so.0 (0x403ee000)
libORBit.so.0 => /usr/lib/libORBit.so.0 (0x403f6000)
libIIOP.so.0 => /usr/lib/libIIOP.so.0 (0x40434000)
libORBitutil.so.0 => /usr/lib/libORBitutil.so.0 (0x40444000)
libnsl.so.1 => /lib/libnsl.so.1 (0x40446000)
libgtkxmhtml.so.1 => /usr/lib/libgtkxmhtml.so.1 (0x4045c000)
libXpm.so.4 => /usr/X11R6/lib/libXpm.so.4 (0x404b9000)
libjpeg.so.62 => /usr/lib/libjpeg.so.62 (0x404c7000)
libpng.so.2 => /usr/lib/libpng.so.2 (0x404e7000)
libz.so.1 => /usr/lib/libz.so.1 (0x40513000)
libc.so.6 => /lib/libc.so.6 (0x40522000)
/lib/ld-linux.so.2 => /lib/ld-linux.so.2 (0x2aaaa000)
```

This program is bringing along support for various graphics formats (libjpeg, libpng, libXpm, and so on), graphical interfaces, sound support, compression support, database support, and several other libraries. Linux makes it possible to easily utilize an existing codebase in your own programs.

See Chapter 9, "Libraries and Linking," for details on building the libraries themselves.

The programmer's gift shop

In addition to the programs discussed already, there are several other small, useful tools on your system that can be useful when building software. Many are part of the GNU binutils package (as are ld and as), but others are from separate packages. Here are some of the tools that can be helpful while you're developing software:

✦ The GNU profiler, gprof, is used to benchmark programs. Gprof has finer granularity than time; it can identify particular functions or sections of code that are bottlenecks.

✦ The debug symbol stripper, strip, is used to remove debugging symbols from a program or object compiled with -g. You can use strip to do this instead of recompiling the program without the debugging information.

✦ The strings program can look inside of binary files and display only the parts that contain plain text.

✦ strace displays the system calls made by a program and the arguments to those calls. The functionality here can overlap somewhat with gdb, but you can get some other useful information from strace as well. A related program is ltrace, which traces library calls.

✦ The makedepend tool, although part of the X11 development suite, can nevertheless be used for many other types of programs. This tool analyzes the code and automatically produces the appropriate dependency lines in a Makefile, saving you from having to update them on a regular basis.

Working with Large Projects

The easiest way to deal with small blocks of C code is to place all the code into a single file and compile this file with gcc. However, when your code size starts to increase, this approach starts to get impractical. Finding the desired line of code within a file containing tens or hundreds of thousands of lines can be difficult. Editors start to become less efficient and more memory-hungry as they must work with large files. Coordinating multiple people working on a development team is difficult when only one file needs to be edited. And recompiling a huge file after making a change to only one line of code is a waste of valuable time.

C provides you with a powerful way to split up your work. By using separate C modules — or functions and data contained in separately compiled .c source files — you can separate your work into logical chunks. Furthermore, each of these chunks can be of a manageable size, making navigation within your program's source simpler. When collaborating with members of a team, what would otherwise be a serious management problem is simplified; as long as team members work on only certain files, synchronizing changes between them becomes easier, especially when a tool such as CVS is used.

There are benefits for the future as well; a good programmer always keeps future uses of code in mind. After the code is separated into modules, assembling these modules into a library can be easy. After being made into a library, use of the code in other projects is trivial as well.

Having said all this, you should note that there could be some downsides to using modules. The use of global variables can be made more difficult, although many would (justly) argue that global variable usages ought to be minimized anyway. If modules are not split at logical places, the result can be more difficult to navigate than the original. However, as long as care is exercised, modules are not difficult.

Note   This book doesn't aim to teach you the intricacies of C; suffice it to say that you will need to use the extern keyword and probably manage a series of .h files for prototypes as well. Here, the aim is to cover those aspects of multiple modules specific to the build system in Linux.

For the sake of discussion, I'll assume that you have three modules as part of your program: io.c, init.c, and compute.c. Most likely, your io.c module handles input and output from the program; init.c, the initialization for the program; and compute.c, whatever computation is necessary. The exact separation of capabilities is not relevant to gcc, but is indeed quite relevant to the programmer.

To compile the entire program the simplistic way, one could use this:

```
$ gcc -Wall -o myprogram io.c init.c compute.c
```

When used like this, gcc compiles each .c file, and then links them all together to form the final product. For small projects, this approach is workable. However, you are still recompiling the entire program every time there is even a minor change, so there is not much advantage for compile time.

The next step is to split the compilation into separate steps. To do this, use the -c option of gcc. The -c option tells gcc that you do not intend to generate the final executable immediately; rather, gcc simply generates an .o file. This .o file contains the compiled code from one .c file only; it is not executable by itself. So, first, you compile the .c files into .o files:

```
$ gcc -Wall -c -o io.o io.c
$ gcc -Wall -c -o init.o init.c
$ gcc -Wall -c -o compute.o compute.c
```

Now there are three .o files that correspond to the three .c files. These are not executable alone; to generate the final executable, you run:

```
$ gcc -o myprogram io.o init.o compute.o
```

Note   -Wall is not specified for the last command. This is because it would have no effect; this final gcc command is not compiling anything—it's simply linking everything together to generate the final executable.

Consider a situation in which you may have modified one line in init.c. Rather than recompile compute.c and io.c as well, you simply can recompile init.c and then relink:

```
$ gcc -Wall -c -o init.o init.c
$ gcc -o myprogram init.o io.o compute.o
```

Some benefit becomes apparent now; only one file has to be recompiled. If your program contains hundreds of files, this advantage can be much more significant than with this particular example. The link process is fairly fast relative to the compilation step, so you come out ahead.

You may be thinking at this point that it is tedious to use four commands to recompile the program instead of only one. Well, if so, you're right. Makefiles, discussed in Chapter 7, "Managing Projects with GNU make," can be used to great advantage to automate this process. Here is a simple Makefile that builds this program:

```
OBJS = io.o init.o compute.o
EXECUTABLE = myprogram
CFLAGS = -Wall
CC = gcc
```

```
# End of configuration options

all: $(EXECUTABLE)

$(EXECUTABLE): $(OBJS)
        $(CC) -o $(EXECUTABLE) $(OBJS)

%.o: %.c
        $(CC) $(CFLAGS) -c -o $@ $<

clean:
        -rm $(OBJS) $(EXECUTABLE) *~
```

Don't worry about the syntax right now; I will cover this in Chapter 7, "Managing Projects with GNU make." There is one thing to note, though. When you look at the lines that are indented from the left, you must use the tab key to indent them. Do not use a series of spaces.

You can modify this Makefile (note that it *must* be named Makefile to work by default) for your own purposes. Generally, you only need to modify the list of .o files in the first line and the executable name on the second line.

Give this Makefile a try. First, delete any existing .o files and your executable; you can also do this by running make clean.

Now, type make and press Enter. Watch what happens:

```
$ make
gcc -Wall -c -o io.o io.c
gcc -Wall -c -o init.o init.c
gcc -Wall -c -o compute.o compute.c
gcc -o myprogram io.o init.o compute.o
```

The make program automatically ran all the commands that you manually ran earlier. Already some timesaving is apparent. Recall the earlier scenario of modifying init.c. Make a modification to that file now and type make again:

```
$ make
gcc -Wall -c -o init.o init.c
gcc -o myprogram io.o init.o compute.o
```

The make program figured out that only one file was modified. So, it recompiled only that one file and then relinked the program. GNU make performed exactly the same actions that you did manually earlier; however, it determined the necessary actions and carried them out without any input from you, saving lots of time.

Using Advanced gcc Options

In addition to the gcc options that control basic file generation, there are also many other options that enable you to fine-tune gcc operations. For instance, you can control everything from where to include the files to the way in which the development tools are invoked.

Specifying search paths

When building a project, gcc has a default search path to use for things like include files and libraries. You will find that you will often need to add components to this path. For instance, if compiling a Tk program, you may need to add an entry to the search path so that gcc can find the header files for Tk that your program uses. Or, if programming for X, you may need to add an entry to the directory search path so that the linker can find the libraries necessary for your program.

The options for adding an entry to the include file search path and the library search path, respectively, are -I and -L. Examples of each option are shown below.

For instance, assume you have a program that wants to include a file named scsi.h. Your system may have this file under /usr/include/scsi, which is not on the default search path. Therefore, you might use:

```
gcc -Wall -I/usr/include/scsi -o myprogram myprogram.c
```

Doing so will enable the preprocessor to find the scsi.h file that your program wants.

A similar concept applies to the search path for libraries. If your program needs to link to the X11 library, for instance, you may need to inform the linker of the location of this library. You can do so by using:

```
gcc -L/usr/X11R6/lib -Wall -o myprogram myprogram.c -lX11
```

Linking with libraries

When writing many programs, you will need to link with libraries. These libraries can be anything from ones that implement mathematical functions to ones that provide support for using a graphical interface in the X Window System. They can be either static or shared; gcc can work with both.

The basic option to use to link in a library with your current program is -l (a lowercase L). This option should be specified at the final link stage of your compile only, which brings together all the .o files. If you are compiling directly from .c source file to a final executable, you should use -l on that gcc command line.

For instance, if you want to use the math library, you would probably include math.h in your program. Then, when compiling, you would need to link in the math library, named simply m. Therefore, a command such as the following would be appropriate:

```
gcc -Wall -o mathprogram mathprogram.c -lm
```

If you want to use the preceding Makefile example with a math program, you could modify it to include the math library in the final link stage, as follows:

```
OBJS = io.o init.o compute.o
EXECUTABLE = myprogram
CFLAGS = -Wall
CC = gcc

# End of configuration options

all: $(EXECUTABLE)

$(EXECUTABLE): $(OBJS)
        $(CC) -o $(EXECUTABLE) $(OBJS) -lm

%.o: %.c
        $(CC) $(CFLAGS) -c -o $@ $<

clean:
        -rm $(OBJS) $(EXECUTABLE) *~
```

With this option, the final link command will be:

```
gcc -o myprogram io.o init.o compute.o -lm
```

If you later wish to use ldd on the generated executable, you will confirm that the math library (libm) has indeed been included. You can add any number of libraries to the gcc command line with -l, and they will all be linked in.

Speeding compilation with pipes

The build process requires many steps — preprocessing, compilation, assembly, and linking to name a few. Normally, gcc handles many aspects of these tasks for you, automatically invoking programs as necessary.

However, by default, this can be slow because there are many temporary files involved. For instance, gcc will create a temporary file holding the output of the preprocessor, another one with the output of the compiler, and perhaps a third with the output of the assembler. Reading and writing these files takes time.

There is another way of communicating that can be more efficient: pipelines. With pipelines, several programs are invoked at once, with the output from one being sent directly to the input of another where possible. Temporary files are avoided with this scheme.

SMP (multiprocessor) machines derive extra benefit from the pipelining system; one process can execute on one processor while another process runs on a separate processor, both simultaneously working on different parts of the build process.

The potential downside to this approach is that more memory is required for the build. Because more processes can be stored in memory, and they must hold some data in RAM as well, the memory requirements increase. In most situations, this is not a problem given today's machines, but it can be difficult—and thus can hurt performance—if you are using an older system or one with little memory to spare.

The pipeline compilation process is specified by giving the `-pipe` option to gcc. After that, gcc takes care of setting up the appropriate pipes. A sample command line might be:

```
gcc -pipe -Wall -O3 -o test2 test2.c
```

The difference in compilation time may not be noticeable on smaller projects. However, with larger projects, the difference can become quite significant.

Peeking at gcc with -v

All of the interactions between the various build programs are normally hidden from view. Their details are generally unimportant and distracting. However, you can request the details to be shown as gcc runs; to do so, you use the `-v` option:

```
$ gcc -v -Wall -O3 -o test2 test2.c
```

When you run this command, gcc displays a lot of details about its build process. Following is the output with commentary:

```
Reading specs from /usr/lib/gcc-lib/i486-linux/egcs-2.91.66/specs
gcc version egcs-2.91.66 Debian GNU/Linux (egcs-1.1.2 release)
```

Thus far, gcc is specifying its version number and where it retrieved some build information. If your display is different from this, the remaining part of the output may differ as well, possibly significantly. This is normal; do not worry if there is a difference.

```
/usr/lib/gcc-lib/i486-linux/egcs-2.91.66/cpp -lang-c -v -undef -D__GNUC__=2 -
D__GNUC_MINOR__=91 -D__ELF__ -Dunix -Di386 -D__i386__ -Dlinux -D__ELF__
-D__unix__ -D__i386__ -D__i386__ -D__linux__ -D__unix -D__i386 -D__linux -
Asystem(posix) -D__OPTIMIZE__ -Wall -Asystem(unix) -Acpu(i386) -Amachine(i386)
-Di386 -D__i386 -D__i386__ -Di486 -D__i486 -D__i486__  test2.c /tmp/ccdiild0.i
```

The preceding output shows where gcc invokes the C preprocessor, cpp. This is all a single command line, and quite a large one at that — be glad that gcc generates it automatically! Most of the options that you see are -D options, telling the preprocessor what symbols should be interpreted as predefined.

```
GNU CPP version egcs-2.91.66 Debian GNU/Linux (egcs-1.1.2 release) (i386
Linux/ELF)
```

Now, the output is coming from the preprocessor. Next, it identifies its version number and then gets down to business:

```
#include "..." search starts here:
#include <...> search starts here:
 /usr/local/include
 /usr/lib/gcc-lib/i486-linux/egcs-2.91.66/include
 /usr/include
End of search list.
```

The preprocessor displays the search path for header (include) files. It first displays any directories for files included with quotation marks, and then the path for those included with angle brackets. There are no additional messages from cpp; the next message is from gcc and indicates the execution of another program as follows:

```
/usr/lib/gcc-lib/i486-linux/egcs-2.91.66/cc1 /tmp/ccdiild0.i -quiet -dumpbase
test2.c -O3 -Wall -version -o /tmp/ccmrFelv.s
```

The cc1 program is the compiler proper; it actually does the grunt work of compiling. Notice that it reads a .i file generated by cpp and generates a .s file for the assembler.

```
GNU C version egcs-2.91.66 Debian GNU/Linux (egcs-1.1.2 release) (i486-linux)
compiled by GNU C version egcs-2.91.66 Debian GNU/Linux (egcs-1.1.2 release).
```

cc1 identifies its version and then displays no additional messages as it proceeds.

```
as -V -Qy -o /tmp/cc5Ux7Gf.o /tmp/ccmrFelv.s
```

The preceding shows how gcc invokes the assembler, telling it to generate an object file, and taking the assembler source file (.s) as input.

```
GNU assembler version 2.9.1 (i486-linux), using BFD version 2.9.1.0.25
```

Next, the assembler identifies its version and then proceeds with no additional output.

```
/usr/lib/gcc-lib/i486-linux/egcs-2.91.66/collect2 -m elf_i386 -dynamic-linker
/lib/ld-linux.so.2 -o test2 /usr/lib/crt1.o /usr/lib/crti.o /usr/lib/gcc-
lib/i486-linux/egcs-2.91.66/crtbegin.o
-L/usr/lib/gcc-lib/i486-linux/egcs-2.91.66 /tmp/cc5Ux7Gf.o -lgcc -lc -lgcc
/usr/lib/gcc-lib/i486-linux/egcs-2.91.66/crtend.o /usr/lib/crtn.o
```

This is the invocation of the linker, which performs the final stage in the build process. Notice some familiar names: ld-linux, the dynamic loader; and -lc, which includes the C library. There are also some unfamiliar names, such as crtbegin.o, which handle certain initializations for the program.

An interesting contrast occurs when you use -pipe for compiling programs:

```
$ gcc -pipe -v -Wall -O3 -o test2 test2.c
Reading specs from /usr/lib/gcc-lib/i486-linux/egcs-
2.91.66/specs
gcc version egcs-2.91.66 Debian GNU/Linux (egcs-1.1.2 release)
```

Thus far, everything is as it was before. However, note the differencein the following example:

```
/usr/lib/gcc-lib/i486-linux/egcs-2.91.66/cpp -lang-c -v -undef -D__GNUC__=2 -
D__GNUC_MINOR__=91 -D__ELF__ -Dunix -Di386 -D__i386__ -Dlinux -D__ELF__
-D__unix__ -D__i386__ -D__i386__ -D__linux__ -D__unix -D__i386 -D__linux -
Asystem(posix) -D__OPTIMIZE__ -Wall -Asystem(unix) -Acpu(i386) -Amachine(i386)
-Di386 -D__i386 -D__i386__ -Di486 -D__i486 -D__i486__ test2.c |
  /usr/lib/gcc-lib/i486-linux/egcs-2.91.66/cc1 -quiet -dumpbase test2.c -O3 -Wall
-version -o - |
  as -V -Qy -o /tmp/cc3vU31B.o -
```

The components are invoked at once by gcc, and gcc sends the output from one program directly to the input of the next program. It invokes the preprocessor, sending its output to cc1, whose output goes to the assembler. Only the link step cannot be performed here, because it requires all files to be ready before linking.

Now, all these programs display their initialization messages:

```
GNU CPP version egcs-2.91.66 Debian GNU/Linux (egcs-1.1.2 release) (i386
Linux/ELF)
#include "..." search starts here:
#include <...> search starts here:
 /usr/local/include
 /usr/lib/gcc-lib/i486-linux/egcs-2.91.66/include
 /usr/include
End of search list.
```

```
GNU C version egcs-2.91.66 Debian GNU/Linux (egcs-1.1.2 release) (i486-linux)
compiled by GNU C version egcs-2.91.66 Debian GNU/Linux (egcs-1.1.2 release).
GNU assembler version 2.9.1 (i486-linux), using BFD version 2.9.1.0.25
```

The compilation and assembly finishes, and execution now moves on to linking. This is the same as seen before:

```
 /usr/lib/gcc-lib/i486-linux/egcs-2.91.66/collect2 -m elf_i386 -dynamic-linker
/lib/ld-linux.so.2 -o test2 /usr/lib/crt1.o /usr/lib/crti.o /usr/lib/gcc-
lib/i486-linux/egcs-2.91.66/crtbegin.o
-L/usr/lib/gcc-lib/i486-linux/egcs-2.91.66 /tmp/cc3vU3lB.o -lgcc -lc -lgcc
/usr/lib/gcc-lib/i486-linux/egcs-2.91.66/crtend.o /usr/lib/crtn.o
```

Being pedantic with ANSI C

When you write code that needs to be portable to nonLinux or nonUNIX platforms, you must adhere to the standards set down in the ANSI C specification. The gcc compiler and Linux environment both add numerous extensions to the language. By default, gcc also doesn't deal with a few undesirable aspects of ANSI C.

You can tell gcc to disable its extensions to ANSI C. This can be useful if you want to check to see if your programs will compile on other platforms. Also, some programs written for pure ANSI C may not compile with the GNU extensions.

You can use the `-ansi` option to enable this type of behavior when compiling your programs. For a step farther, there is the `-pedantic` option. This one disables even more GNU extensions and additional features. Additionally, it generates all warnings that the ANSI C standard mandates, and programs that use nonstandard extensions won't compile.

If you are writing software solely for Linux platforms, these options are not of interest. However, if your program will be running on other platforms (particularly non-UNIX platforms), they can be useful in your development process. Note, however, that some standard code may emit warnings in this situation, so its usefulness may not be as great as you might hope. Using these options does not guarantee that programs will compile elsewhere. They are merely useful guides.

Summary

In this chapter, you learned how to use gcc and its companion programs. In particular, you learned:

✦ The main program to compile your programs is called gcc.

✦ You can invoke gcc with `-W` options to enable useful warnings.

✦ You can enable various levels of optimizations with -0. These optimizations can improve the performance of your program, but writing good code can have an even greater effect.

✦ You can enable the generation of debug symbols with -g or -ggdb3. These enable you to use gdb to track down problems in your code.

✦ There are many tools that work along with gcc to perform such tasks as preprocessing your code, assembling it, and linking the code. Many of these tools are invoked automatically by gcc, but sometimes you may want to invoke them manually.

✦ You can split your programs into modules to decrease recompilation time during development. The GNU make program can automate the build process, and is quite handy in these situations.

✦ When you need to include or link with code not on the standard search paths, you can use -I and -L, respectively.

✦ If you need to use some code from a library, you can do so with the -l option to gcc.

✦ Specifying the -pipe option to gcc often can speed the compilation of your programs because temporary files are no longer necessary.

✦ The -v option enables you to see details about what is going on under the hood of gcc.

✦ The -ansi and -pedantic options turn on additional warnings and greater strictness when compiling your code.

✦   ✦   ✦

Managing Projects with GNU Make

As your programs get larger, the process necessary to build them becomes more complex and time-consuming. The Linux environment provides a tool to help you with this process: GNU make. In this chapter, you'll learn how to use GNU make, what it can do, and how to apply it to your needs.

Introducing GNU Make

If you have ever seen the assembly line for any fairly complex product, such as a car, you know that the process of building that product is detailed, precise, and involved. Everything must be built properly, and all the parts must be linked together to form the final product. If something goes wrong, your car may end up looking more like the surplus materials from an old Pinto plant.

In order to get your new car built properly, managers — both human and computerized — control the process in which it is built. Thus, an element of central control regulates the flow of materials from one area to the next.

Although a problem with the build process in your program probably is not going to cause your next car to have a strange appearance, the same principles apply. With all but the smallest of projects, the build process involves executing dozens, hundreds, or even thousands of commands. If these were all executed manually, the build process would be so long and error-prone that it would be extremely difficult to compile and link your programs.

Therefore, there is an automation system for the assembly line that is the build process for your code. You define the rules that govern how your code is built. The system then applies those rules to build your project.

You define these rules in a file generally named Makefile. You then use a Makefile interpreter, such as GNU make that ships with Linux, to process it and build your project. This program invokes your compilers, linkers, assemblers, and other build programs as necessary to generate a final executable. After you type **make** on the command line, the system automatically examines your rules and the files present on the system and determines exactly what actions need to be taken to completely build your project. These actions could end up spanning thousands of commands, and could even involve parallel processing—a true extension of the assembly line metaphor into the Linux build process.

While you are in the development process, you frequently need to make changes to only a few files in a project, rebuild the program, and then test them. When you use make for your project, the system automatically detects the changes, and then performs actions necessary to update the program with your changes. You don't explicitly tell make what changed; it detects the changes on its own, recompiles only that which is necessary, and re-links your program.

In this section, you will learn how to write these Makefiles and how to use them. As you proceed, you'll even learn how to create intelligent Makefiles that can automatically detect many things about their environment so that you often don't need to tell them even the names of the files that comprise your program!

Principles of Makefiles

At a fundamental level, a Makefile is nothing more than a collection of rules. Each rule defines three things. The first is the file itself. This is the file that will be built when the rule is processed.

The second is the process that you must go through to make files into the final product. For instance, when working with C programs, you must compile a C file (.c) into an object file (.o) first, and then link together all the .o files to generate the final executable. Your rules can define this process.

The third item that you must define is the list of dependencies for each file. These dependencies must be created before you can process a file. For instance, a final executable depends on its .o files. These files, in turn, depend on .c files. In this way, even though you never specifically mention the process to go through from source to executable, the system is smart enough to figure it out.

Dependencies aren't necessarily the files that are built. They can be other arbitrary files. For instance, a C program might list an include file as a dependency. This means that if the include file is updated, the C file will be recompiled to take into account the changes. The dependencies could refer to other rules. For instance, you may require that a configuration scan be performed before the compile begins.

A simple Makefile

Consider a simple start to the world of make. In this example, we'll use the same situation as was featured in the end of Chapter 6, "Welcome to gcc." This code consists of three C source files and one header file.

For compute.c, the source is:

```
extern int someglobal;

int computer(void) {
  return 5 * someglobal;
}
```

For init.c, the source is:

```
#include <stdio.h>
#include "myprogram.h"

int someglobal = 11;

int main(void) {
  foo();
  return 0;
}
```

For io.c, the source is:

```
#include <stdio.h>
#include "myprogram.h"

int foo(void) {
  printf("The value is: %d.\n", computer());
  return 1;
}
```

For the header file, myprogram.h, the source is:

```
int computer(void);
int foo(void);
```

As you can see, this is not terribly complex code. In this chapter, I will focus on how the code is built rather than the code itself.

Next, I'll use a simple Makefile for this code. This Makefile is rather crude, and I'll improve it later in this chapter.

 Caution   You must use the Tab key to indent the lines (as shown in the following example); spaces will not work in this situation. Make considers lines beginning with a tab to be parts of a single rule; lines that do not begin specifically with a tab are parsed differently. If you use spaces instead of a Tab, your Makefile will not work.

Here is the code for the Makefile:

```
# Lines starting with the pound sign are comments.
#

# "all" is the default target. Simply make it point to
# myprogram.

all: myprogram

# Define the components of the program, and how to
# link them together.
# These components are defined as dependencies; that is,
# they must be made up-to-date before the .

myprogram: io.o init.o compute.o
    gcc -o myprogram io.o init.o compute.o

# Define the dependencies and compile information for the three C source
# code files.

compute.o: compute.c
    gcc -Wall -c -o compute.o compute.c

init.o: init.c myprogram.h
    gcc -Wall -c -o init.o init.c

io.o: io.c myprogram.h
    gcc -Wall -c -o io.o io.c
```

Now, you can compile your entire program with a single command at the prompt. The make program first looks for the name to the left of the colon, also called a target (in this example, the target is named all). In this case, all is set to depend on myprogram.

In make, a dependency means that the item on the left of the colon must have been updated at the same time or more recently than *each* item on the right side. In this particular case, all is not the name of an existing file, so it will evaluate myprogram every time make is invoked.

The `myprogram` target then indicates a dependency on three object files. This means that the object files must be up-to-date before you can run the commands necessary to build the final executable named `myprogram`. If any of these object files are newer than the final executable, the final executable is re-built; otherwise, there is no need to do so.

Next, there is an entry for each of the object files. Each entry indicates the dependency on a C source file for the build process. That is, if the specific C source file is updated, the object file must be re-built. Some entries also indicate a header file; the same rule applies there.

The entire build process is based on these rules. Now you can watch as make builds your program:

```
$ make
gcc -Wall -c -o io.o io.c
gcc -Wall -c -o init.o init.c
gcc -Wall -c -o compute.o compute.c
gcc -o myprogram io.o init.o compute.o
```

The commands in the preceding example are executed in the correct order. First, the C source files are compiled into object files. Next, these object files are linked to form the final executable. This ordering is all possible because of the dependencies; the final executable requires that the object files be up-to-date. To make these files current, make must compile the C source code into object code.

Watch what happens if you run make again. This time, because the progam already is compiled and no modifications are made, no compilation is necessary as shown in the following example:

```
$ make
make: Nothing to be done for `all'.
```

When run with already-built code as was done here, make checks to see if all the files are up-to-date. They are, so it exits without doing anything. You can see what happens when one file is modified. You can either load it into your favorite editor and re-save, or you can use the `touch` command, which updates its timestamp to the current time, effectively pretending to have updated the file. Watch what happens when you re-run make after doing this:

```
$ touch io.c
$ make
gcc -Wall -c -o io.o io.c
gcc -o myprogram io.o init.o compute.o
```

This time, make evaluates the dependencies as before. When it reaches io.o, make notices that io.c is newer; io.o must be recompiled. Then, because io.o was recompiled, the program must be re-linked. Make automatically detects these conditions and takes the appropriate actions. Notice that make does not compile the files that have not changed—compute.c and init.c. This saves you time, because the code that does not need recompilation is left alone.

Smarter Makefiles

In this Makefile, there is a lot of repetition. Two things that are repeated are the gcc command line options and the dependency rules for each particular C source file.

To simplify the command line options, you can use variables in your Makefile. This not only reduces the typing (and possible errors) necessary to create your rules, but also enables you to change the rules throughout the entire file by modifying one or two lines. This can be a big win for large files.

Setting variables in a Makefile is similar to doing the same in Bash; you use the equals sign (=) to separate the variable name, on the left, from the new value on the right. To access the contents of the variable later, the syntax is slightly different. With make, you use $(VARIABLE) to access the contents of the variable named VARIABLE.

The following revision of the Makefile incorporates these ideas:

```
# Lines starting with the pound sign are comments.
#

CC=gcc
CFLAGS=-Wall
COMPILE=$(CC) $(CFLAGS) -c

# "all" is the default target. Simply make it point to myprogram.

all: myprogram

# Define the components of the program, and how to link them together.
# These components are defined as dependencies; that is, they must be
# made up-to-date before the code is linked.

myprogram: io.o init.o compute.o
    $(CC) -o myprogram io.o init.o compute.o

# Define the dependencies and compile information for the three C source
# code files.

compute.o: compute.c
    $(COMPILE) -o compute.o compute.c

init.o: init.c myprogram.h
```

```
        $(COMPILE) -o init.o init.c

io.o: io.c myprogram.h
        $(COMPILE) -c -o io.o io.c
```

This revision eliminated the duplication of options such as -Wall on each line. If you want to add optimization to the options, you need to modify only one line — the CFLAGS one — to add the options. You don't need to modify each of the compilation lines.

You might also notice that the COMPILE variable is set based on the contents of two others. There is no problem with using the contents of one variable (or even multiple variables) to set another.

This solution has addressed one of the problems. However, there is still much more that you can do to improve this specific Makefile. For example, you can eliminate the separate listing for each C source file. You can do this by specifying a generic rule for all C source files. Here's a revised version of the Makefile; note that the version in the following example is not completely correct yet:

```
# Lines starting with the pound sign are comments.
#

CC=gcc
CFLAGS=-Wall
COMPILE=$(CC) $(CFLAGS) -c

# "all" is the default target. Simply make it point to myprogram.

all: myprogram

# Define the components of the program, and how to link them together.
# These components are defined as dependencies; that is, they must be
# made up-to-date before the code is linked.

myprogram: io.o init.o compute.o
    $(CC) -o myprogram io.o init.o compute.o

# Define the dependencies and compile information for the three C source
# code files.

%.o: %.c
    $(COMPILE) -o $@ $<
```

The last two lines in this Makefile are the interesting ones; they take the place of all the separate rules that were in the area earlier. Instead of several separate rules, there is a generic rule that indicates that any file ending with .o depends on a file with the same base name, but a .c extension. A rule for compiling these files is then defined. This rule looks much the same as the typical rules used earlier, but there are two unique characters at the end — the $@ and $< operators.

The first operator, $@, is replaced by the name of the target; in this case, the object file. As usual, gcc is told which filename to use for writing its output, and that filename is indicated by $@. The other operator, $<, indicates the file that needs to be compiled; in this case, that file is a C source code file. This bit of information obviously needs to be passed along to gcc as well, and such is done.

As I mentioned earlier, there is a small problem with the Makefile in the preceding example. Recall that two object files listed a C header file along with a source file in their dependency list. This particular Makefile omits that listing, and thus the dependency on the header file will not be recognized by make.

This can be fixed by manually declaring a special dependency for these particular files. Here is a fixed version of this Makefile:

```
# Lines starting with the pound sign are comments.
#

CC=gcc
CFLAGS=-Wall
COMPILE=$(CC) $(CFLAGS) -c

# "all" is the default target. Simply make it point to myprogram.

all: myprogram

# Define the components of the program, and how to link them together.
# These components are defined as dependencies; that is, they must be
# made up-to-date before the code is linked.

myprogram: io.o init.o compute.o
    $(CC) -o myprogram io.o init.o compute.o

# Define a special dependency on a header file.

init.o io.o: myprogram.h

# Specify that all .o files depend on .c files, and indicate how
# the .c files are converted (compiled) to the .o files.

%.o: %.c
    $(COMPILE) -o $@ $<
```

The additional line that starts with init.o demonstrates several important points. First, multiple targets are listed on the left side of the colon; this is indeed an acceptable syntax with make. Second, the line itself defines a dependency but defines no corresponding build rule. This also is acceptable; make realizes that the specified file must be re-built and uses the standard build rule for .o files as defined in the %.o line.

At this point, the new Makefile has reached a point where it performs in exactly the same fashion as the first Makefile presented in this chapter, but with much less effort on your part. With a few more modifications, the Makefile will end up like the one demonstrated in Chapter 6, "Welcome to gcc." Here is that Makefile, with a few slight modifications:

```
# Lines starting with the pound sign are comments.
#
# These things are options that you might need
# to tweak.

OBJS = io.o init.o compute.o
EXECUTABLE = myprogram

# You can modify the below as well, but probably
# won't need to.

CC = gcc
CFLAGS = -Wall
COMPILE = $(CC) $(CFLAGS) -c

# "all" is the default target. Simply make it point to myprogram.

all: $(EXECUTABLE)

# Define the components of the program, and how to link them together.
# These components are defined as dependencies; that is, they must be
# made up-to-date before the code is linked.

$(EXECUTABLE): $(OBJS)
    $(CC) -o $(EXECUTABLE) $(OBJS)

# Add any special rules here.

io.o init.o: myprogram.h

# Specify that all .o files depend on .c files, and indicate how
# the .c files are converted (compiled) to the .o files.

%.o: %.c
    $(COMPILE) -o $@ $<

clean:
    -rm $(OBJS) $(EXECUTABLE) *~
```

Let's analyze this version of the Makefile from start to finish to see how it works. It starts out by declaring two variables that hold information about the components of the program, and then the name of the program itself. With these options, you can easily re-use your Makefile with other projects; you may need to modify these first two lines only!

The next three variables are ones you've seen before; they are exactly the same and have the same purpose in this Makefile. After those variables, you see the all target, which functions the same as it did before; the only difference here is that the executable name is defined by a variable instead of being hard-coded into the rule.

Next, you see a line that begins with $(EXECUTABLE), which defines the rule for the final link step of the program. The difference here, though, is that many more things are used from variables. The executable's name comes from a variable, showing that it is indeed acceptable to use a variable for the name on the left side of a colon. The dependencies are defined by $(OBJS), which expands to a list of the object files that was defined at the top of the file. Then the compilation step uses the name of the compiler as defined in the previous example, as well as the same variables for the executable name and object files.

Next, there is the special rule line covering the dependency on the header file. This is the same line that was used in previous editions of the Makefile. Following that is the generic compilation rule, which is again the same as the one used in previous Makefile versions.

The Makefile ends with a clean target, which makes its first appearance in this version of the Makefile. The purpose of this target is to make a convenient way for you to remove compiled files, editor backup files, and other similar files that may have accumulated during the development process and return to a pristine source tree. This target has no dependencies, and no other targets depend on it. Therefore, there is no way that it can be automatically executed by make.

Tip   The only way to invoke the clean target is by giving an option to make on the command line, as demonstrated in the following example. The single line for the rule's actions, shown above, begins with a dash. This has special meaning to make; it indicates that if the command that is present on that line fails, make should ignore the error and proceed with normal processing. Such an error might occur, for instance, if there were no files that rm needed to delete. The command line itself indicates that the object files, the executable file, and editor backup files (which typically have a trailing tilde) are supposed to be removed.

If you want to remove these files, you can invoke make with the clean target, as shown in the following example:

```
$ make clean
rm io.o init.o compute.o myprogram *~
rm: cannot remove `*~': No such file or directory
make: [clean] Error 1 (ignored)
```

In this particular case, there were no editor backup files to remove, so `rm` complained about that pattern. However, because of the dash, make reports the error but ignores it. You can now test out the new Makefile on your newly cleaned directory if you wish:

```
$ make
gcc -Wall -c -o io.o io.c
gcc -Wall -c -o init.o init.c
gcc -Wall -c -o compute.o compute.c
gcc -o myprogram io.o init.o compute.o
```

Now the program is recompiled with the new, smarter Makefile. This Makefile is much more versatile and effectively scales to larger projects. Furthermore, it can be re-used on additional projects with very few modifications.

Using Intelligent Makefiles

Thus far, you have seen ways to instruct make on how to build your program, what the dependencies for your program are, and similar tasks. GNU make has many more features, however. Rather than giving the information to make manually, you can create an intelligent Makefile that tells the system how to build your program and determine the relevant information automatically. These techniques traditionally are not covered in generic UNIX documentation because they are not portable to other UNIX systems; the extra features used in this section will only work with GNU make. Because Linux distributions use GNU make, you can use these features on any Linux platform safely.

The goal of the intelligent Makefile is to minimize the amount of information that must be given to make prior to building your program.

A good place to start is with the list of object files in your program. Because most users have only one directory for a program, and one program per directory, it seems silly to have to manually specify a list of object files in the Makefile, especially if such a list can be determined based on the files in the current directory. The capability of automatically determining this tidbit of information eliminates the need to manually update the Makefile each time a new file is added to the program or an old file is removed. Furthermore, this enables the Makefile to be much more portable to other projects.

Two variable types

In GNU make, you can use two different types of variables. The first type is commonly used in Makefiles and has been used in the examples you have seen up to now. This kind of variable is re-evaluated each time it is used. That is, if it mentions other variables or functions, those references are not expanded immediately. Rather, they are expanded each time the variable is used. This can be advantageous. For instance, you can specify a variable that references another variable that does not yet exist at the time of the assignment to the first, because the inclusion of the second does not occur until the variable is actually expanded later on.

However, this is not desirable for your purposes,. One reason is, the set of files that match a given wildcard can change each moment while the contents of the Makefile are executed. Another reason is, matching wildcards is a (relatively) slow operation; it's best to perform wildcard matches once and re-use the results in the future.

GNU make has an alternative syntax assigning values to variables specifically geared towards your needs. Simply use := instead of = when assigning a value to a variable. For instance, if you take a line of code from the sample Makefile used in the previous section, you could say:

```
COMPILE := $(CC) $(CFLAGS) -c
```

In that particular Makefile, there is no apparent difference. However, if you consider a situation in which the value of the CC variable might change after this line of code, there is a difference. When you use the normal syntax, the expansion of COMPILE changes as well. When you use this alternative syntax, the value of COMPILE is fixed until you explicitly change it.

Wildcards: problems and solutions

Suppose you want to automatically obtain a list of all the object files in your current directory. This list could be used such that the developer does not have to list those files explicitly in a Makefile.

Your first inclination might be to use a simple wildcard, such as:

```
OBJS = *.o
```

Several problems arise with this approach. For one, the wildcard is evaluated every time something makes reference to the variable. Because the set of object files in the directory obviously can change as components are compiled, this solution can lead to very strange—or even unpredictable—results.

Additionally, this syntax works only if the project is already in a fully compiled state. Before a program is compiled, no object files are in the directory. Thus, the wildcard matches nothing and make thinks that you have a file named literally *.o that you wish to generate. This solution is obviously incorrect.

Furthermore, there is, again, a performance issue where the wildcard has to be evaluated each time it is used, which is a slow operation. Therefore, it is preferable to evaluate the wildcard once only, if possible.

Recalling the discussion of the two types of variables — CC and CFLAGS — you might decide to modify the code to use the alternative syntax instead. Your second attempt could be the following:

```
OBJS := *.o
```

Unfortunately, this is also incorrect. In this particular case, the effect is the same: OBJS is simply set to the string *.o.

Consider a completely different approach: the wildcard function in make. This function causes make to expand a wildcard itself and use the result. Therefore, you could try the following:

```
OBJS = $(wildcard *.o)
```

This time, OBJS will expand to the list of object files each time it is referenced. However, as discussed earlier, when you use normal syntax, there are problems both with a changing list of files and with performance. So, you should use the alternative syntax in this situation; that is:

```
OBJS := $(wildcard *.o)
```

This time, the file list is expanded immediately, and OBJS contains a list of object files — but only if they are present when make is invoked. What you really need is a list of the C source files, and then a way to convert this list into a list of files of the same name, but with an .o extension. Cleverly, the make authors provided a facility for doing this: the patsubst function. Your next step is to put it to use. You might use this first as follows:

```
TEMP := $(wildcard *.c)
OBJS := $(patsubst %.c,%.o,$(TEMP))
```

This is the first syntax example thus far that produces a correct, desired result! Note that the previous example can be rewritten such that the usage of a temporary variable is unnecessary:

```
OBJS := $(patsubst %.c,%.o,$(wildcard *.c))
```

Now you have now reduced the number of lines in the Makefile that require customization to only two: the name of the executable and any special dependencies. Before proceeding to change the file in some more significant ways, here's what it looks like with the wildcard change:

```
# Lines starting with the pound sign are comments.
#
# This is one of two options you might need to tweak.

EXECUTABLE = myprogram

# You can modify the below as well, but probably
# won't need to.

CC = gcc
CFLAGS = -Wall
COMPILE = $(CC) $(CFLAGS) -c
SRCS := $(wildcard *.c)
OBJS := $(patsubst %.c,%.o,$(SRCS))

# "all" is the default target. Simply make it point to myprogram.

all: $(EXECUTABLE)

# Define the components of the program, and how to link them together.
# These components are defined as dependencies; that is, they must be
# made up-to-date before the code is linked.

$(EXECUTABLE): $(OBJS)
    $(CC) -o $(EXECUTABLE) $(OBJS)

# Add any special rules here.

io.o init.o: myprogram.h

# Specify that all .o files depend on .c files, and indicate how
# the .c files are converted (compiled) to the .o files.

%.o: %.c
    $(COMPILE) -o $@ $<

clean:
    -rm $(OBJS) $(EXECUTABLE) *~

explain:
    @echo "The following information represents your program:"
    @echo "Final executable name: $(EXECUTABLE)"
    @echo "Source files:     $(SRCS)"
    @echo "Object files:     $(OBJS)"
```

There's a new target here: explain. This target displays the information that is detected (or, in the case of the executable, supplied) so that you can see what is going to be done. If you run make explain at the command line, you'll receive this output:

```
$ make explain
The following information represents your program:
Final executable name: myprogram
Source files:      compute.c init.c io.c
Object files:      compute.o init.o io.o
```

Note

I want to draw your attention to two things about `explain`. First, there is an at sign (@) at the start of each line. The reason for this is that, normally, make will display each command line prior to executing it. Thus, each line would be displayed twice, which is rather unsightly. The leading at sign suppresses this extra display. Second, all the output is in quotes. This is not strictly necessary in many cases, because echo displays all of its arguments. However, because arguments are space-separated, the extra spaces in the last two lines would not be preserved, and their visual effect would be lost.

Dependency calculations

Now that you have determined the names of all the source and object files in your project automatically, wouldn't it be nice to calculate all their dependencies automatically? This is, in fact, probably more of a benefit for the programmer than automatically figuring out the names of the object files. When dependencies are calculated manually, a programmer must update the Makefile every time it includes another custom file or removes an existing include statement. Calculating dependencies automatically can mean that the Makefile *never* needs to be updated, even when new modules are added to the code that have dependencies on new header files.

Programmers have used many different algorithms over the years to generate these dependencies automatically. There are programs that actually modify the Makefile, such as `makedepend`. Some programmers prefer to generate a giant file containing all the dependencies. GNU make has some features that allow a third option: generating one file per source file, each containing dependency information.

The basic idea is to go through and create a dependency file for each source file with the necessary information. Then, when you use make's `include` directive, these files are read into and parsed as if they're part of the main Makefile already. This approach is beneficial in several ways. First, because there is one dependency file per source file; you can declare a dependency of the dependency file on the *source* file, thus allowing the dependencies to be updated automatically when necessary. Second, because each source file has its dependencies in a separate file, you don't have to update the dependencies for everything when only one file is modified. Finally, you derive benefit from a feature of GNU make's `include` directive.

The dependency files are generated when you use the `-M` output from `gcc`. This option tells the compiler (more specifically, the pre-processor) to suppress the normal actions. Instead, it examines the source file and outputs an actual make rule indicating the dependencies for the given file. This is exactly what is needed here!

The generated rule lists the .o file on the left, followed by the name of the C file and any header files that are included along the way. This is great, but to form a completely correct solution, you need to make the dependency file list all of these files as dependencies also. This way, if a given header file is modified (perhaps to include an additional header file itself), the dependencies are updated as well. Fortunately, a simple call to sed will deal with this.

As a final word of introduction before presenting the updated Makefile, I want to discuss the include operator in GNU make. This operator was originally designed to pull information from other Makefiles into the current one, but GNU make has extended the operator such that it is useful for our purposes as well. Effectively, we will be pulling mini-Makefiles into the master one; each of these smaller files will contain two rules for dependencies.

GNU make's include operator has two useful features. The first is that it automatically rebuilds the files that are included, if necessary. If these files don't exist, or are out-of-date, GNU make looks for a rule to rebuild them in the current Makefile. If such a rule is found, the files are built using the rule.

A second feature is that, if any of these files need to be re-built, make automatically resets itself, allowing all of these files to be loaded in their updated state. Traditional make utilities do not support this sort of reset, meaning that old dependencies may have been used even if newer ones were available.

Listing 7-1 shows a Makefile that automatically generates dependencies and incorporates all of the preceding information.

Note   Listing 7-1 is available online.

Listing 7-1: **Makefile sample**

```
# Lines starting with the pound sign are comments.
#
# This is one of two options you might need to tweak.

EXECUTABLE = myprogram

# You can modify the below as well, but probably
# won't need to.
#

# CC is for the name of the C compiler. CPPFLAGS denotes pre-processor
# flags, such as -I options. CFLAGS denotes flags for the C compiler.
# CXXFLAGS denotes flags for the C++ compiler. You may add additional
```

```
# settings here, such as PFLAGS, if you are using other languages such
# as Pascal.

CC = gcc
CPPFLAGS =
CFLAGS = -Wall -O2
CXXFLAGS = $(CFLAGS)
COMPILE = $(CC) $(CPPFLAGS) $(CFLAGS) -c

SRCS := $(wildcard *.c)
OBJS := $(patsubst %.c,%.o,$(SRCS))
DEPS := $(patsubst %.c,%.d,$(SRCS))

# "all" is the default target. Simply make it point to myprogram.

all: $(EXECUTABLE)

# Define the components of the program, and how to link them together.
# These components are defined as dependencies; that is, they must be
# made up-to-date before the code is linked.

$(EXECUTABLE): $(DEPS) $(OBJS)
    $(CC) -o $(EXECUTABLE) $(OBJS)

# Specify that the dependency files depend on the C source files.

%.d: %.c
    $(CC) -M $(CPPFLAGS) $< > $@
    $(CC) -M $(CPPFLAGS) $< | sed s/\\.o/.d/ > $@

# Specify that all .o files depend on .c files, and indicate how
# the .c files are converted (compiled) to the .o files.

%.o: %.c
    $(COMPILE) -o $@ $<

clean:
    -rm $(OBJS) $(EXECUTABLE) $(DEPS) *~

explain:
    @echo "The following information represents your program:"
    @echo "Final executable name: $(EXECUTABLE)"
    @echo "Source files:     $(SRCS)"
    @echo "Object files:     $(OBJS)"
    @echo "Dependency files:   $(DEPS)"

depend: $(DEPS)
    @echo "Dependencies are now up-to-date."

-include $(DEPS)
```

Having seen this new Makefile, I will review the changes that have been made in it. The first changes occur near the top where variables are declared. There is a greater degree of specialization now; there is a separate CPPFLAGS for pre-processor directives. This is necessary so that only those options can be passed to gcc when it calculates the dependencies; the others should not be passed along when dependencies are being calculated. Additionally, as you'll see shortly when I discuss implicit rules, there can be other benefits to splitting them up in such a way as well.

Another new variable is *DEPS*, which is generated in a fashion similar to *OBJS*, except the dependency files will have a .d extension. So generating a list of dependency files can be done in the same way as generating the list of object files.

Here's an example of the next change that occurs with this rule:

```
$(EXECUTABLE): $(DEPS) $(OBJS)
        $(CC) -o $(EXECUTABLE) $(OBJS)
```

This time, the list of dependency files is also listed. Technically, this is not necessary because make implicitly evaluates those files whenever it starts, but listing them here can be a good reminder that the dependencies do need to be up-to-date when a program is compiled.

Next, there is a new rule that specifies how the dependencies should be calculated. This is a three-line rule:

```
%.d: %.c
        $(CC) -M $(CPPFLAGS) $< > $@
        $(CC) -M $(CPPFLAGS) $< | sed s/\\.o/.d/ > $@
```

The first line specifies that, at a minimum, each dependency file depends on the corresponding C source file, and must be regenerated if that file is modified. The second and third lines list the specific commands used to build the dependency file. The first command simply invokes gcc, and dumps its output directly into the dependency file. The second command again invokes gcc, but this one changes the rule filename from .o to .d and then appends the result to the end of the file. This is done so that the dependency file can be re-built even if all that was modified was a header file included a few levels down, for instance.

The next modification is to the clean target, which lists the dependencies as additional generated files to remove when requested.

> **Note**
>
> One interesting thing to note is that if make clean is run on an already-cleaned directory, the dependency files will be re-built and then promptly deleted:

```
$ make clean
gcc -M io.c > io.d
```

```
gcc -M io.c | sed s/\\.o/.d/ > io.d
gcc -M init.c > init.d
gcc -M init.c | sed s/\\.o/.d/ > init.d
gcc -M compute.c > compute.d
gcc -M compute.c | sed s/\\.o/.d/ > compute.d
rm compute.o init.o io.o myprogram compute.d init.d io.d *~
rm: cannot remove `compute.o': No such file or directory
rm: cannot remove `init.o': No such file or directory
rm: cannot remove `io.o': No such file or directory
rm: cannot remove `myprogram': No such file or directory
rm: cannot remove `*~': No such file or directory
make: [clean] Error 1 (ignored)
```

The reason for this is that the include directive in the Makefile depends on the .d files implicitly. So, after they are built, the file can be processed normally.

After the %.d rule, there is a modification to the explain target that simply displays an extra line of output indicating the names of the dependency files. Then, there is a new target named depend. This target is never invoked directly from another; like clean and explain, it must be invoked from the command line. The depend target is used to re-build the dependency files, if necessary.

The final line of the file is the include directive. The leading dash means to suppress warnings of a file to be included doesn't exist; the file is generated automatically and then included anyway, so the warnings simply amount to junk on-screen. The files to include are those listed by the DEPS variable.

Now that you've seen this Makefile, take a look at what it does with a few sample executions. Starting from a clean directory, you can see all the steps that are taken in order to build the program:

```
$ make
gcc -M io.c > io.d
gcc -M io.c | sed s/\\.o/.d/ > io.d
gcc -M init.c > init.d
gcc -M init.c | sed s/\\.o/.d/ > init.d
gcc -M compute.c > compute.d
gcc -M compute.c | sed s/\\.o/.d/ > compute.d
gcc -Wall -O2 -c -o compute.o compute.c
gcc -Wall -O2 -c -o init.o init.c
gcc -Wall -O2 -c -o io.o io.c
gcc -o myprogram compute.o init.o io.o
```

You can see that it generated the dependency files, and then compiled the program. Here's a look at one of those dependency files:

```
$ cat io.d
io.o: io.c /usr/include/stdio.h /usr/include/features.h \
```

```
/usr/include/sys/cdefs.h /usr/include/gnu/stubs.h \
/usr/lib/gcc-lib/i486-linux/egcs-2.91.66/include/stddef.h \
/usr/lib/gcc-lib/i486-linux/egcs-2.91.66/include/stdarg.h \
/usr/include/bits/types.h /usr/include/libio.h \
/usr/include/_G_config.h /usr/include/bits/stdio_lim.h
myprogram.h
io.d: io.c /usr/include/stdio.h /usr/include/features.h \
/usr/include/sys/cdefs.h /usr/include/gnu/stubs.h \
/usr/lib/gcc-lib/i486-linux/egcs-2.91.66/include/stddef.h \
/usr/lib/gcc-lib/i486-linux/egcs-2.91.66/include/stdarg.h \
/usr/include/bits/types.h /usr/include/libio.h \
/usr/include/_G_config.h /usr/include/bits/stdio_lim.h myprogram.h
```

Note   Your dependency file will probably be different from mine because different distributions or compiler versions use different header files and locations. However, in all cases, you should note an inclusion of stdio.h and myprogram.h.

You can see the two entries generated by the two separate invocations of gcc. The first declares the dependencies of the object file; the second, the same dependencies, but applied to the dependency file itself. Notice that both of them list much more than simply myprogram.h! Also, they are list all of the system header files that are included by the program — or by other system header files that the program includes.

Tip   You can suppress the inclusion of these system header files by using -MM instead of -M in the gcc invocation.

Now, confirm that nothing is recompiled when nothing needs to be. The make program should report that there is nothing to do:

```
$ make
make: Nothing to be done for `all'.
```

Try modifying a file and see what happens now. In this example, touch will be used again:

```
$ touch compute.c
$ make
gcc -M compute.c > compute.d
gcc -M compute.c | sed s/\\.o/.d/ > compute.d
gcc -Wall -O2 -c -o compute.o compute.c
gcc -o myprogram compute.o init.o io.o
```

This time, the system regenerated the dependency file for compute.c and then recompiled the file and rebuilt the final executable. This is essentially the same as had occurred before, with the exception that the dependency file is updated.

Another test would be to modify the .h file and see of two out of the three files get recompiled and their dependency files regenerated:

```
$ touch myprogram.h
$ make
gcc -M io.c > io.d
gcc -M io.c | sed s/\\.o/.d/ > io.d
gcc -M init.c > init.d
gcc -M init.c | sed s/\\.o/.d/ > init.d
gcc -Wall -02 -c -o init.o init.c
gcc -Wall -02 -c -o io.o io.c
gcc -o myprogram compute.o init.o io.o
```

The dependency files are updated, the source is recompiled, and the program is re-linked—everything worked perfectly.

This sort of capability in the Makefile may seem like overkill for a project this small. However, when your projects start to contain dozens, hundreds, or even thousands of modules, maintaining a Makefile can become a big chore. Knowing these techniques enables you to re-use the Makefile in many other situations.

At this point, the Makefile already automatically:

✦ Detects the names of all the C source files in the project.

✦ Determines the names of all the appropriate object files, given the names of those C source files.

✦ Determines the names of the dependency files, given the names of those source files.

✦ Determines the dependencies for each source file and stores them in a file for re-use automatically.

✦ Regenerates these dependencies automatically when necessary.

That's quite a bit of automation! Yet, e more can be done. Notice how the preceding rules apply to C source files only. Of course, the Makefile could be modified trivially so the rules apply to C++ source files only, or with a bit more effort, to Pascal source files only. Athough these modifications are not difficult, think about another alternative for a moment: wouldn't it be great if the system could take the appropriate action automatically based on the particular language in use?

Of course! Now the question is, how can this be done? Several rules rely on files with names ending in .c. You can no longer rely on that sort of rule for other languages.

I'll approach the answer in steps so you can see how the changes progress from one system to another. The first step that can be taken is to use one of make's built-in implicit rules for compilation. Although we haven't used it thus far, GNU make comes with a number of rules that can be applied for compilation purposes. It knows how to compile programs written in C, C++, Pascal, Ada, and many other languages. Instead of manually defining rules for each of these, you simply can use the built-in ones. The info documentation for make describes each of these built-in rules. As an example, the built-in rule for compiling C programs is defined as:

```
$(CC) -c $(CPPFLAGS) $(CFLAGS)
```

Now you can see one of the other benefits of arranging variables as they are in the example Makefile: they fit nicely with the implicit rules. So, what you actually can do is delete from the Makefile the rule for compiling the C program. A few variables are added or modified at the top of the Makefile as well. There is a more specific section for C++ compilation, and there is a separate LINKCC defined. This is the name of the compiler you should use for the final link step; it may be g++ if your program is predominantly C++-based or gcc if it's mostly C-based. It's initially set to equal the C compiler.

Listing 7-2 shows what the Makefile looks like now.

Note　　Listing 7-2 is available online.

Listing 7-2: **Modified Makefile**

```
# Lines starting with the pound sign are comments.
#
# This is one of two options you might need to tweak.

EXECUTABLE = myprogram

# You can modify the below as well, but probably
# won't need to.
#

# CC is for the name of the C compiler. CPPFLAGS denotes pre-processor
# flags, such as -I options. CFLAGS denotes flags for the C compiler.
# CXXFLAGS denotes flags for the C++ compiler. You may add additional
# settings here, such as PFLAGS, if you are using other languages such
# as Pascal.

CPPFLAGS =
LINKCC = $(CC)

CC = gcc
CFLAGS = -Wall -O2
```

```
CXX = g++
CXXFLAGS = $(CFLAGS)


SRCS := $(wildcard *.c)
OBJS := $(patsubst %.c,%.o,$(SRCS))
DEPS := $(patsubst %.c,%.d,$(SRCS))

# "all" is the default target. Simply make it point to myprogram.

all: $(EXECUTABLE)

# Define the components of the program, and how to link them together.
# These components are defined as dependencies; that is, they must be
# made up-to-date before the code is linked.

$(EXECUTABLE): $(DEPS) $(OBJS)
        $(LINKCC) -o $(EXECUTABLE) $(OBJS)

# Specify that the dependency files depend on the C source files.

%.d: %.c
        $(CC) -M $(CPPFLAGS) $< > $@
        $(CC) -M $(CPPFLAGS) $< | sed s/\\.o/.d/ > $@

# Specify that all .o files depend on .c files, and indicate how
# the .c files are converted (compiled) to the .o files.

clean:
        -rm $(OBJS) $(EXECUTABLE) $(DEPS) *~

explain:
        @echo "The following information represents your program:"
        @echo "Final executable name: $(EXECUTABLE)"
        @echo "Source files:      $(SRCS)"
        @echo "Object files:      $(OBJS)"
        @echo "Dependency files:   $(DEPS)"

depend: $(DEPS)
        @echo "Dependencies are now up-to-date."

-include $(DEPS)
```

Notice the absence of any rule explicitly stating how the C code is compiled. Thus far, the Makefile is capable of compiling C++ files but is not capable of identifying them yet because of the wildcard in use.

The wildcard needs a bit more work before it can be used with these different languages. For your information, on Linux, C source files end with .c, and C++ files can end with either .cc or .C. This complicates life a bit, but not terribly.

The first thing you should do is re-work the wildcards. This is what they look like now:

```
SRCS := $(wildcard *.c) $(wildcard *.cc) $(wildcard *.C)
OBJS := $(patsubst %.c,%.o,$(wildcard *.c)) \
    $(patsubst %.cc,%.o,$(wildcard *.cc)) \
    $(patsubst %.C,%.o,$(wildcard *.C))
DEPS := $(patsubst %.o,%.d,$(OBJS))
```

As you can see, the source listing is simply the collection of files with all the different extensions. The object listing has to be more picky, because it has to convert each file type individually. The dependency then is rewritten in terms of the object list, so it doesn't have to do the same thing.

Now, you need a new dependency rule for the files with each new extension that specifies how to generate the dependency file. An example is:

```
%.d: %.C
    $(CXX) -M $(CPPFLAGS) $< > $@
    $(CXX) -M $(CPPFLAGS) $< | sed s/\\.o/.d/ > $@
```

The same will need to occur for .cc files. now your Makefile is language-neutral, and it has support for both C and C++ files. With a few more additions, you could add many other languages as well. Listing 7-3 shows the finished Makefile.

Note   You can find the finished Makefile shown in Listing 7-3 online.

Listing 7-3: **Finished multi-language Makefile**

```
# Lines starting with the pound sign are comments.
#
# These are the two options that may need tweaking

EXECUTABLE = myprogram
LINKCC = $(CC)

# You can modify the below as well, but probably
# won't need to.
#

# CC is for the name of the C compiler. CPPFLAGS denotes pre-
processor
```

```
# flags, such as -I options. CFLAGS denotes flags for the C
compiler.
# CXXFLAGS denotes flags for the C++ compiler. You may add
additional
# settings here, such as PFLAGS, if you are using other
languages such
# as Pascal.

CPPFLAGS =

LDFLAGS =

CC = gcc
CFLAGS = -Wall -O2

CXX = g++
CXXFLAGS = $(CFLAGS)


SRCS := $(wildcard *.c) $(wildcard *.cc) $(wildcard *.C)
OBJS := $(patsubst %.c,%.o,$(wildcard *.c)) \
    $(patsubst %.cc,%.o,$(wildcard *.cc)) \
    $(patsubst %.C,%.o,$(wildcard *.C))
DEPS := $(patsubst %.o,%.d,$(OBJS))

# "all" is the default target. Simply make it point to
myprogram.

all: $(EXECUTABLE)

# Define the components of the program, and how to link them
together.
# These components are defined as dependencies; that is, they
must be
# made up-to-date before the code is linked.

$(EXECUTABLE): $(DEPS) $(OBJS)
    $(LINKCC) $(LDFLAGS) -o $(EXECUTABLE) $(OBJS)

# Specify that the dependency files depend on the C source
files.

%.d: %.c
    $(CC) -M $(CPPFLAGS) $< > $@
    $(CC) -M $(CPPFLAGS) $< | sed s/\\.o/.d/ > $@

%.d: %.cc
    $(CXX) -M $(CPPFLAGS) $< > $@
    $(CXX) -M $(CPPFLAGS) $< | sed s/\\.o/.d/ > $@
```

Continued

Listing 7-3 *(continued)*

```
%.d: %.C
    $(CXX) -M $(CPPFLAGS) $< > $@
    $(CXX) -M $(CPPFLAGS) $< | sed s/\\.o/.d/ > $@

# Specify that all .o files depend on .c files, and indicate how
# the .c files are converted (compiled) to the .o files.

clean:
    -rm $(OBJS) $(EXECUTABLE) $(DEPS) *~

explain:
    @echo "The following information represents your program:"
    @echo "Final executable name: $(EXECUTABLE)"
    @echo "Source files:      $(SRCS)"
    @echo "Object files:      $(OBJS)"
    @echo "Dependency files:   $(DEPS)"

depend: $(DEPS)
    @echo "Dependencies are now up-to-date."

-include $(DEPS)
```

To see how your Makefile works, you can create a zero-byte C++ module. This will have no effect on the program but will go through the motions of compilation and linking. You can use the touch command to create this file, as shown in the following example.

```
$ touch foo.cc
$ make clean
rm compute.o init.o io.o foo.o myprogram compute.d init.d io.d foo.d *~
rm: cannot remove `compute.o': No such file or directory
rm: cannot remove `init.o': No such file or directory
rm: cannot remove `io.o': No such file or directory
rm: cannot remove `foo.o': No such file or directory
rm: cannot remove `myprogram': No such file or directory
rm: cannot remove `*~': No such file or directory
make: [clean] Error 1 (ignored)
```

Depending on whether or not your system is already in the clean state, you may or may not get the same output from make clean. However, from this point on, you should get output much the same as is shown here:

```
$ make explain
g++ -M foo.cc > foo.d
```

```
g++ -M foo.cc | sed s/\\.o/.d/ > foo.d
gcc -M io.c > io.d
gcc -M io.c | sed s/\\.o/.d/ > io.d
gcc -M init.c > init.d
gcc -M init.c | sed s/\\.o/.d/ > init.d
gcc -M compute.c > compute.d
gcc -M compute.c | sed s/\\.o/.d/ > compute.d
The following information represents your program:
Final executable name: myprogram
Source files:      compute.c init.c io.c foo.cc
Object files:      compute.o init.o io.o foo.o
Dependency files:  compute.d init.d io.d foo.d
```

Notice how a different compiler was used to get the dependency information from the C++ module as was used for the C module. On the other hand, it properly identified object and dependency files with the single standard name, which is good.Now try building your project and see if it worked. The build should look like the following example:

```
$ make
gcc -Wall -O2  -c compute.c -o compute.o
gcc -Wall -O2  -c init.c -o init.o
gcc -Wall -O2  -c io.c -o io.o
g++ -Wall -O2  -c foo.cc -o foo.o
gcc -o myprogram compute.o init.o io.o foo.o
```

Everything was executed according to the plan. The C++ program was compiled with the separate compiler (according to a built-in rule), and the C program was compiled with the normal C compiler, again according to a built-in rule.

Building Other Files

Besides programs built from code from C or C++, you can build files from other types of data. For instance, you could build a PostScript file containing the result of processing a LaTeX document. Or, you could build a manpage from the appropriate source code. Some people use make and a pattern language such as m4 to build websites. The make program is versatile enough to handle all of these tasks quite well.

Consider a situation in which you might want to build a website with HTML files that were pre-processed. This pre-processor could be m4, some sort of specialized Web language, or even the C pre-processor.

As a simple example of what can be done with this sort of system, you might have three files. This system builds upon the example in the previous section. One could be a standard inclusion item for your HTML—maybe a header or some macros.

The first file contains some quick macros that can be used with all the pages; name it stdinc.hmac:

```
<!DOCTYPE HTLM PUBLIC "-//W3C//DTD HTML 4.0 Transitional//EN"
 "http://www.w3.org/TR/REC-html40/loose.dtd">

#define _STDHEAD(a) <HEAD><TITLE>a</TITLE></HEAD>

#define _BODYHEAD <H1>myprogram sample information</H1> \
    <P> \
    This is some sample text for your program. \
    This text appears on each generated HTML page that uses \
    the bodyhead macro. \
    <P>
```

The second file is the first one to generate some HTML, page1.mac:

```
#include "stdinc.hmac"
<HTML>
_STDHEAD(Sample Document Page 1)

<BODY>

_BODYHEAD

This is the first page.

/* This text will never appear in the final document. */

</BODY>


</HTML>
```

And now, a third file to generate HTML,:

```
#include "stdinc.hmac"
<HTML>
_STDHEAD(Sample Document Page 2)

<BODY BGCOLOR=#5555FF>

_BODYHEAD

This is the second page.

/* This text will never appear in the final document. */

</BODY>


</HTML>
```

To generate these files, some simple calls to cpp are needed. You can modify the Makefile from above so that it knows how to build all of these files — and even figures out dependencies.

Listing 7-4 shows an updated version of the same intelligent Makefile that was used in Listing 7-3. This time, the Makefile knows how to generate HTML code from the .mac files.

Note Listing 7-4 is available online.

Listing 7-4: **Updated Makefile that generates HTML**

```
# Lines starting with the pound sign are comments.
#
# These are the options that may need tweaking

EXECUTABLE = myprogram
LINKCC = $(CC)
OTHERS = page1.html page2.html
OTHERDEPS = page1.d page2.d

# You can modify the below as well, but probably
# won't need to.
#

# CC is for the name of the C compiler. CPPFLAGS denotes pre-processor
# flags, such as -I options. CFLAGS denotes flags for the C compiler.
# CXXFLAGS denotes flags for the C++ compiler. You may add additional
# settings here, such as PFLAGS, if you are using other languages such
# as Pascal.

CPPFLAGS =

LDFLAGS =

CC = gcc
CFLAGS = -Wall -O2

CXX = g++
CXXFLAGS = $(CFLAGS)


SRCS := $(wildcard *.c) $(wildcard *.cc) $(wildcard *.C)
OBJS := $(patsubst %.c,%.o,$(wildcard *.c)) \
    $(patsubst %.cc,%.o,$(wildcard *.cc)) \
    $(patsubst %.C,%.o,$(wildcard *.C))
DEPS := $(patsubst %.o,%.d,$(OBJS)) $(OTHERDEPS)
```

Continued

Listing 7-4 *(continued)*

```
# "all" is the default target. Simply make it point to myprogram.

all: $(EXECUTABLE) $(OTHERS)

# Define the components of the program, and how to link them together.
# These components are defined as dependencies; that is, they must be
# made up-to-date before the code is linked.

$(EXECUTABLE): $(DEPS) $(OBJS)
    $(LINKCC) $(LDFLAGS) -o $(EXECUTABLE) $(OBJS)

# Specify that the dependency files depend on the C source files.

%.d: %.c
    $(CC) -M $(CPPFLAGS) $< > $@
    $(CC) -M $(CPPFLAGS) $< | sed s/\\.o/.d/ > $@

%.d: %.cc
    $(CXX) -M $(CPPFLAGS) $< > $@
    $(CXX) -M $(CPPFLAGS) $< | sed s/\\.o/.d/ > $@

%.d: %.C
    $(CXX) -M $(CPPFLAGS) $< > $@
    $(CXX) -M $(CPPFLAGS) $< | sed s/\\.o/.d/ > $@

%.d: %.mac
    cpp -M $< | sed s/\\.mac\\.o/.html/ > $@
    cpp -M $< | sed s/\\.mac\\.o/.d/ > $@

%.html: %.mac
    cpp -P < $< > $@

clean:
    -rm $(OBJS) $(EXECUTABLE) $(DEPS) $(OTHERS) *~

explain:
    @echo "The following information represents your program:"
    @echo "Final executable name: $(EXECUTABLE)"
    @echo "Other generated files: $(OTHERS)"
    @echo "Source files:       $(SRCS)"
    @echo "Object files:       $(OBJS)"
    @echo "Dependency files:   $(DEPS)"

depend: $(DEPS)
    @echo "Dependencies are now up-to-date."

-include $(DEPS)
```

Now I'll review the specific additions to the Makefile that generates these files. First, there are two new variables at the top: OTHERS and OTHERDEPS. The OTHERS variable is used to specify additional files that will be generated. The OTHERDEPS variable is used to specify additional dependency files. The reason for this is that there is not a generic rule to determine names of the dependency files given other files with arbitrary names and extensions. Furthermore, many types of files will not even have the capability of generating these dependencies automatically, or generating dependencies may not even make sense with some types of files.

Then, a few lines down, the DEPS variable is updated to include the OTHERDEPS in the list of dependency files. Below that, the all target is also updated to indicate that the additional files need to be compiled.

After that, nothing changes until the following lines:

```
%.d: %.mac
    cpp -M $< | sed s/\\.mac\\.o/.html/ > $@
    cpp -M $< | sed s/\\.mac\\.o/.d/ > $@
```

Here, a dependency file is generated. We can use the same technique as for C and C++ programs neatly, but there is one twist. Because the cpp -M option assumes that the output is named .o, and it is named .html in this case, sed must be used to correct it. Now, you get results like this:

```
page1.html: page1.mac stdinc.hmac
page1.d: page1.mac stdinc.hmac
```

The final modifications include the rule for generating the HTML code, and additional listings of variables in clean and explain.

When you run make on a clean directory now, you get the following messages:

```
$ make
cpp -M page2.mac | sed s/\\.mac\\.o/.html/ > page2.d
cpp -M page2.mac | sed s/\\.mac\\.o/.d/ > page2.d
cpp -M page1.mac | sed s/\\.mac\\.o/.html/ > page1.d
cpp -M page1.mac | sed s/\\.mac\\.o/.d/ > page1.d
g++ -M foo.cc > foo.d
g++ -M foo.cc | sed s/\\.o/.d/ > foo.d
gcc -M io.c > io.d
gcc -M io.c | sed s/\\.o/.d/ > io.d
gcc -M init.c > init.d
gcc -M init.c | sed s/\\.o/.d/ > init.d
gcc -M compute.c > compute.d
gcc -M compute.c | sed s/\\.o/.d/ > compute.d
gcc -Wall -O2  -c compute.c -o compute.o
gcc -Wall -O2  -c init.c -o init.o
gcc -Wall -O2  -c io.c -o io.o
```

```
g++ -Wall -O2  -c foo.cc -o foo.o
gcc -o myprogram compute.o init.o io.o foo.o
cpp -P < page1.mac > page1.html
cpp -P < page2.mac > page2.html
```

Now you can take a look at the generated HTML code. Notice how some elements of the code occur in both output files but are defined once only — in stdinc.hmac. Imagine the possibilities for a large website: the entire look and feel of the site could be modified by making a change to a single macro file and re-running make! Here is the result from processing these two HTML files:

```
$ cat page1.html
<!DOCTYPE HTLM PUBLIC "-//W3C//DTD HTML 4.0 Transitional//EN"
 "http://www.w3.org/TR/REC-html40/loose.dtd">




<HTML>
<HEAD><TITLE> Sample Document Page 1 </TITLE></HEAD>

<BODY>

<H1>myprogram sample information</H1> <P> This is some sample text for your
program. This text appears on each generated HTML page that uses the bodyhead
macro. <P>

This is the first page.



</BODY>


</HTML>
$ cat page2.html
<!DOCTYPE HTLM PUBLIC "-//W3C//DTD HTML 4.0 Transitional//EN"
 "http://www.w3.org/TR/REC-html40/loose.dtd">




<HTML>
<HEAD><TITLE> Sample Document Page 2 </TITLE></HEAD>

<BODY BGCOLOR=#5555FF>
```

```
<H1>myprogram sample information</H1> <P> This is some sample text for your
program. This text appears on each generated HTML page that uses the bodyhead
macro. <P>

This is the second page.


</BODY>


</HTML>
```

Notice several things about this output. First, there are several blank lines in the output at a location where there were no blank lines in the input. The `stdinc.hmac` file causes this. Everything from that file (such as the doctype tag at the start) is passed through literally, except the special declarations like macros. Thus, even blank lines in that file are passed through literally. For HTML files, this is not a problem; you can see that the page displays fine in any HTML browser. Notice, too, that the macro calls in the source files that were expanded; the title, for instance, was a parameter to a macro call.

Using Recursive make

When you are dealing with large projects, you may elect to separate the source into subdirectories based on the particular subsystems that are contained in those parts of the code. When you do this, you can have one large Makefile for the entire project. Alternatively, you may find it more useful to have a separate Makefile for each subsystem. This can make the build system more maintainable because the top-level Makefile does not have to contain the details for the entire program; these can be present solely in each individual directory.

To assist with this sort of configuration, GNU make has several features to help. One is the `MAKE` variable, which can be used to invoke a *recursive make*, and pass along several relevant command-line options. You can use the `-C` option to tell make to enter a specific directory, where it will then process that directory's Makefile.

A recursive make descends into each subdirectory in your project building files. Each subdirectory may, in turn, have additional subdirectories that the build process needs to examine. By designing a recursive make, you end up traversing the entire tree of your project to build all the necessary files.

One way to do that is with this type of syntax:

```
targetname:
    $(MAKE) -C directoryname
```

Note that `targetname` and `directoryname` must be different for this to work. Another option, especially useful if you have large numbers of subdirectories, is to use a loop to enter each of them. This approach will be demonstrated in the example in Listing 7-5.

Another important capability is the communication of variable settings between the master make and the others that it invokes. There are two main ways to do this. The first is to have a file that is included by all of the Makefiles. Another, usually superior, way is to export variables from the top-level make to its child processes.

This is done with the same syntax that Bash uses to export variables to its sub-processes — the `export` keyword. You will want to export options such as the ones that C compiler used, the options passed to it, and the so on. Which files should be compiled will vary between the different directories and thus should not be passed along.

Note that you can actually combine approaches. For instance, you might want to use include files to define make rules, and variable exports to pass along variable contents, using each for its particular strong points.

Another question for you to consider is how to combine the items produced in the subdirectories into the main project. Depending on your specific needs, the subsystems could be completely separate executables, generating libraries, or simply part of your main executable. One popular option is to have a specific directory for the object files — a directory into which all object files are placed. A more modular option is to create a library; you'll learn about that option in Chapter 9, "Libraries and Linking."

Listing 7-5 shows a version of the intelligent Makefile developed before that will act as a top-level Makefile for a project containing two additional subsystems, `input` and `format`.

Note   Listing 7-5 is available online.

Listing 7-5: Top-level recursive Makefile

```
# Lines starting with the pound sign are comments.
#
# These are the options that may need tweaking

EXECUTABLE = myprogram
LINKCC = $(CC)
OTHEROBJS = input/test.o format/formattest.o
OTHERS = page1.html page2.html
OTHERDEPS = page1.d page2.d
```

```
DIRS = input format

# You can modify the below as well, but probably
# won't need to.
#

# CC is for the name of the C compiler. CPPFLAGS denotes pre-processor
# flags, such as -I options. CFLAGS denotes flags for the C compiler.
# CXXFLAGS denotes flags for the C++ compiler. You may add additional
# settings here, such as PFLAGS, if you are using other languages such
# as Pascal.

export CPPFLAGS =

export LDFLAGS =

export CC = gcc
export CFLAGS = -Wall -O2

export CXX = g++
export CXXFLAGS = $(CFLAGS)


SRCS := $(wildcard *.c) $(wildcard *.cc) $(wildcard *.C)
OBJS := $(patsubst %.c,%.o,$(wildcard *.c)) \
    $(patsubst %.cc,%.o,$(wildcard *.cc)) \
    $(patsubst %.C,%.o,$(wildcard *.C))
DEPS := $(patsubst %.o,%.d,$(OBJS)) $(OTHERDEPS)

# "all" is the default target. Simply make it point to myprogram.

all: $(EXECUTABLE) $(OTHERS)

subdirs:
    @for dir in $(DIRS); do $(MAKE) -C $$dir; done

# Define the components of the program, and how to link them together.
# These components are defined as dependencies; that is, they must be
# made up-to-date before the code is linked.

$(EXECUTABLE): subdirs $(DEPS) $(OBJS)
    $(LINKCC) $(LDFLAGS) -o $(EXECUTABLE) $(OBJS) $(OTHEROBJS)

# Specify that the dependency files depend on the C source files.

%.d: %.c
    $(CC) -M $(CPPFLAGS) $< > $@
    $(CC) -M $(CPPFLAGS) $< | sed s/\\.o/.d/ > $@

%.d: %.cc
    $(CXX) -M $(CPPFLAGS) $< > $@
    $(CXX) -M $(CPPFLAGS) $< | sed s/\\.o/.d/ > $@
```

Continued

Listing 7-5 *(continued)*

```
%.d: %.C
    $(CXX) -M $(CPPFLAGS) $< > $@
    $(CXX) -M $(CPPFLAGS) $< | sed s/\\.o/.d/ > $@

%.d: %.mac
    cpp -M $< | sed s/\\.mac\\.o/.html/ > $@
    cpp -M $< | sed s/\\.mac\\.o/.d/ > $@

%.html: %.mac
    cpp -P < $< > $@

clean:
    -rm $(OBJS) $(EXECUTABLE) $(DEPS) $(OTHERS) *~
    @for dir in $(DIRS); do $(MAKE) -C $$dir clean; done

explain:
    @echo "The following information represents your program:"
    @echo "Final executable name: $(EXECUTABLE)"
    @echo "Other generated files: $(OTHERS)"
    @echo "Source files:     $(SRCS)"
    @echo "Object files:     $(OBJS)"
    @echo "Dependency files:   $(DEPS)"
    @echo "Subdirectories:    $(DIRS)"

depend: $(DEPS)
    @for dir in $(DIRS); do $(MAKE) -C $$dir ; done
    @echo "Dependencies are now up-to-date."

-include $(DEPS)
```

Several changes are made to this file from the previous version. First, note the addition of the OTHEROBJS variable; here, the additional generated object files are listed. Then, note how many of the variables are exported. These variables are not defined in the Makefiles in the subdirectories since their value gets passed along from this Makefile. Then, there is a new subdirs target. This target uses a for loop to ensure that the Makefile in each directory gets processed. The leading at sign (@) suppresses the normal output of this command, which can be a bit confusing if you are watching the output of make as it proceeds.

Next, notice that the executable includes an additional dependency on the subdirs target. The remaining changes occur within the clean, explain, and depend targets, each of which is updated to list information about or process the subdirectories.

The Makefile for one of the subdirectories can look like the one shown in Listing 7-6. In this particular example, the file is used for both subdirectories because it detects what needs to be processed automatically.

Note   Listing 7-6 is available online.

Listing 7-6: **Lower-level Makefile**

```
#
# These are the options that may need tweaking

OTHERS =
OTHERDEPS =
DIRS =

# You can modify the below as well, but probably
# won't need to.
#

# CC is for the name of the C compiler. CPPFLAGS denotes pre-processor
# flags, such as -I options. CFLAGS denotes flags for the C compiler.
# CXXFLAGS denotes flags for the C++ compiler. You may add additional
# settings here, such as PFLAGS, if you are using other languages such
# as Pascal.

SRCS := $(wildcard *.c) $(wildcard *.cc) $(wildcard *.C)
OBJS := $(patsubst %.c,%.o,$(wildcard *.c)) \
    $(patsubst %.cc,%.o,$(wildcard *.cc)) \
    $(patsubst %.C,%.o,$(wildcard *.C))
DEPS := $(patsubst %.o,%.d,$(OBJS)) $(OTHERDEPS)

# "all" is the default target. Simply make it point to myprogram.

all: $(OBJS) $(OTHERS) $(DIRS)

#$(DIRS):
#    $(MAKE) -C $<

# Define the components of the program, and how to link them together.
# These components are defined as dependencies; that is, they must be
# made up-to-date before the code is linked.

# Specify that the dependency files depend on the C source files.

%.d: %.c
    $(CC) -M $(CPPFLAGS) $< > $@
    $(CC) -M $(CPPFLAGS) $< | sed s/\\.o/.d/ > $@
```

Continued

Listing 7-6 *(continued)*

```
%.d: %.cc
    $(CXX) -M $(CPPFLAGS) $< > $@
    $(CXX) -M $(CPPFLAGS) $< | sed s/\\.o/.d/ > $@

%.d: %.C
    $(CXX) -M $(CPPFLAGS) $< > $@
    $(CXX) -M $(CPPFLAGS) $< | sed s/\\.o/.d/ > $@

%.d: %.mac
    cpp -M $< | sed s/\\.mac\\.o/.html/ > $@
    cpp -M $< | sed s/\\.mac\\.o/.d/ > $@

%.html: %.mac
    cpp -P < $< > $@

clean:
    -rm $(OBJS) $(EXECUTABLE) $(DEPS) $(OTHERS) *~


explain:
    @echo "The following information represents your program:"
    @echo "Other generated files: $(OTHERS)"
    @echo "Source files:     $(SRCS)"
    @echo "Object files:     $(OBJS)"
    @echo "Dependency files:    $(DEPS)"

depend: $(DEPS)

-include $(DEPS)
```

Note that this file is somewhat smaller than the top-level file. This file does not need to define compiler information, because that information is passed down by the top-level file. Also, this file generates no executable; it simply generates some object files that get linked in by the top-level file.

The example files above use two new files for testing, input/test.cc and format/formattest.c. You can create them by using `mkdir` and `touch`, like so:

```
$ mkdir input format
$ touch input/test.cc
$ touch format/formattest.c
```

When you run make on this file, you get the following output:

```
$ make
cpp -M page2.mac | sed s/\\.mac\\.o/.html/ > page2.d
cpp -M page2.mac | sed s/\\.mac\\.o/.d/ > page2.d
cpp -M page1.mac | sed s/\\.mac\\.o/.html/ > page1.d
cpp -M page1.mac | sed s/\\.mac\\.o/.d/ > page1.d
g++ -M foo.cc > foo.d
g++ -M foo.cc | sed s/\\.o/.d/ > foo.d
gcc -M io.c > io.d
gcc -M io.c | sed s/\\.o/.d/ > io.d
gcc -M init.c > init.d
gcc -M init.c | sed s/\\.o/.d/ > init.d
gcc -M compute.c > compute.d
gcc -M compute.c | sed s/\\.o/.d/ > compute.d
make[1]: Entering directory `/home/username/t/my/input'
g++ -M test.cc > test.d
g++ -M test.cc | sed s/\\.o/.d/ > test.d
make[1]: Leaving directory `/home/username/t/my/input'
make[1]: Entering directory `/home/username/t/my/input'
g++ -Wall -O2  -c test.cc -o test.o
make[1]: Leaving directory `/home/username/t/my/input'
make[1]: Entering directory `/home/username/t/my/format'
gcc -M formattest.c > formattest.d
gcc -M formattest.c | sed s/\\.o/.d/ > formattest.d
make[1]: Leaving directory `/home/username/t/my/format'
make[1]: Entering directory `/home/username/t/my/format'
gcc -Wall -O2  -c formattest.c -o formattest.o
make[1]: Leaving directory `/home/username/t/my/format'
gcc -Wall -O2  -c compute.c -o compute.o
gcc -Wall -O2  -c init.c -o init.o
gcc -Wall -O2  -c io.c -o io.o
g++ -Wall -O2  -c foo.cc -o foo.o
gcc -o myprogram compute.o init.o io.o foo.o input/test.o
format/formattest.o
cpp -P < page1.mac > page1.html
cpp -P < page2.mac > page2.html
```

In this example, make descends into the subdirectories, executes commands there, and then returns to the top level. In fact, this method of using recursion can be used to descend more than one level into subdirectories. Many large projects, such as the Linux kernel, use this method for building.

You also may notice that additional commands descend into the subdirectories as well. The clean target is one such example:

```
$ make clean
rm compute.o init.o io.o foo.o myprogram compute.d init.d io.d foo.d page1.d
page2.d page1.html page2.html *~
rm: cannot remove `*~': No such file or directory
make: [clean] Error 1 (ignored)
make[1]: Entering directory `/home/username/t/my/input'
```

```
rm test.o  test.d  *~
rm: cannot remove `*~': No such file or directory
make[1]: [clean] Error 1 (ignored)
make[1]: Leaving directory `/home/username/t/my/input'
make[1]: Entering directory `/home/username/t/my/format'
rm formattest.o  formattest.d  *~
rm: cannot remove `*~': No such file or directory
make[1]: [clean] Error 1 (ignored)
make[1]: Leaving directory `/home/username/t/my/format'
```

Summary

In this chapter, you learned about automating the build process for your projects by using make. Specifically, the following points were covered:

✦ Building complex projects manually could be time-consuming and error-prone. The make program presents a way to automate the build process.

✦ A Makefile contains the rules describing how a process is to be built.

✦ Each rule describes three things: the file to be built, the files it requires before it can be built, and the commands necessary to build it.

✦ Variables can be used in Makefiles to reduce the need for re-typing of information.

✦ Variables can be either evaluated immediately, or on-the-fly whenever they are used.

✦ Makefiles can be made more reusable by automatically determining things about their environment and the projects they are building. Wildcards are one way to do this.

✦ Manually coding dependencies can be a difficult and time-consuming chore. You can automate this process as well by taking advantage of some features of the pre-processor and some unique syntax in your Makefile.

✦ Make is not limited to dealing only with C or other programming languages. It can also build various other types of files, such as HTML.

✦   ✦   ✦

Memory Management

Managing memory is a fundamental concern to people programming in C. Because C operates on such a low level, you manage memory allocation and removal yourself; that is, the language does not implicitly do this for you. This level of control can mean a performance benefit for your applications. On the other hand, the number of options for managing memory can be daunting, and some algorithms can be complex.

In this chapter, you will see how memory is allocated and managed in C programs under Linux. I'll also look at a topic that is of tremendous importance today — security. You'll see how easy it is to write programs with gaping security holes — and you'll how to write your own programs so that you can avoid these sorts of holes.

You'll also learn how some basic data structures, such as arrays and linked lists, can be applied in Linux programs.

Dynamic versus Static Memory

When you are writing programs in C, there are two ways that you can ask for memory to use for your purposes. The first is *static memory*— memory that the system allocates for you implicitly. The second is *dynamic memory*— memory that you can allocate on request. Let's take a detailed look at each type of memory.

Statically allocated memory

This form of memory is allocated for you by the compiler. Although technically, the compiler may actually allocate and de-allocate memory behind the scenes when variables go in and out of scope, this detail is hidden from you.

The key to this type of memory is that it is always there whenever you are in the relevant area. For instance, an `int` declared at the top of `main()` is always there when you are in `main()`.

Because this memory is always present, static allocation is the only way that you can use variables without manipulating pointers yourself. But the benefit goes deeper than alleviating worries about dereferencing pointers. When dealing with dynamic memory, you have to be extremely careful about how it is used. Because dynamic memory is, essentially, a big chunk of typeless RAM (the functions even return a pointer to `void`), you can access it easily as an integer and then a float — which is not the desired result; safeguards against accidentally doing this are looser.

More important, when you use dynamic memory, you must remember to manually free the memory when you are finished with it. By contrast, you don't have to worry about any of these details when you use memory that is allocated statically.

However, there are some significant drawbacks to using static memory as well. First, a statically allocated item created inside a function is not valid after the function exits, which is a big problem for functions that must return pointers to data such as strings. The following code will not necessarily produce the desired result:

```
char *addstr(char *inputstring) {
  int counter;
  char returnstring[80];

  strcpy(returnstring, inputstring);
  for (counter = 0; counter < strlen(returnstring); counter++) {
    returnstring[counter] += 2;
  }
  return returnstring;
}
```

The problem here is that you return a pointer when you return the `returnstring` item. However, because the memory that holds `returnstring` becomes deallocated after the return of the function, the results can be unpredictable and can even cause a crash. You can observe this behavior by putting the preceding code fragment into a complete program, as shown in this example:

```
#include <stdio.h>
#include <string.h>

char *addstr(char *inputstring);

int main(void) {
  char *str1, *str2;

  str1 = addstr("Hello");
  str2 = addstr("Goodbye");
```

```
    printf("str1 = %s, str2 = %s\n", str1, str2);
    return 0;
}

char *addstr(char *inputstring) {
    int counter;
    char returnstring[80];

    strcpy(returnstring, inputstring);
    for (counter = 0; counter < strlen(returnstring); counter++) {
        returnstring[counter] += 2;
    }

    return returnstring;
}
```

If you compile and run this program, you won't get the output that you might expect. In fact, some gcc versions warn you that an error will result if you return a pointer to memory that goes out of scope:

```
$ gcc -Wall -o ch8-1 ch8-1.c
ch8-1.c: In function `addstr':
ch8-1.c:25: warning: function returns address of local variable
$ ./ch8-1
str1 = , str2 =
```

The preceding example demonstrates one reason to use a dynamically allocated string instead of a statically allocated one: you can return a pointer to such a string because it is not deallocated until you explicitly request it to be.

There is yet another problem in the function. You absolutely must give the returned string a size in the declaration. Here, it is defined to have 80 characters. This may be enough to process a single word but it won't be enough to process 10,000 characters; attempting to do so would cause the program to crash.

Your solution may be to declare returnstring to be 10,001 characters. There are two problems with this approach, however: First, if a string comes along that's 10,100 characters, your program will still crash. Second, it's wasteful to allocate 10,000 characters of space when you're processing 20-character words. To solve these issues, you need dynamically allocated memory.

Dynamically allocated memory

When you use dynamically allocated memory, you control all aspects of its allocation and removal. This means that you allocate the memory when you want it, in the size you want. Similarly, you remove it when you're done with it. This may sound great at first, and it is for many reasons, but it's more complex than that.

Properly managing dynamic memory can be a big challenge when you run large programs. Remembering to free memory when you are done with it can be difficult. If you fail to free memory when you are done with it, your program will silently eat more memory until it cannot either allocate any more or the system crashes because of lack of memory, depending on local security settings. This is obviously a bad thing.

To allocate memory dynamically in C, you use the malloc() function, which is defined in stdlib.h. When you finish using memory, you need to use free() to get rid of it. The argument to malloc() indicates how many bytes of memory you want to allocate; you then get a pointer to that memory. If this pointer is NULL, it means there was an allocation problem and you should be prepared to handle this situation.

Note In C++, you can (and generally should) use the new and delete operators to allocate and remove memory.

Here is the sample program. This program will take your input, add 2 to each character (thus H becomes J), and display the result. It has been rewritten to use dynamic allocation:

```
#include <stdio.h>
#include <string.h>
#include <stdlib.h>

char *addstr(char *inputstring);

int main(void) {
  char *str1, *str2;

  str1 = addstr("Hello");
  str2 = addstr("Goodbye");

  printf("str1 = %s, str2 = %s\n", str1, str2);
  free(str1);
  free(str2);
  return 0;
}

char *addstr(char *inputstring) {
  int counter;
  char *returnstring;

  returnstring = malloc(strlen(inputstring) + 1);
  if (!returnstring) {
    fprintf(stderr, "Error allocating memory; aborting!\n");
    exit(255);
  }
  strcpy(returnstring, inputstring);
  for (counter = 0; counter < strlen(returnstring); counter++) {
    returnstring[counter] += 2;
  }
```

```
    return returnstring;
}
```

When you try to compile and run this program, you no longer get warning
messages and the output is as you would expect:

```
$ gcc -Wall -o ch8-1 ch8-1.c
$ ./ch8-1
str1 = Jgnnq, str2 = Iqqfd{g
```

The behavior in the function call allocates memory and then copies a string into it.
Because there is such a frequent need to do this, there is even a function specialized
for it — strdup( ). You can simplify the program by modifying the function such that
the program reads like this:

```
#include <stdio.h>
#include <string.h>
#include <stdlib.h>

char *addstr(char *inputstring);

int main(void) {
  char *str1, *str2;

  str1 = addstr("Hello");
  str2 = addstr("Goodbye");

  printf("str1 = %s, str2 = %s\n", str1, str2);
  free(str1);
  free(str2);
  return 0;
}

char *addstr(char *inputstring) {
  int counter;
  char *returnstring;

  returnstring = strdup(inputstring);

  if (!returnstring) {
    fprintf(stderr, "Error allocating memory; aborting!\n");
    exit(255);
  }
  for (counter = 0; counter < strlen(returnstring); counter++) {
    returnstring[counter] += 2;
  }

  return returnstring;
}
```

Now that you have a working program, fairly simple in design, I'm going to complicate things a bit. Consider the following code, which has a memory problem:

```c
#include <stdio.h>
#include <string.h>
#include <stdlib.h>

char *addstr(char *inputstring);

int main(void) {
  char *str1, *str2;

  str1 = addstr("Hello");
  str2 = addstr("Goodbye");

  printf("str1 = %s, str2 = %s\n", str1, str2);

  str1 = addstr("Hey!");
  printf("str1 = %s\n", str1);

  free(str1);
  free(str2);
  return 0;
}

char *addstr(char *inputstring) {
  int counter;
  char *returnstring;

  returnstring = strdup(inputstring);

  if (!returnstring) {
    fprintf(stderr, "Error allocating memory; aborting!\n");
    exit(255);
  }
  for (counter = 0; counter < strlen(returnstring); counter++) {
    returnstring[counter] += 2;
  }

  return returnstring;
}
```

If you compile and run the program, you'll see that it appears to run fine. But the program has what is called a memory leak—there is memory allocated that is never freed. Furthermore, after the mistake is made in this program, the memory can never be freed again. The problem is that str1 is assigned a new value—pointing to a new chunk of dynamically allocated memory—before its previous contents are freed. This means that the pointer to the previous chunk is lost. That older area of memory remains allocated, and because the pointer to it is lost, it can never be freed again. This is one type of bug that can easily infest larger programs.

Fortunately, clearing it up is not terribly difficult. You can do so by simply adding `free(str1);` before the new `addstr()` value is assigned to `str1`. In this case, the distinction is somewhat academic, because all memory is returned to the operating system when the program exits. However, you can see the problems that can creep up, especially for long-running programs such as servers. In fact, in the past, some well-known servers have actually restarted themselves periodically to avoid draining system resources because of memory leaks.

Security and Design Concerns

Memory issues are frequently behind security problems in C or C++ code. One key problem is the memory leak, as discussed in the previous section. A heavily loaded server can see its resources eaten up by a program with bad memory leaks, which can result in sluggish performance or even downtime. However, far more insidious problems that can affect your servers. These problems can lead to break-ins, denial of service (DoS) attacks, compromise of some system accounts, and unauthorized modification of data, to name a few.

As I mentioned earlier in this chapter, if more than 80 characters are copied into an area that only has space for an 80-character string, the program will crash. This is generally true. However, if this extra data is carefully crafted, it is possible for a cracker to insert his or her code into your software. This is possible because string copy operations that take the program outside the string buffer's boundaries actually can overwrite memory areas related to the code of your program. It takes a significant technical knowledge of the internal workings of the system and operating system to be able to manage such an attack, but with the proliferation of the Internet, such attackers are becoming more common.

Therefore, it is *vital* that you always make sure that your buffers are sufficiently sized to hold the data placed in them. Remember, too, that even if you plan to deal with data that is only 80 characters long, and even if your program could not possibly have valid input longer than that, a cracker could still send your program longer input. Therefore, you must never assume that your input will be a reasonable length; you must always ensure either that it is or that you use dynamically allocated memory that has a sufficient size to accommodate your input.

The importance of this cannot be overstated. Dozens of bugs in programs, accounting for hundreds or even thousands of security compromises, are attributed to this type of programming error. Also, this is not a problem unique to programming on Linux; it can occur on almost any platform running almost any operating system, including popular non-UNIX PC operating systems.

Because the primary concern for these programs lies with servers, do not assume that you can ignore the problem for other types of software. This type of problem can cause security breaches for setuid or setgid programs just as easily (and perhaps even more so) as for network server software. To summarize, any software that runs with privileges different from the person using it, and accepts input from that person, could have a buffer overflow vulnerability. This includes *a lot* of software — web servers, file transfer servers, mail servers, mail readers, Usenet servers, and also many tools that are included with an operating system.

For your programs, there are two simple but extremely important options for dealing with these problems:

✦ You can choose to use dynamically allocated memory whenever possible, such as the modification made to the sample code presented earlier in this chapter.

✦ You can perform explicit *bounds checking* when reading or processing data, and to reject or truncate data that is too long.

Sometimes, both methods are used. For instance, when arbitrary data is first read into a program, perhaps with fgets(), it may be read in 4K chunks. The data may then be collected and stored in a dynamically allocated area — perhaps a linked list — for later analysis.

The first option has already been demonstrated in the previous section. Now, consider the second option, which uses buffers with a fixed size but are designed to prevent overflows. Here is a version of the code presented in the previous section, modified to work in this fashion:

```
#include <stdio.h>
#include <string.h>
#include <stdlib.h>

void addstr(char *inputstring);

int main(void) {

    addstr("Hello");
    addstr("Goodbye");

    return 0;
}

void addstr(char *inputstring) {
    int counter;
    char printstring[5];

    strncpy(printstring, inputstring, sizeof(printstring));
    printstring[sizeof(printstring) - 1] = 0;
```

```
    for (counter = 0; counter < strlen(printstring); counter++) {
      printstring[counter] += 2;
    }

    printf("Result: %s\n", printstring);
}
```

In this example, a buffer with room for only five characters is allocated. Although this is, no doubt, smaller than you would allocate in most real-life situations, you can easily see the effect of the code in this situation. When you compile and run the code, it does the following:

```
$ gcc -Wall -o ch8-2 ch8-2.c
$ ./ch8-2
Result: Jgnn
Result: Iqqf
```

The string is truncated by the strncpy() call in the function. The next line adds the trailing null character to mark the end of the string. The strncpy() function does not add this null character to the string that was truncated; you must add it yourself. Otherwise the resulting string will be essentially useless because it will not have an end that C/C++ can recognize, or it will end at an incorrect location. The space necessary for this character cuts one character off the maximum size of the string, which is why only four characters were displayed.

This type of algorithm is useful if you know that your data always should be under a certain size, but want to guard against longer data, whether benign or malicious. As you can see, the longer items are modified; if you really expect to deal with data that size, this algorithm is not for you; you are better off with some type of dynamic structure.

Advanced Pointers

Pointers are the keys to many types of data structures in C. Without pointers, you cannot access dynamic memory features at all. They enable you to build complex in-memory systems, giving a great deal of flexibility to deal with data whose quantity—or even type—is unknown when the program is being written.

They are also keys to string manipulation and data input and output in C. A thorough understanding of pointers can help you write better, more efficient programs. This section does not aim to teach you the basics of pointer usage in C. However, it will help you apply your existing skills to some more advanced—and in some cases, unique Linux—topics.

Earlier, I mentioned a situation in which a given algorithm might not be sufficient. A linked list system can help here. When you are reading in data of an unknown size, you have to read it in chunks. This is because the functions that are used to read data must place the data in a certain size of memory area. In this case, you must devise a way to splice together this split data later.

Listing 8-1 is a sample program that does that exactly. It uses `fgets()` to read the data in 9-byte chunks. The buffer size is 10 bytes, but recall that one byte is used for the terminating null character.

Next, a simple linked list is used to store the data. This linked list has one special item: an integer named `iscontinuing`. If this variable has a true value, then it indicates that the current structure does not hold the end of the string; that will be contained in a future element in the linked list. This variable is used later when the data is recalled from memory so that the reading algorithm knows how to re-assemble the data.

Because dynamic memory is used, this code can handle data as small as a few bytes or hundreds of megabytes of memory. Listing 8-1 presents the code.

Note   Listing 8-1 is available online.

Listing 8-1: **Dynamic allocation with linked list**

```c
#include <stdio.h>
#include <stdlib.h>
#include <string.h>

#define DATASIZE 10

typedef struct TAG_mydata {
  char thestring[DATASIZE];
  int iscontinuing;
  struct TAG_mydata *next;
} mydata;

mydata *append(mydata *start, char *input);
void displaydata(mydata *start);
void freedata(mydata *start);

int main(void) {
  char input[DATASIZE];
  mydata *start = NULL;

  printf("Enter some data, and press Ctrl+D when done.\n");

  while (fgets(input, sizeof(input), stdin)) {
```

```
      start = append(start, input);
    }

  displaydata(start);
  freedata(start);
  return 0;
}

mydata *append(mydata *start, char *input) {
  mydata *cur = start, *prev = NULL, *new;

  /* Search through until reach the end of the link, then add a new element. */

  while (cur) {
    prev = cur;
    cur = cur->next;
  }

  /* cur will be NULL now.  Back up one; prev is the last element. */

  cur = prev;

  /* Allocate some new space. */

  new = malloc(sizeof(mydata));
  if (!new) {
    fprintf(stderr, "Couldn't allocate memory, terminating\n");
    exit(255);
  }

  if (cur) {
    /* If there's already at least one element in the list, update its next
       pointer. */
    cur->next = new;
  } else {
    /* Otherwise, update start. */
    start = new;
  }

  /* Now, just set it to cur to make manipulations easier. */

  cur = new;

  /* Copy in the data. */

  strcpy(cur->thestring, input);

  /* If the string ends with \n or \r, it ends the line and thus
     the next struct does not continue. */

  cur->iscontinuing = !(input[strlen(input)-1] == '\n' ||
```

Continued

Listing 8-1 *(continued)*

```
                    input[strlen(input)-1] == '\r');
  cur->next = NULL;

  /* Return start to the caller. */

  return start;
}

void displaydata(mydata *start) {
  mydata *cur;
  int linecounter = 0, structcounter = 0;
  int newline = 1;

  cur = start;
  while (cur) {
    if (newline) {
      printf("Line %d: ", ++linecounter);
    }
    structcounter++;
    printf("%s", cur->thestring);
    newline = !cur->iscontinuing;
    cur = cur->next;
  }
  printf("This data contained %d lines and was stored in %d structs.\n",
      linecounter, structcounter);
}

void freedata(mydata *start) {
  mydata *cur, *next = NULL;

  cur = start;
  while (cur) {
    next = cur->next;
    free(cur);
    cur = next;
  }
}
```

Before I continue, I want to call your attention to the strcpy() call in the append() function. Although I did not perform bounds checking here, the code is not insecure in this case. Bounds checking is not necessary at this location because fgets() guarantees that it will return no more than a 9-byte (plus 1 null byte) string. Nothing is added to that string, so I know that the string passed in to the append() function will be small enough to avoid causing a security hazard.

Furthermore, it is easy to pass the entire group of data between functions. All that they need is a pointer to the start of the linked list, and everything will work well.

When you compile and run this program, you receive the following output:

```
$ gcc -Wall -o ch8-3 ch8-3.c
$  ./ch8-3
Enter some data, and press Ctrl+D when done.
Hi!
This is a really long line that will need to be split.
This is also a fairly long line.
Here
are
several
short
lines
for
testing.
Ctrl+D
Line 1: Hi!
Line 2: This is a really long line that will need to be split.
Line 3: This is also a fairly long line.
Line 4: Here
Line 5: are
Line 6: several
Line 7: short
Line 8: lines
Line 9: for
Line 10: testing.
This data contained 10 lines and was stored in 19 structs.
```

Analyzing this output, you can see that even though the program could process the input in chunks of 10 bytes only, it is still able to re-assemble the data properly. Not only that, but it is able to process 10 lines of input; there is no particular limit. So, although it is safe to do this in this particular case, a modification elsewhere in the program could lead to future problems. Also, a truncation is not acceptable; we want to preserve the data. So I'll show you some alternatives.

There are other, more sensible ways to store the data. With the examples that follow, you will gradually evolve the code until it reaches such a state. The first modification that you can make is a change to the structure's definition. The structure carries space inside for the string. Make the structure carry a pointer to a dynamically allocated area of memory. This has the advantage that its contents can be arbitrarily large. Listing 8-2 shows a revision of the code with this modification.

Note   Listing 8-2 is available online.

Listing 8-2: **Linked list with revised structure**

```c
#include <stdio.h>
#include <stdlib.h>
#include <string.h>

#define DATASIZE 10

typedef struct TAG_mydata {
  char *thestring;
  int iscontinuing;
  struct TAG_mydata *next;
} mydata;

mydata *append(mydata *start, char *input);
void displaydata(mydata *start);
void freedata(mydata *start);

int main(void) {
  char input[DATASIZE];
  mydata *start = NULL;

  printf("Enter some data, and press Ctrl+D when done.\n");

  while (fgets(input, sizeof(input), stdin)) {
    start = append(start, input);
  }

  displaydata(start);
  freedata(start);
  return 0;
}

mydata *append(mydata *start, char *input) {
  mydata *cur = start, *prev = NULL, *new;

  /* Search through until reach the end of the link, then add a new element. */

  while (cur) {
    prev = cur;
    cur = cur->next;
  }

  /* cur will be NULL now.  Back up one; prev is the last element. */

  cur = prev;

  /* Allocate some new space. */

  new = malloc(sizeof(mydata));
```

```
    if (!new) {
      fprintf(stderr, "Couldn't allocate memory, terminating\n");
      exit(255);
    }

    if (cur) {
      /* If there's already at least one element in the list, update its next
         pointer. */
      cur->next = new;
    } else {
      /* Otherwise, update start. */
      start = new;
    }

    /* Now, just set it to cur to make manipulations easier. */

    cur = new;

    /* Copy in the data. */

    cur->thestring = strdup(input);
    if (!cur->thestring) {
      fprintf(stderr, "Couldn't allocate space for the string; exiting!\n");
      exit(255);
    }

    /* If the string ends with \n or \r, it ends the line and thus
       the next struct does not continue. */

    cur->iscontinuing = !(input[strlen(input)-1] == '\n' ||
                          input[strlen(input)-1] == '\r');
    cur->next = NULL;

    /* Return start to the caller. */

    return start;
}

void displaydata(mydata *start) {
  mydata *cur;
  int linecounter = 0, structcounter = 0;
  int newline = 1;

  cur = start;
  while (cur) {
    if (newline) {
      printf("Line %d: ", ++linecounter);
    }
    structcounter++;
    printf("%s", cur->thestring);
    newline = !cur->iscontinuing;
```

Continued

Listing 8-2 *(continued)*

```
    cur = cur->next;
  }
  printf("This data contained %d lines and was stored in %d structs.\n",
         linecounter, structcounter);
}

void freedata(mydata *start) {
  mydata *cur, *next = NULL;

  cur = start;
  while (cur) {
    next = cur->next;
    free(cur->thestring);
    free(cur);
    cur = next;
  }
}
```

The changes that had to be made here cause the memory to be allocated for thestring by a call to strdup(). The only other change necessary is that this memory now must be explicitly freed, so the changes were not extensive.

If you compile and run this code, you'll find that the output is identical to the output from the other version of the code:

```
$ gcc -Wall -o ch8-3 ch8-3.c
$ ./ch8-3
Enter some data, and press Ctrl+D when done.
Hi!
This is a really long line that will need to be split.
This is also a fairly long line.
Here
are
several
short
lines
for
testing.
Ctrl+D
Line 1: Hi!
Line 2: This is a really long line that will need to be split.
Line 3: This is also a fairly long line.
Line 4: Here
Line 5: are
Line 6: several
```

```
Line 7: short
Line 8: lines
Line 9: for
Line 10: testing.
This data contained 10 lines and was stored in 19 structs.
```

From here, the evolution inevitably takes you to a situation in which it is no longer
necessary to split lines between structures. This is because there is now the capability
to store strings of any length in each structure, thanks to dynamic allocation of the
memory for the string. Therefore, the data can be combined as it is being put into the
linked list. Listing 8-3 shows a version of the code that does that exactly.

Note　　　Listing 8-3 is available online.

Listing 8-3: **Linked list with append at insert time**

```c
#include <stdio.h>
#include <stdlib.h>
#include <string.h>

#define DATASIZE 10

typedef struct TAG_mydata {
  char *thestring;
  struct TAG_mydata *next;
} mydata;

mydata *append(mydata *start, char *input, int newline);
void displaydata(mydata *start);
void freedata(mydata *start);

int main(void) {
  char input[DATASIZE];
  mydata *start = NULL;
  int newline = 1;

  printf("Enter some data, and press Ctrl+D when done.\n");

  while (fgets(input, sizeof(input), stdin)) {
    start = append(start, input, newline);
    newline = (input[strlen(input)-1] == '\n' ||
               input[strlen(input)-1] == '\r');
  }

  displaydata(start);
  freedata(start);
  return 0;
}
```

Continued

Listing 8-3 *(continued)*

```
mydata *append(mydata *start, char *input, int newline) {
  mydata *cur = start, *prev = NULL, *new;

  /* Search through until reach the end of the link, then add a new
     element if necessary. */

  while (cur) {
    prev = cur;
    cur = cur->next;
  }

  /* cur will be NULL now.  Back up one; prev is the last element. */

  cur = prev;

  /* Allocate some new space, if necessary. */

  if (newline || !cur) {
    new = malloc(sizeof(mydata));
    if (!new) {
      fprintf(stderr, "Couldn't allocate memory, terminating\n");
      exit(255);
    }

    if (cur) {
      /* If there's already at least one element in the list, update its next
         pointer. */
      cur->next = new;
    } else {
      /* Otherwise, update start. */
      start = new;
    }

    /* Now, just set it to cur to make manipulations easier. */

    cur = new;
    cur->thestring = NULL;    /* Flag it for needing new allocation. */
  } /* (newline || !cur) */

  /* Copy in the data. */

  if (cur->thestring) {
    cur->thestring = realloc(cur->thestring,
                              strlen(cur->thestring) + strlen(input) + 1);
    if (!cur->thestring) {
      fprintf(stderr, "Error re-allocating memory, exiting!\n");
      exit(255);
    }
    strcat(cur->thestring, input);
```

```
    } else {
      cur->thestring = strdup(input);
      if (!cur->thestring) {
        fprintf(stderr, "Couldn't allocate space for the string; exiting!\n");
        exit(255);
      }
    }
  }

  cur->next = NULL;

  /* Return start to the caller. */

  return start;
}

void displaydata(mydata *start) {
  mydata *cur;
  int linecounter = 0, structcounter = 0;

  cur = start;
  while (cur) {
    printf("Line %d: %s", ++linecounter, cur->thestring);
    structcounter++;
    cur = cur->next;
  }
  printf("This data contained %d lines and was stored in %d structs.\n",
         linecounter, structcounter);
}

void freedata(mydata *start) {
  mydata *cur, *next = NULL;

  cur = start;
  while (cur) {
    next = cur->next;
    free(cur->thestring);
    free(cur);
    cur = next;
  }
}
```

You will notice several important things about this code. First of all, you are introduced to a new function: `realloc()`. This function takes an existing block of memory that is already dynamically allocated, allocates a new block of the specified size, initializes the new block to the contents of the old one to the extent possible, frees the old block, and returns a pointer to the new one. Internally, the implementation may be different if your platform allows it, so the pointer may not change necessarily. However, you can still think of it as taking the preceding steps, which are the ones you must take if you do the same thing with your own code.

The code to generate the output is much simpler now. All it has to do is some simple counting and displaying now. There is no longer any need to merge strings together at that point, because they already are merged.

This example probably did not introduce you to new syntax for pointers. Rather, it introduced you to new uses for the syntax you already know. In the next section, I will introduce you to a system that uses pointers to pointers to strings — and with good reason!

Parsing data

When you need to separate data into separate pieces in C, things can start to get tricky. If you don't know the length of the input, or the number of elements that will be present, you inevitably need to use dynamically allocated memory. You need to either use a construct such as a linked list, described in the previous section, or an array of strings. In C, because a string is, itself, an array, and an array is simply a pointer, you end up with a pointer to the start of an array that contains pointers to the start of another array!

Interestingly, you may have already encountered such a situation: the command-line arguments to your program, passed through argv, are passed in such a manner. Here, you'll learn how to create and populate such an item, based on parsing apart a command line.

When you need to separate some data into parts, you normally use strtok(), which is defined in ANSI C. This function takes a string and a delimiter as its arguments. It then changes the delimiter to a NULL in the string, saves the location for the next invocation, and returns a pointer to the start of the first substring. The next time it is called, it returns a pointer to the start of the second substring, and so on until all pieces of the string have been parsed, at which time it returns NULL.

Despite the warning in the manpage (which says "Never use this function!"), strtok() is often the best way to pick apart data in C. However, there are some problems with it. First, it modifies your input string; this can be a bad thing if you want to be able to preserve the original string. Second, because it stores various pointers internally (by using static variables), you must not have a situation in which two parsing operations with strtok() could occur simultaneously. This means that you cannot use it in multithreaded applications. Also, if you use strtok() in main(), in some kind of loop, and inside this loop you call another function that also uses strtok(), things will get messed up because strtok() may think it's operating on the wrong string.

Although I thoroughly warned you not to use this function, see what happens when you try it out! Following is a program that implements parsing with strtok(). More than that, it shows you how certain functions of a shell operate internally by setting up some simple redirection if necessary. You'll learn more about those functions in future chapters.

This code is a fully functional, but rudimentary, shell (see Listing 8-4). Because of the size of the code, I present it here in its entire, final form instead of building up to the final version. Following the code, I describe it and highlight the role that pointers play in this system.

Note   Listing 8-4 is available online.

Listing 8-4: **A rudimentary shell**

```
#include <stdio.h>
#include <string.h>
#include <stdlib.h>
#include <unistd.h>
#include <pwd.h>
#include <fcntl.h>
#include <limits.h>
#include <signal.h>
#include <sys/types.h>
#include <sys/resource.h>
#include <sys/wait.h>

#define MAXINPUTLINE 10240
#define MAXARGS 1024
#define PARSE_NOPIPE -1       /* Default is no pipe */
#define PARSE_USEPIPE -2    /* Using pipes, but FD not yet known */

int background;
static int pipefd[2];

void parse_cmd(char *cmdpart);
void splitcmd(char *cmdpart, char *args[]);
char *expandtilde(char *str);
void freeargs(char *args[]);
void argsdelete(char *args[]);
char *parseredir(char oper, char *args[]);
int checkbackground(char *cmdline);
void stripcrlf(char *temp);
char *gethomedir(void);
char *getuserhomedir(char *user);
void signal_c_init(void);
void waitchildren(int signum);
void parse(char *cmdline);
void striptrailingchar(char *temp, char tc);

int main(void) {
  char input[MAXINPUTLINE];
```

Continued

Listing 8-4 *(continued)*

```
  signal_c_init();

  printf("Welcome to the sample shell!  You may enter commands here, one\n");
  printf("per line.  When you're finished, press Ctrl+D on a line by\n");
  printf("itself.  I understand basic commands and arguments separated by\n");
  printf("spaces, redirection with < and >, up to two commands joined\n");
  printf("by a pipe, tilde expansion, and background commands with &.\n\n");

  printf("\n$ ");

  while (fgets(input, sizeof(input), stdin)) {
    stripcrlf(input);
    parse(input);
    printf("\n$ ");
  }
  return 0;
}

void parse(char *cmdline)
{
  char *cmdpart[2];

  pipefd[0] = PARSE_NOPIPE;     /* Init: default is no pipe */

  background = checkbackground(cmdline);

  /* Separate into individual commands if there is a pipe symbol. */

  if (strstr(cmdline, "|"))
    pipefd[0] = PARSE_USEPIPE;

  /* Must do the strtok() stuff before calling parse_cmd because
     strtok is used in parse_cmd or the functions parse_cmd calls. */

  cmdpart[0] = strtok(cmdline, "|");
  cmdpart[1] = strtok((char *)NULL, "|");
  parse_cmd(cmdpart[0]);
  if (cmdpart[1]) parse_cmd(cmdpart[1]);
}
/* parse_cmd will do what is necessary to separate out cmdpart and run
   the specified command. */

void parse_cmd(char *cmdpart)
{
  int setoutpipe = 0;          /* TRUE if need to set up output pipe
                    after forking */
  int pid;                /* Set to pid of child process */
  int fd;                /* fd to use for input redirection */
```

```
char *args[MAXARGS + 5];
char *filename;              /* Filename to use for I/O redirection */

splitcmd(cmdpart, args);

if (pipefd[0] == PARSE_USEPIPE) {
  pipe(pipefd);
  setoutpipe = 1;
}

pid = fork();
if (!pid) {              /* child */
  if (setoutpipe) {
    dup2(pipefd[1], 1);    /* connect stdout to pipe if necessary */
  }
  if (!setoutpipe && (pipefd[0] > -1)) {
    /* Need to set up an input pipe. */
    dup2(pipefd[0], 0);
  }

  filename = parseredir('<', args);

  if (filename) {    /* Input redirection */
    fd = open(filename, O_RDONLY);
    if (!fd) {
     fprintf(stderr, "Couldn't redirect from %s", filename);
     exit(255);
    }
    dup2(fd, 0);
  }

  if ((filename = parseredir('>', args))) { /* Output redirection */
    fd = open(filename, O_WRONLY | O_CREAT | O_TRUNC, 0666);
    if (!fd) {
     fprintf(stderr, "Couldn't redirect to %s\n", filename);
     exit(255);
    }
    dup2(fd, 1);
  }

  if (!args[0]) {
    fprintf(stderr, "No program name specified.\n");
    exit(255);
  }

  execvp(args[0], args);
  /* If failed, die. */
  exit(255);
} else {              /* parent */
  if ((!background) &&
    (!setoutpipe))
```

Continued

Listing 8-4 *(continued)*

```c
      waitpid(pid, (int *)NULL, 0);
    else
      if (background)
        fprintf(stderr, "BG process started: %d\n", (int) pid);
    if (pipefd[0] > -1) {     /* Close the pipe if necessary. */
      if (setoutpipe)
        close(pipefd[1]);
      else
        close(pipefd[0]);
    }
  } /* if (!pid) */
  freeargs(args);
} /* parse_cmd()  */

/* splitcmd() will split a string into its component parts.

   Since splitcmd() uses strdup, freeargs() should be called on the
   args array after it is not used anymore. */

void splitcmd(char *cmdpart, char *args[])
{
  int counter = 0;
  char *tempstr;

  tempstr = strtok(cmdpart, " ");
  args[0] = (char *)NULL;
  while (tempstr && (counter < MAXARGS - 1)) {
    args[counter] = strdup(expandtilde(tempstr));
    args[counter + 1] = (char *)NULL;
    counter++;
    tempstr = strtok(NULL, " ");
  }
  if (tempstr) {          /* Broke out of loop because of num of args */
    fprintf(stderr, "WARNING: argument limit reached, command may be
truncated.\n");
  }
}


/* expandtilde() will perform tilde expansion on str if necessary. */

char *expandtilde(char *str)
{
  static char retval[MAXINPUTLINE];
  char tempstr[MAXINPUTLINE];
  char *homedir;
  char *tempptr;
  int counter;
```

```
     if (str[0] != '~') return str;       /* No tilde -- no expansion. */
     strcpy(tempstr, (str + 1));          /* Make a temporary copy of the string */
     if ((tempstr[0] == '/') || (tempstr[0] == 0))
       tempptr = (char *)NULL;
     else {                     /* Only parse up to a slash */
       /* strtok() cannot be used here because it is being used in the function
          that calls expandtilde().  Therefore, use a simple substitute. */
       if (strstr(tempstr, "/"))
         *(strstr(tempstr, "/")) = 0;
       tempptr = tempstr;
     }

     if ((!tempptr) || !tempptr[0]) {    /* Get user's own homedir */
       homedir = gethomedir();
     } else {                   /* Get specified user's homedir */
       homedir = getuserhomedir(tempptr);
     }

     /* Now generate the output string in retval. */

     strcpy(retval, homedir);             /* Put the homedir in there */

     /* Now take care of adding in the rest of the parameter */

     counter = 1;
     while ((str[counter]) && (str[counter] != '/')) counter++;

     strcat(retval, (str + counter));

     return retval;
}

/* freeargs will free up the memory that was dynamically allocated for the
   array */

void freeargs(char *args[])
{
  int counter = 0;

  while (args[counter]) {
    free(args[counter]);
    counter++;
  }
}

/* Calculates number of arguments in args */

void calcargc(char *args[], int *argc)
{
  *argc = 0;
  while (args[*argc]) {
```

Continued

Listing 8-4 *(continued)*

```c
    (*argc)++;                /* Increment while non-null */
  }
  (*argc)--;                  /* Decrement after finding a null */
}


/* parseredir will see if it can find a redirection operator oper
   in the array args[], and, if so, it will return the parameter (filename)
   to that operator. */

char *parseredir(char oper, char *args[])
{
  int counter;
  int argc;
  static char retval[MAXINPUTLINE];

  calcargc(args, &argc);

  for (counter = argc; counter >= 0; counter--) {
    fflush(stderr);
    if (args[counter][0] == oper) {
      if (args[counter][1]) {    /* Filename specified without a space */
        strcpy(retval, args[counter] + 1);
        argsdelete(args + counter);
        return retval;
      } else {                   /* Space seperates oper from filename */
        if (!args[counter+1]) {    /* Missing filename */
          fprintf(stderr, "Error: operator %c without filename", oper);
          exit(255);
        }
        strcpy(retval, args[counter+1]);
        argsdelete(args + counter + 1);
        argsdelete(args + counter);
        return retval;
      }
    }
  }
  return NULL;                 /* No match */
}

/* Argsdelete will remove a string from the array */

void argsdelete(char *args[])
{
  int counter = 0;
  if (!args[counter]) return;    /* Empty argument list: do nothing */
  free(args[counter]);
  while (args[counter]) {
```

```
        args[counter] = args[counter + 1];
        counter++;
    }
}

void stripcrlf(char *temp)
{
  while (temp[0] &&
        ((temp[strlen(temp)-1] == 13) || (temp[strlen(temp)-1] == 10))) {
    temp[strlen(temp)-1] = 0;
  }
}

char *gethomedir(void)
{
  static char homedir[_POSIX_PATH_MAX * 2]; /* Just to be safe. */
  struct passwd *pws;

  pws = getpwuid(getuid());
  if (!pws) {
    fprintf(stderr, "getpwuid() on %d failed", (int) getuid());
    exit(255);
  }

  strcpy(homedir, pws->pw_dir);
  return homedir;
}

char *getuserhomedir(char *user)
{
  static char homedir[_POSIX_PATH_MAX * 2]; /* Just to be safe. */
  struct passwd *pws;

  pws = getpwnam(user);
  if (!pws) {
    fprintf(stderr, "getpwnam() on %s failed", user);
    exit(255);
  }

  strcpy(homedir, pws->pw_dir);
  return homedir;
}

void signal_c_init(void)
{
  struct sigaction act;

  sigemptyset(&act.sa_mask);
  act.sa_flags = SA_RESTART;

  act.sa_handler = (void *)waitchildren;
```

Continued

Listing 8-4 *(continued)*

```
  sigaction(SIGCHLD, &act, NULL);
}

void waitchildren(int signum)
{
  while (wait3((int *)NULL,
              WNOHANG,
              (struct rusage *)NULL) > 0) {}
}

/* Check to see whether or not we should run in background */

int checkbackground(char *cmdline)
{
  /* First, strip off any trailing spaces (this has not yet been run
     through strtok) */

  striptrailingchar(cmdline, ' ');

  /* We are looking for an ampersand at the end of the command. */

  if (cmdline[strlen(cmdline)-1] == '&') {
    cmdline[strlen(cmdline)-1] = 0; /* Remove the ampersand from the command */
    return 1;                /* Indicate that this is background mode */
  }
  return 0;
}

void striptrailingchar(char *temp, char tc)
{
  while (temp[0] && (temp[strlen(temp)-1] == tc)) {
    temp[strlen(temp)-1] = 0;
  }
}
```

Analyzing the code

Now I'll go over some of the interesting parts of this program. For now, I'll skip over signals, duplicating file descriptors, and the like because those will be covered in more detail in later chapters such as Chapter 13, "Understanding Signals," and Chapter 14, "Introducing the Linux I/O."

The program starts with a simple loop, asking for input. It first strips the trailing newline character off the input, and then sends it over to be parsed. Then, if there is a pipe symbol, the command line is split into two parts, each of which is processed individually.

The function `parse_cmd()` does much of the processing. One of the first things it does is call `splitcmd()`, which uses `strtok()` — one particular interest here. Notice the definition of args: `char *args[]`. Recall that this is the same as both `char args[][]` and `char **args` — pointer to a pointer to a character.

When `strtok()` is first called, it is passed a string and the separation token; in this case, a space. It returns a pointer to the first part of the string. Then, in the loop, the value returned goes through tilde expansion, is dynamically allocated, and then placed in the args array. Finally, `strtok()` is invoked again. In the second and subsequent invocations, the first parameter should be the null value.

After this goes through, args is an array containing pointers to strings — strings that happen to be the individual arguments parsed from the command line. The end of this array is marked with a null value; otherwise, when reading the array, the software would not know that it has found the last pointer to a string.

After `splitcmd()`, you see the `expandtilde()` function. As its name implies, this function is used to perform tilde expansion on the input. It is called once for each argument and does the following:

1. Checks to see if the argument begins with a tilde (~) character. If not, additional processing is not necessary, and it is returned to the caller unmodified. Otherwise, a copy of the string, excluding the leading tilde (~) character, is made and placed in `tempstr`.

2. Determines whether the tilde should expand to the home directory of the user running the shell, or if a different home directory was specified. If a slash follows the tilde, or nothing at all follows the tilde, the home directory of the user running the shell is used; otherwise, the specific username that is given is the one to use. The `tempptr` variable is set to the username that needs to be used, or `NULL` if that username is the person running the shell.

3. Fetches the appropriate home directory and places it in the `homedir` variable. This value is copied to the return value. A loop then skips past the username specification, if any, and then adds the remainder of the string to the return value.

The `freeargs()` function simply steps through an array, freeing the memory pointed to by the pointers in the array. The `calcargc()` function uses a similar loop, but it is designed to figure out how many entries are in an array. Skipping down a bit, the `argsdelete()` function is another similar one. It removes a string from the middle of the array, and shifts all the remaining elements down so that there is no gap. The `argsdelete()` function does following to remove a string:

1. Verifies that it is given a valid argument to delete; if not, it returns immediately.

2. Frees the memory used by that argument.

3. Moves the remaining elements down the array in its loop.

You use the `stripcrlf()` function to remove the end-of-line character or characters from a given string, if they are present. The loop is fairly straightforward. As long as the string is not zero-length, and there is an end-of-line character at the end of it, remove the last character of the string. The `striptrailingchar()` function is similar to this one.

When you use this code, you should be aware that adequate bounds checking and error checking systems are not necessarily present. There are some cases where the return values of function calls are not checked but should be, and several cases where there are potential buffer overflows. Also, several errors are treated as fatal and simply cause the program to exit. If you are writing something for production use, you want to be less abrupt when an error is encountered, and more stringent with boundary checking. In order to keep the program as simple and small as possible, these things were not always included here.

Now that you've seen the code and analyzed it, it's time to compile and run the program to see if it really works. Notice how some commands do not generate an error, and how wildcards do not work. Listing 8-5 shows a sample session with this shell.

Note   You can find the sample shell session in Listing 8-5 online.

Listing 8-5: **Example shell session**

```
$ gcc -Wall -o  ch8-4 ch8-4.c
$ ./ch8-4
Welcome to the sample shell!  You may enter commands here, one
per line.  When you're finished, press Ctrl+D on a line by
itself.  I understand basic commands and arguments separated by
spaces, redirection with < and >, up to two commands joined
by a pipe, tilde expansion, and background commands with &.


$ echo Hello!
Hello!

$ ls /proc
  1    2    224  240  295  321    cpuinfo       kmsg       partitions  version
  13   200  226  241  296  344    devices       ksyms      pci
  141  206  227  242  297  4      dma           loadavg    scsi
  143  209  228  243  3    486    fb            locks      self
  151  216  229  257  306  487    filesystems   meminfo    slabinfo
  156  219  230  262  316  508    fs            misc       stat
  159  220  231  263  317  510    ide           modules    swaps
  179  221  232  266  318  apm    interrupts    mounts     sys
```

```
186  222  238  290  319  bus       ioports    mtrr   tty
196  223  239  294  320  cmdline   kcore      net    uptime

$ ls /dev/hda*
ls: /dev/hda*: No such file or directory

$ pwd
/home/jgoerzen/rec/private/t/cs6971_3

$ echo ~root
/root

$ cd ~root

$ pwd
/home/username

$ some_nonexistant_command

$ ls /proc | grep in
cmdline
cpuinfo
interrupts
meminfo
slabinfo

$ ls /proc | grep in > foo

$ rev < foo
enildmc
ofniupc
stpurretni
ofnimem
ofnibals

$ rm foo

$ echo "Bye"
"Bye"

$ Ctrl+D
```

You will notice a few things in this example. First, the asterisk was not expanded in the example because wildcards were not implemented. Second, there is no way to change directories because no shell internal commands such as cd were implemented. When a bad command is tried, there is simply no output because no error message is printed at that point; this can be confusing.

Finding Problems

Code problems relating to pointers often can be difficult to track down. If you attempt to dereference a null pointer, for instance, your program will crash and you probably can get good results from analyzing the core file with *gdb* as described in Chapter 10, "Debugging with gdb." However, few pointer problems are as easy to debug as this one.

If you have a problem with a buffer overrun that causes the program to crash, sometimes the stack is so corrupted that the core file produced is not helpful in tracking down the problem; gdb may be unable to determine where the program crashed. In these situations, you often have to trace through the program with gdb until you have pinpointed the location of the problems.

If you are having trouble trying to use pointers that are already freed, or not allocated, one useful tip is to always set the pointer to NULL after it is freed or when it is first defined. This way, you can test for a null value in your code — or, you are guaranteed a crash if you try to dereference it, but this crash should not corrupt the stack, so gdb can easily pinpoint the location of the problem.

Another common problem is memory leaks, which can be much more difficult to track down. These occur when memory is allocated, but not freed when it is no longer needed. Several additional tools can assist you with tracking down these problems. Among them is the FSF (Free Software Foundation) checker program, which may be found at http://www.gnu.org/software/checker/. However, because of the nature of the problem being traced, this program is not compatible with all Linux distributions and works with only one Linux architecture (i386).

Summary

In this chapter, you learned about memory allocation in C under Linux. Specifically, the following topics were covered:

✦ There are two ways to get memory in C: by static allocation, and by dynamic allocation.

✦ Statically allocated memory is easy to work with because the system takes care of allocating and deallocating the memory implicitly.

✦ Statically allocated memory is less flexible than dynamically allocated memory because you must know the size ahead of time, and you cannot change size during program execution.

✦ Dynamic memory is allocated with a call to malloc() and deallocated with a call to free(). In C++, the new and delete keywords can be used for dynamic memory allocation and deallocation.

✦ When you use any type of memory, but especially when you use statically allocated memory that is limited in size, it is extremely important that you do not allow data larger than the buffer size into the buffer. Failure to take note of this issue can lead to security compromises caused by buffer overruns.

✦ Dynamically allocated memory can permit data structures that grow in memory at runtime. You studied examples of linked lists, which have no limits on either the amount of data or the number of elements that they can store. You also studied an array of pointers, which has no limit on the amount of data that it can store but does limit the number of elements.

✦   ✦   ✦

Libraries and Linking

One of the most powerful concepts that we have with modern computer programming languages is the reuse of code. For instance, C gives us functions that enable us to use the same code in many different parts of the program. We also have macros that enable the same thing. You can even link together multiple modules so that you can separate your code and still be able to reuse it.

With libraries on Linux, you can go a step farther. Libraries enable you to share code *between* programs, not just within them. Consider, for instance, a function such as strcat(). This function is used by potentially thousands of programs on your system. Rather than have a separate copy for each of them, you could put a copy of the function into a library that all these programs can use — and in fact, that is done on a Linux system. In this chapter, you will be introduced to the Linux library systems and shown how to use them.

Introduction to Libraries

Libraries in Linux come in two flavors: *static* and *shared* (or dynamic) *libraries*. The static libraries descend from long ago in the history of UNIX but still have a significant place in modern Linux systems. Dynamic libraries are relatively new additions to Linux and other UNIX operating systems, but they present several very useful features.

The core impact of both these library technologies is that they affect the link process of your programs. When you compile a program, the linker (ld) is invoked to generate the final executable. It is responsible for taking code from all your different modules and merging it into a working program.

Static libraries enter this process, at compile time. These libraries are simply packaged-up collections of object files that can be linked into your program. The code in the library is linked into the executable at compile time and always accompanies it.

Dynamic libraries are an entirely different situation. With a dynamic library, all that is added at compile time is a mere hook, which says that when the program is run, it needs to bring in a dynamic library in order to work. Later, when the program is run, the dynamic library is loaded into memory and then the program is allowed to proceed. This method has several advantages and several disadvantages. Among its advantages are memory savings. Rather than requiring each program to have a copy of the library, a single copy is kept on the system. This means that only a single copy of the library needs to be in memory at any given time, and dozens or even hundreds of programs can use that single copy in memory.

Another advantage of using dynamic libraries is that you can upgrade them easily. Consider, for instance, a situation in which a library has a bug that causes programs to crash occasionally. If the library author releases a new version of the library to fix this problem, all that you have to do is compile the new library, install it, and restart your program if it's still running. There's no need to make any modification to the programs that use the library. On the other hand, with static libraries, you have to recompile not only the library itself, but you also have to recompile each and every application that happens to use it. This can be troublesome, especially because it's not possible to determine exactly which static libraries executables might use by simply looking at their binaries.

One other unique feature of dynamic libraries is the capability of overriding the behavior of any dynamic library that you're using. By exploiting this capability, you can, for instance, add features to printf() or more error-checking to unlink(). This is accomplished by preloading your own library in front of another, such as the system's standard libc. You also might replace a different library completely. Users have done this to give dozens of programs in X a more up-to-date feel (xaw3d), or to replace authentication mechanisms.

In addition to the capability of being linked in automatically when a program starts, your program can request that a given library be linked in dynamically—at run time. Several programs, such as Apache and Listar, exploit this capability to allow pluggable modules containing user-defined extensions to the program that are loadable and configurable entirely at run time.

There are some downsides to dynamic libraries, however. First, a program not carrying all its pieces within its own executable can cause potential problems. On modern systems, this risk is usually negligible; however, certain system-recovery tools such as fsck that may run when no dynamic library files are available should not be compiled with shared libraries. Second, conflicts can arise when new versions of a library introduce changes incompatible with previous versions of the shared library. Modern Linux provides methods for dealing with and preventing these problems, but these mechanisms are in the hands of the library authors; if the authors make a mistake (and you do not have source!), you may be stuck with having to recompile your programs anyway. Finally, on register-deprived architectures such as the x86, there may be a performance hit by using dynamic libraries. This is because the optimizer has one less register to use for optimization purposes. This difference is almost always insignificant, but if your program is doing extensive processing inside of dynamic libraries, you might want to benchmark the dynamic library performance and compare it to that of static libraries.

Building and Using Static Libraries

Creating a static library is fairly simple. Essentially, you use the ar program to combine a number of object (.o) files together into a single library, and then run `ranlib` to add some indexing information to that library.

For these examples, I'll start with the safecalls library from Chapter 14, "Introducing the Linux I/O." The code in that chapter is written so that you can use it as a separate module; here, you can use it as a library as well.

To make things more interesting, I'll add a separate file, safecalls2.c that implements two more safe wrappers. Listing 9-1 shows the code for that file.

Note   Listing 9-1 is available online.

Listing 9-1: **safecalls2.c**

```
/* John Goerzen

   This module contains wrappers around a number of system calls and
   library functions so that a default error behavior can be defined.

*/

#include <sys/types.h>
#include <unistd.h>
#include <stdio.h>
#include "safecalls.h"
#include "safecalls2.h"
#include "errno.h"

off_t safelseek(int fildes, off_t offset, int whence) {
  off_t retval;
```

Continued

Listing 9-1 *(continued)*

```
  retval = lseek(fildes, offset, whence);
  if (retval == (off_t) -1)
    HandleError(errno, "lseek", "failed");
  return retval;
}

int safefseek(FILE *stream, long offset, int whence) {
  int retval;

  retval = fseek(stream, offset, whence);
  if (retval == -1)
    HandleError(errno, "fseek", "failed");
  return retval;
}
```

It also has an accompanying .h file, safecalls2.h:

```
/* John Goerzen
 */

#ifndef __SAFECALLS2_H__
#define __SAFECALLS2_H__

#include <stdio.h>          /* required for FILE * stuff */
#include <sys/types.h>
#include <signal.h>

off_t safelseek(int fildes, off_t offset, int whence);
int safefseek(FILE *stream, long offset, int whence);

#endif
```

If you want to use this code in a separate program, you can do so without building a separate library. First, look at the standard usage of the code in a program. The following code purposely triggers an error. The error is trapped in safecalls2.c, which then must call a function in safecalls.c to handle it. Here's the code:

```
#include <stdio.h>
#include <errno.h>

/* The next four are for system-call I/O */

#include <unistd.h>
#include <sys/types.h>
```

```
#include <fcntl.h>
#include "safecalls.h"
#include "safecalls2.h"

int write_buffer(int fd, const void *buf, int count);

int main(void) {
  int outfile;

  /* Open the file */

  outfile = safeopen2("test.dat", O_RDWR | O_CREAT | O_TRUNC, 0640);

  safelseek(1, 10000, SEEK_SET);
  return 0;
}
```

To compile this, you must use a command line such as the following:

```
$ gcc -Wall -o ch9-1 ch9-1.c safecalls.c safecalls2.c
```

Notice that you have to specify all three names on the command line. Now, run the program and observe the result:

```
$ ./ch9-1
*** Error in lseek: failed
*** Error cause: Illegal seek
```

In this case, your "library" consists of two modules only and is not a serious inconvenience. However, some libraries include dozens or hundreds of modules, many megabytes in size. For the purposes of the examples in this chapter, however, I'll use these two files only.

To create an archive, you need to use the ar command to generate it. To avoid confusion, I'll call the library safec. First you must compile to object code by running gcc -c:

```
$ gcc -c -Wall -o safecalls.o safecalls.c
$ gcc -c -Wall -o safecalls2.o safecalls2.c
```

Now, you're ready to build the library file. Use the command to so:

```
$ ar cr libsafec.a safecalls.o safecalls2.o
```

This convention dictates that the name of the library should be preceded by lib and suffixed with .a for static libraries. Before your library is ready to use, you have to add the index symbols:

```
$ ranlib libsafec.a
```

Great! Now you can use your library. If you run your own system, you probably will copy it into /usr/local/lib at this point. Otherwise, you simply can leave it in your current directory. Here's how you compile your program now:

```
$ gcc -L. -Wall -o ch9-1 ch9-1.c -lsafec
```

The `-L.` option tells the linker to look in the current directory, indicated by the dot, for the library. Normally, it looks in the system library directories only. The `-lsafec` requests that the library be pulled in for linking.

Your program is now ready, linked against your static library! You can run it exactly as you ran the program previously.

Before moving on to dynamic libraries, here's a simple Makefile that can be used to automate this process:

```
CFLAGS=-Wall -L.
CC=gcc
OBJS=ch9-1.o
LIBOBJS=safecalls.o safecalls2.o
AR=ar rc

all: ch9-1

ch9-1: $(OBJS) libsafec.a
	$(CC) $(CFLAGS) -o $@ ch9-1.o -lsafec

libsafec.a: $(LIBOBJS)
	$(AR) $@ $(LIBOBJS)
	ranlib $@

%.o: %.c
	$(CC) $(CFLAGS) -c -o $@ $<

clean:
	-rm $(OBJS) $(LIBOBJS) libsafec.a ch9-1
```

In this example, the executable (ch9-1) declares a dependency on the object files as well as the library. The library then declares a dependency on its object files. All of these object files are compiled. The library is built, and finally the executable is built with the library linked in. If you've tried the example commands from earlier in this section, first run make clean so you can see the whole process and then observe the output:

```
$ make
gcc -Wall -L. -c -o ch9-1.o ch9-1.c
gcc -Wall -L. -c -o safecalls.o safecalls.c
gcc -Wall -L. -c -o safecalls2.o safecalls2.c
```

```
ar rc libsafec.a safecalls.o safecalls2.o
ranlib libsafec.a
gcc -Wall -L. -o ch9-1 ch9-1.o -lsafec
```

It's exactly the same process as you went through in the preceding example, only it has been conveniently optimized for you.

At this point, you have completely built and used your static library. Because the library is included in your executable, it's included just as it would have been if you linked the program without using a library. There are no additional issues with using the static library.

Building and Using Dynamic Libraries

Dynamic libraries are a much more powerful and versatile system than the static libraries I discussed in the previous section. This additional flexibility introduces some additional complexity, as you shall see in this section.

Here is a Makefile that you can use to build a program using a dynamic library, and its corresponding library:

```
CFLAGS=-Wall -L.
LIBCFLAGS=$(CFLAGS) -D_REENTRANT -fPIC
CC=gcc
OBJS=ch9-1.o
LIBOBJS=safecalls.o safecalls2.o
AR=ar rc
LIBRARY=libsafec.so.1.0.0
SONAME=libsafec.so.1

all: ch9-1

ch9-1: $(OBJS) $(LIBRARY)
	$(CC) $(CFLAGS) -o $@ ch9-1.o -lsafec

$(LIBRARY): $(LIBOBJS)
	$(CC) -shared -Wl,-soname,$(SONAME) -o $@ $(LIBOBJS) -lc
	ln -sf $@ libsafec.so
	ln -sf $@ $(SONAME)

ch9-1.o: ch9-1.c
	$(CC) $(CFLAGS) -c -o $@ $<

%.o: %.c
	$(CC) $(LIBCFLAGS) -c -o $@ $<

clean:
	-rm $(OBJS) $(LIBOBJS) $(LIBRARY) libsafec.so $(SONAME) ch9-1
```

When you run this Makefile, you get the following output:

```
$ make
gcc -Wall -L. -c -o ch9-1.o ch9-1.c
gcc -Wall -L. -D_REENTRANT -fPIC -c -o safecalls.o safecalls.c
gcc -Wall -L. -D_REENTRANT -fPIC -c -o safecalls2.o safecalls2.c
gcc -shared -Wl,-soname,libsafec.so.1 -o libsafec.so.1.0.0 safecalls.o
safecalls2.o -lc
ln -sf libsafec.so.1.0.0 libsafec.so
ln -sf libsafec.so.1.0.0 libsafec.so.1
gcc -Wall -L. -o ch9-1 ch9-1.o -lsafec
```

Now, I'll review exactly what is being done here. The Makefile begins by compiling the main C file. Next, it compiles the two modules for the library. Notice the special options on those command lines. The -D_REENTRANT causes the preprocessor symbol _REENTRANT to be defined, which activates special behavior in some macros. The -fPIC option enables generation of position-independent code. This is necessary because the libraries are loaded at run time, into a position in memory that is not known at compile time. If you fail to use these options, your library will not necessarily work properly.

After these are compiled, the shared library is linked. The -shared option tells the compiler to generate shared library code. The -Wl option causes the following options to be passed to the linker; in this case, the linker receives -soname libsafec.so.1. The -o option, as usual, specifies the output filename. It then specifies the two object files and explicitly requests that the C library be included. I'll talk about the intricacies of the soname in the next section.

Next, two required symbolic links are created; these will also be specified in the next section. Finally, the executable is linked—incidentally, using the same command as was used before.

To run this executable, you have two options:

✦ You may copy the libsafec.so* files to a directory that is listed in /etc/ld.so.conf and then run the ldconfig utility as root; or

✦ You may run export LD_LIBRARY_PATH=`pwd`, which adds your current directory to the library search path.

These steps are necessary because dynamic libraries are loaded at run time instead of compile time. By default, your current directory is not included in the Run-Time Library (RTL) search path, so you have to specify it manually—exactly as you did with -L. on the command line to gcc. Finally, try running it:

```
$ ./ch9-1
*** Error in lseek: failed
*** Error cause: Illegal seek
```

Success! Your program runs and obligingly issues its customary error message. You've built your first dynamic library!

Using Advanced Dynamic Library Features

As I mentioned before, there's a lot more to dynamic libraries than the benefits inherent in a smaller memory footprint, code sharing, and easier updates. In this section, I'll talk about the mechanisms that enable some of these benefits as well as some additional features of dynamic libraries that you can explore.

The ldd tool

There is a wonderful tool on your system that examines information about shared libraries — ldd. The purpose of ldd is simple: it shows you which libraries your executable requires, and where the dynamic loader manages to find them on your system. Each executable on your system contains a list of the dynamic libraries that it requires to run. When the executable is invoked, the system is responsible for loading these libraries. The ldd tool shows you these details. Consider the following output:

```
$ ldd ./ch9-1
        libsafec.so.1 => /home/jgoerzen/t/libsafec.so.1 (0x40013000)
        libc.so.6 => /lib/libc.so.6 (0x4001d000)
        /lib/ld-linux.so.2 => /lib/ld-linux.so.2 (0x40000000)
```

This output indicates that the sample program requires three shared objects. The first is the shared library built here, libsafec.so.1. The run-time loader found it under the home directory. The second is the system standard C library, which was found under /lib. The final one is the dynamic loader itself; in this case, the absolute path must be embedded in the executable.

The ldd tool can be an extremely useful for diagnostic purposes, to see just how your libraries are being loaded at run time. Additionally, it is useful for educational purposes to see what is going on behind the scenes of your application.

The soname

One of the most important, and often confusing, aspects of shared libraries is the soname — short for shared object name. This is a name embedded in the control data for a shared library (.so) file. As I already mentioned, each of your programs contains a list of the libraries required. The contents of this list are a series of library sonames, which the dynamic loader must find — ldd shows you this process.

The key feature of the soname is that it indicates a certain measure of compatibility. When you upgrade libraries on your system, and the new library has the same soname as the old, it is assumed that programs linked with the old library will still work fine with the newer one. This behavior makes possible the easy bug fixes and upgrades that you get with shared libraries in Linux.

Similarly, if the soname in the new library is different, the assumption is that the two are not compatible. But do not fear — nothing can prevent you from having two copies of the same library on your system at once — one for programs linked against the older version, and another for programs linked against the newer version. It is because of this behavior that modern Linux distributions are so easily capable of running programs compiled against an old version of the C library despite drastic changes to it that would otherwise render the old programs inoperable.

In the Makefile for the example in the "Building and Using Dynamic Libraries" section, I explicitly declared the soname. Convention holds that when the major version number of a library changes, the upgrade is incompatible and the soname should thus be upgraded as well; however, when the minor version numbers change, a soname upgrade is thus unnecessary.

I maintain three files in the library location (typically /usr/lib) for each library. Here is how it was done with this library:

✦ The main file containing the library's code (libsafec.so.1.0.0 in this case) typically has the entire version number of the library. The other two files are symlinks to it. This behavior allows you to have multiple copies of a library with the *same* soname on the system and you can switch between them simply by adjusting two symlinks. Furthermore, it clarifies exactly what library is being invoked by the soname.

✦ The second file has a name that corresponds to the soname of the library, which is a symlink to the main file. In this example, the file is libsafec.so.1. Because the soname does not change except for major changes that are not backwards-compatible, using a symlink here is great. This file *must* exist; it is the one that is used by the dynamic loader to load the library into your programs.

✦ The third file is simply the name of the library, libsafec.so in this case. This file is used solely to compile (or link) programs and is not used by the dynamic loader in any way. This enables you to use syntax such as `-lsafec` to gcc; otherwise, you would have to reference the library by specific path and name. By permitting this compilation convenience, you enable programs to compile easily regardless of the underlying library. Furthermore, the compile/link process is not harmed because the linker extracts the soname from the library's contents.

Now, imagine that you made a major upgrade to the safec library and released safec version 2.0.0. The libsafec.so.1 and libsafec.so.1.0.0 files remain in place unmodified so that the programs already compiled and linked with them continue to run. The new libraries libsafec.so.2 and libsafec.so.2.0.0 are installed alongside them for the use of programs compiled and linked with the new library. Finally, the libsafec.so symbolic link is changed to point to the new version, so that newly compiled programs will use the new library instead of the old one.

Hopefully, you can't help but marvel at the beauty and simplicity of this scheme. For years, one of the most prevalent problems for Windows operating systems has been issues with DLL (their shared library) versioning problems. One application may require one version, and another application may require an older, incompatible version, but the system doesn't provide a good, clean way for both applications to be happy. This means that it is literally impossible to have two programs executing simultaneously with two completely different versions of the libraries loaded (unless you resort to some more drastic steps).

With Linux, each application specifically declares the version that it wants through the use of the soname. Library authors also can declare which versions are compatible with each other, by either retaining or changing the soname, so you end up with no dynamic library versioning conflicts.

Thanks to this versatile shared library system, Linux programmers use them extensively. It's not at all uncommon to find Linux installations containing hundreds, perhaps even thousands, of shared libraries. These libraries exist for doing everything from reading from JPEG files to processing ZIP archives. Most are used by dozens of programs on the system. This reduces development time for programmers, decreases resource utilization for you, and provides for an easier and less-intrusive upgrade path.

The dynamic loader

The Linux dynamic loader (also known as the dynamic linker) is invoked automatically when your program is invoked. Its job is to ensure that all the libraries that your program needs are loaded into memory, in their proper version. The dynamic loader, named either ld.so or ld-linux.so, depending on your Linux libc version, must complete its job with little outside interaction. However, it does accept some configuration information in environment variables and in configuration files.

The file /etc/ld.so.conf defines the locations of the standard system libraries. This is taken as a search path for the dynamic loader. For the changes there to take effect, you must run the ldconfig tool as root. This updates the /etc/ls.so.cache file, which is actually the one used internally by the loader.

You can use several environment variables to control the behavior of the dynamic loader (see Table 9-1).

Table 9-1
Dynamic Loader Environment Variables

Variable	Purpose
LD_AOUT_LIBRARY_PATH	The same function as LD_LIBRAY_PATH but for the deprecated a.out binary format.
LD_AOUT_PRELOAD	The same function as LD_PRELOAD, but for the deprecated a.out binary format.
LD_KEEPDIR	Applicable to a.out libraries only; causes the directory that may be specified with them to be ignored.
LD_LIBRARY_PATH	Adds additional directories to the library search path. Its contents should be a colon-separated list of directories in the same fashion as the PATH variable for executables. This variable is ignored if you invoke a setuid or setgid program.
LD_NOWARN	Applicable to a.out libraries only; causes warnings about changing version numbers to be suppressed.
LD_PRELOAD	Causes additional user-defined libraries to be loaded before the others such that they have an opportunity to override or redefine the standard library behavior. Multiple entries can be separated by a space. For programs that are setuid or setgid, only libraries also marked as such will be preloaded. A systemwide version also can be specified in /etc/ld.so.perload, which is not subject to this restriction.

Notice how several options relate to a.out. The a.out binary format was used before the current one (ELF). No current distribution uses a.out anymore, so these a.out options are intended for unique circumstances only.

Working with LD_PRELOAD

One of the most unique features of the shared library system in Linux is the LD_PRELOAD item described in Table 9-1. This enables you to replace any function called in any library that the program uses with your own version. This kind of power is extremely wide-ranging and can be used for everything from adding new features to correcting bugs. Sometimes, it may be used to swap in an entirely different behavior for something—for instance, to use a different type of encryption for passwords in an authentication system.

Listing 9-2 shows some code that intercepts the call to safelseek() in our wayward program and instead writes some data out to screen.

Note   Listing 9-2 is available online.

Listing 9-2: **Sample Code for LD_PRELOAD**

```c
#include <dlfcn.h>
#include <stdio.h>
#include <sys/types.h>
#include <unistd.h>

#include "safecalls.h"
#include "safecalls2.h"

/* Declare a wrapper around lseek. */

off_t lseek(int fildes, off_t offset, int whence) {
  /* A pointer to the "real" lseek function.  Static so it only
     has to be filled in once.*/

  static off_t (*funcptr)(int, off_t, int) = NULL;

  if (!funcptr) {
    funcptr = (off_t (*)(int, off_t, int)) dlsym(RTLD_NEXT, "lseek");
  }

  if (fildes == 1) {          /* Error condition is occuring */
    fprintf(stderr, "Hey!  I've trapped an attempt to lseek on fd 1.  I'm\n");
    fprintf(stderr, "returning you a fake success indicator.\n");
    return offset;
  } else {             /* Otherwise, pass it through. */
    fprintf(stderr, "OK, passing your lseek through.\n");
    return (*funcptr)(fildes, offset, whence);
  }
}

/* And one around safeopen2, just for kicks. */

int safeopen2(const char *pathname, int flags, mode_t mode) {
  static int (*funcptr)(const char *, int, mode_t) = NULL;

  if (!funcptr) {
    funcptr = (int (*)(const char *, int, mode_t)) dlsym(RTLD_NEXT,
                        "safeopen2");
  }

  fprintf(stderr, "I'm passing along a safeopen2() call now.\n");
  return (*funcptr)(pathname, flags, mode);
}
```

Name this code interceptor.c. Before demonstrating how it is used, I'll examine how it works.

The code begins by declaring a function named lseek() — this will intercept calls to the standard function of that name. This new function must have the exact same prototype as the standard one, which it does. Inside the function, the first variable declaration is a rather odd-looking one. It is a pointer to a function of a type that returns off_t and takes an int, an off_t, and an int — a function of the lseek variety, in this case. In the function, the first thing to do is see if that variable is set yet. If not, you need to do so.

This variable is used if you want to pass along the call to the wrapper function all the way to the standard one. If you simply want to intercept a function call with no intention of ever passing the call back to the standard one, you have no need for this sort of trickery.

At this point, you need to know the address of the lseek() function in the standard libraries. The dlsym() function can tell you. The RTLD_NEXT argument tells dlsym() to look only in the libraries loaded after this one for the specified symbol. The function returns its address, which is stored away for later use.

Next, the function checks to see if it received a request to lseek on the file descriptor 1 — the error in the program. If so, it prints a warning message and then returns a code that indicates a successful seek — all without ever calling the real lseek() function or moving any file position indicator.

If the file descriptor is not 1, the normal processing mode is assumed. The function calls the real lseek() (as stored in funcptr), passes along the arguments, and returns the result back to the caller.

The wrapper around safeopen2() works in a similar way. It finds the address of the real function and saves it. Then it adds its own special behavior before passing all the necessary information on to the real function.

Here is how you compile this library, assuming you named it interceptor.c:

```
$ gcc -shared -Wl,-soname,libinterceptor.so.0 -o
libinterceptor.so.0.0.0 interceptor.c -ldl -lc
$ ln -s libinterceptor.so.0.0.0 libinterceptor.so.0
```

The -ldl line in the preceding example brings in functions from the dl library, which happens to contain the implementation of dlsym that is necessary in this program.

Now you're ready to experiment. Remember that you must set LD_LIBRARY_PATH as described in the "Building and Using Dynamic Libraries" section if you aren't copying libraries into your system directory.

```
$ export LD_PRELOAD=libinterceptor.so.0
$ ./ch9-1
I'm passing along a safeopen2() call now.
Hey!  I've trapped an attempt to lseek on fd 1.  I'm
returning you a fake success indicator.
```

Also take note of the new output from ldd:

```
$ ldd ./ch9-1
        libinterceptor.so.0 => /home/jgoerzen/t/libinterceptor.so.0 (0x40014000)
        libsafec.so.1 => /home/jgoerzen/t/libsafec.so.1 (0x40016000)
        libc.so.6 => /lib/libc.so.6 (0x4001f000)
        libdl.so.2 => /lib/libdl.so.2 (0x400fa000)
        /lib/ld-linux.so.2 => /lib/ld-linux.so.2 (0x40000000)
```

You can see the inclusion of the interceptor library even though this was not specified when the program was compiled. Moreover, the libdl library is included because libinterceptor requires it. Now, be sure that you unset LD_PRELOAD or else you will mess up other applications!

```
$ unset LD_PRELOAD
```

Using dlopen

Another powerful library function that you can use is dlopen(). This function will open a new library and load it into memory. This function primarily is used to load in symbols from libraries whose names you do not know at compile time. For instance, the Apache web server uses this capability to load in modules at run time that provide certain extra capabilities. A configuration file controls the loading of these modules. This mechanism prevents the need to recompile every time a module should be added or deleted from the system.

You can use dlopen() in your own programs as well. The dlopen() function is defined in dlfcn.h and is implemented in the dl library. It takes two parameters: a filename and a flag. The filename can be the soname of the library as we have been using thus far in our examples. The flag indicates whether or not the library's dependencies should be evaluated immediately. If set to RTLD_NOW, they are evaluated immediately; otherwise, if set to RTLD_LAZY, they are evaluated when necessary. Additionally, you can specify RTLD_GLOBAL, which causes libraries that may be loaded later to have access to the symbols in this one.

After the library is loaded, you can pass along the handle returned by `dlopen()` as the first parameter to `dlsym()` to retrieve the addresses of the symbols in the library. With this information, you can dereference the pointers to functions as we did in the in Listing 9-2 example and call the functions in the loaded library.

Summary

In this chapter, you learned about static and dynamic libraries in Linux. Specifically, you learned:

✦ You can use two different types of libraries in Linux: static and dynamic.

✦ Static libraries are loaded into the executable when it is compiled. Dynamic libraries are loaded when the executable is run.

✦ Dynamic libraries are more powerful but are also much more complex.

✦ Static libraries are built by compiling code normally to object files, putting them in an ar archive, and then running `ranlib`. They are linked in with the `-l` option on the command-line.

✦ Dynamic libraries are built by compiling with `-fPIC -D_REENTRANT`. Then, the object files are linked together with `gcc -share` and the soname specified with a command such as `-Wl,-soname,libname-4`.

✦ The dynamic linker, ld-linux.so, can be controlled by several different environment variables and system-wide configuration files.

✦ You can use `LD_LIBRARY_PATH` to add directories to the standard library search path.

✦ The `LD_PRELOAD` option enables you to override functions in the standard libraries.

✦ ✦ ✦

Debugging with gdb

One of the most frequent tasks that any programmer must face, no matter how good, is the task of debugging. When your program compiles, it may not run properly. Perhaps it crashes completely. Or it simply might not perform some function correctly. Maybe its output is suspect, or it doesn't seem to prompt for the correct input. Whatever the case, tracking down these problems, especially with a large program, can be the most difficult part of the journey towards developing a correct fix. Here's where *gdb* (the GNU debugger) enters the picture. This program is a debugger — a system that helps you find bugs in software.

In this chapter, you will learn about using gdb to debug your C and C++ programs. Although gdb does have support for other compiled languages, these are by far the most common ones that it is used with. You'll learn about the basic features of gdb and how it can be used to step through your code as it runs. Then you'll learn some more advanced features for running programs, such as ways to display data, set breakpoints, or set watches. Finally, the chapter will explain how you can analyze a core dump to find out what caused a program to crash.

The Need for gdb

The point of gdb is to help you out of a bind. Without such a tool, you are at a serious disadvantage. To track down some bugs, you may have to add voluminous statements to generate special output from your program. For some programs, such as network daemons, this isn't possible at all; they have to resort to other methods such as logging. Sometimes the very act of adding special code to help find a bug may effect the bug itself. And finally, you have no methods of performing post-mortem analysis of programs that have crashed and generated a core dump.

With gdb, you get all of these features, and more. You can step through your code, line by line, as it executes. As you do this, you can see the logic flow, watch what happens to your variables and data, and see how various instructions effect the program. Another timesaving feature enables you to set breakpoints. These enable your program to execute normally until a certain condition is reached. This condition could be that a variable has taken on a certain value, or even that a certain place in the code has been reached.

The gdb feature set includes other useful options. For one, gdb enables you to analyze a core file generated by a program that has crashed. By doing so, you can figure out what caused the crash, find out the last instruction called before the crash, examine all variables prior to the crash, and examine the stack (provided it was not damaged by the crash) prior to the point that the program exited. Another option is that gdb can attach itself to an already running process — a feature great for debugging network servers, programs that fork, or ones that need to run for some time prior to encountering a situation that triggers a bug.

You can use gdb without modifying your code; simply ask gcc to generate some additional information, and you are ready to go. You simply load up your program inside gdb, and you can step through it. Alternatively, you can start with a core dump to see exactly what happened.

As an example, consider this code from Chapter 6, "Welcome to gcc":

```
#include <stdio.h>

int main(void) {
    int input = 0;
    printf("Enter an integer: ");
    scanf("%d", input);
    printf("Twice the number you supplied is %d.\n", 2 * input);
    return 0;
}
```

When you run the program, you get:

```
$ ./crash
Enter an integer: 5
Segmentation fault
```

This isn't particularly helpful. All that you know is that the program runs fine until it tries to read input. From these messages only, you don't know whether the program crashes at that point or later. With gdb, you can trace through your code as it executes, line by line, to watch what happens and to pinpoint the location of a problem. With the Linux core dump feature, you can also analyze the results from gdb after a program exits, even if it wasn't running under gdb when it crashes.

Stepping Through Your Code

Using gdb to step through your code is one of the most commonly used features of the debugger. When you do this, you can get an inside look at how your program is functioning. You can see which commands it's executing, what the variables are, and many more details.

Debugging tutorial

Start with a simple program that doesn't have any bugs in it. This gives you a chance to see how to trace through your code. Then, you'll see how to apply this knowledge to tracking down bugs.

Here is the source code for the first example program:

```c
#include <stdio.h>

int getinput(void);
void printmessage(int counter, int input);

int main(void) {
  int counter;
  int input;

  for (counter = 0; counter < 200; counter++) {
    input = getinput();
    if (input == -1) exit(0);
    printmessage(counter, input);
  }
  return 0;
}

int getinput(void) {
  int input;

  printf("Enter an integer, or use -1 to exit: ");
  scanf("%d", &input);
  return input;
}

void printmessage(int counter, int input) {
  static int lastnum = 0;

  counter++;

  printf("For number %d, you entered %d (%d more than last time)\n",
         counter, input, input - lastnum);
  lastnum = input;
}
```

Before moving on to an example of this code, I want to highlight two things about it for those who are newer to the C language. First, notice how both the main() and printmessage() functions contain a variable named counter. Inside the printmessage() function, commands operate on the local counter variable— not the one from main(). This variable is initially set to hold the same value as the one in main(), however, because it is passed in during the function call.

The second thing to notice at this point is the static int declaration inside the printmessage() function. This indicates that, even when that variable falls out of scope when the function exits, its value should be preserved for the next invocation of the function.

Having taken note of this, you should try to compile and run the program now. Recall from Chapter 6, "Welcome to gcc," that -ggdb3 includes the maximum amount of debugging information in an executable, so you should compile with that option. For example:

```
$ gcc -ggdb3 -o ch10-1 ch10-1.c
$ ./ch10-1
Enter an integer, or use -1 to exit: 215
For number 1, you entered 215 (215 more than last time)
Enter an integer, or use -1 to exit: 300
For number 2, you entered 300 (85 more than last time)
Enter an integer, or use -1 to exit: 100
For number 3, you entered 100 (-200 more than last time)
Enter an integer, or use -1 to exit: 5
For number 4, you entered 5 (-95 more than last time)
Enter an integer, or use -1 to exit: -1
```

From this output, you should have no trouble seeing that this program is a fairly straightforward one, and its actions are, likewise, straightforward. Now, take a look at it in the debugger. I'll show you some interaction with gdb in the following example and then explain what happened.

```
$ gdb ch10-1
GNU gdb 4.18
Copyright 1998 Free Software Foundation, Inc.
GDB is free software, covered by the GNU General Public License, and you are
welcome to change it and/or distribute copies of it under certain conditions.
Type "show copying" to see the conditions.
There is absolutely no warranty for GDB.  Type "show warranty" for details.
This GDB was configured as "alphaev56-unknown-linux-gnu"...
(gdb)
```

The first thing that occurs here is an invocation of gdb. The debugger loads, and comes up with the sample program ready to use. Although some output from gdb may be different from this example, you do not worry about this; the differences will be in areas that are not relevant to your purposes.

The main interface to gdb is the (gdb) prompt. At this prompt, you enter your commands for gdb. The first thing you should do is set a breakpoint for the start of the main() function. A breakpoint indicates that gdb should stop executing a program at that point to give you a chance to step through it. Setting a breakpoint at main() enables you to start tracing execution at that point. So, go ahead and set the breakpoint as follows:

```
(gdb) break main
Breakpoint 1 at 0x1200004a8: file ch10-1.c, line 6.
```

The debugger confirms that the breakpoint is set, and shows you the location. Now it's time run the program:

```
(gdb) run
Starting program: /home/jgoerzen/t/ch10-1
Breakpoint 1, main () at ch10-1.c:6
6         int main(void) {
```

Your program begins executing, and then immediately hits the breakpoint for the main() function. The gdb debugger indicates that breakpoint 1 has been hit, and then displays the next line of code to be executed.

To step through your code, you normally start with the step command. This executes one line of code:

```
(gdb) step
main () at ch10-1.c:10
10         for (counter = 0; counter < 200; counter++) {
(gdb) s
11             input = getinput();
(gdb) Enter
getinput () at ch10-1.c:18
18        int getinput(void) {
```

The step command is used here to execute three lines of code. The first step executed line 6 of the program. Then, a gdb shortcut is used. With gdb, you can abbreviate commands in many cases. In this situation, the s is used as a shortcut for the step command. After stepping past line 10, the loop is entered. Stepping on line 11 causes execution to go into the getinput() function. Notice another shortcut here—simply pressing Enter causes the previous command (a step, in this case) to be executed again as follows:

```
(gdb) s
getinput () at ch10-1.c:21
21             printf("Enter an integer, or use -1 to exit: ");
(gdb) s
22             scanf("%d", &input);
(gdb) print input
$1 = 1439424
```

You may be wondering why there is no output on-screen after stepping past line 21, which displays a prompt. The reason is the buffering used by printf() and the other similar functions. The prompt appears when scanf() is executed.

Another new concept is demonstrated here: displaying values of variables. After stepping past line 21, I asked gdb to display the contents of the variable named input. Because this request occurs prior to reading in a value for that variable with scanf(), the content of the variable is essentially random. Now, step through the scanf(). Predicting the result, you should see the prompt from the earlier printf() displayed, and input read from the terminal. Take a look and see if that really happens:

```
(gdb) s
Enter an integer, or use -1 to exit: 150
23              return input;
```

Indeed it does! The scanf() is executed, the prompt is displayed, and input is read from the terminal. The following example confirms that the value of the input variable has changed:

```
(gdb) print input
$2 = 150
```

Because the program is ready to return a value, stepping at this point shortly goes back to the main() function as shown in the following example:

```
(gdb) s
24          }
(gdb) s
main () at ch10-1.c:12
12              if (input == -1) exit(0);
```

Now take a look at a new command: display:

```
(gdb) display counter
1: counter = 0
(gdb) display input
2: input = 150
(gdb) s
13              printmessage(counter, input);
2: input = 150
1: counter = 0
```

At first glance, display appears to act the same as print acted before. However, there is a difference. When you use display, the values of those variables are shown each time the debugger stops the program pending your instructions. This means that when you step through a program, those values are displayed after each line of code. And in fact, you can see this. After stepping over line 12, gdb first displays the line of code that will be executed by the next command, and then the values of those two variables. Watch what happens when you step into the `printmessage()` function:

```
(gdb) s
printmessage (counter=0, input=150) at ch10-1.c:26
26       void printmessage(int counter, int input) {
(gdb) s
printmessage (counter=0, input=150) at ch10-1.c:29
29           counter++;
(gdb) disp counter
3: counter = 0
```

The debugger no longer is displaying the values of `counter` and `input`. Why? Well, the reason is that the `counter` and `input` variables that it displayed beforehand are now out of scope—they cannot be accessed from within `printmessage()`. This function does contain variables named `counter` and `input`, but these variables, although named the same, are actually different. The debugger is now asked to display counter:

```
(gdb) s
31           printf("For number %d, you entered %d (%d more than
last time)\n",
3: counter = 1
(gdb) s
For number 1, you entered 150 (150 more than last time)
33           lastnum = input;
3: counter = 1
(gdb) s
34       }
3: counter = 1
```

While stepping through this code, you can watch as the value of `counter` is incremented. Then, line 31 displays the values of these two variables. The `lasnum` variable is set, and then the function is ready to return:

```
(gdb) s
main () at ch10-1.c:10
10           for (counter = 0; counter < 200; counter++) {
2: input = 150
1: counter = 0
```

Notice how gdb is saying that counter is zero again. This is because the value of this `counter` variable in `main()` never changed; only the one in `printmessage()` was modified. Now step through an entire iteration of the loop so you can see it all together:

```
(gdb) s
11           input = getinput();
```

```
2: input = 150
1: counter = 1
(gdb) s
getinput () at ch10-1.c:18
18       int getinput(void) {
(gdb) s
getinput () at ch10-1.c:21
21          printf("Enter an integer, or use -1 to exit: ");
(gdb) s
22          scanf("%d", &input);
(gdb) s
Enter an integer, or use -1 to exit: 12
23          return input;
(gdb) s
24       }
(gdb) s
main () at ch10-1.c:12
12           if (input == -1) exit(0);
2: input = 12
1: counter = 1
(gdb) s
13              printmessage(counter, input);
2: input = 12
1: counter = 1
(gdb) s
printmessage (counter=1, input=12) at ch10-1.c:26
26       void printmessage(int counter, int input) {
3: counter = 1
(gdb) s
printmessage (counter=1, input=12) at ch10-1.c:29
29          counter++;
3: counter = 1
(gdb) s
31          printf("For number %d, you entered %d (%d more than
last time)\n",
3: counter = 2
(gdb) s
For number 2, you entered 12 (-138 more than last time)
33          lastnum = input;
3: counter = 2
(gdb) s
34       }
3: counter = 2
(gdb) s
main () at ch10-1.c:10
10           for (counter = 0; counter < 200; counter++) {
2: input = 12
1: counter = 1
```

That was a lot of work—and a lot of information. Note a few things, though. First, gdb remembers your display requests, and when it enters the printmessage() function, it again starts displaying the counter variable present in that scope. Second, many of these messages are repetitious. If you already know how your functions work, or that they work correctly, there is no need to step into them.

To avoid stepping through functions that you don't need to review, gdb has a command called next. The next command acts like step, with the exception that it will not trace into your functions. Following is an example of a loop using next:

```
(gdb) next
11              input = getinput();
2: input = 12
1: counter = 2
(gdb) n
Enter an integer, or use -1 to exit: 10
12              if (input == -1) exit(0);
2: input = 10
1: counter = 2
(gdb) n
13              printmessage(counter, input);
2: input = 10
1: counter = 2
(gdb) n
For number 3, you entered 10 (-2 more than last time)
10          for (counter = 0; counter < 200; counter++) {
2: input = 10
1: counter = 2
```

The difference here is quite significant! You are no longer forced to wade through functions that you may consider irrelevant. So, this can be a great time-saver if you know where your problems lie. Many users use both next and step while debugging their programs; doing so is perfectly fine.

Before proceeding to the next section, exit gdb as follows:

```
(gdb) quit
The program is running.  Exit anyway? (y or n) y
```

Debugging other processes

Developers sometimes face the special need to debug processes that are already running. This might be the case when a process cannot be started from inside the debugger. For instance, the process may be started by the inetd super-server or at boot time. Or, perhaps the process needs to run for some time before you can look at it. Maybe a program that is inside a debugger doesn't know how to invoke the process.

In any of these cases, attaching gdb to the process after it is started may be your best (or only) option for debugging. Your debugger provides you with two ways to do this. You can specify the numeric PID of the process on the gdb command line, or you can use the attach command while already in gdb.

I will review this type of capability by using the example in Listing 10-1. You will need to open two X windows for this example, or use two different virtual consoles because you'll be interacting with two separate interfaces. In your first window, start up the program as you normally would:

```
$ ./ch10-2
Enter a string, or leave blank when done: Hi!
```

Now, leave this program running. In a second window, the first thing you need to do is determine the process ID (PID) of the running process. You can do that with the following command:

```
$ ps ax | grep ch10-2 | grep -v grep
  532 pts/1     S       0:00 ./ch10-2
```

This command says to list all processes, search for lines that contain the text ch10-2, and eliminate the lines that contain the text grep. The far-left number is the process ID to use. Most likely, your number will be different than this one; substitute your number for mine in the following examples.

With this piece of information, you are ready to invoke gdb on the already running process. You can do so by typing gdb ch10-2 532 on the command line, as shown in the following example. Again, replace the number 532 with your particular PID value:

```
$ gdb ch10-2 532
GNU gdb 4.18
Copyright 1998 Free Software Foundation, Inc.
GDB is free software, covered by the GNU General Public License, and you are
welcome to change it and/or distribute copies of it under certain conditions.
Type "show copying" to see the conditions.
There is absolutely no warranty for GDB.  Type "show warranty" for details.
This GDB was configured as "i686-pc-linux-gnu"...

/home/jgoerzen/t/532: No such file or directory.
Attaching to program: /home/jgoerzen/t/ch10-2, process 532
Reading symbols from /lib/libc.so.6...done.
Reading symbols from /lib/ld-linux.so.2...done.
0x400b8884 in read () from /lib/libc.so.6
```

In the preceding example, the line that begins with "Attaching to program" confirms that gdb managed to successfully attach itself to the program.

At this point, the question to ask is — where in the program is the execution? The debugger tells you; the last line indicates that it's in a read() call. The program doesn't contain a read() call; in fact, this call occurs from within the C library, as the debugger indicates. It's probably more useful to obtain a backtrace and find out where the execution is in your own code. I'll discuss the backtrace in the following example in more detail when you get a chance to analyze core dumps:

```
(gdb) bt
#0  0x400b8884 in read () from /lib/libc.so.6
#1  0x400ff66c in __DTOR_END__ () from /lib/libc.so.6
#2  0x4006bbb9 in _IO_new_file_underflow () from /lib/libc.so.6
#3  0x4006cd11 in _IO_default_uflow () from /lib/libc.so.6
#4  0x4006cc30 in __uflow () from /lib/libc.so.6
#5  0x40068fd5 in _IO_getline_info () from /lib/libc.so.6
#6  0x40068f86 in _IO_getline () from /lib/libc.so.6
#7  0x40068790 in fgets () from /lib/libc.so.6
#8  0x80485d7 in getinput () at ch10-2.c:35
#9  0x8048537 in main () at ch10-2.c:19
```

The first eight stack frames (numbered zero through seven) in this particular case occur inside the C library. Go ahead and step so that you can return to your own code:

> **Note**
>
> Your debugger may not show the frames from the C library (numbered zero through seven above), or it may show different frames depending on your library version. This variation is normal; if you do not have the debugging libraries installed (they are optional and may not be installed by default), you will not see these extra frames. Therefore, you will also not need to step until returning to your own code as shown in the example below.

```
(gdb) s
Single stepping until exit from function read,
which has no line number information.
```

At this point, gdb appears to hang. It hasn't really, but I'll examine exactly what is going on beneath the hood. When you attach to the process, the process is inside the read() system call. This is not where you send a debugger when working on some ordinary code. Furthermore, several more stack frames occur inside the C library. Again, these are not areas that you will trace into — and, in fact, you can't trace into them unless you have special versions of the library.

When you ask gdb to step while the process is deep within those frames, gdb simply executes the code until control returns to your software. This means that gdb executes code until the fgets() function returns. The gdb program is now waiting for the return from fgets(). The function will not return until you type something in the other window. Do so now:

```
Enter a string, or leave blank when done: Makefile
```

At this point, you'll notice activity in your own gdb window. For now, keep pressing the S key until you get back to your own area. The output may be different on your system and you may need to press s a different number of times, but the idea is the same. Because gdb cannot trace the code in these areas, it simply executes it and lets you know when it changes stack frames:

```
0x4006c311 in _IO_file_read () from /lib/libc.so.6
(gdb) s
Single stepping until exit from function _IO_file_read,
which has no line number information.
0x4006bbb9 in _IO_new_file_underflow () from /lib/libc.so.6
(gdb) s
Single stepping until exit from function
_IO_new_file_underflow,
which has no line number information.
0x4006cd11 in _IO_default_uflow () from /lib/libc.so.6
(gdb) s
Single stepping until exit from function _IO_default_uflow,
which has no line number information.
0x4006cc30 in __uflow () from /lib/libc.so.6
(gdb) s
Single stepping until exit from function __uflow,
which has no line number information.
0x40068fd5 in _IO_getline_info () from /lib/libc.so.6
(gdb) s
Single stepping until exit from function _IO_getline_info,
which has no line number information.
0x40068f86 in _IO_getline () from /lib/libc.so.6
(gdb) s
Single stepping until exit from function _IO_getline,
which has no line number information.
0x40068790 in fgets () from /lib/libc.so.6
(gdb) s
Single stepping until exit from function fgets,
which has no line number information.
getinput () at ch10-2.c:36
36              input[strlen(input)-1] = 0;
```

You have now returned to your own code. For future reference, you might note that you can set a temporary breakpoint with tbreak (see the section on breakpoints later in this chapter) for line 36, and then use the continue command to proceed to this location.

Now, you might notice that the program in the other window appears to be stalled. That is correct; the code there is executing only as you permit it. Go ahead and tell gdb to execute code until the return from the getinput() function:

```
(gdb) finish
Run till exit from #0  getinput () at ch10-2.c:36
```

```
0x8048537 in main () at ch10-2.c:19
19              svalues[counter] = getinput();
Value returned is $1 = (struct TAG_datastruct *) 0x8049b00
```

The debugger enables the program to execute until the end of the getinput()
function. For good measure, confirm that you can examine variables at this point:

```
(gdb) s
20              if (!svalues[counter]) break;
(gdb) print svalues[counter]->string
$2 = 0x8049b10 "Makefile"
```

The variable display is successful. Continue stepping through the code for a
few instructions:

```
(gdb) s
21              maxval = counter;
(gdb) s
18              for (counter = 0; counter < 200; counter++) {
(gdb) s
19              svalues[counter] = getinput();
(gdb) s
getinput () at ch10-2.c:34
34              printf("Enter a string, or leave blank when done: ");
(gdb) s
35              fgets(input, 79, stdin);
(gdb) s
```

At this point, you have returned to the input area. As before, gdb is waiting for the
code that reads your input to execute. Type something in the application window.
In the following example, I typed **gdb**:

```
Enter a string, or leave blank when done: gdb
```

After doing so, gdb returns with a prompt. Now use continue to tell gdb to let the
program finish executing:

```
36              input[strlen(input)-1] = 0;
(gdb) continue
Continuing.
```

The application window displays another prompt. Press Enter to leave it blank and
enable the program to terminate:

```
Enter a string, or leave blank when done: Enter
This structure has a checksum of 798.  Its string is:
Makefile
```

The program exits and the shell prompt returns. Meanwhile, in gdb's window, you see:

```
Program exited normally.
(gdb)
```

In other words, gdb confirms that the program successfully exited.

Displaying Data

In the previous section, I gave you a tour of using gdb to step through your programs, and I introduced you to many features of gdb. One of them is the capability of displaying data from your program. Here, you'll learn more details about these capabilities and how to use them.

Using the print and display commands

The two most commonly used commands for displaying data are print and display. These commands are more powerful than simple integer value displays. Listing 10-1 shows you a program that contains some more complex data structures. This program uses structures, arrays of pointers, and other more tricky data structures.

Note   Listing 10-1 is available online.

Listing 10-1: **Example for debugging: ch10-2.c**

```c
#include <stdio.h>
#include <stdlib.h>
#include <string.h>

typedef struct TAG_datastruct {
  char *string;
  int checksum;
} datastruct;

datastruct *getinput(void);
void printmessage(datastruct *todisp);

int main(void) {
  int counter;
  int maxval = 0;
  datastruct *svalues[200];

  for (counter = 0; counter < 200; counter++) {
```

```
      svalues[counter] = getinput();
      if (!svalues[counter]) break;
      maxval = counter;
   }

   printmessage(svalues[maxval / 2]);

   return 0;
}

datastruct *getinput(void) {
   char input[80];
   datastruct *instruct;
   int counter;

   printf("Enter a string, or leave blank when done: ");
   fgets(input, 79, stdin);
   input[strlen(input)-1] = 0;
   if (strlen(input) == 0)
     return NULL;
   instruct = malloc(sizeof(datastruct));
   instruct->string = strdup(input);
   instruct->checksum = 0;
   for (counter = 0; counter < strlen(instruct->string); counter++) {
     instruct->checksum += instruct->string[counter];
   }
   return instruct;
}

void printmessage(datastruct *todisp) {
   printf("This structure has a checksum of %d.  Its string is:\n",
          todisp->checksum);
   puts(todisp->string);
}
```

It's would be useful to examine the normal output of this program before examining it with the debugger.

Here's a sample execution:

```
$ ./ch10-2
Enter a string, or leave blank when done: Hello
Enter a string, or leave blank when done: This is the second line.
Enter a string, or leave blank when done: This is the third
Enter a string, or leave blank when done: gdb is interesting
Enter a string, or leave blank when done: Hmm...!
Enter a string, or leave blank when done: Enter
This structure has a checksum of 1584.  Its string is:
This is the third
```

Examining the code, you can see that there is a datastruct in which data is stored. The main() function contains an array of pointers to such structs. Note that this array is not an array of structs itself; rather it is an array of pointers to structs. Thus, there is a loop that is used to populate this array with data. In this loop, the getinput() function is called. This function returns a pointer to a struct, which is then placed into the array. If the pointer is null, the loop exits before filling all 200 elements. Otherwise, the maxval variable is set to the current array index. Finally, an element near the middle of the populated array is selected for printing. The pointer is passed to printmessage(), which displays the information. After that, the program exits.

Here is an example of how gdb is capable of accessing the data in this program:

```
$ gcc -ggdb3 -Wall -o ch10-2 ch10-2.c
$ gdb ch10-2
GNU gdb 4.18
Copyright 1998 Free Software Foundation, Inc.
GDB is free software, covered by the GNU General Public License, and you are
welcome to change it and/or distribute copies of it under certain conditions.
Type "show copying" to see the conditions.
There is absolutely no warranty for GDB.  Type "show warranty" for details.
This GDB was configured as "alphaev56-unknown-linux-gnu"...
(gdb) break main
Breakpoint 1 at 0x1200005b8: file ch10-2.c, line 15.
(gdb) run
Starting program: /home/jgoerzen/t/ch10-2

Breakpoint 1, main () at ch10-2.c:15
15          int maxval = 0;
```

Thus far, this has been standard fare for starting a program in a debugger. Suppose you wish to examine the contents of the svalues array at this point. Your first inclination, no doubt, would be to use print svalues. Give it a try:

```
(gdb) print svalues
$2 = {0x0, 0x0, 0x0, 0x0, 0x20000013490, 0x2000011dd90, 0x3e8, 0x3e8, 0x3e8,
  0x3e8, 0x2000011dd88, 0x120000040, 0x0 <repeats 13 times>, 0x1, 0x0, 0x0,
  0x0, 0x11ffff558, 0x0, 0x1, 0x0, 0x120000190, 0x0, 0x0, 0x0, 0x2000011e168,
  0x2000033e1c0, 0x20000347290, 0x0, 0x2000011e168, 0x2000, 0x20000347290,
  0x3e8, 0x0, 0x20000010210, 0x2000001ea00, 0x20000151b58, 0x20000343560,
  0x2000033e1c0, 0x340, 0x0, 0x11ffff750, 0x0, 0x2000011e168,
  0xffffffffffffffff, 0x20000347290, 0x2000014fa58, 0x20000341bd8,
  0x200003474b8, 0x200003474a8, 0x200003476a8, 0x11ffff7a0, 0x20000010210,
  0x2000001ea00, 0x20000150ac0, 0x200003428d0, 0x0, 0x2000011e168, 0x0,
```

This sort of thing continues for several more pages. At this point the values are random memory contents, and mean essentially nothing. To confirm this, you can try dereferencing a pointer as follows:

```
(gdb) print svalues[0]->checksum
Cannot access memory at address 0x8.
```

If you attempt to access that value in your program at this point in its execution, it will segfault (crash because of a memory access problem). Step through the program a bit so that you can have some useful data to work with:

```
(gdb) s
18          for (counter = 0; counter < 200; counter++) {
(gdb) s
19              svalues[counter] = getinput();
(gdb) s
getinput () at ch10-2.c:29
29      datastruct *getinput(void) {
(gdb) s
getinput () at ch10-2.c:34
34          printf("Enter a string, or leave blank when done: ");
(gdb) s
35          fgets(input, 79, stdin);
(gdb) s
Enter a string, or leave blank when done: Hello.
36          input[strlen(input)-1] = 0;
```

Take a look at the contents of the input string now:

```
(gdb) print input
$3 = "Hello.\n\000_\003\000 \001", '\000' <repeats 11 times>,
"\001\000\000\000\000\002\000\000Ø_\021\000\000\002\000\000\b\r\001\000\000\002\
000\0000\r\000\000\000\002\000\000\002\000\000\000\000\000\000\000xŧ\021\000\000
\002\000\000\000\000\000\000\000\000\000"
```

This may seem rather strange for output of a string that should contain only one word. There is a simple explanation, however. Recall that in C, strings are merely arrays. The data placed into the string overwrites the memory near the start only; it does not touch the remaining parts of the string. After the newline character (\n), a null character (\000) is inserted. The null character indicates the end of the string in C; this precise behavior is used by the following line to strip off the newline character:

```
(gdb) s
37          if (strlen(input) == 0)
(gdb) print input
$4 = "Hello.\000\000_\003\000 \001", '\000' <repeats 11 times>,
"\001\000\000\000\000\002\000\000Ø_\021\000\000\002\000\000\b\r\001\000\000\002\
000\0000\r\000\000\000\002\000\000\002\000\000\000\000\000\000\000xŧ\021\000\000
\002\000\000\000\000\000\000\000\000\000"
```

Notice that the \n is gone; it was replaced by \000. You also can use familiar constructs from the language being debugged to access arrays. For instance:

```
(gdb) print input[0]
$5 = 72 'H'
```

This print command is used to display the single character (H) at the start of the string—the first element of the array. Step through the program a bit further:

```
(gdb) s
39        instruct = malloc(sizeof(datastruct));
(gdb) s
40        instruct->string = strdup(input);
(gdb) s
41        instruct->checksum = 0;
(gdb) s
42        for (counter = 0; counter < strlen(instruct->string); counter++) {
```

Now take a look at the contents of the instruct variable. Your first inkling might be to use the following:

```
(gdb) print instruct
$6 = (datastruct *) 0x120100f80
```

This isn't particularly useful; because instruct is a pointer, gdb obligingly displays the data—its memory address. Perhaps it would be more useful to examine the data of the structure pointed to by the variable:

```
(gdb) print *instruct
$7 = {string = 0x120100fa0 "Hello.", checksum = 0}
```

Yes, dereferencing the pointer produces useful results! The debugger obligingly displays the different items in the struct, and their contents. You also can use standard C syntax to drill deeper. For instance:

```
(gdb) print instruct->string[0]
$8 = 72 'H'
```

Continue stepping through the code:

```
(gdb) s
43           instruct->checksum += instruct->string[counter];
(gdb) s
42        for (counter = 0; counter < strlen(instruct->string); counter++) {
(gdb) s
43           instruct->checksum += instruct->string[counter];
```

This loop is particularly uninteresting. Continue with the function until it exits by using the finish command in gdb. Here is the resulting output:

```
(gdb) finish
Run till exit from #0  getinput () at ch10-2.c:43
0x1200005d8 in main () at ch10-2.c:19
19           svalues[counter] = getinput();
Value returned is $9 = (datastruct *) 0x120100f80
```

Stepping now assigns the relevant value to the appropriate spot in the array of pointers. Take another look at the array:

```
(gdb) print svalues
$10 = {0x120100f80, 0x0, 0x0, 0x0, 0x20000013490, 0x2000011dd90, 0x3e8, 0x3e8,
  0x3e8, 0x3e8, 0x2000011dd88, 0x120000040, 0x0 <repeats 13 times>, 0x1, 0x0,
  0x0, 0x0, 0x11ffff558, 0x0, 0x1, 0x0, 0x120000190, 0x0, 0x0, 0x0,
  0x2000011e168, 0x2000033e1c0, 0x20000347290, 0x0, 0x2000011e168, 0x2000,
  0x20000347290, 0x3e8, 0x0, 0x20000010210, 0x2000001ea00, 0x20000151b58,
  0x20000343560, 0x2000033e1c0, 0x340, 0x0, 0x11ffff750, 0x0, 0x2000011e168,
```

Notice how the first value in this example, 0x120100f80, is identical to the value returned when you used the finish command. Good!

Examining memory

While learning about print and display in the previous section, you saw many memory addresses. Although you can often dereference pointers to access them, sometimes you want to drill down to a lower level. To do this, gdb provides a command named x. The syntax of x is

```
x/format address
```

where format specifies how many items should be displayed, followed by how the memory should be displayed. Following is an example from the already-running program:

```
(gdb) print *svalues[0]
$12 = {string = 0x120100fa0 "Hello.", checksum = 546}
(gdb) x/2c 0x120100fa0
0x120100fa0:    72 'H'   101 'e'
```

Here, determining the memory address is the first thing that is done. In this case, it is 0x120100fa0. The address will be different in your situation; simply use the address given to you in the examples. Then, gdb is asked to display two characters starting at that address, which it does.

```
(gdb) x/1s 0x120100fa0
0x120100fa0:    "Hello."
```

In this example, gdb is asked to display one string from that location, which gives the entire word. The various formats supported by x are summarized in Table 10-1. Note that when using the numeric items, you can specify a size after the item. For instance, x/5xb will print the hexadecimal values of five bytes.

Table 10-1
Gdb x Command Formats

Character	Meaning
A	Address (pointer)
B	Displays the corresponding item by bytes
C	Char
D	Decimal
F	Float
g	Displays the corresponding item by giant words (8 bytes)
h	Displays the corresponding item by half-words
o	Octal
s	String
t	Binary (raw characters)
u	Unsigned (decimal)
w	Displays the correspinding item by words
x	Hexadecimal

Using the printf command

Another way to display data in gdb is by using its built-in `printf` command. Like the `printf()` function in C, this command accepts a format specifier and various arguments. Here's an example of how the `printf` command is used:

```
(gdb) printf "%2.2s", (char *)0x120100fa0
He(gdb)
```

As you see, you also can access memory directly by using gdb's `printf` command. Note, though, that the output was unfortunately not suffixed with a newline character, so the output and the prompt run together. Better add a newline character as you do in C, such as:

```
(gdb) printf"%2.2s\n", (char *)0x120100fa0
He
```

Better! But `printf` is even more powerful than that. Consider this bit of code:

```
(gdb) printf "%d\n", 100 * svalues[0]->checksum
54600
```

As you can see, you can evaluate simple expressions here. This is not limited to `printf`, but `printf` often proves to be an ideal place in which to use them.

Using the set command

In addition to displaying variables, you can modify them. This can be useful if, for instance, you spot your program doing something wrong with variables, but wish to reset them to the correct value and continue tracing execution. Alternatively, you may purposely prefer to set variables to certain values to be able to determine whether or not your code is capable of dealing with them. Consider this example:

```
(gdb) print svalues[0]->checksum
$1 = 546
(gdb) set variable svalues[0]->checksum = 2000
(gdb) print svalues[0]->checksum
$2 = 2000
```

You can see that gdb has modified the value of the variable. If you run the program, the variable will remain with the new value.

Using Breakpoints and Watches

Often when debugging a large program, you may have some idea of where to locate a problem. Stepping through the entire program, even skipping function calls, could be prohibitive. A better solution, then, is to use breakpoints or watches.

These are used to interrupt execution of a program when a certain condition becomes true. This condition could be: that a variable is set to a certain value, that execution of the program reaches a certain point, or even that a certain arbitrary expression becomes true.

Setting breakpoints

The simplest way to set breakpoints is with the `break` command. With this command, you simply specify a location in the code at which execution should be interrupted and control should be given to you and the debugger. For example:

```
$ gdb ch10-2
GNU gdb 4.18
Copyright 1998 Free Software Foundation, Inc.
GDB is free software, covered by the GNU General Public License, and you are
welcome to change it and/or distribute copies of it under certain conditions.
Type "show copying" to see the conditions.
There is absolutely no warranty for GDB.  Type "show warranty" for details.
```

```
This GDB was configured as "alphaev56-unknown-linux-gnu"...
(gdb) break ch10-2.c:21
Breakpoint 1 at 0x1200061c: file ch10-2.c, line 21.
(gdb) break printmessage
Breakpoint 2 at 0x120000848: file ch10-2.c, line 48.
```

In this example, two breakpoints are set — one on line 21 of the program and another on line 48. The debugger automatically finds the location of the start of the function in the second case. If you run the program now, it will execute until it gets to the breakpoint:

```
(gdb) run
Starting program: /home/jgoerzen/t/ch10-2
Enter a string, or leave blank when done: Hello!

Breakpoint 1, main () at ch10-2.c:21
21          maxval = counter;
```

The program is invoked and proceeds to run until it encounters the first breakpoint. At this point, you are free to do whatever you need to do to continue debugging the program. Perhaps you will step through the code, or examine the contents of some variables. When you are done, you can issue a continue command, which causes execution to resume until a breakpoint is reached again or the program exits.

```
(gdb) s
18          for (counter = 0; counter < 200; counter++) {
(gdb) s
19              svalues[counter] = getinput();
(gdb) continue
Continuing.
Enter a string, or leave blank when done: Hello!

Breakpoint 1, main () at ch10-2.c:21
21          maxval = counter;
(gdb) continue
Continuing.
Enter a string, or leave blank when done: Enter

Breakpoint 2, printmessage (todisp=0x100000002) at ch10-2.c:48
48      void printmessage(datastruct *todisp) {
```

In this situation, gdb is asked to continue twice, and does so both times until another breakpoint is reached. If you continue a third time, gdb continues until the program exits:

```
(gdb) continue
Continuing.
This structure has a checksum of 533.  Its string is:
Hello!

Program exited normally.
```

You can also set a conditional breakpoint, one that only triggers if some other condition is true. This can be particularly useful if a problem only occurs when certain values are set to variables, such as in the following example:

```
$ gdb ch10-2
GNU gdb 4.18
Copyright 1998 Free Software Foundation, Inc.
GDB is free software, covered by the GNU General Public License, and you are
welcome to change it and/or distribute copies of it under certain conditions.
Type "show copying" to see the conditions.
There is absolutely no warranty for GDB.  Type "show warranty" for details.
This GDB was configured as "alphaev56-unknown-linux-gnu"...
(gdb) break 21
Breakpoint 1 at 0x12000061c: file ch10-2.c, line 21.
```

Here, the program is loaded and a breakpoint is set for line 21. Now, you apply a condition to the breakpoint. Notice how gdb assigned a number to the breakpoint—it is breakpoint 1. To apply a condition to it, you specify which breakpoint, and then the expression that must be true in order for execution to be interrupted:

```
(gdb) condition 1 svalues[counter]->checksum > 700
(gdb) run
Starting program: /home/jgoerzen/t/ch10-2
Enter a string, or leave blank when done: Hi
Enter a string, or leave blank when done: Hello
Enter a string, or leave blank when done: How are you?

Breakpoint 1, main () at ch10-2.c:21
21              maxval = counter;
```

Now the program will continue running until the condition becomes true, as it will only when a sufficiently large string is encountered. After the expression becomes true, the breakpoint takes effect, and the execution is interrupted.

The GNU debugger also provides a capability called temporary breakpoints. These are breakpoints that are hit only once. That is, as soon as the breakpoint is triggered, it is automatically deleted. Note that it is possible to assign a condition to a temporary breakpoint exactly as you can to a standard one.

The command to set up a temporary breakpoint is tbreak, as shown in the following example. This output uses the code for ch10-4.c, printed in the Core dump analysis section:

```
$ gdb ch10-4
GNU gdb 4.18
Copyright 1998 Free Software Foundation, Inc.
GDB is free software, covered by the GNU General Public License, and you are
welcome to change it and/or distribute copies of it under certain conditions.
Type "show copying" to see the conditions.
There is absolutely no warranty for GDB.  Type "show warranty" for details.
This GDB was configured as "i686-pc-linux-gnu"...
```

```
(gdb) tbreak 43
Breakpoint 1 at 0x8048647: file ch10-4.c, line 43.
(gdb) run
Starting program: /home/jgoerzen/t/ch10-4
Enter a string, or leave blank when done: Hello!
getinput () at ch10-4.c:43
43              instruct->checksum += instruct->string[counter];
(gdb) continue
Continuing.
Enter a string, or leave blank when done: Hi!
Enter a string, or leave blank when done: Enter
```

Notice how the breakpoint was triggered only once, even though the program passed through that section of code many more times. Interestingly enough, this tbreak command is the same as the following two commands:

```
break 43
enable delete 1
```

This requests that a breakpoint should be created, and that breakpoint 1 should be deleted after it is triggered.

Setting watches

You can cause execution of a program to be aborted when a certain condition becomes true by using *watches*. You can set an arbitrary expression to be watched with the watch command. When this expression becomes true, the execution is immediately interrupted. That is, watches are not tied to interrupting execution at any particular point in the program; rather, they interrupt excecution whenever the expression turns true.

Because watches are not tied to a specific part of code, and thus are evaluated at arbitrary times, if any of the variables used in the watch go out of scope, the watch expression no longer can be evaluated. Breakpoint conditionals do not have this particular problem because they are evaluated only at fixed placed in the code.

Here's a quick look at some code you can use to examine watches, named ch10-3.c:

```c
#include <stdio.h>

int main(void) {
    int counter;
    for (counter = 0; counter < 30; counter++) {
        if (counter % 2 == 0) {
            printf("Counter: %d\n", counter);
        }
    }
}
```

When run, the result is fairly simple:

```
$ gcc -ggdb3 -o ch10-3 ch10-3.c
$ ./ch10-3
Counter: 0
Counter: 2
Counter: 4
Counter: 6
Counter: 8
Counter: 10
Counter: 12
Counter: 14
Counter: 16
Counter: 18
Counter: 20
Counter: 22
Counter: 24
Counter: 26
Counter: 28
```

If you start this program inside gdb, you will have an opportunity to set a particular watchpoint to interrupt execution halfway through, for instance:

```
$ gdb ch10-3
GNU gdb 4.18
Copyright 1998 Free Software Foundation, Inc.
GDB is free software, covered by the GNU General Public License, and you are
welcome to change it and/or distribute copies of it under certain conditions.
Type "show copying" to see the conditions.
There is absolutely no warranty for GDB.  Type "show warranty" for details.
This GDB was configured as "alphaev56-unknown-linux-gnu"...
```

So gdb is started in normal fashion. Observe what happens if a watch is set at this particular point:

```
(gdb) watch counter > 15
No symbol "counter" in current context.
```

This is because execution has not reached the main() function yet, and as such, the counter variable is not in scope yet. Step through the code until it is.

```
(gdb) break main
Breakpoint 1 at 0x120000428: file ch10-3.c, line 3.
(gdb) run
Starting program: /home/jgoerzen/t/ch10-3

Breakpoint 1, main () at ch10-3.c:3
3        int main(void) {
(gdb) s
5            for (counter = 0; counter < 30; counter++) {
(gdb) s
6                if (counter % 2 == 0) {
```

Now that we are in scope of the relevant variable, try to set the watch again:

```
(gdb) watch counter > 15
Hardware watchpoint 2: counter > 15
```

And try running the program:

```
(gdb) continue
Continuing.
#0  main () at ch10-3.c:6
6               if (counter % 2 == 0) {
Counter: 0
Counter: 2
Counter: 4
Counter: 6
Counter: 8
Counter: 10
Counter: 12
Counter: 14
Hardware watchpoint 2: counter > 15

Old value = 0
New value = 1
0x8048418 in main () at ch10-3.c:5
5               for (counter = 0; counter < 30; counter++) {
```

And so the execution of the program is interrupted by the specified watch expression. This expression is can be thought of as being continuously evaluated until its truth value changes.

Here's a look at a situation in which a watch will not work. I'll refer to the ch10-2.c code again for this example:

```
$ gdb ch10-2
GNU gdb 4.18
Copyright 1998 Free Software Foundation, Inc.
GDB is free software, covered by the GNU General Public License, and you are
welcome to change it and/or distribute copies of it under certain conditions.
Type "show copying" to see the conditions.
There is absolutely no warranty for GDB.  Type "show warranty" for details.
This GDB was configured as "i686-pc-linux-gnu"...
(gdb) break getinput
Breakpoint 1 at 0x80485b9: file ch10-2.c, line 34.
(gdb) run
Starting program: /home/jgoerzen/t/ch10-2

Breakpoint 1, getinput () at ch10-2.c:34
34          printf("Enter a string, or leave blank when done: ");
(gdb) s
35          fgets(input, 79, stdin);
```

```
(gdb) s
Enter a string, or leave blank when done: Hi
36        input[strlen(input)-1] = 0;
(gdb) s
37        if (strlen(input) == 0)
(gdb) s
39        instruct = malloc(sizeof(datastruct));
(gdb) s
40        instruct->string = strdup(input);
(gdb) s
41        instruct->checksum = 0;
(gdb) s
42        for (counter = 0; counter < strlen(instruct->string); counter++) {
(gdb) watch instruct->checksum > 750
Hardware watchpoint 2: instruct->checksum > 750
```

Now a watchpoint is set. However, see what happens when execution continues:

```
(gdb) continue
Continuing.
#0  getinput () at ch10-2.c:42
42        for (counter = 0; counter < strlen(instruct->string); counter++) {
Watchpoint 2 deleted because the program has left the block in
which its expression is valid.
0x8048537 in main () at ch10-2.c:19
19        svalues[counter] = getinput();
```

Immediately when the relevant variable goes out of scope, the watch expression cannot be evaluated, and gdb informs you of this.

Therefore, you can see that both breakpoints and watches have their uses, but neither is necessarily a solution for every problem.

Core Dump Analysis

When your programs crash, you want to find out why. Sometimes, you can't run gdb on the program to trace its execution. Perhaps the program is running on someone else's computer, or it is timing-sensitive and manually stepping through it would cause unacceptable delays.

So what can you do in a case like this? Well, you can, in many cases, determine the cause of a crash even after a program has ended. This capability comes thanks to Linux's *core dump* facility. When your program crashes, Linux can create a core file from it. This file contains a copy of the process's memory and other information about it. With this information, gdb can enable you to find out details about what the program was doing when it crashed.

Before we begin analyzing core dumps, first you need to make sure that they are enabled on your account. Some distributions or system administrators may disable core dumps by default. You can enable them by running this command:

```
$ ulimit -c unlimited
```

Having done that, you can work with these core files. Consider the code in Listing 10-2, which contains a small modification from the ch10-4.c code in use earlier.

Note　　Listing 10-2 is available online.

Listing 10-2: **Example with a bug**

```c
#include <stdio.h>
#include <stdlib.h>
#include <string.h>

typedef struct TAG_datastruct {
  char *string;
  int checksum;
} datastruct;

datastruct *getinput(void);
void printmessage(datastruct *todisp);

int main(void) {
  int counter;
  int maxval = 0;
  datastruct *svalues[200];

  for (counter = 0; counter < 200; counter++) {
    svalues[counter] = getinput();
    if (!svalues[counter]) break;
    maxval = counter;
  }

  printmessage(svalues[maxval * 2]);

  return 0;
}

datastruct *getinput(void) {
  char input[80];
  datastruct *instruct;
  int counter;

  printf("Enter a string, or leave blank when done: ");
  fgets(input, 79, stdin);
```

```
    input[strlen(input)-1] = 0;
    if (strlen(input) == 0)
      return NULL;
    instruct = malloc(sizeof(datastruct));
    instruct->string = strdup(input);
    instruct->checksum = 0;
    for (counter = 0; counter < strlen(instruct->string); counter++) {
      instruct->checksum += instruct->string[counter];
    }
    return instruct;
}

void printmessage(datastruct *todisp) {
    printf("This structure has a checksum of %d.  Its string is:\n",
           todisp->checksum);
    puts(todisp->string);
}
```

Now, compile and run the program. This time, when you run it, you won't be
running it inside gdb; it will be running on its own:

```
$ gcc -ggdb3 -o ch10-4 ch10-4.c
$ ./ch10-4
Enter a string, or leave blank when done: Hi!
Enter a string, or leave blank when done: I like Linux.
Enter a string, or leave blank when done: How are you today?
Enter a string, or leave blank when done: Enter
This structure has a checksum of -1541537728.  Its string is:
Segmentation fault (core dumped)
```

Obviously, something is seriously wrong here. Because the printed checksum is
incorrect, the program crashed. To see what happened, the first thing you should
do is load the core file into gdb. You do this as follows:

```
$ gdb ch10-4 core
GNU gdb 4.18
Copyright 1998 Free Software Foundation, Inc.
GDB is free software, covered by the GNU General Public License, and you are
welcome to change it and/or distribute copies of it under certain conditions.
Type "show copying" to see the conditions.
There is absolutely no warranty for GDB.  Type "show warranty" for details.
This GDB was configured as "i686-pc-linux-gnu"...
Core was generated by `./ch10-4'.
Program terminated with signal 11, Segmentation fault.
Reading symbols from /lib/libc.so.6...done.
Reading symbols from /lib/ld-linux.so.2...done.
#0  0x8048686 in printmessage (todisp=0x0) at ch10-4.c:49
49          printf("This structure has a checksum of %d.  Its string is:\n",
```

Already, you have some clues to determine the problem. The debugger notes that the program crashed from a segmentation fault, and that it can trace the problem to a call to printf(). This is already more information than you may sometimes have, but I'll go into more detail.

From here, a good first step is to find out exactly where in the program the system was prior to the crash. You can do this by getting a stack backtrace using either the bt or info stack commands. The following example shows the output:

```
(gdb) bt
#0  0x8048686 in printmessage (todisp=0x0) at ch10-4.c:49
#1  0x804858e in main () at ch10-4.c:24
```

Here, gdb is telling you what the last line to be executed in each function is. The interesting one is in frame zero (the frame numbers are on the left), on line 49. This is the line highlighted by gdb in the above example.

Something else is interesting. Notice that it says todisp is zero when printmessage() was called. Because todisp is a pointer, it should never be zero. You can verify its state by using print:

```
(gdb) print todisp
$1 = (struct TAG_datastruct *) 0x0
```

So, now you have deduced that the problem is not with printmessage(), but rather with its invocation. To examine its call in main(), you need to change the active stack frame to frame 1, which is in main():

```
(gdb) frame 1
#1  0x804858e in main () at ch10-4.c:24
24              printmessage(svalues[maxval * 2]);
```

Now in frame 1, you can examine the variables in main(). Here, you should look at several variables to ensure that they seem valid:

```
(gdb) print counter
$2 = 3
(gdb) print maxval
$3 = 2
(gdb) print svalues[1]
$4 = (struct TAG_datastruct *) 0x8049b00
(gdb) print *svalues[1]
$5 = {string = 0x8049b10 "I like Linux.", checksum = 1132}
```

Thus far, everything is in order. Now look at the value that is being passed in to printmessage():

```
(gdb) print svalues[maxval * 2]
$6 = (struct TAG_datastruct *) 0x0
```

There is a definite problem there! This time, take another look at `svalues`, dereferencing the pointer:

```
(gdb) print *svalues[maxval * 2]
Cannot access memory at address 0x0.
```

Now you have pinpointed the problem. The expression `svalues[maxval * 2]` is looking outside the range of those items in `svalues` that already had pointers stored.

Although this kind of analysis of core dumps can be extremely useful, it is not foolproof. If the stack was corrupted before the program completely crashed, you may not be able to get much useful data at all. In those cases, you are probably limited to tracing through the program. However, in many cases, core dump analysis can prove quite useful.

Here's a look at another program. This is the example from the printing and displaying data section in this chapter. Consider two separate invocations of the program:

```
$ ./ch10-2
Enter a string, or leave blank when done: Hello!
Enter a string, or leave blank when done: I enjoy Linux.
Enter a string, or leave blank when done: Gdb is interesting!
Enter a string, or leave blank when done: Enter
This structure has a checksum of 1260.  Its string is:
I enjoy Linux.
$ ./ch10-2
Enter a string, or leave blank when done: Enter
Segmentation fault (core dumped)
```

The program crashed after the second invocation. You can load up gdb to find out what happened. After doing so, you can formulate a fix. Start by loading the program in gdb:

```
$ gdb ch10-2 core
GNU gdb 4.18
Copyright 1998 Free Software Foundation, Inc.
GDB is free software, covered by the GNU General Public License, and you are
welcome to change it and/or distribute copies of it under certain conditions.
Type "show copying" to see the conditions.
There is absolutely no warranty for GDB.  Type "show warranty" for details.
This GDB was configured as "i686-pc-linux-gnu"...
Core was generated by `./ch10-2'.
Program terminated with signal 11, Segmentation fault.
Reading symbols from /lib/libc.so.6...done.
Reading symbols from /lib/ld-linux.so.2...done.
#0  0x8048696 in printmessage (todisp=0x0) at ch10-2.c:49
49          printf("This structure has a checksum of %d.  Its string is:\n",
```

As before, start with a backtrace. Notice, though, where gdb says todisp=0x0; this is a clue that some invalid value got passed in to the printmessage() function:

```
(gdb) bt
#0  0x8048696 in printmessage (todisp=0x0) at ch10-2.c:49
#1  0x804859e in main () at ch10-2.c:24
```

Indeed, the suspicions are confirmed. Switch to frame number 1 and get some context:

```
(gdb) frame 1
#1  0x804859e in main () at ch10-2.c:24
24          printmessage(svalues[maxval / 2]);
(gdb) list
19              svalues[counter] = getinput();
20              if (!svalues[counter]) break;
21              maxval = counter;
22          }
23
24          printmessage(svalues[maxval / 2]);
25
26          return 0;
27      }
28
```

The debugger obligingly displays a list of the code surrounding the call to printmessage(). At this point, take a look at the values of the variables involved in the call to that function:

```
(gdb) print maxval
$1 = 0
(gdb) print svalues[maxval / 2]
$2 = (struct TAG_datastruct *) 0x0
```

From this, you can see that maxval is set to zero, which is not incorrect. In fact, this can happen legitimately if the user supplies only one line of input; that intput will have an index of zero. However, the problem is that maxval also is set to zero if there is no input at all. Because of this, you can't test maxval to see whether or not a result should be displayed. One solution to this dilemma is to initialize maxval to -1. This will never be a value that you will see as an array index, so there is no chance of it being mistaken for a legitimate index into your array. With that in mind, you can test maxval to see whether or not you ought to print out some data. Listing 10-3 shows a version of the code with this fix.

Listing 10-3: **Fixed example code**

```
#include <stdio.h>
#include <stdlib.h>
#include <string.h>

/* ch10-2.c: Fixed version of the code. */

typedef struct TAG_datastruct {
  char *string;
  int checksum;
} datastruct;

datastruct *getinput(void);
void printmessage(datastruct *todisp);

int main(void) {
  int counter;
  int maxval = -1;
  datastruct *svalues[200];

  for (counter = 0; counter < 200; counter++) {
    svalues[counter] = getinput();
    if (!svalues[counter]) break;
    maxval = counter;
  }

  if (maxval > -1) {
    printmessage(svalues[maxval / 2]);
  } else {
    printf("No input received; nothing to display.\n");
  }

  return 0;
}

datastruct *getinput(void) {
  char input[80];
  datastruct *instruct;
  int counter;

  printf("Enter a string, or leave blank when done: ");
  fgets(input, 79, stdin);
  input[strlen(input)-1] = 0;
  if (strlen(input) == 0)
    return NULL;
  instruct = malloc(sizeof(datastruct));
  instruct->string = strdup(input);
  instruct->checksum = 0;
  for (counter = 0; counter < strlen(instruct->string); counter++) {
```

Continued

Listing 10-3 *(continued)*

```
    instruct->checksum += instruct->string[counter];
  }
  return instruct;
}

void printmessage(datastruct *todisp) {
  printf("This structure has a checksum of %d.  Its string is:\n",
         todisp->checksum);
  puts(todisp->string);
}
```

If you run this code now, you'll notice no problems at all:

```
$ ./ch10-2
Enter a string, or leave blank when done: Hello!
Enter a string, or leave blank when done: I enjoy Linux.
Enter a string, or leave blank when done: Gdb is interesting!
Enter a string, or leave blank when done: Enter
This structure has a checksum of 1260.  Its string is:
I enjoy Linux.
$ ./ch10-2
Enter a string, or leave blank when done: Enter
No input received; nothing to display.
```

Command Summary

The gdb debugger contains a large assortment of commands available for your use. You can find information about these commands while in gdb by using the help command. For your benefit, many of the most useful commands are listed in Table 10-2, along with their syntax and a description of their purpose and use.

Table 10-2
gdb Debugger Commands

Command	Arguments	Description
Attach	Filename PID	Attaches to the specified process or the specified file for debugging purposes.
Awatch	expression	Interrupts your program whenever the given expression is accessed—that is, whenever it is either read from or written to.

Command	Arguments	Description
break | hbreak	Line-number Function-name *Address	Causes program execution to be interrupted at the specified location, which may be a line number, a function name, or an address preceded by an asterisk. If the command specified is hbreak, then it requests hardware support for the breakpoint. This support is not necessarily available on all platforms.
Bt	[full]	Displays a listing of all stack frames active at the present time. If full is specified, local variables from each frame present are also displayed. You can interact with a given frame by using the frame command.
Call	function	Performs a call to the specified function in your program. The arguments should be the function name along with the parameters, if necessary, using the syntax of the language of the program being debugged.
catch catch	[exception]	Causes program execution to be interrupted when the named exception is caught, or when any exception is caught if the name is omitted.
catch exec		Causes program execution to be interrupted when the program attempts to call a member of the exec series of functions.
catch exit		Causes execution to be interrupted when a process is almost ready to exit.
catch fork		Causes execution to be interrupted when there is a call to fork().
catch signal	[name]	Causes program execution to be interrupted when the specified signal name is received by the program. If no signal name is specified, it interrupts execution when any signal is received.
catch start		Causes process execution to be interrupted when a new process is about to be created.
catch stop		Causes the execution to be interrupted (as it were) just prior to the program's termination.
catch throw	[exception]	Causes process execution to be interrupted when some code throws an exception. If a specific exception is named, it only has this effect when the thrown exception is the one being watched for.

Continued

Table 10-2 *(continued)*

Command	Arguments	Description
catch vfork		Interrupts the program's execution when vfork() is called.
cd	directory	Changes the current working directory for both the debugger and the program being debugged to the indicated directory.
clear	[Line-Number] [Function-Name] [*Address]	Removes the breakpoint from the specified location. If no location is specified, it removes any breakpoints set for the current line of the program's execution.
commands	[number] (see description)	Lists gdb commands to be executed when the specified breakpoint is hit. If no breakpoint is specified, it applies to the most recently set breakpoint. See gdb's help commands option for details on specifying the list of commands to gdb.
condition	number expression	Applies the specified expression as a condition to the breakpoint with the number specified. When this syntax is used, the breakpoint only causes execution interruption if the given expression evaluates to true when the breakpoint is encountered.
continue	[count]	Causes the program execution to continue until another event is encountered to interrupt such execution. If the optional count is specified, it causes the breakpoint (if any) that caused the last execution interruption to be ignored for the specified number of iterations over it.
delete breakpoints	[number [number ...]]	Deletes the specified breakpoints, or all breakpoints if no breakpoint numbers are specified.
delete display	[number [number ...]]	Deletes the specified display requests, or all such requests if no numbers are specified.
delete tracepoints	[number [number ...]]	Deletes the specified tracepoints, or all tracepoints if no numbers are specified.
detach		Causes gdb to detach from a process, which proceeds to execute normally. If gdb is debugging a file, gdb proceeds to ignore the file.

Command	Arguments	Description
directory	directory	Indicates that the specified directory should be added to the beginning of the search path used for locating files containing source code for the program being debugged.
disable <breakpoints | display | tracepoints>	[number [number ...]]	Prevents the specified item from being acted upon, or all items of the specified type if the number is omitted.
display	expression	Like print, but causes the expression to be displayed each time the execution stops and returns control to gdb.
enable	[number [number ...]]	Enables the specified breakpoints (after a prior disable command), or all breakpoints if no numbers are specified.
enable delete	[number [number ...]]	Enables the specified breakpoint (or all breakpoints), but it will be deleted after the breakpoint is triggered once.
enable <display | tracepoints>	[number [number ...]]	Re-enables the specified display or tracepoint items, after a prior disable command. If no numbers are specified, all display or tracepoint items will be re-enabled.
enable once	number [number ...]	Enables specified breakpoint for one encounter. When the breakpoint is triggered, it becomes disabled again automatically.
finish		Continues execution until a breakpoint is encountered or the current function returns to its caller.
frame	number	Selects the specified stack frame for examination or manipulation. See the bt command to find out the numbers available.
help	[topic [topic...]]	Displays help, optionally on a specific (specified) topic.
info	name	Displays information about the debugger and the program being debugged. See help info inside gdb for a listing of the information that can be displayed.

Continued

Table 10-2 *(continued)*

Command	Arguments	Description
list	- [File:]Line-Number [File:]Function-Name *Address	Displays specified lines of source code. With no arguments, it displays at least ten lines after the most recently displayed source code line. With a single dash, it displays ten lines prior to the preceeding display. With one argument, specifying a line number, function name, or address, it begins display at that location and continues for approximately ten lines. Two arguments, each of those types, indicate start and end ranges; the output could span more than ten lines in this case. Either the line number or the function can be preceeded by a filename and a colon.
next	[count]	Causes the program to step through a line (as with the step command). However, unlike step, called functions are executed without being traced into. The optional argument is a repeat count and defaults to one.
print	expression	Displays the result from evaluating the specified expression. A typical usage is to display the contents of variables.
printf	format, [expression [. expression]]	Displays information using the syntax of `printf()` in C. The arguments are the format string and then any necessary arguments, separated by commas.
ptype	type	Displays the type of the indicated element.
pwd		Displays the current working directory of your process being debugged, which is also the current working directory of gdb.
quit		Exits the gdb debugger.
run	[command-line arguments]	Starts executing the program to be debugged. If any arguments are specified, they are passed to the program as command-line arguments. The run command understands wildcards and I/O redirection, but not piping.
set	variable-name value	Sets the specified internal gdb variable to the indicated value. For a list of the variables that can be set, use `help set` in gdb.
set variable	variable-name value	Sets the specified program variable to the indicated value.
show	name	Displays the item requested by the argument. For a complete list, use `help show` in gdb.

Command	Arguments	Description
until	[File:]Linux-Number] [[File:] Function-Name] [*Address]	Continues execution until the program reaches a source line greater than the current one. If a location is specified (using the same syntax as break), execution continues until that location is reached.
x	/CountType [Size] Address	Displays a dump of memory at the specified address, showing a certain number of elements of the specified type. For details, type help x from inside gdb or see the Examining Memory section in this chapter.
xbreak	Function-name *Address	Sets a breakpoint to trigger on exit from the function with the specified name or address.

In this chapter, you were introduced to many gdb commands. There remain yet more commands that you can use while debugging your programs. If you require more details about these commands, you may consult the documentation internal to gdb (with the help command) or the info documentation provided with gdb.

Summary

In this chapter, you learned how to use gdb to find bugs in your code. Specifically, you learned:

✦ Tracking down bugs in code can be difficult. The GNU Debugger, gdb, is a tool that you can use to make the task much easier.

✦ You can use gdb as a tool to step through your code, often line-by-line. When you invoke gdb, you simply tell it the name of the program to be debugged, and it will load it into the debugger.

✦ You can use the break command to set a breakpoint, which is a location at which the debugger interrupts program execution so you may inspect the program. One thing to do when debugging from the start of the progam is to set a breakpoint at the main() function, with the command break main.

✦ You also can use tbreak to set a temporary breakpoint, one that is deleted automatically after it has been triggered once.

✦ You can examine the contents of your variables by using the print command. The display command is similar, although display asks the debugger to display the result of the expression each time execution is interrupted instead of once only.

✦ The `step` and `next` commands enable you review your code one line at a time. They differ in that the `next` command executes your functions without stepping into them.

✦ You use the `bt` command to obtain a stack backtrace. This is particularly useful when working with core dumps or attaching to an already-running process.

✦ You can set watches with the `watch` command. Watchpoints interrupt execution when the value of an expression changes. Beware of scope issues, though.

✦ You use the `continue` command to ask the program to resume execution after it was interrupted, perhaps by a breakpoint or a watchpoint.

✦ Linux can dump useful information about a crash to a file called `core` when a program crashes. The debugger can use this file to help you piece together why the program crashed.

✦ In addition to the commands discussed in this chapter, gdb has a wide array of commands that you can use. Many are highlighted in Table 10-2. Also, you can get information on gdb from its `help` command.

✦   ✦   ✦

The Linux Model

Files, Directories, and Devices

Linux provides a powerful concept of access to data, one that is probably not new to you but has some new twists. In Linux, access to virtually any aspect of the system, ranging everywhere from on-disk files to scanners, is accomplished through the file and directory structure. The idea is to make it possible for you to access as much as possible through a single, unified interface.

In this chapter, you'll first find out how Linux manages your files so that you can understand what information is available and how to ask for it. After that, you will learn about the different input/output systems available on Linux, the similarities and differences between them, and when to use each. Finally, you will learn about "special" files — things that may look like a file but really represent something entirely different.

The Nature of Files

The Linux operating system organizes your data into a system of files and directories. This system is, at the highest level, much the same as that used in other operating systems, even though Linux has its own terminology (for instance, "directories" in Linux mean the same thing as "folders" in Windows). If you have used other UNIX systems, you may already be familiar with the terminology used with Linux as it is essentially the same as that used for other UNIX operating systems. As with any modern operating system, your programs can open, read from, write to, close, and modify files. By using the appropriate system calls, you can do the same for directories.

What about the devices on your Linux system, though? How could a program communicate with a scanner to bring in images? How would a sound editor play your files on your sound card? How does a disk partitioning utility talk to your hard drive?

The answer to all of these questions lies in the special files in your Linux file system. With Linux, you can use a single set of system calls, and thus a single interface, for basic file access, scanner access, hard drive access, Internet communication, communication with pipes and FIFOs, printer access, and many more functions.

Fundamentally, three items relate to the treatment of files in Linux. These are the directory structure, the inode, and the file's data itself.

The *directory structure* exists for each directory on the system. This structure contains a list of the entries in the directory. Each entry contains a name and an inode number. The name enables access from programs, and the inode number provides a reference to information about the file itself.

The *inode* holds information about the file. It does not hold the file's name or directory location, given that these details are part of the directory structure. Rather, the inode holds information such as the permissions of the file, the owner of the file, the file size, the last modified time for the file, the number of hard links to the file, quota information about the file, special flags relating to the file, and many other details. Because Linux permits hard links to files, which essentially allow multiple filenames to refer to a single block of data on disk, putting the filename in the inode just doesn't make sense, because multiple filenames may reference the same inode.

The third area, the file's *data,* is in a location (or locations) specified in the inode. Some file system entries, such as FIFOs and device special files, do not have a data area on the disk. Both files and directories do have data areas.

Your programs can get information from the directory structure by using the opendir() functions. The stat() system call is used to get information from an inode. The file's data can be accessed through normal file operation functions such as fgets() and open(). Finally, if you are dealing with a symbolic link, readlink() can give you the location it points to.

stat() and lstat()

The stat() and lstat() functions provide the primary interface to the information stored in the inode information for a file. They fill a structure of type struct stat with information. The fields of this structure are defined in the stat(2) manpage. If you include sys/stat.h, you also get access to macros used for interpreting that data. The program in Listing 11-1 displays all data provided by these functions.

The difference between the two functions is that lstat() will not follow a symbolic link, instead returning information about the link itself. The stat() function, on the other hand, will trace symbolic links until the end of the chain, as most functions do. The code in Listing 11-1 uses both functions.

Note   Listing 11-1 is available online.

Listing 11-1: **Demonstration of stat() and lstat(): ch11-1.c**

```c
#include <stdio.h>
#include <sys/stat.h>
#include <unistd.h>
#include <errno.h>
#include <stdarg.h>
#include <time.h>
#include <limits.h>

void printinfo(const struct stat sbuf, const char *name);
void pline(const char *desc, const char *fmt, ...);
void pbool(const char *desc, int cond);
char *myctime(const time_t *timep);

int main(int argc, char *argv[]) {
  struct stat sbuf;

  if (argc != 2) {
    printf("Syntax: %s filename\n", argv[0]);
    return(1);
  }

  /* First, look at the file.  If it's a link, gives information about
     the link. */

  printf("Information for file %s:\n\n", argv[1]);
  if (lstat(argv[1], &sbuf) == -1) {
    perror("lstat failed");
    return(2);
  }

  printinfo(sbuf, argv[1]);

  if (S_ISLNK(sbuf.st_mode)) {
    printf("\n-----------------------------------\n");
    printf("Information for file pointed to by link\n\n");

    if (stat(argv[1], &sbuf) == -1) {
      perror("stat on link failed");
      return(3);
    }

    printinfo(sbuf, "");
  }
  return 0;
}

void printinfo(const struct stat sbuf, const char *name) {
  pline("Device", "%d", sbuf.st_dev);
  pline("Inode", "%d", sbuf.st_ino);
```

Continued

Listing 11-1 *(continued)*

```
pline("Number of hard links", "%d", sbuf.st_nlink);
pbool("Symbolic link", S_ISLNK(sbuf.st_mode));
if (S_ISLNK(sbuf.st_mode)) {
  char linkname[PATH_MAX * 2];
  int length;

  length = readlink(name, linkname, sizeof(linkname) - 1);
  if (length == -1) {
    perror("readlink failed");
  }

  linkname[length] = 0;
  pline("Link destination", linkname);
}

pbool("Regular file", S_ISREG(sbuf.st_mode));
pbool("Directory", S_ISDIR(sbuf.st_mode));
pbool("Character device", S_ISCHR(sbuf.st_mode));
pbool("Block device", S_ISBLK(sbuf.st_mode));
pbool("FIFO", S_ISFIFO(sbuf.st_mode));
pbool("Socket", S_ISSOCK(sbuf.st_mode));

printf("\n");

pline("Device type", "%d", sbuf.st_rdev);
pline("File size", "%d", sbuf.st_size);
pline("Preferred block size", "%d", sbuf.st_blksize);
pline("Length in blocks", "%d", sbuf.st_blocks);
pline("Last access", "%s", myctime(&sbuf.st_atime));
pline("Last modification", "%s", myctime(&sbuf.st_mtime));
pline("Last change", "%s", myctime(&sbuf.st_ctime));

printf("\n");

pline("Owner uid", "%d", sbuf.st_uid);
pline("Group gid", "%d", sbuf.st_gid);
pline("Permissions", "0%o", sbuf.st_mode &
      (S_ISUID | S_ISGID | S_ISVTX | S_IRWXU | S_IRWXG | S_IRWXO));
pbool("setuid", sbuf.st_mode & S_ISUID);
pbool("setgid", sbuf.st_mode & S_ISGID);
pbool("sticky bit", sbuf.st_mode & S_ISVTX);
pbool("User    read permission", sbuf.st_mode & S_IRUSR);
pbool("User   write permission", sbuf.st_mode & S_IWUSR);
pbool("User execute permission", sbuf.st_mode & S_IXUSR);
pbool("Group    read permission", sbuf.st_mode & S_IRGRP);
pbool("Group   write permission", sbuf.st_mode & S_IWGRP);
pbool("Group execute permission", sbuf.st_mode & S_IXGRP);
pbool("Other    read permission", sbuf.st_mode & S_IROTH);
```

```
    pbool("Other   write permission", sbuf.st_mode & S_IWOTH);
    pbool("Other execute permission", sbuf.st_mode & S_IXOTH);

}

void pline(const char *desc, const char *fmt, ...) {
  va_list ap;

  va_start(ap, fmt);
  printf("%30s: ", desc);
  vprintf(fmt, ap);
  printf("\n");
}

void pbool(const char *desc, int cond) {
  pline(desc, cond ? "Yes" : "No");
}

char *myctime(const time_t *timep) {
  char *retval;

  retval = ctime(timep);

  retval[strlen(retval) - 1] = 0;     /* strip off trailing \n */
  return (retval + 4);                /* strip off leading day of week */
}
```

Before you run this code, I'd like to make some observations about the code itself. First, the `pline()` function uses the variable argument list support in C, which is why it looks somewhat strange if you haven't used that support before. Also, `perror()` is simply a function that displays the supplied error text and then the reason for the error.

 Cross-Reference You can find details about the `pline()` function in Chapter 14, "Introducing the Linux I/O."

When the program begins, it first runs `lstat()` on the supplied file. If this call to `lstat()` is successful, the information for that file is printed. If the supplied filename was a symbolic link, the program runs `stat()` on it and then displays the information for the file pointed to by the link.

The `printinfo()` function is responsible for displaying the information retrieved from the `stat()` or `lstat()` call. It starts by printing out some numbers. Then, if the file is a symbolic link, `readlink()` is run on it to get the destination of the link, which is then displayed. Then, parts of the `st_mode` field in the structure are displayed. This field is a big bitfield, meaning that you can use binary AND operations to isolate individual parts. The S_IS* macros are effectively isolating parts, and this is done manually later on. The stat(2) manpage indicates the actual values of each of these, but you are encouraged to use the macros whenever possible to ensure future compatibility and portability.

After displaying the times, owner, and group, the code again displays information gathered from st_mode. You can see it pick out a permission number in the same format that you can supply to chmod. Then, it isolates each individual permission bit and displays it for you. For instance, the value sbuf.st_mode & S_IRUSR will evaluate to true if the user read permission bit is set, or false if it is not. From the code example, you can see exactly how to find out all of this information for your own programs.

Let's take a look at some examples of the type of data that the program can generate. First, here's the result when looking at a plain file from /etc:

```
$ ./ch11-1 /etc/exports
Information for file /etc/exports:

                   Device: 770
                    Inode: 36378
     Number of hard links: 1
            Symbolic link: No
             Regular file: Yes
                Directory: No
         Character device: No
             Block device: No
                     FIFO: No
                   Socket: No

              Device type: 0
                File size: 115
     Preferred block size: 4096
         Length in blocks: 2
              Last access: Jun  3 13:31:41 1999
        Last modification: Oct  4 22:34:01 1998
              Last change: Jun  2 19:27:17 1999

                Owner uid: 0
                Group gid: 0
              Permissions: 0644
                   setuid: No
                   setgid: No
               sticky bit: No
User      read permission: Yes
User     write permission: Yes
User   execute permission: No
Group     read permission: Yes
Group    write permission: No
Group  execute permission: No
```

```
Other    read permission: Yes
Other   write permission: No
Other execute permission: No
```

From this output, you can observe many interesting things about the file system. First, you get the device number. This is not often useful in user-mode programs, but one potential use is to determine whether two files are on the same file system. This can be useful because certain operations, such as moving files with `rename()` or setting a hard link, only work if both files are on the same file system. Comparing these values from two different files can tell you whether you're dealing with a single file system.

Next, you get the inode number, which is of little immediate use but can be useful if you are looking at the file system at a low level. Then, you get the hard link count. In Linux, each directory entry that references this file is considered to be a hard link. Therefore, for a normal file, this value is typically 1. For directories, the value will always be at least 2. The reason is that each directory contains an entry named ., which is a hard link to itself, as well as an entry named .., which is a hard link to its parent. Therefore, because of the link to itself, each directory will have a hard link count of at least 2. If the directory has any subdirectories, the count will be greater because of the links to the parent in each subdirectory.

The remaining lines in the first section indicate what type of file you are dealing with. In this case, it's a regular file, so that is the only bit turned on.

The next section displays some information about the file that you might sometimes get from `ls`. You get the file's size and dates. The `ls` program uses the last modification value as its default date to display. The last change value refers to the date of the last modification to the inode itself (for instance, a change in ownership of the file). The last access corresponds to the last read from the file.

The preferred block size has no implications for many programs. For regular file systems, though, it can be useful. This indicates that the system likes to perform input or output from the file in chunks of data of this size. Usually, your data will be of arbitrary size, and you will just ignore this value. However, consider a case in which you are copying data from one file to another file — perhaps 200 megabytes of data. The operation is simple: read some data, write it out, and repeat until you have read and written all of the data. But how big of a buffer do you use? That is, how much data should you read and write with each call? Well, this value is telling you the answer — you should use a 4096-byte buffer, or perhaps some multiple of that value.

The last block of text is for the permission settings on the file. The uid and gid values come from separate entries; all the other ones come from `st_mode`. The predefined macros for analyzing these entries are used here; you can conveniently test for read, write, and execute permissions for each of the three categories (user, group, and other). Also, there are macros to test for setuid, setgid, and the sticky bit.

Now let's take a look at an example that demonstrates both symbolic links and a block device. Listing 11-2 shows /dev/cdrom, which, on my system, is a symbolic link to /dev/hdc.

Note   Listing 11-2 is available online.

Listing 11-2: **Sample execution of ch11-1**

```
$ ./ch11-1 /dev/cdrom
Information for file /dev/cdrom:

                     Device: 770
                      Inode: 53538
      Number of hard links: 1
             Symbolic link: Yes
          Link destination: hdc
              Regular file: No
                 Directory: No
          Character device: No
              Block device: No
                      FIFO: No
                    Socket: No

                Device type: 0
                  File size: 3
        Preferred block size: 4096
           Length in blocks: 0
                Last access: Sep  4 07:25:24 1999
          Last modification: Sep  4 07:25:24 1999
                Last change: Sep  4 07:25:24 1999

                  Owner uid: 0
                  Group gid: 0
                Permissions: 0777
                     setuid: No
                     setgid: No
                 sticky bit: No
User      read permission: Yes
User     write permission: Yes
User   execute permission: Yes
Group     read permission: Yes
Group    write permission: Yes
Group  execute permission: Yes
Other     read permission: Yes
Other    write permission: Yes
Other  execute permission: Yes

----------------------------------
Information for file pointed to by link
```

```
                 Device: 770
                  Inode: 52555
 Number of hard links: 1
          Symbolic link: No
           Regular file: No
              Directory: No
       Character device: No
           Block device: Yes
                   FIFO: No
                 Socket: No

            Device type: 5632
              File size: 0
   Preferred block size: 4096
        Length in blocks: 0
            Last access: Jun  2 13:38:47 1999
      Last modification: Feb 22 21:42:19 1999
            Last change: Jun 18 12:09:31 1999

              Owner uid: 0
              Group gid: 29
            Permissions: 0771
                 setuid: No
                 setgid: No
             sticky bit: No
 User      read permission: Yes
 User     write permission: Yes
 User   execute permission: Yes
 Group     read permission: Yes
 Group    write permission: Yes
 Group  execute permission: Yes
 Other     read permission: No
 Other    write permission: No
 Other  execute permission: Yes
```

Listing 11-2 shows several things. First of all, you see how the symbolic link is handled. The lstat() call provides information in st_mode that indicates that the file is a link, and then readlink() indicates its destination.

Note   However, note that the code does not run stat() on the information returned by readlink(). There are several reasons for that. First, note that the link did not have an absolute path in it. This is perfectly valid, and the operating system has no problem with this syntax. However, if you were to manually use this value, you would have to ensure that you either took care of the directory issue yourself or changed into the directory of the link before working with it. By using the first file, you avoid the problem. Furthermore, you can have multiple levels of symbolic links on a Linux system. The stat() call will go through all of them and display the results of the final destination.

The final file, /dev/hdc in Listing 11-2, is a block special device file. This means that it corresponds to a special driver in the kernel, and accessing it means that you are accessing a particular device directly. In this case, it is an IDE device, but it could also correspond to a tape drive, SCSI port, scanner, or other such device. A block device is one whose communication is done in blocks of data, usually of a fixed size. For instance, a tape drive might require that all communication is done in chunks that are 1 kilobyte in size. A hard drive might require 512-byte blocks. The following code shows an example of the information that is given for a special file such as /dev/ttyS0:

```
$ ./ch11-1 /dev/ttyS0
Information for file /dev/ttyS0:

                        Device: 770
                         Inode: 53353
         Number of hard links: 1
                 Symbolic link: No
                  Regular file: No
                     Directory: No
              Character device: Yes
                  Block device: No
                          FIFO: No
                        Socket: No

                   Device type: 1088
                     File size: 0
          Preferred block size: 4096
              Length in blocks: 0
                   Last access: Aug 15 14:03:27 1999
             Last modification: Aug 15 14:06:24 1999
                   Last change: Aug 15 14:06:27 1999

                     Owner uid: 0
                     Group gid: 20
                   Permissions: 0660
                        setuid: No
                        setgid: No
                    sticky bit: No
User        read permission: Yes
User       write permission: Yes
User     execute permission: No
Group       read permission: Yes
Group      write permission: Yes
Group    execute permission: No
Other       read permission: No
Other      write permission: No
Other    execute permission: No
```

The preceding output is an example of a character device, /dev/ttyS0 — the first serial communications port on your system. Aside from the special appearance in the first section, this may appear to be a zero-byte file. However, reading from or writing to it will actually cause you to read from or write to your computer's serial port!

The following program output presents the results of displaying the information about a directory:

```
$ ./ch11-1 /usr
Information for file /usr:

                     Device: 773
                      Inode: 2
      Number of hard links: 17
             Symbolic link: No
              Regular file: No
                 Directory: Yes
          Character device: No
              Block device: No
                      FIFO: No
                    Socket: No

               Device type: 0
                 File size: 1024
       Preferred block size: 4096
           Length in blocks: 2
               Last access: Jun  3 07:29:42 1999
         Last modification: Aug 12 21:03:47 1999
               Last change: Aug 12 21:03:47 1999

                 Owner uid: 0
                 Group gid: 0
               Permissions: 0755
                    setuid: No
                    setgid: No
                sticky bit: No
User     read permission: Yes
User    write permission: Yes
User  execute permission: Yes
Group    read permission: Yes
Group   write permission: No
Group execute permission: Yes
Other    read permission: Yes
Other   write permission: No
Other execute permission: Yes
```

The preceding output highlights an important facet of file system storage on Linux: a directory has an inode just like any other file. It also has data, just like any other file. The difference lies in the mode flag that tells the operating system that it is dealing with a directory (with specially formatted directory information) instead of just a normal file. The directory contents are written automatically by the operating system when the directory's contents are modified—for instance, when files are created or deleted. It is not possible to manually modify a directory. However, one common requirement for programs is to be able to read information about a directory, which is described in the following section.

opendir(), readdir(), and friends

In order to read the contents of a directory, you need to open a directory handle. This is done by calling opendir() with the name of the directory you wish to examine. After calling this function, you can use many others to examine the directory. Chief among them is readdir(), which lets you retrieve directory entries one at a time. You can also use telldir(), which gives you a position in the directory. A companion to telldir() one is seekdir(), which lets you reposition inside the directory. The rewinddir() function returns to the beginning of the directory, and closedir() closes your directory handle. Finally, scandir() iterates over the directory structure, running one of your functions on each entry, much like standard file I/O calls.

The following program enables you to go through a directory and display a listing similar to ls. This program is written in Perl, which offers the same functions for these things as C, with syntax that is quite similar. Its name is ch11-2.pl:

```perl
#!/usr/bin/perl -w

# Perl's unless is an inverse if.  That is, unless(a) is the same as
# if (!(a)).

unless ($ARGV[0]) {
  die "Must specify a directory."
}

# -d is a Perl shorthand.  It does a stat() on the passed filename, and
# then looks at the mode.  If the filename is a directory, it returns true;
# if not, it returns false.

unless (-d $ARGV[0]) {
  die "The filename supplied was not a directory."
}

# This is the same as DIRHANDLE = opendir("filename") in C.
# In C, you can use DIR *DIRHANDLE; to declare the variable.

opendir(DIRHANDLE, $ARGV[0]) or die "Couldn't open directory: $!";

# In C, readdir() returns a pointer to struct dirent, whose members are
# defined in readdir(3).  In Perl, returns one file in scalar context,
# or all remaining filenames in list context.

while ($filename = readdir(DIRHANDLE)) {
  print "$filename\n";
}

closedir(DIRHANDLE);
```

To make this program executable, you need to use chmod. Go ahead and do that now, and then run it:

```
$ chmod a+x ch11-2.pl
$ ./ch11-2.pl /usr
.
..
lost+found
bin
sbin
lib
doc
man
share
dict
games
include
info
src
X11R6
local
openwin
i486-linuxlibc1
```

There you have it — a basic usage of readdir(). The program was able to present you with a listing similar to ls of all files in the directory. Let's take it a step farther and get a recursive listing of the directory. This means that a directory, and all its subdirectories, should be listed. Here's the code for such a program:

```perl
#!/usr/bin/perl -w

# Perl's unless is an inverse if.  That is, unless(a) is the same as
# if (!(a)).

unless ($ARGV[0]) {
  die "Must specify a directory."
}

# -d is a Perl shorthand.  It does a stat() on the passed filename, and
# then looks at the mode.  If the filename is a directory, it returns true;
# if not, it returns false.

unless (-d $ARGV[0]) {
  die "The filename supplied was not a directory."
}

dircontents($ARGV[0], 1);

sub dircontents{
  my ($startname, $level) = @_;
```

```
    my $filename;
    local *DH;                      # Ensure that the handle is locally-scoped

# This is the same as DH = opendir("filename") in C.
# In C, you can use DIR *DH; to declare the variable.

    unless(opendir(DH, $startname)) {
      warn "Couldn't open directory $startname: $!";
      return undef;
    }

    # In C, readdir() returns a pointer to struct dirent, whose members are
    # defined in readdir(3).  In Perl, returns one file in scalar context,
    # or all remaining filenames in list context.

    while ($filename = readdir(DH)) {
      print(' ' x (3 * ($level - 1)), "$filename\n");
      if ($filename ne '.' &&
          $filename ne '..' &&
          ! -l "$startname/$filename" &&
          -d "$startname/$filename") {
        dircontents("$startname/$filename", $level + 1);
      }
    }

    closedir(DH);
}
```

There are several important things to note about this code. First, you need to determine whether or not each file is a directory; you also need to see whether or not it should be descended into. At first, you might think that a simple call to -d is sufficient (or a call to stat() in C). However, this is not the case. The reason? Every directory has . and .. entries. If you continuously scan those, you'll get in an endless loop, scanning the same directory over and over. Therefore, those special entries are excluded. Then, there is a problem with symbolic links. Recall that -d is equivalent to doing a stat() call, which follows links. If there is a symbolic link that points to ., for instance, then the same problem will arise as before: an endless loop. So, if the file is not a special one corresponding to the current directory or its parent, is not a symbolic link, and is a directory, then it is descended. Also, the previous fatal error of being unable to open a directory is transformed into a mere warning—if there is a problem, such as permission denied, somewhere along the tree, it's better to just ignore that part of the tree than to completely exit the program. This is what is done in the dircontents subroutine in the previous code, although this example also issues a warning.

Also notice that the program adds $startname to the start of the filename whenever checking or descending into a directory. The reason is that the filename is always relative. So, for instance, if the person running the program is in a home directory and requests information about /usr, and the program encounters a directory named bin, it needs to ask for /usr/bin, not just bin—which would produce the bin directory in the user's home directory.

Running this revised version on /usr produces over 65,000 lines of output on my laptop; enough to fill over 900 pages with filenames. Listing 11-3 shows the revised version on a smaller directory area: /etc/X11.

Note   Listing 11-3 is available online.

Listing 11-3: Example processing /etc/X11

```
$ ./ch11-2.pl /etc/X11
.
..
Xsession.options
Xresources
   .
   ..
   xbase-clients
   xterm
   xterm~
   xfree86-common
   tetex-base
window-managers
fvwm
   .
   ..
   system.warnings
   update.warn
   pre.hook
   default-style.hook
   system.fvwm2rc
   init.hook
   restart.hook
   init-restart.hook
   main-menu-pre.hook
   main-menu.hook
   menudefs.hook
   post.hook
xinit
   .
   ..
   xinitrc
wm-common
   .
   ..
xview
   .
   ..
   textswrc
   ttyswrc
   text_extras_menu
```

Continued

Listing 11-3 *(continued)*

```
XF86Config
WindowMaker
    .
    ..
    background.menu
    menu.prehook
    menu
    menu.ca
    menu.cz
    menu.da
    menu.de
    menu.el
    menu.es
    menu.fi
    menu.fr
    menu.gl
    menu.he
    menu.hr
    menu.hu
    menu.it
    menu.ja
    menu.ko
    menu.nl
    menu.no
    menu.pt
    menu.ru
    menu.se
    menu.sl
    menu.tr
    menu.zh_CN
    menu.zh_TW.Big5
    plmenu
    plmenu.dk
    plmenu.fr
    plmenu.hr
    plmenu.zh_CN
    wmmacros
    menu.posthook
    menu.hook
    plmenu.da
    plmenu.it
    appearance.menu
Xsession
fonts
    .
    ..
    100dpi
        .
        ..
```

```
    xfonts-100dpi.alias
misc
    .
    ..
    xfonts-base.alias
    xfonts-jmk.alias
75dpi
    .
    ..
    xfonts-75dpi.alias
Speedo
    .
    ..
    xfonts-scalable.scale
Type1
    .
    ..
    xfonts-scalable.scale
xserver
    .
    ..
    SecurityPolicy
XF86Config~
Xmodmap
Xserver
afterstep
    .
    ..
    menudefs.hook
Xserver~
Xloadimage
window-managers~
```

Listing 11-3 demonstrates how the program is able to descend into directories.
Thanks to the level information passed along, it's also possible to indent the
contents of a directory to make a visually appealing output format.

I/O Methods

When you are performing input or output with files on a Linux system, there are
two basic ways to do it in C: stream-based I/O or system call I/O. C++ also has a
more object-oriented stream system, which is similar in basic purpose to the
stream-based I/O in C. The stream-based I/O is actually implemented in the C
library as a layer around the system call functions. The stream I/O adds additional
features, such as formatted output, input parsing, and buffering to increase
performance.

However, for some tasks, you need to use system call I/O. For instance, if you are writing a network server, you need to use the system calls to at least establish your connection. Moreover, you often need to do the same when you need to work with select() or other advanced I/O tasks — generally, ones that deal with things other than files.

How can you tell the difference? As a general rule, the stream functions have names beginning with an f, whereas the system call versions do not. For instance, you have fopen, fread, fwrite, and fclose as opposed to open, read, write, and close. Also, the stream functions deal with a FILE * handle, whereas the system call versions deal with an integer file descriptor.

As a note, this difference is only relevant for C and similar languages. Most languages do not provide two separate systems for doing I/O as is done with C.

Stream I/O

This is the typical I/O system as you have learned with C in general. Stream-based I/O gives you access to the library's extra functions for formatting output, such as fprintf(), and parsing input, such as fscanf(). Here's a sample program:

```
#include <stdio.h>
#include <errno.h>

#define ITERATIONS 9000000

int main(void) {
    int number;
    char writestring[100];
    int counter;
    int size;
    FILE *output;

    printf("Please enter a number: ");
    scanf("%d", &number);

    number /= 2;

    printf("Writing %d copies of %d to a file.\n", ITERATIONS, number);
    output = fopen("testfile", "wb");
    if (!output) {
        perror("Can't open output file");
        exit(255);
    }

    sprintf(writestring, "%d", number);
    size = strlen(writestring);
```

```
for (counter = 0; counter < ITERATIONS; counter++) {
  fwrite(writestring, size, 1, output);
}

fclose(output);
return 0;
}
```

The stream I/O functions automatically create the output file if it doesn't exist. In this case, fopen() automatically creates the file if it does already exist. Then, several copies of a number are written out to the file. Note that no error-checking is done on the writes or the close, which is not something that you should let slip by in production code. When I time this execution, the program takes about seven seconds to run — this result will be important later when looking at system call I/O.

One feature of stream I/O is that I/O is buffered — that is, the system call to actually carry out the operation isn't issued until a certain amount of data has been queued up, or a newline character is encountered. Because a system call can be expensive in terms of performance, this behavior can really help to speed up your program.

However, it can also introduce some problems. You may want to make sure that your data is written out immediately. Or, if you need to mix system-call I/O with stream I/O in your program, you need to make sure that both are always written out immediately, or else the output may be mixed up.

A function to use to do that is called fflush(). This function takes as a parameter a specific file handle, and it will completely carry out any pending I/O for your file handle. A flush is implicitly carried out for you whenever you try to read input, or when you write out a newline character.

System call I/O

When you need to interact with the I/O subsystem on a lower level, you will need to use system call I/O. Usually, you will not need to do this when dealing with files or general I/O. However, when dealing with network sockets, devices, pipes, FIFOs, or other special types of communication, system call I/O may be the only reasonable way to work.

Here is a version of the previous program, rewritten to use system call I/O for actually writing out to a file:

```
#include <stdio.h>
#include <errno.h>
#include <sys/types.h>
#include <sys/stat.h>
#include <fcntl.h>
#include <unistd.h>
```

```
#define ITERATIONS 9000000

int main(void) {
  int number;
  char writestring[100];
  int counter;
  int size;
  int output;

  printf("Please enter a number: ");
  scanf("%d", &number);

  number /= 2;

  printf("Writing %d copies of %d to a file.\n", ITERATIONS,
number);
  output = open("testfile", O_CREAT | O_TRUNC);
  if (!output) {
    perror("Can't open output file");
    exit(255);
  }

  sprintf(writestring, "%d", number);
  size = strlen(writestring);

  for (counter = 0; counter < ITERATIONS; counter++) {
    write(output, writestring, size);
  }

  close(output);
  return 0;
}
```

Note Notice that the parts of the program that interact with the user are still written to use stream I/O. Using stream I/O for these tasks is much easier because you get the convenience of using calls such as `printf()` to format your output.

The code looks quite similar to that which used stream I/O. A file is opened, data is written to it in a loop, and then the file is closed. The difference is that this example uses the system call I/O functions instead of the stream I/O functions. For a simple program like this, there is really no reason to go this route, but you can see that the basic idea is the same, even if the functions are different.

Because there is no buffering before making a system call when you use this type of I/O, the performance of this program is quite a bit worse. In fact, it takes almost three times as long to run with system call I/O as it does with stream I/O. The lesson: stream I/O gives you performance benefits in many cases, if it is versatile enough for your needs.

On another note, some of these functions do not guarantee that they will write out all the data you requested at once, even if there is no error. You will generally not see this behavior when dealing with files, but it can become more common when dealing with a network, as the operating system is forced to split the data into blocks for transmission. Here's a function that you can use in your programs to ensure that all the data is written properly:

```
/*
    This function writes certain number of bytes from "buf" to a file
    or socket descriptor specified by "fd". The number of bytes is
    specified by "count". "fd" SHOULD BE A DESCRIPTOR FOR A FILE,
    OR A PIPE OR TCP SOCKET. It returns the number of bytes written
    or -1 on error.
*/

int write_buffer(int fd, char *buf, int count)
{
    char *pts = buf;
    int  status = 0, n;

    if (count < 0) return (-1);

    while (status != count) {
        n = write(fd, pts+status, count-status);
        if (n < 0) return (n);
        status += n;
    }
    return (status);
}
```

Along the same lines, the functions do not guarantee that they will read as much information as you have asked for either. Therefore, if you know in advance that you are expecting information of a fixed size, you may find it useful to have a function to read data until that size is reached. Here is such a function that you can use:

```
/*
    This function reads certain number of bytes from a file or socket
    descriptor specified by "fd" to "buf". The number of bytes is
    specified by "count". "fd" SHOULD BE A DESCRIPTOR FOR A FILE,
    OR A PIPE OR TCP SOCKET. It returns number of bytes read
    or (<0) on error.
*/

int read_buffer(int fd, char *buf, int count)
{
    char *pts = buf;
    int  status = 0, n;

    if (count < 0) return (-1);

    while (status != count) {
        n = read(fd, pts+status, count-status);
```

```
        if (n < 0) return n;
        status += n;
    }
    return (status);
}
```

If you use this function, take care to make sure that your buffer is at least `count` characters long. If you don't, your program could crash.

Special Files

You have seen how to interact with standard files already. However, some entities on your Linux system appear to be files but are not really files at all. These are sometimes called "special" files.

Special files can be of many different types. Often, they correspond to actual devices on the system, as is the case with many of the files in /dev. When you read from or write to one of these files, you are actually communicating with some device that is attached to your system! So, you can, for instance, communicate with the first serial port by opening /dev/ttyS0.

Other special files can be FIFOs (also known as named pipes). These are used to communicate between two processes on the system. When you open one of these files, you will actually be exchanging data with another process on the same system.

 You can find more details about FIFO files in Chapter 17, "Using Pipes and FIFOs."

Finally, there is the /proc file system. This area contains information about your system, which devices are connected to it, and which processes are running on the system. Many programs, such as `ps`, get the information they need to run from /proc.

Summary

In this chapter, you learned about how files are dealt with internally in Linux. Specifically, you learned:

✦ The file system consists of one inode per file.

✦ Directory information is stored on the file system as a directory special file.

✦ You can access information from the inode with `stat()` and `lstat()`.

✦ You can read the destination of a symbolic link with `readlink()`.

✦ Directory information can be found with `opendir()` and its relatives.

✦ Many different types of entries are present on a Linux file system, such as files, directories, devices, FIFOs, and sockets.

✦ C provides two types of I/O for your use: system call I/O and stream I/O.

✦   ✦   ✦

Processes in Linux

One of the most important ideas about the Linux
environment is that of the process. In this chapter, I'll
show you what processes are all about. After that, I'll discuss
some basics of dealing with processes in Linux, how to
manage these processes, and how to get information back
from them. This chapter concludes with an overview of
synchronization issues and security issues relating to
processes.

Understanding the Process Model

The process model in Linux undercuts everything that your
program does, from loading it into memory, to running it, and
to handling its exit. Moreover, processes manage multiple
programs, enable these programs to run at once, and
much more.

Before examining processes, it may be useful to look at an
analogy. Imagine a warehouse full of boxes — each box
representing a process. The contents of each box are
prevented from mixing with the contents of another box. A
box may contain many pages of paper — as a process might
contain many pages of memory. The boxes probably are
marked with labels on the outside, identifying who the box
belongs to and what is in it. Similarly, processes have information that identify the user that owns the process and the
program that's running in the process.

Finally, somebody manages the entire operation. In the
physical world, if you're in a military situation or perhaps
a certain chicken restaurant chain, this person is called a
colonel. In Linux, the part of the system that manages the
processes is likewise the *kernel*.

Introducing Process Basics

In this section, I'll discuss the big picture of processes. There are a few exceptions to some of the rules in this section, such as if you're using shared memory or threading, but the principles discussed in this section still hold unless you knowingly make some changes.

Every program running on your system is running in its own *process*. In fact, every copy of every program running has its own process. That is, if you start up an editor twice, without closing the first invocation before starting the second, you'll have two processes running that editor.

A process has the following attributes associated with it:

✦ PID (Process ID)

✦ Memory area

✦ File descriptors

✦ Security information

✦ Environment

✦ Signal handling

✦ Resource scheduling

✦ Synchronization

✦ State

Each process has a unique numeric process ID, better known as the PID. Each PID occurs only once on the system at any given moment, but if your system remains online for long enough, they are reused eventually. The PID is the primary way of identifying a particular process.

Each process also has a memory area associated with it. This area holds the code for the program that is running in that process. It also holds the data (variables) for that particular program. Any change that you make in the variables or memory of one process is restricted to that process. The operating system prevents these changes from affecting other processes, which is a major source of Linux's stability relative to some other operating systems. One errant process can crash itself but the rest of the system will continue unharmed.

Processes also have file descriptors associated with them. You were introduced already to the three default file descriptors: standard input, standard output, and standard error. These file descriptors are opened by default for your program in most situations. Any other file descriptors that you might open (for instance, if you open a file) or any changes that you make to the default ones take effect in your process only. No other processes on the system are directly effected. Of course, if other processes are reading the data you are writing, there is an effect; however, the file descriptors of one process are not modified by a change in another.

Some security information is associated with processes as well. At a minimum, processes record the user and the group of the person that owns the process, which, generally, is the person that started it. As you'll see later, there can be much more security information to deal with in some special situations.

There is an environment that goes with each process. This environment holds things such as environment variables and the command line used to invoke the program that is running in the process.

A process can send and receive signals, and act based on them. These enable standard execution to be interrupted to carry out a special task. Signal reception is based on security of the process.

Cross-Reference

For more details, see the discussion of signals in Chapter 13, "Understanding Signals."

A process is also the unit for scheduling system resources for access. For instance, if 20 programs are running on a system with a single CPU, the Linux kernel alternates between each of them, giving them each a small amount of time to run, and then rapidly switching to the next. Thus, each process gets a small *time slice*, but because it gets these frequently, it seems as if the system is actually managing to run all 20 processes simultaneously. In systems with more than one CPU, the kernel decides which process should run on which CPU, and manages multitasking issues between them. A process can have certain values, such as a priority level, that modify how much time a process gets from the CPU or how big its time slice is. The security settings of the process govern access to the priority level.

Synchronization with other programs is also done on a per-process level. Processes may request and check for locks on certain files to ensure that only one process is modifying the file at any given time. Processes also may use shared memory or semaphores to communicate with and synchronize between each other. I'll discuss some synchronization issues in this chapter.

Cross-Reference

Chapter 14, "Introducing the Linux I/O," covers file locking in more detail and Chapter 16, " Shared Memory and Semaphores," covers shared memory/ semaphores in more detail.

Finally, each process has a state. It may be running, waiting to be scheduled for running, or sleeping—that is, not processing anything because it's waiting for an event to occur, such as user input or the release of a lock.

Starting and Stopping Processes

When you want to create a new process in Linux, the basic call to do this is fork(). This is, incidentally, one of the few calls in Linux that are able to return twice; you'll see why next.

When you fork a process, the system creates another process running the same program as the current process. In fact, the newly created process, called the *child process*, has all the data, connections, and so on as the *parent process* and execution continues at the same place. The single difference between the two is the return value from the fork() system call, which returns the PID of the child to the parent and a value of 0 to the child. Therefore, common practice is to examine the return value of the call in both processes, and do different things based on it.

Basic forking

I'll start out with a basic program. The following code will simply fork a process and each of these processes will print a message, and then exit:

```
#include <stdio.h>
#include <unistd.h>
#include <sys/types.h>

int main(void) {
  pid_t pid;

  pid = fork();

  if (pid == 0) {
    printf("Hello from the child process!\n");
  } else if (pid != -1) {
    printf("Hello from the parent.  I've forked process %d.\n", pid);
  } else {
    printf("There was an error with forking.\n");
  }
}
```

This code will fork. If the return value is 0, it means that the current process is the child from the fork. If the value is not -1, it means that the fork was successful and the return value indicates the PID of the new process. On the other hand, if the value is -1, then the fork failed.

When you run this program, you will get two messages — one from the parent and one from the child. Because these are separate processes, these messages appear in essentially a random order. If you run the program several times, you'll get the messages in both orders. For instance, here are sample executions from my system:

```
$ ./ch12-1
Hello from the parent.  I've forked process 458.
Hello from the child process!
$ ./ch12-1
Hello from the child process!
Hello from the parent.  I've forked process 460.
```

The reason for getting two messages is that the two separate processes can have their CPU time scheduled in any order, because they really are running as separate programs now.

Executing other programs

Besides forking, you'll often have a need to invoke other programs. This is done with the exec family of functions. When you run exec, your process's current image is replaced with that of the new program. That is, if your call to an exec function is successful, the call will never return — a different program will run in its place in your process.

Sometimes this may be what you want. Sometimes you may prefer both processes to continue executing. Or, you may prefer the parent to wait until the child is finished executing — the behavior of, for instance, the Linux shell.

An Example of exec()

I'll start with an example of a program in which the program in the process is completely replaced by the child:

```c
#include <stdio.h>
#include <unistd.h>

int main(void) {

    printf("Hello, this is a sample program.\n");
    execlp("ls", "ls", "/proc", NULL);
    printf("This code is running after the exec call.\n");
    printf("You should never see this message unless exec failed.\n");
    return 0;
}
```

This is a fairly simple program. It starts out by displaying a message on the screen. Then, it calls one of the exec family of functions. The l in the name means to use an argument list passed to it, and the p means to search the path. The first argument is the name of the program to run. The remaining arguments are passed to it as argv. Recall that argv[0] is conventionally the name of the program, so the program name is duplicated. The next argument contains a directory list. The final argument, a null pointer, tells the system that it reached the end of the argument list, and must be present.

Unless the exec call fails, you will never see the remaining information because the code for this program will be replaced completely by that for the program being executed. To that end, try running it to verify the result:

```
$ ./ch12-2
Hello, this is a sample program.
1     198  250  267  323  347  4        filesystems  meminfo     slabinfo
114   2    255  268  324  348  404      fs           misc        stat
116   200  259  272  325  349  5        ide          modules     swaps
124   201  260  277  328  350  apm      interrupts   mounts      sys
129   204  261  285  329  354  bus      ioports      mtrr        tty
132   208  262  286  333  357  cmdline  kcore        net         uptime
14    209  263  290  343  360  cpuinfo  kmsg         partitions  version
143   241  264  3    344  391  devices  ksyms        pci
152   243  265  317  345  392  dma      loadavg      scsi
160   247  266  322  346  396  fb       locks        self
```

Indeed you can see that the program image in memory is replaced by the program image of ls. None of the messages at the end of the original program are displayed.

Details of exec()

The system provides you with many options for executing new programs. The manpages list the following options for syntax:

```
int execl(const char *file, const char *arg, ...);
int execlp(const char *file, const char *arg, ...);
int  execle(const char *file, const char *arg , ..., char *const envp[]);
int execv(const char *file, char *const argv[]);
int execvp(const char *file, char *const argv[]);
int execve(const char *file, char *const argv[], char *const envp[]);
```

These calls are all prototyped in unistd.h. Each of these commands begins with the name of the program to execute. The ones containing a p — execlp() and execvp() — will search the PATH for the file if it cannot be located immediately. With all other functions, this should be the full path to the file. Relative paths are permissible, but with all of these functions, you should use an absolute path whenever possible for security reasons.

The three ll functions — execl(), execlp(), and execle() — take a list of the arguments for the program on the command line. After the last argument, you must specify the special value NULL. For instance, you might use the following to invoke ls:

```
    execl("/bin/ls", "/bin/ls", "-l", "/etc", NULL);
```

This is the same as running the shell command ls -l /etc. Notice that, for this and all the functions, the first (zeroth, to the executed process) argument should be the name of the program. This is usually the same as the specified filename.

The vv functions — execv( ), execvp( ), and execve( ) — use a pointer to an array of strings for the argument list. This is the same format as is passed in to your program in argv in main( ). The last item must be NULL. Here is how you might write the same command in the previous example with execv( ):

```
char *arguments[4];

arguments[0] = "/bin/ls";
arguments[1] = "-l";
arguments[2] = "/etc";
arguments[3] = NULL;

execv("/bin/ls", arguments);
```

This type of syntax is particularly useful when you do not know in advance how many arguments you will need to pass to the new program. You can build up your array on the fly, and then use it for the arguments.

The e functions — execle( ) and execve( ) — enable you to customize the specific environment variables received by your child process. These functions are not usually used, which enables the new process to inherit the same environment that the current one has. However, if you specify the environment, it should be in a pointer to an array of pointers to strings, exactly like the arguments. This array also must be terminated by NULL.

When an exec...( ) call succeeds, the new program inherits none of the code or data from your current program. Signals and signal handlers are cleared. However, the security information and the PID of the process are retained. This includes the uid of the owner of the process, although setuid or setgid may change this behavior. Furthermore, file descriptors remain open for the new program to use.

Waiting for processes

You must consider several very important things when you are dealing with multiple processes. One of them is to clean up after a child process exits. In the example of forking thus far in this chapter, this was not done because the parent exited almost immediately and thus the init process inherited the problem and took care of it. However, if both processes need to hang around for awhile, you need to take care of these issues yourself.

The problem is this: when a process exits, its entry in the process table does not completely go away. This is because the operating system is waiting for a parent process to fetch some information about why the child process exited. This could include a return value, a signal, or something else along those lines. A process whose program terminated but still remains because its information was not yet collected is dubbed a zombie process. Here's a quick example of this type of process:

```c
#include <stdio.h>
#include <unistd.h>
#include <sys/types.h>

int main(void) {
  pid_t pid;

  pid = fork();

  if (pid == 0) {
    printf("Hello from the child process!\n");
    printf("The child is exiting now.\n");
  } else if (pid != -1) {
    printf("Hello from the parent, pid %d.\n", getpid());
    printf("The parent has forked process %d.\n", pid);
    sleep(60);
    printf("The parent is exiting now.\n");
  } else {
    printf("There was an error with forking.\n");
  }
}
```

There is now a `sleep` call in the parent to delay its exit for a minute so you can examine the state of the system's process table in another window. When you run the program, you will see this:

```
$ ./ch12-3
Hello from the parent, pid 448.
Hello from the child process!
The child is exiting now.
The parent has forked process 449.
```

Now, in a separate window or terminal, take the process ID of the child. In this case, it is 449. Find its entry with a command like this:

```
$ ps aux | grep 449 | grep -v grep
jgoerzen   449 0.0  0.0     0     0 pts/0    Z    08:18   0:00 [ch12-3
<defunct>]
```

You should observe two things here. First, note that the state of the process is indicated as Z—that is, a zombie process. As another reminder to you, `ps` also indicates that the process is defunct, meaning the same thing.

To clear out this defunct process, you need to wait on it, even if you don't care about its exit information. You can use a family of `wait` calls, some of which I'll go over in this section.

Family of wait Calls

First, let's look at an example. Listing 12-1 is an example of a modified version of a previous program that waits for the child to exit.

Note   Listing 12-1 is available online.

Listing 12-1: **First wait() example**

```
#include <stdio.h>
#include <unistd.h>
#include <stdarg.h>
#include <time.h>
#include <sys/types.h>
#include <sys/wait.h>

int tprintf(const char *fmt, ...);

int main(void) {
  pid_t pid;

  pid = fork();

  if (pid == 0) {
    tprintf("Hello from the child process!\n");
    tprintf("The child is exiting now.\n");
  } else if (pid != -1) {
    tprintf("Hello from the parent, pid %d.\n", getpid());
    tprintf("The parent has forked process %d.\n", pid);
    waitpid(pid, NULL, 0);
    tprintf("The child has stopped.  Sleeping for 60 seconds.\n");
    sleep(60);
    tprintf("The parent is exiting now.\n");
  } else {
    tprintf("There was an error with forking.\n");
  }
  return 0;
}

int tprintf(const char *fmt, ...) {
  va_list args;
  struct tm *tstruct;
  time_t tsec;

  tsec = time(NULL);
  tstruct = localtime(&tsec);
```

Continued

Listing 12-1 *(continued)*

```
printf("%02d:%02d:%02d %5d| ",
       tstruct->tm_hour,
       tstruct->tm_min,
       tstruct->tm_sec,
       getpid());

va_start(args, fmt);
return vprintf(fmt, args);
}
```

This code introduces a new function, `tprintf()`, which will be useful in the examples in the rest of this chapter. It presents an interface similar to that of `printf()` to the caller but internally it prints out the current time and the current PID before displaying the message. In this way, you can track the progress through the program in time.

The body of the code has a new call, one to `waitpid()`. This causes the execution of the parent to be put on hold until the forked child process has exited. When the child process exits, the parent gathers up its exit information and then continues to execute. Here is the output you'll get from running this program:

Note   Some things may appear in a different order, depending on whether the parent or the child will be capable of displaying its output first.

```
$ ./ch12-4
14:58:27   358| Hello from the parent, pid 358.
14:58:27   359| Hello from the child process!
14:58:27   358| The parent has forked process 359.
14:58:27   359| The child is exiting now.
14:58:27   358| The child has stopped.  Sleeping for 60 seconds.
14:59:27   358| The parent is exiting now.
```

If you use a `ps` command, as in the preceding example, while the parent is sleeping, you would see that there is no longer any zombie process waiting to be collected. Rather, `waitpid()` call picks up the information and allows it to be removed from the process table.

If you plan to fork many processes, it would be easier on you if you don't have to specifically wait for each one, assuming your parent is supposed to continue executing. Therefore, you can have a signal handler that automatically waits for any child process when it exits, meaning that you don't have to explicitly code any such wait yourself. Listing 12-2 shows a modification of the code from Listing 12-1 to do exactly that.

Cross-Reference For more details on signals and signal handlers, see Chapter 13, "Understanding Signals."

Note Listing 12-2 is available online.

Listing 12-2: **Signal handler for waiting**

```
#include <stdio.h>
#include <unistd.h>
#include <stdarg.h>
#include <time.h>
#include <sys/types.h>
#include <sys/wait.h>
#include <signal.h>

int tprintf(const char *fmt, ...);
void realsleep(int seconds);
void waitchildren(int signum);

int main(void) {
  pid_t pid;

  pid = fork();

  if (pid == 0) {
    tprintf("Hello from the child process!\n");
    tprintf("The child is sleeping for 15 seconds.\n");
    realsleep(15);
    tprintf("The child is exiting now.\n");
  } else if (pid != -1) {
    /* Set up the signal handler. */
    signal(SIGCHLD, (void *)waitchildren);

    tprintf("Hello from the parent, pid %d.\n", getpid());
    tprintf("The parent has forked process %d.\n", pid);
    tprintf("The parent is sleeping for 30 seconds.\n");
    realsleep(30);
    tprintf("The parent is exiting now.\n");
  } else {
    tprintf("There was an error with forking.\n");
  }
  return 0;
}
```

Continued

Listing 12-2 *(continued)*

```
int tprintf(const char *fmt, ...) {
  va_list args;
  struct tm *tstruct;
  time_t tsec;

  tsec = time(NULL);
  tstruct = localtime(&tsec);

  printf("%02d:%02d:%02d %5d| ",
         tstruct->tm_hour,
         tstruct->tm_min,
         tstruct->tm_sec,
         getpid());

  va_start(args, fmt);
  return vprintf(fmt, args);
}

void waitchildren(int signum) {
  pid_t pid;

  while ((pid = waitpid(-1, NULL, WNOHANG)) > 0) {
    tprintf("Caught the exit of child process %d.\n", pid);
  }
}

void realsleep(int seconds) {
  while (seconds) {
    seconds = sleep(seconds);
    if (seconds) {
      tprintf("Restarting interrupted sleep for %d more seconds.\n", seconds);
    }
  }
}
```

There are several implementation details to go over here. First of all, notice that the sleep() call can return before its time is up if a signal arrives that is not ignored by your code. Therefore, you have to watch for this. If this occurs, sleep() will return the number of seconds remaining, so a simple wrapper around it will take care of this problem.

Then, take note of the signal() call in the parent area. This indicates that whenever the parent process receives SIGCHLD, the waitchildren() function is invoked. That function is an interesting one, even though it has only two lines of code.

Its first line sets up a loop. As long as waitpid() continues finding child processes that have exited, the loop continues executing. For each process, a message is displayed. In your programs, you probably will eliminate the message and thus have an empty loop body. The -1 value is used for the PID in the call to waitpid() so that any child process will be found; inside the signal handler, you don't necessarily know exactly which process exited or even which processes are your children. The signal handler doesn't care about the exit status of the child, so it passes NULL for that value. Finally, it uses WNOHANG. This way, after all exited child processes are waited upon, it returns a different code that breaks the loop, instead of simply blocking execution of the parent until another process decides to exit.

Details of wait

There are a number of variants of the wait functions in Linux, just as there are a number of variants of the exec calls. Each call has its own special features and syntax. The various wait functions are declared as follows:

```
pid_t wait(int *status)
pid_t waitpid(pid_t pid, int *status, int options);
pid_t wait3(int *status, int options, struct rusage *rusage);
pid_t wait4(pid_t pid, int *status, int options,
            struct rusage *rusage);
```

The first two calls require the inclusion of sys/types.h and sys/wait.h, and the last two require those as well as sys/resource.h. Each of these functions returns the PID of the process that exited, 0 if they were told to be non-blocking and no matching process was found, and -1 if there was an error. By default, these functions block the caller until there is a matching child that has exited and has not been waited upon yet. This means that execution of the parent process will be suspended until the child process exits. Of course, if there are child processes that have already exited (which would make them zombies), the wait functions can return right away with information from one of them, without blocking execution in the parent.

If the status parameter is NULL, it is ignored. Otherwise, information is stored there. Linux defines a number of macros, shown in Table 12-1, that can be used with an integer holding the status result to determine what exactly happened. These macros are called, for instance, as WIFEXITED(status).

Note   Note that the macros take the integer as the parameter, not a pointer to it as does the function.

Table 12-1
Macros Used with Integers

Macro	Meaning
WEXITSTATUS	Returns the exit code that the child process returned, perhaps through a call to `exit()`. Note that the value from this macro is not usable unless WIFEXITED is true.
WIFEXITED	Returns true if the child process in question exited normally.
WIFSIGNALED	Returns a true value if the child process exited because of a signal. If the child process caught the signal and then exited by calling something like `exit()`, this will not be true.
WIFSTOPPED	Returns a true value if the WUNTRACED value is specified in the options parameter to `waitpid()` and the process in question causes `waitpit()` to return because of that.
WSTOPSIG	Gets the signal that stops the process in question, if WIFSTOPPED is true.
WTERMSIG	Gets the signal that terminates the process in question, if WIFSIGNALED is true.

Several of these functions take a parameter named `options`. It is formed by using a bitwise or (with the | operator) of various macros. If you wish to use none of these special options, simply use a value of 0. Linux defines two options, WNOHANG and WUNTRACED. WNOHANG means that the call should be non-blocking. That is, it should return immediately even if no child exited instead of holding up execution of the parent until a child does exit. WUNTRACED returns information about child processes that are stopped, whereas normally these would be ignored.

For `waitpid()`, the `pid` option can have some special meanings as well. If its value is -1, then `waitpid()` waits for any child process. If the value is greater than 0, then it waits for the process with that particular PID. Values of 0 or strictly less than -1 refer to process groups, which are used for sending signals and terminal control and are generally used only in special-purpose applications such as shells.

The `wait3()` and `wait4()` calls are used if you need to get process accounting information from the child. If the `rusage` parameter is NULL, this extra information is ignored; otherwise, it is stored into the structure pointed to. This sort of accounting information is rarely needed by the parent; you can find the definition of the `rusage` structure in /usr/include/sys/resource.h or /usr/include/bits/resource.h.

Combining forces

You may have noticed that the shell on Linux exhibits behavior that I haven't quite covered. When you run a program in the shell, the shell is dormant while the program executes, and then it returns back to life exactly where you left off, and with the same PID to boot.

This cannot be done solely with calls to exec functions; those would replace the shell completely. It also can't be done with a fork() call and then an exec, because the shell would continue executing while the called program executes simultaneously! The solution is to have your program fork, then have the parent wait on the exit of the child. Meanwhile, the child should call exec to load up the new program. Listing 12-3 shows an example of this technique.

Note   Listing 12-3 is available online.

Listing 12-3: **Forking with exec and wait**

```
#include <stdio.h>
#include <unistd.h>
#include <stdarg.h>
#include <time.h>
#include <sys/types.h>
#include <sys/wait.h>
#include <unistd.h>
#include <stdlib.h>

int tprintf(const char *fmt, ...);
void waitchildren(int signum);

int main(void) {
  pid_t pid;

  pid = fork();

  if (pid == 0) {
    tprintf("Hello from the child process!\n");
    setenv("PS1", "CHILD \\$ ", 1);
    tprintf("I'm calling exec.\n");
    execl("/bin/sh", "/bin/sh", NULL);
    tprintf("You should never see this because the child is already gone.\n");
  } else if (pid != -1) {

    tprintf("Hello from the parent, pid %d.\n", getpid());
    tprintf("The parent has forked process %d.\n", pid);
```

Continued

Listing 12-3 *(continued)*

```
      tprintf("The parent is waiting for the child to exit.\n");
      waitpid(pid, NULL, 0);
      tprintf("The child has exited.\n");
      tprintf("The parent is exiting.\n");
   } else {
      tprintf("There was an error with forking.\n");
   }
   return 0;
}

int tprintf(const char *fmt, ...) {
   va_list args;
   struct tm *tstruct;
   time_t tsec;

   tsec = time(NULL);
   tstruct = localtime(&tsec);

   printf("%02d:%02d:%02d %5d| ",
          tstruct->tm_hour,
          tstruct->tm_min,
          tstruct->tm_sec,
          getpid());

   va_start(args, fmt);
   return vprintf(fmt, args);
}
```

This code invokes the shell. Before it does, it sets the PS1 environment variable. If your shell is Bash, this will change the prompt for the child. Here is a sample interaction with the program.

Note In Bash, the symbol $$ refers to the PID of the current process.

```
$ ./ch12-6
16:40:25    482| Hello from the parent, pid 482.
16:40:25    483| Hello from the child process!
16:40:25    483| I'm calling exec.
16:40:25    482| The parent has forked process 483.
16:40:25    482| The parent is waiting for the child to exit.
CHILD $ echo Hi, I am PID $$
Hi, I am PID 483
CHILD $ ls -d /proc/i*
```

```
/proc/ide   /proc/interrupts   /proc/ioports
CHILD $ exit
16:41:31    482| The child has exited.
16:41:31    482| The parent is exiting.
```

As you can see from the output, the parent is blocked while the child is executing—precisely the desired behavior. As soon as the child exits, the parent continues along on its way.

Using Return Codes

In the previous section where I covered `wait` functions, there is information on a few macros that deal with the return code of a child process. This is the value that is returned from the argument to `exit()` or returned from an instance of `return` while in `main()`.

Generally, Linux programs are expected to return 0 for success and some value greater than 0 on failure. Many programs, particularly shell scripts and utilities, use these numbers for information. For instance, the make utility checks the return code of all the programs it invokes, and if there is a failure, it will normally halt the make so that the problem can be corrected. Shell scripts can use `if` and operators, such as `&&`, to change their behavior depending on whether or not a given command succeeded or failed.

The exit code makes more sense for some programs than for others. For instance, if the `ls` program is given a name of a single directory to list, and that directory does not exist, clearly an error occurs and it is the duty of `ls` to report the error and return an appropriate exit code. On the other hand, if your application is a GUI one, you might inform the user of the error and then continue executing, rather than exit immediately with an error code.

Returning exit codes is simple, as you've seen; you simply have your program pass a nonzero value to a call to `exit()`. Catching the codes is not hard either. Listing 12-4 shows a version of the previous program that displays some information about the cause for termination of the executed program.

Note   Listing 12-4 is available online.

Listing 12-4: **Reading return codes**

```
#include <stdio.h>
#include <unistd.h>
```

Continued

Listing 12-4 *(continued)*

```
#include <stdarg.h>
#include <time.h>
#include <sys/types.h>
#include <sys/wait.h>
#include <unistd.h>
#include <stdlib.h>

int tprintf(const char *fmt, ...);
void waitchildren(int signum);

int main(void) {
  pid_t pid;
  int status;

  pid = fork();

  if (pid == 0) {
    tprintf("Hello from the child process!\n");
    setenv("PS1", "CHILD \\$ ", 1);
    tprintf("I'm calling exec.\n");
    execl("/bin/sh", "/bin/sh", NULL);
    tprintf("You should never see this because the child is already gone.\n");
  } else if (pid != -1) {

    tprintf("Hello from the parent, pid %d.\n", getpid());
    tprintf("The parent has forked process %d.\n", pid);
    tprintf("The parent is waiting for the child to exit.\n");
    waitpid(pid, &status, 0);
    tprintf("The child has exited.\n");
    if (WIFEXITED(status)) {
      tprintf("The child exited normally with code %d.\n",
          WEXITSTATUS(status));
    }
    if (WIFSIGNALED(status)) {
      tprintf("The child exited because of signal %d.\n",
          WTERMSIG(status));
    }
    tprintf("The parent is exiting.\n");
  } else {
    tprintf("There was an error with forking.\n");
  }
  return 0;
}

int tprintf(const char *fmt, ...) {
  va_list args;
  struct tm *tstruct;
  time_t tsec;
```

```
    tsec = time(NULL);
    tstruct = localtime(&tsec);

    printf("%02d:%02d:%02d %5d| ",
        tstruct->tm_hour,
        tstruct->tm_min,
        tstruct->tm_sec,
        getpid());

    va_start(args, fmt);
    return vprintf(fmt, args);
}
```

This program uses several of the macros documented earlier to figure out why the child exited, and then to figure out more information about its exit. I will use a few sample invocations of the program so that you can see what it manages to do. Here is the output from the first example:

```
$ ./ch12-7
18:32:14    523| Hello from the parent, pid 523.
18:32:14    524| Hello from the child process!
18:32:14    524| I'm calling exec.
18:32:14    523| The parent has forked process 524.
18:32:14    523| The parent is waiting for the child to exit.
CHILD $ exit
exit
18:32:18    523| The child has exited.
18:32:18    523| The child exited normally with code 0.
18:32:18    523| The parent is exiting.
```

In this case, the child process, which is the shell, exited normally — returning code zero to the parent. Next you can see that other codes can get passed along. When you specify a number as a parameter to exit on the command line, this number is returned as the shell's exit status. In the following example, you can see how the parent process detected the new exit code:

```
$ ./ch12-7
18:33:30    525| Hello from the parent, pid 525.
18:33:30    526| Hello from the child process!
18:33:30    526| I'm calling exec.
18:33:30    525| The parent has forked process 526.
18:33:30    525| The parent is waiting for the child to exit.
CHILD $ exit 5
exit
18:33:32    525| The child has exited.
18:33:32    525| The child exited normally with code 5.
18:33:32    525| The parent is exiting.
```

As you can see, the parent capable of detecting that a different code was returned this time. Finally, here's an example of termination by signal:

```
$ ./ch12-7
18:34:35    527| Hello from the parent, pid 527.
18:34:35    528| Hello from the child process!
18:34:35    528| I'm calling exec.
18:34:35    527| The parent has forked process 528.
18:34:35    527| The parent is waiting for the child to exit.
CHILD $ echo My pid is $$
My pid is 528
CHILD $ kill 528
CHILD $ kill -9 528
18:34:44    527| The child has exited.
18:34:44    527| The child exited because of signal 9.
18:34:44    527| The parent is exiting.
```

In this example, the child process first displays its PID. Then, it sends itself SIGTERM. However, the shell either has a handler for or is set to ignore SIGTERM, so nothing happens. Then the process is sent SIGKILL (number 9). This signal cannot be caught, and so the process inevitably dies. The parent detects that the child exited because of a signal and displays the signal number that caused the exit.

Synchronizing Actions

Sometimes it is necessary for two or more processes to be capable of synchronizing their actions with each other. Perhaps they both need to write to a file, but only one should ever be writing to the file at any given moment to avoid potential corruption. Or, maybe a parent process needs to wait until a child process accomplishes a given task before continuing. There are many different ways of synchronizing actions. You might use file locking (described in Chapter 14), signals (Chapter 13), semaphores (Chapter 16), a pipe or FIFO (Chapter 17), or sockets (Chapters 18 and 19). Some of these actions, such as file locking and semaphores, are designed specifically for synchronization uses. The remaining items are general-purpose communication tools that you also can use for the specific purpose of inter-process synchronization.

For instance, you might have a process fork off a child to handle a specific task so that both can continue operating separately from each other. The child might exit later when it's done, which automatically sends a catchable SIGCHLD signal to the parent.

You must deal with several issues relative to synchronization that span any particular method used to implement it. This is a somewhat tricky topic and it helps to be familiar with the issues surrounding it.

Synchronization issues are often among the most difficult to track down when bugs crop up. A given program may operate perfectly for tens of thousands of executions, and then suddenly its own data files get corrupted, and you have to figure out why. If the program is one that can ever be run with two processes at once, you have to be aware of synchronization issues. Any program such as a CGI automatically has to deal with these issues, as do most network server applications.

Atomic versus non-atomic operations

Sometimes you perform a task that either needs to be completed entirely or fail entirely without the possibility of any other process to run a similar instruction at the same time. For instance, if you want to append data to the end of a file, you need to seek to the end and then perform a write. If two processes are appending data to the end of a file, though, what happens is the second process writes data between the time the first does a seek and does a write.

This happens because the seek/write operation is not atomic. If that operation were atomic, then both seek and the write would take place before any other process is allowed to write data to the file (or at least to the end of it). Linux provides a way to do this. It's called the *append mode*, in which any write is preceded automatically by an atomic seek to the end of the file.

The append mode is discussed in Chapter 14, "Introducing the Linux I/O System."

Here's another example. Consider a case in which you have software that generates serial numbers for a product. You want to assign these numbers sequentially, so you have a small file that simply holds the next number to use. When you need a new serial number, you open up the file, read its contents, seek back to the start, and write out a value one larger than the current one. However, being a successful company, you have several people assigning these numbers all at once. What happens if one process reads the value, but another reads the same value before the first has had a chance to increment it? The result is that two products receive the same serial number, which is clearly a bad situation.

The answer to this problem is that the entire operation of reading the number, seeking back to the start of the file, and writing the result needs to be atomic; no other instances of the application should be able to interact with the file while you are. Linux provides a capability called *file locking* that enables you to deal with such a situation.

Chapter 14, "Introducing the Linux I/O System," covers the file locking capability.

Deadlock

Consider the following situation. There are two files, A and B, that your process needs to access. It needs to do things to both of them without interference, so it requests a lock on file A, and when this lock is granted, it requests a lock on file B.

A separate process has the same requirements, but it requests a lock on file B and then a lock on file A. There is a potential for deadlock in this situation. Consider what would happen if the first process receives its lock on file A, and then the second process receives its lock on file B. In such a case, the first process will try to lock file B while the second process tries to lock file A. Neither process will be able to ever move forward because of this situation. Both processes will be completely locked until one of them is killed.

This problem is dubbed *deadlock*, and it occurs when synchronization attempts to go haywire, causing two or more processes to be stalled, each waiting for the other to do something. Like other synchronization problems, this one can be difficult to diagnose. Fortunately, though, you can attach gdb to an already-running, hung process and figure out where it is encountering trouble. If it's inside a call to a synchronization function such as flock(), you can bet that you have a deadlock problem.

You can take some steps to prevent deadlock from occurring. For one, try to avoid locking multiple resources at once. This is one of the most common causes of deadlock. If you absolutely must do this, take care to always lock them in the same order. Failing to do so is an invitation for deadlock to occur, which is not good. When you release resources, release them in an order opposite from which you requested them.

Race conditions

The examples of synchronization problems—the incrementing counter problem, deadlock, the append problem, and so on—are all instances of a more general class of problem called the *race condition*. A race condition occurs any time you have an operation whose outcome depends solely on the order in which processes at a critical part of code are scheduled for execution by the kernel. That is, two processes race to complete something.

Note   Race conditions can also occur with situations other than two processes competing for a resource. You could also have this occur within one process, such as with callback functions in Perl/Tk, or due to a logic error in a single process. However, the most widely encountered problem deals with multiple processes racing for access to a single resource.

Now I will examine the examples earlier in this section. The incrementing counter problem is an example of a race condition. If the first process is capable of completing its increment and writing the result back out before the second process reads anything then everything will be fine. On the other hand, if the second process reads its value before the first has a chance to finish, the data becomes corrupted.

In addition to some of the races highlighted above, other race conditions exist that are commonly encountered in Linux systems. One of them is the so-called *tmp race*, which is a serious security problem in many shell scripts.

On Linux systems, the /tmp directory is a place for storing temporary files. Typically, it is cleaned out when the system boots, or it is cleaned periodically by a cron job. The /tmp directory is used as scratch space for all sorts of different programs that need a space to shove data temporarily. The /tmp is a world-writable directory, which means that it allows any user with an account on the system to place files or directories there.

So far, this is fine. However, any user with an account on the system also can place symbolic links there. This is fine as well, unless users become malicious about it.

Suppose the system administrator of a Linux system routinely runs a program that writes data out to a file named /tmp/mydata. If one of the users with an account on the system notices this, the user maliciously might create a symbolic link named /tmp/mydata pointing to the file /etc/passwd. The next time the system administrator runs the program, it will open up /etc/mydata for writing. However, being a symbolic link, it will open up /etc/passwd, truncate the file, and replace it with the temporary data! This will mean that nobody, including the sytem adminstrator, will be able to log on to the system — a major problem! Note that the same is applicable to other users on the system. An attacker might create a symbolic link to, for instance, somebody's mail inbox, destroying its entire contents of a program running as the other user tried to open the symbolic link for writing.

Some users thought of this problem, and decided that they would try to thwart the potential attacker by checking to see if the file /tmp/mydata exists before opening it, perhaps by attempting to stat it. Perhaps this might work, but not always. If an attacker manages to create the file between the time the program checked for its existence and the time the program opened it, the same vulnerability exists. Attackers have been able to do this too.

 Cross-Reference For more details about stat(), see Chapter 11, "Files, Directories, and Devices."

So you must defeat this type of attack. One way is to use mkdir() to create a directory in /tmp. With mkdir(), you can specify the permissions on the directory, which are set in an atomic fashion when the directory is created, so you can prevent anyone else from creating files in it. When you're done, simply remove the directory and continue on your way.

Another way is to avoid the use of /tmp altogether. Perhaps you can store your files in the home directory of a calling user, or you might be able to redesign your program to avoid the need for temporary files altogether. There are other solutions that can provide you with an atomic operation, but these are some of the easiest to understand and implement.

Spinning and busy waiting

Spinning is not solely a synchronization issue but frequently is enountered as such. A program is said to be spinning if it is running through a loop without apparently making progress. A specific example of this is the busy wait, in which a program continually runs through a loop waiting for a certain event to occur.

For example, on some old PCs, one reads input from the keyboard by repeatedly polling the keyboard to see if there is any data there to read. This is, of course, possible on Linux by using non-blocking reads. However, doing so is a very bad idea; you eat up lots of CPU resources that could otherwise go to other processes, and makes yourself out to be a resource hog.

Linux provides the programmer with many capabilities specifically designed to help avoid the need to busy wait. Among your alternatives to busy waits are setting signal handlers to invoke when a certain event occurs, using the `select()` call for multiplexing across I/O channels, and simply having better algorithm design. Some users might insert a command like `sleep(1)` each time through the loop, claiming that it is no longer busy waiting. In reality, it still is busy waiting, except less CPU resources are consumed because the program does not consume resources while sleeping.

Understanding Security

One of the most confusing aspects of the process model on Linux is that of security. I'll start by covering the basics and then I'll go into more detail about the process security model.

Basics

In its most simple (and most common) case, each Linux process essentially holds two values: a uid and a gid. These values are used by the Linux kernel to determine what the process can do, and in some cases, what can be done to the process.

As an example, if you try to open a file, your process's uid is compared with the uid of the file owner. If they are the same, you can open the file. If not, you need some additional permissions, such as group or world permission, to be able to open the file. Similarly, if you want to send a signal to a process, the recipient process must have the same uid as the sending process. In this way, the system prevents people from causing unwanted effects in each other's processes.

When you log in to a Linux system, your uid and gid values are set (by the login program, typically) and then the shell's process is invoked. Because the uid and gid are values that are passed along through both fork() and exec(), any programs that you start inherit these same values.

Internals

The system described previously sounds pretty simple, and it is. Most programs live out their lives with a single uid and gid value only. However, there are really eight such values, plus another, somewhat of a maverick one, as you'll see next. Table 12-2 lists the eight values associated with a process.

<table>
<tr><td colspan="3">Table 12-2
Per-Process Security Attributes</td></tr>
<tr><td>*Attribute*</td><td>*Meaning*</td><td>*Functions*</td></tr>
<tr><td>real user ID</td><td>The uid of the person that invoked this process.</td><td>getuid(), setuid(), setruid(), setreuid()</td></tr>
<tr><td>effective user ID</td><td>The user ID under which the process is currently running, for the purpose of evaluating permissions.</td><td>geteuid(), setuid(), seteuid(), setreuid()</td></tr>
<tr><td>filesystem user ID</td><td>The user ID that is used solely for evaluating permissions of file system access. In almost all cases, this is identical to the effective user ID.</td><td>setfsuid() sets this value specifically. It is also implicitly set by any call changing the effective uid, such as setuid(), seteuid(), and setreuid().</td></tr>
<tr><td>Saved user ID</td><td>The original effective user ID of the process that is set when the program running in the process is first invoked.</td><td>setuid(), but only if the process's effective uid is that of the superuser.</td></tr>
</table>

Continued

Table 12-2 (continued)		
Attribute	**Meaning**	**Functions**
`real group ID`	The uid of the primary group of the user that invoked this process.	`getgid()`, `setgid()`, `setrgid()`, `setregid()`
`effective group ID`	The primary group ID under which the process is currently running.	`getegid()`, `setgid()`, `setegid()`, `setregid()`
`filesystem group ID`	The primary group ID under which file system accesses are authenticated against. In almost all circumstances, this is identical to the effective user ID.	`setfsgid()` sets this value specifically. Also, it is set implicitly by any call changing the effective gid, such as `setgid()`, `setegid()`, and `setregid()`.
`saved group ID`	The original effective group ID of the process that is set when the program running in the process is first invoked.	`setgid()`, but only if the process's effective uid is the superuser.

Don't worry about the specific meanings of all these attributes right now; I'll go into these later when I discuss the Linux `setuid()` and `setgid()` mechanism. What you can learn from this table is that the process security model in Linux is much more complex than a single uid and a single gid. Each process may have these eight different values. One may indicate, for instance, a certain uid to be used for file system access. Other activities, such as sending and receiving signals, may be authenticated based on a different uid. There are many different functions that you can use to change these values, each having some fairly complex invocation rules.

In Table 12-2, note that the `filesystem user ID` and `filesystem group ID` values are features unique to Linux. Other operating systems do not necessarily have those features, so their use is discouraged unless you specifically must modify the file system uid without modifying the effective uid, which is an extremely rare requirement. Furthermore, Linux implements these functions according to the POSIX saved IDs specification; other, particularly older, operating systems may not have as many features or behave in the same manner as Linux in this regard. Therefore, if you need to port code using setuid or setgid features to or from Linux, make certain that you check the documentation on both platforms to ensure that your actions have the desired effect.

When a normal process is invoked, all four of the user ID values and all four of the group ID values are set to a single value: the uid of the process and the gid of the process, respectively. A great majority of programs on your system act in this fashion.

However, some programs have more complex requirements. When such a program is started, the real uid and real gid of the process are saved. The remaining three fields for both the gid and the uid are set to the new values. After this is done, it is possible to switch back and forth between permission sets.

Besides these eight values, there is a ninth attribute to be considered as well: the supplementary group list. This is a list of additional groups, beyond the user's login group, to which the user is considered a member, as defined in /etc/group. The contents of this list can only be changed by a process whose effective uid is that of the superuser (0), and even then, changing the value of this list (except in some cases to completely zero it out) is not recommended. You get the contents of the list by using getgroups() and it can be set with setgroups() or initgroups(). Because this list does not change across setuid or setgid changes, it can be ignored for the remainder of the discussion on setuid and setgid, and their roles in the Linux security model.

setuid and setgid

Most programs on Linux are content with working under the permissions of the user that runs them. However, there are some situations in which other permissions are necessary.

Consider, for example, a game that maintains a high-scores file. You do not want people to be capable of arbitrarily editing the file, because doing so gives them the opportunity to cheat and record whatever scores they like. So you need to restrict permissions on the file such that normal accounts don't have write access to it.

But what about the game program itself? It needs to have write access, but it doesn't have such access because it's running under the permissions of the user running it. To get around this problem, you can make the game setuid. This means that, when the game starts, it will run under the permissions of some other user, and it will be capable of freely flipping between the two permission sets while running. In other words, this enables the game to run as the normal user for most of its life, but flip to the special uid when it needs to write to the file.

To make a program setuid, you turn on the setuid bit of its file in the file system, and chown the file to the user that it should be setuid to. Similarly, to make a program setgid, you turn on the setgid bit of its file in the file system, and chgrp the file to the group that it should be setgid to. When such a program is invoked, the saved ID, effective ID, and file system ID are all set to the new value; only the real ID indicates the original person who runs it.

Depending on your perspective, the setuid/setgid mechanism could be the single greatest mistake in the entire 30-year history of UNIX, or a feature that permits modern applications to function. Most people take a more moderate approach and view setuid/setgid as a necessary evil that should be avoided whenever possible, but one that does have a certain place on the system.

setuid- and setgid-Related Functions

I'm going to give you a summary of all the different functions that effect the process's permission settings on a Linux system so that you can better understand what the examples are doing. After that, there is an extremely important discussion on the security implications of using these functions, and tips to avoid problems. The setuid/setgid feature of Linux is one of the most frequent sources of security bugs, especially when combined with other problems such as buffer overflows, so extreme caution must be exercised when writing setuid/setgid software.

Table 12-3 lists all the setuid- and setgid-related functions in Linux. The Modifies column indicates what values the function can modify. The May Change To column indicates the possible values that may be used when changed. Note that if the effective uid is 0, for the superuser, any of these values may be changed to *anything*. The Returns column indicates the value returned by the function, and the Notes column indicates special notes about a function.

These functions require the inclusion of unistd.h and sys/types.h. They are prototyped as follows:

```
uid_t getuid(void);
gid_t getgid(void);
int   setuid(uid_t uid);
int   setgid(gid_t gid);
uid_t geteuid(void);
gid_t getegid(void);
int   seteuid(uid_t euid);
int   setegid(gid_t egid);
int   setreuid(uid_t ruid, uid_t euid);
int   setregid(gid_t rgid, gid_t egid);
int   setfsuid(uid_t fsuid);
int   setfsgid(uid_t fsgid);
```

Table 12-3
Process setuid/setgid Functions

Function	Modifies	May Change To	Returns	Notes
getuid	n/a	n/a	Real uid.	
getgid	n/a	n/a	Real gid.	
setuid	Real uid (if run by superuser), effective uid, file system uid, saved uid (if and only if run by the superuser).	Real uid, effective uid, saved uid.	0 on success, –1 on failure.	Behaves as seteuid() unless running as superuser.
setgid	Real gid, effective gid, file system gid, saved gid (if and only if run by the superuser).	Real gid, effective gid, saved gid.	0 on success, –1 on failure.	Behaves as setegid() unless running as superuser.
geteuid	n/a	n/a	The current effective uid of the process.	
getegid	n/a	n/a	The current effective gid of the process.	
seteuid	Effective uid, file system uid.	Real uid, effective uid, saved uid.	0 on success, –1 on failure.	
setegid	Effective gid, file system gid.	Real gid, effective gid, saved gid.	0 on success, –1 on failure.	
setreuid	Real uid, effective uid, file system uid.	Real uid, effective uid, saved uid.	0 on success, –1 on failure.	Some Linux documentation incorrectly states that this function is capable of modifying the saved uid. The file system uid is set to the new effective uid.

Continued

Table 12-3 (continued)

Function	Modifies	May Change To	Returns	Notes
setregid	Real gid, effective gid, file system gid.	Real gid, effective gid, saved gid.	0 on success, −1 on failure.	Some Linux documentation incorrectly states that this function is capable of modifying the saved gid. The file system gid is set to the new effective gid.
setfsuid	File system uid.	Effective uid, real uid, saved uid, file system uid.	Previous file system uid value on success, current file system uid value on failure.	Should be avoided except in extreme situations.
setfsgid	File system gid.	Effective gid, real gid, saved gid, file system gid.	Previous file system gid value on success, current file system gid value on failure.	Should be avoided except in extreme situations.

Use of setuid- and setgid-Related Functions

Now that you've seen what the various functions are, here is an example of how to use them. Listing 12-5 demonstrates how to open a file normally only openable by root. To do this, the program must run setuid to root, as I will explain later.

Note   Listing 12-5 is available online.

Listing 12-5: **Sample setuid program**

```c
#include <stdio.h>
#include <unistd.h>
#include <stdarg.h>
#include <time.h>
#include <sys/types.h>
#include <sys/stat.h>
#include <fcntl.h>
#include <unistd.h>
#include <stdlib.h>
#include <errno.h>

int tprintf(const char *fmt, ...);
void enhancedperms(void);
void normalperms(void);
void tryopen(void);

int ruid, euid;

int main(void) {

  /* FIRST THING: save of uid values and IMMEDIATELY ditch extra permissions.
   */

  ruid = getuid();
  euid = geteuid();
  normalperms();

  /* If the two values were equal, the program wasn't set setuid in the
     filesystem (or was just run by root in the first place).  */

  if (ruid == euid) {
    tprintf("Warning: This program wasn't marked setuid in the filesystem\n");
    tprintf("or you are running the program as root.\n");
  }

  tryopen();
```

Continued

Listing 12-5 *(continued)*

```
    enhancedperms();
    tryopen();
    normalperms();

    tprintf("Exiting now.\n");
    return 0;
}

int tprintf(const char *fmt, ...) {
    va_list args;
    struct tm *tstruct;
    time_t tsec;

    tsec = time(NULL);
    tstruct = localtime(&tsec);

    printf("%02d:%02d:%02d %5d| ",
            tstruct->tm_hour,
            tstruct->tm_min,
            tstruct->tm_sec,
            geteuid());

    va_start(args, fmt);
    return vprintf(fmt, args);
}

void enhancedperms(void) {
    if (seteuid(euid) == -1) {
        tprintf("Failed to switch to enhanced permissions: %s\n",
            sys_errlist[errno]);
        exit(255);
    } else {
        tprintf("Switched to enhanced permissions.\n");
    }
}

void normalperms(void) {
    if (seteuid(ruid) == -1) {
        tprintf("Failed to switch to normal permissions: %s\n",
            sys_errlist[errno]);
        exit(255);
    } else {
        tprintf("Switched to normal permissions.\n");
    }
}

void tryopen(void) {
    char *filename = "/etc/shadow";
```

```
   int result;

   result = open(filename, O_RDONLY);
   if (result == -1) {
     tprintf("Open failed: %s\n", sys_errlist[errno]);
   } else {
     tprintf("Open was successful.\n");
     close(result);
   }
}
```

This program is designed to show you how setuid can effect the program. When the program begins, it runs with the enhanced (0) effective uid. The first thing it does is it saves off the real and effective uids, and then it immediately gets rid of the enhanced uid. Notice that throughout the program, it uses the extra permissions as little as possible, immediately reverting to the real uid when done.

The program tries to open the /etc/shadow file, which should exist on most Linux systems. Only root should be capable of opening this file; its permissions prevents other users from being capable of doing so. Compile and test this program first without marking it setuid in the file system:

```
$ gcc -Wall -o ch12-8 ch12-8.c
$ ./ch12-8
09:26:47  1000| Switched to normal permissions.
09:26:47  1000| Warning: This program wasn't marked setuid in the filesystem.
09:26:47  1000| Open failed: Permission denied
09:26:47  1000| Switched to enhanced permissions.
09:26:47  1000| Open failed: Permission denied
09:26:47  1000| Switched to normal permissions.
09:26:47  1000| Exiting now.
```

Notice that this program displays its effective uid at the start of each line instead of displaying its process ID. My personal uid is 1000; yours may be different. Recall that programs that are not marked setuid have all four uid values set to the same thing. So when this program thinks it's switching to the ehnahced permissions (based on the saved effective uid), really it is not making any change at all. Therefore, both open attempts fail.

To mark the program setuid to root, you need to log in as or su to root. Here's how you might do that:

```
$ su
Password: Your Password
# chown root ch12-8
# chmod u+s ch12-8
# exit
```

Now, back at your normal account, try running the program again. Notice the difference in the results this time:

```
$ ./ch12-8
09:30:25 1000| Switched to normal permissions.
09:30:25 1000| Open failed: Permission denied
09:30:25    0| Switched to enhanced permissions.
09:30:25    0| Open was successful.
09:30:25 1000| Switched to normal permissions.
09:30:25 1000| Exiting now.
```

This time, the program's effective uid did change when it called seteuid(). Moreover, the call to open() successfully managed to open the file for reading because the program was running as root at the time. Notice how the same call failed between the time the program gave up its extra permissions and it reclaimed them.

If you glance at Table 12-3, you'll notice that, if your effective uid is 0, the setuid() function can be used to change the effective, real, and saved uids. You can do this to remove any possibility of your process regaining the enhanced (or any other) permissions permanently. If you are not running with an effective uid of 0, you cannot possibly ditch these permissions permanently.

Listing 12-6 shows a modification of the code to demonstrate that. Notice that the program dies when it tries to regain root permissions after they were permanently revoked.

Note Listing 12-6 is available online.

Listing 12-6: **Revoking permissions**

```c
#include <stdio.h>
#include <unistd.h>
#include <stdarg.h>
#include <time.h>
#include <sys/types.h>
#include <sys/stat.h>
#include <fcntl.h>
#include <unistd.h>
#include <stdlib.h>
#include <errno.h>

int tprintf(const char *fmt, ...);
void enhancedperms(void);
void normalperms(void);
void permnormalperms(void);
void tryopen(void);
```

```
int ruid, euid;

int main(void) {

  /* FIRST THING: save of uid values and IMMEDIATELY ditch extra permissions.
   */

  ruid = getuid();
  euid = geteuid();
  normalperms();

  /* If the two values were equal, the program wasn't set setuid in the
     filesystem.  */

  if (ruid == euid) {
    tprintf("Warning: This program wasn't marked setuid in the filesystem.\n");
  }

  tryopen();

  /* Try to open with enhanced permissions. */

  enhancedperms();
  tryopen();

  /* Print out the info while using enhanced permissions. */
  tprintf("Real uid = %d, effective uid = %d\n", getuid(), geteuid());

  /* Permanently switch to normal permissions and display the information. */
  permnormalperms();
  tprintf("Real uid = %d, effective uid = %d\n", getuid(), geteuid());

  tprintf("Now, I'll try to go back to enhanced permissions.\n");
  enhancedperms();
  tryopen();
  normalperms();

  tprintf("Exiting now.\n");
  return 0;
}

int tprintf(const char *fmt, ...) {
  va_list args;
  struct tm *tstruct;
  time_t tsec;

  tsec = time(NULL);
```

Continued

Listing 12-6 *(continued)*

```
  tstruct = localtime(&tsec);

  printf("%02d:%02d:%02d %5d| ",
       tstruct->tm_hour,
       tstruct->tm_min,
       tstruct->tm_sec,
       geteuid());

  va_start(args, fmt);
  return vprintf(fmt, args);
}

void enhancedperms(void) {
  if (seteuid(euid) == -1) {
    tprintf("Failed to switch to enhanced permissions: %s\n",
        sys_errlist[errno]);
    exit(255);
  } else {
    tprintf("Switched to enhanced permissions.\n");
  }
}

void normalperms(void) {
  if (seteuid(ruid) == -1) {
    tprintf("Failed to switch to normal permissions: %s\n",
        sys_errlist[errno]);
    exit(255);
  } else {
    tprintf("Switched to normal permissions.\n");
  }
}

void tryopen(void) {
  char *filename = "/etc/shadow";
  int result;

  result = open(filename, O_RDONLY);
  if (result == -1) {
    tprintf("Open failed: %s\n", sys_errlist[errno]);
  } else {
    tprintf("Open was successful.\n");
    close(result);
  }
}

void permnormalperms(void) {
  if (setuid(ruid) == 01) {
    tprintf("Failed to permanently switch to normal permissions: %s\n",
```

```
        sys_errlist[errno]);
    exit(255);
  } else {
    tprintf("Permanently switched to normal permissions.\n");
  }
}
```

Like the previous program (see Listing 12-5), when this program starts, it automatically has the enhanced permissions because it is marked setuid in the file system. Like the previous one, it removes these permissions as soon as possible. It tries to open the file, and then attains the enhanced permissions and tries to open the file a second time. This program then permanently removes the enhanced permissions from its process. As an exercise, it tries to recapture those permissions, but this will fail and the program will exit.

Here is what the execution of the program looks like if properly marked setuid:

```
$ ./ch12-9
10:12:21  1000|  Switched to normal permissions.
10:12:21  1000|  Open failed: Permission denied
10:12:21     0|  Switched to enhanced permissions.
10:12:21     0|  Open was successful.
10:12:21     0|  Real uid = 1000, effective uid = 0
10:12:21  1000|  Permanently switched to normal permissions.
10:12:21  1000|  Real uid = 1000, effective uid = 1000
10:12:21  1000|  Now, I'll try to go back to enhanced permissions.
10:12:21  1000|  Failed to switch to enhanced permissions: Operation not
permitted
```

As before, if you run the program without marking it setuid, all of these requests will succeed but will have no effect. Here is the output of such an execution:

```
$ ./ch12-9
10:12:01  1000|  Switched to normal permissions.
10:12:01  1000|  Warning: This program wasn't marked setuid in the filesystem.
10:12:01  1000|  Open failed: Permission denied
10:12:01  1000|  Switched to enhanced permissions.
10:12:01  1000|  Open failed: Permission denied
10:12:01  1000|  Real uid = 1000, effective uid = 1000
10:12:01  1000|  Permanently switched to normal permissions.
10:12:01  1000|  Real uid = 1000, effective uid = 1000
10:12:01  1000|  Now, I'll try to go back to enhanced permissions.
10:12:01  1000|  Switched to enhanced permissions.
10:12:01  1000|  Open failed: Permission denied
10:12:01  1000|  Switched to normal permissions.
10:12:01  1000|  Exiting now.
```

setuid/setgid side effects

Because these systems introduce extra capability for programs to access files, some other subsystems are affected if you choose to make your program setuid or setgid. Generally, this takes the form of disabling a certain behavior for security reasons.

Behavior Across exec()

When you want to execute another program, you need to be aware of what happens. Not all of this is documented in manpages for the exec functions, so there is a chance that the behavior may change eventually.

When you call exec on a program, it copies the real and effective uid and gid values from the existing process first. Then, it checks for setuid or setgid bits and makes changes to effective permissions as warranted. Finally, it copies the effective uid and effective gid to the saved uid and saved gid, respectively.

This means that the permissions for the executed program depend on exactly how the permissions in your program were set prior to the call. If the effective uid (or gid) is the same as the real uid (or gid) in your program, meaning that presumably you either permanently or temporarily removed the enhanced permissions, the called program will have no access at all to enhanced permissions.

On the other hand, if your effective uid (or gid) is set to an enhanced value at the time you call exec, the called program will have this as its effective uid and saved uid — essentially behaving as if it were setuid, even if it is not.

Therefore, it is highly recommended that you drop additional permissions by calling seteuid() prior to executing another program. Additionally, you can find some more security warnings about exec() in the next section.

Impact on ld-linux.so

This effects you only if you are manipulating shared libraries.

Cross-Reference   See Chapter 9, "Libraries and Linking," for more details on shared libraries.

The Linux dynamic loader disables certain behavior if it is being called to link a setuid or setgid program. It ignores the LD_PRELOAD environment variable. If it does not, this would enable the user to override library calls with others that potentially could run with the extended permissions of the setuid program, which would be a big security risk.

The loader also ignores the `LD_LIBRARY_PATH` and `LD_AOUT_LIBRARY_PATH` environment variables for a similar reason. In this case, users could provide trojan libraries that would pretend to be real ones but could abuse the extra permissions of a setuid program.

Impact on fork()

When you call `fork()`, all of the uid and gid information is copied to the child process. Therefore, immediately after the fork, the permission information is identical between the parent and child process. If your child (or, for that matter, the parent) process is doing something for which it does not need the extra permissions, you should remove (permanently, if possible) these permissions from the process.

Staying secure with setuid/setgid

In addition to introducing some powerful capabilities, setuid and setgid also introduce an amazing potential for problems. In addition to the security ideas presented here that are specifically applicable to the setuid and setgid programs, there are other security principles that you should also be familiar with and apply.

 The other security principles that you should apply are mentioned in Chapter 27, "Understanding Security and Code." The security issues that relate to the buffer overflow problem are of particular importance.

Most of these tips operate on the principle of least permission. This means that your software should always be written such that, at any given moment, it has the least possible permissions required to accomplish a given task.

Don't setuid to root

One of the most dangerous things you possibly could do is make a program setuid to root. Sometimes, there is no way around it and the program must be setuid to root. However, if at all possible, avoid this.

Consider the example of the game program that needs to write out its score file. Instead of making the program setuid to root, a wise programmer instead creates a special user on the system and makes the program setuid to that user. That way, if there is a flaw in the game's code or a security violation occurs, the potential harm is far less.

Another option is to create a group for the program to use and make it setgid to that group.

Remove Extra Permissions Immediately

Immediately after you save away the necessary information, you should ditch the extra permissions. Later on in your program, you should reclaim them only when doing so is necessary for proper operation of the program. Furthermore, you should remove the extra permissions permanently if possible, and as soon as possible.

Doing so can help prevent damage that may occur from a bug in your program or a security breach involving your program. Even if you are certain that your program is secure and bug-free, it doesn't hurt to be cautious just in case you may have overlooked something.

Never Use execlp() or execvp()

If you run a program that is setuid, you should absolutely never use these functions. The reason is that they rely on the PATH that is passed in to you by the user running the program. Consider what might happen if you run execlp() on ls, but the PATH starts with an entry pointing to that user's home directory. If you run the program with full permissions, all that the user has to do is place a custom ls binary somewhere on the PATH before the system's copy of ls, and instantly the user can get custom code to run with extra permissions.

Because of this problem, you should always use absolute pathnames when you want to use exec for something new from a setuid program. The only time that you should consider execlp() is if you completely drop your enhanced permissions, either temporarily or permanently. Even so, as a precaution, you should avoid it if possible.

Never Invoke a Shell or Use System()

Another thing that you should avoid is executing a shell. Shells grab many things from the environment, and if they are passed material from the user, it is possible to convince them to do undesired things with their extended permissions. For instance, a historic way to exploit this would be to embed something such as, ; rm -rf /etc in input (such as a filename) to a setuid program. If the program uses a shell or calls system() for it, the shell will see the semicolon, treat it as a command separator, and then proceed to delete all of the /etc directory if the program is run setuid to root.

Because the system() library call is implemented in terms of a call to the shell, you should avoid it as well. Along the same lines, you should double-check any input that you send to an executed program while it is setuid. Your checks should make sure that only sensible and expected types of input are passed through. If you are using Perl, its taint-checking features will help identify these problems for you. Additionally, if you are using Perl, you should avoid the backtick and glob items because both of them are also implemented in terms of the shell.

Close File Descriptors

This one is a simple but important tip. If you have a program that is setuid, and the program used this to its advantage to open a file to which it would otherwise not have had access (or had less access), these extra permissions stay with that file descriptor even if you subsequently relinquish your enhanced permissions. Therefore, you should always close such file descriptors as soon as possible. In no case should you `exec` another program without first closing any such file descriptors in your own program because your own file descriptors and their permissions are passed on to the executed program. Imagine, for instance, a program that reads /etc/shadow and then executes another program. If the first program does not close the file descriptor for /etc/shadow, the second can read the contents of that file even if it is not invoked with any other special permissions.

Beware of the umask

Although your programs should be specifying explicitly good and secure permissions when files or directories are created via calls to `open()` or `mkdir()`, sometimes they aren't. When you run setuid, you may prefer to create files that the normal user invoking your program cannot read from or write to. However, if you are a bit sloppy and the original invoker is tries to obtain access to these files, the original user's umask may be set such that your program creates the file with incorrect permissions while setuid. A quick fix is to manually issue a call such as `umask(022)` to reset it to a more normal value.

Watch for Deadly Signals

As you'll learn in the Sending Signals section of Chapter 13, "Understanding Signals," your process can only receive signals from another process whose effective uid is the same as yours, or from the superuser. However, when you are running a program that is setuid, your effective uid may change from moment to moment as execution progresses. Signals can be sent that may make your program dump core or die in some cases, and you should be extremely cautious with them.

Note that this is the original impetus for the creation of the file system uid and gid on Linux. The Linux NFS server wanted to setuid to a *less* privileged uid than it would normally use (root). However, when it did that, it could become vulnerable to signals sent to it by the owner of such an account. Therefore, it simply sets the file system uid to avoid this problem.

Heed General Security Principles

Earlier in this chapter, I touched on the /tmp race problem. Be careful about this in your own programs if they are setuid. Also, take note of all the security issues mentioned in Chapter 27, "Understanding Security and Code"; they become even more important in a program that is setuid or setgid.

Avoid setuid/setgid Entirely

Another way to help ensure the security of your programs is to avoid the usage of setuid or setgid code entirely. Some alternatives that may work for you might be implementing a client/server pair. The server could run with the necessary permissions from the start, and the client could run without setuid, asking the server for the specific information that it needs. Although this is not always a viable alternative, it can be for some tasks. You have a large number of options to choose among.

Cross-Reference   See Chapters 17 through 19 for details on some of the options.

Some would argue that avoiding setuid/setgid entirely is your best option. It may well turn out to be, but there can still be cases when setuid/setgid permissions are practically unavoidable.

Summary

In this chapter, you learned about the Linux process model. Specifically, you learned:

✦ Each process is its own separate space, providing only certain well-defined ways to communicate with other processes.

✦ Because each process has its own memory area, one errant process cannot cause another one to crash as well; the worst it can do is cause itself to terminate.

✦ Each process is associated with information, such as its environment, file descriptors, scheduling information, and security information.

✦ To create a new process, you use `fork()`. This call creates a copy of the existing process, and both processes then continue to execute simultaneously.

✦ To run another program, you use `exec()`. This call replaces the program running in the current process with a different program; your current program ceases to exist unless the call fails for some reason.

✦ Processes leave around certain information after they terminate. If you don't clean it up, it can use up valuable space in the process table.

✦ You can wait either until a process exits or clean up the information from an already exited process by using one of the `wait()` family of functions.

✦ If you want your process to continue when starting a new one, you should fork and then execute the new program.

✦ You can find out why a process exited by examining the status information from one of the `wait()` functions.

✦ Synchronization between processes is a tricky but important topic.

✦ An atomic operation cannot be interrupted by another similar operation.

✦ Deadlock occurs when two or more processes are waiting for each other to release some resource.

✦ Race conditions occur when random flukes of scheduling influence whether or not your code will work.

✦ Busy waiting occurs when your program continuously polls for an event to occur instead of waiting to be told of it.

✦ Each process has a set of eight ID values plus a list of groups.

✦ You can manipulate these values and groups in setuid or setgid programs, but doing so can be dangerous.

✦   ✦   ✦

Understanding Signals

◆ ◆ ◆ ◆

In This Chapter

The use of signals

Signal handlers

Signal sending

Signals and
system calls

Dangers of signal
handlers

◆ ◆ ◆ ◆

Signals are a way of informing a process that an event
has occurred. In this chapter, you will learn about the
mechanics of signals. Then, you'll learn about signal handlers,
which are used to allow the execution of your program to be
diverted to a special function when a signal is received. After
that, you will find out how to transmit signals, the interaction
between signals and system calls, and some potential pitfalls
that may arise from the use of signals.

The Use of Signals

Linux offers you many different ways to enable processes to
communicate between each other. Processes might use an
Internet socket to communicate with a process on a computer
in a different country. Or, they might use a pipe to communicate
with a process on the same computer.

Signals are also a form of communication, but they are designed
to solve a different problem. Rather than sending data from place
to place, a signal is sent to a process to inform it that a certain
event occurred. For instance, if I am running a program and press
Ctrl+C, the process receives SIGINT — the interrupt signal. By
default, this causes the process to terminate. However, if the
process is something like an editor, I might want something else
to occur. So, I can have the process catch the SIGINT signal and
do something specific when it occurs. That is, no matter where
in the code the program is, when it receives SIGINT, it will
immediately execute the handler for it. In the case of an editor,
the handler might save the user's file and then exit. Or, it might
ask for confirmation to exit. Finally, it may just ignore SIGINT
altogether.

Signals can be useful in other ways as well. Suppose that you are doing some complex calculations, perhaps in a tight loop, that take several hours to complete. Every 30 seconds, you'd like to inform the operator of the status of the program. You don't update it every time through the loop, because this would significantly slow down the program. However, without signals, you have to poll the system time every time through the loop. Although faster than doing I/O (input or output) every time, it is still a performance burden.

Rather than polling the system, you can ask the operating system to send you a signal 30 seconds in the future. You then continue with your calculations, never needing to bother to check the time. After 30 seconds, the operating system sends your process a signal. This causes your program to jump to the signal handler, which might print out the status information and ask for another signal to be sent 30 seconds later.

As another example, if you are communicating with another process with something like a pipe, and that process suddenly exits, your process will be sent a SIGPIPE signal informing you of this. If one of your process's child processes exits, you'll receive a SIGCHLD signal, possibly an indication that you should wait on the child process.

Cross-Reference   Chapter 12, "Processes in Linux," cover waiting on the child process.

Signal Handlers

Normally, when your process receives a signal, the system will take action on it. This could mean just ignoring the signal, or it could mean terminating your process. If you want something else to occur, you can register a handler for any particular signal.

When your process receives a signal, if you have a handler set for that signal, the handler function is called immediately. This occurs regardless of where the execution point is in your code; when your program receives a signal, it is sent to the handler immediately.

When you register a signal handler, you use the signal(2) call. There are two signals you cannot catch: SIGSTOP and SIGKILL. All others can have handlers registered for them.

Two special signal handlers are also available: SIG_IGN, which ignores the signal completely; and SIG_DFL, which restores the system default behavior when a given signal is received.

Basic handlers

Here's an example of a program that sets a handler for SIGTERM rather than let the program die when that signal is received:

```c
#include <stdio.h>
#include <signal.h>
#include <stdarg.h>
#include <time.h>
#include <unistd.h>
#include <sys/types.h>

int tprintf(const char *fmt, ...);
void sighandler(int signum);

int main(void) {
char buffer[200];

  if (signal(SIGTERM, &sighandler) == SIG_ERR) {
    tprintf("Couldn't register signal handler.\n");
  }

  while (1) {
    fgets(buffer, sizeof(buffer), stdin);
    tprintf("Input: %s", buffer);
  }
  return 0;
}

int tprintf(const char *fmt, ...) {
  va_list args;
  struct tm *tstruct;
  time_t tsec;

  tsec = time(NULL);
  tstruct = localtime(&tsec);

  printf("%02d:%02d:%02d %5d| ",
         tstruct->tm_hour,
         tstruct->tm_min,
         tstruct->tm_sec,
         getpid());

  va_start(args, fmt);
  return vprintf(fmt, args);
}

void sighandler(int signum) {
  tprintf("Caught signal SIGTERM.\n");
}
```

As you run this program, it will simply echo back your input to you. Now, in a separate window, use `kill` *pid* to send it a SIGTERM signal. Each line of output conveniently contains the pid for your use. Instead of terminating on the spot, it prints out a message and continues. After printing the message, the code resumes whatever it was doing before (in this case, probably waiting for input). You can exit the program by using Ctrl+C. Here's some sample output:

```
$ ./ch13-1
Hi!
20:19:02   764| Input: Hi!
I'll send you a signal now.
20:19:10   764| Input: I'll send you a signal now.
20:19:13   764| Caught signal SIGTERM.
You got it!
20:19:48   764| Input: You got it!
```

You can also have multiple signals delivered to a single handler. Moreover, you can also have multiple handlers in your program. Listing 13-1 shows a program that uses both of these methods.

Note   Listing 13-1 is available online.

Listing 13-1: A Multi-signal handler

```
#include <stdio.h>
#include <signal.h>
#include <string.h>
#include <stdarg.h>
#include <time.h>
#include <unistd.h>
#include <sys/types.h>

int tprintf(const char *fmt, ...);
void sighandler(int signum);
void continuehandler(int signum);
char buffer[200];

int main(void) {

    /* Initialize buffer in case someone interrupts the program before
        assigning anything to it. */

    strcpy(buffer, "None\n");

    if (signal(SIGTERM, &sighandler) == SIG_ERR) {
        tprintf("Couldn't register signal handler for SIGTERM.\n");
```

```
  }

  if (signal(SIGINT, &sighandler) == SIG_ERR) {
    tprintf("Couldn't register signal handler for SIGINT.\n");
  }

  if (signal(SIGCONT, &continuehandler)  == SIG_ERR) {
    tprintf("Couldn't register signal handler for SIGCONT.\n");
  }

  while (1) {
    fgets(buffer, sizeof(buffer), stdin);
    tprintf("Input: %s", buffer);
  }
  return 0;
}

int tprintf(const char *fmt, ...) {
  va_list args;
  struct tm *tstruct;
  time_t tsec;

  tsec = time(NULL);
  tstruct = localtime(&tsec);

  printf("%02d:%02d:%02d %5d| ",
         tstruct->tm_hour,
         tstruct->tm_min,
         tstruct->tm_sec,
         getpid());

  va_start(args, fmt);
  return vprintf(fmt, args);
}

void sighandler(int signum) {
  tprintf("Caught signal %d.\n", signum);
}

void continuehandler(int signum) {
  tprintf("Continuing.\n");
  tprintf("Your last input was: %s", buffer);
}
```

This time, the program catches two more signals. SIGTERM and SIGINT will both be handled by the `sighandler()` function. SIGCONT will be handled by the `continuehandler()` function. Give this program a try to see how it works:

```
$ ./ch13-2
Hello.
10:12:49   443| Input: Hello.
This is another test.
10:12:52   443| Input: This is another test.
Ctrl+C
10:12:53   443| Caught signal 2.
```

Notice that Ctrl+C will no longer exit the program. You can also go into another window and send it SIGTERM by running kill *pid*, where *pid* is the process ID of the sample program, (443) in this example. When you do so, the process will show:

```
10:14:55   443| Caught signal 15.
```

Next, you can try suspending the process with Ctrl+Z:

```
This is some more input.
10:15:30   443| Input: This is some more input.
Ctrl+Z
[1]+  Stopped                    ./ch13-2
$ ls -d /proc/i*
/proc/ide  /proc/interrupts  /proc/ioports
$ fg
./ch13-2
10:15:44   443| Continuing.
10:15:44   443| Your last input was: This is some more input.
```

So, you can cause the program to stop (which sends it an uncatchable SIGSTOP signal). Then, you might do something else, such as run ls. When you're ready to continue again, the program receives SIGCONT. When it does, the handler conveniently shows you your last input to help you remember where you left off. Other programs might redraw the screen or take other actions to restore context, if necessary.

Notice that even if the program is stopped, it can still receive signals queued for examination upon continuing as shown in this example (watch what happens when the program returns):

```
Here is some more input.
10:24:01   443| Input: Here is some more input.

[1]+  Stopped                    ./ch13-2
$ kill 443
$ kill -INT 443
$ fg
./ch13-2
10:24:15   443| Continuing.
10:24:15   443| Your last input was: Here is some more input.
10:24:15   443| Caught signal 15.
10:24:15   443| Caught signal 2.
```

Because this program catches the standard signals used to kill it, it's a bit harder to convince to terminate. You'll need to send it SIGKILL (number 9), which is uncatchable. In this example, you can use `kill -9 443` to achieve the desired result.

Blocking signals

Sometimes you may prefer to delay the delivery of signals to your program. Instead of having them be totally ignored or having them interrupt your flow of execution by calling a handler, you may want the signal to be blocked for the moment but still delivered later. You might be executing some timing-critical piece of code, or the signal may cause confusion for the user.

In our particular case, consider the situation in which SIGTERM is received in the middle of entering a string. The program will display a message immediately, and the screen will display a confusing message. Rather than doing this, it would be better to notify the user of the signal reception later, after each line of input.

Listing 13-2 shows a program that will do just that for two out of the three signals that the program catches.

Note   Listing 13-2 is available online.

Listing 13-2: **Blocking signals**

```
#include <stdio.h>
#include <signal.h>
#include <stdarg.h>
#include <time.h>
#include <string.h>
#include <unistd.h>
#include <sys/types.h>

int tprintf(const char *fmt, ...);
void sighandler(int signum);
void continuehandler(int signum);
char buffer[200];

int main(void) {

   sigset_t blockset;

   /* Initialize buffer in case someone interrupts the program
before
      assigning anything to it. */

   strcpy(buffer, "None\n");
```

Continued

Listing 13-2 *(continued)*

```
  if (signal(SIGTERM, &sighandler) == SIG_ERR) {
    tprintf("Couldn't register signal handler for SIGTERM.\n");
  }

  if (signal(SIGINT, &sighandler) == SIG_ERR) {
    tprintf("Couldn't register signal handler for SIGINT.\n");
  }

  if (signal(SIGCONT, &continuehandler)  == SIG_ERR) {
    tprintf("Couldn't register signal handler for SIGCONT.\n");
  }

  sigemptyset(&blockset);
  sigaddset(&blockset, SIGTERM);
  sigaddset(&blockset, SIGINT);

  while (1) {
    sigprocmask(SIG_BLOCK, &blockset, NULL);
    fgets(buffer, sizeof(buffer), stdin);
    tprintf("Input: %s", buffer);
    sigprocmask(SIG_UNBLOCK, &blockset, NULL);
  }
  return 0;
}

int tprintf(const char *fmt, ...) {
  va_list args;
  struct tm *tstruct;
  time_t tsec;

  tsec = time(NULL);
  tstruct = localtime(&tsec);

  printf("%02d:%02d:%02d %5d| ",
         tstruct->tm_hour,
         tstruct->tm_min,
         tstruct->tm_sec,
         getpid());

  va_start(args, fmt);
  return vprintf(fmt, args);
}

void sighandler(int signum) {
  tprintf("Caught signal %d.\n", signum);
}

void continuehandler(int signum) {
```

```
        tprintf("Continuing.\n");
        tprintf("Your last input was: %s", buffer);
    }
```

Let's look at how this code works its magic. First, we declare a variable of type sigset_t. This is the generic signal set type that holds a set of signals. Down below, it is initialized to be the empty set. Then, two signals, those we will eventually want to block, are added to the set by the calls to sigaddset(). In order to actually block the signals, the sigprocmask() function is called with a SIG_BLOCK parameter. After this call, the input is read and printed. Then, sigprocmask() is called again, but this time with a SIG_UNBLOCK parameter. If any signals were pending but not delivered due to the previous block, they will all be delivered and handled before sigprocmask() returns to the caller. Therefore, any pending signals are handled at this time.

Note that you can also use SIG_SETMASK for sigprocmask(). The other two options (SIG_BLOCK and SIG_UNBLOCK)add or subtract entries from the process's signal mask; this one sets it to an absolute value. Therefore, the first call, to block some signals, could be the same. The one to remove blocking could use SIG_SETMASK with an empty set to achieve the same effect.

When the loop resets to the top, the relevant signals are once again blocked before input is read. In this way, the signals are always blocked while input is being read from the terminal but are allowed to be delivered once for each time through the loop.

Before looking at a sample session of code, you should be aware of a special case when Ctrl+C is pressed to send SIGINT or Ctrl+Z is pressed to send SIGSTOP. You already know that the terminal, by default, sends input to the programs in line-sized chunks. Internally, the terminal driver keeps a buffer of input before delivering it to the program, so that the terminal driver can handle backspace correction and the like. Pressing Ctrl+C or Ctrl+Z will erase the contents of the buffer, so when you press one of these keys, even though the screen may not reflect it, the buffer is being erased. You'll be able to see that behavior in the following example:

```
$ ./ch13-1
This is a normal line of input.
14:57:15   676| Input: This is a normal line of input.
I am sending SIGINT here Ctrl+C in the middle of this line.
14:57:35   676| Input:  in the middle of this line.
14:57:35   676| Caught signal 2.
Now I will send SIGSTOP at the end of this line Ctrl+Z
[1]+  Stopped                 ./ch13-3
$ fg
./ch13-3
```

```
14:58:04    676| Continuing.
14:58:04    676| Your last input was:  in the middle of this line.
and now I'll type another line.
14:58:10    676| Input: and now I'll type another line.
```

Now watch what happens when you send SIGTERM from another window. Nothing.
However, after you type another line of input, the program indicates that it received
SIGTERM:

```
Here is some more input.
14:59:44    676| Input: Here is some more input.
14:59:44    676| Caught signal 15.
```

You can also check to see what signals are pending (waiting for delivery due to
being blocked) without causing the signals to actually be delivered. Listing 13-3
demonstrates one way to do that, as an add-on to the application.

Note   Listing 13-3 is available online.

Listing 13-3: **Pending signals**

```
#include <stdio.h>
#include <signal.h>
#include <stdarg.h>
#include <time.h>
#include <string.h>
#include <unistd.h>
#include <sys/types.h>

int tprintf(const char *fmt, ...);
void sighandler(int signum);
void continuehandler(int signum);
char buffer[200];

int main(void) {

  sigset_t blockset, pending;
  int pendingcount;

  /* Initialize buffer in case someone interrupts the program before
     assigning anything to it. */

  strcpy(buffer, "None\n");

  if (signal(SIGTERM, &sighandler) == SIG_ERR) {
    tprintf("Couldn't register signal handler for SIGTERM.\n");
  }
```

```
    if (signal(SIGINT, &sighandler) == SIG_ERR) {
      tprintf("Couldn't register signal handler for SIGINT.\n");
    }

    if (signal(SIGCONT, &continuehandler)  == SIG_ERR) {
      tprintf("Couldn't register signal handler for SIGCONT.\n");
    }

    sigemptyset(&blockset);
    sigaddset(&blockset, SIGTERM);
    sigaddset(&blockset, SIGINT);

    while (1) {
      sigprocmask(SIG_BLOCK, &blockset, NULL);
      fgets(buffer, sizeof(buffer), stdin);
      tprintf("Input: %s", buffer);

      /* Process pending signals. */

      sigpending(&pending);
      pendingcount = 0;
      if (sigismember(&pending, SIGINT)) pendingcount++;
      if (sigismember(&pending, SIGTERM)) pendingcount++;
      if (pendingcount) {
        tprintf("There are %d signals pending.\n", pendingcount);
      }

      /* Deliver them. */

      sigprocmask(SIG_UNBLOCK, &blockset, NULL);
    }
    return 0;
}

int tprintf(const char *fmt, ...) {
  va_list args;
  struct tm *tstruct;
  time_t tsec;

  tsec = time(NULL);
  tstruct = localtime(&tsec);

  printf("%02d:%02d:%02d %5d| ",
         tstruct->tm_hour,
         tstruct->tm_min,
         tstruct->tm_sec,
         getpid());

  va_start(args, fmt);
  return vprintf(fmt, args);
}
```

Continued

Listing 13-3 *(continued)*

```
void sighandler(int signum) {
  tprintf("Caught signal %d.\n", signum);
}

void continuehandler(int signum) {
  tprintf("Continuing.\n");
  tprintf("Your last input was: %s", buffer);
}
```

The `sigpending()` function fills in a signal set just like one that was manually created earlier. You can then use `sigismember()` to test to see whether a particular entry in the signal is set. This information is checked to see if any signals were pending. In our situation, the algorithm presented is sufficient. Note, though, that there is a race condition in the code. If a new signal arrives that is blocked between the time that `sigpending()` is run and the time that the print statement is run, the displayed count can be incorrect. The handlers will still be run when they are unblocked, even if the program displays the incorrect output.

Advanced handlers

Linux provides another way to define handlers: `sigaction()`. This function enables you to be more precise about what happens when a given signal is received. The `sigaction()` function is defined as follows:

```
int sigaction(int signum,  const  struct  sigaction  *act, struct sigaction
*oldact);
```

To use this function, you pass it a signal number, a pointer to a signal action structure, and a pointer to a structure to fill in with the old information, which may be NULL if you don't care about the old information.

The structure has the following definition:

```
    struct sigaction {
      void (*sa_handler)(int);
      void (*sa_sigaction)(int, siginfo_t *, void *);
      sigset_t sa_mask;
      int sa_flags;
    }
```

You can specify a standard signal handler as with `signal()` in the `sa_handler` field. Alternatively, if you specify SA_SIGINFO in the `sa_flags` area, you may specify a handler in `sa_sigaction` instead. This handler is passed more information about the signal received, as you will learn later in this section.

The `sa_mask` field is a signal set indicating which signals should be automatically blocked when the signal handler for this signal is executing. These are automatically unblocked when the signal handler returns. By default, the signal for this handler is automatically included, but this default behavior can be suppressed by specifying `SA_NODEFER` or `SA_NOMASK` in the `sa_flags` area.

You may use a value of 0 for `sa_flags` to use all the default options. If you prefer to set flags, the value can be attained by taking the bitwise OR of the available flags shown in Table 13-1.

Table 13-1
Flag and Their Meanings

Flag	Meaning
SA_NOCLDSTOP	Indicates that, if the specified signal is SIGCHLD, the signal should only be delivered when a child process is terminated, not when one stops.
SA_NODEFER	Suppresses automatic blocking of the signal handler's own signal while the signal handler is executing.
SA_NOMASK	Same as SA_NODEFER.
SA_ONESHOT	After the specified signal handler has been called once, the signal handler is automatically restored to SIG_DFL.
SA_RESETHAND	Same as SA_ONESHOT.
SA_RESTART	Enables automatic restart of the system calls that would not normally automatically restart after receiving this signal.
SA_SIGINFO	Specifies that you will specify the signal handler with sa_sigaction instead of sa_handler.

You also need to be aware of the second and third parameters to the signal handler specified with `sa_sigaction`. Of them, `siginfo_t` is a structure, which is defined as follows:

```
siginfo_t {
    int       si_signo;   /* Signal number */
    int       si_errno;   /* An errno value */
    int       si_code;    /* Signal code */
    pid_t     si_pid;     /* Sending process ID */
    uid_t     si_uid;     /* Real user ID of sending process */
    int       si_status;  /* Exit value or signal */
    clock_t   si_utime;   /* User time consumed */
    clock_t   si_stime;   /* System time consumed */
    sigval_t  si_value;   /* Signal value */
    int       si_int;     /* POSIX.1b signal */
    void *    si_ptr;     /* POSIX.1b signal */
```

```
    void *   si_addr;   /* Memory location that caused fault */
    int      si_band;   /* Band event */
    int      si_fd;     /* File descriptor */
}
```

Not all of these members will be set for every signal or for every method of sending a signal. For instance, si_addr only makes sense for signals such as SIGSEGV and SIGBUS that indicate a problem at a specific address. The possible values for si_code are defined in Table 13-2.

Table 13-2
Possible Values for si_code

Code	Meaning	Valid For
BUS_ADRALN	An address alignment problem has occurred.	SIGBUS only
BUS_ADRERR	There was an access attempt to a machine address that does not exist.	SIGBUS only
BUS_OBJERR	An error specific for this particular object occurred.	SIGBUG only
CLD_CONTINUED	A child process, currently stopped, has received SIGCONT.	SIGCHLD only
CLD_DUMPED	A child process terminated with an error that generally causes a core dump.	SIGCHLD only
CLD_EXITED	A child process has exited.	SIGCHLD only
CLD_KILLED	A child process has been killed.	SIGCHLD only
CLD_STOPPED	A child process has been stopped by SIGSTOP or similar.	SIGCHLD only
CLD_TRAPPED	A child being traced has encountered a trap.	SIGCHLD only
FPE_FLTDIV	There was an attempt to perform a floating-point divide by zero.	SIGFPE only
FPE_FLTINV	An invalid floating-point operation was attempted.	SIGFPE only
FPE_FLTOVF	A floating-point overflow condition has been detected.	SIGFPE only
FPE_FLTRES	The floating-point operation result may be rounded.	SIGFPE only
FPE_FLTSUB	An out-of-range floating-point subscript was used.	SIGFPE only
FPE_FLTUND	A floating-point underflow condition has been detected.	SIGFPE only
FPE_INTDIV	There was an attempt to perform an integer divide by zero.	SIGFPE only

Code	Meaning	Valid For
FPE_INTOVF	An integer overflow condition has been detected.	SIGFPE only
ILL_BADSTK	A stack error has occurred.	SIGILL only
ILL_COPROC	An illegal coprocessor operation was attempted.	SIGILL only
ILL_ILLADR	An illegal addressing mode error occurred.	SIGILL only
ILL_ILLOPC	An illegal opcode error occurred.	SIGILL only
ILL_ILLOPN	An illegal operand error occurred.	SIGILL only
ILL_ILLTRP	An illegal trap error occurred.	SIGILL only
ILL_PRVOPC	An illegal attempt to use a privileged opcode occurred.	SIGILL only
ILL_PRVREG	An illegal attempt to access a privileged register occurred.	SIGILL only
POLL_ERR	An error has occurred with one of the watched descriptors.	SIGPOLL only
POLL_HUP	The remote end of one of the watched descriptors has been closed.	SIGPOLL only
POLL_IN	Data is available for reading on one of the watched descriptors.	SIGPOLL only
POLL_MSG	It is now possible to read a message from one of the watched descriptors.	SIGPOLL only
POLL_OUT	It is now possible to write data to one of the watched descriptors.	SIGPOLL only
POLL_PRI	It is now possible to read high-priority input data from one of the watched descriptors.	SIGPOLL only
SEGV_ACCERR	An access error has occurred due to lack of permission to access the requested address.	SIGSEGV only
SEGV_MAPERR	A mapping error has occurred.	SIGSEGV only
SI_ASYNCIO	Asynchronous (non-blocking) I/O has finished.	All signals
SI_KERNEL	The kernel generated this signal.	All signals
SI_MESGQ	Message queue state changed.	All signals
SI_QUEUE	The signal came from sigqueue.	All signals
SI_TIMER	A timer expired, causing the signal to be sent.	All signals
SI_USER	Signal was user-generated by this or another process. See "Signal Sending" later in this chapter.	All signals
TRAP_BRKPT	A process breakpoint has been reached.	SIGTRAP only
TRAP_TRACE	A process trace condition has occurred.	SIGTRAP only

Considering this additional information that can be delivered to the application, let's rewrite it to take advantage of it. Listing 13-4 presents a new version that uses `sigaction` to catch its signals.

Note   Listing 13-4 is available online.

Listing 13-4: **Example with sigaction**

```
#include <stdio.h>
#include <signal.h>
#include <stdarg.h>
#include <time.h>
#include <unistd.h>
#include <string.h>
#include <sys/types.h>

#if defined(__linux__) && !defined(SI_KERNEL)
#define SI_KERNEL 0x80
#endif


int tprintf(const char *fmt, ...);
void sighandler(int signum, siginfo_t *info, void *extra);
void continuehandler(int signum, siginfo_t *info, void *extra);
char buffer[200];

int main(void) {
  struct sigaction act;
  sigset_t blockset, pending;
  int pendingcount;

  /* Initialize buffer in case someone interrupts the program before
     assigning anything to it. */

  strcpy(buffer, "None\n");

  /* Set some values to apply to all the signals. */

  sigemptyset(&blockset);
  act.sa_mask = blockset;
  act.sa_flags = SA_SIGINFO;

  /* Two signals use the same handler. */
  act.sa_sigaction = &sighandler;
  if (sigaction(SIGTERM, &act, NULL) == -1) {
    tprintf("Couldn't register signal handler for SIGTERM.\n");
  }
  if (sigaction(SIGINT, &act, NULL) == -1) {
    tprintf("Couldn't register signal handler for SIGINT.\n");
  }
```

```
  /* A different handler for the third. */
  act.sa_sigaction = &continuehandler;
  if (sigaction(SIGCONT, &act, NULL) == -1) {
    tprintf("Couldn't register signal handler for SIGCONT.\n");
  }

  /* blockset is still the empty set. */

  sigaddset(&blockset, SIGTERM);
  sigaddset(&blockset, SIGINT);

  while (1) {
    sigprocmask(SIG_BLOCK, &blockset, NULL);
    fgets(buffer, sizeof(buffer), stdin);
    tprintf("Input: %s", buffer);

    /* Process pending signals. */

    sigpending(&pending);
    pendingcount = 0;
    if (sigismember(&pending, SIGINT)) pendingcount++;
    if (sigismember(&pending, SIGTERM)) pendingcount++;
    if (pendingcount) {
      tprintf("There are %d signals pending.\n", pendingcount);
    }

    /* Deliver them. */

    sigprocmask(SIG_UNBLOCK, &blockset, NULL);
  }
  return 0;
}

int tprintf(const char *fmt, ...) {
  va_list args;
  struct tm *tstruct;
  time_t tsec;

  tsec = time(NULL);
  tstruct = localtime(&tsec);

  printf("%02d:%02d:%02d %5d| ",
         tstruct->tm_hour,
         tstruct->tm_min,
         tstruct->tm_sec,
         getpid());

  va_start(args, fmt);
  return vprintf(fmt, args);
}
```

Continued

Listing 13-4 *(continued)*

```
void sighandler(int signum, siginfo_t *info, void *extra) {
  tprintf("Caught signal %d from ", signum);
  switch (info->si_code) {
    case SI_USER: printf("a user process\n");
                  break;
    case SI_KERNEL: printf("the kernel\n");
                    break;
    default: printf("something strange\n");
  }
}

void continuehandler(int signum, siginfo_t *info, void *extra) {
  tprintf("Continuing.\n");
  tprintf("Your last input was: %s", buffer);
}
```

The structure of this program is fundamentally the same as of the other signal-using programs I have discussed so far. It registers a signal handler for three signals, handles blocks, and the like. However, it uses the advanced sa_sigaction feature of sigaction().

Signal Sending

To send a signal is fairly easy. You need to know two pieces of information: which signal to send, and what process to send it to. You can find a list of the available signals in the signal(7) manpage. You may only send signals to processes that you own, or if you are running as root, you may send signals to any process. You can also request a signal to be sent to yourself at a certain point in the future. Let's first look at the basics.

You can send a signal to yourself by calling raise(). It takes a single parameter, the signal number to send. Listing 13-5 shows an example that causes the program to terminate by SIGKILL when the user types in **exit** as the input.

Note   Listing 13-5 is available online.

Listing 13-5: **Example of sending a signal**

```
#include <stdio.h>
#include <signal.h>
#include <stdarg.h>
```

```
#include <time.h>
#include <string.h>
#include <unistd.h>
#include <sys/types.h>
#include <string.h>

int tprintf(const char *fmt, ...);
void sighandler(int signum);
void continuehandler(int signum);
char buffer[200];

int main(void) {

  sigset_t blockset, pending;
  int pendingcount;

  /* Initialize buffer in case someone interrupts the program before
     assigning anything to it. */

  strcpy(buffer, "None\n");

  if (signal(SIGTERM, &sighandler) == SIG_ERR) {
    tprintf("Couldn't register signal handler for SIGTERM.\n");
  }

  if (signal(SIGINT, &sighandler) == SIG_ERR) {
    tprintf("Couldn't register signal handler for SIGINT.\n");
  }

  if (signal(SIGCONT, &continuehandler)  == SIG_ERR) {
    tprintf("Couldn't register signal handler for SIGCONT.\n");
  }

  sigemptyset(&blockset);
  sigaddset(&blockset, SIGTERM);
  sigaddset(&blockset, SIGINT);

  while (1) {
    sigprocmask(SIG_BLOCK, &blockset, NULL);
    fgets(buffer, sizeof(buffer), stdin);
    tprintf("Input: %s", buffer);

    /* Process pending signals. */

    sigpending(&pending);
    pendingcount = 0;
    if (sigismember(&pending, SIGINT)) pendingcount++;
    if (sigismember(&pending, SIGTERM)) pendingcount++;
    if (pendingcount) {
      tprintf("There are %d signals pending.\n", pendingcount);
    }
```

Continued

Listing 13-5 *(continued)*

```
    /* Deliver them. */

    sigprocmask(SIG_UNBLOCK, &blockset, NULL);

    /* Exit if requested. */

    if (strcmp(buffer, "exit\n") == 0) {
      raise(SIGKILL);
    }
  }
  return 0;
}

int tprintf(const char *fmt, ...) {
  va_list args;
  struct tm *tstruct;
  time_t tsec;

  tsec = time(NULL);
  tstruct = localtime(&tsec);

  printf("%02d:%02d:%02d %5d| ",
         tstruct->tm_hour,
         tstruct->tm_min,
         tstruct->tm_sec,
         getpid());

  va_start(args, fmt);
  return vprintf(fmt, args);
}

void sighandler(int signum) {
  tprintf("Caught signal %d.\n", signum);
}

void continuehandler(int signum) {
  tprintf("Continuing.\n");
  tprintf("Your last input was: %s", buffer);
}
```

When the program runs, and you type in **exit**, the program will send itself a SIGKILL signal, which will cause it to exit. Of course, in this case, you could just as easily call exit(), but sometimes you need to send yourself another signal—for instance, to invoke an alarm handler before an alarm is due.

You can also send a signal to another process. The function to do this is kill(2). This function takes two parameters: the pid of the process to send the signal to, and the signal to send.

These two functions are fairly self-explanatory and uninteresting. More interesting is the alarm(2) function, which arranges for your process to receive a signal at a specified point of time in the future. The single argument to alarm() is the number of seconds in the future at which the SIGALRM signal should be sent to your process. Whenever you call alarm(), any previously requested alarms (but not pending blocked SIGALRM signals!) are canceled, and the time remaining on one of these previous requests is returned. Listing 13-6 shows a version of the program that will automatically exit after thirty seconds of inactivity.

Note   Listing 13-6 is available online.

Listing 13-6: **Example with inactivity timeout**

```
#include <stdio.h>
#include <signal.h>
#include <stdarg.h>
#include <time.h>
#include <string.h>
#include <unistd.h>
#include <sys/types.h>
#include <string.h>

int tprintf(const char *fmt, ...);
void sighandler(int signum);
void continuehandler(int signum);
void alarmhandler(int signum);
char buffer[200];

int main(void) {

  sigset_t blockset, pending;
  int pendingcount;

  /* Initialize buffer in case someone interrupts the program before
     assigning anything to it. */

  strcpy(buffer, "None\n");

  if (signal(SIGTERM, &sighandler) == SIG_ERR) {
    tprintf("Couldn't register signal handler for SIGTERM.\n");
  }
```

Continued

Listing 13-6 *(continued)*

```
  if (signal(SIGINT, &sighandler) == SIG_ERR) {
    tprintf("Couldn't register signal handler for SIGINT.\n");
  }

  if (signal(SIGCONT, &continuehandler)  == SIG_ERR) {
    tprintf("Couldn't register signal handler for SIGCONT.\n");
  }

  if (signal(SIGALRM, &alarmhandler) == SIG_ERR) {
    tprintf("Couldn't register signal handler for SIGALRM.\n");
  }

  sigemptyset(&blockset);
  sigaddset(&blockset, SIGTERM);
  sigaddset(&blockset, SIGINT);

  while (1) {
    sigprocmask(SIG_BLOCK, &blockset, NULL);
    alarm(30);
    fgets(buffer, sizeof(buffer), stdin);
    tprintf("Input: %s", buffer);

    /* Process pending signals. */

    sigpending(&pending);
    pendingcount = 0;
    if (sigismember(&pending, SIGINT)) pendingcount++;
    if (sigismember(&pending, SIGTERM)) pendingcount++;
    if (pendingcount) {
      tprintf("There are %d signals pending.\n", pendingcount);
    }

    /* Deliver them. */

    sigprocmask(SIG_UNBLOCK, &blockset, NULL);

    /* Exit if requested. */

    if (strcmp(buffer, "exit\n") == 0) {
      raise(SIGKILL);
    }
  }
  return 0;
}

int tprintf(const char *fmt, ...) {
  va_list args;
  struct tm *tstruct;
```

```
    time_t tsec;

    tsec = time(NULL);
    tstruct = localtime(&tsec);

    printf("%02d:%02d:%02d %5d| ",
           tstruct->tm_hour,
           tstruct->tm_min,
           tstruct->tm_sec,
           getpid());

    va_start(args, fmt);
    return vprintf(fmt, args);
}

void sighandler(int signum) {
  tprintf("Caught signal %d.\n", signum);
}

void continuehandler(int signum) {
  tprintf("Continuing.\n");
  tprintf("Your last input was: %s", buffer);
}

void alarmhandler(int signum) {
  tprintf("No activity for 30 seconds, exiting.\n");
  exit(0);
}
```

The program requests an alarm for 30 seconds in the future immediately before
reading a line of input. Each time a line is read, the alarm is reset immediately prior.
You can now see the effects by running the program:

```
$ ./ch13-7
Hello.
18:44:51  1100| Input: Hello.
This is a test.
18:44:56  1100| Input: This is a test.
I'll now wait for 30 seconds.
18:44:59  1100| Input: I'll now wait for 30 seconds.
18:45:29  1100| No activity for 30 seconds, exiting.
$
```

This is one of several options for requesting a signal in the future. You can also
use the setitimer() function, which gives you more control and precision. It is
defined as follows, with the header in sys/time.h:

```
int setitimer(int which, const struct itimerval *value, struct itimerval
*ovalue);
```

The `which` parameter can take three options:

1. The first is `ITIMER_REAL`, which causes your timer to count time according to system clock. It will send the SIGALRM signal when the time has expired, just as the `alarm()` function will, so you cannot really use the two of these together.

2. The second option is `ITIMER_PROF`, which counts time whenever your program is executing. The SIGPROF signal is sent when it has expired.

3. The final option is `ITIMER_VIRTUAL`, which tracks time only when the process is executing in user mode. When it expires, SIGVTALRM is sent.

The `itimerval` structure is defined as follows:

```
struct itimerval {
  struct timeval it_interval; /* next value */
  struct timeval it_value;    /* current value */
};
```

The `it_value` field specifies the amount of time until the next triggering of the alarm. If it is zero, the alarm is disabled. The `it_interval` field specifies a value to which the alarm should be reset to after each time it is triggered; if it is zero, the alarm will only be triggered once. The structure that it uses is defined as:

```
struct timeval {
  long tv_sec;                /* seconds */
  long tv_usec;              /* microseconds */
};
```

So you can see that you get more precision with this function than `alarm()`, although keep in mind that the time required to set the alarm, that to deliver the signal, and the time taken up by other processes on the system may affect the accuracy of the signal.

So, you might be able to rewrite your program to use this type of timer as shown in Listing 13-7.

Note Listing 13-7 is available online.

Listing 13-7: **Example using setitimer()**

```
#include <stdio.h>
#include <signal.h>
#include <stdarg.h>
#include <time.h>
#include <string.h>
#include <sys/time.h>
#include <unistd.h>
```

```
#include <sys/types.h>
#include <string.h>

int tprintf(const char *fmt, ...);
void sighandler(int signum);
void continuehandler(int signum);
void alarmhandler(int signum);
char buffer[200];

int main(void) {

  struct itimerval itimer;
  sigset_t blockset, pending;
  int pendingcount;

  /* Initialize buffer in case someone interrupts the program before
     assigning anything to it. */

  strcpy(buffer, "None\n");

  if (signal(SIGTERM, &sighandler) == SIG_ERR) {
    tprintf("Couldn't register signal handler for SIGTERM.\n");
  }

  if (signal(SIGINT, &sighandler) == SIG_ERR) {
    tprintf("Couldn't register signal handler for SIGINT.\n");
  }

  if (signal(SIGCONT, &continuehandler)  == SIG_ERR) {
    tprintf("Couldn't register signal handler for SIGCONT.\n");
  }

  if (signal(SIGALRM, &alarmhandler) == SIG_ERR) {
    tprintf("Couldn't register signal handler for SIGALRM.\n");
  }

  sigemptyset(&blockset);
  sigaddset(&blockset, SIGTERM);
  sigaddset(&blockset, SIGINT);

  itimer.it_interval.tv_usec = 0;
  itimer.it_interval.tv_sec = 0;

  itimer.it_value.tv_usec = 0;
  itimer.it_value.tv_sec = 30;

  while (1) {
    sigprocmask(SIG_BLOCK, &blockset, NULL);
    setitimer(ITIMER_REAL, &itimer, NULL);
    fgets(buffer, sizeof(buffer), stdin);
    tprintf("Input: %s", buffer);
```

Continued

Listing 13-7 *(continued)*

```
    /* Process pending signals. */

    sigpending(&pending);
    pendingcount = 0;
    if (sigismember(&pending, SIGINT)) pendingcount++;
    if (sigismember(&pending, SIGTERM)) pendingcount++;
    if (pendingcount) {
      tprintf("There are %d signals pending.\n", pendingcount);
    }

    /* Deliver them. */

    sigprocmask(SIG_UNBLOCK, &blockset, NULL);

    /* Exit if requested. */

    if (strcmp(buffer, "exit\n") == 0) {
      raise(SIGKILL);
    }
  }
  return 0;
}

int tprintf(const char *fmt, ...) {
  va_list args;
  struct tm *tstruct;
  time_t tsec;

  tsec = time(NULL);
  tstruct = localtime(&tsec);

  printf("%02d:%02d:%02d %5d| ",
         tstruct->tm_hour,
         tstruct->tm_min,
         tstruct->tm_sec,
         getpid());

  va_start(args, fmt);
  return vprintf(fmt, args);
}

void sighandler(int signum) {
  tprintf("Caught signal %d.\n", signum);
}

void continuehandler(int signum) {
  tprintf("Continuing.\n");
  tprintf("Your last input was: %s", buffer);
```

```
}

void alarmhandler(int signum) {
  tprintf("No activity for 30 seconds, exiting.\n");
  exit(0);
}
```

Signals and System Calls

When you decide to register a signal handler for some signals, the semantics of some system calls can be modified. The system calls that can block "forever"— (those that can read from the network or a terminal, and those that wait for other events) are included. Normally, they are not affected by signals. However, if you register a handler, the operating system can assume that you want the system call interrupted when a signal arrives. When this occurs, the system call will exit with a failure code and set errno to EINTR.

Sometimes this can be a desired behavior, but sometimes you may prefer to inhibit this behavior. You can do so by setting the SA_RESTART flag on the signal when its handler is registered with sigaction().

Caution

If you don't set this flag, your code may incorrectly interpret a signal as a failure in a system call. Worse, if you're assuming that a system call will succeed (reading from the terminal, for instance) and instead it fails, data corruption in your program can occur. Therefore, if you're using these signals, you need to be aware of the potential consequences.

For these reasons, many users prefer to use sigaction() in programs such that the semantics of signal delivery can be more tightly controlled.

Dangers of Signal Handlers

In addition to the potential problems with system calls, you may encounter other dangers in using signal handlers.

First, it is possible for a new signal to arrive while your program is already executing a signal handler. In this case, the existing signal handler's execution is interrupted, and it is called a second time. After the second execution finishes, the first resumes, and when it finishes, the program begins executing again. Keep this in mind especially if you are using static variables; you should take advantage of sigaction's capability to automatically block signals while in a handler in this situation.

Another potential concern arises when you use the fork() or exec() functions. Keep in mind that when you use the fork() function, signal handlers and masks are propagated to the child process, but pending signals are not. When you execute a new program, all the signals are reset to SIG_DFL.

It is possible to prevent the default behavior, such as an exit, for some signals. However, this can have unfortunate side-effects. Users may be confused when they can't kill a process. The process may be ignoring signals that are warning it of an impending system shutdown, and thus may be avoiding a chance to save data before a crash.

You can also use the longjmp() and siglongjmp() functions to jump out of a signal handler. While this is possible, this is not necessarily a good idea. If you try to use one of these functions to escape from SIGABORT, your program will exit anyway.

Summary

In this chapter, you learned about the following aspects of signals:

✦ Signals are sent to a process when a certain event occurs.

✦ A process may catch a signal and direct it to a special signal handler that takes some action when it is received.

✦ You can use signal() to register a handler for a signal, restore the default behavior, or tell the operating system to ignore the signal.

✦ You can find a list of available signals on your machine by running kill -l. You can also find a list in signal(7).

✦ If you use sigaction(), you can more tightly control the delivery of signals and let your handlers receive more detailed information about the signals they are called upon to process.

✦ A signal can be delivered to your own process by using raise() or to other processes by using kill().

✦ You can use alarm() and setitimer() to request signals be automatically delivered to your process at some time in the future.

✦   ✦   ✦

Introducing the Linux I/O System

I n this chapter, you'll be introduced to the I/O and
communication subsystems on Linux. You'll find that,
in Linux, you'll use many of the items documented here
to do everything from reading from files and terminals to
communicating over the Internet with a computer in a
different country. Linux tries to present you with a unified
interface to the I/O system wherever possible. Therefore, not
only can a single set of code read from a disk file as easily as it
can read from a network connection, but also you can access
things such as hardware devices and system ports with the
same interface.

Library versus System Call

In Linux, you will frequently encounter two different ways
of handling input and output (I/O) on the system. The first
involves directly using system calls. These calls include such
items as open(), read(), write(), and socket(). The
second involves using the ANSI C library calls such as
fopen(), fread(), fwrite(), and fprintf().

The difference between these two ways of I/O handling goes
deeper than simply having a different name. The C library
calls, commonly known as the stream I/O calls, are actually
wrappers around the system calls. Therefore, they technically
don't add any features to your program that you could not
write yourself.

However, stream I/O calls provide a number of conveniences
that are extremely beneficial to your programs. For one, they
automatically buffer output, minimizing the need to call the
system calls and improving performance. Second, you have

convenience functions such as `fprintf()` that enable you to format output and write it out all at once. Finally, they take care of some details of system calls for you, such as handling system calls that have been interrupted by a signal.

Cross-Reference   See Chapter 13, "Understanding Signals," for details on system calls.

Although these features are great for many programs, they can be a hindrance for others. For example, the stream I/O functions do not have some features necessary for communicating over a network. Moreover, the buffering tends to make network communication difficult because it can interfere with the protocol being used. Sometimes you may need more control than they give you, and thus you may need to use the system calls directly.

Considering these different sets of requirements, people often prefer to use stream I/O for terminal and file interaction, and system call I/O for network and pipe use. It is easy to use both methods in a single program, as long as you use only one method for any given file descriptor. In fact, you can use both methods for a single file descriptor as well, but such usage requires extreme care and can be difficult.

You can mix and match between the two features — the `fileno()` function gives you the file descriptor for a stream and the `fdopen()` function opens a stream based on an already open file descriptor. Note, though, that it is generally unwise to use both methods simultaneously.

In this chapter, I'll use both methods. I'll start by showing you programs that do the same thing written using each method to give you a basis for comparison.

Stream I/O

Stream I/O is the method taught in many C textbooks and classes because it is a portable way to do I/O. System call I/O may not necessarily be portable to non-Linux or non-UNIX platforms, especially if it contains more advanced system call I/O features.

One of the features of stream I/O is its built-in buffering, which can be a performance win for your applications. However, be aware that data that you write with one of these functions is not written out immediately. If you are writing out information such as status messages, network communication, or the like, you can use the `fflush()` call to flush it all out immediately.

Here is a fairly basic program that uses stream I/O functions; notice that this program does no error-checking at all (which is a problem that I'll address shortly):

```
#include <stdio.h>
#include <string.h>
```

```
#include <stdlib.h>

void stripcrlf(char *temp);

int main(void) {
  FILE *outfile;
  char input[80];

  printf("Select output filename: ");
  fgets(input, sizeof(input), stdin);
  stripcrlf(input);

  outfile = fopen(input, "w");

  printf("Please enter some numbers.  Use -1 when you want to exit.\n");

  do {
    fgets(input, sizeof(input), stdin);
    fwrite(input, strlen(input), 1, outfile);
    stripcrlf(input);
    fprintf(outfile, "New: %d\n",
        atoi(input) * 5 + (20 * 100) - 12);
  } while (atoi(input) != -1);
  fclose(outfile);
  return 0;
}

void stripcrlf(char *temp)
{
  while (strlen(temp) && temp[0] &&
        ((temp[strlen(temp)-1] == 13) || (temp[strlen(temp)-1] == 10))) {
    temp[strlen(temp)-1] = 0;
  }
}
```

This program reads in a filename and opens it up for writing. Then it enters a loop, reading some numbers. It writes out the number, and then a new number is generated based on the existing one to the file. The program continues doing so until -1 is supplied, at which time it writes it out, closes the output file, and exits.

Next, I'll add some error-checking to the program. As it is, the program would never know if the data it's trying to write out simply disappears into the ether. To make sure that the I/O calls are successful, the program needs to check the return values for them. Listing 14-1 shows the revised program, which has these checks.

Note   Listing 14-1 is available online.

Listing 14-1: **Revised program to check return values of I/O**

```c
#include <stdio.h>
#include <string.h>
#include <stdlib.h>
#include <errno.h>

void stripcrlf(char *temp);

int main(void) {
  FILE *outfile;
  char input[80];

  printf("Select output filename: ");
  fgets(input, sizeof(input), stdin);
  stripcrlf(input);

  outfile = fopen(input, "w");
  if (!outfile) {
    printf("Error opening output file: %s\n",
        sys_errlist[errno]);
    exit(255);
  }

  printf("Please enter some numbers.  Use -1 when you want to exit.\n");

  do {
    fgets(input, sizeof(input), stdin);
    if (fwrite(input, strlen(input), 1, outfile) != 1) {
      printf("Error writing: %s\n",
          sys_errlist[errno]);
      exit(255);
    }
    stripcrlf(input);
    if (fprintf(outfile, "New: %d\n",
        atoi(input) * 5 + (20 * 100) - 12) < 1) {
      printf("Error writing: %s\n",
          sys_errlist[errno]);
      exit(255);
    }
  } while (atoi(input) != -1);
  fclose(outfile);
  return 0;
}

void stripcrlf(char *temp)
{
  while (strlen(temp) && temp[0] &&
      ((temp[strlen(temp)-1] == 13) || (temp[strlen(temp)-1] == 10))) {
    temp[strlen(temp)-1] = 0;
  }
}
```

This time, the program checks more return codes. It still does not check fgets(), printf(), and fclose(). Also, the error-checking for fprintf() is imperfect; because I don't know an exact count of the amount of data it will be writing, I can't specifically check its return value for matching that count. The following section presents an alternative approach that uses system call I/O instead of stream I/O.

System call I/O

The same task can be accomplished by using system call I/O instead of stream I/O. Listing 14-2 presents a modified version of the previous program using system call I/O for the output to a file and stream I/O for reading and writing from the terminal. This is a model that is not infrequently encountered; especially when stream I/O is used for reading from the terminal and system call I/O for interaction with a network connection.

Note   Listing 14-2 is available online.

Listing 14-2: **Example with stream I/O**

```
#include <stdio.h>
#include <string.h>
#include <stdlib.h>
#include <errno.h>

/* The next four are for system call I/O */

#include <unistd.h>
#include <sys/types.h>
#include <sys/stat.h>
#include <fcntl.h>

void stripcrlf(char *temp);
int write_buffer(int fd, const void *buf, int count);

int main(void) {
  int outfile;
  char input[80];
  char buffer[80];

  printf("Select output filename: ");
  fgets(input, sizeof(input), stdin);
  stripcrlf(input);

  outfile = open(input, O_WRONLY | O_CREAT | O_TRUNC, 0640);

  if (outfile == -1) {
    printf("Error opening output file: %s\n",
```

Continued

Listing 14-2 *(continued)*

```
          sys_errlist[errno]);
     exit(255);
  }

  printf("Please enter some numbers.  Use -1 when you want to exit.\n");

  do {
    fgets(input, sizeof(input), stdin);
    if (write_buffer(outfile, input, strlen(input)) < 0) {
      printf("Error writing: %s\n",
          sys_errlist[errno]);
      exit(255);
    }
    stripcrlf(input);

    sprintf(buffer, "New: %d\n",
        atoi(input) * 5 + (20 * 100) - 12);

    if (write_buffer(outfile, buffer, strlen(buffer)) < 0) {
      printf("Error writing: %s\n",
          sys_errlist[errno]);
      exit(255);
    }
  } while (atoi(input) != -1);
  close(outfile);
  return 0;
}

void stripcrlf(char *temp) {
  while (strlen(temp) && temp[0] &&
      ((temp[strlen(temp)-1] == 13) || (temp[strlen(temp)-1] == 10))) {
    temp[strlen(temp)-1] = 0;
  }
}

/*
   This function writes certain number bytes from "buf" to a file
   or socket descriptor specified by "fd". The number of bytes is
   specified by "count". It returns the number of bytes written,
   or <0 on error.
*/

int write_buffer(int fd, const void *buf, int count)
{
  const void *pts = buf;
  int  status = 0, n;

  if (count < 0) return (-1);
```

```
  while (status != count) {
    n = write(fd, pts+status, count-status);
    if (n < 0) return (n);
    status += n;
  }
  return (status);
}
```

Now I'll review the changes. First, outfile is replaced with an integer file descriptor instead of a FILE *. Second, the opening of the output file is different. Although the call is more involved, it does give much more flexibility, and an opportunity to assign permissions automatically as it is opened (that is the function of the last argument).

You can call open() two ways; it is defined like this:

```
int open(const char *pathname, int flags);
int open(const char *pathname, int flags, mode_t mode);
```

In general, when you are using the O_CREAT flag, you should take care to specify a mode. In all other situations, specifying it is unnecessary and the specification will be ignored if present. Table 14-1 lists the valid values for flags. Note that you must specify exactly one of O_RDONLY, O_WRONLY, or O_RDWR. The remaining flags are optional and can be or'd with one of the above three flags to generate the final value.

Table 14-1
Flag Values

Flag	Meaning
O_APPEND	Causes all writes to take place after a seek to the end of the file, which takes place atomically with the actual write. This behavior is not guaranteed across network file systems.
O_CREAT	Creates the requested file with the specified mode (with umask applied) if it does not already exist.
O_EXCL	Causes open to fail if the file already exists when used with O_CREAT. This behavior is not guaranteed across network file systems, however.
O_NDELAY	Same as O_NONBLOCK.
O_NOCTTY	Prevents a terminal special device from automatically becoming your process's controlling terminal if you try to open it.

Continued

Table 14-1 *(continued)*

Flag	Meaning
O_NOFOLLOW	Mandates that the final name in the supplied filename not be a symbolic link.
O_NONBLOCK	Indicates that the file should be opened with non-blocking semantics on later I/O calls dealing with this descriptor.
O_RDONLY	Opens the file for reading only.
O_RDWR	Opens the file for reading and writing.
O_SYNC	Forces an immediate commit to the physical device when writing data to this descriptor.
O_TRUNC	Causes the file's existing contents to be deleted on open, if the file exists.
O_WRONLY	Opens the file for writing only.

Next, notice the call to write_buffer(). Instead of simply calling write(), the program instead calls this special function, which I'll go over next. Also notice that I use sprintf() to generate the output string. For the ultimate in speed, I might write my own integer-to-string conversion routine to add on later, but for this program, this sprintf() call will be fine.

Now take a look at the write_buffer() function. This function is necessary because write() does not guarantee that it will write out all that you request at once. It may write out half of it, or as little as one byte. It does guarantee that it will write at least one byte before returning unless there is an error.

Therefore, you need to restart the write() call if some bytes remain unwritten. That way, you are guaranteed that, if write_buffer() returns with no error code, then the write is a success. This function begins by validating its input. It then proceeds to enter a loop. In the status variable, it keeps a count of how many bytes were written thus far; this is of course initialized to 0. After each write, the value of n is examined. If it indicates an error, the error code is returned. Otherwise, it is a count of bytes written, which is added to the value in status. If status still is not up to size, it continues writing until it is.

Now, how about using system call I/O for the terminal interaction as well? Using it to write out to the terminal is trivial; using it to read is a bit more difficult. Before you begin, you need to know three standard values — file descriptor 0 corresponds to standard input, 1 to standard output, and 2 to standard error. I'll use the first two values in the program shown in Listing 14-3.

Note   Listing 14-3 is available online.

Listing 14-3: **System call I/O for terminal interaction**

```
#include <stdio.h>
#include <string.h>
#include <stdlib.h>
#include <errno.h>

/* The next four are for system call I/O */

#include <unistd.h>
#include <sys/types.h>
#include <sys/stat.h>
#include <fcntl.h>

void stripcrlf(char *temp);
int write_buffer(int fd, const void *buf, int count);
int read_buffer(int fd, void *buf, int count);
int readnlstring(int socket, char *buf, int maxlen);
int readdelimstring(int socket, char *buf, int maxlen, char delim);
void exiterror(char *message, int errnum);

const char *MESSAGE_filename = "Select output filename: ";
const char *MESSAGE_numbers =
"Please enter some numbers.  Use -1 when you want to exit.\n";

int main(void) {
  int outfile;
  char input[80];
  char buffer[80];

  /* Write the prompt for filename and read in the filename. */

  write_buffer(1, MESSAGE_filename, strlen(MESSAGE_filename));
  readnlstring(0, input, sizeof(input));

  /* Open the file */

  outfile = open(input, O_WRONLY | O_CREAT | O_TRUNC, 0640);

  if (outfile == -1) {
    exiterror("Error opening output file: ", errno);
  }

  /* Write the basic instructions. */

  write_buffer(1, MESSAGE_numbers, strlen(MESSAGE_numbers));

  do {
    /* Read a line of input. */
    readnlstring(0, input, sizeof(input));
```

Continued

Listing 14-3 *(continued)*

```
  /* Write it out with trailing newline. */
  if (write_buffer(outfile, input, strlen(input)) < 0) {
    exiterror("Error writing: ", errno);
  }
  if (write_buffer(outfile, "\n", 1) < 0) {
    exiterror("Error writing: ", errno);
  }

  sprintf(buffer, "New: %d\n",
      atoi(input) * 5 + (20 * 100) - 12);
  if (write_buffer(outfile, buffer, strlen(buffer)) < 0) {
    exiterror("Error writing: ", errno);
  }
} while (atoi(input) != -1);
close(outfile);
return 0;
}

void stripcrlf(char *temp) {
  while (strlen(temp) && temp[0] &&
    ((temp[strlen(temp)-1] == 13) || (temp[strlen(temp)-1] == 10))) {
    temp[strlen(temp)-1] = 0;
  }
}

/*
   This function writes certain number bytes from "buf" to a file
   or socket descriptor specified by "fd". The number of bytes is
   specified by "count". It returns the number of bytes written,
   or <0 on error.
*/

int write_buffer(int fd, const void *buf, int count) {
  const void *pts = buf;
  int  status = 0, n;

  if (count < 0) return (-1);

  while (status != count) {
    n = write(fd, pts+status, count-status);
    if (n < 0) return (n);
    status += n;
  }
  return (status);
}

int read_buffer(int fd, void *buf, int count) {
  void *pts = buf;
```

```
    int  status = 0, n;

    if (count < 0) return (-1);

    while (status != count) {
      n = read(fd, pts+status, count-status);
      if (n < 1) return n;
      status += n;
    }
    return (status);
}

int readnlstring(int socket, char *buf, int maxlen) {
    return readdelimstring(socket, buf, maxlen, '\n');
}

int readdelimstring(int socket, char *buf, int maxlen, char delim) {
    int status;
    int count = 0;

    while (count < maxlen - 1) {
      if ((status = read_buffer(socket, buf+count, 1)) < 1) {
        printf("Error reading.\n");
        return -1;
      }
      if (buf[count] == delim) {            /* Found the delimiter */
        buf[count] = 0;
        return 0;
      }
      count++;
    }
    buf[count] = 0;
    return 0;
}

void exiterror(char *message, int errnum) {
    write_buffer(1, message, strlen(message));
    write_buffer(1, sys_errlist[errnum], strlen(sys_errlist[errnum]));
    write_buffer(1, "\n", 1);
    exit(255);
}
```

The code for this program sure has become larger! I'll go over the pieces here. The main() function is fairly similar to its previous state. A few common messages are given now in constants so that taking their length becomes easier for use with write_buffer().A readnlstring() function that reads a single line (terminated by the newline character) using system call I/O is the rough equivalent of fgets() in the stream I/O world.

Displaying the error message on exit is now more complex, so that task now has its own function, exiterror(). The only remaining function from the standard I/O library now is sprintf(), and it doesn't perform any I/O directly.

The new read_buffer() function performs the same function as the write_buffer() does, so make sure that a certain number of bytes are read in before returning to its caller. Then there is the readdelimstring() function, for which readnlstring() is a simple wrapper. The purpose of readdelimstring() is to be capable of reading in data separated by a specific delimiter—in this case, a newline character. The readdelimstring() function reads in the string, chops off the delimiter, and saves the result. This function is not terribly efficient as is but making it more efficient would require a much more complex algorithm, and it is plenty fast for our purposes here. The key to the inefficiency is that it reads data in chunks of one byte at a time.

Error Conditions

One of the most important aspects of dealing with input and output in any program is the proper detection and handling of errors. Although your program may encounter no error at all for almost 100 percent of the time that it runs, the occasion on which something does go wrong is often the most likely to cause data corruption and problems in your program. The cause for a failure could be something such as a user entering a wrong filename, a disk filling up, a network link going down, or even a bug in another program that you're piping data to.

The first step toward preventing data loss from I/O errors is to take proper steps to identify these error conditions when they occur. For instance, you need to properly check the return values of calls to open() to make sure that the files really are open as you requested. You should check the return values of calls to write() to make sure that a disk did not fill up while you were writing your data out. You should check the return value of close() to be sure that all the data is capable of being physically written to disk without any physical media problem.

Many programmers ignore the return values of close(), intentionally or unintentionally. Especially prevalent is a tendency to not check the return value of calls to fclose() or close()—notice that the examples in this chapter represent a somewhat typical approach to error-checking: input from the terminal or output to it is not really checked. One can often assume that the terminal is functional if the program is executing; however, programs that may have information piped to or from them cannot make this assumption.

Another concern is the actual data coming in. Even if you check to make sure that reads are successful, you may not check to ensure that the data read is as you expect it to be. For instance, in the program in Listing 14-3, the input was not checked to ensure it was actually a number—or even that it was not a blank line. In this particular program, that won't cause any serious harm because it's simply for demonstration purposes—the result in the output file really doesn't matter. However, sometimes this can be a big issue. For instance, if you are expecting a first and a last name on a line, and get only a first name, a sorting function may fail because there is no value for the last name.

Using a wrapper library

As you saw in Listing 14-3, checking for errors after every call can be tedious—and, at a certain point, so annoying that some developers opt to forsake proper error-checking during development. To help make error-checking easier for programs, I wrote a module that consists of some functions that wrap around the actual calls. These functions automatically check for problems, and if one is detected, an appropriate error is printed automatically. The functions in the wrapper can also exit the program automatically, or raise a signal that can be caught. It will write to stderr by default, but this can be changed to a different file handle to enable it to write to a log file, or to a pipe that is connected to another process that does the actual logging, for instance:

```
The code for this module comes in two files: a header file and a C source file.
Here is the header file, safecalls.h.:

#ifndef __SAFECALLS_H__
#define __SAFECALLS_H__

#include <stdio.h>          /* required for FILE * stuff */
#include <sys/stat.h>         /* required for struct stat stuff */
#include <sys/types.h>
#include <signal.h>
#include <unistd.h>


#ifndef __SAFECALLS__C__
FILE *SafeLibErrorDest
#endif

char *safestrdup(const char *s);
char *safestrncpy(char *dest, const char *src, size_t n);
char *safestrcat(char *dest, const char *src, size_t n);
int safekill(pid_t pid, int sig);
char *safegetenv(const char *name);
int safechdir(const char *path);
int safemkdir(const char *path, mode_t mode);
int safestat(const char *file_name, struct stat *buf);
int safeopen(const char *pathname, int flags);
int safeopen2(const char *pathname, int flags, mode_t mode);
int safepipe(int filedes[2]);
int safedup2(int oldfd, int newfd);
```

```
int safeexecvp(const char *file, char *const argv[]);
int saferead(int fd, void *buf, size_t count);
int safewrite(int fd, const char *buf, size_t count);
int safeclose(int fd);
FILE *safefopen(char *path, char *mode);
size_t safefread(void *ptr, size_t size, size_t nmemb, FILE *stream);
char *safefgets(char *s, int size, FILE *stream);
size_t safefwrite(void *ptr, size_t size, size_t nmemb, FILE *stream);
int safefclose(FILE *stream);
int safefflush(FILE *stream);
void *safemalloc(size_t size);
void HandleError(int ecode, const char *const caller,
        const char *fmt, ...);


#endif
```

Listing 14-4 shows the C source file, safecalls.c.

Note   Listing 14-4 is available online.

Listing 14-4: **safecalls.c, a wrapper**

```
/* This module contains wrappers around a number of system calls and
   library functions so that a default error behavior can be defined.

*/

#include <stdio.h>
#include <stdlib.h>
#include <string.h>
#include <sys/types.h>
#include <sys/stat.h>
#include <fcntl.h>
#include <unistd.h>
#include <malloc.h>
#include <signal.h>
#include <errno.h>
#include <stdarg.h>

#define __SAFECALLS_C__
#include "safecalls.h"

/* The first two are automatically set by HandleError.  The third you can
   set to be the file handle to which error messages are written.  If
   NULL, is taken to be stderr. */

const char *SafeLibErrorLoc;
int SafeLibErrno = 0;
FILE *SafeLibErrorDest = NULL;
```

```c
char *safestrdup(const char *s)
{
  char *retval;

  retval = strdup(s);
  if (!retval)
    HandleError(0, "strdup", "dup %s failed", s);
  return retval;
}

char *safestrncpy(char *dest, const char *src, size_t n)
{
  if (strlen(src) >= n)
    HandleError(0, "strncpy", "Attempt to copy string \"%s\"\n"
                    "to buffer %d bytes long", src, (int) n);
  return strncpy(dest, src, n);
}

char *safestrcat(char *dest, const char *src, size_t n)
{
  if ((strlen(src) + strlen(dest)) >= n)
    HandleError(0, "strcat", "Attempt to strcat too big a string");
  return strncat(dest, src, n - 1);
}


int safekill(pid_t pid, int sig)
{
  int retval;

  retval = kill(pid, sig);
  if (retval == -1)
    HandleError(errno, "kill", "kill (pid %d, sig %d) failed", (int) pid, sig);
  return retval;
}


char *safegetenv(const char *name)
{
  char *retval;

  retval = getenv(name);
  if (!retval)
    HandleError(errno, "getenv", "getenv on %s failed", name);
  return retval;
}

int safechdir(const char *path)
{
  int retval;
```

Continued

Listing 14-4 *(continued)*

```
  retval = chdir(path);
  if (retval == -1)
    HandleError(errno, "chdir", "chdir to %s failed", path);
  return retval;
}

int safemkdir(const char *path, mode_t mode)
{
  int retval;

  retval = mkdir(path, mode);
  if (retval == -1)
    HandleError(errno, "mkdir", "mkdir %s failed", path);
  return retval;
}

int safestat(const char *file_name, struct stat *buf)
{
int retval;
  retval = stat(file_name, buf);
  if (retval == -1)
    HandleError(errno, "stat", "Couldn't stat %s", file_name);
  return retval;
}

int safeopen(const char *pathname, int flags)
{
int retval;
  if ((retval = open(pathname, flags)) == -1) {
    HandleError(errno, "open", "open %s failed", pathname);
  }
  return retval;
}

int safeopen2(const char *pathname, int flags, mode_t mode)
{
  int retval;

  retval = open(pathname, flags, mode);
  if (retval == -1)
    HandleError(errno, "open2", "Open %s failed", pathname);
  return retval;
}

int safepipe(int filedes[2])
{
  int retval;
```

```
    retval = pipe(filedes);
    if (retval == -1)
      HandleError(errno, "pipe", "failed");
    return retval;
}

int safedup2(int oldfd, int newfd)
{
  int retval;

  retval = dup2(oldfd, newfd);
  if (retval == -1)
    HandleError(errno, "dup2", "failed");
  return retval;
}

int safeexecvp(const char *file, char *const argv[])
{
  int retval;

  retval = execvp(file, argv);
  if (retval == -1)
    HandleError(errno, "execvp", "execvp %s failed", file);
  return retval;
}

int saferead(int fd, void *buf, size_t count)
{
  int retval;

  retval = read(fd, buf, count);
  if (retval == -1)
    HandleError(errno, "read",
        "read %d bytes from fd %d failed", (int) count, fd);
  return retval;
}

int safewrite(int fd, const char *buf, size_t count)
{
  int retval;

  retval = write(fd, buf, count);
  if (retval == -1)
    HandleError(errno, "write",
        "write %d bytes to fd %d failed", (int) count, fd);
  return retval;
}

int safeclose(int fd)
{
  int retval;
```

Continued

Listing 14-4 *(continued)*

```
  retval = close(fd);

  if (fd == -1) {
    HandleError(errno, "close", "Possible serious problem: close failed");
  }
  return retval;
}

FILE *safefopen(char *path, char *mode)
{
  FILE *retval;

  retval = fopen(path, mode);
  if (!retval)
    HandleError(errno, "fopen", "fopen %s failed", path);
  return retval;
}

size_t safefread(void *ptr, size_t size, size_t nmemb, FILE *stream)
{
  size_t retval;

  retval = fread(ptr, size, nmemb, stream);
  if (ferror(stream))
    HandleError(errno, "fread", "failed");
  return retval;
}

char *safefgets(char *s, int size, FILE *stream) {
  char *retval;

  retval = fgets(s, size, stream);
  if (!retval)
    HandleError(errno, "fgets", "failed");
  return retval;
}

size_t safefwrite(void *ptr, size_t size, size_t nmemb, FILE *stream)
{
  size_t retval;

  retval = fread(ptr, size, nmemb, stream);
  if (ferror(stream))
    HandleError(errno, "fwrite", "failed");
  return retval;
}

int safefclose(FILE *stream)
{
  int retval;
```

```
  retval = fclose(stream);
  if (retval != 0)
    HandleError(errno, "fclose", "Possibly serious error: fclose failed");
  return retval;
}

int safefflush(FILE *stream)
{
  int retval;

  retval = fflush(stream);
  if (retval != 0)
    HandleError(errno, "fflush", "fflush failed");
  return retval;
}

void *safemalloc(size_t size)
{
  void *retval;

  retval = malloc(size);
  if (!retval)
    HandleError(0, "malloc", "malloc failed");
  return retval;
}

void HandleError(int ecode, const char *const caller,
        const char *fmt, ...) {

  va_list fmtargs;
  struct sigaction sastruct;
  FILE *of = (SafeLibErrorDest) ? SafeLibErrorDest : stderr;

  /* Safe these into global variables for any possible signal handler. */

  SafeLibErrorLoc = caller;
  SafeLibErrno = ecode;

  /* Print the error message(s) */

  va_start(fmtargs, fmt);

  fprintf(of, "*** Error in %s: ", caller);
  vfprintf(of, fmt, fmtargs);
  va_end(fmtargs);
  fprintf(of, "\n");
  if (ecode) {
    fprintf(of, "*** Error cause: %s\n", strerror(ecode));
  }

  /* Exit if no signal handler.  Otherwise, raise a signal. */
```

Continued

Listing 14-4 *(continued)*

```
sigaction(SIGUSR1, NULL, &sastruct);
if (sastruct.sa_handler != SIG_DFL) {
  raise(SIGUSR1);
} else {
  exit(254);
}
}
```

I'll examine how this code works. A function is created in the safecalls.c file for each function that should be wrapped. This function calls the *real* one, passing along the appropriate arguments. It checks to see if there is any error. If so, it calls HandleError, passing along errno (if applicable; 0 otherwise) and a printf-style format string.

HandleError, then, receives this information. It uses C's variable argument support to be able to pass the format string and any other items to vfprintf(). HandleError saves the first two arguments in global variables — this way, if you have a signal handler, you can examine those variables for a hint as to what is going on — or perhaps to decide how to handle the situation.

Then, HandleError prints out the error messages. If no signal handler is registered for SIGUSR1 (or more precisely, the handler is not the default; SIG_IGN still causes it to raise the signal), the HandleError function simply terminates the program. Otherwise, it will raise that signal and then return.

Note   What is being done is a simplistic form of exception handling. If you are using a language that already has exception handling capabilities, such as C++ or Perl, you can avoid the mess of using a signal handler and simply throw an exception.

If you want to add more functions to this program, doing so is not hard; you simply can add a function in the safecalls.c file, following the form used by the others. When you've done that, add the prototype to the safecalls.h file and you're ready!

All of these functions are completely interoperable and interchangeable with their standard counterparts. You can use the normal ones when you want to omit error-checking or prefer to handle the error-checking yourself.

Using a wrapper library with your own program

To use this wrapper system with your own programs, you simply need to include the header file in your program and use the equivalent safe version of the system calls. If you want to customize the error behavior, you can register a signal handler for SIGUSR1. Listing 14-5 shows a modified version of the previous example program, designed to work with these safecalls.c functions.

Note   Listing 14-5 is available online.

Listing 14-5: **Sample usage of safecalls.c**

```c
#include <stdio.h>
#include <string.h>
#include <stdlib.h>
#include <errno.h>

/* The next four are for system call I/O */

#include <unistd.h>
#include <sys/types.h>
#include <sys/stat.h>
#include <fcntl.h>
#include "safecalls.h"

void stripcrlf(char *temp);
int write_buffer(int fd, const void *buf, int count);
int read_buffer(int fd, void *buf, int count);
int readnlstring(int socket, char *buf, int maxlen);
int readdelimstring(int socket, char *buf, int maxlen, char delim);
void exiterror(char *message, int errnum);

const char *MESSAGE_filename = "Select output filename: ";
const char *MESSAGE_numbers = "Please enter some numbers.  Use -1 when you want
to exit.\n";

int main(void) {
  int outfile;
  char input[80];
  char buffer[80];

  /* Write the prompt for filename and read in the filename. */

  write_buffer(1, MESSAGE_filename, strlen(MESSAGE_filename));
  readnlstring(0, input, sizeof(input));

  /* Open the file */

  outfile = safeopen2(input, O_WRONLY | O_CREAT | O_TRUNC, 0640);

  /* Write the basic instructions. */

  write_buffer(1, MESSAGE_numbers, strlen(MESSAGE_numbers));
```

Continued

Listing 14-5 *(continued)*

```
  do {
    /* Read a line of input, */
    readnlstring(0, input, sizeof(input));

    /* Write it out with trailing newline. */
    write_buffer(outfile, input, strlen(input));
    write_buffer(outfile, "\n", 1);

    sprintf(buffer, "New: %d\n",
        atoi(input) * 5 + (20 * 100) - 12);

    write_buffer(outfile, buffer, strlen(buffer));
  } while (atoi(input) != -1);
  safeclose(outfile);
  return 0;
}

void stripcrlf(char *temp) {
  while (strlen(temp) && temp[0] &&
    ((temp[strlen(temp)-1] == 13) || (temp[strlen(temp)-1] == 10))) {
    temp[strlen(temp)-1] = 0;
  }
}

/*
   This function writes certain number bytes from "buf" to a file
   or socket descriptor specified by "fd". The number of bytes is
   specified by "count". It returns the number of bytes written,
   or <0 on error.
*/

int write_buffer(int fd, const void *buf, int count) {
  const void *pts = buf;
  int   status = 0, n;

  if (count < 0) return (-1);

  while (status != count) {
    n = safewrite(fd, pts+status, count-status);
    if (n < 0) return (n);
    status += n;
  }
  return (status);
}

int read_buffer(int fd, void *buf, int count) {
  void *pts = buf;
  int   status = 0, n;
```

```
    if (count < 0) return (-1);

  while (status != count) {
    n = saferead(fd, pts+status, count-status);
    if (n < 1) return n;
    status += n;
  }
  return (status);
}

int readnlstring(int socket, char *buf, int maxlen) {
  return readdelimstring(socket, buf, maxlen, '\n');
}

int readdelimstring(int socket, char *buf, int maxlen, char delim) {
  int status;
  int count = 0;

  while (count < maxlen - 1) {
    if ((status = read_buffer(socket, buf+count, 1)) < 1) {
      printf("Error reading.\n");
      return -1;
    }
    if (buf[count] == delim) {            /* Found the delimeter */
      buf[count] = 0;
      return 0;
    }
    count++;
  }
  buf[count] = 0;
  return 0;
}

void exiterror(char *message, int errnum) {
  write_buffer(1, message, strlen(message));
  write_buffer(1, sys_errlist[errnum], strlen(sys_errlist[errnum]));
  write_buffer(1, "\n", 1);
  exit(255);
}
```

To compile this program, you'll need to run:

```
$ gcc -Wall -o ch14-05 ch14-05.c safecalls.c
```

Now watch what happens when you run it and try, for instance, to give it a bad filename:

```
$ ./ch14-05
Select output filename: /tmp/no/such/file/exists
*** Error in open2: Open /tmp/no/such/file/exists failed
*** Error cause: No such file or directory
```

So, you didn't have to make any test at all in the main program for this error; it was caught, dealt with, and caused the program to exit. This simplifies your task significantly!

Advanced I/O

You should be familiar with several more advanced concepts as I proceed into more detailed descriptions of the I/O system on Linux.

To make the most of this section, you should review the material presented in Chapter 11, "Files, Directories, and Devices."

Sparse files

An interesting thing occurs when you attempt to seek past the end of a file in Linux. If you do this, you cause the file to grow. If you then write data at this new location, you leave a hole between the end of the previous data and the start of the new data.

What goes into that hole then? The answer is: nothing. You might have a 10-byte write, seek 10MB into it, and write another 10 bytes. The file will show up as being over 10MB but really uses only 1 or 2KB of disk space because of the hole.

When you try to read into this hole, the operating system generates a stream of NULL characters for you. It looks as if there is really data there (albeit a large chunk of NULLs), but there really isn't.

Sparse files may occur more frequently with certain file types. Examples might include core dumps, some types of binaries, some types of libraries, and so on. Particularly, this is likely to happen to files that are intended to be memory-mapped as executable.

Listing 14-6 shows a quick program that creates such a sparse file.

Listing 14-6 is available online.

Listing 14-6: **Creating a sparse file**

```
#include <stdio.h>
#include <string.h>
#include <stdlib.h>
#include <errno.h>
```

```
/* The next four are for system call I/O */

#include <unistd.h>
#include <sys/types.h>
#include <sys/stat.h>
#include <fcntl.h>
#include "safecalls.h"

int write_buffer(int fd, const void *buf, int count);

int main(void) {
  int outfile;

  /* Open the file */

  outfile = safeopen2("test.dat", O_WRONLY | O_CREAT | O_TRUNC, 0640);

  write_buffer(outfile, "Hi", 2);
  lseek(outfile, 10485760, SEEK_SET);
  write_buffer(outfile, "Hi", 2);

  safeclose(outfile);
  return 0;
}

/*
   This function writes a certain number of bytes from "buf" to a file
   or socket descriptor specified by "fd". The number of bytes is
   specified by "count". It returns the number of bytes written,
   or <0 on error.
*/

int write_buffer(int fd, const void *buf, int count) {
  const void *pts = buf;
  int  status = 0, n;

  if (count < 0) return (-1);

  while (status != count) {
    n = safewrite(fd, pts+status, count-status);
    if (n < 0) return (n);
    status += n;
  }
  return (status);
}
```

To compile this program, you might want to use a command such as:

```
$ gcc -Wall -o ch14-6 ch14-6.c safecalls.c
```

You need to specifically mention safecalls.c on your call to gcc. If you don't, the code for the wrapper will not be included and the program will fail to link.

This program writes out Hi, seeks 10MB into the file, and writes out the same string again. After you run it, you get the following file:

```
$ ls -l test.dat
-rw-r-----   1 jgoerzen jgoerzen 10485762 Oct 12 05:47 test.dat
```

This is normal. But check the actual disk space usage:

```
$ ls -s test.dat
   4 test.dat
```

This file used only four blocks (each block is 1K by default on Linux)! Therefore you can see that the file is indeed sparse.

Non-blocking I/O

Normally, when you perform I/O, the function you call waits before returning until the data has been read or entered into the buffer for writing. This often means that you must wait on a device or person before the operating will return. This waiting can sometimes take a long time — even days, if a person gets up and leaves the terminal.

Occasionally, you may want to perform an operation such as, "give me some data if there is any that's ready." You can achieve this by using non-blocking I/O. With non-blocking I/O, the function calls return immediately, whether or not they actually performed the requested action.

Non-blocking I/O is available only with system call I/O. You can enable it by specifying O_NONBLOCK in the flags to the open call. After this, when you call an I/O function that would normally block, you will receive an error value from your call. The global variable errno will be set to EAGAIN because the operation cannot yet be completed.

You can use this type of support to work with a queuing mechanism, when you are working with many file descriptors, and so on. However, for many of these tasks, you should probably use select() or poll() instead for modern applications.

These settings are separate from the blocking/non-blocking options for file locking, although they serve the same basic purpose.

Memory-Mapped I/O

One of the most fascinating capabilities of Linux is memory-mapped I/O. This feature enables you to literally map a file into a memory region. When you access that memory, as with a standard pointer, the appropriate operation is performed automatically on the underlying file.

There are two main reasons that you might prefer to use memory-mapped I/O instead of standard system call or stream I/O. The first involves speed. If you are reading data in bulk, you will find that using memory-mapped I/O is faster. The reason is that this prevents the system from having to perform additional memory copies of data from kernel to user space, as is necessary when using more conventional functions.

The other reason is that you may prefer to have an interface to the file of this type. This sort of interface lends itself to certain types of features. For instance, you can pass around pointers into the file, which act like normal memory to functions but really are referencing the data on-disk.

There are some disadvantages to using this method. For one, when you map a part of the file into memory, you must define a specific size ahead of time. This size cannot shrink or expand. Therefore, adding data to files can be tricky when you use this type of method to do it. Also, you can only memory-map regular files and other seekable things like them. You cannot memory-map a socket, a pipe, or anything of that sort because they are inherently unseekable.

To write out to a file, you must first generate it. You can do so quickly by generating a sparse file as was done in Listing 14-6. Listing 14-7 shows a program that uses memory-mapped I/O to write data into a file.

Note   Listing 14-7 is available online.

Listing 14-7: **Example of memory-mapped I/O**

```
#include <stdio.h>
#include <string.h>
#include <stdlib.h>
#include <errno.h>
#include <sys/mman.h>

/* The next four are for system call I/O */
#include <unistd.h>
#include <sys/types.h>
#include <sys/stat.h>
```

Continued

Listing 14-7 *(continued)*

```
#include <fcntl.h>
#include "safecalls.h"

int write_buffer(int fd, const void *buf, int count);

int main(void) {
  int outfile;
  char *mapped;
  char *ptr;

  /* Open the file */

  outfile = safeopen2("test.dat", O_RDWR | O_CREAT | O_TRUNC, 0640);

  lseek(outfile, 1000, SEEK_SET);
  safewrite(outfile, "\0", 1);
  mapped = mmap(NULL, 1000, PROT_READ | PROT_WRITE, MAP_SHARED,
        outfile, 0);
  if (!mapped) {
    printf("mmap failed.\n");
  }

  ptr = mapped;
  printf("Please enter a number: \n");
  fgets(mapped, 80, stdin);

  ptr += strlen(mapped);
  sprintf(ptr, "Your number times two is: %d\n",
      atoi(mapped) * 2);
  printf("Your number times two is: %d\n",
      atoi(mapped) * 2);

  msync(mapped, 1000, MS_SYNC);
  munmap(mapped, 1000);

  safeclose(outfile);
  return 0;
}

/*
   This function writes certain number bytes from "buf" to a file
   or socket descriptor specified by "fd". The number of bytes is
   specified by "count". It returns the number of bytes written,
   or <0 on error.
*/

int write_buffer(int fd, const void *buf, int count) {
  const void *pts = buf;
  int   status = 0, n;

  if (count < 0) return (-1);
```

```
while (status != count) {
  n = safewrite(fd, pts+status, count-status);
  if (n < 0) return (n);
  status += n;
}
return (status);
}
```

I'll go over the code for this program. This program uses the safecalls library, so you will need to specify it on your gcc command as you did for the code in Listing 14-6. This program begins normally enough by opening up a file for output. It seeks 1000 bytes into it, and writes out a single byte—a quick-and-easy way to make the file look like it's 1000 bytes long for mmap(). Then, there is the call to mmap(). The first argument is a suggested location for the memory block. There is no guarantee that mmap() will use that location, and so it is usually set to NULL. The second argument is the number of bytes from the file that should be mapped into your process's address space. The third argument specifies the permissions for this area in memory. The options and their meanings are in the following table:

Option	Meaning
PROT_EXEC	The information in the memory area contains machine code and may be executed. This is very rarely seen in user-mode applications.
PROT_NONE	No type of access is permitted.
PROT_READ	Read access to the mapped area is permitted.
PROT_WRITE	Write access to the mapped area is permitted.

The fourth argument defines the flags for the memory map. Three such flags are available. At least one of MAP_SHARED or MAP_PRIVATE must be specified; the MAP_FIXED flag is optional and may be specified in combination with either of the others. The flags and their meanings are in the following table:

Flag	Meaning
MAP_FIXED	Causes mmap() to return with an error if it is unable to use the suggestion for the memory location of the mapped area.
MAP_PRIVATE	Any modifications made to the mapped area will not be written back to the disk file.
MAP_SHARED	If writing is permitted, changes to the mapped area in memory will be reflected by the appropriate change to the file.

The fifth argument to mmap() describes the file descriptor whose contents should be mapped into memory. In the example in Listing 14-7, that file descriptor is the one corresponding to the test file. The sixth argument indicates the offset into that file at which the mapped region begins. In this case, the mapped region starts at the very beginning of the file. However, if you prefer to map only data later on in the file instead, you may use this option to specify where to start.

Now that the memory is mapped, you can use the variable named mapped to access it. This variable is a pointer to the start of the memory-mapped region. You can thus access the file directly by accessing this variable. Notice how the call to fgets() uses this variable as the name of its buffer. This means that as soon as the data is read from the keyboard, it's already on its way out for being written to the file, simply by virtue of the fact that it was placed directly into the mapped area of memory.

Then there's a helper variable, ptr, which advances past the point of the initial read so that it's easy to keep track of where more data should be placed. After that, sprintf() is called to write the data out to the file. This may seem odd, but remember that writing the data out to the area that ptr is pointing to effectively writes it out to the file! For convenience, there's also a call to printf() that enables you to see exactly what was written out.

After the program is done writing, it needs to do three things: synchronize the mmapped area, unmap it, and close the file. The synchronization step is necessary because, like with system call I/O, mmap does not always write data out to disk automatically. However, unlike the system call I/O, calling munmap() (the rough equivalent of close) does not cause the pending data to be flushed to disk. Therefore, you must do that manually to ensure that everything gets written.

To do this, you simply call msync, passing it the pointer to the start of the mapped region, the length, and some flags. You should set exactly one of MS_ASYNC or MS_SYNC; the remaining one is optional. The following table lists the flags and their meanings:

Flag	Meaning
MS_ASYNC	Causes the synchronization to be performed asynchronously. That is, the write is set to occur but msync() may return to its caller before the write is complete.
MS_SYNC	Forces the write to be performed synchronously. The msync() function will not return until the write is complete.
MS_INVALIDATE	Tells the system to inform any process that has mapped this region of the file that the data in the file has changed, forcing a reload of fresh data into the buffers for these other mappings.

Finally, after synchronizing the memory, the memory is unmapped with a call to `munmap()`. Again, this takes two arguments: the pointer to the start of the mapped region and its length. After you call `munmap()`, that region may no longer be accessible and definitely will not be tied to the contents of the file.

select() and poll()

Thus far in our programming examples, you've only encountered a need to read from or write to a single file descriptor or stream at a time. For most programs, this is how their lifespan is spent — reading some data, processing it, writing back out the result. However, some programs — particularly network applications — often need to monitor more than one file descriptor at a time. For instance, a network client for an interactive chat needs to be capable of monitoring both the user's keyboard for input to send to the remote user and the network for data to be displayed locally.

With the mechanisms we have studied thus far, there is no good way to do this. You might elect to use non-blocking I/O and poll each file descriptor. However, this gets you into trouble with busy waiting. So, perhaps you decide to insert a `sleep()` call. If you do this, you are still busy waiting, but its effects are diminished. However, this also adversely affects performance, possibly even to such a degree that the program is no longer usable for interactive chat.

You might consider something along the lines of using blocking I/O for local input and non-blocking I/O for network input, effectively polling the network for information every time the local user types a message. This is essentially the approach used by a number of the more simplistic network clients out there, such as the one for FTP. However, for interactive chat, this is not exactly a good idea — it causes unacceptable delays when trying to carry on a conversation.

The select() function

What you need is a function that keeps an eye on a set of file descriptors for you and blocks until something occurs with at least one of them. Well, Linux provides exactly such a function for your use: `select()`. You give the `select()` function three sets of file descriptors to watch. When something relevant to your process occurs on one of the watched descriptors, the call returns and you are told which file descriptor (or descriptors) are ready for action from you.

This interface means an excellent solution to the problem mentioned previously. You no longer have to worry about how you will possibly get data in from both of the descriptors because the operating system automatically handles those details and informs you only when at least one of them is ready to give you some information.

Listing 14-8 shows the code for a program that demonstrates the usage of the `select()` call.

Note   Listing 4-8 is availablkloe online.

Listing 14-8: **Example of select()**

```c
/*
  Chapter 14 example program 8

  Here we demonstrate the use of select().

*/

#include <stdio.h>
#include <stdlib.h>
#include <time.h>
#include "safecalls.h"

int write_buffer(int fd, const void *buf, int count);

int pipes[2];            /* [0] for reading, [1] for writing */

int child(void);
int parent(void);

int main(void) {
  pid_t pid;
  safepipe(pipes);

  pid = fork();

  if (pid == 0)
    return child();

  if (pid > 0)
    return parent();

  return 255;
}

/* The thild process will just send some random data over to the parent
   every 10 seconds. */

int child(void) {
  char buffer[80];

  close(pipes[0]);         /* Get rid of unneeded pipe */
  srand(time(NULL));

  do {
    sleep(10);
    sprintf(buffer, "Message %d\n", rand());
  } while (write_buffer(pipes[1], buffer, strlen(buffer)) != -1);
```

```
    return 0;
}

int parent(void) {
  char buffer[100];
  fd_set readfds;

  close(pipes[1]);        /* Get rid of unneeded pipe */
  printf("You may enter some data.  I'll read it and data from the\n");
  printf("other process and display each.\n\n");

  while(1) {
    FD_ZERO(&readfds);
    FD_SET(0, &readfds);              /* standard input */
    FD_SET(pipes[0], &readfds);      /* child process */

    select(pipes[0] + 1, &readfds, NULL, NULL, NULL);

    if (FD_ISSET(0, &readfds)) {
      buffer[saferead(0, buffer, sizeof(buffer) -1)] = 0;
      printf("You typed: %s\n", buffer);
    }

    if (FD_ISSET(pipes[0], &readfds)) {
      buffer[saferead(pipes[0], buffer, sizeof(buffer) -1)] = 0;
      printf("Child sent: %s\n", buffer);
    }
  }
}

/*
   This function writes certain number bytes from "buf" to a file
   or socket descriptor specified by "fd". The number of bytes is
   specified by "count". It returns the number of bytes written,
   or <0 on error.
*/

int write_buffer(int fd, const void *buf, int count) {
  const void *pts = buf;
  int  status = 0, n;

  if (count < 0) return (-1);

  while (status != count) {
    n = safewrite(fd, pts+status, count-status);
    if (n < 0) return (n);
    status += n;
  }
  return (status);
}
```

To compile this program, you may use a command like this:

```
$ gcc -Wall -o ch14-8 ch14-8.c safecalls.c
```

This program is divided into two separate parts: the parent and the child. The program forks near the beginning, but only after first establishing a pipe.

 Note   Pipes are covered in detail in Chapter 17, "Using Pipes and FIFOs." For the moment, though, all that you need to know is that a pipe is a method of communicating from one process to another—when one process writes to a pipe, the other process can read the data from it.

The child process does nothing but put data in the pipe. Every 10 seconds, the child process puts data into the pipe consisting of some text and a randomly generated numeric message.

The parent is somewhat more complex. It begins by displaying some brief help text to the screen. Then, it enters its main loop. The select() call operates on sets of file descriptors, which are defined in fd_set variables. There are several macros to use to manipulate these sets. FD_ZERO clears all descriptors, FD_CLR clears one specific descriptor, FD_SET adds one descriptor, and FD_ISSET tests whether the given descriptor is set in the set. After running select(), the input sets themselves are modified. In this case, I just rebuild them every time through the loop. If you have more than two descriptors to watch, you may prefer to make a copy of the sets and then simply restore from the copy for each call to select().

The arguments for select() start with the number of the highest descriptor in any set, plus 1. After that, there is a pointer to the set of descriptors to watch for reading, a pointer to the set to watch for writing, and a pointer to the set to watch for errors. Finally, there is a pointer to a struct timeval indicating the maximum time to wait for an event to occur. Because we don't have a time limit and don't care about the writing or error conditions, those three parameters are left to NULL. Because standard input is 0, the other file descriptor must be higher, so one plus standard input's number is the value for the first parameter.

After the call to select() returns, you know that data is ready to be received on at least one, and perhaps both, of the descriptors being watched. The set of descriptors is tested to see exactly which one has received data. For each particular option, if it has received some data, this data is read in. Notice that I don't use read_buffer() here. The reason is that a hit from select indicates that there is some data waiting—in this case, probably not enough to fill up the entire buffer. Therefore, simply using a standalone read() call (or a saferead(), which does the same thing) is best. It probably will not fill the buffer—but this way, the program does not block waiting for data to arrive on this single descriptor.

Because this method is used, you need to be aware that the strings read in from read() are not null-terminated. Therefore, you need to do that yourself.

Conveniently, the return value from `read()` indicates the number of bytes read, so it makes a nice index into the string for the purposes of appending a trailing null character.

Before giving this program a try, I want to give you one final caution. The terminal driver does not deliver data to programs as you type them; rather, it waits until you press Enter and then delivers your entire line all at once. Therefore, if input arrives from the child process while you are in the middle of a line on the parent, the results can be visually confusing as your input line will be interrupted on-screen but not interrupted with its input. By using a system such as ncurses, you can partition off the screen to avoid this problem, but that would unnecessarily complicate this particular program.

Here is some sample output:

```
$ ./ch14-08
You may enter some data.  I'll read it and data from the
other process and display each.

Hello!
You typed: Hello!

This is some sample input.
You typed: This is some sample input.

Child sent: Message 591369805

It looks like the client is working.
You typed: It looks like the client is working.

Child sent: Message 133889111

Bye.
You typed: Bye.

Ctrl-C
```

You can see that the program was indeed capable of receiving and immediately processing messages from both the keyboard and the other process.

The poll( ) function

In addition to using `select()`, you can use the `poll()` call. It does the same sort of thing—it waits for activity on a specified set of file descriptors. However, its semantics may make it easier to work with in some situations. Listing 14-9 shows a rewrite of this code to use `poll()` instead of `select()`.

Note   Listing 14-9 is available online.

Listing 14-9: **Example of poll()**

```c
/*
  Chapter 14 example program 9

  Here we demonstrate the use of poll().

*/

#include <stdio.h>
#include <stdlib.h>
#include <time.h>
#include <sys/poll.h>
#include "safecalls.h"

int write_buffer(int fd, const void *buf, int count);

int pipes[2];            /* [0] for reading, [1] for writing */

int child(void);
int parent(void);

int main(void) {
  int pid;
  safepipe(pipes);

  pid = fork();

  if (pid == 0)
    return child();

  if (pid > 0)
    return parent();

  return 255;
}

/* The thild process will just send some random data over to the parent
   every 10 seconds. */

int child(void) {
  char buffer[80];

  close(pipes[0]);         /* Get rid of unneeded pipe */
  srand(time(NULL));

  do {
    sleep(10);
    sprintf(buffer, "Message %d\n", rand());
  } while (write_buffer(pipes[1], buffer, strlen(buffer)) != -1);
```

```
    return 0;
}

int parent(void) {
  char buffer[100];
  struct pollfd pfds[2];

  close(pipes[1]);        /* Get rid of unneeded pipe */
  printf("You may enter some data.  I'll read it and data from the\n");
  printf("other process and display each.\n\n");

  pfds[0].fd = 0;
  pfds[0].events = POLLIN;
  pfds[1].fd = pipes[0];
  pfds[1].events = POLLIN;

  while(1) {
    poll(pfds, 2, 0);

    if (pfds[0].revents && POLLIN) {
      buffer[saferead(0, buffer, sizeof(buffer) -1)] = 0;
      printf("You typed: %s\n", buffer);
    }

    if (pfds[1].revents && POLLIN) {
      buffer[saferead(pipes[0], buffer, sizeof(buffer) -1)] = 0;
      printf("Child sent: %s\n", buffer);
    }
  }
}

/*
   This function writes certain number bytes from "buf" to a file
   or socket descriptor specified by "fd". The number of bytes is
   specified by "count". It returns the number of bytes written,
   or <0 on error.
*/

int write_buffer(int fd, const void *buf, int count) {
  const void *pts = buf;
  int  status = 0, n;

  if (count < 0) return (-1);

  while (status != count) {
    n = safewrite(fd, pts+status, count-status);
    if (n < 0) return (n);
    status += n;
  }
  return (status);
}
```

There are no changes to the child implementation for this program, but there are some changes to the main loop of the parent process. The poll() function takes an array of structures, which are defined as follows:

```
struct pollfd {
    int fd;           /* file descriptor; -1 to ignore */
    short events;     /* requested events */
    short revents;    /* returned events */
};
```

Each entry specifies the file descriptor. In the events field, you specify which events you want to trigger. When one gets triggered, the function returns and fills out the revents field showing which one (or which ones) triggered. Table 14-2 lists and describes the various events.

Table 14-2
Events for poll()

Event	Meaning	Valid For
POLLERR	An error occurred on this file descriptor.	revents only
POLLHUP	A hangup condition occurred.	revents only
POLLIN	You can read data on this file descriptor.	events and revents
POLLNVAL	The specified file descriptor is not valid.	revents only
POLLOUT	You can write data now on this file descriptor.	events and revents
POLLPRI	There is high-priority data to read.	events and revents
POLLRDBAND	Data from a non-normal band can be read.	events and revents
POLLRDNNORM	Normal-priority data can be read.	events and revents
POLLWRBAND	You can write data to a nonzero band.	events and revents
POLLWRNORM	Same as POLLOUT.	events and revents

The second parameter to poll() is a count of the number of structures in the array; in the example in Listing 14-9, that number is 2. The final value is a timeout, measured in milliseconds. The 0 value disables the timeout, so that is what is used.

After poll() returns, the remaining logic is the same as that for select: find out which descriptors have some action pending and work with it. In this case, that means checking to see whether POLLIN is set on each of the descriptors. If it is, go ahead and read the data in as before.

This example is a fairly simple one. However, bear in mind that for things such as network servers, select() and poll() give you a great deal of flexibility and room to expand your server. These can be an alternative to multi-process servers, which sometimes can consume more resources than a single-process multiplexing server that uses select() or poll().

Advisory Locking

One of the most common problems on a multitasking operating system such as Linux is synchronization between two processes. A specific instance of these problems is synchronizing access to files. On a system where you easily might have a dozen copies of a program running at once, if they all want to write to a single file, the potential for corruption to that file is significant.

There needs to be some way for processes to coordinate their accesses to files. This method needs to work not only for different instances of a single program but between different programs as well.

The answer on Linux is called *advisory file locking*. This means that programs call a function provided by the operating system to coordinate their accesses. It is called advisory because programs that are not aware of or do not take into account the file locks will not be prevented from accessing the file; systems that prevent access from any process at all implement mandatory locking. Either method works and each has its own unique advantages and disadvantages. Linux now has experimental optional mandatory locking, but the advisory locking is far more prevalent and is more portable to other UNIX operating systems as well.

You can use many different functions for locking in Linux and UNIX systems — flock(), fcntl(), and lockf() are among them. In this section, I'll describe flock(). In Linux, these are all interfaces around the same underlying code, so there is not a large amount of difference, save some feature difference between them.

When you want to lock a file with flock, you have a choice of two different lock types: a shared lock and an exclusive lock. With a *shared lock*, multiple processes can have a shared lock on a file. If you request an *exclusive lock*, no other process may have a lock on the file at all. Therefore, with these semantics, you typically use a shared lock for systems that are reading or an exclusive lock for systems that are writing. This is because simply reading from a file does not conflict with other processes that are doing the same. However, there are problems when two processes try to write at once, or when a process tries to read from a section that another process is writing to — the reading process may get the old data, the new data, or a combination of both.

Listing 14-10 presents a sample program that demonstrates file locking. You can start this program up multiple times to see what it does.

 Note   Listing 14-10 is available online.

Listing 14-10: **Example of locking**

```c
#include <stdio.h>
#include <sys/file.h>
#include <sys/types.h>
#include <sys/stat.h>
#include <fcntl.h>

#include "safecalls.h"

void display(int fd);
void add(int fd);
int flockwrapper(int fd, int operation);
int write_buffer(int fd, const void *buf, int count);
int read_buffer(int fd, void *buf, int count);

int main(void) {
  int input;
  int fd;

  fd = safeopen2("ch14-10.dat", O_CREAT | O_RDWR, 0640);

  printf("Select: \n");
  printf("1. Display file\n");
  printf("2. Add to file\n");
  printf("\nYour selection: ");
  scanf("%d", &input);

  switch (input) {
    case 1: display(fd);
            break;
    case 2: add(fd);
            break;
    default: printf("Invalid selection.  Exiting.\n");
  }
  return 0;
}

/* Display the files.  Request a lock such that processes writing won't
   be able to do that while I'm reading.  */

void display(int fd) {
  int data;

  flockwrapper(fd, LOCK_SH);
  while (read_buffer(fd, &data, sizeof(int)) > 0) {
    printf("Data: %d\n", data);
  }
  close(fd);
}
```

```
/* Add new entries.  Request a lock to block everything else. */

void add(int fd) {
  int data;

  flockwrapper(fd, LOCK_EX);
  lseek(fd, 0, SEEK_END);

  do {
    printf("Enter a number (-1 when done): ");
    scanf("%d", &data);
    write_buffer(fd, &data, sizeof(int));
  } while (data != -1);
  close(fd);
}

int flockwrapper(int fd, int operation) {
  printf("Obtaining %s lock on fd %d\n",
      (operation & LOCK_SH) ? "shared" : "exclusive",
      fd);
  if (flock(fd, operation | LOCK_NB) != -1) return 0;
  printf("Another process has a lock; please wait until it is released.\n");
  return flock(fd, operation);
}

/*
   This function writes certain number bytes from "buf" to a file
   or socket descriptor specified by "fd". The number of bytes is
   specified by "count". It returns the number of bytes written,
   or <0 on error.
*/

int write_buffer(int fd, const void *buf, int count) {
  const void *pts = buf;
  int  status = 0, n;

  if (count < 0) return (-1);

  while (status != count) {
    n = safewrite(fd, pts+status, count-status);
    if (n < 0) return (n);
    status += n;
  }
  return (status);
}

int read_buffer(int fd, void *buf, int count) {
  void *pts = buf;
  int  status = 0, n;

  if (count < 0) return (-1);
```

Continued

Listing 14-10 *(continued)*

```
while (status != count) {
  n = saferead(fd, pts+status, count-status);
  if (n < 1) return n;
  status += n;
}
return (status);
}
```

This program can do two things: display the contents of a file and add data to it. I use the appropriate type of file locking to demonstrate how to do so. When displaying data, the program requests a shared lock. This shared lock enables other processes to read the data at the same time. Because an exclusive lock is used for writing when adding to the file, no other processes are allowed access.

There is a wrapper around flock() that exploits the non-blocking option. It uses this wrapper so that it can display a message if there is going to be a delay, so that the user knows what is going on. The LOCK_NB option indicates a non-blocking lock. One other option that has not been used is LOCK_UN, which releases a lock. Note that closing a file or exiting the process automatically releases a lock.

Try running this program in a window. You can compile and start it up like this:

```
$ gcc -Wall -o ch14-10 ch14-10.c safecalls.c
$ ./ch14-10
Select:
1. Display file
2. Add to file

Your selection: 2
Obtaining shared lock on fd 3
Enter a number (-1 when done): 1
Enter a number (-1 when done): 2
Enter a number (-1 when done): 3
```

Now, without exiting the program in Listing 14-10, fire up another copy in another window or terminal. Take a look and see what happens when you try to read:

```
$ ./ch14-10
Select:
1. Display file
2. Add to file

Your selection: 1
Obtaining shared lock on fd 3
Another process has a lock; please wait until it is released.
```

If you open up yet a third process for the purpose of writing, you'll get something similar:

```
$ ./ch14-10
Select:
1. Display file
2. Add to file

Your selection: 2
Obtaining shared lock on fd 3
Another process has a lock; please wait until it is released.
```

Now, if you go back to the first process and type -1 to cause it to exit, you'll see that one of the other processes will obtain a lock. If the second one gets the lock first, it displays the file and exits immediately, and then the third gets the lock for writing. Otherwise, the third asks you for data, and when it is done, the second process displays the file.

Beware of deadlock problems when using file locking. Some programs may lock many files at once. A general hint is to always lock files in the same order, and release locks in the opposite order in which you acquired them.

Summary

In this chapter, you learned about input and output (I/O) on Linux. Specifically, you learned:

✦ Two different types of basic I/O in Linux are library (stream) I/O and system call I/O.

✦ Stream I/O is buffered automatically before the system call level and operates with FILE * variables.

✦ System call I/O is a more low-level interface, and often requires more coding on your part to achieve the same as stream I/O. However, many functions possible with system call I/O are not available with stream I/O.

✦ Handling of error conditions in your programs is one of the most important things you can do to ensure data integrity in your software.

✦ One way to handle errors conveniently is to use wrappers around functions that might fail.

✦ You can create sparse files, or files with holes in them, by seeking past the end of a file and writing data there.

✦ You can use non-blocking I/O when you prefer to have a function return immediately, whether it has executed your request or not.

✦ Memory-mapped I/O enables you to access files as you would normally access memory.

✦ The `select()` and `poll()` functions enable your program to request that the system watch several descriptors for activity and inform you when a request event occurs on at least one of them.

✦ You can use advisory locking to coordinate access to files to prevent data corruption.

✦   ✦   ✦

Looking at Terminals

This chapter covers the aspect of Linux that deals with terminals. This is a very large system, dealing with many different types of devices and requirements. It encompasses the xterm emulator for X, hardware terminals, modems, kernel terminal drivers, terminal emulation, pseudo-terminals, and more.

The modern Linux approach to terminals derives from that in the early versions of UNIX. Back in the early days of UNIX, one might frequently use a console connected via a serial connection (possibly even a modem) to communicate with the system, run programs, and the like. Therefore, the system needs to keep track of some basic attributes of the line, such as the signaling rate (expressed in bps), some link characteristics, and the like.

As more vendors released terminals, each invented their own command set for their terminals. This command set enables the terminals to understand commands from applications requesting them to erase some text, reposition the cursor on the screen, display bold or inverse video, and so on. Linux needs a way to be able to generalize terminal access; writing several thousand different applications, one for each terminal type, is simply not practical. Therefore, Linux uses a capabilities database known as terminfo for storing what each terminal is capable of and how to invoke the features on it. For programmers, a library such as ncurses handles the details of working with the terminfo database; all you have to do is issue library calls to perform actions.

Applications also need some preprocessing to be done by the kernel on their behalf. For instance, consider how much work it would be if you had to manually process backspace characters each time you tried to read input from the terminal. To solve this problem, the UNIX and Linux systems include, by default, some simple line-editing support in the terminal drivers in the kernel. This enables the user to type in input line by line, taking advantage of the Backspace key to make corrections, and then feed the result to you when a complete line of input is ready. Some programs, however, need this behavior to be turned off. For instance, an editor can't wait until Enter is pressed to handle three presses of the up arrow; it should handle this immediately. Similarly, a Backspace key may have more significance in an editor than in traditional line-editing mode. It may be able, for instance, to delete an entire block if one is selected.

Another concern is: what happens when someone presses one of the "special keys"? The answer is that the terminal driver must intercept the keystroke, parse the input, and send an appropriate signal to the process if necessary.

In your user programs, you need to be able to understand different terminal signals for particular events. For instance, different terminals send a different code for the left arrow press. Your programs may need to be able to interpret these keypresses and, if so, you'll need to know how to deal with the input. Fortunately, ncurses and the terminfo system come to your rescue yet again, as they also describe the information that the terminal itself sends.

In some cases, you may want to be able to provide the terminal driver features for devices that are not really a terminal. For instance, a person telnetting into your system will want to be able to use terminal driver features such as line editing with the Backspace key while logged in. These features, however, are provided in the kernel terminal driver and require a terminal device on which to operate. This is where pseudo-terminals come in. They provide a way for programs to pretend to be a real terminal and thus play nicely with the system.

Terminal Attributes

With all this power and diversity, it should come as no surprise that manipulating terminals can be a complex process. The primary way to do this is through tcgetarttr() and tcsetattr(). Dozens of flags are available; in fact, the manpage spends seven whole pages summarizing the available flags and control items.

Both tcgetattr() and tcsetattr() use a struct termios. This structure is defined as follows:

```
struct termios {
  tcflag_t c_iflag;        /* input modes */
  tcflag_t c_oflag;        /* output modes */
  tcflag_t c_cflag;        /* control modes */
  tcflag_t c_lflag;        /* local modes */
  cc_t c_cc[NCCS];         /* control chars */
};
```

The traditional way to set terminal attributes in this way is to first call `tcgetattr()` to populate this structure, make necessary changes, and then call `tcsetattr()` to put the new items into effect. Listing 15-1 shows an example that puts the terminal into raw mode, and then reads one character at a time.

Note   Listing 15-1 is available online.

Listing 15-1: **Sample of raw mode, ch15-1.c**

```c
#include <termios.h>
#include <unistd.h>
#include <stdio.h>

int main(void) {
  int input;

  struct termios save, current;

  tcgetattr(0, &save);
  current = save;

  current.c_lflag &= ~ICANON;
  current.c_lflag &= ~ECHO;

  current.c_cc[VMIN] = 1;
  current.c_cc[VTIME] = 0;

  tcsetattr(0, TCSANOW, &current);

  printf("Enter some text, Q to stop.\n");
  while ((input = getc(stdin)) != 'Q') {
    printf("You typed: %c\n", input);
  }

  tcsetattr(0, TCSANOW, &save);

  printf("Terminal values back to default.\n");
  printf("Try some text again, Q to stop.\n");
  while ((input = getc(stdin)) != 'Q') {
    printf("You typed: %c\n", input);
  }

  return 0;

}
```

Run this program and note the result. If you type **Hello** (not shown in the following program run because it doesn't echo the first time), it will display the message immediately as you press the keys. The second instance of the loop will wait until the entire line has been input before processing any of it. Here's the output:

```
$ ./ch15-1
Enter some text, Q to stop.
You typed: H
You typed: e
You typed: l
You typed: l
You typed: o
You typed: !
Terminal values back to default.
Try some text again, Q to stop.
Hi!
You typed: H
You typed: i
You typed: !
You typed:

ByeQ
You typed: B
You typed: y
You typed: e
```

It is extremely important that you always reset your terminal to the default state upon exit. If you don't, the user's shell and future programs may be confused and display improperly. This is the reason for saving the terminal state information at the beginning and restoring it later.

The terminal attributes are separated into four categories: input, output, control, and local attributes. In this program, only the local attributes are considered relevant, although any of the others could have been modified as well. The &= syntax means to perform a bitwise AND on the variable and the rvalue (the value to the right of the equals sign), and to assign the result back to the variable. In this case, we are wanting to shut off a bit, so the bitwise AND is used to remove a single bit from the bitmask. If you wanted to add on some bits, you could use |= NAME to do that (no leading ~ this time).

This bitwise AND syntax is used to remove two bits: echo and canonical. Turning off canonical mode turns off the standard line editing. This step is necessary if your program is to be able to read one line at a time from the terminal. Echo is turned off as well because having the output appear would only lead to confusion, and the input is displayed soon enough anyway.

That brings us to the termios structure member c_cc. This is used to control how data is sent to the calling program. When there is no longer a line break to fall back upon, how does the terminal driver know when to send data to the process? Because reading from the input a character at a time can (and frequently is) inefficient in most cases, you can set this variable to a minimum value and/or time after which data is returned. For instance, you could cause it to return whatever data is still pending after 10 seconds waiting. Or, as in this case, you can ask it to return after a certain number of characters have been read.

Attributes are available for control for virtually every aspect of the terminal driver. These include speed, flow control, byte size, handling of lowercase characters (some extremely old terminals did not support lowercase letters), control characters (you can prevent Ctrl+C from having any effect or remap it to a different character), and many other attributes. However, as most programs that are interested in these attributes also present a full-screen terminal interface, such attributes are usually modified through the interface of a system such as `ncurses`.

Many of the more intricate details of `tcsetattr()` and `tccgetattr()` are automatically handled for your convenience and sanity by libraries such as ncurses. However, if you don't quite need the power and size of ncurses, you can use these functions to control the terminal as well.

Pseudo-terminals

Sometimes it is necessary for a program to interject itself in the line of communication between a program and its final output device. This could be the case, for instance, for a telnet daemon — instead of writing data to a terminal, the program will need to send data across a network. The UNIX program `script`, which makes a log of your actions, acts in the same fashion as well.

You can't simply use pipes, because pipes lack functions that programs need, and they are not bidirectional. A program needs to be able to find out information about its environment — its window size, its terminal emulation, and so on — that are not available with a pipe. This is where the pseudo-terminals enter the picture. These devices look and act like real terminals, but in reality, they are not.

In this chapter, I am going to present you with a custom version of the "script" program. This program will create a pseudo-terminal, fork, and exec your shell. On the parent side, the program will need to pass standard input on to the client and pass standard output on to both the screen and a file. This is done by forking *again*, to create one handler for each direction. Thus, the entire system will make up three processes. Listing 15-2 shows the source code.

Note Listing 15-2 is available online.

Listing 15-2: **Example script replacement**

```
#include <pty.h>
#include <stdio.h>
#include <sys/types.h>
#include <sys/stat.h>
#include <fcntl.h>
#include <unistd.h>
#include <errno.h>
#include <sys/ioctl.h>
#include "safecalls.h"

int masterfd, output, execpid, childpid;
struct termios origsettings;


void slave(void);
void master(void);
void master_frompty(void);
void master_topty(void);
int write_buffer(int fd, const void *buf, int count);
void catchchildren(int signum);


int main(void) {
  struct winsize size;

  tcgetattr(0, &origsettings);
  ioctl(0, TIOCGWINSZ, (void *) &size);

  output = safeopen2("mytypescript", O_CREAT | O_WRONLY | O_TRUNC, 0600);

  execpid = forkpty(&masterfd, NULL, &origsettings, &size);

  switch (execpid) {
    case 0: slave(); break;
    case -1: HandleError(errno, "forkpty", "failure"); break;
    default: master(); break;
  }
  return 0;
}

/* Here is the process to handle the slave side.  The slave PTY has
   already been set to be the controlling terminal, so all that's left
   to do is exec. */

void slave(void) {
  printf("Starting process, use exit to return...\n");
  if (execl("/bin/sh", "/bin/sh", NULL) == -1) {
    HandleError(errno, "execl", "failure to exec /bin/sh");
```

```
    }
  }

/* Master needs to set it up to copy in two directions: from stdin to
   the pty and from the pty to stdout and the file. */

void master(void) {
  childpid = fork();
  if (childpid == -1) {
    HandleError(errno, "fork", "failed to fork second child");
    return;
  }

  if (childpid == 0) {
    master_frompty();
    return;
  }

  /* Set up signal handlers to exit and kill off other process if any
     one of the other processes dies. */

  signal(SIGCHLD, &catchchildren);

  master_topty();
}

void master_frompty(void) {
  char buffer[2000];
  ssize_t size;

  while ((size = read(masterfd, buffer, sizeof(buffer))) > 0) {
    write_buffer(output, buffer, size);
    write_buffer(1, buffer, size);
  }
}

void master_topty(void) {
  char buffer[2000];
  ssize_t size;
  struct termios newt;

  newt.c_iflag &= ~(ICRNL | INPCK | ISTRIP | IXON | BRKINT | IXOFF | IXANY |
                    INLCR | IGNBRK);
  newt.c_oflag &= ~OPOST;
  newt.c_lflag &= ~(ECHO | ICANON | NOFLSH | ISIG | IEXTEN);
  newt.c_cflag |= CS8;
  newt.c_cflag &= ~CSIZE;

  newt.c_cc[VMIN] = 1;
```

Continued

Listing 15-2 *(continued)*

```
  newt.c_cc[VTIME] = 0;

  tcsetattr(0, TCSANOW, &newt);

  while ((size = read(0, buffer, sizeof(buffer))) > 0) {
    write_buffer(masterfd, buffer, size);
  }
}

int write_buffer(int fd, const void *buf, int count) {
  const void *pts = buf;
  int   status = 0, n;

  if (count < 0) return (-1);

  while (status != count) {
    n = safewrite(fd, pts+status, count-status);
    if (n < 0) return (n);
    status += n;
  }
  return (status);
}

void catchchildren(int signum) {
  kill(execpid, SIGTERM);
  kill(childpid, SIGTERM);
  tcsetattr(0, TCSANOW, &origsettings);
  printf("Process exited; back to normal!\n");
  exit(0);
}
```

To compile this program, you will need to use a command like the following:

```
$ gcc -Wall -o myscript myscript.c -lutil
```

You need to link in the util library because it is where `forkpty()` is defined. Other than that, there is nothing special that needs to be done to compile this program.

Let's go over the code for this program. It begins by grabbing the terminal settings for this terminal and its window size with calls to `tcgetattr()` and `ioctl()`. These settings are to be used for two purposes. First, for the new process created in `forkpty()`, the terminal (the pty slave) will be initialized with these settings. The `forkpty()` call will automatically handle this task based on the pointers to `origsettings` and `size` that are passed in. Then, in `master_topty()` (described in the following text), the parent process's terminal will have to be modified, and it will need to be reset to its original value upon exit.

After grabbing the settings, the output file is opened with a call to `safeopen2()`. After that, the ptys are created and the process forks all at once by calling `forkpty()`. For this to work, two ptys are created. One is the master, which the master processes monitor. The other is the slave pty, which is hooked up to the slave process.

If the process is the slave, the `slave()` function is invoked. This function prints out a message and then execs the shell. That is the end of our code for the slave.

If the process is the master, it forks again. This is done to create one process to handle communication in each direction. That is, there will be one process to handle copying from the input to the terminal and another to handle copying from the terminal to the output file and the screen. The child process of this fork invokes the `master_frompty()` function. The parent process registers a signal handler for SIGCHLD events. This is to clean up after exited processes as covered in Chapter 13, "Understanding Signals." Then, the parent process invokes `master_topty()`.

The `master_frompty()` function copies data from the pty to two destinations: the output file and the screen. The screen is represented by standard output, which is file descriptor number 1. Therefore, it uses two `write_buffer()` calls for each read: one to write to the file and one to write to standard output.

The `master_topty()` cal needs to do some terminal initialization before it is ready to handle data. It needs to set the terminal to a mode such that it gets data in as raw a form as possible. The reason is that some programs in the slave (for instance, a text editor) may require this. Since the slave has its own terminal, with its own driver, it will do its own line buffering, so there is no need for the master to continue to do so. After setting these attributes, it enters a loop to copy the data from standard input (file descriptor 0) to the slave's terminal.

Ncurses

The name *ncurses* stands for new curses, meaning that is a new, improved, and completely compatible reimplementation of the standard curses library. The ncurses program enables full-screen I/O with your programs.

The idea is that you can create full-screen applications, such as editors, dialog utilities, and the like, by using ncurses. You may also want to investigate Perl/Tk or Gnome as you make your decisions for an interface for your program. There are some impressive advantages for using ncurses, though.

Chief among these advantages is speed. The simple truth is that no GUI interface can ever even come close to the speed of a full-screen ncurses-based one. The reason is that a text-mode interface requires far less data to generate the image. Whereas an X interface requires fonts, cursors, and bitmaps, and it sends many graphics commands down the wire, an ncurses interface requires none of that; it is simply text with a few commands to relocate or change a bit of the attribute information. This becomes extremely important when running applications remotely over the Internet. X does support remote execution of applications; however, most Internet links today are not sufficiently fast and latency-free to run most X applications at a satisfactory speed.

One advantage over command-line interfaces is that an ncurses interface can enable the user to fill out forms, browse the Web, and the like—all without requiring a graphical interface.

The ncurses approach has some downsides too, however. For one, many users tend to use terminal emulators with imperfect or downright broken terminal emulation, as is the case, for instance, with the standard telnet program that ships with Windows. These users may get confused when their own terminal emulators do not make sense of the data being sent.

Also, the GUI is able to display more data and in a more powerful way. Graphics, icons, buttons, and the like all provide assistance when your application is inherently graphical. For instance, if you had to write a paint program, you would probably prefer to work in a GUI environment than with ncurses.

Several Linux vendors have embraced or will shortly embrace installation and configuration tools based on ncurses or one of its derivatives. This can only be good; often, the initial installation phase is working from a single floppy disk, and space is so tight that there is no way that X would fit onto that disk. However, a simple, easy-to-understand interface is also of paramount importance (beginning users are the ones that need this more than anyone) at install time. Confuse people, and your product fails.

I'll show you modified versions of two programs that I wrote some years ago. Both use ncurses; the first is written in C, and the second is written in Perl. From the first example, you'll be able to see just how much more professional your interface can look if you cleared the screen and did not require an Enter keypress for menu selections. The second example, in Perl, uses the Perlmenu package and the Curses binding for Perl (both available from CPAN and `http://www.perl.com/CPAN-local/modules/`).

Tip   Some Linux distributions may come with both Perl's Curses package and the Perlmenu system available for install. If you are using such a distribution, you may want to install that version instead of the one from CPAN, as your distribution's software will usually be easier to install. In Debian GNU/Linux, the relevant packages are named libncurses-perl and perlmenu.

The first application presented below illustrates basic interaction with curses. It was written way back when I was first learning about writing sort algorithms; I've stripped out all but three from the code. The basic idea is that you run the genrandom program (which it also builds) to create a file full of random integers. Then, you load that file into this program, which gives you an interface to select a sort algorithm, a function to verify that everything was properly sorted, and so on.

This program comes in three pieces: a simple Makefile, the main code, and a program to generate a file with many random integers in it. First, here's the Makefile:

```
CC=gcc
CFLAGS := -Wall -O3
LINK := $(CC)
EXECS = genrandom ch15-2

all: $(PROGRAM)
    @if [ "x$(PROGRAM)" = "x" ]; then \
        for PNAME in $(EXECS); do $(MAKE) PROGRAM=$$PNAME; done; \
    fi

$(PROGRAM): $(PROGRAM).o
    $(LINK) -o $@ $< -lncurses

$(PROGRAM).o: $(PROGRAM).c
    $(CC) $(CFLAGS) -c -o $@ $<

clean:
    -rm $(EXECS) *.o *~
```

Next, the file to generate random numbers, genrandom.c:

```
/*
    genrandom will create a text file with the following specifications:
     * The first line will contain the number of integers
     * Each following line will contain a randomly generated integer,
       up to the number of integers specified on the first line
*/

#include <stdio.h>
#include <sys/time.h>
#include <limits.h>
#include <stdlib.h>

int main(int argc, char *argv[])
{
unsigned long num, counter;
FILE *outfile;
int seed;
```

```
  if (argc < 2) {
    printf("Syntax: genrandom filename\n");
    printf("It will write the numbers to the filename passed, and the\n");
    printf("line will contain the number of integers written.\n");
    exit(255);
  }
  printf("Enter number of lines to create: ");
  scanf("%lu", &num);
  outfile = fopen(argv[1], "wt");
  if (!outfile) exit(255);
  fprintf(outfile, "%lu\n", num);
  seed = (int)(time(NULL) / (ULONG_MAX / INT_MAX));
  printf("Using seed %d\n", seed);
  srandom(seed);
  for (counter = 1; counter <= num; counter++) {
    fprintf(outfile, "%d\n", (int)(random() / (LONG_MAX / INT_MAX)));
    if (!(counter % 10000))          /* printf is S L O W when dealing
                          with thousands of calls */
      printf("Wrote %lu of %lu numbers, %d%%\r", counter, num, (int)(100 *
counter / num));
  }
  fclose(outfile);
  printf("\n");                      /* Add terminating newline */
  return 0;
}
```

Note that the preceding program does not actually use curses. Listing 15-3 shows the code that does.

Note   Listing 15-3 is available online.

Listing 15-3: **Example usage of curses**

```
/* Include some standard stuff... */

#include <stdio.h>
#include <string.h>
#include <sys/time.h>
#include <malloc.h>
#include <limits.h>
#include <stdlib.h>
#include <memory.h>
#include <signal.h>

/* Curses is used for interactive operation */

#include <curses.h>
```

```
/* Standard macros */

#ifndef TRUE
#define TRUE 1
#endif

#ifndef FALSE
#define FALSE 0
#endif

#ifndef NULL
#define NULL 0
#endif

/* Type used for the array */

typedef int typearray;

/* Defines for type of array in memory */
#define ARRAYTYPE_NONE 0
#define ARRAYTYPE_UNSORTED 1
#define ARRAYTYPE_SORTED 2

/* Defines for type of sort */
#define INSERTIONSORT 1
#define MERGESORT 2
#define HEAPSORT 3

/* Some global information */

int isinteratvive = TRUE;             /* True if running interactively */
typearray* globalarray = NULL;        /* Main array, used for sorting */
unsigned long arraysize = 0;          /* Size of main array....This is
                                         stored in a very big number so
                                         that very large arrays can be
                                         accommodated. */

time_t start = 0;                     /* Start time, in seconds */
int is_firstline_size = TRUE;         /* True if the first line of file
                                         is number of elements in the
                                         file */

int arraytype = ARRAYTYPE_NONE;       /* Type of array in memory */
char defoutput[80];                   /* Default output file/viewer */
char definput[80];                    /* Default input file */
int sorttype = HEAPSORT;

/* Function prototypes */
void mainmenu(void);
void readitin(void);
void reset(void);
```

Continued

Listing 15-3 *(continued)*

```
void toggleint(int *togglevar, int min, int max);
void runsort(void);
    void insertionsort(void);
    void mergesort(unsigned long first, unsigned long last);
    void heapsort(void);
void writeoutput(void);
    void changeviewer(void);
void checkvalidity(void);
void setinputfile(void);
void mergesort_merge(unsigned long first, unsigned long last);
void heapsort_buildheap(unsigned long heapsize);
void heapsort_heapify(unsigned long node);
void heapsort_heapsort(unsigned long node);
void heapsort_swap(unsigned long index1, unsigned long index2);

int main(void) {

    /* Curses may cause program to die with SIGSEGV or other signal if the
       TERM variable is incorrectly set.  This is due to a bug in some versions
       of curses.  The above message will appear only for an instant if
       curses works correctly because the screen will be cleared with a curses
       call. */

    initscr(); cbreak(); clear(); refresh();      /* Set up curses */
    printw("\n Notes on operation:\n");
    printw(" * If you are using a file in which the first line denotes the\n");
    printw("   number of elements in the file, and thus should *not* be\n");
    printw("   included in any sort, you will need to select option 3 before\n");
    printw("   doing anything else.\n\n");
    printw(" * Put license/copyright thing here perhaps.\n\n");
    printw("Press any key to continue.");
    refresh();
    getch();
    clear();
                        /* Do some initialization */
    strcpy(defoutput, "|less");
    strcpy(definput, "INPUTINT.TXT");
    sigblock(sigmask(SIGPIPE));    /* Ignore the SIGPIPE signal --
                                      Otherwise program would terminate
                                      if user ends the viewer before
                                      all data had been sent through
                                      the pipe */



    mainmenu();
    endwin();                           /* End curses */
    if (globalarray) free(globalarray);  /* If the array is still allocated,
                                            free it. */
```

```
    return 0;
}

void mainmenu(void)
{
int selection = 0;
int maxy, maxx;

  getmaxyx(stdscr, maxy, maxx);
  do {
    clear();
    move(maxy - 1, 0);
    attron(A_REVERSE);
    printw("  Sometimes a status bar goes here.  ");
    attroff(A_REVERSE);
    move(0, 0);
    printw("Main Menu\n");
    printw("0. Exit program\n");
    switch (arraytype) {
      case ARRAYTYPE_NONE:
        printw("Cannot sort [no data in memory]\n");
        break;
      case ARRAYTYPE_UNSORTED:
        printw("Sort the array\n");
        break;
      case ARRAYTYPE_SORTED:
        printw("No sort necessary [data loaded and sorted]\n");
        break;
    }
    switch (arraytype) {
      case ARRAYTYPE_NONE: printw("   Cannot sort (no data loaded into
memory)\n"); break;
      case ARRAYTYPE_UNSORTED: printw("2. Sort the array\n"); break;
      case ARRAYTYPE_SORTED: printw("   No sort necessary (data already
sorted)\n"); break;
    }
    printw("3. Toggle method of determining size of array to hold data\n");
    printw("   Current: ");
    if (is_firstline_size)
      printw("[First line of input denotes size of data]\n");
    else
      printw("[Count lines in file before sorting]\n");
    if (arraytype)
      printw("4. View or output sorted data\n");
    else
      printw("   There must be data in memory before it can be viewed.\n");
    printw("5. Change output file or viewer [%s]\n", defoutput);
    if (arraytype == ARRAYTYPE_SORTED)
```

Continued

Listing 15-3 *(continued)*

```
      printw("6. Check validity of sorted array\n");
    else
      printw("   Array not yet sorted; validity test unavailable.\n");
    printw("7. Set type of sort: ");
    switch (sorttype) {
      case INSERTIONSORT: printw("[insertion sort]\n"); break;
      case MERGESORT: printw("[merge sort]\n"); break;
      case HEAPSORT: printw("[heap sort]\n"); break;
    }
    printw("8. Set input filename [%s]\n", definput);
    refresh();
    noecho();                             /* Turn off echo */
    selection = getch();
    echo();
    switch (selection) {
      case '1':                          /* Load data into memory */
            if (arraytype) reset();           /* Reset if data in memory */
            readitin();
            arraytype = ARRAYTYPE_UNSORTED;
            break;
      case '2': if (arraytype == ARRAYTYPE_UNSORTED) runsort(); break;
      case '3': toggleint(&is_firstline_size, 0, 1); break;
      case '4': if (arraytype) writeoutput(); break;
      case '5': changeviewer(); break;
      case '6': if (arraytype == ARRAYTYPE_SORTED) checkvalidity(); break;
      case '7': toggleint(&sorttype, INSERTIONSORT, HEAPSORT); break;
      case '8': setinputfile(); break;
    }
                  /* Other cases either exit program
                     or are ignored */
  } while (selection != '0');
}

void readitin(void)
{
unsigned long counter;
FILE *infile;
int tempbuffer, fscanfresult;
  arraysize = 0;
  clear();
  infile = fopen(definput, "rt");
  if (!infile) {
    printw("Error opening input file %s.  Data not read.\n", definput);
    printw("Press any key...");
    refresh();
    getch();
    return;
  }
```

```
   printw("Reading data...\n"); refresh();
   if (!is_firstline_size) {
     printw("Counting lines:\n");
     infile = fopen(definput, "rt");
     while (!feof(infile)) {
        if ((!feof(infile)) && (fscanf(infile, "%d", &tempbuffer))) arraysize++;
        if (!(arraysize % 10000)) {  /* It goes faster if screen not updated
                                          for every single line...here it is updated
                                          every 10000 lines */
          printw("Got %lu lines\r", arraysize);
          refresh();
        }
     }
     arraysize--;                    /* The above code, using fscanf, always
                                        will yield one greater than the actual
                                        size due to a quirk in fscanf.  Here
                                        this is compensated for. */

     rewind(infile);                 /* Reset to the beginning */
     clearerr(infile);
   } else                            /* First line denotes size */
     if (!fscanf(infile, "%lu", &arraysize)) arraysize = 0;
   if (arraysize)
     printw("There are %lu integers in the data file.\n", arraysize);
   else {
     printw("Empty or corrupted data file, read failed.\n");
     printw("Press any key...\n");
     refresh();
     getch();
     fclose(infile);
     return;
   }
   refresh();
   /* Now allocate the array in dynamic memory */
   globalarray = calloc(arraysize, sizeof(typearray));
   if (!globalarray) {
     printw("Could not allocate memory.  Press any key to continue.\n");
     refresh();
     getch();
     fclose(infile);
     return;
   }

   for (counter = 0; counter < arraysize; counter++) {
     if (!(counter % 10000)) {
       printw("Read %lu of %lu elements, %d percent done\r",
              counter, arraysize, (int)(100 * counter / arraysize));
       refresh();
     }
```

Continued

Listing 15-3 *(continued)*

```
    do
      fscanfresult = fscanf(infile, "%d", globalarray + counter);
    while (!fscanfresult && !feof(infile));
    if (feof(infile)) {
      printw("Unexpected end of file, read aborted.  Memory freed.\n");
      printw("Counter = %d\n", counter);
      printw("Press any key.\n");
      refresh();
      free(globalarray);
      globalarray = NULL;
      getch();
      return;
    }
  }

  arraytype = ARRAYTYPE_UNSORTED;
}

void reset(void)                   /* Reset state of program */
{
  if (globalarray) {
    free(globalarray);
    globalarray = NULL;
  }
  arraytype = ARRAYTYPE_NONE;
  arraysize = 0;
}

void toggleint(int *togglevar, int min, int max)
{
  if (++*togglevar > max) *togglevar = min;
}


void runsort(void)
{
  clear();
  start = time(NULL);
  printw("Running sort: ");
  switch (sorttype) {
    case INSERTIONSORT: printw("insertion sort....\n"); refresh();
                        insertionsort(); break;
    case MERGESORT: printw("merge sort...\n"); refresh();
                    mergesort(0, arraysize-1); break;
    case HEAPSORT: printw("heap sort...\n"); refresh(); heapsort(); break;
  }
  arraytype = ARRAYTYPE_SORTED;
  printw("Elapsed time was: %lu seconds\n", time(NULL) - start);
```

```
    printw("Please note: Other processes on a multi-tasking operating system\n");
    printw("may have an effect on the amount of time a given sort takes.\n");
    printw("\nPress any key to continue.");
    refresh();
    getch();
}

void insertionsort(void)
{
register unsigned long x, y;
int temp_holder;

  for (x = 1; x < arraysize; x++) {
    temp_holder = *(globalarray + x);
    y = x;
    while (y > 0 && temp_holder < *(globalarray + y - 1)) {
      *(globalarray + y) = *(globalarray + y - 1);
      y--;
    }
    *(globalarray + y) = temp_holder;
  }
}

void mergesort(unsigned long first, unsigned long last)
{
    /* the 1 is added to the value because, for instance, if you
       have an array with 2 elements, first is 0, last is 1,
       then last - first = 1, but space is really needed for 2.
    */
unsigned long mid;
  if (first < last) {            /* If they're the same, don't bother */
    mid = (first + last) / 2;
    mergesort(first, mid);
    mergesort(mid+1, last);
    mergesort_merge(first, last);
  }
}

void mergesort_merge(unsigned long first, unsigned long last)
{
typearray *temparray = calloc(last - first + 1, sizeof(typearray));
unsigned long mid = (first + last) / 2;
unsigned long position = 0, left = first, right = mid + 1;

  if (!temparray) {
    printw("FATAL ERROR IN mergesort(): COULD NOT ALLOCATE ENOUGH MEMORY\n");
    printw("FOR TEMPORARY ARRAY.  ABORTING.\n");
    refresh();
```

Continued

Listing 15-3 *(continued)*

```
   exit(255);
 }

 while ((left <= mid) && (right <= last))    /* Run the loop as long
                                                as both left and right
                                                portions of the array
                                                contain data */
   if (*(globalarray + left) < *(globalarray + right))
     *(temparray + position++) = *(globalarray + left++);
   else
     *(temparray + position++) = *(globalarray + right++);

 /* Now copy any remaining elements into temparray */

 /* Because of the "&&" above, only one of the below will execute. */

 while (left <= mid)
   *(temparray + position++) = *(globalarray + left++);
 while (right <= last)
   *(temparray + position++) = *(globalarray + right++);

 /* Now copy temparray back into globalarray */

 memcpy(globalarray + first, temparray,
        (last - first + 1) * sizeof(typearray));

 /* And free the memory used by temparray */

 free(temparray);

}

/* Variables for heapsort funtions */

unsigned long heapsize;

void heapsort(void)
{
  heapsize = arraysize;              /* Initialize it */
  printw("heapsort: building the heap\n");
  refresh();
  heapsort_buildheap(heapsize);
  printw("heapsort: sorting the heap\n");
  refresh();
  heapsort_heapsort(heapsize);
}

void heapsort_buildheap(unsigned long heapsize)
```

```
{
unsigned long node;

  /* Because an unsigned item is used here, the heapify function has to
     be called once later....because node should never go below 0 */

  for (node = heapsize / 2; node > 0; node--)
    heapsort_heapify(node);
  heapsort_heapify(0);
}

void heapsort_heapify (unsigned long node)
{
unsigned long left = (node + 1) * 2 - 1,
              right = (node + 1) * 2,
              largest;     /* Index of largest */

  if ((left < heapsize) &&
      (*(globalarray + left) > *(globalarray + node)))
    largest = left;
  else
    largest = node;

  if ((right < heapsize) &&
      (*(globalarray + right) > *(globalarray + largest)))
    largest = right;

  if (largest != node) {
    heapsort_swap(node, largest);
    heapsort_heapify(largest);
  }

}


void heapsort_heapsort(unsigned long node)
{

unsigned long i;

  for (i = node - 1; i >= 1; --i) {
    heapsort_swap(0, i);
    --heapsize;
    heapsort_heapify(0);
  }
}

void heapsort_swap(unsigned long index1, unsigned long index2)
{
```

Continued

Listing 15-3 *(continued)*

```
typearray tempholder;
  tempholder = *(globalarray + index1);
  *(globalarray + index1) = *(globalarray + index2);
  *(globalarray + index2) = tempholder;
}

void writeoutput(void)
{
FILE *outfile;
int ispipe = FALSE;
unsigned long counter;
  if (defoutput[0] != '|')
    outfile = fopen(defoutput, "wt");
  else {
    clear(); refresh();          /* Clear the screen before piping */
    outfile = popen(defoutput + 1, "w");
    ispipe = TRUE;
  }
  if (!outfile) {
    printw("Error opening output file!  Press any key to continue...\n");
    refresh();
    getch();
    return;
  }
  for (counter = 0; counter < arraysize; counter++) {
    if (fprintf(outfile, "%d\n", *(globalarray + counter)) == EOF) {
      clear();
      if (ispipe) {              /* Viewer/program exited early */
        printw("Pipe closed before all data could be sent.\n");
        pclose(outfile);
      } else {                   /* Some sort of disk error */
        printw("Error writing data to file!\n");
        fclose(outfile);
      }
      printw("Press any key.\n");
      refresh();
      getch();
      return;
    }
  }
  if (ispipe) pclose(outfile);
    else fclose(outfile);
  clear();
  printw("Write/view successful.\n");
  printw("Press any key...\n");
  refresh();
  getch();
}
```

```
void changeviewer(void)
{
  clear();
  printw("Here you can set the file to write output to, or a viewer to use.\n");
  printw("To write the output to a file, just enter the filename.  To pipe\n");
  printw("the output to a program, use the pipe character (|) followed by\n");
  printw("the command line to use to invoke the program.  For instance, to\n");
  printw("use the less file viewer, type in \"|less\" (w/o the quotes).\n");
  printw("Enter your selection: ");
  refresh();
  nocbreak();               /* Re-enables things like backspace! */
  getstr(defoutput);
  cbreak();                 /* Back to "raw" mode for curses */
}

void checkvalidity(void)
{
unsigned long counter;
int last = INT_MIN;         /* Init to lowest possible value */
  clear();
  printw("Performing check on sorted data to ensure it is correctly sorted.\n");
  for (counter = 0; counter < arraysize; counter++) {
    if (*(globalarray + counter) < last)
      printw("Item %lu (%d) less than item %lu (%d)\n",
             counter, *(globalarray + counter),
             counter - 1, *(globalarray + counter - 1));
    else
      if (counter % 10000 == 0) {
        printw("Item %lu OK\r", counter);
        refresh();
      }
    last = *(globalarray + counter);          /* Reset it for next time */
  }
  printw("Scan finished.  Problems in sorted data, if any, are shown above.\n");
  printw("If no problems are shown above, sorted data has been sorted\n");
  printw("correctly.\n\n");
  printw("Press any key to continue.\n");
  refresh();
  getch();
}

void setinputfile(void)
{
  clear();
  printw("Input filename: ");
  refresh();
  nocbreak(); getstr(definput); cbreak();
}
```

Because this is a large and somewhat complex system, I'd like to lead you through what it looks like to the user before you take a look at its internals. First, you'll want to use genrandom to get some random numbers. It will ask you how many to make; the answer depends on your system. On my 366MHz laptop, one million lines sort in about eight seconds; the same number of lines sort in under one second on a 600MHz Alpha machine. You may prefer to use fewer lines if you have a slower machine or more if you have a faster machine. I ran it like this:

```
$ ./genrandom data.txt
Enter number of lines to create: 1000000
Wrote 1000000 of 1000000 numbers, 100%
```

Next, fire up the main program by running the program in Listing 15-3. After the intro screen, you'll get a main screen. Press 8 to pick the filename and enter **data.txt**. Then, your screen will look like this:

```
Main Menu
0. Exit program
1. Load data into memory [no data in memory]
   Cannot sort (no data loaded into memory)
3. Toggle method of determining size of array to hold data
   Current: [First line of input denotes size of data]
   There must be data in memory before it can be viewed.
5. Change output file or viewer [|less]
   Array not yet sorted; validity test unavailable.
7. Set type of sort: [heap sort]
8. Set input filename [data.txt]




        Sometimes a status bar goes here.
```

The program offers you options that can be toggled. You can put number 1, then number 2 to watch as it uses a progress indicator in curses. Let's take a look at how it works, with an eye toward the interaction with ncurses.

Its interaction with the ncurses system begins with this line of code:

```
initscr(); cbreak(); clear(); refresh();      /* Set up curses */
```

This code accomplishes four things. First, the curses system is initialized, which must be done before you can use it for anything else. Second, the program disables the line buffer with the call to `cbreak()`. The effect is the same as the calls to `tcsetattr()` in Listing 15-2. Next, it clears the screen. Finally, it calls `refresh()`.

With ncurses, before *any* changes take effect, you must call `refresh()`. This may seem like a pain, but in reality it is an advantage, because it gives ncurses a chance to optimize for your terminal. For instance, if your program moves the cursor first to line 5, then to line 18, line 6, line 9, and line 7 in that order, this is a lot of moving. The program could reorder it to go to the line 18, then to line 5, and just print the remaining ones in order with no explicit repositioning required. It also lets you draw things on the screen without letting the user know that you've already started to draw them.

Next, you see a series of `printw()` calls. These are the curses equivalent of `printf()` for the standard output. Again remember that they do not take effect until another call to `refresh()`. In curses, you may create mini-windows inside your screen, each with its own virtual coordinate system; `wprintw()` will let you target an arbitrary window. The default window is `stdscr`, and it's all that's used in this program.

The program then calls `getch()`. Because the terminal is in `cbreak()` mode, the effect is that pressing any key on the keyboard causes the program to go to the next menu immediately.

It then calls `mainmenu()` to display the menu, and then—quite important—calls `endwin()` to reset the terminal to its natural state and clean up after ncurses. Never exit a program without calling that function!

Inside `mainmenu()` itself, the first thing you see is a call to `getmaxyx`, a macro. It will give you the dimensions of the terminal window in which it is running, independent of any particular virtual window. These values are saved. Then, the main menu loop is entered. First, it clears the screen. Then it moves the cursor to the very last line on the screen at the left edge. It turns on reverse video, prints a message, and then turns reverse video back off. After doing that, it returns to the upper-left corner and proceeds to display the main menu.

Then, it turns off echo before reading the selection (it could be unsightly otherwise), reads the input, and then reenables echo because it may be needed later for reading data from the user.

Notice that in `changeviewer()`, the program calls `nocbreak()`. If it didn't do this, you wouldn't be able to see your text as you type it! It then calls `getstr()`, which is actually insecure because it does not have a maximum size limitation; `getnstr()` is better. However, because this program is not running setuid or setgid, it is not of concern in this particular situation. After reading the input, it returns to cbreak mode.

Notice the calls to `attron()` and `attroff()`. These calls cause a specified terminal attribute to be enabled or disabled. You can use `attron()` and `attroff()` to set these things one at a time. Or you can use `attrset()` to set them all at once; just use a bitwise OR to combine the values. Table 15-1 lists the possible values for this option.

Table 15-1
Attributes for ncurses

Name	Meaning
A_ALTCHARSET	Specifies a terminal's alternate character set.
A_BLINK	Specifies blinking mode. Not all terminals support a blink; some will use a separate color to indicate blinking.
A_BOLD	Specifies bold text mode.
A_DIM	Causes the text to be dim.
A_INVIS	Specifies invisible mode.
A_NORMAL	Special item that resets everything to normal mode. Generally only used with `attrset()`.
A_PROTECT	Specifies protected mode.
A_REVERSE	Specifies inverse video mode.
A_STANDOUT	Specifies highlighting, the exact method of which is terminal dependent. This often means bold, or a combination of bold and underlining.
A_UNDERLINE	Specifies underline mode. Some terminals cannot display underline and may instead use a separate color or bold to indicate it.
COLOR_PAIR(x)	Uses specified color; see the discussion on color later in this section.

Many terminals support these attributes. On the other hand, many more modern terminals are geared more toward color. For instance, the Linux text console by default supports color but not underline mode. The xterm terminal in Linux's X graphical interface supports both. The ncurses library does include support for color on the terminal. Listing 15-4 features a sample program that demonstrates this support.

Note   Listing 15-4 is available online.

Listing 15-4: **Example of color with ncurses**

```
#include <curses.h>

void doexit(int exitcode);

int main(void) {
  initscr(); cbreak(); noecho();
  start_color();
  clear();
  if (!has_colors()) {
    printw("I'm sorry, but your terminal does not allow color changes.\n");
    doexit(255);
  }

  init_pair(1, COLOR_RED, COLOR_BLACK);
  attrset(COLOR_PAIR(1));
  printw("Here's something in a nice red.  Maybe useful for a warning\n");
  printw("message.\n\n");
  attrset(COLOR_PAIR(1) | A_BOLD);
  printw("Notice how you can get bright colors by adding the A_BOLD\n");
  printw("attribute.\n\n");
  init_pair(2, COLOR_WHITE, COLOR_BLUE);
  attrset(COLOR_PAIR(2));
  printw("Here's white on blue.\n");
  attrset(COLOR_PAIR(2) | A_BOLD);
  printw("And this is a lighter white on blue.\n\n");

  init_pair(3, COLOR_YELLOW, COLOR_BLACK);
  attrset(COLOR_PAIR(3));
  printw("Notice that the \"dark\" yellow appears brown on some terminals.\n");
  attrset(COLOR_PAIR(3) | A_BOLD);
  printw("But it becomes yellow when the bright version is used.\n\n");
  attrset(COLOR_PAIR(0));
  printw("Press any key to watch what happens when a pair is redefined.\n");
  refresh();
  getch();
  init_pair(1, COLOR_GREEN, COLOR_BLACK);
  attrset(COLOR_PAIR(1));
  printw("Notice the existing text printed to the screen with this\n");
  printw("pair is not modified, but this new text has the new color.\n");

  attrset(A_NORMAL);
  printw("You can use A_NORMAL or COLOR_PAIR(0) to return to\n");
  printw("the terminal's default color.\n\n");

  doexit(0);
```

Continued

Listing 15-4 *(continued)*

```
  return 0;               /* to suppress warning */
}

void doexit(int exitcode) {
  printw("Press any key to exit.\n");
  refresh();
  cbreak();
  noecho();
  getch();
  endwin();
  exit(exitcode);
}
```

To compile this code, you may use gcc as normal, with one exception: you will need to add -lncurses to the end of your commmand line. This flag will tell the compiler to link with the ncurses library.

The idea here is that, first, color support must be initialized. Then, you should test to see if your terminal supports color. If not, usually you would resort to using more conventional attributes such as bold and underline. Because this program is specifically about color, exit if the terminal doesn't support it.

Then, to use color, you first need to initialize a color pair. Each pair consists of two attributes: a foreground color and a background color. To actually use the pair, you use its number as an argument to COLOR_PAIR(x) inside of one of the attribute-setting functions such as attrset().

Switching gears a bit, here is a program that uses Perlmenu. Perlmenu is a library layered on top of the Curses library for Perl, which is simply a Perl binding for the familiar C library. As such, you can use Curses and Perlmenu commands in a program that uses Perlmenu. And, if you're curious about how Perlmenu draws its items, you can simply look at its source code.

The program here is a scaled-down version of a quick application to help track grades on assignments. It uses Perlmenu to achieve a pleasant interface, with scrolling, highlighting, and so on—more full-featured than the sample C program in Listing 15-4. This is largely because Perlmenu can handle all of these details automatically, freeing the programmer to concentrate on higher levels of interface and program design.

This program consists of one main Perl script and several sample data files that you can play with. Listing 15-5 shows the script.

Listing 15-5: **Using curses in Perl**

```perl
#!/usr/bin/perl

$HEADER = 'Chapter 15 Example 5';

BEGIN { $Curses::OldCurses = 1; }
use Curses;
use perlmenu;

&menu_prefs(0, 0, 0, "", "n", 0, 1);

$window = &initscr();
&menu_curses_application($window);

# A few subs to automate curses access

sub cprintw {
    printw @_;
    refresh;
}

# Main program starts here

&scrheader;

cprintw "Loading data, please wait...";
&loaddata;
cprintw "\nDone.\n";

&mainmenu;
endwin();

sub scrheader {
    clear; refresh;
    attron(A_BOLD);
    cprintw "$HEADER\n\n";
    attroff(A_BOLD);
    refresh;
}

sub loaddata {
    cprintw "students...";
    &loaddata_students;
    cprintw "grades...";
    &loaddata_grades;
    cprintw "assignments...";
    &loaddata_assignments;
```

Continued

Listing 15-5 *(continued)*

```perl
        cprintw "categories...";
        &loaddata_categories;
}

sub loaddata_students {
    open SFILE, "<students" or die "Couldn't open students file";
    foreach (<SFILE>) {
        chomp;
        ($id, $name) = /(.+?)[\s;:]+(.*)/;
        $students{$id} = $name;
    }
}

sub loaddata_grades {
    open GFILE, "<grades" or return;
    foreach (<GFILE>) {
        chomp;
        ($id, $name) = /(.+?)[\s;:]+(.*)/;
        $grades{$id} = $name;
    }
}

sub loaddata_categories {
    $catnum = 0;
    open CFILE, "<categories" or die "Couldn't open categories file";

    foreach (<CFILE>) {
        chomp;
        ($catnam, $pcat) = /(.+?)[;:](.+)/;
        $catlist[$catnum] = $catnam;
        $catprint{$catnam} = $pcat;
        $catnum++;
    }
}

sub loaddata_assignments {
    $anum = 0;
    open AFILE, "<assignments" or die "Couldn't open assignments file";
    foreach (<AFILE>) {
        chomp;
        ($c, $a, $p) = /(.+?)[\s;:](.+?)[;:]+(.*)/;
        $categories[$anum] = $c;
        $assignments[$anum] = $a;
        $possible[$anum] = $p;
        $anum++;
    }
}

sub mainmenu {
    while (1) {
        &menu_init(1, "Main Menu", 0, "$HEADER", "Press q to quit");
```

```
        &menu_quit_routine("endwin");
        &menu_item("Add grades", "add");
        &menu_item("View/Modify grades", "view");
        &menu_item("Generate report", "report");
        $choice = &menu_display("");

        SWITCH: {
            if ($choice eq "add") {
                &assignmenu(1);
                last SWITCH;
            }
            if ($choice eq "view") {
                &usermenu(1);
                last SWITCH;
            }
            if ($choice eq "report") {
                &scrheader;
                cprintw("Report generator not in this sample.\n\n");
                cprintw "Press Enter to continue.\n";
                <STDIN>;
                last SWITCH;
            }
        }
    }
}


# argument:
#    1 if should call usermenu; 0 otherwise.

sub assignmenu{
    my $adefault = 0;
while (1) {
    if ($_[0] == 0) {
        &parsegrades;          # Make sure grades for menu are current
    }
    &menu_init(1, "Select assignment", 0,
        ($_[0]) ? "(Add Grades)" :
                "User: $students{$curstudent} ($curstudent)");
    for ($i = 0; $i < $anum; $i++) {
        if ($_[0]) {            # Selecting before user
            &menu_item(sprintf("%-35s %-3s possible",
                            $assignments[$i],
                            $possible[$i]), $i);
        } else {                   # Selecting AFTER user
            &menu_item(sprintf("%-35s %-3s of %-3s",
                            $assignments[$i],
                            $curgrades[$i],
                            $possible[$i]), $i);
        }
    }
```

Continued

Listing 15-5 *(continued)*

```perl
    my $topline = 0;
    if ($adefault > 0) {
        $topline = 1;
        $adefault--;
    }
    $curassign = &menu_display("", $topline, $adefault);
    if ($curassign eq "%UP%") { return; }
    $adefault = $curassign + 1;
    if ($adefault >= ($anum)) { $adefault = 0; }

    if ($_[0]) {
        &usermenu(0);
    } else {
        &parsegrades;
        &setgrade;
    }
 }                  # while (1)
}

# argument:
#    a. 1 if should call assignmenu; 0 otherwise.

sub usermenu {
    my $udefault = 0;
    my $z = 0;
    while (1) {
        &menu_init(1, "Select a user", 0,
                    (! $_[0]) ? "Assignment: $assignments[$curassign]"
                              : "(View/Modify)");
        $z = 0;
        foreach (sort keys %students) {
            if ($_[0] == 0) {
                $curstudent = $_;
                &parsegrades;
                $_ = $curstudent;
                &menu_item(sprintf("%-15s %-30s %-3s of %-3s",
                                   $_,
                                   $students{$_},
                                   $curgrades[$curassign],
                                   $possible[$curassign]), "$_:$z");
            } else {
                &menu_item(sprintf("%-15s %s",$_,$students{$_}), "$_:$z");
            }
            $z++;
        }
        my $topline = 0;
        if ($udefault > 0) {
            $topline = 1;
            $udefault--;
        }
        $curstudent = &menu_display("", $topline, $udefault);
```

```
            if ($curstudent eq "%UP%") {
                return;
            }

            ($curstudent, $udefault) = $curstudent =~ /(.+?):(.+)/;

            # Find the proper setting for udefault

            $udefault++;              # Add 1
            if ($udefault >= (scalar(keys %students))) {
                $udefault = 0;
            }

            &parsegrades;
            if ($_[0]) {
                &assignmenu(0);
            } else {
                &setgrade;
            }
        }
    }
}

# Sets the grade

sub setgrade {
    &scrheader;

    cprintw("Id: $curstudent\n");
    cprintw("Student: $students{$curstudent}\n");
    cprintw("Assignment: $curassign,
$assignments[$curassign];$possible[$curassign] possible\n\n");
    cprintw("Current grade: $curgrades[$curassign]\n");
    cprintw("New grade: ");

    my $foo;
    getstr($foo);
    $curgrades[$curassign] = $foo;
    chomp $curgrades[$curassign];
    &setgrades;
    &writegrades;
}

# Generate a curgrades array with this student's current grades

sub parsegrades {
    @curgrades = $grades{$curstudent} =~ m/(\d*),/g;
}

# Convert the curgrades array back to the comma-delimited format

sub setgrades {
```

Continued

Listing 15-5 *(continued)*

```
    $grade = "";

    for ($i = 0; $i < $anum; $i++) {
        $grade .= "$curgrades[$i],";
    }

    $grades{$curstudent} = $grade;
}

# Write the grades file

sub writegrades {
    open GFILE, ">grades" or die "Couldn't write to grades file";
    foreach (sort keys %students) {
        print(GFILE sprintf("%-8s %s\n", $_, $grades{$_}));
    }
    close GFILE;
}
```

Here is the first sample data file, named assignments:

```
Computers:Slide-Rule in C:30
Computers:Coffee Pot Robot:30
Computers:Language Assimilator in Perl:50
Physics:Electricity and Water:30
Physics:Magnetic Fields, Floppies, and Refrigerators:50
Linux:Benchmark System:30
Linux:AI Assignment Grader:200
```

Here is the second sample data file, named categories:

```
Computers
Physics
Linux
```

And this is the final one, students:

```
1003    Herman Hollerith
2001    Dave
1002    Blaise Pascal
3141    Isaac Newton
1970    Ken Thompson
9876    Niklaus Wirth
2023    Linus Torvalds
```

When you run the program, you get a main menu with three items: add grades, view/modify grades, and generate a report. If you pick Add Grades, by using the arrow keys to move the highlight, you then get a menu listing the different assignments on the system, along with the number of possible points on each. Pick one of these and you see a list of students. Select one and you can assign the grade immediately to that person.

The program's interface details are all handled by Perlmenu; all that it has to do is tell Perlmenu what the menus are and what goes in them, and Perlmenu then will draw the menus with Curses.

This is convenient for several reasons. First, it frees you from having to deal with the low-level details of having to worry about exactly where to position the cursor, how to draw the menus, and the like. Second, you can actually look at the code for Perlmenu to find out how it works relative to the curses library — this can be useful if you want to write your own programs in curses. Finally, you can extend Perlmenu (perhaps by adding color support) so that, though its basic framework is still available to help you, it can draw things in a different way.

Summary

In this chapter, we discussed terminal interaction. Specifically, the following were covered:

✦ Terminals can be real hardware devices or virtual terminals. They are referenced by entries in /dev.

✦ Terminals have attributes governing their modes, which specify things such as the state of echo and line buffering.

✦ Pseudo-terminals let you set up a program to process that data going to and from a given terminal. They do so by pretending to be a real terminal.

✦ To present full-screen interfaces, you use the curses/ncurses library.

✦ This library includes support for things such as cursor relocation, colors, attribute settings, and windowing.

✦ In Perl, you also have the option of using the Perlmenu library, which handles the lower-level ncurses interactions for you.

✦   ✦   ✦

Talking to the World

Shared Memory and Semaphores

Linux provides several different ways for you to communicate between the processes on your system. One of these ways is shared memory, which I'll cover in this chapter. I'll show you where shared memory is useful and in what situations you might want to use another technique. Then, I'll talk about the synchronization issues that arise with shared memory, and how to use semaphores to deal with them. I'll close with some sample programs that actually use shared memory and semaphores to communicate.

Uses of Shared Memory

Shared memory is generally regarded as the lowest level of communication possible between two processes on a Linux system. Shared memory allows two or more processes to share a block of memory. Normally, in Linux, each process has its own data area, completely separate from all others on the system. However, this shared memory support allows processes to request from the system a region of memory that they all have access to.

Raw shared memory would theoretically be the fastest way of communicating between two processes. The first can simply read data in and place it directly into shared memory; the second can then read the data directly from the shared memory segment. What's more, a given shared memory segment can be used by more than two processes, enabling a sort of "broadcast" of data to many processes on the system. In practice, things are rarely that simple; synchronization issues are extremely important when dealing with shared memory.

Even with just this one simple example, synchronization plays a part. First, there has to be some way for the second process to know when the first is done placing data into the shared memory segment. Your solution might be to have a byte somewhere that is set to 1 when there's data to be picked up. This means that the client must busy-wait until that byte changes—a very poor solution. Then there are issues about how the first process knows when the second has picked up the data, such that more can be inserted into the area.

To handle these synchronization issues, most users rely on *semaphores,* which were introduced to work with just these sorts of situations. Semaphores enable you to implement a sort of locking for arbitrary events. They're not tied to files, or even to memory; they can be used for any purpose.

Shared memory and semaphores are both a part of the SYSV IPC (System V interprocess communication) subsystem. For this reason, you'll see that the process of requesting them, some details of usage, and the process of releasing them when done are similar. You may be interested to note that SYSV IPC also includes a third facility, message queues. However, these are outdated and rarely used anymore because of the more modern, flexible, and faster options available with things such as pipes and FIFOs.

Synchronization with Semaphores

Before you can even start to do anything useful with shared memory, you need to be able to properly synchronize your accesses to it. This is where semaphores enter the scene. Semaphores are a shared resource that enables you to synchronize access to any resource, not just shared memory. However, semaphores are most commonly used alongside applications that use shared memory.

I'll start with the code in Listing 16-1. This code has some problems that I'll clean up as I go along.

 Note   Listing 16-1 is available online.

Listing 16-1: **First semaphore example**

```
#include <stdio.h>
#include <sys/types.h>
#include <sys/ipc.h>
#include <sys/sem.h>
#include <sys/shm.h>
#include <stdlib.h>
```

```
#include <errno.h>
#include <string.h>

int semheld = 0;

void release(int id);
void request(int id);

/* The union for semctl may or may not be defined for us.  This code, defined
   in Linux's semctl() manpage, is the proper way to attain it if necessary. */

#if defined(__GNU_LIBRARY__) && !defined(_SEM_SEMUN_UNDEFINED)
/* union semun is defined by including <sys/sem.h> */
#else
/* according to X/OPEN we have to define it ourselves */
union semun {
  int val;                    /* value for SETVAL */
  struct semid_ds *buf;       /* buffer for IPC_STAT, IPC_SET */
  unsigned short int *array;  /* array for GETALL, SETALL */
  struct seminfo *__buf;      /* buffer for IPC_INFO */
};
#endif


int main(int argc, char *argv[]) {
  int id;
  union semun sunion;

  /* No arguments: "server". */
  if (argc < 2) {
    /* Request a semaphore. */
    id = semget(IPC_PRIVATE, 1, SHM_R | SHM_W);

    /* Initialize its resource count to 1. */

    sunion.val = 1;
    semctl(id, 0, SETVAL, sunion);
  } else {
    /* Open up the existing one. */
    id = atoi(argv[1]);
    printf("Using existing semaphore %d.\n", id);
  }

  if (id == -1) {
    printf("Semaphore request failed: %s.\n", strerror(errno));
    return 0;
  }

  printf("Successfully allocated semaphore id %d\n", id);

  while (1) {
```

Continued

Listing 16-1 *(continued)*

```
    int selection;
    printf("\nStatus: %d resources held by this process.\n", semheld);
    printf("Menu:\n");
    printf("1. Release a resource\n");
    printf("2. Request a resource\n");
    printf("3. Exit this process\n");
    printf("Your choice: ");

    scanf("%d", &selection);

    switch(selection) {
      case 1: release(id); break;
      case 2: request(id); break;
      case 3: exit(0); break;
    }
  }

  return 0;
}

void release(int id) {
  struct sembuf sb;

  if (semheld < 1) {
    printf("I don't have any resources; nothing to release.\n");
    return;
  }

  sb.sem_num = 0;
  sb.sem_op = 1;
  sb.sem_flg = 0;

  semop(id, &sb, 1);
  semheld--;

  printf("Resource released.\n");
}

void request(int id) {
  struct sembuf sb;

  if (semheld > 0) {
    printf("I already hold the resource; not requesting another one.\n");
    return;
  }

  sb.sem_num = 0;
  sb.sem_op = -1;
```

```
    sb.sem_flg = 0;

    printf("Requesting resource...");
    fflush(stdout);

    semop(id, &sb, 1);
    semheld++;

    printf(" done.\n");
}
```

To compile this program, you may use a command such as this:

```
    $ gcc -Wall -o ch16-1 ch16-1.c
```

Let's take a look at how this program works, and then watch it in action. The program begins in main(). There are two ways to start it: one is without any command-line parameters. In this case, it creates a new semaphore in the system and displays its ID. The second is by specifying the ID of the semaphore already created by the first process.

Note   The semaphore ID is unique on the entire system; if the ID is valid in one process, it will work in any other process as well, assuming that these other processes have permission to access that semaphore. Contrast this with the behavior of the file descriptor, whose number is specific to a given process and means nothing anywhere else.

The semaphore is created by calling semget(). The arguments to this function are a key, the number of semaphores, and flags. The key is used if you are attempting to locate an already created semaphore but don't know its ID. Hopefully your program and another will have agreed beforehand on a unique ID. However, this method is not recommended because there is nothing to guarantee that the key really was generated by your program. Therefore, usually IPC_PRIVATE is used here. This causes the OS to ignore the key and create a new semaphore for you. It is then your job to communicate the ID to the other process. You might do this by forking after you create it, by writing it to a file or pipe, or through some other means.

The second argument to semget() is an entry for the number of semaphores to create. It is possible to use multiple semaphores; this is sometimes necessary if multiple resources or operations need to be synchronized at once; it is more convenient to use multiple semaphore under the same ID because you can request certain operations to be atomic.

Finally, there are the flags. Valid flags include IPC_CREAT and IPC_EXCL, which function as O_CREAT and O_EXCL do for open(2). Additionally, you can specify permissions SHM_R or SHM_W for user read and write permissions, (SHM_R > 3) or (SHM_W > 3) for group read and write permissions, and (SHM_R > 6) or (SHM_W > 6) for world read and write permissions.

Next we need to initialize the semaphore. Basically, semaphores are initialized to the number of units of the resource that are available. In most cases, this will be 1, but it could be a value larger than that. When a process wants to obtain a lock, it decrements this value by 1. If the value is already 0, the process is blocked until some other process releases a lock and the value is incremented. So, we first have to set our semaphore to 1.

This is done by calling semctl(). This is a generic control function used mainly to set up or inquire about a given semaphore. It is not a general-use function for your program to use when the semaphore is being manipulated; rather, it should be used only when the semaphores are being initially configured.

One of the arguments is a union. This is an interesting situation because originally the standard was that the OS would not declare the union but that you had to do so yourself. However, some people decided that it would be easier to have the OS declare it as is done with virtually everything else on the system. This caused errors compiling programs that assumed the definition did not already exist, so it was removed. This is the reason for the strange-looking compiler code; it checks to see whether or not the semaphore is defined, and if it is not, it defines it here.

The first argument to semctl() is the ID of the semaphore on which you want to operate. The second argument indicates which semaphore in the set to use. Because this example program has only one such semaphore, the number 0 (corresponding to the first one) is used. The third argument is a command. Its possible values are summarized in Table 16-1.

Table 16-1
Options for semctl()

Command	Meaning
GETALL	Places the values for each semaphore in the set into an array specified by arg.array.
GETNCNT	Returns the number of processes waiting on a lock for the given semaphore.
GETPID	Returns the PID of the process that last completed an operation with semop() on the given semaphore.

Command	Meaning
GETVAL	Returns the value of the specified semaphore.
GETZCNT	Returns the number of processes waiting for the semaphore's value to be 0.
IPC_RMID	Causes the semaphore to be removed immediately.
IPC_SET	Sets some internal values of the semaphore as indicated by the struct semid_ds that arg.buf points to.
IPC_STAT	Gets status information and puts it into the structure whose address is indicated at arg.buf.
SETALL	Sets the values for all the semaphore in the set, using those specified in arg.array.
SETVAL	Sets the value for the one specific semaphore indicated.

In the event that the ID number was passed on the command line, the process simply needs to read that in and use it.

Then, the program enters the main menu. Normally, the program would lock the resource before using it and unlock it afterward; here, however, you'll notice that because no actual resource is locked, the program keeps track of its own use of the semaphore. In this way, it can prevent potential strangeness if the user might, for instance, try to decrement the semaphore from a process that does not have a lock on the semaphore.

The real fun occurs in request() and release(). Let's look at the request() function (at the end of the program) first. It begins by checking how many semaphores are held already; if any are, it displays an error and returns. Otherwise, request() fills the members of the sembuff structure indicating what they will do. It says that the semaphore should be decremented. Because it is at a maximum of 1, this will indicate to future processes that the resource is in use, and they'll have to wait for it to become available.

The request() function executes this action by filling out the structure and calling semop(). The structure is defined as:

```
struct sembuf {
  short sem_num;  /* semaphore number: 0 = first */
  short sem_op;   /* semaphore operation */
  short sem_flg;  /* operation flags */
}
```

Here, the semaphore number indicates which semaphore to operate upon within the semaphore set. The operation indicates what should be done to it. A positive number indicates that value should be added, indicating a release of resources. A negative number subtracts that value from the semaphore, indicating a consumption of resources. Two flags are available for sem_flg: SEM_UNDO and IPC_NOWAIT. If SEM_UNDO is specified, and if the process exits without releasing consumed resources, these resources will be freed by the operating system. If IPC_NOWAIT is specified, the call will be nonblocking.

You can pass an array of such structures to the semop() function. If you do so, the last argument should be a count of the number of structures in your array; otherwise, you can leave it at 1 for a single modification.

Unless IPC_NOWAIT is indicated, the call will block until all requested operations can be performed. In the request function, a message is printed and then flushed so that it appears immediately. The semop() function is invoked, the internal count is incremented, and it returns.

The release() function does just about the same thing: it releases the resource by calling semop(), except this time it uses a positive number in sb.sem_op.

Notice that there is no attempt to release resources or delete the semaphore as the program exits. Unlike such things as file descriptors and file locks, semaphores and shared memory neither release resources nor delete themselves when a process exits. I'll remedy that in a future version of this code.

Let's look at some sample output. You will need two terminals available. On the first terminal, run this program:

```
$ ./ch16-1
Successfully allocated semaphore id 770

Status: 0 resources held by this process.
Menu:
1. Release a resource
2. Request a resource
3. Exit this process
Your choice: 2
Requesting resource... done.

Status: 1 resources held by this process.
Menu:
1. Release a resource
2. Request a resource
3. Exit this process
Your choice: 2
I already hold the resource; not requesting another one.

Status: 1 resources held by this process.
Menu:
```

```
1. Release a resource
2. Request a resource
3. Exit this process
Your choice:
```

You have requested a resource in this process, and you have confirmed that the process will detect an attempt to request two resources. Note the semaphore ID printed out at the top; in this example, it's 770. Now, start up a second process, passing that number on the command line:

```
$ ./ch16-1 770
Using existing semaphore 770.
Successfully allocated semaphore id 770

Status: 0 resources held by this process.
Menu:
1. Release a resource
2. Request a resource
3. Exit this process
Your choice: 2
Requesting resource...
```

The process is now blocked until the other process releases the resource. In the other window, press 1 to release a resource. The first window will show no resources held; the second will show 1 held. In the first, go ahead and request a resource again. Now the first window will block. In the second process, press 3 to exit. Notice that the lock in the first process is not released; the program does not automatically release resources upon exit. There is now no way to recover from this problem; you'll have to press Ctrl+C to terminate the first process.

This is not the only problem. The other is that the semaphore resource still exists in the computer, taking up memory. Try running this at the prompt:

```
$ ipcs
```

```
------ Shared Memory Segments --------
key        shmid      owner      perms      bytes      nattch     status

------ Semaphore Arrays --------
key        semid      owner      perms      nsems      status
0x00000000 770        jgoerzen   600        1

------ Message Queues --------
key        msqid      owner      perms      used-bytes messages
```

Even though both processes have exited, the resource remains. You'll have to manually remove it:

```
$ ipcrm sem 770
resource deleted
```

Now, let's fix some of the problems in the program so that it is more robust. Listing 16-2 presents a new version of the code.

Note   Listing 16-2 is available online.

Listing 16-2: **Revised semaphore example**

```c
#include <stdio.h>
#include <sys/types.h>
#include <sys/ipc.h>
#include <sys/sem.h>
#include <sys/shm.h>
#include <stdlib.h>
#include <errno.h>
#include <string.h>
#include <signal.h>

int semheld = 0;
int master = 0;
int id = 0;

void release(int id);
void request(int id);
void delete(void);

/* The union for semctl may or may not be defined for us.  This code, defined
   in Linux's semctl() manpage, is the proper way to attain it if necessary. */

#if defined(__GNU_LIBRARY__) && !defined(_SEM_SEMUN_UNDEFINED)
/* union semun is defined by including <sys/sem.h> */
#else
/* according to X/OPEN we have to define it ourselves */
union semun {
  int val;                    /* value for SETVAL */
  struct semid_ds *buf;       /* buffer for IPC_STAT, IPC_SET */
  unsigned short int *array;  /* array for GETALL, SETALL */
  struct seminfo *__buf;      /* buffer for IPC_INFO */
};
#endif


int main(int argc, char *argv[]) {
  union semun sunion;

  /* No arguments: "server". */
  if (argc < 2) {
    /* Request a semaphore. */
```

```
      id = semget(IPC_PRIVATE, 1, SHM_R | SHM_W);

    if (id != -1) {
      /* Delete the semaphore when exiting. */
      atexit(&delete);

      /* Initialize its resource count to 1. */

      sunion.val = 1;
      if (semctl(id, 0, SETVAL, sunion) == -1) {
        printf ("semctl failed: %s\n", strerror(errno));
        exit(255);
      }
    }
    master = 1;
  } else {
    /* Open up the existing one. */
    id = atoi(argv[1]);
    printf("Using existing semaphore %d.\n", id);
  }

  if (id == -1) {
    printf("Semaphore request failed: %s.\n", strerror(errno));
    return 0;
  }


  printf("Successfully allocated semaphore id %d\n", id);

  while (1) {
    int selection;
    printf("\nStatus: %d resources held by this process.\n", semheld);
    printf("Menu:\n");
    printf("1. Release a resource\n");
    printf("2. Request a resource\n");
    printf("3. Exit this process\n");
    printf("Your choice: ");

    scanf("%d", &selection);

    switch(selection) {
      case 1: release(id); break;
      case 2: request(id); break;
      case 3: exit(0); break;
    }
  }

  return 0;
}

void release(int id) {
```

Continued

Listing 16-2 *(continued)*

```
  struct sembuf sb;

  if (semheld < 1) {
    printf("I don't have any resources; nothing to release.\n");
    return;
  }

  sb.sem_num = 0;
  sb.sem_op = 1;
  sb.sem_flg = SEM_UNDO;

  if (semop(id, &sb, 1) == -1) {
    printf("semop release error: %s\n", strerror(errno));
    exit(255);
  }
  semheld--;

  printf("Resource released.\n");
}

void request(int id) {
  struct sembuf sb;

  if (semheld > 0) {
    printf("I already hold the resource; not requesting another one.\n");
    return;
  }

  sb.sem_num = 0;
  sb.sem_op = -1;
  sb.sem_flg = SEM_UNDO;

  printf("Requesting resource...");
  fflush(stdout);

  if (semop(id, &sb, 1) == -1) {
    printf("semop release error: %s\n", strerror(errno));
    exit(255);
  }
  semheld++;

  printf(" done.\n");
}

void delete(void) {
  printf("Master exiting; deleting semaphore.\n");
  if (semctl(id, 0, IPC_RMID, 0) == -1) {
    printf("Error releasing semaphore.\n");
  }
}
```

This code is improved in several ways. For one, there is now error handling to make sure that the return values of functions are appropriate. Without error handling, the processes might think that they have a lock on a resource even if they do not because of an error.

Also, an atexit() handler has been registered. In this example, the "master" will delete the semaphore when it is finished with it. For a more complex use of semaphores, stay tuned; the shared memory applications that follow make more demanding use of them.

Tip   Although the atexit() handler is called for normal termination, it is not called when there is a Ctrl+C event. You might want to add a signal handler for that situation. For more details on signal handlers, see Chapter 13, "Understanding Signals."

Communicating with Shared Memory

Shared memory is literally a block of memory accessible to multiple processes. In this section, I'll build up a small client/server application that uses shared memory to pass messages between two such processes.

Shared memory requires a synchronization method in order to be useful. For this purpose, semaphores are almost always selected. Therefore, we can begin to implement a program by extending the previous example.

The program here, at the moment, works with only two processes. Later, it will be updated to work with any number of processes. The idea is that the client reads some input from a user and sends the data to the server; the server then prints it out.

You might initially think of using an algorithm like this for the server:

```
locksem(semid, 0);
printf("Message received: %s\n", buffer);
unlocksem(semid, 0);
```

And something like this for the client:

```
locksem(semid, 0);
fgets(buffer, sizeof(buffer), stdin);
unlocksem(semid, 0);
```

In these examples, locksem() locks the semaphore and unlocksem() unlocks it. However, there is a serious problem with these functions. Consider the server side first. What if, between the time the server unlocks and the time it relocks the semaphore, the client has not been scheduled for execution? The server will print the message twice. This is not desirable at all. The same could happen on the client side: it could ask for the message twice.

In order to solve the problem, you need two semaphores: one for reading and one for writing. Listing 16-3 shows just such a system.

Note   Listing 16-3 is available online.

Listing 16-3: **Shared memory example**

```
#include <stdio.h>
#include <sys/types.h>
#include <sys/ipc.h>
#include <sys/sem.h>
#include <sys/shm.h>
#include <stdlib.h>
#include <errno.h>
#include <string.h>
#include <signal.h>
#include "safecalls.h"

/* The union for semctl may or may not be defined for us.  This code, defined
   in Linux's semctl() manpage, is the proper way to attain it if necessary. */

#if defined(__GNU_LIBRARY__) && !defined(_SEM_SEMUN_UNDEFINED)
/* union semun is defined by including <sys/sem.h> */
#else
/* according to X/OPEN we have to define it ourselves */
union semun {
  int val;                    /* value for SETVAL */
  struct semid_ds *buf;       /* buffer for IPC_STAT, IPC_SET */
  unsigned short int *array;  /* array for GETALL, SETALL */
  struct seminfo *__buf;      /* buffer for IPC_INFO */
};
#endif

#define SHMDATASIZE 1000
#define BUFFERSIZE (SHMDATASIZE - sizeof(int))

#define SN_EMPTY 0
#define SN_FULL  1

int DeleteSemid = 0;

void server(void);
void client(int shmid);
void delete(void);
void sigdelete(int signum);
void locksem(int semid, int semnum);
void unlocksem(int semid, int semnum);
```

```
void waitzero(int semid, int semnum);
void clientwrite(int shmid, int semid, char *buffer);

int safesemget(key_t key, int nsems, int semflg);
int safesemctl(int semid, int semnum, int cmd, union semun arg);
int safesemop(int semid, struct sembuf *sops, unsigned nsops);
int safeshmget(key_t key, int size, int shmflg);
void *safeshmat(int shmid, const void *shmaddr, int shmflg);
int safeshmctl(int shmid, int cmd, struct shmid_ds *buf);


int main(int argc, char *argv[]) {

  /* No arguments: "server". */
  if (argc < 2) {
    server();
  } else {
    client(atoi(argv[1]));
  }
  return 0;
}

void server(void) {
  union semun sunion;
  int semid, shmid;
  void *shmdata;
  char *buffer;

  /* First thing: generate the semaphore. */

  semid = safesemget(IPC_PRIVATE, 2, SHM_R | SHM_W);

  DeleteSemid = semid;

  /* Delete the semaphore when exiting. */
  atexit(&delete);
  signal(SIGINT, &sigdelete);

  /* Initially empty should be available and full should not be. */

  sunion.val = 1;
  safesemctl(semid, SN_EMPTY, SETVAL, sunion);
  sunion.val = 0;
  safesemctl(semid, SN_FULL, SETVAL, sunion);

  /* Now allocate a shared memory segment. */

  shmid = safeshmget(IPC_PRIVATE, SHMDATASIZE, IPC_CREAT | SHM_R | SHM_W);

  /* Map it into memory. */
```

Continued

Listing 16-3 *(continued)*

```
  shmdata = safeshmat(shmid, 0, 0);

  /* Mark it to automatically delete when the last holding process exits. */

  safeshmctl(shmid, IPC_RMID, NULL);

  /* Write the semaphore id to its beginning. */
  *(int *)shmdata = semid;

  buffer = shmdata + sizeof(int);

  printf("Server is running with SHM id ** %d **\n",
         shmid);

  /****************************************************************
    MAIN SERVER LOOP
    ****************************************************************/

  while (1) {
    printf("Waiting until full...");
    fflush(stdout);
    locksem(semid, SN_FULL);
    printf(" done.\n");

    printf("Message received: %s\n", buffer);
    unlocksem(semid, SN_EMPTY);
  }
}

void client(int shmid) {
  int semid;
  void *shmdata;
  char *buffer;

  shmdata = safeshmat(shmid, 0, 0);

  semid = *(int *)shmdata;
  buffer = shmdata + sizeof(int);

  printf("Client operational: shm id is %d, sem id is %d\n",
         shmid,
         semid);

  while (1) {
    char input[3];

    printf("\n\nMenu\n1. Send a message\n");
    printf("2. Exit\n");
```

```
      fgets(input, sizeof(input), stdin);

      switch(input[0]) {
        case '1': clientwrite(shmid, semid, buffer); break;
        case '2': exit(0); break;
      }
    }

}


void delete(void) {
  printf("\nMaster exiting; deleting semaphore %d.\n", DeleteSemid);
  if (semctl(DeleteSemid, 0, IPC_RMID, 0) == -1) {
    printf("Error releasing semaphore.\n");
  }
}

void sigdelete(int signum) {
  /* Calling exit will conveniently trigger the normal
     delete item. */

  exit(0);
}

void locksem(int semid, int semnum) {
  struct sembuf sb;

  sb.sem_num = semnum;
  sb.sem_op = -1;
  sb.sem_flg = SEM_UNDO;

  safesemop(semid, &sb, 1);
}

void unlocksem(int semid, int semnum) {
  struct sembuf sb;

  sb.sem_num = semnum;
  sb.sem_op = 1;
  sb.sem_flg = SEM_UNDO;

  safesemop(semid, &sb, 1);
}

void waitzero(int semid, int semnum) {
  struct sembuf sb;

  sb.sem_num = semnum;
  sb.sem_op = 0;
  sb.sem_flg = 0;                /* No modification so no need to undo */
```

Continued

Listing 16-3 *(continued)*

```c
  safesemop(semid, &sb, 1);
}

void clientwrite(int shmid, int semid, char *buffer) {
  printf("Waiting until empty...");
  fflush(stdout);
  locksem(semid, SN_EMPTY);
  printf(" done.\n");

  printf("Enter message: ");
  fgets(buffer, BUFFERSIZE, stdin);
  unlocksem(semid, SN_FULL);
}

int safesemget(key_t key, int nsems, int semflg) {
  int retval;

  retval = semget(key, nsems, semflg);
  if (retval == -1)
    HandleError(errno, "semget", "key %d, nsems %d failed", key, nsems);
  return retval;
}

int safesemctl(int semid, int semnum, int cmd, union semun arg) {
  int retval;

  retval = semctl(semid, semnum, cmd, arg);
  if (retval == -1)
    HandleError(errno, "semctl", "semid %d, semnum %d, cmd %d failed",
                semid, semnum, cmd);
  return retval;
}

int safesemop(int semid, struct sembuf *sops, unsigned nsops) {
  int retval;

  retval = semop(semid, sops, nsops);
  if (retval == -1)
    HandleError(errno, "semop", "semid %d (%d operations) failed",
                semid, nsops);
  return retval;
}

int safeshmget(key_t key, int size, int shmflg) {
  int retval;

  retval = shmget(key, size, shmflg);
  if (retval == -1)
    HandleError(errno, "shmget", "key %d, size %d failed", key, size);
  return retval;
}
```

```
void *safeshmat(int shmid, const void *shmaddr, int shmflg) {
  void *retval;

  retval = shmat(shmid, shmaddr, shmflg);
  if (retval == (void *) -1)
    HandleError(errno, "shmat", "shmid %d failed", shmid);
  return retval;
}

int safeshmctl(int shmid, int cmd, struct shmid_ds *buf) {
  int retval;

  retval = shmctl(shmid, cmd, buf);
  if (retval == -1)
    HandleError(errno, "shmctl", "shmid %d, cmd %d failed",
                shmid, cmd);
  return retval;
}
```

There are many things to go over about this code. This time, I want you to see
how it works before using it. Before continuing, you need the safecalls.c file
from Chapter 14, "Introducing the Linux I/O." This program actually uses only
its HandleError function, so if you don't want to type or download it all, you
can make do with just that.

Then, compile this program like this:

```
$ gcc -Wall -o ch16-3 ch16-3.c safecalls.c
```

After this, you are ready to start up a server process. Here's what you need to type
at the prompt:

```
$ ./ch16-3
Server is running with SHM id ** 126724 **
Waiting until full...
```

The server will continue running until you press Ctrl+C; it will not want any more
input from you now.

Next, you can start up a client process. To do so, give it the SHM ID that the server
printed out on its command line. For instance, in this example, I'd type:

```
$ ./ch16-4 126724
Client operational: shm id is 126724, sem id is 3330


Menu
1. Send a message
2. Exit
```

The client looks up the shared memory segment, reads the semaphore ID, and then presents you with the main menu. Pick option 1 to send a message:

```
1
Waiting until empty... done.
Enter message: Hello, this is a test!


Menu
1. Send a message
2. Exit
```

The client sent the message. On the server side, you'll see this response:

```
Waiting until full... done.
Message received: Hello, this is a test!

Waiting until full...
```

This occurs each time you send it a message. Now, you can go ahead and exit the client and press Ctrl+C to exit the server, or experiment a bit more if you wish. When you exit the server, it automatically deletes its semaphore as before.

Now let's take a look at the code and find out what makes this program tick. We begin by declaring two constants: SN_EMPTY and SN_FULL. These are used to access particular semaphores inside the semaphore set. This time, instead of only one semaphore in the set, there are two. Next are prototypes for many different functions in the program.

As you arrive at main(), things are fairly simple: main() either calls the server function or passes along the integer conversion of the argument to the client function. After doing that, it returns a success code to its caller.

The first thing the server() function does is create a new semaphore. This is done exactly as was done before. The ID is saved in DeleteSemid, and atexit() is called. This time, because pressing Ctrl+C exits the server, a signal handler is registered as well. This deletes the semaphore when the program exits by SIGINT.

Next, the two semaphores in the semaphore set are initialized. The first, SN_EMPTY, is initialized to 1. The SN_FULL semaphore is initialized to zero, meaning that a process must explicitly unlock it before another one can get a lock in it.

Now the shared memory segment is allocated. The SHMDATASIZE value was defined at the top of the program to be 1000 bytes. It is created, and an ID is returned. In order to actually access the shared memory, it has to be mapped into memory — the job of shmat(). This function takes an ID, a recommended address, and flags. The last two parameters are rarely used; this program just sets them to zero.

Because shared memory has a concept of being attached, the kernel can keep a usage counter. Unlike semaphores, you can request that shared memory be automatically deleted when the last process using it terminates. That is what is done with the call to `safeshmctl()`.

At this point, there was a decision. The server could have printed out the IDs for both the semaphore and the shared memory for the client to use. Instead, we are a bit sneaky about it: only the ID for the shared memory is printed; the ID for the semaphore is written into the shared memory itself. Because this value never changes, and the server is guaranteed to write to it before clients do (clients don't even know the ID of the shared memory yet), there's no need to worry about locking it. I cast the `void *` variable `shmdata` to an `int *` variable, dereference it, and assign the semaphore ID to it. Then, the variable `buffer` (which will be used for the rest of the program) is initialized to point to the shared memory area, just past this semaphore ID. The server prints out the shared memory ID and then enters its main loop.

The server waits until the client signals that the buffer is full (by unlocking the `SN_FULL` semaphore). When that is done, the server gets the lock, displays the message, and then unlocks the `SN_EMPTY` semaphore for the client.

You may want to think of the locking and unlocking as wait and signal operations, respectively. When you lock a semaphore, you are waiting until it is available. In this program, when you unlock it, you are signaling the other process that it has become available.

Now you arrive at the `client()` function. It gets the shared memory ID passed in from `main()`. The `client()` function first reads the semaphore ID and then sets `buffer` — similar to what was done in the `server()` function. Then, it enters its main loop. It offers to read from the terminal or exit. If you choose to read, it calls `clientwrite()`; otherwise, it exits.

The `delete()` and `sigdelete()` functions are already fairly familiar or trivial enough; we'll skip them. The `locksem()` and `unlocksem()` functions are the equivalents of the `request()` and `return()` functions in the earlier example. The `waitzero()` function is not used by this program but is included for completeness if you want to use this code somewhere else. Its purpose is to block until the semaphore's value is zero (that is, until someone has obtained a lock on it) but not modify the semaphore itself.

After these functions, you find the implementation of `clientwrite()`. It's quite similar to the `server()` function. It waits until it can lock `SN_EMPTY`, reads the message from the keyboard, and then unlocks `SN_FULL`. Notice that for performance reasons you would normally move the `fgets()` call before the `locksem()` call, but it is here for demonstration purposes, as I'll explain shortly.

After these functions, you see the implementations of the safe wrappers around calls, which are used for error detection. These are written in the same fashion as those described in Chapter 14.

Now you have seen this program, but it is not very robust. It supports only one client and one server. Let's rewrite it so that this restriction is removed. We'll rename what is now the client to the "producer" and what is now the server to the "consumer." Many computer science textbooks address the *producer/consumer problem*, of which this is an instance.

Consider the benefits of the code in Listing 16-4. You can write a system that institutes a job processing system. Any number of processes may queue jobs. Servers to process them may enter or leave the system at any time. You can even implement a queue simply by modifying Listing 16-4 to have a larger buffer and handle a situation of adding new entries at an offset into the shared memory (which is not terribly difficult).

Note   Listing 16-4 is available online.

Listing 16-4: **Revised shared memory example**

```
#include <stdio.h>
#include <sys/types.h>
#include <sys/ipc.h>
#include <sys/sem.h>
#include <sys/shm.h>
#include <stdlib.h>
#include <errno.h>
#include <string.h>
#include <signal.h>
#include "safecalls.h"

/* The union for semctl may or may not be defined for us.  This code, defined
   in Linux's semctl() manpage, is the proper way to attain it if necessary. */

#if defined(__GNU_LIBRARY__) && !defined(_SEM_SEMUN_UNDEFINED)
/* union semun is defined by including <sys/sem.h> */
#else
/* according to X/OPEN we have to define it ourselves */
union semun {
  int val;                    /* value for SETVAL */
  struct semid_ds *buf;       /* buffer for IPC_STAT, IPC_SET */
  unsigned short int *array;  /* array for GETALL, SETALL */
  struct seminfo *__buf;      /* buffer for IPC_INFO */
};
#endif
```

```
#define SHMDATASIZE 1000
#define BUFFERSIZE (SHMDATASIZE - sizeof(int))

#define SN_EMPTY 0
#define SN_FULL  1
#define SN_LOCK  2

int DeleteSemid = 0;

void consumer(int shmid);
void producer(int shmid);
int masterinit(void);
char *standardinit(int shmid, int *semid);
void delete(void);
void sigdelete(int signum);
void locksem(int semid, int semnum);
void unlocksem(int semid, int semnum);
void waitzero(int semid, int semnum);
void producerwrite(int shmid, int semid, char *buffer);

int safesemget(key_t key, int nsems, int semflg);
int safesemctl(int semid, int semnum, int cmd, union semun arg);
int safesemop(int semid, struct sembuf *sops, unsigned nsops);
int safeshmget(key_t key, int size, int shmflg);
void *safeshmat(int shmid, const void *shmaddr, int shmflg);
int safeshmctl(int shmid, int cmd, struct shmid_ds *buf);


int main(int argc, char *argv[]) {
char selection[3];
int shmid;
  /* No arguments: "master */
  if (argc < 2) {
    shmid = masterinit();
  } else {
    shmid = atoi(argv[1]);
  }

  printf("Shall I be a [C]onsumer or a [P]roducer process? ");
  fgets(selection, sizeof(selection), stdin);

  switch(selection[0]) {
    case 'p':
    case 'P': producer(shmid); break;
    case 'c':
    case 'C': consumer(shmid); break;
    default:  printf("Invalid choice; exiting.\n");
  }
  return 0;
}
```

Continued

Listing 16-4 *(continued)*

```c
void consumer(int shmid) {
  int semid;
  char *buffer;

  buffer = standardinit(shmid, &semid);

  printf("Consumer operational: shm id is %d, sem id is %d\n",
         shmid,
         semid);

  while (1) {
    printf("Waiting until full... ");
    fflush(stdout);
    locksem(semid, SN_FULL);
    printf("done; ");

    printf("waiting for lock... ");
    fflush(stdout);
    locksem(semid, SN_LOCK);
    printf("done.\n");

    printf("Message received: %s\n", buffer);
    unlocksem(semid, SN_LOCK);
    unlocksem(semid, SN_EMPTY);
  }
}

void producer(int shmid) {
  int semid;
  char *buffer;

  buffer = standardinit(shmid, &semid);

  printf("Producer operational: shm id is %d, sem id is %d\n",
         shmid,
         semid);

  while (1) {
    char input[3];

    printf("\n\nMenu\n1. Send a message\n");
    printf("2. Exit\n");

    fgets(input, sizeof(input), stdin);

    switch(input[0]) {
      case '1': producerwrite(shmid, semid, buffer); break;
      case '2': exit(0); break;
```

```
      }
    }
}

char *standardinit(int shmid, int *semid) {
  void *shmdata;
  char *buffer;

  shmdata = safeshmat(shmid, 0, 0);

  *semid = *(int *)shmdata;
  buffer = shmdata + sizeof(int);

  return buffer;
}

int masterinit(void) {
  union semun sunion;
  int semid, shmid;
  void *shmdata;

  /* First thing: generate the semaphore. */

  semid = safesemget(IPC_PRIVATE, 3, SHM_R | SHM_W);

  DeleteSemid = semid;

  /* Delete the semaphore when exiting. */
  atexit(&delete);
  signal(SIGINT, &sigdelete);

  /* Initially empty should be available and full should not be.
     The lock will also be available initially. */

  sunion.val = 1;
  safesemctl(semid, SN_EMPTY, SETVAL, sunion);
  safesemctl(semid, SN_LOCK, SETVAL, sunion);
  sunion.val = 0;
  safesemctl(semid, SN_FULL, SETVAL, sunion);

  /* Now allocate a shared memory segment. */

  shmid = safeshmget(IPC_PRIVATE, SHMDATASIZE, IPC_CREAT | SHM_R | SHM_W);

  /* Map it into memory. */

  shmdata = safeshmat(shmid, 0, 0);

  /* Mark it to delete automatically when the last holding process exits. */

  safeshmctl(shmid, IPC_RMID, NULL);
```

Continued

Listing 16-4 *(continued)*

```
  /* Write the semaphore id to its beginning. */
  *(int *)shmdata = semid;

  printf(" *** The system is running with SHM id %d \n",
         shmid);

  return shmid;
}


void delete(void) {
  printf("\nMaster exiting; deleting semaphore %d.\n", DeleteSemid);
  if (semctl(DeleteSemid, 0, IPC_RMID, 0) == -1) {
    printf("Error releasing semaphore.\n");
  }
}

void sigdelete(int signum) {
  /* Calling exit will conveniently trigger the normal
     delete item. */

  exit(0);
}

void locksem(int semid, int semnum) {
  struct sembuf sb;

  sb.sem_num = semnum;
  sb.sem_op = -1;
  sb.sem_flg = SEM_UNDO;

  safesemop(semid, &sb, 1);
}

void unlocksem(int semid, int semnum) {
  struct sembuf sb;

  sb.sem_num = semnum;
  sb.sem_op = 1;
  sb.sem_flg = SEM_UNDO;

  safesemop(semid, &sb, 1);
}

void waitzero(int semid, int semnum) {
  struct sembuf sb;

  sb.sem_num = semnum;
```

```
    sb.sem_op = 0;
    sb.sem_flg = 0;            /* No modification so no need to undo */

    safesemop(semid, &sb, 1);
}

void producerwrite(int shmid, int semid, char *buffer) {
    printf("Waiting until empty... ");
    fflush(stdout);
    locksem(semid, SN_EMPTY);

    printf("done; waiting for lock...\n");
    fflush(stdout);
    locksem(semid, SN_LOCK);


    printf("Enter message: ");
    fgets(buffer, BUFFERSIZE, stdin);

    unlocksem(semid, SN_LOCK);
    unlocksem(semid, SN_FULL);
}

int safesemget(key_t key, int nsems, int semflg) {
    int retval;

    retval = semget(key, nsems, semflg);
    if (retval == -1)
        HandleError(errno, "semget", "key %d, nsems %d failed", key, nsems);
    return retval;
}

int safesemctl(int semid, int semnum, int cmd, union semun arg) {
    int retval;

    retval = semctl(semid, semnum, cmd, arg);
    if (retval == -1)
        HandleError(errno, "semctl", "semid %d, semnum %d, cmd %d failed",
                    semid, semnum, cmd);
    return retval;
}

int safesemop(int semid, struct sembuf *sops, unsigned nsops) {
    int retval;

    retval = semop(semid, sops, nsops);
    if (retval == -1)
        HandleError(errno, "semop", "semid %d (%d operations) failed",
                    semid, nsops);
    return retval;
}
```

Continued

Listing 16-4 *(continued)*

```
int safeshmget(key_t key, int size, int shmflg) {
  int retval;

  retval = shmget(key, size, shmflg);
  if (retval == -1)
    HandleError(errno, "shmget", "key %d, size %d failed", key, size);
  return retval;
}

void *safeshmat(int shmid, const void *shmaddr, int shmflg) {
  void *retval;

  retval = shmat(shmid, shmaddr, shmflg);
  if (retval == (void *) -1)
    HandleError(errno, "shmat", "shmid %d failed", shmid);
  return retval;
}

int safeshmctl(int shmid, int cmd, struct shmid_ds *buf) {
  int retval;

  retval = shmctl(shmid, cmd, buf);
  if (retval == -1)
    HandleError(errno, "shmctl", "shmid %d, cmd %d failed",
                shmid, cmd);
  return retval;
}
```

The code is now complete! You simply start up one process, which allocates the shared memory and semaphore. Then, you can start up as many other processes as you wish, of either type, and add them into the system simply by passing them the shared memory ID. To really see how things work, you need to start up at least two producers and two consumers. There is a lot of internal reshuffling of code to make things a bit better suited to the producer/consumer model. There is a new semaphore, SN_LOCK. Using this semaphore makes the program a full-fledged producer/consumer solution. Although this current scheme does not require that, it is there as an example for you should you have a system that would benefit from buffers.

Summary

In this chapter, you learned about shared memory and semaphores. Specifically, you learned:

✦ Shared memory can be very fast, but access can be complicated due to synchronization requirements.

✦ Both shared memory and semaphores are examples of parts of the SYSV IPC (System V interprocess communication) system, and so they are created in similar ways.

✦ Semaphores are used to provide resource synchronization. Resources are said to be available if the semaphore is positive, or unavailable if it is zero.

✦ Semaphores cannot be automatically deleted when the program exits, so you should use `atexit()` or signal handlers to make sure that they are deleted.

✦ You can use `SEM_UNDO` to cause the resources requested by a process to be released, but the semaphore itself will not be.

✦ Each semaphore allocated actually contains a customizable amount of semaphores under a single ID.

✦ Shared memory is usually implemented with semaphores as the synchronization method.

✦ When you have a shared memory ID, you must attach it to your process with `shmat()`.

✦   ✦   ✦

Using Pipes and FIFOs

As I continue our discussion of communication on Linux, I now turn away from shared memory and toward file descriptor–based communication. Pipes are provided for your use for setting up lines of communication between two processes on your local machine. Instead of using open(2) to create a pipe, you use pipe(2). After that, however, you use standard system calls such as read(2) and write(2), just as you would with a more "normal" file descriptor.

 For more information on using system-call input and output, please see the information in Chapter 14, "Introducing the Linux I/O."

Pipes are intended solely for communication between two processes. When you create a pipe, you actually get two file descriptors — one for reading and one for writing. Any data that is written to the write side of the descriptor can later be read back from the read side.

Compared with the shared memory and semaphore system, pipes are a far easier method to use for communication between processes. Pipes can be a bit slower, and unlike shared memory, you cannot use a single pipe for more than two processes. Instead you might have to use a solution such as setting up a line of pipes (a pipeline) to shuttle data from one process to the next, which will certainly be slower. On the other hand, because pipes are used as standard file descriptors, they are the method of choice for communication between two processes that use file descriptor I/O already. For instance, this is the type of device that the shell implements to handle pipelines created with | in the shell, because any terminal I/O is ultimately implemented in terms of file descriptors.

Another advantage is that pipes function much like their more complex big brother, the TCP/IP socket suite. You can start out with using communication only locally, and then later graduate to using TCP/IP sockets to permit communication on the Internet. Some parts of your code will have to be modified — especially the initialization code — but as long as you are doing basic reads and writes on file descriptors, the bulk of your code should still be operational even with this completely different method of communication. Most communication in Linux, in fact, occurs with the file descriptor model; this chapter and the two chapters following it focus entirely on communication with this model, and pipes are a fitting introduction to it.

A FIFO is a particular type of pipe that has a presence in the file system. It is used to allow processes to establish a connection with each other without requiring them to have previously forked, a limitation of standard pipes which you shall see in the text that follows.

Setting Up Pipes

To create a pipe, you must first simply call pipe(2). The function will create the file descriptor pair and place them in a two-element array for your use. After this, you need to cause communication to occur between processes. The standard approach is to call pipe(2), obtain your descriptors, and then use the fork() system call. Each end will close one of the descriptors. For instance, if the child process will do the writing and the parent the reading, the child process should close the reading end of the pipe and the parent should close the writing end.

Listing 17-1 shows a sample program to create a pipe and then communicate over it. Notice how it must fork and then the two processes use the pipe file descriptors that were opened before the fork.

Note   Listing 17-1 is available online.

Listing 17-1: **Pipe example**

```
#include <stdio.h>
#include <unistd.h>
#include <errno.h>
#include <stdarg.h>
#include <time.h>

#include "safecalls.h"

#define FD_READ 0
```

```
#define FD_WRITE 1

void parent(int pipefds[2]);
void child(int pipefds[2]);
int write_buffer(int fd, const void *buf, int count);
int read_buffer(int fd, void *buf, int count);
int readnlstring(int socket, char *buf, int maxlen);
int readdelimstring(int socket, char *buf, int maxlen, char delim);
int tprintf(const char *fmt, ...);
pid_t safefork(void);

int main(void) {
  int pipefds[2];

  safepipe(pipefds);
  if (safefork())
    parent(pipefds);
  else
    child(pipefds);

  return 0;
}

void parent(int pipefds[2]) {
  char buffer[100];
  /* First, close the descriptors that the parent doesn't need.
     Since the parent will not be reading from the terminal -- only
     the child will -- close off standard input as well. */

  close(pipefds[FD_WRITE]);
  close(0);

  tprintf("The parent is ready.\n");

  /* Now wait for data, and display it. */

  while (readnlstring(pipefds[FD_READ], buffer, sizeof(buffer)) >= 0) {
    tprintf("Received message: %s\n", buffer);
  }
  tprintf("No more data; parent exiting.\n");
  safeclose(pipefds[FD_READ]);
}

void child(int pipefds[2]) {
  char buffer[100];

  /* First, close the descriptor that the child doesn't need. */
```

Continued

Listing 17-1 *(continued)*

```
    close(pipefds[FD_READ]);

    tprintf("The child is ready.\n");

    tprintf("Enter message (Ctrl+D to exit): ");
    while (fgets(buffer, sizeof(buffer), stdin) != NULL) {
      tprintf("Transmitting message: %s\n", buffer);
      write_buffer(pipefds[FD_WRITE], buffer, strlen(buffer));
      tprintf("Enter message (Ctrl+D to exit): ");
    }
    tprintf("Client exiting.\n");
    safeclose(pipefds[FD_WRITE]);
}

/*
   This function writes a certain number of bytes from "buf" to a file
   or socket descriptor specified by "fd". The number of bytes is
   specified by "count". It returns the number of bytes written,
   or <0 on error.
*/

int write_buffer(int fd, const void *buf, int count) {
  const void *pts = buf;
  int   status = 0, n;

  if (count < 0) return (-1);

  while (status != count) {
    n = safewrite(fd, pts+status, count-status);
    if (n < 0) return (n);
    status += n;
  }
  return (status);
}

int read_buffer(int fd, void *buf, int count) {
  void *pts = buf;
  int   status = 0, n;

  if (count < 0) return (-1);

  while (status != count) {
    n = saferead(fd, pts+status, count-status);
    if (n < 1) return n;
    status += n;
  }
  return (status);
}
```

```
int readnlstring(int socket, char *buf, int maxlen) {
  return readdelimstring(socket, buf, maxlen, '\n');
}

int readdelimstring(int socket, char *buf, int maxlen, char delim) {
  int status;
  int count = 0;

  while (count < maxlen - 1) {
    if ((status = read_buffer(socket, buf+count, 1)) < 1) {
      printf("Error reading: EOF in readdelimstring()\n");
      return -1;
    }
    if (buf[count] == delim) {          /* Found the delimiter */
      buf[count] = 0;
      return 0;
    }
    count++;
  }
  buf[count] = 0;
  return 0;
}

int tprintf(const char *fmt, ...) {
  va_list args;
  struct tm *tstruct;
  time_t tsec;

  tsec = time(NULL);
  tstruct = localtime(&tsec);

  printf("%02d:%02d:%02d %5d| ",
         tstruct->tm_hour,
         tstruct->tm_min,
         tstruct->tm_sec,
         getpid());

  va_start(args, fmt);
  return vprintf(fmt, args);
}

pid_t safefork(void) {
  pid_t retval;

  retval = fork();
  if (retval == -1)
    HandleError(errno, "fork", "failed");
  return retval;
}
```

To compile this program, you'll need the safecalls.c and safecalls.h files from Chapter 14, "Introducing the Linux I/O." Then run gcc with the arguments shown to compile:

```
$ gcc -Wall -o ch70-1 ch17-1.c safecalls.c
```

The program begins by defining some macros for the read and write sides of the descriptors to make things easier to remember later. Then, inside main(), the pipe is created, and the results are stored in pipefds(). After doing that, the program forks, each side going to its respective function.

In the parent() function, the write descriptor is closed. Because the child will be the only one reading from standard input, it closes the read descriptor on its end. Then, the parent reads strings from the input descriptor of the pipe and displays them. Finally, it will close its end of the pipe and exit.

The child similarly closes the reading end of the pipe, which it will not be using. Then it enters a loop reading data from the keyboard. After reading each line of input, it prints a message, writes it to the pipe, and repeats the loop.

Note that because both processes are writing to the same terminal, some strangeness is bound to occur unless they carefully synchronize their actions. One way to address this problem is to use a semaphore for locking display to the screen. Another way is to open a second pipeline for the server to communicate an acknowledgment of receipt to the client. The client can wait for this message to arrive before displaying its output.

The program in Listing 17-1 will successfully communicate with the server. However, because we do not synchronize the result from the server (pipes are one way) and both processes are sharing a single terminal, the result can be a bit confusing. Let's take a look at the output anyway:

```
$ ./ch17-1
13:51:31    337| The parent is ready.
13:51:31    338| The child is ready.
13:51:31    338| Enter message (Ctrl+D to exit): Hello!
13:51:34    338| Transmitting message: Hello!

13:51:34    338| Enter message (Ctrl+D to exit): 13:51:34    337|
Received message: Hello!
This is another message
13:51:41    338| Transmitting message: This is another message

13:51:41    338| Enter message (Ctrl+D to exit): 13:51:41    337|
Received message: This is another message
Ctrl+D
13:51:55    338| Client exiting.
Error reading: EOF in readdelimstring()
13:51:55    337| No more data; parent exiting.
```

Situations such as this are rare where both processes are writing to the same terminal. In this case, you can solve the problem simply by eliminating some of the prompting on the client side.

There's another problem: the server is getting an error condition when it tries to read at the end. Specifically, what's happening is it has detected that the other end has closed the pipe, and thus that there is no more data to read. This is not really an error, just an event, but the function is expecting to be able to read until a newline. One solution here is to change the protocol a bit such that the client informs the server when it is exiting. Another option is to modify the function that is generating the error message so that it remains silent when an end-of-file condition occurs.

Listing 17-2 shows a rewritten version of the program in Listing 17-1 that takes these things into consideration.

Note   Listing 17-2 is available online.

Listing 17-2: **Revised pipe example**

```
#include <stdio.h>
#include <unistd.h>
#include <errno.h>
#include <stdarg.h>
#include <time.h>

#include "safecalls.h"

#define FD_READ 0
#define FD_WRITE 1

void parent(int pipefds[2]);
void child(int pipefds[2]);
int write_buffer(int fd, const void *buf, int count);
int read_buffer(int fd, void *buf, int count);
int readnlstring(int socket, char *buf, int maxlen);
int readdelimstring(int socket, char *buf, int maxlen, char delim);
int tprintf(const char *fmt, ...);
pid_t safefork(void);

int main(void) {
  int pipefds[2];

  safepipe(pipefds);
  if (safefork())
```

Continued

Listing 17-2 *(continued)*

```
    parent(pipefds);
  else
    child(pipefds);

  return 0;
}

void parent(int pipefds[2]) {
  char buffer[100];
  /* First, close the descriptors that the parent doesn't need.
     Since the parent will not be reading from the terminal -- only
     the child will -- close off standard input as well. */

  close(pipefds[FD_WRITE]);
  close(0);

  tprintf("The parent is ready.\n");

  /* Now wait for data, and display it. */

  while (read_buffer(pipefds[FD_READ], buffer, 1) > 0) {
    if (buffer[0] == 'E') {
      tprintf("Received exit code from child.\n");
      break;
    }
    if (buffer[0] == 'M') {
      readnlstring(pipefds[FD_READ], buffer, sizeof(buffer));
      tprintf("Received message: %s\n", buffer);
    } else {
      tprintf("Received unknown action code.\n");
    }
  }
  tprintf("Parent exiting.\n");
  safeclose(pipefds[FD_READ]);
}

void child(int pipefds[2]) {
  char buffer[100];

  /* First, close the descriptor that the child doesn't need. */

  close(pipefds[FD_READ]);

  tprintf("The child is ready.  Enter messages, or Ctrl+D when done.\n");

  while (fgets(buffer, sizeof(buffer), stdin) != NULL) {
    /* Send a message code and then the message. */
    write_buffer(pipefds[FD_WRITE], "M", 1);
```

```
      write_buffer(pipefds[FD_WRITE], buffer, strlen(buffer));
   }
   write_buffer(pipefds[FD_WRITE], "E", 1);
   tprintf("Client exiting.\n");
   safeclose(pipefds[FD_WRITE]);
}

/*
   This function writes certain number bytes from "buf" to a file
   or socket descriptor specified by "fd". The number of bytes is
   specified by "count". It returns the number of bytes written,
   or <0 on error.
*/

int write_buffer(int fd, const void *buf, int count) {
   const void *pts = buf;
   int  status = 0, n;

   if (count < 0) return (-1);

   while (status != count) {
     n = safewrite(fd, pts+status, count-status);
     if (n < 0) return (n);
     status += n;
   }
   return (status);
}

int read_buffer(int fd, void *buf, int count) {
   void *pts = buf;
   int  status = 0, n;

   if (count < 0) return (-1);

   while (status != count) {
     n = saferead(fd, pts+status, count-status);
     if (n < 1) return n;
     status += n;
   }
   return (status);
}

int readnlstring(int socket, char *buf, int maxlen) {
   return readdelimstring(socket, buf, maxlen, '\n');
}

int readdelimstring(int socket, char *buf, int maxlen, char delim) {
   int status;
```

Continued

Listing 17-2 *(continued)*

```
   int count = 0;

   while (count < maxlen - 1) {
     if ((status = read_buffer(socket, buf+count, 1)) < 1) {
       printf("Error reading: EOF in readdelimstring()\n");
       return -1;
     }
     if (buf[count] == delim) {              /* Found the delimiter */
       buf[count] = 0;
       return 0;
     }
     count++;
   }
   buf[count] = 0;
   return 0;
}

int tprintf(const char *fmt, ...) {
  va_list args;
  struct tm *tstruct;
  time_t tsec;

  tsec = time(NULL);
  tstruct = localtime(&tsec);

  printf("%02d:%02d:%02d %5d| ",
         tstruct->tm_hour,
         tstruct->tm_min,
         tstruct->tm_sec,
         getpid());

  va_start(args, fmt);
  return vprintf(fmt, args);
}

pid_t safefork(void) {
  pid_t retval;

  retval = fork();
  if (retval == -1)
    HandleError(errno, "fork", "failed");
  return retval;
}
```

This time, before the child sends anything to the parent, it sends a one-character code indicating what's going on. This code will be M (to indicate a message follows) or E (to indicate that the client is exiting). The parent receives this code, and if it is an E, it won't even try to read a message; it will break out of its loop immediately.

Watch what happens when this version of the program is run:

```
$ ./ch17-2
15:46:50    786| The parent is ready.
15:46:50    787| The child is ready.  Enter messages, or Ctrl+D when done.
Hello!
15:46:52    786| Received message: Hello!
This is another test.
15:46:56    786| Received message: This is another test.
Ctrl+D
15:46:58    787| Client exiting.
15:46:58    786| Received exit code from child.
15:46:58    786| Parent exiting.
```

Implementing Redirection

Sometimes it would be nice for your program to invoke another one, but instead of having the output of this other program go to the terminal, have it go to your program for additional processing. Or, you might prefer to be able to supply custom input to one of these other programs such that they read their input from your program instead of from the keyboard. You can do this by using the fork() and exec() calls; first, however, you need to change the child process.

The system provides a function called dup2() that allows you to copy a file descriptor to another number. Because, for instance, standard output is always number 1, if you copy your pipe file descriptor over the terminal file descriptor that normally resides at position 1, any output from the child process will go to the parent instead. Listing 17-3 shows a program that does just such a thing.

Note   Listing 17-3 is available online.

Listing 17-3: **Using redirection**

```
#include <stdio.h>
#include <unistd.h>
#include <errno.h>
#include <stdarg.h>
```

Continued

Listing 17-3 *(continued)*

```
#include <time.h>

#include "safecalls.h"

#define FD_READ 0
#define FD_WRITE 1

void parent(int pipefds[2]);
void child(int pipefds[2]);
int write_buffer(int fd, const void *buf, int count);
int read_buffer(int fd, void *buf, int count);
int readnlstring(int socket, char *buf, int maxlen);
int readdelimstring(int socket, char *buf, int maxlen, char delim);
int tprintf(const char *fmt, ...);
pid_t safefork(void);

int main(void) {
  int pipefds[2];

  safepipe(pipefds);
  if (safefork())
    parent(pipefds);
  else
    child(pipefds);

  return 0;
}

void parent(int pipefds[2]) {
  char buffer[100];
  /* First, close the descriptors that the parent doesn't need.
     Since the parent will not be reading from the terminal -- only
     the child will -- close off standard input as well. */

  close(pipefds[FD_WRITE]);
  close(0);

  tprintf("The parent is ready.\n");

  /* Now wait for data, and display it. */

  while (readnlstring(pipefds[FD_READ], buffer, sizeof(buffer)) >= 0) {
    tprintf("Received message: %s\n", buffer);
  }
  tprintf("No more data; parent exiting.\n");
  safeclose(pipefds[FD_READ]);
}
```

```
void child(int pipefds[2]) {
  /* First, close the descriptor that the child doesn't need. */

  close(pipefds[FD_READ]);

  tprintf("The child is ready.\n");
  safedup2(pipefds[FD_WRITE], 1);
  execlp("ls", "ls", "/proc/self", NULL);
  tprintf("Exec failed, exiting\n");
}

/*
   This function writes a certain number of bytes from "buf" to a file
   or socket descriptor specified by "fd". The number of bytes is
   specified by "count". It returns the number of bytes written,
   or <0 on error.
*/

int write_buffer(int fd, const void *buf, int count) {
  const void *pts = buf;
  int   status = 0, n;

  if (count < 0) return (-1);

  while (status != count) {
    n = safewrite(fd, pts+status, count-status);
    if (n < 0) return (n);
    status += n;
  }
  return (status);
}

int read_buffer(int fd, void *buf, int count) {
  void *pts = buf;
  int   status = 0, n;

  if (count < 0) return (-1);

  while (status != count) {
    n = saferead(fd, pts+status, count-status);
    if (n < 1) return n;
    status += n;
  }
  return (status);
}

int readnlstring(int socket, char *buf, int maxlen) {
```

Continued

Listing 17-3 *(continued)*

```c
  return readdelimstring(socket, buf, maxlen, '\n');
}

int readdelimstring(int socket, char *buf, int maxlen, char delim) {
  int status;
  int count = 0;

  while (count < maxlen - 1) {
    if ((status = read_buffer(socket, buf+count, 1)) < 1) {
      return -1;
    }
    if (buf[count] == delim) {              /* Found the delimiter */
      buf[count] = 0;
      return 0;
    }
    count++;
  }
  buf[count] = 0;
  return 0;
}

int tprintf(const char *fmt, ...) {
  va_list args;
  struct tm *tstruct;
  time_t tsec;

  tsec = time(NULL);
  tstruct = localtime(&tsec);

  printf("%02d:%02d:%02d %5d| ",
         tstruct->tm_hour,
         tstruct->tm_min,
         tstruct->tm_sec,
         getpid());

  va_start(args, fmt);
  return vprintf(fmt, args);
}

pid_t safefork(void) {
  pid_t retval;

  retval = fork();
  if (retval == -1)
    HandleError(errno, "fork", "failed");
  return retval;
}
```

This program is similar to the first example. The extra error message has been removed from the function now, however, given that we no longer have control over the protocol because another application is generating the data being sent to the parent.

The parent receives the output of the ls command over the pipe and displays this output with its own additional messages before each line. Thus, you'll get output that looks something like this:

```
$ ./ch17-3
15:57:33   838| The parent is ready.
15:57:33   839| The child is ready.
15:57:33   838| Received message: cmdline
15:57:33   838| Received message: cwd
15:57:33   838| Received message: environ
15:57:33   838| Received message: exe
15:57:33   838| Received message: fd
15:57:33   838| Received message: maps
15:57:33   838| Received message: mem
15:57:33   838| Received message: root
15:57:33   838| Received message: stat
15:57:33   838| Received message: statm
15:57:33   838| Received message: status
15:57:33   838| No more data; parent exiting.
```

If you would prefer instead to send data as input to the child, you need only keep the writer open on the parent and the read descriptor open on the child, and use the dup2() call on that descriptor to descriptor number 0 on the child. Note also that the stream I/O system provides a function named popen() that performs a similar task but uses system() and stream I/O for its communication. This may be appropriate in some cases, but not necessarily in all situations.

Addressing Communication Issues

As you have seen, pipes are not bi-directional; that is, data can flow through pipes in only one direction. This could be fine in many cases. However, sometimes you might prefer to have bi-directional communication between processes. In these situations, you have two options. One is to open two sets of file descriptors (for a total of four) between the parent and the child: one set for communication in one direction and another for communication in the other direction. Another option is to use a different type of communication that works bidirectionally, such as a socket. I discuss sockets in Chapters 18 and 19.

Some people may try to use pipes for communication within a single process. This is almost always a bad idea and can result in deadlock. The reason is that a write to a pipe will not necessarily return until there is a corresponding read from the other end. However, your process cannot do so because it is still trying to write. A better solution might be to simply use an internal buffer for storage of the data that you need to pass along.

Another problem is that there is no way, with a standard pipe, to be able to open it save by a single process before a fork. This means that arbitrary processes cannot connect to it later, which is no doubt a bad thing. In order to address this issue, you'd use FIFOs.

Using FIFOs

FIFO stands for "first in, first out"—the first data to be written to the FIFO is the first to be read out later. A FIFO (also known as *named pipe*) is a special kind of pipe; it has an entry in the file system. This entry is created with the mkfifo(3) library call or the mkfifo(1) shell command. After it has been created, any process with proper permissions can open it. Reads from the resulting file descriptor will read data from whatever program connected to write to it. No data is actually stored on the disk for this type of entry; it is solely there as a way for two programs to rendezvous without one having to have forked off the second.

After your programs are done using the FIFO, you will need to remove it. The FIFO is not automatically removed from the file system by the system. You can use the standard unlink() call to remove the FIFO.

Listing 17-4 shows a rewrite of the program in Listing 17-2 to use a FIFO. If started without command-line parameters, it will create a FIFO and then read from it. Otherwise, it will hook up to the existing FIFO whose location is specified on the command line and write to it.

Note   Listing 17-4 is available online.

Listing 17-4: **Sample usage of FIFOs**

```
#include <stdio.h>
#include <unistd.h>
#include <errno.h>
#include <stdarg.h>
#include <time.h>
#include <sys/types.h>
#include <sys/stat.h>
#include <fcntl.h>
```

```
#include "safecalls.h"

void parent(char *argv[]);
void child(char *argv[]);
int write_buffer(int fd, const void *buf, int count);
int read_buffer(int fd, void *buf, int count);
int readnlstring(int socket, char *buf, int maxlen);
int readdelimstring(int socket, char *buf, int maxlen, char delim);
int tprintf(const char *fmt, ...);
pid_t safefork(void);

int main(int argc, char *argv[]) {

  if (argc < 2)
    parent(argv);
  else
    child(argv);

  return 0;
}


void parent(char *argv[]) {
  char buffer[100];
  int fd;
  /* Close standard input.  Don't need it. */

  close(0);

  /* Create the FIFO and open it. */

  if (mkfifo("ch17-fifo", 0600) == -1)
    HandleError(errno, "mkfifo", "failed to create ch17-fifo");

  tprintf("The server is listening on ch17-fifo.\n");

  /* This will block until someone else connects to write. */

  fd = safeopen("ch17-fifo", O_RDONLY);

  tprintf("Client has connected.\n");

  /* Now wait for data, and display it. */

  while (readnlstring(fd, buffer, sizeof(buffer)) >= 0) {
    tprintf("Received message: %s\n", buffer);
  }
  tprintf("No more data; parent exiting.\n");
```

Continued

Listing 17-4 *(continued)*

```
   safeclose(fd);

   /* Delete the FIFO. */

   unlink("ch17-fifo");
}

void child(char *argv[]) {
   int fd;
   char buffer[100];

   fd = safeopen(argv[1], O_WRONLY);

   tprintf("The client is ready.  Enter messages, or Ctrl+D when done.\n");

   while (fgets(buffer, sizeof(buffer), stdin) != NULL) {
     write_buffer(fd, buffer, strlen(buffer));
   }
   tprintf("Client exiting.\n");
   safeclose(fd);

}

/*
   This function writes a certain number of bytes from "buf" to a file
   or socket descriptor specified by "fd". The number of bytes is
   specified by "count". It returns the number of bytes written,
   or <0 on error.
*/

int write_buffer(int fd, const void *buf, int count) {
   const void *pts = buf;
   int   status = 0, n;

   if (count < 0) return (-1);

   while (status != count) {
     n = safewrite(fd, pts+status, count-status);
     if (n < 0) return (n);
     status += n;
   }
   return (status);
}

int read_buffer(int fd, void *buf, int count) {
   void *pts = buf;
   int   status = 0, n;
```

```
    if (count < 0) return (-1);

  while (status != count) {
    n = saferead(fd, pts+status, count-status);
    if (n < 1) return n;
    status += n;
  }
  return (status);
}

int readnlstring(int socket, char *buf, int maxlen) {
  return readdelimstring(socket, buf, maxlen, '\n');
}

int readdelimstring(int socket, char *buf, int maxlen, char delim) {
  int status;
  int count = 0;

  while (count < maxlen - 1) {
    if ((status = read_buffer(socket, buf+count, 1)) < 1) {
      return -1;
    }
    if (buf[count] == delim) {            /* Found the delimiter */
      buf[count] = 0;
      return 0;
    }
    count++;
  }
  buf[count] = 0;
  return 0;
}

int tprintf(const char *fmt, ...) {
  va_list args;
  struct tm *tstruct;
  time_t tsec;

  tsec = time(NULL);
  tstruct = localtime(&tsec);

  printf("%02d:%02d:%02d %5d| ",
         tstruct->tm_hour,
         tstruct->tm_min,
         tstruct->tm_sec,
         getpid());

  va_start(args, fmt);
```

Continued

Listing 17-4 *(continued)*

```
  return vprintf(fmt, args);
}

pid_t safefork(void) {
  pid_t retval;

  retval = fork();
  if (retval == -1)
    HandleError(errno, "fork", "failed");
  return retval;
}
```

Here is a sample result from running this code. First the parent side:

```
$ ./ch17-4
17:29:54  1035| The server is listening on ch17-fifo.
17:29:58  1035| Client has connected.
17:30:05  1035| Received message: Hello, this is a message.
17:30:07  1035| Received message: Here's another one.
17:30:11  1035| Received message: I'm done sending messages now.
17:30:11  1035| No more data; parent exiting.
```

And now from the client side:

```
$ ./ch17-4 ch17-fifo
17:29:58  1036| The client is ready.  Enter messages, or Ctrl+D when done.
Hello, this is a message.
Here's another one.
I'm done sending messages now.
Ctrl+D
17:30:11  1036| Client exiting.
```

Summary

In this chapter, you learned about using pipes and FIFOs to communicate between processes. The following topics were discussed:

✦ A pipe is a unidirectional interprocess communication mechanism that uses file descriptors and standard system-call I/O to do most functions.

✦ A FIFO is a named pipe; that is, it has an entry in the file system although no data is stored in the file system to accompany a named pipe.

✦ To use a pipe, you get an array of two file descriptors, then fork.

✦ You can use dup2(2) to copy a pipe's descriptor in place of standard input, output, or error to redirect the input or output of another program before using `exec()` to start it.

✦ To use a FIFO, one process needs to run `mkfifo()`. Then, both processes need to open it; one for reading and one for writing.

✦ The FIFO entry in the file system does not disappear by itself; you have to unlink it when you're done with it.

✦   ✦   ✦

Internet Sockets

In Chapter 17, you learned about pipes as a method for
communicating between processes residing on a single
machine. In this chapter, I'll introduce you to TCP sockets,
which are used to communicate with processes that may
reside on different machines.

This capability gives you an amazingly powerful tool. You can
now exchange data with processes on other machines, letting
you accomplish tasks such as distributed or parallel processing
and true client/server applications. Moreover, you can set up
information servers, such as Web servers, by using these calls.
The networking that Linux uses natively for LAN purposes is
the same as the networking used by the Internet, unlike some
other operating systems. You have a complete, full-featured
suite of tools for handling Internet communications in Linux.

Along with all this power, though, comes a significant amount
of added complexity. Dealing with a network introduces a
significant number of variables and wildcards that are not
present when you are communicating solely with another
process on your local machine. In order to deal with these
situations, you will have to go to some extra effort to ensure
the correctness of your program.

An Introduction to TCP/IP

In order to have a clear understanding of how your programs
work, and why the system calls behave as they do, you need to
understand a few details about the underlying communication
mechanism, the problems the designers of TCP faced, and how
they resolved them. Although it's technically possible to write
a program without this understanding, you'll most likely write
far better code if you know a bit about the inner workings of
the system.

The problems

As networks have evolved, the need has arisen for a way to organize communication across them. Because Internet communication may pass through many different connections and routers, the communication method must be robust enough to detect failures. Because a single wire may hold communication between multiple processes on a computer, or even multiple computers, there has to be a way to share the wire with different computers and processes while still ensuring that data sent to or from one particular process is kept separate from data from all the others. The systems need to be sure not to send data faster than the recipient can process it. For communication to be reliable, there needs to be a way to confirm that the remote machine has received a given transmission.

Another problem is with the network itself. The protocol has to deal with network failures in a proper way, without causing data loss. This can be very tricky because the very nature of a network failure means a communication loss occurs, in which the remote end cannot necessarily be told to clean up after a problem.

The protocol has to be able to deal with situations that arise without interrupting the network communication, if possible. For instance, if a network connection is overloaded (more data is being sent than it can accommodate), it will have to drop some data. A good protocol should be resilient in the face of this; it should detect the loss and resend the lost data.

The solutions

In order to provide a communication method to address these issues, designers crafted a layered stack of protocols based upon IP, the Internet Protocol. As a developer, you are most interested in TCP, the Transmission Control Protocol, which is used for most Internet communication.

TCP is a packet protocol. This means that when you send data from your program, no matter how large it is, it is separated into small packets for transport. These packets typically are no larger than one or two kilobytes. Each packet is stamped with some control information: which computer sent the packet, which port sent the packet (more on ports is in the Addressing section below), which computer the packet is going to, and which port the packet is going to. There is also some extra control information, a sequence number, and a checksum, which is used to ensure that the data in the packet has not been corrupted.

The sequence number is important because sometimes packets may be delivered out of order. Most programs are extremely sensitive to order of data and could not deal with this sort of problem. Therefore, TCP will automatically encode an order number, and the receiving computer will automatically reassemble the packets in the correct order and discard duplicates.

Additionally, this packet mechanism permits multiplexing of the network connection — that is, a single connection can be shared between multiple processes. This is possible because each packet sent is identified with the sending and receiving information.

When a system receives an intact TCP packet, it sends back an acknowledgment to the sender. The sender will continue trying to send packets until it receives such an acknowledgment. This behavior means that communication can get through (albeit slowly) even if some packet loss occurs, as may be the case with an overloaded network connection. Additionally, it allows the sender to pace itself such that it does not transmit data at a speed faster than the recipient can process it, in that the sender can refrain from sending new data until receipt of most of the older data has been acknowledged.

Moreover, because the packets are stamped with the sender's address, if there is a network error along the way, the sender can sometimes be informed about it and return an error to the application. Of course, things do not always happen this way (sometimes the error communication can't reach your program due to this very failure).

Finally, in order to establish communication, the two processes must first agree to communicate with each other; otherwise, there's no point in sending data across the network. With TCP, this is done with the so-called three-way handshake.

Let's look at an analogy to help you understand the issues: a chess game played by mail. When you start, you need to confirm that you will be playing the game, and figure out such issues as who will take the first move. For the sake of this discussion, let's assume that it normally takes about a day for your letters to be delivered and perhaps two weeks to contemplate each move.

You might take the first move, and send off a letter to your friend with the move. Knowing the postal service, you never trust the letter to get there; it could get lost, misdirected, crushed, folded, spindled, or mutilated — you just never know. Because your friend may take some time before sending you the next move, you need to confirm the receipt of the one you sent. Therefore, your friend will mail you back an acknowledgment confirming receipt of the information you sent. If you don't receive this acknowledgment in the expected timeframe (perhaps two days), you can resend the information, thinking that the postal service has lost your letter.

There is another possibility: the postal service may have lost the acknowledgment. If this is the case, you need to make sure to number your moves, because your friend may receive two copies of this one. You don't want someone else to mistake the information as your *next* move, so you agree on a system of numbering. If either of you receives more than one copy of a single item, you send an acknowledgment for each but only read the first. That way, in case the acknowledgment was lost, your friend knows you received the information, but you will not process (read) it twice.

There's another thing to consider: what if you're a much better chess player than your friend? Well, you might anticipate your opponent's moves, and decide to go ahead and send along your moves before even hearing what the other moves are. For chess, this is a bit of a stretch of the analogy, but please bear with me anyway. So you might write five letters, and want to send them all to your opponent — properly numbered, of course. But your opponent's mailbox can only hold three letters, and if the postal service tries to jam more letters in the mailbox, you can be sure that some will be lost or arrive in an unreadable state.

Your solution is to use flow control — wait for acknowledgments for previous information before sending new information. In this case, you could send at most three letters ahead of the recipient, based on the arrival of the acknowledgments. This three-letter limit is known as a *sliding window*; that is, at any given time, there may be a window of three packets in transit.

Notice also how the postal service implements something analogous to multiplexing: the resources of the mail delivery trucks are shared between all the packets being transferred. In the same way, the resources of the network are shared between all the packets being electronically transferred.

Just as the postal service can accidentally drop your letter out the back of a truck or spill coffee all over it, so too an electronic network can drop your packets or corrupt them. The communication method that you may use with a chess game is not unlike that used with TCP. Because TCP guarantees that your data will arrive intact and in the proper order unless a catastrophic failure prevents it, it is termed a *reliable* protocol. With TCP, data gets through correctly or not at all.

A note about jargon

Because communication across a network can be complex, you should grow familiar with some jargon specific to this system. First, when we say server in relation to TCP/IP networking, we usually refer to a *server process*, although sometimes this could mean the actual computer that runs that process. TCP/IP lends itself to a client/server programming model, but aside from the initial connection, there is nothing that requires this method be used.

A similar situation is true for the client: the word could apply to the client machine, but more often, to the client process. Again, this distinction may or may not be relevant after the initial connection has been established.

Unique Challenges of TCP/IP

You have already been introduced to some of the challenges facing people who use a distributed network for communication. The deceptively simple problem that the network does not always deliver data reliably means some rather complex interactions occur with your programs. You have to be able to deal with long delays as TCP resends packets that may have been dropped. You have to deal with network outages that could interrupt communication between your program and the remote. You have to deal with a situation in which the remote process or computer may crash.

As an example, let's consider a simple problem. Programs on various computers need to get a unique identifier from a central location. Identifiers must not be used twice, and they must all be used in sequence (there should be no gaps). They may be used to generate unique customer IDs or something similar.

So, you decide to write a server that takes a request for an ID and gives out the next available item. Normally, this is easy. The server gives out an ID, and then the client machines will use it for whatever purpose is necessary. However, what happens if a network failure occurs as this is going on? The server has no way of knowing whether or not the client actually received the ID — a lack of an acknowledgment could be because the network went down before the ID was received by the client or because it went down after it was received by the client but before the acknowledgment was transmitted. There is no easy solution to this problem; the server is left in an unfortunate situation of not knowing what to do with a given ID.

Although there are ways that you can reduce the problem, a better option may be to just prevent it from occurring in the first place. Perhaps you should make the server both generate and process the ID, meaning that a network failure would not prevent a generated ID from being used.

Protocols

When you send data from computer to computer with TCP/IP, you have to send it in such a way that the computer on the remote end understands what you're trying to communicate. For instance, if you are writing a networked chess game, you need to have an agreed-upon way of encoding the chess moves into a form that can be communicated between the two machines, and decoding the data from the network such that the program can process it.

In a stacked system such as TCP/IP, there are already other protocols at work that you don't even have to worry about. There are signaling protocols that define the voltages, signaling speeds, and the like used by the physical medium such as Ethernet or a modem. There is the TCP/IP suite, itself a collection of protocols built upon an existing physical protocol set. All of these exist to support your own application with its own protocol.

The protocol that's right for you can vary depending on what your program does and what sort of data it needs to communicate. Although TCP, at its lower level, splits your data stream into packets, you are never told and have no control over where this occurs, in that the packets are reassembled for you. When you read data from the network, you have no inherent indication of when the sending computer is finished sending a block of data. Contrast this with reading from a terminal, which (by default) returns data to your program one line at a time. Reading the same line, say a 70-character line, from the network may result in a chunk of 2 bytes, one of 60 bytes, and then one of 8 bytes — there is no way to know beforehand. Therefore, you must develop a way of communicating between your two processes such that they each know when they've received a full block of data.

There are many different ways to do this. One of the most common is to send a fixed-length size indicator before sending the data itself. This size indicator is then read in its entirety by the recipient. The recipient then reads data in the amount indicated from the network, thus ensuring that it gets the entire communication and nothing more. Using this method has the advantage that it is fairly simple to code on both ends, which can be a big plus. A disadvantage is that it generally prevents users from being able to connect directly to your server and type commands to it, which can be useful for debugging.

Another common method is to use a certain end-of-request marker. Many protocols used on the Internet, such as SMTP for mail and HTTP for Web traffic, use this method and use the carriage return or linefeed (something like \n) as their end-of-request marker. From the perspective of the program sending the data, this is an extremely simple way to go. However, for the recipient, the task is a bit more difficult. The input must be processed, scanned for this marker. Some programs simply read from the network one byte at a time when using this type of protocol. Although this leads to easy coding, it is quite slow, and a more complex buffering system often has to be worked out. Additionally, there is another potential problem: what if the request itself needs to contain the marker character? In some cases, this will never occur. However, it's quite possible in some other cases. In these situations, you actually have to encode the usage of the character in the data, and decode this usage on the recipient side. Therefore, if you are transmitting binary data across the network, you cannot use the marker character method unless you perform what could be costly processing on both ends to encode the data.

Another option is only useful in some situations, such as a chess game. If your requests are always the same size, then you can simply have each side read data in blocks of that size. In chess, you always have a source square and a destination square for your move—so you could simply always send data in this certain size. The program on the other end would know about it and would read data in chunks of that fixed size.

The issue of identifying the start and end of a request or response is only part of the issue of communication, but it is frequently the most tricky. Another issue is that of sending binary data. Sometimes you may prefer to, for instance, send an integer in binary form instead of using something like `sprintf()` to convert it to text and then parse it back to binary on the remote. Doing so is faster and easier, although it again does make it difficult to talk to the server manually. There is a trick, though: different platforms use different internal representations for binary data such as integers. To overcome this problem, designers have devised a *network byte order* for these things, which is a standard representation for the data over the network. The data is converted into the network byte order, sent across the network, and converted to the appropriate local representation on the other end. The functions to do that include `htonl()` and `htons()` for converting from host to network order, and `ntohl()` and `ntohs()` for converting from network to host order.

Addressing

One issue that you never had to worry about when dealing with pipes is addressing. You never needed to worry about it because the issue simply did not exist—you were always talking to the local machine, so there was no need to find out the location of a remote one. Furthermore, because you would get the descriptors and then fork, there was no need to be able to locate a particular process on a machine.

With the Internet, this is somewhat more difficult. You have several issues to contend with. First of all, you have to be able to identify the remote machine. Internally, the Internet Protocol uses a 32-bit number (up to 15 characters long in dotted-quad form) that uniquely identifies each host on the Internet. In the not-so-distant future, 64-bit addresses will be used, which will provide four billion times more addresses (for a total address space of roughly 18 quintillion or $1.8 * 10 \char`^ 19$ unique addresses). Although machines like to deal with numeric addresses, us humans are quite different. It's much easier for us to remember a name than a 12-digit number. Moreover, it is useful to structure addressing hierarchically for larger organizations, just as snail mail addressing is hierarchical (country, state, city, city region, street, building number, and sometimes even the unit inside that building). To achieve this hierarchical arrangement, there is a distributed database for resolving names into numeric addresses, collectively known as the Domain Name System (RFC 1591). To access the Domain Name System (DNS), you can use the library call `gethostbyname()`. You typically use this call to do things such as resolve `www.idgbooks.com` into an address such as `38.170.216.15`.

This is only half of the puzzle. The second part is identifying the proper process with which to communicate on the remote (server) machine, after you have identified the remote machine. Consider the fact that there could easily be dozens of processes on the remote waiting for connections. One could be an HTTP (Web) server, another could be FTP, and a third could be a telnet server. If you want to connect to the Web server, you surely don't want to communicate with the FTP or telnet server instead. Moreover, on your own machine, you may have several copies of a Web browser that you want to run at once. You need the results from Web servers to be directed to the proper process locally. In other words, you need to be able to uniquely identify processes on each end of the communication.

However, the next question becomes: how can you do this? You might first think that you could use process IDs; just direct a packet to a specific machine and process. Unfortunately, there are several problems. First, if you're connecting to a server, how do you know what process ID it has? PIDs are assigned in such a way that the server is never guaranteed to have the same PID. Besides, some programs need to open up multiple connections. Web browsers, for instance, do this so that they can download multiple graphics at once while loading a page. If you refer to an endpoint of communication by just a machine name and process ID, you lose the ability to separate out the data for the two different connections within the same process. This is obviously unacceptable.

To solve this problem, designers came up with the notion of *ports*. A port is simple. For a client process, when it opens up a connection to a server, the system will allocate it the next available port (there are thousands possible). The client doesn't care which port it gets; it just needs one. This is a unique identifier corresponding to a single endpoint of communication. When packets arrive from the server, they are sent to that port on the client's machine. The kernel knows which process is using that port, and more important, which socket is using it, and sends the data to the proper place.

On the server, the situation is somewhat different. The port can't be picked entirely randomly; there has to be a way for the client to identify the server for connection. The typical method for this is to agree on a particular port beforehand. The server will begin listening on this port, and the client will connect to that port on the server.

There is a system allowing symbolic names for these predefined port names — also known as services — permitting them to be looked up instead of hard-coded into a program. This is similar in concept, albeit much less sophisticated, to the Domain Name System. To perform a symbolic lookup, you typically use the getservbyname() library call.

There is one additional twist to the issue of ports. Linux enforces a rule that only the root user is able to open a socket with a port number less than 1024. This prevents applications from hijacking system services and masquerading as a legitimate server. Unless your program will be running as root and specifically needs this protection, your server should use a port number greater than 1024. You might want to also consult your /etc/services file to make sure you are not choosing a number that is already taken by a well-known service. On the client side, you'll randomly be assigned a number greater than 1024 if not running as root, so there is nothing to worry about there.

Client-Side Connections

In this section, I'm going to provide for you what is probably the smallest and most simple program. If you really stretch the definition, you could even call this a Web browser. The program connects to a Web server, requests a single document, and displays the result. Listing 18-1 shows a copy of the source code to this sample program. Note that the greater part of the code is used to establish a connection instead of actually do the communication. When you run the program, you'll need to give it two arguments: a server name and a port name or number. I'll show you an example of running it after presenting the code.

Note   Listing 18-1 is available online.

Listing 18-1: **Sample web client**

```
#include <string.h>
#include <sys/types.h>
#include <sys/socket.h>
#include <netdb.h>
#include <errno.h>
#include <arpa/inet.h>
#include "safecalls.h"

#define PROTOCOL "tcp"
#define REQUEST "GET / HTTP/1.0\n\n"

int write_buffer(int fd, const void *buf, int count);

int main(int argc, char *argv[]) {
  int sockid;
  struct servent *serviceaddr;
  struct hostent *hostaddr;
  struct protoent *protocol;
  struct sockaddr_in socketaddr;
  char buffer[1024];
  int count;

  /******** Step 1: resolve names and generate the socket structure. */
```

Continued

Listing 18-1 *(continued)*

```
/* First, initialize the socketaddr. */
bzero((char *) &socketaddr, sizeof(socketaddr));
socketaddr.sin_family = AF_INET;

/* Resolve the service name. */

serviceaddr = getservbyname(argv[2], PROTOCOL);
if (!serviceaddr) {
  HandleError(0, "getservbyname", "service resolution failed");
}
socketaddr.sin_port = serviceaddr->s_port;

/* Resolve the host name. */

hostaddr = gethostbyname(argv[1]);
if (!hostaddr) {
  HandleError(0, "gethostbyname", "host resolution failed");
}

memcpy(&socketaddr.sin_addr, hostaddr->h_addr, hostaddr->h_length);

/* Resolve the protocol name. */

protocol = getprotobyname(PROTOCOL);
if (!protocol) {
  HandleError(0, "getprotobyname", "protocol resolution failed");
}
/* Note: using SOCK_STREAM below since this is only TCP. */

/********* Step 2: Create the socket for this end. */

sockid = socket(PF_INET, SOCK_STREAM, protocol->p_proto);
if (sockid < 0) {
  HandleError(errno, "socket", "couldn't create socket");
}

/********* Step 3: Connect the socket to the server.  (Almost done!) */

if (connect(sockid, &socketaddr, sizeof(socketaddr)) < 0) {
  HandleError(errno, "connect", "connect call failed");
}

/*******************************************************************/

/* The channel for communication to the server has now been established.
   Now, request the document at the server root. */

write_buffer(sockid, REQUEST, strlen(REQUEST));
```

```
   /* Request has been sent.  Read the result. */

   while ((count = saferead(sockid, buffer, sizeof(buffer) - 1))) {
     write_buffer(1, buffer, count);
   }

   return 0;
}

int write_buffer(int fd, const void *buf, int count) {
   const void *pts = buf;
   int   status = 0, n;

   if (count < 0) return (-1);

   while (status != count) {
     n = safewrite(fd, pts+status, count-status);
     if (n < 0) return (n);
     status += n;
   }
   return (status);
}
```

Let's step through this code and watch what it does. The first step is the biggest —
it is responsible for gathering information and using it to fill out the sockaddr_in
structure. First, it initializes the structure to all nulls and sets the protocol family
to indicate the Internet protocol. Next, it resolves the service name. After that, it
queries the DNS for the host name. This action is a little strange in that the result
needs to be copied into the structure by using memcpy(); the reason is that the
types are incompatible for a direct assignment. Finally, the protocol entry is found.

With step 2, a socket is created. The socket is a special-purpose file descriptor.
Each side uses a socket for communication. This call does not actually connect it
to the remote; rather, it creates an entry for the socket in the system. Finally, with
step 3, the socket is actually connected. At this point, the TCP handshake occurs
and the two machines begin talking to each other.

After the socket has been created, you can refer to it as with any other file
descriptor. You'll note that, unlike pipes, the socket is bidirectional — it is both
written to and read from. A request is sent, which will obtain the top page from a
Web server. After sending the request, the program enters a loop reading data
until the Web server closes the connection. The data read is simply printed out
to the screen.

To compile the program, you'll need the safecalls.c and safecalls.h files from Chapter 14, "Introducing the Linux I/O." You can then compile with a command like this:

```
$ gcc -Wall -o ch18-1 ch18-1.c safecalls.c
```

When you run the program, it expects two parameters: the name of a server and the name of a protocol. For the protocol, you should use HTTP, as it's designed to communicate with a Web server. Here's an example of running the program:

```
$ ./ch18-1 www.apache.org http
HTTP/1.1 200 OK
Date: Thu, 28 Oct 1999 03:31:07 GMT
Server: Apache/1.3.10-dev (Unix) ApacheJServ/1.0 PHP/3.0.6
Content-Location: index.html
Vary: negotiate
TCN: choice
Last-Modified: Tue, 05 Oct 1999 16:43:47 GMT
Connection: close
Content-Type: text/html

<!DOCTYPE HTML PUBLIC "-//W3C//DTD HTML 3.2 Final//EN">
<HTML>
 <HEAD>
  <TITLE>Apache Project Development Site</TITLE>
 </HEAD>
```

To be sure, there is actually far more output than this; you can see for yourself that the entire HTML source for this front page is returned. You can also experiment with trying other servers, although you should be aware that you'll only be able to request the root page, because the program isn't sophisticated enough to request other pages.

Server-Side Connections

Setting up a connection for a server is a bit more complex than doing the same for a client. In order to form a server, you actually need to use two file descriptors. The first is designed solely to listen for connections. After a connection is received, a second is created to deal with the communication. As you'll see in a bit, this mechanism is necessary to support a server that can handle multiple connections. Listing 18-2 presents the source code for a first attempt at a server.

Note   Listing 18-2 is available online.

Listing 18-2: **Sample server**

```c
#include <string.h>
#include <sys/types.h>
#include <sys/socket.h>
#include <netdb.h>
#include <errno.h>
#include <arpa/inet.h>
#include "safecalls.h"

#define PROTOCOL "tcp"
#define SERVICE 7797
#define WELCOME "You have connected to the counting server.  Welcome!\n"

int write_buffer(int fd, const void *buf, int count);
int readnlstring(int socket, char *buf, int maxlen);
int read_buffer(int fd, void *buf, int count);
int readdelimstring(int socket, char *buf, int maxlen, char delim);

int main(void) {
  int listensock, workersock;
  struct protoent *protocol;
  struct sockaddr_in socketaddr;
  char buffer[1024];
  char size[100];
  int addrlen;
  int trueval = 1;

  /******** Step 1:  generate the socket structure and resolve names. */

  bzero((char *) &socketaddr, sizeof(socketaddr));
  socketaddr.sin_family = AF_INET;
  socketaddr.sin_addr.s_addr = INADDR_ANY;
  socketaddr.sin_port = htons(SERVICE);


  /* Resolve the protocol name. */

  protocol = getprotobyname(PROTOCOL);
  if (!protocol) {
    HandleError(0, "getprotobyname", "protocol resolution failed");
  }
  /* Note: using SOCK_STREAM below since this is only TCP. */

  /********* Step 2: Create the master socket */

  listensock = socket(PF_INET, SOCK_STREAM, protocol->p_proto);
  if (listensock < 0) {
    HandleError(errno, "socket", "couldn't create socket");
```

Continued

Listing 18-2 *(continued)*

```
/********* Step 3: Bind it to a port. */

if (bind(listensock, &socketaddr, sizeof(socketaddr)) < 0) {
  HandleError(errno, "bind", "couldn't bind to port %d", SERVICE);
}

/* Let others connect to it immediately upon exit. */

setsockopt(listensock, SOL_SOCKET, SO_REUSEADDR, &trueval, sizeof(trueval));

/********* Step 4: Listen for connections. */

if (listen(listensock, 0) < 0) {
  HandleError(errno, "listen", "couldn't listen on port %d", SERVICE);
}

printf("Listening for a connection...\n");

/********* Step 5: Accept a connection from the client. */

workersock = accept(listensock, &socketaddr, &addrlen);
if (workersock < 0) {
  HandleError(errno, "accept", "couldn't open worker socket");
}

/********* Ready to communicate! */

printf("Received connection from a client at ");
printf("%s port %d\n", inet_ntoa(socketaddr.sin_addr),
       ntohs(socketaddr.sin_port));

write_buffer(workersock, WELCOME, strlen(WELCOME));

while(readnlstring(workersock, buffer, sizeof(buffer)) >= 0) {
  sprintf(size, "Size: %d\n", strlen(buffer) - 1);
  write_buffer(workersock, size, strlen(size));
  if (strncmp(buffer, "exit", 4) == 0) break;
}

printf("Shutting down.\n");

safeclose(workersock);
safeclose(listensock);

return 0;
}

int write_buffer(int fd, const void *buf, int count) {
```

```
     const void *pts = buf;
     int  status = 0, n;

     if (count < 0) return (-1);

     while (status != count) {
       n = safewrite(fd, pts+status, count-status);
       if (n < 0) return (n);
       status += n;
     }
     return (status);
}

int read_buffer(int fd, void *buf, int count) {
     void *pts = buf;
     int  status = 0, n;

     if (count < 0) return (-1);

     while (status != count) {
       n = saferead(fd, pts+status, count-status);
       if (n < 1) return n;
       status += n;
     }
     return (status);
}


int readnlstring(int socket, char *buf, int maxlen) {
     return readdelimstring(socket, buf, maxlen, '\n');
}

int readdelimstring(int socket, char *buf, int maxlen, char delim) {
     int status;
     int count = 0;

     while (count < maxlen - 1) {
       if ((status = read_buffer(socket, buf+count, 1)) < 1) {
         return -1;
       }
       if (buf[count] == delim) {              /* Found the delimiter */
         buf[count] = 0;
         return 0;
       }
       count++;
     }
     buf[count] = 0;
     return 0;
}
```

There is a five-step connection process in this situation. The first step initializes the socket address structure. In this case, we know the port number (defined as 7797) ahead of time, so there is no need to do a lookup on that. The protocol is still looked up, but notice that there is no need to look up a host — that's because the clients look up the server, not the other way around.

With step 2, you create the master, or listening, socket. As with the client, the socket can't actually do anything until it is connected to something useful. Therefore, we need a few more steps to get everything into gear.

In step 3, the socket is bound to a port on the server machine. This registers the socket as using that port with the operating system; it is the step immediately prior to a listen. After that, as a convenience, the SO_REUSEADDR option is set. Normally, when your program exits, the system may prevent another program from binding to the same port for a few seconds; if you're going to be experimenting with this program, it's useful to inhibit that behavior so you can restart the server immediately. In step 4, the system is told to listen for connections.

Beginning with step 5, these actions can be repeated for every server in the system. Many servers will handle multiple requests and might fork after the call to accept. Some might instead loop, resetting themselves and then using accept() to get new connections. The accept() call will wait until a client connection request is received. When such a request is received, it returns a new file descriptor — a worker socket — through which all the communication to the client must take place. Additionally, if its second parameter is not NULL, it will fill out details about this connection in the sockaddr_in structure pointed to by the argument. These details are printed out in the code.

The communication itself is fairly straightforward; the program reads a string terminated by a newline character and sends a string containing the size back to the client. It does this until the client closes the connection (causing readnlstring() to return a value less than 1) or until the supplied string begins with "exit."

Now, let's try this program out. First, start the server. Then, you can use telnet to connect to it. If you are not live on a network, you can use telnet localhost 7797 to connect from your own machine. If you are, you can use any machine on your network (or the entire Internet if you are properly connected to it) to connect to your new server; simply substitute the server's host name for localhost in the example. Here is a sample interaction from the client side:

```
$ telnet localhost 7797
Trying 127.0.0.1...
Connected to localhost.
Escape character is '^]'.
You have connected to the counting server.  Welcome!
Hello!
```

```
Size: 6
This is a test of the new server.
Size: 33
1
Size: 1
2
Size: 1
9
Size: 1
10
Size: 2
bye
Size: 3
exit
Size: 4
Connection closed by foreign host.
```

The server worked! It accepted the connection, handled the data, and sent the result back to the client. In the window running the server process, you'll see something like this:

```
$ ./ch18-2
Listening for a connection...
Received connection from a client at 127.0.0.1 port 1399
Shutting down.
```

The server listened for a connection, informed you when it received one, and then shut down when requested. Notice that every time you connect, a different port number will be reported. This is because the port number for the client is assigned by the operating system as mentioned before.

This server works, but it has some limitations. For one, it can handle only one client at a time. This is not really acceptable. Imagine a Web server that could handle only one client at a time–if there were a large file that took 20 minutes to download, no pages would be served until it was completely transferred! In almost every case, you want your server to be able to handle multiple requests at once. A second problem is that the server would exit after handling only one request. Again, this is no doubt not what you really want; a server that only handles one request is most often not very useful.

One solution to these problems is to have the server fork off when it gets a connection request from a child. Listing 18-3 shows a version of the code that does just that.

 Note   Listing 18-3 is available online.

Listing 18-3: **Sample server code that forks**

```
#include <string.h>
#include <sys/types.h>
#include <sys/socket.h>
#include <sys/resource.h>
#include <sys/wait.h>
#include <netdb.h>
#include <errno.h>
#include <arpa/inet.h>
#include <signal.h>
#include "safecalls.h"

#define PROTOCOL "tcp"
#define SERVICE 7797
#define WELCOME "You have connected to the counting server.  Welcome!\n"

int write_buffer(int fd, const void *buf, int count);
int readnlstring(int socket, char *buf, int maxlen);
int read_buffer(int fd, void *buf, int count);
int readdelimstring(int socket, char *buf, int maxlen, char delim);
void waitchildren(int signum);
pid_t safefork(void);

static int connectioncount = 0;

int main(void) {
  int listensock, workersock;
  struct protoent *protocol;
  struct sockaddr_in socketaddr;
  char buffer[1024];
  char size[100];
  int addrlen;
  int trueval = 1;
  struct sigaction act;

  /* Initialize the signal handler. */

  sigemptyset(&act.sa_mask);
  act.sa_flags = SA_RESTART;
  act.sa_handler = (void *)waitchildren;
  sigaction(SIGCHLD, &act, NULL);

  /******** Step 1:  generate the socket structure and resolve names. */

  bzero((char *) &socketaddr, sizeof(socketaddr));
  socketaddr.sin_family = AF_INET;
  socketaddr.sin_addr.s_addr = INADDR_ANY;
  socketaddr.sin_port = htons(SERVICE);
```

```
/* Resolve the protocol name. */

protocol = getprotobyname(PROTOCOL);
if (!protocol) {
  HandleError(0, "getprotobyname", "protocol resolution failed");
}
/* Note: using SOCK_STREAM below since this is only TCP. */

/********* Step 2: Create the master socket */

listensock = socket(PF_INET, SOCK_STREAM, protocol->p_proto);
if (listensock < 0) {
  HandleError(errno, "socket", "couldn't create socket");
}

/********* Step 3: Bind it to a port. */

if (bind(listensock, &socketaddr, sizeof(socketaddr)) < 0) {
  HandleError(errno, "bind", "couldn't bind to port %d", SERVICE);
}

/* Let others connect to it immediately upon exit. */

setsockopt(listensock, SOL_SOCKET, SO_REUSEADDR, &trueval, sizeof(trueval));

/********* Step 4: Listen for connections. */

if (listen(listensock, 0) < 0) {
  HandleError(errno, "listen", "couldn't listen on port %d", SERVICE);
}

printf("The server is active.  You may terminate it with Ctrl-C.\n");


while (1) {
  workersock = accept(listensock, &socketaddr, &addrlen);
  if (workersock < 0) {
    HandleError(errno, "accept", "couldn't open worker socket");
  }

  connectioncount++;

  if (safefork()) {              /* parent process */
    safeclose(workersock);       /* don't need this socket for the parent */
    printf("Received connection from a client at ");
    printf("%s port %d\n", inet_ntoa(socketaddr.sin_addr),
           ntohs(socketaddr.sin_port));
    printf("There are %d clients active.\n", connectioncount);
  } else {                       /* child process */
    safeclose(listensock);
```

Continued

Listing 18-3 *(continued)*

```
    write_buffer(workersock, WELCOME, strlen(WELCOME));

    while(readnlstring(workersock, buffer, sizeof(buffer)) >= 0) {
      sprintf (size, "Size: %d\n", strlen(buffer) - 1);
      write_buffer(workersock, size, strlen(size));
      if (strncmp(buffer, "exit", 4) == 0) break;
    }

    safeclose(workersock);
    exit(0);
    }
  }

  printf("Shutting down.\n");

  safeclose(listensock);

  return 0;
}

int write_buffer(int fd, const void *buf, int count) {
  const void *pts = buf;
  int  status = 0, n;

  if (count < 0) return (-1);

  while (status != count) {
    n = safewrite(fd, pts+status, count-status);
    if (n < 0) return (n);
    status += n;
  }
  return (status);
}

int read_buffer(int fd, void *buf, int count) {
  void *pts = buf;
  int  status = 0, n;

  if (count < 0) return (-1);

  while (status != count) {
    n = saferead(fd, pts+status, count-status);
    if (n < 1) return n;
    status += n;
  }
```

```
    return (status);
  }

int readnlstring(int socket, char *buf, int maxlen) {
  return readdelimstring(socket, buf, maxlen, '\n');
}

int readdelimstring(int socket, char *buf, int maxlen, char delim) {
  int status;
  int count = 0;

  while (count < maxlen - 1) {
    if ((status = read_buffer(socket, buf+count, 1)) < 1) {
      return -1;
    }
    if (buf[count] == delim) {          /* Found the delimiter */
      buf[count] = 0;
      return 0;
    }
    count++;
  }
  buf[count] = 0;
  return 0;
}

void waitchildren(int signum) {
  while (wait3((int *)NULL,
               WNOHANG,
               (struct rusage *)NULL) > 0) {
    connectioncount--;
    printf("A client disconnected.\n");
    printf("There are %d clients active.\n", connectioncount);
  }
}

pid_t safefork(void) {
  int retval;

  retval = fork();

  if (retval == -1) {
    HandleError(errno, "fork", "fork failed");
  }
  return retval;
}
```

This program simply continues accepting connections as long as it continues to run. When a connection comes in, the program forks a copy of itself to process the connection and immediately goes back to accepting new connections. In this way, each connection can be processed in its own process, without blocking other connections from coming in and being processed. Altogether, this is a big win for the server.

A Network Library

As you write network programs, you'll find that you are repeating many tasks over and over. A library of networking calls can help you write programs faster, to be able to reuse more code, and to reduce bugs that may be introduced by reimplementing code. Here is the code for the library. Some functions in it have not yet been discussed; they'll be covered in the next chapter. After presenting the code for the library, I'll explain a few details to you and demonstrate a rewrite of an earlier program in this chapter using the new library.

First, look at Listing 18-4, the header file, networkinglib.h.

Note   Listing 18-4 is available online.

Listing 18-4: **Network library header: networkinglib.h**

```
/* Don't include this file twice... */
#ifndef __NETWORKINGLIB_H__
#define __NETWORKINGLIB_H__

#include <sys/types.h>
#include <sys/socket.h>
#include <netinet/in.h>
#include <netdb.h>
#include <arpa/inet.h>
#include <string.h>
#include <fcntl.h>
#include <stdio.h>
#include <malloc.h>
#include <errno.h>              /* errno global variable */
#include "safecalls.h"

#ifndef  INADDR_NONE
#define  INADDR_NONE 0xffffffff
#endif

#ifndef COPY_BUFSIZE
```

```
#define COPY_BUFSIZE 10*1024          /* Buffer size for copies is 10K */
#endif

/* Basic reading and writing */
int read_buffer(int fd, char *buf, int count);
int write_buffer(int fd, char *buf, int count);

/* String/delimited reading and writing */

int writestring(int sockid, char *str);
int readstring(int sockid, char *buf, int maxlen);
int readnlstring(int sockid, char *buf, int maxlen);
int readdelimstring(int sockid, char *buf, int maxlen, char delim);

/* Integer reading and writing */

int read_netulong(int fd, uint32_t *value);
int write_netulong(int fd, const unsigned long int value);

/* Data copy */

int copy(int in, int out, unsigned long maxbytes);

/* Reverse DNS lookups and friends */

char *getmyfqdn(void);
char *getfqdn(const char *host);

/* Network initialization */

void socketaddr_init(struct sockaddr_in *socketaddr);
int socketaddr_service(struct sockaddr_in *socketaddr,
            const char *service, const char *proto);
int socketaddr_host(struct sockaddr_in *socketaddr,
            const char *host);
int resolveproto(const char *proto);
int prototype(const char *proto);
int clientconnect(const char *host, const char *port, const char *proto);
int serverinit(const char *port, const char *proto);

/* Miscellaneous */

void stripcrlf(char *temp);

#endif
```

And now, Listing 18-5 shows the code itself, networkinglib.c.

Note   Listing 18-5 is available online.

Listing 18-5: **Net work library: networkinglib.c**

```
/*
Library for:
 * general networking
 * sockets, pipes, etc.
 * unbuffered I/O
 * other items relating to the above

by John Goerzen, Linux Programming Bible
*/

#include <ctype.h>
#include <stdlib.h>
#include "networkinglib.h"

static int checkstring(const char *string);

/* checkstring() is a private function used only by this library.  It checks
    the passed string.  It returns false if there are no nonnumeric
    characters  in the string, or true if there are such characters. */

static int checkstring(const char *string) {
int counter;
  for (counter = 0; counter < strlen(string); counter++)
    if (!(isdigit(string[counter])))
      return 1;
  return 0;
}

/* Send a string, including terminating null.  readdelimstring() could be
    perfect for reading it on the other end.  And in fact, readstring()
    uses just that. */

int writestring(int sockid, char *str) {
  return write_buffer(sockid, str, strlen(str) + 1);
}

/* Reads a string from the network, terminated by a null. */

int readstring(int sockid, char *buf, int maxlen) {
  return readdelimstring(sockid, buf, maxlen, 0);
}

/* Reads a string terminated by a newline */

int readnlstring(int sockid, char *buf, int maxlen) {
  return readdelimstring(sockid, buf, maxlen, '\n');
}
```

```
/* Reads a string with an arbitrary ending delimiter. */

int readdelimstring(int sockid, char *buf, int maxlen, char delim) {
  int count = 0, status;

  while (count <= maxlen) {
    status = saferead(sockid, buf+count, 1);
    if (status < 0) return status;
    if (status < 1) {
      HandleError(0, "readdelimstring", "unexpected EOF from socket");
      return status;
    }
    if (buf[count] == delim) {              /* Found the delimiter */
      buf[count] = 0;
      return 0;
    }
    count++;
  }
  return 0;
}

/* Copies data from the in to the out file descriptor.  If numsize
   is nonzero, specifies the maximum number of bytes to copy.  If
   it is 0, data will continue being copied until in returns EOF. */

int copy(int in, int out, unsigned long maxbytes) {
  char buffer[COPY_BUFSIZE];
  int indata, remaining;

  remaining = maxbytes;

  while (remaining || !maxbytes) {
    indata = saferead(in, buffer,
             (!remaining || COPY_BUFSIZE < remaining) ? COPY_BUFSIZE
               : remaining);
    if (indata < 1) return indata;
    write_buffer(out, buffer, indata);
    if (maxbytes) remaining -= indata;
  }
  return (0);
}


/*
   This function will write a certain number of bytes from the buffer
   to the descriptor fd.  The number of bytes written are returned.
   This function will not return until all data is written or an error
   occurs.
*/
```

Continued

Listing 18-5 *(continued)*

```
int write_buffer(int fd, char *buf, int count) {
  int   status = 0, result;

  if (count < 0) return (-1);

  while (status != count) {
    result = safewrite(fd, buf + status, count - status);
    if (result < 0) return result;
    status += result;
  }
  return (status);
}

/*
   This function will read a number of bytes from the descriptor fd.  The
   number of bytes read are returned.  In the event of an error, the
   error handler is returned.  In the event of an EOF at the first read
   attempt, 0 is returned.  In the event of an EOF after some data has
   been received, the count of the already-received data is returned.
*/

int read_buffer(int fd, char *buf, int count) {
  char *pts = buf;
  int   status = 0, n;

  if (count < 0) return (-1);

  while (status != count) {
    n = saferead(fd, pts+status, count-status);
    if (n < 0) return n;
    if (n == 0) return status;
    status += n;
  }
  return (status);
}

/* Reads a uint32 from the network in network byte order.

   A note on the implementation: because some architectures cannot
   write to the memory of the integer except all at once, a character
   buffer is used that is then copied into place all at once. */

int read_netulong(int fd, uint32_t *value) {
  char buffer[sizeof(uint32_t)];
  int status;

  status = read_buffer(fd, buffer, sizeof(uint32_t));
  if (status != sizeof(uint32_t)) {
```

```
      HandleError(0, "read_netulong", "unexpected EOF");
      return -1;
    }
  bcopy(buffer, (char *)value, sizeof(uint32_t));
  *value = ntohl(*value);
  return (0);
}

/* Write an unsigned long in network byte order */

int write_netulong(int fd, const unsigned long int value) {
  char buffer[sizeof(uint32_t)];
  uint32_t temp;
  int status;

  temp = htonl(value);
  bcopy((char *)&temp, buffer, sizeof(temp));
  status = write_buffer(fd, buffer, sizeof(temp));
  if (status != sizeof(temp)) return -1;
  return (0);
}

/* Returns the fully qualified domain name of the current host. */
char *getmyfqdn(void) {
  char hostname[200];
  gethostname(hostname, sizeof(hostname));
  return getfqdn(hostname);
}

/* Returns the fully qualified domain name of an arbitrary host. */
char *getfqdn(const char *host) {
  struct hostent *hp;
  static char fqdn[200];

  hp = gethostbyname(host);
  if (!hp)
    return (char *)NULL;
  safestrncpy(fqdn, (hp->h_aliases[0]) ? hp->h_aliases[0] : hp->h_name,
            sizeof(fqdn));
  return fqdn;
}

void socketaddr_init(struct sockaddr_in *socketaddr) {
  bzero((char *) socketaddr, sizeof(*socketaddr));
  socketaddr->sin_family = AF_INET;
}

int socketaddr_service(struct sockaddr_in *socketaddr,
                       const char *service, const char *proto) {
  struct servent *serviceaddr;
```

Continued

Listing 18-5 *(continued)*

```
/* Need to allow numeric as well as textual data. */

/* 0: pass right through. */

if (strcmp(service, "0") == 0)
  socketaddr->sin_port = 0;
else {                              /* nonzero port */
  serviceaddr = getservbyname(service, proto);
  if (serviceaddr) {
    socketaddr->sin_port = serviceaddr->s_port;
  } else {                         /* name did not resolve, try number */
    if (checkstring(service)) { /* and it's a text name, fail. */
      HandleError(0, "socketaddr_service", "no lookup for %s/%s",
                  service, proto);
      return -1;
    }
    if ((socketaddr->sin_port = htons((u_short)atoi(service))) == 0) {
      HandleError(0, "socketaddr_service", "numeric conversion failed");
      return -1;
    }
  }
}

return 0;
}

int socketaddr_host(struct sockaddr_in *socketaddr,
                    const char *host) {
  struct hostent *hostaddr;
  hostaddr = gethostbyname(host);
  if (!hostaddr) {
    HandleError(0, "socketaddr_host", "gethostbyname failed for %s", host);
    return -1;
  }

  memcpy(&socketaddr->sin_addr, hostaddr->h_addr, hostaddr->h_length);
  return 0;
}

int resolveproto(const char *proto) {
  struct protoent *protocol;
  protocol = getprotobyname(proto);
  if (!protocol) {
    HandleError(0, "resolveproto", "getprotobyname failed for %s", proto);
    return -1;
  }

  return protocol->p_proto;
}
```

```
int prototype(const char *proto) {
  if (strcmp(proto, "tcp") == 0) return SOCK_STREAM;
  if (strcmp(proto, "udp") == 0) return SOCK_DGRAM;
  return -1;
}

int clientconnect(const char *host, const char *port, const char *proto) {
  struct sockaddr_in socketaddr;
  int sockid;

  socketaddr_init(&socketaddr);
  socketaddr_service(&socketaddr, port, proto);
  socketaddr_host(&socketaddr, host);

  sockid = socket(PF_INET, prototype(proto), resolveproto(proto));
  if (sockid < 0) {
    HandleError(errno, "clientconnect", "socket failed");
    return -1;
  }

  if (connect(sockid, &socketaddr, sizeof(socketaddr)) < 0) {
    HandleError(errno, "clientconnect", "connect failed");
    return -1;
  }

  return sockid;
}

int serverinit(const char *port, const char *proto) {
  struct sockaddr_in socketaddr;
  int mastersock;
  int trueval = 1;

  socketaddr_init(&socketaddr);
  socketaddr.sin_addr.s_addr = INADDR_ANY;
  socketaddr_service(&socketaddr, port, proto);

  mastersock = socket(PF_INET, prototype(proto), resolveproto(proto));
  if (mastersock < 0) {
    HandleError(errno, "serverinit", "couldn't create socket");
    return -1;
  }

  if (bind(mastersock, &socketaddr, sizeof(socketaddr)) < 0) {
    HandleError(errno, "serverinit", "bind to port %d failed",
                socketaddr.sin_port);
    return -1;
  }

  setsockopt(mastersock, SOL_SOCKET, SO_REUSEADDR, &trueval, sizeof(trueval));
```

Continued

Listing 18-5 *(continued)*

```
  if (prototype(proto) == SOCK_STREAM) {
    if (listen(mastersock, 5) < 0) {
      HandleError(errno, "serverinit", "listen on port %d failed",
                  socketaddr.sin_port);
      return -1;
    }
  }

  return mastersock;
}

/* Removes CR and LF from the end of a string. */
void stripcrlf(char *temp)
{
  while (strlen(temp) &&
         ((temp[strlen(temp)-1] == 13) || (temp[strlen(temp)-1] == 10))) {
    temp[strlen(temp)-1] = 0;
  }
}
```

You'll find that this code is mostly the same as the code you have already seen.
There are some modifications to allow it to work in more situations, such as when
HandleError() does not cause program termination. The service resolving
routine will now allow you to specify numeric port names, so you can, for
instance, substitute 80 for HTTP for a Web server.

Included below are rewrites of the first and third examples from this chapter, now
designed to use the library. Notice how easy establishing a network connection
suddenly becomes, and how easy communication can be as well. Here is a rewrite
of the simple client:

```
#include <string.h>
#include <sys/types.h>
#include <sys/socket.h>
#include <netdb.h>
#include <errno.h>
#include <arpa/inet.h>
#include "safecalls.h"
#include "networkinglib.h"

#define PROTOCOL "tcp"
#define REQUEST "GET / HTTP/1.0\n\n"

int main(int argc, char *argv[]) {
  int sockid;
```

```
    sockid = clientconnect(argv[1], argv[2], "tcp");

    /* The channel for communication to the server has now been
established.
        Now, request the document at the server root. */

    write_buffer(sockid, REQUEST, strlen(REQUEST));

    /* Request has been sent.  Read the result. */

    copy(sockid, 1, 0);

    return 0;
}
```

The program is now far shorter and a lot easier to understand. Because all of the work is shoved off to the network library, you can make the program work with a lot less code used itself. To compile, you can use:

```
$ gcc -Wall -o newclient newclient.c networkinglib.c
```

The server program gets a benefit as well, although because it is a bit more complex, the difference is not quite as apparent—however, it still sheds almost 100 lines as shown in Listing 18-6.

Note   Listing 18-6 is available online.

Listing 18-6: **Revised network library code**

```
#include <string.h>
#include <sys/types.h>
#include <sys/socket.h>
#include <sys/resource.h>
#include <sys/wait.h>
#include <errno.h>
#include "safecalls.h"
#include "networkinglib.h"

#define PROTOCOL "tcp"
#define SERVICE "7797"
#define WELCOME "You have connected to the counting server.  Welcome!\n"

void waitchildren(int signum);
pid_t safefork(void);

static int connectioncount = 0;
```

Continued

Listing 18-6 *(continued)*

```c
int main(void) {
  int mastersock, workersock;
  struct sigaction act;
  struct sockaddr_in socketaddr;
  int addrlen;
  char buffer[1024];
  char size[100];

  /* Initialize the signal handler. */

  sigemptyset(&act.sa_mask);
  act.sa_flags = SA_RESTART;
  act.sa_handler = (void *)waitchildren;
  sigaction(SIGCHLD, &act, NULL);

  mastersock = serverinit(SERVICE, PROTOCOL);

  printf("The server is active.  You may terminate it with Ctrl-C.\n");

  while (1) {
    workersock = accept(mastersock, &socketaddr, &addrlen);
    if (workersock < 0) {
      HandleError(errno, "accept", "couldn't open worker socket");
    }

    connectioncount++;

    if (safefork ()) {                    /* parent process */
      safeclose(workersock);              /* don't need this socket for the parent */
      printf("Received connection from a client at ");
      printf("%s port %d\n", inet_ntoa(socketaddr.sin_addr),
             ntohs(socketaddr.sin_port));
      printf("There are %d clients active.\n", connectioncount);
    } else {                              /* child process */
      safeclose(mastersock);
      write_buffer(workersock, WELCOME, strlen(WELCOME));

      while(readnlstring(workersock, buffer, sizeof(buffer)) >= 0) {
        sprintf(size, "Size: %d\n", strlen(buffer) - 1);
        write_buffer(workersock, size, strlen(size));
        if (strncmp(buffer, "exit", 4) == 0) break;
      }

      safeclose(workersock);
      exit(0);
    }
  }
}
```

```
    printf("Shutting down.\n");

    safeclose(mastersock);

    return 0;
}

void waitchildren(int signum) {
  while (wait3((int *)NULL,
               WNOHANG,
               (struct rusage *)NULL) > 0) {
    connectioncount--;
    printf("A client disconnected.\n");
    printf("There are %d clients active.\n", connectioncount);
  }
}

pid_t safefork(void) {
  int retval;

  retval = fork();

  if (retval == -1) {
    HandleError(errno, "fork", "fork failed");
  }
  return retval;
}
```

Summary

In this chapter, you were introduced to communication via TCP/IP. Specifically, I covered these points:

✦ TCP/IP allows you to communicate between different machines instead of just different processes on a single machine.

✦ TCP/IP uses a packet transmission method that allows multiplexing and resilience in the face of some packet loss.

✦ One challenge that faces you as a programmer is identifying endpoints of requests (addressing).

✦ Each endpoint of a TCP connection is identified by an IP address and a port number.

✦ The Domain Name System (DNS) is used to convert host names into IP addresses.

✦ Connecting from a client involves looking up the service, looking up the server's IP address, initializing a few other details, and then connecting the socket to the server.

✦ Connecting from a server involves looking up the service, initializing a few details, binding to a port, listening on that port, and accepting connections. A server will use at least two sockets: one for listening for new connections and one for actually interacting with clients.

✦ A library of network routines is often helpful to streamline the design of your programs.

✦   ✦   ✦

Advanced TCP/IP Sockets

In Chapter 18, you learned about the basics of writing programs that interact with each other over a network. In this chapter, you will learn about two more advanced topics that relate to networking. The first introduces you to a new way to write your server: multiplexing with select() or poll(). The second new topic introduces the connectionless User Datagram Protocol (UDP).

Server Design and Multiplexing

In the example of a server in the Chapter 18, the server forks off a new copy of itself to deal with every client connection. This is often an algorithm that works well. However, there are times when a more sophisticated variant of it would work better or when a different algorithm entirely would be better.

There are several potential problems that you might encounter with the algorithm used in the server in Chapter 18. First, it is vulnerable to a denial of service attack; an attacker could strike up a huge number of connections, causing the server to fork until all the system memory is exhausted. This problem is easily addressed by refusing to fork if the connection count exceeds a certain value; the connections could be refused at that point. Another problem is that, for large and complex servers, forking can be an expensive operation. Finally, if your server has light computation or large amounts of data, you may be able to attain better performance by switching between requests inside your server instead of asking the operating system to do task switching for you.

This last option is often implemented in terms of a polling mechanism based upon select() or poll(). Sometimes, this can be a great opportunity. For instance, the Boa Web server has proved itself to be faster than forking Web servers in many situations due to its tight internal mechanism wrapped around select(). However, this mechanism is not always appropriate. For one thing, the requirements for buffering can be extremely complex. Because you must never attempt to read more data than is immediately available, you need to have a buffer area set aside for each file descriptor that you'll potentially read from, into which you can store partial results. Not only that, but sometimes bits of the next request may come along with the end of the current one—or even several more. Therefore, dealing with a single-process multiplexing server like this is no easy task.

Steps can be taken to shore up servers that use the forking model. For one thing, you might consider preforking—that is, forking off some processes at the beginning of the server's life span and simply having them continue running. They won't exit after a connection has been serviced; they'll just wait for more to arrive. This saves on the overhead of forking new processes, but you still have the overhead of task switching.

What follows is an example of the server from Chapter 18, "Internet Sockets," rewritten to use select() instead of forking. First, Listing 19-1 shows the code for a new buffering library, queue.c.

Note   Listing 19-1 is available online.

Listing 19-1: **Server with select() multiplexing, queue.c**

```
#include <string.h>
#include <stdlib.h>
#include "safecalls.h"
#include "queue.h"

static struct qtype *qstart = NULL;
static struct qtype *qend = NULL;

#ifndef TRUE
#define TRUE 1
#endif

#ifndef FALSE
#define FALSE 0
#endif

/* enq() is the heart of the queue system.  It accepts a pointer to a string
that contains null-terminated raw data that arrived over the network
connection.  It splits the data up into individual commands, and queues them.
*/
```

```
int addtoqueue(int id, char *data) {
  struct qtype *item;
  int iscompleted = 0;
  char *substring = data, *endloc = data;
  char *newdata = NULL;              /* To hold new data */

  while ((endloc = strstr(substring, "\n"))) {
    /* While there are still newlines to process... */
    iscompleted = 1;
    *(endloc) = 0;
    item = findincomplete(id);
    if (item->data) {
      /* We are finishing data for this item. */
      newdata = safemalloc(strlen(item->data) + strlen(substring) + 2);
      if (!newdata) return 0;
      strcpy(newdata, item->data);
      strcat(newdata, substring);
      free(item->data);
      item->data = newdata;
    } else {
      item->data = safestrdup(substring);
      if (! item->data) return 0;
    }
    item->iscomplete = TRUE;
    substring = (char *)(endloc + 1);
  }

  /* At this point:
     - substring could point to a null character, if we just finished
       a terminating newline and are at the end of the string
     - substring could point to a valid part of the data.  In this case,
       there is partial data remaining. */

  if (*substring) {        /* More data. */
    item = findincomplete(id);

    /* Same code as above.... almost! */

    if (item->data) {
      /* We are finishing data for this item. */
      newdata = safemalloc(strlen(item->data) + strlen(substring) + 2);
      if (!newdata) return 0;
      strcpy(newdata, item->data);
      strcat(newdata, substring);
      free(item->data);
      item->data = newdata;
    } else {
      item->data = safemalloc(strlen(substring) + 2);
      if (!item->data) return 0;
```

Continued

Listing 19-1 *(continued)*

```
      strcpy(item->data, substring);
    }

    item->iscomplete = FALSE;
  }

  return TRUE;
}

struct qtype *deqany(void) {
  struct qtype *item = qstart;

  while (item) {
    if (item->iscomplete)
      return deqptr(item);          /* deqptr() just returns item */
    item = item->next;
  }
  return (struct qtype *)NULL;
}

struct qtype *deqid(int id) {
  struct qtype *item = qstart;

  while (item) {
    if ((item->id == id) && (item->iscomplete))
      return deqptr(item);
    item = item->next;
  }
  return (struct qtype *)NULL;
}

struct qtype *deqptr(struct qtype *pointer) {

  struct qtype *previtem = qstart;
  if (!qstart) return (struct qtype *)NULL;  /* empty queue! */
  if (qstart == pointer) {     /* first item in queue */
    qstart = pointer->next;
    if (qend == pointer)     /* only item in queue */
      qend = qstart;
  } else while ((previtem) && (previtem->next != pointer))
    previtem = previtem->next;
  if (!previtem) return previtem;

  /* OK, now...previtem is the item immediately preceding the one do be
     dequeued. */

  previtem->next = pointer->next;
  if (qend == pointer) qend = previtem;
```

```
      return pointer;
}

int deleteallid(int id) {

   struct qtype *item = qstart, *next;
   while (item) {
      next = item->next;              /* Must save it because item may be deleted! */
      if (item->id == id)
         if (!deleteitem(item)) return FALSE;
      item = next;
   }
   return TRUE;
}

int deleteitem(struct qtype *item) {
   /* Dequeue */

   if (!deqptr(item)) return FALSE;

   /* De-allocate memory. */
   if (item->data) free(item->data);
   free(item);

   return TRUE;
}

struct qtype *findincomplete(int id) {

   struct qtype *item = qstart;
   while (item) {
      if ((item->id == id) && (!(item->iscomplete))) return item;
      item = item->next;
   }
   /* Not found; create a new one for 'em. */

   item = createitem();
   item->id = id;
   return item;
}

struct qtype *createitem(void) {

   struct qtype* item;
   item = allocq();
   if (!item) return item;           /* error condition */
```

Continued

Listing 19-1 *(continued)*

```
/* Insert into the queue. */

if (!qend) {                          /* Queue is empty */
  qstart = qend = item;
} else {
  qend->next = item;
  qend = item;
}

/* Set up reasonable defaults. */

item->next = (struct qtype *)NULL;
item->data = (char *)NULL;
item->iscomplete = FALSE;
item->id = 0;

return item;
}

struct qtype *allocq(void) {
  return (struct qtype *)malloc(sizeof(struct qtype));
}
```

You'll also need its header file, queue.h, which appears in Listing 19-2.

Note   Listing 19-2 is available online.

Listing 19-2: **Header file queue.h**

```
/*
   header file for queue implementations
   */

#ifndef __QUEUE_H__
#define __QUEUE_H__

struct qtype {                     /* Each entry in queue will be of this type */
  char *data;
  int iscomplete;                  /* TRUE if it is a complete line
                                      no entry will ever have more than one line
                                   */
  struct qtype *next;              /* Pointer to next entry
                                      the queue is implemented as a linked list */
```

```
    int id;                          /* Unique ID (socket number works here) */
} ;


/*********** FUNCTIONS ***********/

/* Add data to the queue. */
int addtoqueue(int id, char *data);

/* Will dequeue and return the first completed item in the queue.
   NULL is returned if there are no completed items in the queue.
   Data is NOT de-allocated. */
struct qtype *deqany(void);

/* Will dequeue and return the first item matching the given id.  NULL is
   returned if no *completed* items match the given id. */
struct qtype *deqid(int id);

/* Will dequeue the item pointed to.  Used internally by queue.c.  Returns
   pointer. Memory not freed. */
struct qtype *deqptr(struct qtype *pointer);

/* Will DELETE all items associated with the given id.  Will also de-allocate
   memory, etc. */
int deleteallid(int id);

/* Will DELETE only the item pointed to.  Will free memory. */
int deleteitem(struct qtype *item);

/* Will find any incomplete one matching the given id.
   If there are no matching items, will return a pointer to a new queue
   entry to be filled in. */
struct qtype *findincomplete(int id);

/* Will return a pointer to a new, empty queue entry that is already
   properly linked into the chain. */
struct qtype *createitem(void);

struct qtype *allocq(void);

#endif                   /* __QUEUE_H__ */
```

Listing 19-3 shows the program that uses this buffering library.

Note   Listing 19-3 is available online.

Listing 19-3: **Main server code, ch19-1.c**

```c
#include <string.h>
#include <sys/types.h>
#include <sys/socket.h>
#include <sys/resource.h>
#include <sys/wait.h>
#include <errno.h>
#include "safecalls.h"
#include "networkinglib.h"
#include "queue.h"

#define PROTOCOL "tcp"
#define SERVICE "7797"
#define WELCOME "You have connected to the counting server.  Welcome!\n"

int main(void) {
  int mastersock, workersock;
  char buffer[1024];
  char sizebuf[100];
  int nfds = getdtablesize();
  struct qtype *item;

  fd_set orig_fdset, fdset;
  int counter, size;

  mastersock = serverinit(SERVICE, PROTOCOL);

  printf("The server is active.  You may terminate it with Ctrl-C.\n");

  FD_ZERO(&orig_fdset);
  FD_SET(mastersock, &orig_fdset);

  while (1) {
    /* Restore watch set as appropriate. */
    bcopy(&orig_fdset, &fdset, sizeof(orig_fdset));

    select(nfds, &fdset, (fd_set *)0, (fd_set *)0,
           (struct timeval *)0);
    if (FD_ISSET(mastersock, &fdset)) {
      /* New connection! */
      printf("Received connection from a client.\n");
      workersock = accept(mastersock, NULL, NULL);
      FD_SET(workersock, &orig_fdset);
      write_buffer(workersock, WELCOME, strlen(WELCOME));
    }

    /* Data on existing connection.  Add to the queue. */

    for (counter = 0; counter < nfds; counter++) {
```

```
        if ((counter != mastersock) && FD_ISSET(counter, &fdset)) {
            size = saferead(counter, buffer, sizeof(buffer) -1);
            buffer[size] = 0;          /* add trailing null */
            addtoqueue(counter, buffer);
        }
    }

    /* Process items in the queue. */

    while ((item = deqany())) {
        sprintf(sizebuf, "Size: %d\n", strlen(item->data) - 1);
        write_buffer(item->id, sizebuf, strlen(sizebuf));
        if (strncmp(buffer, "exit", 4) == 0) {
            safeclose(item->id);
            FD_CLR(item->id, &orig_fdset);
        }
        deleteitem(item);
    }
}
safeclose(mastersock);
}
```

To compile this, you'll need to use a command like this:

```
$ gcc -Wall -o ch19-1 ch19-1.c queue.c safecalls.c networkinglib.c
```

This program is based upon select; for more details on it, see Chapter 14, "Introducing the Linux I/O." The basic idea is simple: read from whatever socket is ready to be read from, shove the items on the queue, and process whichever ones are ready. However, for simplicity's sake, this program is really more simply done than it could be. For one thing, it doesn't detect when the client has disconnected without using exit(). Also, it should be using a queueing system for writing data as well; the write_buffer() calls are definitely a potential bottleneck if the network cannot transmit the data as fast as the program can write it.

It's not altogether uncommon to need to do multiplexing from the client side as well. Most frequently, this need arises when dealing with both network input and keyboard input. For instance, an IRC client needs to be able to read from both whenever there is data ready; blocking on either one could cause some problems. Therefore, you can use select() or poll() to simply watch both the socket and standard input. With this mechanism, and a bit of the same queuing as used in the preceding program (Listings 19-1 through 19-3), you can achieve a higher quality of user interaction in your client-side programs.

User Datagram Protocol

Like TCP, the User Datagram Protocol (UDP) is based on the Internet Protocol (IP). However, there are significant differences between UDP and TCP. UDP is an unreliable protocol; that is, packets may be lost, delivered out of order, delivered twice, and so on. With UDP, you are expected to take care of these things for yourself. The benefit to UDP is that, especially for one-time communication over networks that are generally reliable, overhead is lower (sometimes significantly so) compared to TCP due to the relaxing of requirements to keep the data intact.

UDP does guarantee that, if a packet gets through to your application, the data in that packet is correct, so you do not need to do your own error detection. You can use `connect()` just as with TCP to connect to a remote host. However, unlike with TCP, you can use a single socket to communicate with multiple remotes with UDP; simply reconnect to a different one or use the UDP-specific `sendmsg()` function.

UDP implementations in the kernel perform no buffering; if your program is using buffers that are not large enough to accommodate the input, for instance, the input will simply be dropped. You are solely responsible for splitting your communications into packets before sending them out the door and onto the wire, rather than relying on the underlying protocol to do this for you.

Summary

In this chapter, you read about some more advanced networking concepts:

✦ The algorithm that causes a server to fork a new copy of itself for each client connection has some problems and is not always the best option.

✦ You can avoid forking entirely by writing a single-process multiplexing server using `select()` or `poll()`.

✦ If you go this route, you introduce some complex buffering issues that you have to take care of. The example program here demonstrates how to take care of the most important of them, but you may often need to buffer output as well.

✦ Multiplexing can also be useful for a client that needs to read from both the network and the keyboard.

✦ UDP offers an alternative to TCP for programs needing high speed but that can withstand some packet loss.

✦   ✦   ✦

The Glue: Perl

Introducing Perl

A book on Linux programming cannot be complete without a look at Perl. Perl has, in recent years, become the language of choice for many scripting and data processing tasks. In this chapter, you will be introduced to Perl. The chapter begins by explaining the design behind Perl—what problems it is used to solve, and how it can work with the system. In the First Steps section, I'll present some sample Perl code and explain how it works. After that, I will cover four different aspects of Perl: data structures, subroutines, flow control, and object-oriented programming.

Perl Design Philosophy

Perl is one of the most fascinating languages available for Linux today. It is often described as a "glue language"—that is, Perl is very good at communicating with all sorts of other systems and languages and is frequently used to automate communication between them. For instance, Perl can talk both to Web servers using CGI and to SQL database servers using DBI. Not surprisingly, Perl is a frequently used language for making databases available on the Web.

Perl draws its syntax from many sources. You'll find that the basic syntax resembles C to a large degree—semicolons end statements, braces delimit blocks, and so on. However, added on to this C-based syntax is a large assortment of features from various other languages such as sed, awk, grep, various shells, and even C++. Add into this melting pot of languages additional features unique to Perl, such as transparent database tie-ins, built-in associative arrays (hashes), enhanced regular expressions, and the like, and you get an amazingly versatile and powerful language.

The overall philosophy of this design is "don't constrain the programmer." You get a tremendous amount of freedom in Perl. The documentation that accompanies it, for instance, demonstrates three completely different ways of implementing a case statement in Perl. When you are parsing data, you can just as easily parse one line at a time, or ask Perl to slurp the entire file into memory and then parse the result. You can use variable interpolation (as with a shell) to generate strings, or you can use `sprintf()` as in C to do that — or you can use both. And these are but a few examples of the flexibility of Perl.

Perl's quoting is another example of flexibility. As when shell programming, you have different quotes depending on what you want to be interpolated, but you also have ways to automatically parse strings as certain types of quoted material, split them up, and assign them to arrays.

Perl's object-oriented features are a fairly new addition to the language. They're not as mature as the object-oriented features in a language such as Java, notably missing data hiding and powerful inheritance features. Nevertheless, Perl approaches OOP (Object-Oriented Programming) in a completely unique way, as you will see in the OOP Features section at the end of this chapter.

Perl modules can plug into the interpreter at run time and can be written either in Perl or in another language such as C. Therefore, you can extend Perl with anything that you can write in Perl as well as anything you can write in another language such as C or C++. Developers have used this module capability to write a large number of modules that you can plug in to your Perl system. To name just a few examples, Perl includes modules or integrated support for HTML parsing, XML parsing, compression, graphical user interfaces, SQL database communication, date/time manipulation, socket-level I/O, MIME, synchronization with PalmPilot devices, sound, database usage, serialization and deserialization of arbitrary objects, embedded Perl inside other programs such as Web servers, communication with servers such as FTP and SMTP, and many more programming needs. Therefore, not only is Perl a powerful glue language, but it also is a powerful automation language.

All of this power and flexibility does come at a price: it can be somewhat difficult to learn the language or to read others' code until you've been using Perl a lot.

Cross-Reference   For more details, see *Programming Perl*, second edition; *Linux(r) Programming* (IDG Books Worldwide, ISBN 1-55828-507-5); and *Discover Perl 5* (IDG Books Worldwide, ISBN 0-7645-3076-3).

Variables

In Perl, "normal" (scalar) variables that hold a single value are named, and they are *always* accessed with a leading dollar sign. For instance, the following is a bit of Perl:

```
$x = 5;
$y = $x * 2;
```

This code causes the scalar variable x to be assigned the value 5. It also causes the scalar y to be assigned twice the value of x.

Note   Notice the dollar signs are used every time the scalar variable is accessed.

As in the shell, variables in Perl can be interpolated into strings. For instance, you can use the following:

```
print "The value of y is $y.\n";
printf "I can also display it with printf: %d\n", $y;
```

In Perl, whether the internal value of a scalar is a string or a numeric value is not relevant. If it's a string and you attempt to perform an arithmetic operation on it, it will be converted to a numeric value as necessary. Similarly, if you need a string representation of a value, it will be converted to a string as appropriate. All of this takes place behind the scenes, which is very handy for reading in and parsing data. There is no need to specifically convert the data read in from a keyboard or file into an integer or floating-point format; Perl automatically does it for you when necessary. Here is a sample of this conversion:

```
$x = "5";
$y = $x * 2;
```

The previous code is still quite valid and will produce the same result as the preceding example. The string containing the digit 5 is simply converted into a number when necessary.

There are actually four types of variables in Perl: scalars, lists (or arrays), hashes (or associative arrays), and subroutines. Besides strings and numbers as described in the preceding paragraphs, a scalar in Perl can also hold a reference, which is similar in concept to a pointer in C. Each type of variable has its own unique prefix character, as shown in Table 20-1.

Table 20-1
Variables and Prefix Characters

Variable Type	Prefix
scalar	$
list	@
subroutine	&
hash	%

These namespaces are kept separate. That is, $x is not the same as @x.

Tip   This can be the source of some confusion with Perl. To make things simpler, generally it is best to keep the names unique.

Arrays

Perl arrays are quite powerful. They automatically shrink or expand as data is added to or removed from them, so there is no need to predefine the size of your arrays. Setting one up can be as simple as:

```
@myarray = ('Hi, this is the first element', 'second',
            'third', 'last');
```

You can pass around the entire array to functions (called subroutines in Perl) by calling it @myarray. You can also access individual elements of the array, using an index starting with 0. For instance:

```
print $myarray[0];
```

This will display Hi, this is the first element on your screen. Notice that you use a dollar sign ($) instead of the at sign (@) when you are accessing just one element of the array instead of the array in aggregate. The reason is that the dollar sign is always used when accessing a scalar value, and each individual element of an array is a scalar. Note also that $myarray[0] and $myarray refer to two entirely different variables: The first indicates the first element in the array named @myarray. The second indicates the contents of the scalar named $myarray.

Hashes

Like arrays, hashes are used to store separate pieces of data in one place. However, this is really where the similarity ends. Whereas an array is indexed by a numeric value, a hash is indexed by a key. This key is something that you can pick. It can be any word, a phrase, whatever—just so long as it's unique within a given hash.

If you are used to programming in C, think of a Perl hash as somewhat of a dynamic structure, one to which you can add and remove variables at will. You can set up a hash by assigning all the values at once, as shown in the following examples:

```
%myhash = ('color' => 'purple', 'size' => 'large',
           'location' => 'Alaska');

%myhash2 = (red => 0xff0000,
            green => 0x00ff00,
            blue => 0x0000ff);

%myhash3 = ('city', 'Seattle', 'weather', 'wet',
            'cars', 2);
```

This sets up three separate hashes. As you might have deduced from this example, Perl's syntax for creating hashes is fairly flexible. In the first one, we see that the attribute color is set to purple, size to large, and location to Alaska. In the second one, the key red is set to have the value 0xff0000, and so on. In the final one, the key city is set to be Seattle, weather to wet, and so forth.

The => operator provides you with some useful shortcuts. For one, you are able to omit the quotes on the key (the value to the *left* of the operator) if you prefer. This is done with the %myhash2 example above. Also, it provides a nice visual indication of the mapping from a key to a value. Note that the reason that the values to the right of the operator are not quoted in the second example is because they're numeric instead of string data, not due to any special feature of this operator.

The third example shows that you can use a simple list of elements to set up a hash. The elements are taken as a key followed by a value, for as many elements as are present. This could make an interesting way for you to create a hash based on the contents of an array.

Now that your hash is set up, you'll want to access its data. You can do that as shown in these examples:

```
print $myhash2{'red'};
print $myhash3{city};
$myhash1{size} = 'microscopic';
$somekey = 'gray';
$myhash2{$somekey} = 0xa5a5a5;
```

So, you can see that you access the individual elements by using the curly brace syntax. As before, you can omit the quotes on the key name if it consists solely of regular characters. You can also use a variable for the key name (or the data for that matter). You can also assign to individual elements using this syntax, and in fact, you could build your entire hash this way if you prefer.

Note   An array stores its elements in a set order. A hash is unordered; generally, it is used by accessing specific keys directly. You can request all its elements, but there is no guarantee that you'll get them back in the same order that you put them in. In fact, you probably won't.

First Steps

Now that we've talked about a few Perl basics, it's time to start into some Perl programs. First, any Perl program needs to begin with a line indicating the location of the Perl interpreter, as with shell scripts. This line is generally the following (it may vary slightly if your system has the Perl interpreter in a different location):

```
#!/usr/bin/perl
```

Note that this is the same situation as you have with executable shell scripts. Additionally, though, many users prefer to enable warnings in Perl, similar to warnings from gcc. This can be done by extending the first line:

```
#!/usr/bin/perl -w
```

Now, when you create a Perl script, you need to mark it executable. Like shell scripts, you use chmod to do that. You can use the following command to do so:

```
chmod a+x myscript.pl
```

 Tip   If you don't want to go to the effort to make your script executable, you can also invoke a program on the command line. For instance, you may use `perl myscript.pl` to invoke this program.

Now let's try a simple program:

```
#!/usr/bin/perl -w

print "Please type something: ";
$input = <STDIN>;
chomp $input;
print "You typed: '$input'\n";
```

Analyzing the code, it starts out with a standard invocation of Perl. It then proceeds to read a line of input from standard input, the terminal. When used in a scalar context, <STDIN> reads and returns one line of input. Here, that line is placed in the $input variable. The next line of code, calling chomp, removes the newline character that is at the end of the input string. Then, the program prints out a string with the result, and then exits.

In the paragraph above, I mentioned *scalar context*. Perl has a system whereby functions can determine what type of data the caller expects them to return. In this case, when the caller expects a single item (a *scalar*) to be returned, <STDIN> returns a single line. If you used it in a situation where the caller wanted an array, for instance @AllLines = <STDIN>, the <STDIN> operator would return an array containing all lines in the file. It returns one line per array element. You can then see that the operator behaves differently in scalar and in array context.

You can read in a large amount of data at once. For instance, you can use <STDIN> in an array context to do that. Here is an example::

```
#!/usr/bin/perl -w

@input = <STDIN>;

$counter = 0;
```

```
foreach $key (sort @input) {
  chomp $key;
  $counter++;
  print "Line $counter: \"$key\"\n";
}
```

This code reads input until end-of-file is reached, storing it all in the array @input. A counter is initialized to zero. The code then initializes a counter to zero, which it uses later to count the number of lines. The foreach foreach loop executes once for each item in the @input array.

Note   Note that the sort function sorts @input.

Each pass through the loop, the $key scalar variable holds the current element in the @input array. The chomp function removes the trailing newline character (to avoid extra blank lines in our output) and the counter is incremented. The print statement prints out the current line number and the text of the line. Here's an example of running this code:

```
$ chmod a+X ch20-1.pl
$ ./ch20-1.pl
good
morning
this
is
a
test
of
some
perl
sorting
code.
Ctrl+D
Line 1: "a"
Line 2: "code."
Line 3: "good"
Line 4: "is"
Line 5: "morning"
Line 6: "of"
Line 7: "perl"
Line 8: "some"
Line 9: "sorting"
Line 10: "test"
Line 11: "this"
```

The program worked as expected. It read some input into an array and displayed that array, sorted, with line numbers.

As described in Chapter 3, "Working with Regular Expressions," Perl has extensive support for regular expressions. Here is a sample use of them:

```
#!/usr/bin/perl -w

while ($inputline = readinput()) {
  ($key, $value) = $inputline =~ /^([^=]+)=(.+)$/;
  if ($key && $value) {
    $hash{$key} = $value;
  } else {
    print "Bad input, try again.\n";
  }
}

foreach $key (sort keys %hash) {
  print "$key is set to the value $hash{$key}\n";
}

sub readinput {
  print "Enter a key=value pair, or type END when done: ";
  $input = <STDIN>;
  return undef unless $input;
  chomp $input;

  return undef if $input =~ /^END$/i;

  return $input;
}
```

Let's go over this code. First, there is a main loop. It calls the readinput subroutine. That subroutine prompts the user to enter some data—a key and a value separated by an equal sign—and then checks to see if it is time to exit. If the input line is empty, or it matches the word "end," this is the end of the input. When this is the case, undef is returned to the caller, indicating that the function has nothing to return. This is similar to NULL in C in some situations.

Notice the shortcut notation in Perl:

```
return undef unless $input;
```

is the same as:

```
unless ($input) {
  return undef;
}
```

Note that, unlike C, Perl requires braces with the preceding syntax even if they enclose only one statement. The preceding shortcut is also the same as:

```
if (!$input) {
  return undef;
}
```

Also, when you simply evaluate a string like this, not even comparing it to anything, the result will be false if the scalar holds undef or a zero-length string, or true otherwise. Therefore, it is a great way to check if valid input is still forthcoming.

Let's look at another spot of code in that function before returning to the main program. You see the following:

```
return undef if $input =~ /^END$/i;
```

Rewriting this code results in the following code:

```
if ($input =~ /^END$/i) {
  return undef;
}
```

Now, let's look at it. This is a regular expression match. The =~ sign says that the pattern on the right should be applied to the scalar on the left. So, you get a true result if the input matches the word end, in a case-insensitive fashion (because of the trailing i flag) or a false result otherwise.

Back in the main program, there is a similar use:

```
($key, $value) = $inputline =~ /^([^=]+)=(.+)$/;
```

In this case, the return value feature of parentheses in a regular expression is exploited. The first string to be returned would be any text up until the first equal sign in the string, and the second string is all text after that equal sign. This pattern is applied to $inputline. The regular expression matching operator returns a list corresponding to each element on the right.

In Perl, a list can actually be an lvalue—that is, appear on the left side of an assignment operator. Each item from the right will be placed into the corresponding location on the left. Therefore, $key holds the value from the first parenthesis match, and $value the text from the second. Then, there is another if test performed. If either or both of these strings are not matched, the corresponding variable will be set to undef. This indicates that the regular expression did not properly match and that the input was corrupt. The code detects this and issues a warning message if that occurs, or stuffs the data into the hash otherwise.

Then, you see this code:

```
foreach $key (sort keys %hash) {
```

which can be rewritten in a more C-like form as:

```
foreach $key (sort(keys(%hash))) {
```

As you might guess, the keys item returns an array of all the keys in the hash, in no particular order. This list is then sorted before it is passed along for use in the foreach loop.

Let's give the program a whirl:

```
$ chmod a+x ch20-2.pl
$ ./ch20-2.pl
Enter a key=value pair, or type END when done: Hi!
Bad input, try again.
Enter a key=value pair, or type END when done: greeting=Hi!
Enter a key=value pair, or type END when done: os=Linux
Enter a key=value pair, or type END when done: equal sign==
Enter a key=value pair, or type END when done: language=perl
Enter a key=value pair, or type END when done: color=magenta
Enter a key=value pair, or type END when done: some long key=some long value
Enter a key=value pair, or type END when done: end
color is set to the value magenta
equal sign is set to the value =
greeting is set to the value Hi!
language is set to the value perl
os is set to the value Linux
some long key is set to the value some long value
```

From this example, you can see that the key for a hash may be several words long, as is the case for the key named equal sign here. Additionally, the data can have any value, and the input error-detection code does work. Perl also allows you to open and work with arbitrary files. Here is an example of doing so:

```
#!/usr/bin/perl -w

print "Enter a filename: ";
$filename = <STDIN>;
chomp $filename;

open OUTFILE, ">$filename" or
  die "Couldn't open output file: $!";

print "Enter a number: ";
$number = <STDIN>;
print OUTFILE $number * 3, "\n";

close OUTFILE;
```

This code first prompts the user for a filename, reads it, and strips off the trailing newline. Then, it tries to open the file named for writing. The > sign in open means to open the file for writing; if it is omitted, the file is opened for reading only. You can also use the > sign to open a file for appending. The OUTFILE file handle is set up for this file. If the open call fails, it returns an error condition. When it does this, the or operator steps in and the die command is run. This command displays an error message and then causes the program to terminate. The error message to be displayed in this case contains $!, which holds the error result from the last failed operation—like errno in C.

After opening the file, the user is prompted for a number, which is read and then written. Note that in this case, there is no chomp on the input. The reason is that the input will be converted to a number anyway (because it is multiplied by three), so there is no need to explicitly remove the trailing newline character.

Also note that there is no comma after the filehandle name in the `print` call. This is different from the syntax in C, and from the syntax of many other things in Perl. The code will not work if you insert a comma at that place.

Data Structures

Earlier in this chapter, you were introduced to some of the different types of variables that are to be found in Perl. Here, we'll go into more detail on each of them, but I'll first introduce you to references in Perl.

References

Perl does not have direct hardware-level pointer support as is present in C. However, it does have references, which perform essentially the same function — with some added flexibility as well.

In Perl, the operator to create a reference is the backslash (\). This is roughly the same as the address-of (&) operator in C. The dereferencing operator is the dollar sign. You can create a reference to any type of variable, and even a few other types of entities as well. Let's examine a few examples of using references:

```
@array = (1, 1, 2, 3, 5, 8);
$arrayref = \@array;

foreach $key (@$arrayref) {
  print "$key\n";
}
```

In this code snippet, an array is created. We then create a reference to it and save the reference in a variable. Inside the `foreach` statement, the dereferenced value is used. Notice that the at sign is still used even when dealing with a reference — this is because you are still dealing with a list value after dereferencing it.

You can also create similar things with hashes:

```
%hash = (key1 => 1, key2 => 2, key3 => 3);
$hashref = \%hash;

foreach $key (sort keys %$hashref) {
  print "$key = $$hashref{$key}\n";
}
```

Note the double dollar sign. This is used because one dollar sign causes the dereference of the reference. The other indicates that a scalar value is being accessed, as usual with a hash. Perl defines a shortcut for this situation, similar to the C -> operator:

```
#!/usr/bin/perl -w

%hash = (key1 => 1, key2 => 2, key3 => 3);
$hashref = \%hash;

foreach $key (sort keys %$hashref) {
  print "$key = $hashref->{$key}\n";
}
```

The so-called arrow operator (->) indicates that the preceding item is to be dereferenced. This trick actually applies to arrays as well, but it is used more frequently with hashes.

So, where are these references useful? Well, there are numerous situations. Sometimes, you may want to pass along a large data structure—say an array or hash—to functions. As I will explain shortly, references are often much better for passing these types than passing the data by value. Perl's object-oriented features are almost always used with references, another important use for references.

In C, dealing with pointers can be tricky. You have to worry about allocating and freeing memory, keeping track of sizes of allocated memory, and the like. References in Perl have no such problem. Perl automatically allocates memory for you when you need it, and automatically frees memory when there are no variables or references pointing to it anymore. This mechanism, called a garbage collector, makes life with Perl references a lot easier than with C.

Anonymous references

You can also create references to so-called anonymous data—that is, data that has never before been assigned to a variable. As usual, Perl gives you several ways to do so, and I'll highlight the easiest and most frequently used ones here. Here is a script that demonstrates all of these uses:

```
#!/usr/bin/perl -w

$scalarref = \"Hi";
$arrayref = [1, 2, 3, 4, 5, 6, 7, 8, 9, 10, 11, 12];
$hashref = {key1 => 1, key2 => 2, key3 => 3};

print "$$scalarref\n";

foreach $key (@$arrayref) {
```

```
    print "Array: $key\n";
  }

foreach $key (sort keys %$hashref) {
  print "Hash: $key = $hashref->{$key}\n";
  }
```

Creating a reference to an anonymous scalar is trivial: simply use a backslash before the scalar's value. To create a reference to an anonymous array, you simply use brackets instead of parentheses to build the array. Note that \(1, 2, 3) is not the same as [1, 2, 3]; the former is in fact treated as (\1, \2, \3) — an array of three references, instead a reference to an array with three elements.

Likewise, to create an anonymous hash, you use braces instead of the normal parenthesis syntax. By using this syntax, you can create references to arrays and hashes from scratch — without ever needing to have an actual variable hold the data.

When you run the preceding code, you get the following output:

```
Hi
Array: 1
Array: 2
Array: 3
Array: 4
Array: 5
Array: 6
Array: 7
Array: 8
Array: 9
Array: 10
Array: 11
Array: 12
Hash: key1 = 1
Hash: key2 = 2
Hash: key3 = 3
```

So everything did work as expected.

Symbolic references

In addition to the standard reference behavior described previously, Perl also provides another capability for references: symbolic references, somewhat analogous to symbolic links in the Linux file system.

This capability allows you to actually dereference a string. The string is taken to be the name of a variable or subroutine, which is then referred to as appropriate. This can be a great way to eliminate ugly case statements based on input if you are expecting certain values to arrive; simply dereference a string as a symbolic reference and use that!

```
$foo = 2;
$name = "foo";
$foo += 3;

print "$$name\n";
```

In this particular example, using a symbolic reference was not an advantage. However, it could have been had you read $name from the keyboard. In general, you should not use symbolic references unless you are in a situation in which standard references will not work.

Arrays

In the previous section, you were briefly introduced to arrays. Now, we'll go into more detail, describing some features and quirks of Perl arrays, and then showing an example of arrays in action.

First, we need to cover an important concept: how do you combine two arrays? Well, it turns out that in Perl, this is as simple as (@arr1, @arr2) — the result will be an array consisting of all elements from the first array, followed by all elements from the second. Note that the preceding syntax does not return an array containing two embedded arrays as it might in some other languages. To do that, you need to use array references. Note that this behavior makes it absolutely necessary to use references if you want to pass more than one array to a subroutine.

Another feature is the capability to find out how many elements are in your array. To do this, you use $#arr1, for instance. Perl actually returns the index of the last element in the array, and because it starts counting at zero, you just need to add 1 to the result to get a count of the number of elements present. Note that if you are using an array reference, you would use a syntax such as $#$arrayref — just think of the $# as replacing the @ in this situation.

Note   Perl actually provides a variable named $[that can be used to change the index of the first element in an array (and the first character in a substring). It is rarely used because it is a very easy way to cause confusion and thus is highly discouraged, but if you use it, you will have to modify your length calculations appropriately because your indexing will not start at zero.

Now, on to arrays of arrays — also known as multidimensional arrays. These are supported in Perl, but with a twist: you use operators that deal with references to arrays. The bracket syntax still makes it look like you're dealing with traditional multidimensional arrays and, in fact, you can treat them either in that way or as arrays of references. Here is a program that creates, and then displays, such an array:

```perl
#!/usr/bin/perl -w

$arrayref = [1, 3, [500, 600, 700], 8, 9, [1000, 1100, [2000, 2100] ], 10];

printit($arrayref, 0);

sub printit {
  my ($ref, $count) = @_;
  my $key;
  my $counter = 0;

  foreach $key (@$ref) {
    print " " x ($count * 3);
    if (ref $key) {
      printf "%3d: nested array:\n", $counter;
      printit($key, $count + 1);
    } else {
      printf "%3d: %d\n", $counter, $key;
    }
    $counter++;
  }
}

print "\n\$arrayref->[5][2][0] = $arrayref->[5][2][0]\n";
```

This code begins by setting up a reference to an array. This array contains not only some typical elements, but also references to additional arrays. These can be accessed as if they are multidimensional arrays. Then, the code invokes the printit() function.

This subroutine takes two parameters: a reference to an array and a count of how far indented each line should be. We'll go into more detail on these items in the section on subroutines, later in this chapter.

The function iterates over the list by using foreach—as you have seen several times already. For each element, it starts by printing out an appropriate amount of space. The x operator means to copy the string on the left for the number of repetitions indicated by the expression on the right. Next, the program tests the key value to see if it is a reference. If it is a reference, the program is dealing with a nested array (in this situation; it could also be a reference to an embedded hash, scalar, or whatever if you are working with a different program). In this case, the subroutine displays a message and then calls itself to process the nested array. If the key value is not a nested array, its value is simply displayed. Finally, the element counter is incremented.

At the very end of the program, there is a print statement, displaying a single value from the array. It illustrates how you can access a single nested value and, in fact, shows that the syntax is quite like that of languages such as C. Here you can see the complete output from this program:

```
$ ./ch20-5.pl
  0: 1
  1: 3
  2: nested array:
      0: 500
      1: 600
      2: 700
  3: 8
  4: 9
  5: nested array:
      0: 1000
      1: 1100
      2: nested array:
          0: 2000
          1: 2100
  6: 10

$arrayref->[5][2][0] = 2000
```

In Chapter 11, "Files, Directories, and Devices," a similar recursive algorithm was used to display a directory listing. It did its job, but there could be a problem — if you need to access the listing in your program, particularly if you need to do so more than once, the Chapter 11 code had no way to save the results. Let's now rewrite that code to use nested arrays — and use the printing code from right here to display the result. Listing 20-1 shows an example of code that uses arrays to hold the data.

Note   Listing 20-1 is available online.

Listing 20-1: **Example of nested arrays**

```perl
#!/usr/bin/perl -w

# Perl's unless is an inverse if.  That is, unless(a) is the same as
# if (!(a)).

unless ($ARGV[0]) {
  die "Must specify a directory."
}

# -d is a Perl shorthand.  It does a stat() on the passed filename, and
# then looks at the mode.  If the filename is a directory, it returns true;
# if not, it returns false.

unless (-d $ARGV[0]) {
  die "The filename supplied was not a directory."
}
```

```perl
  my $dirs = dircontents($ARGV[0]);
  printit($dirs, 0);

  sub dircontents{
    my $startname = shift @_;
    my $filename;
    my $retval = [];              # Initialize with an empty array reference
    local *DH;                    # Ensure that the handle is locally scoped

# This is the same as DH = opendir("filename") in C.
# In C, you can use DIR *DH; to declare the variable.

    unless(opendir(DH, $startname)) {
      warn "Couldn't open directory $startname: $!";
      return undef;
    }

    # In C, readdir() returns a pointer to struct dirent, whose members are
    # defined in readdir(3).  In Perl, returns one file in scalar context,
    # or all remaining filenames in list context.

    while ($filename = readdir(DH)) {
      if ($filename ne '.' &&
          $filename ne '..' &&
          ! -l "$startname/$filename" &&
          -d "$startname/$filename") {
        push(@$retval, dircontents("$startname/$filename"));
      } else {
        push(@$retval, $filename);
      }
    }

    closedir(DH);
    return $retval;
  }

sub printit {
  my ($ref, $count) = @_;
  my $key;
  my $counter = 0;

  foreach $key (@$ref) {
    print " " x ($count * 3);
    if (ref $key) {
      printf "%3d: subdirectory\n", $counter;
      printit($key, $count + 1);
    } else {
      printf "%3d: %s\n", $counter, $key;
    }
    $counter++;
  }
}
```

The code in Listing 20-1 is quite similar to both the code from Chapter 11 and the earlier example (ch20-5.pl). This time, however, the filenames are pushed onto the array instead of being displayed. First, let's look at this line, which is used if the file being examined is not a directory:

```
push(@$retval, $filename);
```

This causes the current filename to be placed at the end of the array. Notice that the push operator expects an array, and not a reference to one, as its first argument. Also, you can pass more than one value to push at once — even another array — and all those values will be added to the end of your current array.

Now let's take a look at the command used when the system is processing a file that is a directory. That code is:

```
push(@$retval, dircontents("$startname/$filename"));
```

This calls the function itself on the subdirectory. The call returns a reference to an array, which is then pushed onto the end of the current array — just as needed to form an array of the same type as used previously.

However, there is a problem: the filename information for this directory is lost — it is never placed onto the array. In the next section, we'll go over nested hashes, which present a solution for this problem. Let's take a look at the output, which will demonstrate the problem:

```
$ ./ch20-6.pl /etc/modutils
  0: .
  1: ..
  2: aliases
  3: paths
  4: subdirectory
     0: .
     1: ..
     2: i386
     3: m68k.amiga
     4: m68k.atari
     5: m68k.generic
     6: m68k.mac
     7: alpha
  5: pcmcia
  6: setserial
```

Nested hashes

Now that you've seen the possibilities of references, and nested arrays, it's time to move on to another topic: nested hashes. As you saw in the commentary about Listing 20-1, there was a problem with the array. We really want to store at least two pieces of data for each file. You could use a separate array for the second piece of data, but that gets clumsy. Furthermore, to find a given file, you have to manually search the array. With a nested hash, you can traverse the hash just as you traverse a directory tree! We'll first look at a simple port of the existing code to use a hash, and then take a look at adding some more features to it that are made possible by hashes. Listing 20-2 shows code that uses hashes to store the data.

Note   Listing 20-2 is available online.

Listing 20-2: **Example of hashes**

```
#!/usr/bin/perl -w

# Perl's unless is an inverse if.  That is, unless(a) is the same as
# if (!(a)).

unless ($ARGV[0]) {
  die "Must specify a directory."
}

# -d is a Perl shorthand.  It does a stat() on the passed filename, and
# then looks at the mode.  If the filename is a directory, it returns true;
# if not, it returns false.

unless (-d $ARGV[0]) {
  die "The filename supplied was not a directory."
}

my $dirs = dircontents($ARGV[0]);
printit($dirs, 0);

sub dircontents{
  my $startname = shift @_;
  my $filename;
  my $retval = {};          # Initialize with an empty hash reference
  local *DH;                # Ensure that the handle is locally-scoped

# This is the same as DH = opendir("filename") in C.
# In C, you can use DIR *DH; to declare the variable.

  unless(opendir(DH, $startname)) {
    warn "Couldn't open directory $startname: $!";
    return undef;
  }

# In C, readdir() returns a pointer to struct dirent, whose members are
# defined in readdir(3).  In Perl, returns one file in scalar context,
# or all remaining filenames in list context.
```

Continued

```
  while ($filename = readdir(DH)) {
    if ($filename ne '.' &&
    $filename ne '..' &&
    ! -l "$startname/$filename" &&
    -d "$startname/$filename") {
      $retval->{$filename} = dircontents("$startname/$filename");
    } else {
      $retval->{$filename} = 1;
    }
  }

  closedir(DH);
  return $retval;
}

sub printit {
  my ($ref, $count) = @_;
  my $key;
  my $counter = 0;

  foreach $key (sort keys %$ref) {
    print " " x ($count * 3);
    if (ref $ref->{$key}) {
      printf "%3d: subdirectory %s\n", $counter, $key;
      printit($ref->{$key}, $count + 1);
    } else {
      printf "%3d: %s\n", $counter, $key;
    }
    $counter++;
  }
}
```

Not much has changed in this code. Instead of pushing strings onto an array, we now insert strings into a hash. You can traverse this hash by path; for instance, if you started at root, you could use $ref->{etc}->{X11}->{xdm}->{Xstartup} to get to the entry for /etc/X11/xdm/Xstartup—nested, similar to the filesystem.

Notice that if it is not dealing with a directory, the program really has no meaningful value to insert, so it simply inserts the value 1. You could, however, be storing much more information. Consider the following example: instead of simply having each hash entry point to either a subdirectory hash or a useless value, why not have each hash entry point to another hash holding some useful information? Perhaps this would be some information such as the file's size, modification date, and so on. Then, if the particular file in question is a directory, an extra field in the hash can indicate that. Note that what we are building here is essentially a file object—and you'll see another rewrite of this code to use it as such later on in this chapter. For now, though, we'll proceed without adding object-oriented features to the program. Listing 20-3 shows the code for the added features.

Note   Listing 20-3 is available online.

Listing 20-3: **Revised hash example**

```
#!/usr/bin/perl -w

# Perl's unless is an inverse if.  That is, unless(a) is the same as
# if (!(a)).

unless ($ARGV[0]) {
  die "Must specify a directory."
}

# -d is a Perl shorthand.  It does a stat() on the passed filename, and
# then looks at the mode.  If the filename is a directory, it returns true;
# if not, it returns false.

unless (-d $ARGV[0]) {
  die "The filename supplied was not a directory."
}

my $dirs = dircontents($ARGV[0]);
printit($dirs, 0);

sub dircontents{
  my $startname = shift @_;
  my $filename;
  my $retval = {};          # Initialize with an empty hash reference
  local *DH;                # Ensure that the handle is locally scoped

# This is the same as DH = opendir("filename") in C.
# In C, you can use DIR *DH; to declare the variable.

  unless(opendir(DH, $startname)) {
    warn "Couldn't open directory $startname: $!";
    return undef;
  }

  # In C, readdir() returns a pointer to struct dirent, whose members are
  # defined in readdir(3).  In Perl, returns one file in scalar context,
  # or all remaining filenames in list context.
```

Continued

Listing 20-3 *(continued)*

```perl
  while ($filename = readdir(DH)) {
    $retval->{$filename} = { name => $filename,
                            size => -s "$startname/$filename",
                            age => -M "$startname/$filename"};
    if ($filename ne '.' &&
        $filename ne '..' &&
        ! -l "$startname/$filename" &&
        -d "$startname/$filename") {
      $retval->{$filename}->{subdir} = dircontents("$startname/$filename");
    }
  }

  closedir(DH);
  return $retval;
}

sub printit {
  my ($ref, $count) = @_;
  my $key;
  my $counter = 0;

  foreach $key (sort keys %$ref) {
    print " " x ($count * 3);
    if (exists($ref->{$key}->{subdir})) {
      printf "%3d: subdirectory %s (%d bytes)\n", $counter, $key,
             $ref->{$key}->{size};
      printit($ref->{$key}->{subdir}, $count + 1);
    } else {
      printf "%3d: %s (%d bytes)\n", $counter, $key, $ref->{$key}->{size};
    }
    $counter++;
  }
}
```

Now things start to get interesting! At the heart of it all is this:

```perl
    $retval->{$filename} = { name => $filename,
                            size => -s "$startname/$filename",
                            age => -M "$startname/$filename"};
```

This code creates a reference to an anonymous hash. This hash contains the file's name (so you don't have to pass along the hash key separately), its size, and its age. Then, if there is a subdirectory, an additional item named subdir is added to the hash, the value of which is a reference to a hash for that subdirectory. Thus, to get to the information for the same /etc/X11/xdm/Xstartup file as described earlier, you'd now need to use $ref->{etc}->{subdir}->{X11}->{subdir}->{xdm}->{subdir}->{Xstartup}. This is clearly more typing; on the other hand, you now have more useful information in the hash. When the information is being printed out, it too has to trace through this additional level to get to some information; however, that information was not available at all before. Here is the output of running this revised code:

```
$ ./ch20-8.pl /etc/modutils
  0: . (1024 bytes)
  1: .. (6144 bytes)
  2: aliases (1259 bytes)
  3: subdirectory arch (1024 bytes)
      0: . (1024 bytes)
      1: .. (1024 bytes)
      2: alpha (35 bytes)
      3: i386 (35 bytes)
      4: m68k.amiga (623 bytes)
      5: m68k.atari (624 bytes)
      6: m68k.generic (251 bytes)
      7: m68k.mac (277 bytes)
  4: paths (1161 bytes)
  5: pcmcia (37 bytes)
  6: setserial (487 bytes)
```

Subroutines and Scope

Like C, Perl offers functions. In Perl, they are called subroutines — you've already seen examples of them in this chapter. Let's dive in and take a look at the details.

Perl subroutines can be called with a syntax similar to the syntax for internal functions, but there are a few extra twists that you haven't seen yet. Here are examples of calling a subroutine named mysub:

```
mysub();
mysub(1, 2, 3);
mysub("abcde", "xyz");
&mysub;
```

The first example invokes the subroutine without passing any arguments. The second passes it three integers, and the third passes it two strings. The final example invokes it with the use of the older ampersand notation. This notation is rarely needed today, but may still be used.

If your subroutines take parameters, these parameters are passed in using the @_ array. Generally the first thing you will want to do is save the contents of that array for later use. If you are expecting only one argument, a typical way to do that is:

```
my $arg = shift @_;
```

This removes the argument from the front of the array and returns it, for assignment to your variable. If you are expecting multiple arguments, you might do this:

```perl
my ($scalar1, $scalar2, $scalar3, @remainder) = @_;
```

This code will take the first three arguments and place them into the corresponding scalar variable. Any remaining arguments (perhaps from an array) will be placed into the array. These variables can then be used later.

Notice the my keyword that occurs here. This is a scoping operator. This operator indicates that the variables being created should exist in the namespace of only the current subroutine—which is a very good thing. Otherwise, your subroutines may inadvertently overwrite variables used by the main program, or even by other invocations of your own subroutine! Because the function used in the earlier example program was recursive, this was a requirement; otherwise, the variables would definitely get overwritten.

Whenever you use any variable in a subroutine, whether or not it was passed in, you should declare it my unless there is a strong reason not to. In fact, it's not a bad idea to do that in all your code; getting into the habit can be good, and you can help isolate variables between different modules.

Subroutines in Perl return values just as they do in C. If no explicit return statement is present, the return value of a subroutine is simply the return value of the last statement run.

Calling a subroutine in Perl 5 is done just as it is in C, with parenthesis. You might occasionally see code that uses the & sign to call subroutines. This is mostly—but not always—a holdover from days of earlier Perl versions.

One interesting thing that you can do with subroutines is create references to them—for instance, $ref = \&sub. Moreover, you can even use an anonymous subroutine, as demonstrated in this example:

```perl
#!/usr/bin/perl -w

my $subref = sub {
  my $arg = shift @_;
  print "Hello, I am an anonymous sub ($arg)!\n"
};

&$subref("really");
```

Here, you set up a reference to an anonymous subroutine. This subroutine takes a single argument and prints out a message with that argument embedded in it. The reference is then dereferenced and the value displayed. This is one case where the ampersand (&) is required—this code will not work without it.

You are now able to pass along arbitrary code as parameters to functions, with interesting results. Perl/Tk makes extensive use of this feature. In our previous code examples, for instance, you might pass along a custom subroutine for printing out the information for any given file, so that you can use a single function to walk through the list and prepare for printing, but with a custom output format.

Cross-Reference   Chapter 24, "GUIs with Perl/TK," covers Perl/TK.

There is another note about subroutines with which you should be aware. In Chapter 8, "Memory Management," I warned you never to return a pointer to a local variable in C. You do not have this problem with Perl; you may freely return references to local variables. The reason is that even though the local variable may disappear from the namespace after the subroutine exits, if there is something pointing to it, its data will not. This is due to Perl's garbage collection mechanism, which will ensure that nothing is removed until it is no longer being used. Therefore, you do not have to worry about variables going out of scope after they (or rather, pointers to them) have been indicated for being returned to the caller.

Flow Control

Like C, Perl provides a variety of methods for various loops and conditionals. Many of them function in a manner similar to their C equivalents. For instance, the `if` operator in Perl works in almost the same way—the difference is that Perl requires braces around the action, whereas C makes them optional. Perl's version, though, has another syntax, as demonstrated in the following line of code:

```
print "Hi\n" if ($shouldprint);
```

In this example, if the conditional is true, the `print` statement is executed; otherwise, it is skipped. Perl also provides an `unless` statement, which is essentially an `if` but with an implied not. You can use it just as the `if` statement with both syntax varieties, as shown in this example:

```
print "Hi\n" unless ($skipPrint);
```

This would display the message unless the variable is true, presumably asking for the message to be skipped.

You have already seen examples of Perl's `foreach` statement. This takes a variable and a list of items. The variable is set to the value of each item in the list, in order, and the supplied code is executed once per item. As an example, it was used earlier in this chapter in this context:

```
foreach $key (sort keys %$hashref) {
  print "Hash: $key = $hashref->{$key}\n";
}
```

This caused Perl to set $key to each key in the hash, one key at a time, and to execute the print command for each such key.

Perl also supports a C-style for loop, which looks almost identical to the C version. Here's a quick example of one such loop:

```
for ($a = 0; $a < 200; $a++) {
  print "$a\n";
}
```

Perl doesn't have a built-in case statement but does offer several alternatives from which to choose. One of the more popular ones involves using a particular feature of the for statement to temporarily set Perl's default variable, $_, to the variable you're tying to match—great for regular expressions. Unlike in C, the example that follows doesn't require just numbers to match, it can use any arbitrary expression to obtain a match:

```
SWITCH: for ($foo) {
  /abc/         && do { print "alpha\n"; last; };
  /xyz/         && do { print "ending\n"; last; };
  $foo == 2         && do { print "second\n"; last; };
  die "Couldn't match input to switch.";
}
```

Because the = = operator requires two arguments, you can't omit $foo there, but you can omit $foo with the regular expressions with this syntax. The die call at the end is the default, which is called if nothing matches. This can, of course, be omitted if you prefer.

OOP Features

One interesting addition to Perl is support for object-oriented programming (OOP). This support is implemented in a unique way and is built atop Perl modules.

Perl modules are used for more than just OOP; they make it easy to add new functionality to Perl programs by bringing in third-party modules (libraries). The Comprehensive Perl Archive Network, CPAN, has a repository of modules available online. You can see it at http://www.perl.com/CPAN-local/. In this book, in fact, we use some modules from CPAN in later chapters.

Cross-Reference

In Chapter 22, "CGI Programming," I use CGI.pm. Chapter 23, "SQL Databases with DBI," I use the DBI module, and, in Chapter 24, "GUIs with Perl/Tk," I use the Tk module. There are thousands more available for your use as well.

Each object in Perl, with its corresponding classes, is defined in a Perl module file. This means that they live in a separate namespace from the main program and thus don't have (direct) access to your program's main variables. Making such access more difficult is a good thing, though — it helps to encourage writing reusable objects that do not depend on certain things being present in the main program for their functionality.

An object is created by using the bless operator; bless is given a reference and a class name. Typically, a Perl module that implements an object will define a new subroutine that will create such a reference, bless it, and return it to the caller. Perl also defines new syntaxes that can be used for calling methods for the object.

If you call a generic method, you can use a syntax such as Classname->new() or new Classname() to call a generic subroutine from the class. When you use this syntax, Perl automatically passes the name of the object to the subroutine as its first argument. After you have an object, you should use, for example, $object->display() to invoke methods. When an object is called this way, Perl automatically passes the reference to the object as the first parameter to any subroutine.

As an example of object-oriented programming, I'll take the example of a directory traversal program from earlier and reimplement it with objects. This example will require two files. The first is ch20-10.pl, included in Listing 20-4.

Note Listing 20-4 is available online.

Listing 20-4: **Example code: ch20-10.pl**

```perl
#!/usr/bin/perl -w

require FileObject;

# Perl's unless is an inverse if.  That is, unless(a) is the same as
# if (!(a)).

unless ($ARGV[0]) {
  die "Must specify a directory."
}

# -d is a Perl shorthand.  It does a stat() on the passed filename, and
# then looks at the mode.  If the filename is a directory, it returns true;
# if not, it returns false.

unless (-d $ARGV[0]) {
  die "The filename supplied was not a directory."
}
```

Continued

Listing 20-4 *(continued)*

```perl
my $dirs = dircontents($ARGV[0]);
printit($dirs, 0);

sub dircontents{
  my $startname = shift @_;
  my $filename;
  my $retval = {};              # Initialize with an empty hash reference
  local *DH;                    # Ensure that the handle is locally scoped

# This is the same as DH = opendir("filename") in C.
# In C, you can use DIR *DH; to declare the variable.

  unless(opendir(DH, $startname)) {
    warn "Couldn't open directory $startname: $!";
    return undef;
  }

  # In C, readdir() returns a pointer to struct dirent, whose members are
  # defined in readdir(3).  In Perl, returns one file in scalar context,
  # or all remaining filenames in list context.

  while ($filename = readdir(DH)) {
    my $object = new FileObject($startname);
    $object->populate($filename);
    if ($object->{isdir}) {
      $object->setsubdir(dircontents("$startname/$filename"));
    }
    $retval->{$filename} = $object;
  }

  closedir(DH);
  return $retval;
}

sub printit {
  my ($ref, $count) = @_;
  my $key;

  foreach $key (sort keys %$ref) {
    $ref->{$key}->display($count);
    if ($ref->{$key}->{isdir}) {
      printit($ref->{$key}->{subdir}, $count + 1)
    }
  }
}
```

The second required file is FileObject.pm (see Listing 20-5). Note that this second file does not need to be marked executable nor does it need the bangpath on the first line. This is because it is not called directly; rather, it is loaded by Perl after parsing the `require` statement in file ch20-10.pl.

Note Listing 20-5 is available online.

Listing 20-5: **Example code: FileObject.pm**

```perl
package FileObject;

sub new {
  my ($class, $startfile, $filename) = @_;
  my $self = {startfile => $startfile};
  bless($self, $class);

  if ($filename) {
    $self->populate($filename);
  }

  return $self;
}

sub populate {
  my ($self, $filename) = @_;

  $self->{size} = -s $self->{startfile} . "/$filename";
  $self->{age} = -M "$self->{startfile}/$filename";
  $self->{name} = $filename;
  if ($filename ne '.' &&
      $filename ne '..' &&
      ! -l "$self->{startfile}/$filename" &&
      -d "$self->{startfile}/$filename") {
    $self->{isdir} = 1;
  } else {
    $self->{isdir} = 0;
  }
}

sub setsubdir {
  my ($self, $subdir) = @_;

  unless ($self->{isdir}) {
    die "Attempt to set subdirectory on non-directory!";
  }

  $self->{subdir} = $subdir;
}
```

Continued

Listing 20-5 *(continued)*

```perl
sub display {
  my ($self, $level) = @_;
  $level = 0 unless $level;

  print " " x (3 * $level);
  printf "%s%s (%d bytes)\n",
         ($self->{isdir} ? "directory " : ""),
         $self->{name},
         $self->{size};
}

1;
```

Now that you have both parts of the code, let's go over them and examine what it is that they do. The main part, ch20-10.pl, first says `require FileObject`. This causes Perl to load in the FileObject.pm file as a separate package. Inside `dircontents`, there is a loop as before that runs `readdir`. This time, however, the first thing that's done inside the loop is to generate a new object, passing along the `startname` (which is the path of the object that it needs to use for `stat`). Then, it calls `$object->populate($filename)`, which tells the object to set all of its internal data structures based on the passed name — that is, get its size, age, and the like and take note of them. If the object is a directory, its contents are set as such; otherwise, the object is fine as is. Finally, the object is added to the main hash. Note how much cleaner this has made the `while` loop — the object essentially knows how to find out details about itself, so there is no need to do that in the main loop!

Likewise, the subroutine to display the objects is similarly compacted to just four lines of actual code. The key is that it calls the object's `display` method, which does the grunt work of displaying the object to the screen.

In FileObject.pm, the first thing that the code does is declare itself to be a Perl package named `FileObject`. It then defines its methods. The first method, `new`, starts by generating an anonymous hash and saving it into `$self`. It takes note of the passed starting position as the initial entry in that hash. Then it blesses `$self`, using the implicitly passed class name. If a filename was passed in as well, it goes ahead and calls the `populate` method; otherwise, that is left to the caller to do later. Finally, it returns the newly created object to the caller.

The `populate` subroutine is used to find out information about the object. As with all the remaining subroutines in this file, `$self` is passed automatically by Perl as the first parameter. The subroutine fills out various fields in its object. The setsubdir function performs a similar duty, although note that it has a consistency check. If someone tries to set a subdirectory on an object that is not a directory, an error is emitted.

Next, the display subroutine displays the object on the screen. This is fairly straightforward, using code similar to that used in earlier versions of the code.

Finally, you see the two characters at the end of the file: 1;. They are there because Perl wants to know if your module loaded properly. If your module has not, Perl will abort compilation of your program. If it has loaded properly, Perl continues with its normal execution. This value is simply the last value evaluated by the module. Because this module has no initialization code that could possibly fail, it simply says 1 so that Perl gets a true value from it.

Let's run this final version of the code over /etc/X11 so that you can see that it does indeed work to traverse several directories deep (see Listing 20-6).

Note   Listing 20-6 is available online.

Listing 20-6: **Sample output**

```
$ chmod a+x ch20-10.pl
$ ./ch20-10.pl /etc/X11
. (1024 bytes)
.. (6144 bytes)
directory WindowMaker (2048 bytes)
    . (2048 bytes)
    .. (1024 bytes)
    appearance.menu (553 bytes)
    background.menu (1170 bytes)
    menu (8164 bytes)
    menu.ca (10101 bytes)
    menu.cz (4189 bytes)
    menu.da (9164 bytes)
    menu.de (4126 bytes)
    menu.el (8731 bytes)
    menu.es (4331 bytes)
    menu.fi (7204 bytes)
    menu.fr (9238 bytes)
    menu.gl (3799 bytes)
    menu.he (6958 bytes)
    menu.hook (29056 bytes)
    menu.hr (7312 bytes)
    menu.hu (7925 bytes)
    menu.it (4048 bytes)
    menu.ja (7570 bytes)
    menu.ko (8423 bytes)
```

Continued

Listing 20-6 *(continued)*

```
     menu.nl (3223 bytes)
     menu.no (7008 bytes)
     menu.posthook (0 bytes)
     menu.prehook (0 bytes)
     menu.pt (7812 bytes)
     menu.ru (4548 bytes)
     menu.se (7561 bytes)
     menu.sl (7645 bytes)
     menu.tr (6512 bytes)
     menu.zh_CN (7233 bytes)
     menu.zh_TW.Big5 (7361 bytes)
     plmenu (4461 bytes)
     plmenu.da (9069 bytes)
     plmenu.dk (11409 bytes)
     plmenu.fr (4830 bytes)
     plmenu.hr (5694 bytes)
     plmenu.it (4684 bytes)
     plmenu.zh_CN (3376 bytes)
     wmmacros (2397 bytes)
XF86Config (20488 bytes)
Xloadimage (842 bytes)
Xmodmap (547 bytes)
directory Xresources (1024 bytes)
     . (1024 bytes)
     .. (1024 bytes)
     tetex-base (126 bytes)
     xbase-clients (36 bytes)
     xfree86-common (349 bytes)
     xterm (895 bytes)
Xserver (249 bytes)
Xsession (3672 bytes)
Xsession.options (235 bytes)
directory afterstep (1024 bytes)
     . (1024 bytes)
     .. (1024 bytes)
     menudefs.hook (36511 bytes)
directory fonts (1024 bytes)
     . (1024 bytes)
     .. (1024 bytes)
     directory 100dpi (1024 bytes)
        . (1024 bytes)
        .. (1024 bytes)
        xfonts-100dpi.alias (3154 bytes)
     directory 75dpi (1024 bytes)
        . (1024 bytes)
        .. (1024 bytes)
        xfonts-75dpi.alias (3066 bytes)
     directory Speedo (1024 bytes)
        . (1024 bytes)
        .. (1024 bytes)
        xfonts-scalable.scale (564 bytes)
```

```
           directory Type1 (1024 bytes)
              . (1024 bytes)
              .. (1024 bytes)
              xfonts-scalable.scale (1075 bytes)
           directory misc (1024 bytes)
              . (1024 bytes)
              .. (1024 bytes)
              xfonts-base.alias (9940 bytes)
              xfonts-jmk.alias (5424 bytes)
        directory fvwm (1024 bytes)
           . (1024 bytes)
           .. (1024 bytes)
           default-style.hook (309 bytes)
           init-restart.hook (357 bytes)
           init.hook (409 bytes)
           main-menu-pre.hook (259 bytes)
           main-menu.hook (385 bytes)
           menudefs.hook (36642 bytes)
           post.hook (121 bytes)
           pre.hook (253 bytes)
           restart.hook (97 bytes)
           system.fvwm2rc (15195 bytes)
           system.warnings (3462 bytes)
           update.warn (199 bytes)
        window-managers (338 bytes)
        directory wm-common (1024 bytes)
           . (1024 bytes)
           .. (1024 bytes)
        directory xinit (1024 bytes)
           . (1024 bytes)
           .. (1024 bytes)
           xinitrc (188 bytes)
        directory xserver (1024 bytes)
           . (1024 bytes)
           .. (1024 bytes)
           SecurityPolicy (2929 bytes)
        directory xview (1024 bytes)
           . (1024 bytes)
           .. (1024 bytes)
           text_extras_menu (703 bytes)
           textswrc (2409 bytes)
           ttyswrc (444 bytes)
```

Summary

In this chapter, you received a quick introduction to the Perl programming language. Specifically, you learned:

✦ Perl is a "glue language," doing a good job of tying together data coming from many different sources.

✦ Perl's syntax largely resembles that of C but also includes numerous features from shell, awk, sed, grep, and various other UNIX tools or languages.

✦ Perl supports four main types of variables: scalars, lists, hashes, and subroutines.

✦ References are available, which are similar in concept to pointers in C.

✦ All memory allocation and deallocation in Perl is done automatically.

✦ By using references, you can build complex data structures such as nested arrays or nested hashes.

✦ The my operator is important to enforce local scoping rules in subroutines.

✦ Perl features object-oriented functionality as an addition to its package system.

✦   ✦   ✦

Manipulating Data with Perl

Now that you have learned some basics of Perl, it's time to address an area that is one of Perl's greatest strengths: its data manipulation support. In this chapter, you will learn how to get data into your Perl programs, process the data once you have it, implement some persistent storage mechanisms, and generate output from your programs.

Reading Data

Perl provides you with several different ways to get data into your program. Because many Perl programs are written to read data from line-oriented files such as text files, it's no surprise that Perl has operators designed for just such uses.

The main such operator is the angle-bracket operator, which reads line-oriented data from a machine. When used in a scalar context, it returns one line of input. When used in a list context, it continues reading data into memory until EOF (end of file) is reached, and it returns a list whose elements are the lines in the file. Like some similar functions in C, this operator does not strip off the trailing newline; Perl's chomp function is great for this.

You can also use this operator in a loop. The following code is an illustration of a very common usage of the angle-bracket operator in a loop:

```
#!/usr/bin/perl -w

my $counter = 1;
while (my $line = <STDIN>) {
   chomp $line;
   print "Line $counter: $line\n";
   $counter++;
}
```

As long as the `<STDIN>` continues to return data, the `while` loop will continue to run. The newline is removed by `chomp`, the line is printed, and you get output. For instance:

```
$ ls /etc/X11 | ./ch21-1.pl
Line 1: WindowMaker
Line 2: XF86Config
Line 3: Xloadimage
Line 4: Xmodmap
Line 5: Xresources
Line 6: Xserver
Line 7: Xsession
Line 8: Xsession.options
Line 9: afterstep
Line 10: fonts
Line 11: fvwm
Line 12: window-managers
Line 13: wm-common
Line 14: xinit
Line 15: xserver
Line 16: xview
```

You can also open arbitrary files for reading. For instance, here's a simple program to count the number of lines in a file:

```
#!/usr/bin/perl -w

print "Enter a filename: ";
chomp ($filename = <STDIN>);

open INFILE, $filename or
  die "Couldn't open file $filename: $!\n";

$counter = 0;

while (<INFILE>) {
  $counter++;
}

print "Lines: $counter\n";
```

This program prompts for a filename. Note the shortcut on line 4—the input is chomped while it is being read in.

Some programs, especially programs like CGI programs, and some utility scripts, need to read data from the process's environment variables. This can be done by accessing the special `%ENV` hash. The keys of this hash are the environment variable names, and their values are, of course, the contents of the variables themselves. For instance, `$ENV{PATH}` corresponds to the system's current search path for your process. You can both read from and write to these items just as you would any other hash.

You can also read arguments passed on the command line. Perl has an @ARGV array that functions in a manner similar to argv in C. However, Perl does not include the name of the script in the array. Furthermore, there is no argc; you can access that information with $#ARGV.

As a special feature, you can have your program read through lines of any files specified on the command line, one after another. Perl will automatically open them and feed them to your program. And if one of the items on the line is a single dash, Perl will read standard input at that point—essentially mimicking the behavior of cat:

```
#!/usr/bin/perl -w

$counter = 0;

while (<>) {
  $counter++;
}

print "Lines: $counter\n";
```

You can run this program, for instance, like this:

```
$ ./ch21-2.pl /etc/passwd /etc/group /etc/X11/XF86Config
Lines: 700
```

Tip   Notice the <> operator in the example Perl program immediately above. This operator reads input a line at a time, just like <STDIN> did. However, the difference is that <> will read input from each file specified on the command line for the program. In this case, it read input from /etc/passwd, /etc/group, and /etc/X11/XF86Config before finally returning an end of file indication. If no files are specified on the command like, <> reverts to <STDIN>.

Parsing and Processing Data

One of the most powerful features of Perl is its capability to easily pick apart data and process it. In Chapter 3, "Working with Regular Expressions," you learned about the power of regular expressions. Perl integrates regular expressions into the language, and they form an important part of it. You can use them for string comparisons—but comparisons much more powerful than simply determining whether two strings are equal. With regular expressions, you get to indicate precisely how nearly equal strings have to be to be considered a match. Furthermore, these regular expressions can be engineered by your own software on the fly—that is, any string can be a regular expression.

In Chapter 3, I introduced a pattern testing program named `pattest`. Here is its code:

```
#!/usr/bin/perl

while (1) {
  print "Enter pattern";
  print ", or . to re-use previous," if ($LASTREGEXP);
  print " or leave empty to exit:\n";
  print "> ";
  $REGEXP = <STDIN>;
  chomp $REGEXP;
  if ($REGEXP eq '.') {
    $REGEXP = $LASTREGEXP;
  }
  exit (0) unless ($REGEXP);
  print "Enter string to match";
  print " or . to re-use previous" if ($LASTSTRING);
  print ":\n";
  print "> ";
  $STRING = <STDIN>;
  chomp $STRING;
  if ($STRING eq '.') {
    $STRING = $LASTSTRING;
  }

  $LASTREGEXP = $REGEXP;
  $LASTSTRING = $STRING;

  @MATCHES = $STRING =~ /$REGEXP/;
  if ($#MATCHES > -1) {
    print "Successful match!\n";
    print "There were " . ($#MATCHES + 1) . " strings returned: \n";
    $counter = 0;
    foreach $MATCH (@MATCHES) {
      $counter++;
      print "String $counter: $MATCH\n";
    }
  } else {
    print "There was not a successful match.\n";
  }
  print "\n\n";
}
```

Let's take a look at this code. First, the program starts with `while(1)` — this means that the loop will continue forever — although there is an exit `condition` (`exit (0) unless ($REGEXP);`)in it. Then, the user is prompted for a pattern. If the data entered is simply a period, then the program uses the previously entered value. If the regular expression supplied is empty, the program exits. The program similarly prompts for a string to match, and again, it can reuse the last one if desired. Then, we come to this line:

```
@MATCHES = $STRING =~ /$REGEXP/;
```

This code causes the regular expression to be applied to the input string. If any items were returned, they are placed into that array, which is then displayed. Then, the cycle repeats.

You can make this a more useful program by being able to pipe data to it — perhaps in a fashion similar to grep (see Chapter 4); but this way, you get Perl's regular expression support instead of grep's. Here's a revised version of the code:

```
#!/usr/bin/perl -w

$pattern = shift @ARGV;

while ($string = <>) {
  chomp $string;
  @matches = $string =~ /$pattern/;

  if ($#matches > -1) {
    print "Match: (";
    print join(', ', @matches);
    print ")\n";
  }
}
```

This code is indeed much shorter, but it may be more useful than the other. Consider, for instance, using it to isolate a permission string and file size from an ls listing:

```
$ ls -l /etc/X11 | ./pattest '^(\S+)\s+\d+\s+\D+\s+(\d+)'
Match: (drwxr-xr-x, 2048)
Match: (-rw-r--r--, 20488)
Match: (-rw-r--r--, 842)
Match: (-rw-r--r--, 547)
Match: (drwxr-xr-x, 1024)
Match: (-rw-r--r--, 249)
Match: (-rwxr-xr-x, 3672)
Match: (-rw-r--r--, 235)
Match: (drwxr-xr-x, 1024)
Match: (drwxr-xr-x, 1024)
Match: (drwxr-xr-x, 1024)
Match: (-rw-r--r--, 338)
Match: (drwxr-xr-x, 1024)
Match: (drwxr-xr-x, 1024)
Match: (drwxr-xr-x, 1024)
Match: (drwxr-xr-x, 1024)
```

Using split

Another use for parsing is to split apart a string based on a certain delimiter.
This function is more or less the inverse of the regular expression match. Instead
of specifying the text to match, you specify a regular expression indicating the
text *not* to match. When you are parsing data that has a fixed separator, split is
ideal. Examples include the passwd file (a colon separator), English text (a space
separator between words), comma-delimited files, and even some forms of
column-based output. Here is a rewrite of pattest that uses split:

```perl
#!/usr/bin/perl -w

$pattern = shift @ARGV;

while ($string = <>) {
  chomp $string;
  @matches = split(/$pattern/, $string);

  if ($#matches > -1) {
    print "Match: (";
    print join(', ', @matches);
    print ")\n";
  }
}
```

You can take a look at how this code works by again working with a directory
listing, using it (recall that because the space is a shell metacharacter, it needs
to be quoted on the command line):

```
$ ls -l /etc/X11 | ./splittest ' '
Match: (total, 41)
Match: (drwxr-xr-x, , , 2, root, , , , , root, , , , , , , , , 2048, Sep, 11,
10:40, WindowMaker)
Match: (-rw-r--r--, , , 1, root, , , , , root, , , , , , , , , 20488, Jul, 20,
15:26, XF86Config)
Match: (-rw-r--r--, , , 1, root, , , , , root, , , , , , , , , 842, Apr, , 5,
, 1998, Xloadimage)
Match: (-rw-r--r--, , , 1, root, , , , , root, , , , , , , , , 547, May, 27,
07:40, Xmodmap)
Match: (drwxr-xr-x, , , 2, root, , , , , root, , , , , , , , , 1024, Sep, 15,
16:05, Xresources)
```

This type of output continues on. What is happening is that each space is matched
separately. You can achieve a more useful result by using a regular expression that
matches one or more spaces. Here's a revised version of the preceding code:

```
$ ls -l /etc/X11 | ./splittest ' +'
Match: (total, 41)
Match: (drwxr-xr-x, 2, root, root, 2048, Sep, 11, 10:40, WindowMaker)
Match: (-rw-r--r--, 1, root, root, 20488, Jul, 20, 15:26, XF86Config)
Match: (-rw-r--r--, 1, root, root, 842, Apr, 5, 1998, Xloadimage)
Match: (-rw-r--r--, 1, root, root, 547, May, 27, 07:40, Xmodmap)
```

```
Match: (drwxr-xr-x, 2, root, root, 1024, Sep, 15, 16:05, Xresources)
Match: (-rw-r--r--, 1, root, root, 249, Jun, 2, 20:36, Xserver)
Match: (-rwxr-xr-x, 1, root, root, 3672, Aug, 26, 21:50, Xsession)
Match: (-rw-r--r--, 1, root, root, 235, May, 27, 07:52, Xsession.options)
Match: (drwxr-xr-x, 2, root, root, 1024, Sep, 11, 10:40, afterstep)
Match: (drwxr-xr-x, 7, root, root, 1024, Jun, 2, 19:34, fonts)
Match: (drwxr-xr-x, 2, root, root, 1024, Sep, 11, 10:40, fvwm)
Match: (-rw-r--r--, 1, root, root, 338, Aug, 31, 19:30, window-managers)
Match: (drwxr-xr-x, 2, root, root, 1024, May, 13, 19:42, wm-common)
Match: (drwxr-xr-x, 2, root, root, 1024, Aug, 31, 19:40, xinit)
Match: (drwxr-xr-x, 2, root, root, 1024, Aug, 31, 19:41, xserver)
Match: (drwxr-xr-x, 2, root, root, 1024, Jun, 18, 12:08, xview)
```

Using grep

Another useful function in Perl is named `grep`. Its function is similar to the well-known command by that name: to check each element in an array for a match on a certain pattern, and return a list of corresponding elements. You can easily rewrite the preceding code to use `grep`—in fact, you can write your own simple version of the `grep` command in Perl in just a very few lines of code:

```
#!/usr/bin/perl -w

$pattern = shift @ARGV;

foreach $match (grep(/$pattern/, <>)) {
  print $match;
}
```

This short bit of code does what hundreds or even thousands of lines would do in other languages—thanks to Perl's built-in regular expression support. Take a look at the results:

```
$ ls -l /etc/X11 | ./mygrep X
-rw-r--r--  1 root     root        20488 Jul 20 15:26 XF86Config
-rw-r--r--  1 root     root          842 Apr  5  1998 Xloadimage
-rw-r--r--  1 root     root          547 May 27 07:40 Xmodmap
drwxr-xr-x  2 root     root         1024 Sep 15 16:05 Xresources
-rw-r--r--  1 root     root          249 Jun  2 20:36 Xserver
-rwxr-xr-x  1 root     root         3672 Aug 26 21:50 Xsession
-rw-r--r--  1 root     root          235 May 27 07:52 Xsession.options
```

This code behaves almost exactly like the `grep` command! Notice that you can also rewrite it with a little bit more effort by implementing the functionality of Perl's `grep` function yourself. Here's a version of the program that does the same as the preceding version, but without using `grep`:

```
#!/usr/bin/perl -w

$pattern = shift @ARGV;
```

```
foreach $match (<>) {
  print $match if $match =~ /$pattern/;
}
```

Running this program gives the same results as before, as you can see here:

```
$ ls -l /etc/X11 | ./mygrep X
-rw-r--r--   1 root     root        20488 Jul 20 15:26 XF86Config
-rw-r--r--   1 root     root          842 Apr  5  1998 Xloadimage
-rw-r--r--   1 root     root          547 May 27 07:40 Xmodmap
drwxr-xr-x   2 root     root         1024 Sep 15 16:05 Xresources
-rw-r--r--   1 root     root          249 Jun  2 20:36 Xserver
-rwxr-xr-x   1 root     root         3672 Aug 26 21:50 Xsession
-rw-r--r--   1 root     root          235 May 27 07:52 Xsession.options
```

Storing Data

Another common concern when writing programs is how to use persistent storage for data. With small, simple programs, simply writing data out to a text file and reading it back in the next time the program runs may be sufficient. However, consider a situation in which you have ten thousand—or ten million—records. This process may not be a practical solution in that case. Or consider a case in which you have nested arrays or hashes as described in Chapter 20, "Introducing Perl." In this situation, a flat text file may require a complex format and some significant work to recreate the structures in memory when reading it back in.

Perl provides features for both of these problems, and more. For the problem of storing large amounts of data, Perl enables you to transparently tie structures such as hashes to an on-disk database. This means that any access to those structures actually takes place from disk, freeing you from the constraints of available memory and enabling you to obtain a convenient persistent storage method at the same time.

For the problem of storing complex structures, Perl provides the Data Dumper, which can take any Perl structure and generate a string representation of it. This string representation is actually valid Perl, so your Perl program can read it back in later and (with a few exceptions) recreate the in-memory contents exactly as they were before writing the data out—automatically.

You can even combine these two methods and store output from the Data Dumper in a database. Additionally, Perl is capable of communicating with numerous SQL database servers if your data storage needs require something more robust. This topic will be discussed in Chapter 23, "SQL Databases with DBI"; for now, we'll concentrate on the simpler ways to store data. Although both methods involve a database, the two are significantly different. The database type being described in this chapter is useful if you have simple key/value pairs that need to be stored, as with a hash. A SQL database could be more useful if your data is more complex or if you need data analysis or query tools in the database engine.

Using databases

Perl provides you with a wonderful capability to extend your programs to provide fast, persistent storage for data structures such as hashes — with almost no changes to your code. This is accomplished by using Perl's tie operator. After you use tie, operations such as reading or writing from your hash actually take place from an on-disk database. Because the database is on the disk instead of in memory, the data can be reloaded into your program later. Not only that, but because the data is on disk, you can potentially deal with much more data than would fit into memory.

Note   Perl provides tie-ins to several different database engines. In this chapter, I'll use the Berkeley db system for the examples. This is standard on many current Linux distributions, but if you are running a custom version of Perl or an older distribution, you may not have this. Therefore, you may need to replace every occurrence of DB_File with SDBM_File. Also, be aware that sdbm has a 1K per-record size limit, whereas the Berkeley db system does not.

Of course, these features can come at a price: disk access can be significantly slower than memory access, although operating system caching often helps. Also, certain things cannot be stored in a database — at least not if you expect them to be able to be reloaded later. These include items such as references or object associations. So, these databases are best suited to storing scalar data.

As a demonstration of how to modify a program to store its data in a database, let's take a program from an earlier chapter and modify it for use with a database (see Listing 21-1). The first version will simply add a database tie-in, but it will have a few problems. We'll analyze the problems and then fix the code to work better.

Listing 21-1: **Example of tie**

```
#!/usr/bin/perl -w

use DB_File;

my %dirs = ();

tie(%dirs, "DB_File", "Dirs.hash") or die "Couldn't tie: $!\n";

# Perl's unless is an inverse if.  That is, unless(a) is the same as
# if (!(a)).

unless ($ARGV[0]) {
  print "Displaying saved data:\n";
  printit(\%dirs, 0);
  exit 0;
}
```

Continued

Listing 21-1 *(continued)*

```
# -d is a Perl shorthand.  It does a stat() on the passed filename and
# then looks at the mode.  If the filename is a directory, it returns true;
# if not, it returns false.

unless (-d $ARGV[0]) {
  die "The filename supplied was not a directory."
}

dircontents($ARGV[0], \%dirs);
printit(\%dirs, 0);

untie(%dirs);

sub dircontents{
  my ($startname, $retval) = @_;
  my $filename;
  $retval = {} unless ($retval);
  local *DH;                  # Ensure that the handle is locally scoped

# This is the same as DH = opendir("filename") in C.
# In C, you can use DIR *DH; to declare the variable.

  unless(opendir(DH, $startname)) {
    warn "Couldn't open directory $startname: $!";
    return undef;
  }

  # In C, readdir() returns a pointer to struct dirent, whose members are
  # defined in readdir(3).  In Perl, returns one file in scalar context,
  # or all remaining filenames in list context.

  while ($filename = readdir(DH)) {
    if ($filename ne '.' &&
        $filename ne '..' &&
        ! -l "$startname/$filename" &&
        -d "$startname/$filename") {
      $retval->{$filename} = dircontents("$startname/$filename");
    } else {
      $retval->{$filename} = 1;
    }
  }

  closedir(DH);
  return $retval;
}

sub printit {
  my ($ref, $count) = @_;
```

```
  my $key;
  my $counter = 0;

  foreach $key (sort keys %$ref) {
    print " " x ($count * 3);
    if (ref $ref->{$key}) {
      printf "%3d: subdirectory %s\n", $counter, $key;
      printit($ref->{$key}, $count + 1);
    } else {
      printf "%3d: %s\n", $counter, $key;
    }
    $counter++;
  }
}
```

This program was modified very little to use a tied hash. One change actually ties the hash to the database, and a corresponding change allows the subroutine to directly work on this hash. It is, of course, possible to assign to the entire hash at once, but by working on individual hash elements, its existing contents are not replaced unless you're using a duplicate key. Therefore, it's possible to store multiple directory trees in the database at once. However, these modifications are not quite sufficient, as you can see from running the program:

```
$ ./ch21-2.pl   /etc/X11
   0: .
   1: ..
   2: WindowMaker
   3: XF86Config
   4: Xloadimage
   5: Xmodmap
   6: Xresources
   7: Xserver
   8: Xsession
   9: Xsession.options
  10: afterstep
  11: fonts
  12: fvwm
  13: window-managers
  14: wm-common
  15: xinit
  16: xserver
  17: xview
```

The problem here is that the program no longer recognizes directories as such. The reason is that the following test fails:

```
    if (ref $ref->{$key}) {
```

Interestingly, if you comment out the line that ties the database to the hash, the program works fine. The reason is that the hash can no longer store a real reference if tied to a database because the database doesn't support this. Instead, the reference is converted into a string (containing essentially some useless numbers) for storage into the databases. Thus, when the subroutine tries to check if the value stored in the database is a reference, it gets a negative result. Note that you can display the saved contents of the database by running this program with no arguments — the program indicates that it's displaying the saved data and then proceeds to give you output exactly like normal.

In order to fix this problem, you need to modify the code such that it doesn't need to store references in the main hash. This means that you can't store things recursively any longer — perhaps you just need to take a different approach. Listing 21-2 shows a version of the code that stores data without using nested hashes, thus avoiding that problem.

Listing 21-2: **Revised tie example**

```
#!/usr/bin/perl -w

use DB_File;

my %dirs = ();

tie(%dirs, "DB_File", "Dirs.hash") or die "Couldn't tie: $!\n";

# Perl's unless is an inverse if.  That is, unless(a) is the same as
# if (!(a)).

unless ($ARGV[0]) {
  print "Displaying saved data:\n";
  printit(\%dirs, 0);
  exit 0;
}

# -d is a Perl shorthand.  It does a stat() on the passed filename and
# then looks at the mode.  If the filename is a directory, it returns true;
# if not, it returns false.

unless (-d $ARGV[0]) {
  die "The filename supplied was not a directory."
}

dircontents($ARGV[0], \%dirs);
printit(\%dirs, 0);
```

```
untie(%dirs);

sub dircontents{
  my ($startname, $retval) = @_;
  my $filename;
  $retval = {} unless ($retval);
  local *DH;                    # Ensure that the handle is locally scoped

# This is the same as DH = opendir("filename") in C.
# In C, you can use DIR *DH; to declare the variable.

  unless(opendir(DH, $startname)) {
    warn "Couldn't open directory $startname: $!";
    return undef;
  }

  # In C, readdir() returns a pointer to struct dirent, whose members are
  # defined in readdir(3).  In Perl, returns one file in scalar context,
  # or all remaining filenames in list context.

  while ($filename = readdir(DH)) {
    if ($filename ne '.' &&
      $filename ne '..' &&
      ! -l "$startname/$filename" &&
      -d "$startname/$filename") {
      dircontents("$startname/$filename", $retval);
    } else {
      $retval->{"$startname/$filename"} = -s "$startname/$filename";
    }
  }

  closedir(DH);
  return %$retval;
}

sub printit {
  my ($ref, $count) = @_;
  my $key;
  my $counter = 0;

  foreach $key (sort keys %$ref) {
    print " " x ($count * 3);
      printf "%3d: %s (%d bytes)\n", $counter, $key, $ref->{$key};
    $counter++;
  }
}
```

This time, instead of hashes being nested for directories, entire pathnames are stored as the keys for the hash. Now there's no need to have nested hashes, and the subroutine to print the results could actually be modified to parse the pathnames to determine indentation if desired. To take a look at the results, first you need to remove the existing Dirs.hash file so that data from a previous version of the program does not creep into this one. Then, try the program:

```
$ rm Dirs.hash
$ ./ch21-3.pl /etc/X11
  0: /etc/X11/. (1024 bytes)
  1: /etc/X11/.. (6144 bytes)
  2: /etc/X11/WindowMaker/. (2048 bytes)
  3: /etc/X11/WindowMaker/.. (1024 bytes)
  4: /etc/X11/WindowMaker/appearance.menu (553 bytes)
  5: /etc/X11/WindowMaker/background.menu (1170 bytes)
  6: /etc/X11/WindowMaker/menu (8164 bytes)
  7: /etc/X11/WindowMaker/menu.ca (10101 bytes)
  8: /etc/X11/WindowMaker/menu.cz (4189 bytes)
  9: /etc/X11/WindowMaker/menu.da (9164 bytes)
 10: /etc/X11/WindowMaker/menu.de (4126 bytes)
 11: /etc/X11/WindowMaker/menu.el (8731 bytes)
```

The output actually continues for many more lines on my system but is truncated here; you can see that directories are properly being traversed. However, there is a downside. Recall that the system was able to store not only size but also information such as age in a nested hash. Not only that, but it could also store an object there. Well, this sort of thing is now impossible because you can only store a string in the hash.

However, there is a solution — have a subroutine that generates a string representation of the data, and another that converts the string back to a hash. Doing this is sometimes referred to as *serialization* of data. Serialization can be annoying, but if you use something like Perl's object-oriented features, it can be implemented in a fashion that is not terribly cumbersome. Listing 21-3 shows a version of the FileObject code that adds support for serialization.

Listing 21-3: FileObject.pm: an object with serialization

```perl
package FileObject;

# Can be invoked with:
#    startfile
#    startfile, filename
#    serialform

sub new {
  my ($class, $startfile, $filename) = @_;
```

```perl
  my $self = {startfile => $startfile};
  bless($self, $class);

  if ($startfile =~ m'^///') {
    $self->deserialize($startfile);
  } elsif ($filename) {
    $self->populate($filename);
  }

  return $self;
}

sub populate {
  my ($self, $filename) = @_;

  $self->{size} = -s $self->{startfile} . "/$filename";
  $self->{age} = -M "$self->{startfile}/$filename";
  $self->{name} = $filename;
  if ($filename ne '.' &&
      $filename ne '..' &&
      ! -l "$self->{startfile}/$filename" &&
      -d "$self->{startfile}/$filename") {
    $self->{isdir} = 1;
  } else {
    $self->{isdir} = 0;
  }
}

sub deserialize {
  my ($self, $serialform) = @_;

  $serialform =~ s'^///'';

  ($self->{startfile},
   $self->{size},
   $self->{age},
   $self->{name},
   $self->{isdir}) = split('\|', $serialform);
}

sub serialize {
  my $self = shift @_;

  return "///" . join('|', $self->{startfile},
                           $self->{size},
                           $self->{age},
                           $self->{name},
                           $self->{isdir});
}

sub setsubdir {
```

Continued

Listing 21-3 *(continued)*

```perl
  my ($self, $subdir) = @_;

  unless ($self->{isdir}) {
    die "Attempt to set subdirectory on non-directory!";
  }

  $self->{subdir} = $subdir;
}
sub display {
  my ($self, $level) = @_;
  $level = 0 unless $level;

  print " " x (3 * $level);
  printf "%s%s (%d bytes)\n",
         ($self->{isdir} ? "directory " : ""),
         "$self->{startfile}/$self->{name}",
         $self->{size};
}

1;
```

Listing 21-4 is the Perl program to accompany the previous code. It has been modified to use serialization as well.

Listing 21-4: Example usage of FileObject

```perl
#!/usr/bin/perl -w

use DB_File;
require FileObject;

my %dirs = ();

tie(%dirs, "DB_File", "Dirs.hash") or die "Couldn't tie: $!\n";

# Perl's unless is an inverse if.  That is, unless(a) is the same as
# if (!(a)).

unless ($ARGV[0]) {
  print "Displaying saved data:\n";
  printit(\%dirs, 0);
  exit 0;
}

# -d is a Perl shorthand.  It does a stat() on the passed filename and
```

```perl
# then looks at the mode.  If the filename is a directory, it returns true;
# if not, it returns false.

unless (-d $ARGV[0]) {
  die "The filename supplied was not a directory."
}

dircontents($ARGV[0], \%dirs);
printit(\%dirs, 0);

untie(%dirs);

sub dircontents{
  my ($startname, $retval) = @_;
  my $filename;
  $retval = {} unless ($retval);
  local *DH;                    # Ensure that the handle is locally scoped

# This is the same as DH = opendir("filename") in C.
# In C, you can use DIR *DH; to declare the variable.

  unless(opendir(DH, $startname)) {
    warn "Couldn't open directory $startname: $!";
    return undef;
  }

  # In C, readdir() returns a pointer to struct dirent, whose members are
  # defined in readdir(3).  In Perl, returns one file in scalar context,
  # or all remaining filenames in list context.

  while ($filename = readdir(DH)) {
    my $object = new FileObject($startname);
    $object->populate($filename);
    if ($object->{isdir}) {
      dircontents("$startname/$filename", $retval);
    }
    $retval->{"$startname/$filename"} = $object->serialize();
  }

  closedir(DH);
  return %$retval;
}

sub printit {
  my ($ref, $count) = @_;
  my $key;
  my $counter = 0;

  foreach $key (sort keys %$ref) {
    my $object = new FileObject($ref->{$key});
    $object->display($count);
  }
}
```

Examining the code, you can see that FileObject.pm contains some new code. There is a subroutine called `serialize` that generates a simple string based on the contents of the object. As a special identifier, it starts this string out with three slashes so that it is easily distinguishable from others. Then it joins together various data from the object, separated by the pipe symbol.

Note   The pipe symbol, and even the three leading slashes, are valid characters in the file system, so this code can fail if files containing such codes are encountered. Solutions to this problem could be a further encoding of the strings (perhaps in a hexadecimal notation), selection of alternative characters, or encoding length information and then the strings themselves.

An accompanying `deserialize` function does the opposite—it first strips off the leading slashes and then splits the input into the original parts. The new function has been modified as well with a handy shortcut: if it is called with a serialized version of the object (which it can detect from the leading slashes), it initializes the object to its deserialized form. Thus, the `printit` function in the main program can simply create an object for each entry in the database and ask the object to display itself.

Note that the subdir information is not stored in the serialized string. The reason is that this information is simply a reference, and as you know, references cannot be stored in a database. However, because the object is not being used in a nested fashion in this program anyway, that limitation is not a problem.

If you want to try out this program, go ahead and do so. As usual, first remove the Dirs.hash file. Then try the program. Here is an example of the results after a second execution of the program, where it is called to display the data it saved the first time:

```
$ ./ch21-4.pl
Displaying saved data:
/etc/X11/. (1024 bytes)
/etc/X11/.. (6144 bytes)
directory /etc/X11/WindowMaker (2048 bytes)
/etc/X11/WindowMaker/. (2048 bytes)
/etc/X11/WindowMaker/.. (1024 bytes)
/etc/X11/WindowMaker/appearance.menu (553 bytes)
/etc/X11/WindowMaker/background.menu (1170 bytes)
/etc/X11/WindowMaker/menu (8164 bytes)
/etc/X11/WindowMaker/menu.ca (10101 bytes)
/etc/X11/WindowMaker/menu.cz (4189 bytes)
```

Again, this output continues for over a hundred additional lines, but you can see the point. The data, including full filename and size, has been saved in the database and can be recalled without having to traverse the directory tree again.

Using the Data Dumper

You saw earlier in this chapter all the hoops that were necessary to be able to store complex data structures in a database. Perl offers a way to ease those problems, though: the Data Dumper, known in Perl as `Data::Dumper`. This piece of code takes something — almost anything — and effectively serializes the entire object. What's more impressive, though, is that the serial representation of the object is actually executable Perl code. Thus, to load in such a serialized version and recreate the original, all you have to do is run `eval` over it. Thus, this type of code may be ideal for the dilemma of nested hashes as you have already seen.

However, there are some downsides as compared to the database format. First, the Data Dumper does not provide a tie interface, so this sort of access can not happen automatically. Second, the Data Dumper is not well-suited to dealing with large amounts of data, because it must store everything in memory (and even two copies in memory, for a brief time). Thus, it cannot really be used as a way of manipulating large amounts of data by using a hard drive. If you want to serialize data in a security-conscious environment, for instance as a network server, you will not want to use the Data Dumper, because restoring the data allows people to run arbitrary Perl code in the input, a security hazard. Finally, Data Dumper can be somewhat slow compared to a database. So it's mostly useful for saving data between program executions — perhaps as a Save operation in your program.

That said, usage of the Data Dumper is extremely easy; serializing even a large and complex data structure (such as one that contains objects) or nested hashes is not difficult. Listing 21-5 shows a revised Perl program. It also requires a FileObject.pm file; either the final version from Chapter 20 or the version presented in the previous section here will work fine.

Listing 21-5: **Using the Data Dumper**

```perl
#!/usr/bin/perl -w

use Data::Dumper;
require FileObject;

# Perl's unless is an inverse if.  That is, unless(a) is the same as
# if (!(a)).

unless ($ARGV[0]) {
  my $datastr;
  my $dirs;

  print "No argument found, displaying information from Dirs.dump!\n";

  open DUMPFILE, "Dirs.dump" or die "Couldn't read from Dirs.dump: $!\n";
```

Continued

Listing 21-5 *(continued)*

```perl
    $datastr = join('', <DUMPFILE>);
    eval $datastr;
    printit($dirs, 0);
    exit 0;
}

# -d is a Perl shorthand.  It does a stat() on the passed filename and
# then looks at the mode.  If the filename is a directory, it returns true;
# if not, it returns false.

unless (-d $ARGV[0]) {
  die "The filename supplied was not a directory."
}

my $dirs = dircontents($ARGV[0]);
open DUMPFILE, ">Dirs.dump" or die "Couldn't open Dirs.dump: $!\n";
my $dump = new Data::Dumper([$dirs], ['dirs']);
$dump->Indent(1);
print DUMPFILE $dump->Dump;

sub dircontents{
  my $startname = shift @_;
  my $filename;
  my $retval = {};           # Initialize with an empty hash reference
  local *DH;                 # Ensure that the handle is locally scoped

# This is the same as DH = opendir("filename") in C.
# In C, you can use DIR *DH; to declare the variable.

  unless(opendir(DH, $startname)) {
    warn "Couldn't open directory $startname: $!";
    return undef;
  }

  # In C, readdir() returns a pointer to struct dirent, whose members are
  # defined in readdir(3).  In Perl, returns one file in scalar context,
  # or all remaining filenames in list context.

  while ($filename = readdir(DH)) {
    my $object = new FileObject($startname);
    $object->populate($filename);
    if ($object->{isdir}) {
      $object->setsubdir(dircontents("$startname/$filename"));
    }
    $retval->{$filename} = $object;
  }

  closedir(DH);
```

```
    return $retval;
}

sub printit {
  my ($ref, $count) = @_;
  my $key;

  foreach $key (sort keys %$ref) {
    $ref->{$key}->display($count);
    if ($ref->{$key}->{isdir}) {
      printit($ref->{$key}->{subdir}, $count + 1)
    }
  }
}
```

Looking at the code, take note of a new use statement at the top that brings in the
Data Dumper. Instead of aborting when no argument is passed, the program then
instead loads the saved data and displays it. To do that, the program first opens
Dirs.dump for reading. The file is then read in and stored in $datastr. The join
call here simply joins together all the strings in the array that represents the whole
file that the angle-bracket operator returns. The eval function is invoked, which
actually parses the input string as Perl code — inside this code, the $dirs variable
is set. The information is then printed out and the program exits.

If an argument was present, the reference to a hash ($dirs) is built exactly as
before. Then the output dump file is opened for writing. A new object is created.
The parameters to new are a reference to an array containing all the items to dump
and a second reference to an array containing their names; this second reference to
an array is optional. Because only one thing is being dumped, it ($dirs) is passed
as the sole element in the first array and its name as the sole element in the second.
After that, the output indentation style is set, and then the data is dumped. Note
that nothing is even displayed in this situation; the only way to get a display from
this code is to run it with no arguments, forcing it to load its data from the saved
file. Try running it the first time:

```
$ ./ch21-5.pl /etc/X11
```

The program traverses the specified directory and saves its results. If you're
curious, you can actually look at these results — they're plain ASCII. Here are the
first few lines from that file on my system; these lines may be different on yours:

```
$dirs = {
  'fvwm' => bless( {
    'subdir' => {
      'default-style.hook' => bless( {
        'name' => 'default-style.hook',
```

```
    'isdir' => '0',
    'size' => 309,
    'age' => '109.185381944444',
    'startfile' => '/etc/X11/fvwm'
}, 'FileObject' ),
'init.hook' => bless( {
    'name' => 'init.hook',
    'isdir' => '0',
    'size' => 409,
    'age' => '109.185381944444',
    'startfile' => '/etc/X11/fvwm'
}, 'FileObject' ),
```

Note that the system completely understood the nested object, even taking care to bless the objects as they are recreated. Everything was preserved, down to the last detail. You can check on the results of reading the data back in:

```
$ ./ch21-5.pl
No argument found, displaying information from Dirs.dump!
/etc/X11/. (1024 bytes)
/etc/X11/.. (6144 bytes)
directory /etc/X11/WindowMaker (2048 bytes)
    /etc/X11/WindowMaker/. (2048 bytes)
    /etc/X11/WindowMaker/.. (1024 bytes)
    /etc/X11/WindowMaker/appearance.menu (553 bytes)
    /etc/X11/WindowMaker/background.menu (1170 bytes)
    /etc/X11/WindowMaker/menu (8164 bytes)
    /etc/X11/WindowMaker/menu.ca (10101 bytes)
    /etc/X11/WindowMaker/menu.cz (4189 bytes)
    /etc/X11/WindowMaker/menu.da (9164 bytes)
```

This information once again continues for over one hundred lines. You can see from here that the data was read back in properly. It was able to be printed out with absolutely no modification to that code whatsoever — something that took more work with the database.

The Data Dumper really is that simple to use. In most cases, it is able to make a perfect representation of your information in a string, which can be restored by simply running eval on the string.

Data Dumper options

In the sample code in Listing 21-5, there was a line that told the Data Dumper how to indent its output. There are several options available to you in this fashion. These are set with the syntax $obj->Item(newvalue) — although some of them make the new value optional. Table 21-1 lists the options that you may set for Data Dumper.

Table 21-1 Data: Dumper Options	
Option	**Meaning**
Bless	If for some reason you prefer to use a function other than bless when restoring objects, you can pass its name as a string to this configuration option.
Deepcopy	When using objects containing references, it's possible to have more than one reference pointing to the same data. With this option, the dumped data will try to minimize this behavior. Usually, you prefer the dumped data to be as much like the original as possible, so the default is 0, but you can set it to 1 to enable this other behavior.
Freezer	If you want something special to be done to your objects before they are dumped, you can use this option to indicate a particular method name. If you specify a method with Freezer, that method will be run immediately before the Data Dumper dumps the object in question. See also the Toaster option.
Indent	Determines how the output from the Dumper will be indented. The options are 0, 1, 2, and 3.Option 0 causes there to be no indentation. In fact, there will be no white space at all — everything will be on one single line.
	Option 1 causes the indentation to be similar to ($level * 2) — that is, the indentation value for each level is constant. This is often useful if option 2 produces output that is too wide to conveniently work with.
	Option 2 (the default) indents each line such that it lines up with various items on the preceding line. This has the effect of generally indenting things more, but for objects without much nested data, it can be more readable than option 1.
	Option 3 adds comments to the output indicating the index of each value in an array. Other than that, it is like option 2.
Names	Replaces Data Dumper's list of the names of the objects to dump. If no value is specified, it simply returns the existing settings.
Pad	Causes each line to begin with the specified string. The default is to use no pad.
Purity	Setting this value to 1, instead of the default of 0, causes the Data Dumper to go to more effort to recreate various sets of references. Option 0 is sufficient for most situations, but if you have a complex network of references, you may need to try option 1.

Continued

Table 21-1 (continued)	
Option	**Meaning**
Quotekeys	When this option is set to 1, keys for a hash are always enclosed in single quotes. When it is set to 0, keys are not quoted unless necessary. The default is 1.
Terse	When set to 1, causes the Data Dumper to generate output that may be more easily parsable by hand, but may not necessarily form legal Perl code. The default is 0.
Toaster	Like the Freezer option, except the specified method is called immediately after the data is restored. As a special additional requirement, this method must also return $self.
Useqq	When set to 1, causes Data Dumper to use double quotes instead of single quotes for strings. The Data Dumper will escape any characters necessary for this usage. This option is not yet available in all implementations and may slow down both the dump and the restore process.
Values	Replaces the Data Dumper's list of the objects to dump. If no value is specified, it simply returns the existing settings.
Varname	Changes the standard variable name used for generating names for variables whose names have not been passed to the Data Dumper. The default is VAR.

Output and Special Concerns

You have already seen many scripts that generate output in one form or another. Some may simply display messages on the screen; others save data into files. Here, we'll go into some more detail on these items and on dealing with files themselves.

Basic output

The most basic way to generate output in Perl is to use print to display data on standard output, the terminal. Because Perl provides you with variable interpolation (the capability to put the contents of a variable directly inside a string), this is often all that is necessary. There is frequently no need to use something as complex as C's printf() in Perl.

Using print is simple. It takes one or more strings as arguments and displays them to standard output, one after another. Perl's print does not automatically add a newline at the end of the text; you need to use \n in your string to do that.

For more rigorous printing needs, Perl has printf. This function works the same as its C counterpart — it takes a format string and then zero or more additional items, depending on the format string. Perl supports most all the syntax of the

C version, except for the asterisk operator, which is unnecessary in Perl due to string interpolation.

Output to files or commands

In order to write data to arbitrary files, you first need to open the files as in C. With Perl, you use the open command. Its first argument is a file handle that should be created for the file, and the second argument is a string indicating the access type and the filename. For instance, to open a file for writing, you could use:

```
open(FILEHANDLE, ">filename");
```

There are also other options that you can use. For instance, you can open a file in append mode by using a syntax like this:

```
open(FILEHANDLE, ">filename");
```

Options for open

You can even send output to, or read input from, arbitrary commands. Table 21-2 presents a list of the most common options that you can pass to Perl's open.

<table>
<tr><th colspan="3">Table 21-2
Options for open</th></tr>
<tr><th>Option</th><th>Location</th><th>Meaning</th></tr>
<tr><td><</td><td>start</td><td>Opens the file for reading. If omitted, this is the default behavior.</td></tr>
<tr><td>></td><td>start</td><td>Opens the file for writing. If the file already exists, its contents will be erased. If the file does not already exist, it will be created.</td></tr>
<tr><td>></td><td>start</td><td>Opens the file for writing in append mode. All data will be added to the end of the file. If the file does not already exist, it will be created.</td></tr>
<tr><td>+<</td><td>start</td><td>Opens the file for both reading and writing.</td></tr>
<tr><td>+></td><td>start</td><td>Also opens the file for both reading and writing, but will destroy any data already in the file. Therefore, +< is generally preferable.</td></tr>
<tr><td>|</td><td>start</td><td>Opens a pipe to the program specified after the pipe character. Data written to the file handle will be sent directly to the program.</td></tr>
<tr><td>|</td><td>end</td><td>Opens a pipe from the program specified before the pipe character. Reads on the file handle will read data directly from the program.</td></tr>
</table>

Once you have opened a file handle, you can use standard functions like `print` and `printf` to write to it. Simply specify the file handle on the line for those functions. Note, however, that you should *not* put a comma after the file handle. As an example, all of these forms are valid ways to do this:

```
print FILEHANDLE "Hi", " there\n";
print(FILEHANDLE "Good", " morning\n");
print FILEHANDLE ("How", " are you?\n");
printf FILEHANDLE "%s\n", "Hello";
```

Passing file handles

File handles are somewhat unique in Perl, as they do not behave like regular variables. However, they still do have an entry in the Perl namespace, so they can be passed — but with a unique syntax. To pass a file handle, you can use the `\*FILEHANDLE` syntax. To deal with the file handle in the function, then, you just use the variable that you stored the passed value in. Here is an example:

```
#!/usr/bin/perl -w

open HANDLE, ">blah.txt" or die "Couldn't open file: $!";

printit(\*HANDLE);

sub printit {
  my $fh = shift @_;

  print $fh "Hi!\n";
}
```

The system was able to write out to that file handle successfully. Inside the `printit` subroutine, you can use `$fh` just as you would have used `HANDLE` in the main program. You can also pass the file handle from `printit` to another subroutine; simply pass `$fh` to it.

It's also possible to read from a file handle passed in such a manner. The following program, for instance, tells a subroutine to read from standard input:

```
#!/usr/bin/perl -w

readit(\*STDIN);

sub readit {
  my $fh = shift @_;
  my $text;

  while ($text = <$fh>) {
    print "You typed: $text";
  }
}
```

Scoping file handles

Another problem that could arise is that you need file handles to be valid only in a particular subroutine—normally, they are global to each package in your program. We needed this sort of functionality, for instance, with the recursive function in the example program. Whenever a subroutine opens a file for its own private use, it really ought to keep the file handle private.

You keep the handle private by declaring the typeglob for the file handle local; my will not work for this particular situation. For example:

```
local *FILEHANDLE;

open(FILEHANDLE, ">file.txt");
```

Cross-Reference For more information on my, see the Subroutines and Scope section in Chapter 20, "Introducing Perl."

This code snippet will force the handle named FILEHANDLE to be valid only in the current subroutine (or ones that it calls). It will not be visible once the subroutine returns, or if a called subroutine also declares a local item named FILEHANDLE.

Summary

In this chapter, you learned about dealing with data in Perl. Specifically, you learned:

✦ You can use the angle-bracket operator with a file handle to read lines from the file. For instance, <STDIN> will read lines from standard input.

✦ The %ENV hash contains the process's environment variables.

✦ Basic regular expression operators, split, and grep can all be used to find or parse data.

✦ You can store information in a local database by tying a hash to the database.

✦ Thus tying a hash enables you to both have persistent storage and use data greater than will fit into memory at once.

✦ Databases can only store scalar information, so nested structures cannot be stored in them.

✦ The Data Dumper can dump a perfect representation of nearly all data structures, but it is slower than databases and loads all the data into memory at once.

✦ You can use basic functions like `print` and `printf` to write data out to files.

✦ To pass a file handle, use `\*FILEHANDLE`.

✦ To make a file handle created in a subroutine local, use `local *FILEHANDLE` before opening it.

✦   ✦   ✦

CGI Programming

Today, the World Wide Web has become an increasingly important part of the Internet, responsible for everything from providing documentation to taking online orders for products. Originally, the Web was made up of static data—that is, files on disk. However, as technology evolved, newer ways of getting information to the web browser were developed. This chapter deals with a way of generating information on-the-fly to present to the browser. This information may be calculated based on information the browser sent to the server before, such as the results of a search request. Or it may be customized in some way for a particular user. Maybe it is used to display a screen that always has a summary of special sales for today. It might be used to generate content based on a database— perhaps a current temperature or weather forcast, or inventory information for a product.

CGI and the Web

As far as web browsers are concerned, this sort of dynamically generated content is no different from any other. It's still made up of HTML code, and is sent to the browser in exactly the same way. The difference, then, is on the server side. Instead of simply sending a file that contains HTML to the browser, the server invokes a program. This program then generates the HTML that is sent to the browser.

Sometimes certain things need to be communicated between the server and the program that runs. This might include the data supplied in an input form, the IP address of the remote host, and so on. This is where the Common Gateway Interface (CGI) comes in: it defines how these data is passed between the server and the program, and lets you use the same program with many different servers—or a program written in any number of different languages with your servers.

You can, of course, write a program in any language that manually parses the information passed to you with CGI. However, Perl offers you several CGI libraries that do these tasks for you, thus freeing you up to concentrate on the things that are specific to your CGI scripts.

Several different CGI libraries are available with Perl. In this chapter, I will use CGI.pm, which actually ships with some current Perl distributions. This is a full-featured and robust library that is used by many people for their scripts.

Note In order to run the CGI examples in this chapter on your own machine, you'll need a working web server and a CGI directory within that server that is capable of running your scripts. The exact way of configuring this varies depending on the web server you're running; consult your server documentation for details. Unlike the other Perl scripts we've dealt with thus far, CGI scripts are executed by the web server, not directly by you. You simply need to move them in place, mark them executable, and then pull up the URL that corresponds to your script by using a web browser.

While there is no requirement that CGI scripts receive data from a user, a common use for CGI scripts is to receive input from a web-based form and generate the appropriate result. This could mean saving the data in a file, e-mailing it to someone, or simply displaying requested information back to the browser.

Your forms will ask for information from the reader, and will pass the results in to your CGI script. Your script can then retrieve the information from the CGI object and use it to generate a reply.

Writing CGI Scripts

It's time to begin writing some CGI scripts. I'll start with a fairly basic one that simply displays a greeting—a classical "Hello World" example:

```perl
#!/usr/bin/perl -Tw

$| = 1;

use CGI qw(:standard);

print header;

print start_html('Hello World!');
print "Hello, World!<P>";
print "Greetings from process $$\n";

print end_html;
```

When you look at this Perl code, you'll notice the first line already contains something new: -T. This option enables Perl's taint mode. In this mode, any data that comes from an unsecure source — as input in a CGI script, from an environment variable, from a file, and so on — is not allowed to be used in an insecure area until is has been validated by your program. Taint checking is a great way to make sure that your scripts are as secure as possible.

Tip You may have noticed a new syntax in the above example: qw(:standard). The qw operator is Perl's quote-by-word operator. That means that you can specify several items inside the parentheses, separated by a space. Perl will convert these items into the elements of an array. This handy shortcut is frequently used with CGI.pm.

Then, by setting $|, you disable the output caching in the Perl I/O routines. For a script such as this, this is not really necessary. However, if your scripts take a little while to run (for instance, when displaying search results), it's useful to give users partial information as soon as possible.

Next there is a line that brings in the CGI library and various standard variables and functions such as header and start_html. The HTTP header is printed next, followed by the HTML header, and a message. Then, there is a message containing the process ID to display — just so you can see that the content is dynamic. Each time you reload the page, this value changes.

Finally, the HTML closing tags are printed, and then the script exits. The following is the code that it generates:

```
<!DOCTYPE HTML PUBLIC "-//IETF//DTD HTML//EN">
<HTML><HEAD><TITLE>Hello World!</TITLE>
</HEAD><BODY>Hello, World!<P>Greetings from process 1331
</BODY></HTML>
```

The first two lines, and up until the start of the message, are generated by start_html. The last line is generated by the last line in the program. When viewed in a web browser, it appears as follows:

```
Hello, World!

Greetings from process 1331
```

With a few modifications, you can make this program interactive. Here's a modified version:

```
#!/usr/bin/perl -Tw

$| = 1;

use CGI qw(:standard);
```

```perl
my $q = new CGI;

print header;
print start_html('Hello World!');

if ($q->param('message')) {
  print "Hello, World!<P>";
  print "Greetings from process $$\n<P>\n";
  print "Your message was:\n<FONT COLOR=blue>";
  print $q->param('message');
  print "</FONT>\n";
} else {
  print <<'EOF';
Please enter a message:<P>
<FORM METHOD=POST>
<input type="text" name="message" size=30>
<BR>
<input type="submit" name="submit" value="Go">
</FORM>
EOF
}

print end_html;
```

This time, when you first invoke the CGI script, it displays a form asking for a message. It does this because there was no item named message passed in to the CGI the first time that you run it. However, when you fill out that field on the form and click Go, the text that you type is sent along as the message value, which can be accessed with $q->param('message') in this case. Therefore, the logic is fairly straightforward — if there is a message, display it; if not, ask for it. Note that the initial form contains nothing dynamic; that is, you could embed it in a standard HTML file if you prefer.

To go a bit farther, make the code such that the user can switch between the entry and the display screens at will, and that the CGI program can keep track of some data while this is being done:

```perl
#!/usr/bin/perl -Tw

$| = 1;

use CGI qw(:standard);

my $q = new CGI;

print header;
print start_html('Hello World!');

my $count = $q->param('count') ? $q->param('count') : 1;
```

```
if ($q->param('mode') eq 'display') {
  print "Hello, World!<P>";
  print "Greetings from process $$\n<P>\n";
  print "Message number $count:\n<FONT COLOR=blue>";
  print $q->param('message');
  print "</FONT>\n<P>\n";
  print <<"EOF";
  <FORM METHOD=POST>
EOF
  print '<input type="hidden" name="count" value="';
  print $count + 1;
  print '">';
  print <<"EOF";

  <input type="submit" name="submit" value="Enter another message">
  </FORM>
EOF
} else {
  print <<"EOF";
  Please enter message number $count:<P>
  <FORM METHOD=POST>
  <input type="text" name="message" size=30>
  <input type="hidden" name="count" value="$count">
  <input type="hidden" name="mode" value="display">
  <BR>
  <input type="submit" name="submit" value="Go">
  </FORM>
EOF
}


print end_html;
```

This time, there are two screens, both with dynamic content, and both with forms. Several things are tracked between the screens. The first is a message count. If the CGI is invoked with no count, the variable $count is set to 1; otherwise, it's set to the value that was passed in. Then, if no mode parameter was passed to the CGI, it displays a default screen, which is the message inputthat occurs after the else. Note that, in addition to having an input field for the text, there are two hidden fields as well. These enable the form to pass along data to the CGI when the form is submitted without the user having to supply it. Thus, we pass along the count automatically — there's no need for the user to have to worry about it. Also, we pass along a mode value that tells the script that it should go into a display mode instead of asking for a message.

When the script is run with a mode parameter set to display, it displays a standard Hello World message. But after that, it generates another form. This form has no opportunity for input; it just contains a hidden field. This field contains the value of count, plus one. This way, when the user clicks the submit button, the count will be incremented for the next message.

To make it easier for the user, it might be nice to be able to suggest the last message as a default for the text input area the next time it's displayed. It's possible to do that with the existing framework, but it can get a bit ugly to have to do all of this manually. Fortunately, the CGI library provides a nice way to build forms automatically. What's more, the form elements automatically set their defaults to the current value, instantly making the form friendly for users. Here's a version of the code that does essentially the same as the preceding example, but has been rewritten to use the CGI libraries form functions (from here on, I'll use these functions in code in this chapter):

```perl
#!/usr/bin/perl -Tw

$| = 1;

use CGI qw(:standard);

my $q = new CGI;

print header;
print start_html('Hello World!');

my $count = $q->param('count') ? $q->param('count') : 1;

if ($q->param('mode') eq 'display') {
  print "Hello, World!<P>";
  print "Greetings from process $$\n<P>\n";
  print "Message number $count:\n<FONT COLOR=blue>";
  print $q->param('message');
  print "</FONT>\n<P>\n";
  print $q->startform(-method => 'POST');
  print $q->hidden(-name => 'count', -default => $count + 1,
                   -override => 1), "\n";
  print $q->hidden(-name => 'message'), "\n";
  print $q->submit('submit', 'Enter another message'), "\n";
  print $q->endform;
} else {
  print "Please enter message number $count:<P>\n";
  print $q->startform(-method => 'POST');
  print $q->textfield(-name => 'message', -size => 30), "\n";
  print $q->hidden(-name => 'count', -value => $count), "\n";
  print $q->hidden(-name => 'mode', -value => 'display'), "\n<BR>\n";
  print $q->submit('submit', 'Go'), "\n";
  print $q->endform;
}


print end_html;
```

Notice how much cleaner this code is. Not only is it shorter than the previous version, but it does more. Let's take a look at how the code is working. As before, I'll begin the analysis with the default screen, the code for which occurs after the else statement. The familiar prompt asks for a message. Then, there is the start of a form. The first item in the form is a text entry field of size 30—the same as was used before. Because the CGI library uses defaults, if there is a value for message passed in to the script, it automatically sets the default here. Next, the count value is placed in a hidden field. The default mechanism would work here, too, except on the first time — you have to pass in the value there because no previous value for count was passed in. Then there is a hidden field for the mode setting, a submit button, and the end of the form.

Looking at the code for the display screen, again there is the familiar code displaying the message in blue. Then there is the form, which starts out with a hidden field for the count. This time, the default has to be set explicitly. What's more, because we are changing the value of this item, you need to tell the CGI library to override the normal default; otherwise, the normal default takes precedence over the one in your script. Following that, there is another hidden field with the message. This is so that the entry screen has something to show for the default. Notice once again that you don't have to say explicitly what the field's contents are because the CGI library automatically sets the default based on what was passed in to the script. Finally, there is a submit button and the end of the form.

Many CGI scripts run in a sequential mode order. That is, they display a page of information, and then successive ordered pages based on the input that went before. This is common in online ordering and payment systems, database interfaces, and so on. Listing 22-1 extends the simple message-display program to run in this sort of system.

Note Listing 22-1 is available online.

Listing 22-1: **CGI script with multiple pages**

```perl
#!/usr/bin/perl -Tw

# Turn off output buffering.

$| = 1;

# Bring in the CGI library.

use CGI qw(:standard);

# Create a new CGI object.
my $q = new CGI;

# Print the HTTP header.

print header;

# Select a default mode.
```

Continued

Listing 22-1 *(continued)*

```perl
my $mode = "mode_" . ($q->param('mode') || 'start');

# Eliminate something invalid.

unless ($mode =~ /^mode_[a-zA-Z]+$/) {
  $mode = 'mode_error';
}

# Call the subroutine that handles that mode.

&$mode();

# End the HTML.

print end_html;

### program exits here ###

sub mode_start {
  print start_html('Welcome to Message Displayer');
  print <<'EOF';
Welcome to the Message Displayer!  Through this program, you will get
to compose a message and select how it will be displayed on-screen.
<P>
EOF
  print ContinueButton('EnterMessage');
}

sub mode_EnterMessage {
  print start_html('Message Displayer: Enter Message');
  print <<'EOF';
Now is the time to enter the message to display.  You will have
options to configure it later.
<P>
EOF

  # Generate a form to use to enter the message.

  print $q->startform(-method => 'POST');
  print "Your message:\n<BR>\n";
  print $q->textarea(-name => 'message',
                     -rows => 10,
                     -columns => 40);
  print "<BR>";
  print ContinueButton('SelectColor', 1);
  print $q->endform;
}

sub mode_SelectColor {
  # If there was no message, jump back to that mode.
```

```perl
    unless ($q->param('message')) {
      return mode_EnterMessage();
    }

    # Now start this one.

    # Here are the colors for the list.

    my @colors = ('red', 'green', 'blue', 'yellow', 'black', 'white',
                  'orange', 'pink', '#FFFFFF', '#AC0000', '#FF00FF');

    # Start the HTML and display the existing message.

    print start_html('Message Displayer: Select Color');
    print <<"EOF";
You now need to select the color for your message.  Your message is:
<HR>
EOF
    print $q->param('message');
    print "<HR>\n";

    # Start the form.

    print $q->startform(-method => 'POST');

    # Display the list.
    print $q->scrolling_list(-name => 'color',
                             -values => \@colors,
                             -size => 4,
                             -default => 'blue');
    print "<P>\n";

    # Display the button to use to continue to the next step.
    print ContinueButton('SelectFont', 1);
    print $q->endform;
}

sub mode_SelectFont {
    # If no message or color, jump back a level.
    # This is for error-checking.
    unless ($q->param('message') && $q->param('color')) {
      return mode_SelectColor();
    }

    # Now start this one.
    print <<EOF;
Now that you have selected your message and its color, you get to select some
attributes for it.  You may select none, all, or any number in between.
<P>
Attributes:
<BR>
```

Continued

Listing 22-1 *(continued)*

```
EOF
  print $q->startform(-method => 'POST');
  print $q->checkbox_group(-name => 'font',
                           -values => ['bold', 'italic', 'underline',
                                       'large', 'small'],
                           -linebreak => 'true');
  print ContinueButton('Confirm', 1);
  print $q->endform;
}

sub mode_Confirm {
  # If no message or color, jump back a level.
  unless ($q->param('message') && $q->param('color')) {
    return mode_SelectColor();
  }

  # Now start this one.

  print <<"EOF";
Here is the data you have submitted for processing.  If you believe this is
correct, click Continue to view your message.
<P>
<TABLE WIDTH="100%" BORDER>
EOF
  print "<TR><TD><B>Message</B><TD>", $q->param('message'), "\n";
  print "<TR><TD><B>Color</B><TD>", $q->param('color'), "\n";
  print "<TR><TD><B>Attributes</B><TD>";
  if ($q->param('font')) {
    print join(', ', $q->param('font'));
  } else {
    print "None";
  }
  print "\n</TABLE>\n";

  print ContinueButton('finish');
}

sub mode_finish {
  # If no message or color, jump back a level.
  unless ($q->param('message') && $q->param('color')) {
    return mode_SelectColor();
  }

  # Now start this one.

  my @closetags;

  print <<'EOF';
Here is your message:
```

```
<HR>
EOF
  print '<font color="', $q->param('color'), '">';
  unshift @closetags, '</FONT>';

  InsertAttr('bold', '<B>', '</B>', \@closetags);
  InsertAttr('italic', '<I>', '</I>', \@closetags);
  InsertAttr('underline', '<U>', '</U>', \@closetags);
  InsertAttr('large', '<FONT SIZE="+2">', '</FONT>', \@closetags);
  InsertAttr('small', '<FONT SIZE="-2">', '</FONT>', \@closetags);
  print $q->param('message');

  # Display the closing tags.
  print join('', @closetags);

  print "\n<HR>\nThanks for using Message Displayer!\n";
}

sub InsertAttr {
  my ($val, $start, $end, $arr) = @_;

  # unshift is used instead of push below because we want the values
  # to be inserted at the start of the array since they have to be
  # displayed in the inverse order that the were added.

  if (isinarr($val, $q->param('font'))) {
    print $start;
    unshift @$arr, $end;
  }
}


sub mode_error {
  print start_html('Error');

  print "I'm sorry, there was an error.  Please use your browser's back\n";
  print "button and retry the operation.\n";
}

# This sub displays the button that takes the user to the next mode.

sub ContinueButton {
  my ($mode, $suppressform) = @_;
  my $retval = "";
  unless ($suppressform) {
    $retval = $q->startform(-method => 'POST') . "\n";
  }

  # Copy everything except the mode.
  $retval .= CopyParams('mode') . "\n";
```

Continued

Listing 22-1 *(continued)*

```perl
    # Insert the item for this mode.
    $retval .= $q->hidden(-name => 'mode', -value => $mode,
                          -override => 1) . "\n";
    $retval .= $q->submit('submit', 'Continue') . "\n";
    unless ($suppressform) {
      $retval .= $q->endform . "\n";
    }
    return $retval;
}

# This is used to generate hidden fields to pass along the current values
# to the next invocation.  The parameters are an array of values to *not*
# pass along.

sub CopyParams {
    my @keysToIgnore = @_;
    unshift @keysToIgnore, 'submit';
    my $retval = "";
    my $parameter;

    foreach $parameter ($q->param) {
      if (!isinarr($parameter, @keysToIgnore)) {
        $retval .= $q->hidden(-name => $parameter,
                              -value => [$q->param($parameter)],
                              -override => 1) . "\n";
      }
    }

    return $retval;
}

# Returns true if the search term is found as an element in the array, or
# false if not.

sub isinarr {
    my ($search, @array) = @_;
    my $thisvalue;

    foreach $thisvalue (@array) {
      return 1 if ($thisvalue eq $search);
    }
    return 0;
}
```

This program may seem complex, but if you analyze it in small chunks, perhaps it can be demystified a bit.

The program starts in a fairly standard way, by bringing in the CGI library, printing a header, and so on. These three commands do that:

```
use CGI qw(:standard);
my $q = new CGI;
print header;
```

Then it generates a string that is used to select which subroutine to use. This is done by generating a string that is used as a soft reference, and then invoking it as a subroutine with that name. So, there is one subroutine for each mode in the program. After the specified subroutine runs, the HTML footer is printed and the program exits. Here is the code that sets the $mode variable and calls the indicated subroutine:

```
my $mode = "mode_" . ($q->param('mode') || 'start');
unless ($mode =~ /^mode_[a-zA-Z]+$/) {
  $mode = 'mode_error';
}
&$mode();
```

The first mode is named start, and is set as the default if no mode is specified, as may be the case if the CGI script were just starting. It displays a short welcome message and a continue button. This button takes the person to the next mode.

This next mode, EnterMessage, asks the user to supply a message. When Continue is pressed, the script is invoked again, with the mode parameter indicating to go into the color selection area. Here's the code for the form generated in the EnterMessage mode:

```
print $q->startform(-method => 'POST');
  print "Your message:\n<BR>\n";
  print $q->textarea(-name => 'message',
                     -rows => 10,
                     -columns => 40);
  print "<BR>";
  print ContinueButton('SelectColor', 1);
  print $q->endform;
```

The same framework is used for picking colors, selecting fonts, and confirming the input. That is, there is a prompt for data and a confirmation button that takes the user to the next mode in sequence. Then, the final message is displayed.

The ContinueButton subroutine is responsible for generating the HTML for the Continue button. It can either generate the entire form or live within another form. This program uses it within another form in all but the very first screen. It adds a hidden value for the next mode, and then copies the hidden values for anything passed into this invocation of the script.

The CopyParams subroutine is responsible for doing this copying. Its parameters are the list of parameters to not copy, possibly because they will be overridden by something else. Take special note of the way the hidden field is created here. The value that it is set to is passed in as a reference to an anonymous array, whose elements are returned by $q->param. The reason for this is that sometimes, there may be multiple values for a single parameter. For instance, the attribute selection screen may return values of font set to both bold and italic. If only one of these is passed through, the remainder of the information is lost. By using this syntax, all the values are preserved for the next invocation of the script.

Finally, the isinarr subroutine determines whether a given element is in an array. This is a useful all-around function that you'll probably find a use for even in non-CGI programs. Here's its source code:

```
sub isinarr {
  my ($search, @array) = @_;
  my $thisvalue;

  foreach $thisvalue (@array) {
    return 1 if ($thisvalue eq $search);
  }
  return 0;
}
```

Perl's CGI library is quite extensive; its manual page, which is mostly reference material, goes on for over 50 pages. For more information about various other features, such as other form elements, or the arguments to use with them, please consult the CGI manpage on your Linux system, or use perldoc CGI.

Dealing with Connectionless Issues

One of the problems facing programmers of CGI scripts is that the communication between the web browser and the web server is essentially connectionless. That is, the browser requests some information, receives a response, and then disconnects. No connection is maintained between the two. Moreover, a CGI script starts, executes, and finishes once for each connection. So, any variables you set in your script, of course, will not be set the next time the script is run.

Many scripts need a way to carry information along from one page to another. The example in the previous section needed this to carry the message from the first to the last screen. Other common needs are with online ordering systems, to keep track of a shopping cart contents or payment information; or search engines, to keep track of the query through multiple result pages.

One way of doing this is to pass around all the information in hidden form fields. This method is simple and easy to implement. However, it has some downsides. If the data being saved is large, you can annoy your users by making them re-upload it for each click they make. Not only that, but if you want to pass around this data outside a form (such as with a standard link), it is somewhat difficult.

One solution to this problem is to generate a unique identification number or string at the first page. Only this identification information is passed along in the form from screen to screen; the submitted data are stored on the server, presumably in a database. This eliminates the problem with large data but instantly requires more server resources and a more complex script. It is possible to use this with both standard links and forms, because the data for the standard link is fairly simple. However, you have to remember to pass it along with each link.

Another option is to store this identification information or various other small items in a cookie. An advantage here is that you do not have to worry about passing the information from screen to screen because the user's browser does this for you. However, beware! Cookies are inherently unreliable and there's little you can do about that because they're outside of your control. Many proxy servers intercept cookies and block them from being set. Current browsers have options to disable cookie support, and some current browsers don't have cookie support at all. Therefore, although cookies are quite useful in theory, in practice, their usefulness is somewhat limited.

One approach is to use cookies if available and fall back on hidden form fields if necessary. This enables you to use the elegance of cookies if possible, and to still present a useful interface if they're not available.

Some people choose to use cookies solely for noncritical functions. For instance, visitors to a site may be capable of selecting the background color for the site, and this selection could be saved in their browsers as a cookie for any CGI script on the site to follow. Although this may be a nice feature, it's certainly not critical, and the added effort to implement it without cookies may not be worth it.

When passing along any but the most trivial of information from one connection to the next, the second and third methods here require some type of database storage on the server. In these situations, you may want to look at a Perl tied database if your server is small. Beware, though, that you need to lock your database file lest it be corrupted by two CGIs writing to it at once!

See Chapter 14, "Introducing the Linux I/O," for more details on file locking. Perl implements `flock` with the same syntax as the C call, so you should find locking in Perl easy to use after using it in C.

For more serious needs, or servers that are under a higher load, a full-fledged SQL database is probably called for. Some sites already have such a database in place, such as Oracle. If you do not, don't worry; several Open Source database servers are available for free and have relatively easy installation procedures.

See Chapter 23, "SQL Databases with DBI," for more details on using SQL databases within Perl.

Solving Performance Issues

As I've already mentioned, the CGI script is started fresh for each request that comes in. This is fine for CGI scripts that are not used frequently (many times per minute). However, on a highly loaded server, this can significantly bog down the processor. This effect only becomes worse if there is a SQL database backend for your script, because establishing a connection to one of these databases typically can take a little bit of time.

One solution is to use Apache's `mod_perl` support. This module actually embeds a Perl interpreter inside the web server itself. This means that your scripts can be loaded, compiled, and initialized once but yet still serve all the connection requests to them. This can be a major performance win for heavily loaded sites.

However, it also means that your scripts must be written in a much more careful way. Variables left around, files left open, and so on, are not disposed of automatically when a page is sent because your script really doesn't exit in those cases. Therefore, although it's possible to have code that works both with and without the `mod_perl` environment, it can be a bit tricky. For more details, visit `http://perl.apache.org/`.

There are other options. One is to use a small C program as the CGI. This C program might open a socket to the real Perl script, pass it the information, and pass the response back to the browser. In this situation, there is still a fork and an exec, but the small C program will have a much lower startup time. A final option is to use FastCGI support, which implements an idea similar to the above.

Summary

In this chapter, you learned about writing CGI scripts for dynamic web page creation. Specifically, you learned:

✦ CGI scripts offer you a way to become more interactive with visitors to your web site.

✦ Although CGI programs can be written in any language, Perl's CGI library makes an easy and powerful way to do so.

✦ Your scripts can receive input from the user by using forms.

✦ State information can be passed to your script by using hidden form fields.

✦ Other solutions, such as SQL databases and cookies, also can be helpful in preserving state information.

✦ An embedded Perl interpreter in your web server can provide a boost for performance.

✦   ✦   ✦

SQL Databases with DBI

◆ ◆ ◆ ◆

In This Chapter

Introducing
databases

First steps with DBI

Using SQL

Using databases in
applications

◆ ◆ ◆ ◆

As a glue language, one of the most crucial features
of Perl lies in Perl's ability to access data stored in
databases. Since more and more data is stored in ever-growing
databases, it's essential that Perl provides the glue to get at
your data. Perl does this through a series of add-on modules,
designed to access.

This chapter covers the DBI, or database interface, series of
Perl modules, modules that provide the glue to talk to many
different databases such as Oracle or Informix. DBI goes further,
though, in providing a consistent interface to access all these
disparate systems. That makes your job a lot easier and really
helps when you need to convert data from one database to
another, for example.

The DBI module itself provides the consistent interface. Then,
to access a particular database, such as Oracle, you make use
of a special database driver, or DBD module, DBD::Oracle in
this case.

Introducing Databases

As discussed in Chapter 21, "Manipulating Data with Perl," data
storage is often one of the trickiest parts of writing a large
application. Perl provides tie-ins to some simple databases, but
often this is simply not sufficient. Your application may need
something more powerful. Perhaps the database needs to reside
on a computer separate from your application. Or perhaps you
need to be able to have many different processes — or even
computers — access the data in the database at once. You may
need to work with certain subsets of the data, or to be able to
retrieve information using more than one key. Finally, maybe
you need a relational database so that you can join together
information from multiple tables into a single coherent result.

SQL databases provide you with these capabilities. SQL, short for Structured Query Language, is itself only a query language, but it forms a standard front end to many heavy-duty databases such as Oracle, mySQL, PostgreSQL, and Informix. Each database manufacturer starts with SQL as a base and then adds on some unique features. Thus, SQL is similar but not identical across different databases.

More important, though, are several other ideas inherent in modern SQL databases. First, there is a separation between your process and the database server. This means that the server can just as easily be running on your own machine as it can be running on a machine down the hall or across the country. These database servers can be accessed across the network.

Another important feature is that the database servers themselves can do some basic data analysis for you, thanks to the power of SQL. The server evaluates your SQL requests and sends the result back to you.

There are several different ways to access these SQL databases in Perl. One way is to use vendor-specific libraries. However, these are implemented differently for each vendor, meaning that a change to a different SQL database server later could be extremely difficult due to a change in the underlying API.

There is a better way, though. You can use the database interface, or DBI, module. DBI provides a universal front end for SQL databases. It uses a driver architecture such that each different database type supported in Perl has its own database driver, or DBD.

Your applications are written using routines from DBI. DBI then converts these to appropriate lower-level calls to a database library through the use of a DBD. This driver or library encodes the request for transmission to the database server. The server, which may or may not be on your own computer, handles the request and sends the result back. The DBD parses the result, and your application fetches it through DBI routines. Thus, even though the communications protocol and library may be significantly different for each database, you can use almost identical calls for them in Perl.

To be able to run the examples in this chapter, you'll need three pieces of software: the DBI library, a SQL database supported by DBI, and the DBD for your chosen database. Debian GNU/Linux ships with all of these; other distributions may or may not have all of those pieces. If you need the DBI or DBD software, you can download it from `http://www.symbolstone.org/technology/perl/DBI/index.html`. In this chapter, I'll be using the PostgreSQL RDBMS for the examples. This is a Free SQL database that runs well on Linux. If you do not have it already, you may find it at `http://www.postgresql.org/`.

Tip   If you need help with installing DBI, you may consult the README file that comes with the DBI package. The DBI site also contains some documentation on the topic.

Note Other SQL databases supported by DBI, such as mySQL or Oracle, will work fine as well, although some examples may have to be modified slightly to work with them, especially with the connect calls and certain data types.

I'll assume before proceeding that you have installed all of the software previously described already and have it in a working condition. These examples are written with version 1.12 of DBI; if you have an older version and encounter difficulties, consider upgrading your DBI (and perhaps DBD as well) to the latest version.

First Steps with DBI

When you work with DBI, the general order of code is as follows. You will first connect to the database server, possibly passing along some authentication information. This will give you a database handle. Then you'll generate queries and use DBI's `prepare` method to ready them for query. After doing this, you'll receive a statement handle, which can be used to fetch the results of that one particular query. When you have all the results, you'll be finished with the statement handle. You may prepare and retrieve many more items during your program's lifetime. When your program is finished, you'll disconnect from the database and exit.

Listing 23-1 shows one program that reads SQL commands from the operator, sends these commands to the database, and returns the result. Note that this code is actually a bit more complex than most that you'll deal with because it doesn't know in advance what will be returned. However, you'll be able to use this program throughout the rest of the chapter to send commands directly to the SQL server without having to write a separate program to send each one.

Note Most databases include such a tool already; however, their interfaces vary significantly. For instance, PostgreSQL includes psql, and Oracle includes sqlplus.

Note Listing 23-1 is available online.

Listing 23-1: Using the DBI module

```perl
#!/usr/bin/perl -w

use DBI;                    # DBI library
use DBD::Pg;                # Postgres driver

my $DBUSER = $ENV{USER};
my $DBNAME = $DBUSER;
```

Continued

Listing 23-1 *(continued)*

```perl
# Connect to the database.

my $dbh = DBI->connect("dbi:Pg:dbname=$DBNAME", "", "") or die
  "Couldn't connect to database: " . DBI::errstr;

# Loop to read from terminal.

my $input;
my $querystr = '';
printmessage();

while ($input = <STDIN>) {
  chomp $input;                # Strip off trailing CR
  $input =~ s/\s+$//g;         # Strip off other trailing whitespace
  if ($input =~ /;$/) {        # If ends with a semicolon...
    $input =~ s/;$//;          # Strip off the semicolon
    $querystr .= $input;       # Append to the query string
    runquery($querystr);       # Run the query
    $querystr = '';            # Reset querystring for next iteration
    printmessage();            # Print instructions
  } else {
    $querystr .= "$input ";    # Append to query string
  }
}

$dbh->disconnect;

sub printmessage {
  print <<EOF;

Enter your query here.  After each query, enter a semicolon at the end of the
last line or on a line by itself.  When you're finished with the program,
press Ctrl+D.

EOF
}

sub runquery {
  my $querystr = shift @_;
  my $rowcount;

  print "\n";

  my $sth = $dbh->prepare($querystr);
  unless ($sth) {
    print "Prepare FAILED: " . $dbh->errstr . "\n";
    return;
  }

  my $executeresult = $sth->execute();
  if (!$executeresult) {
```

```
     print "Execute FAILED: " . $dbh->errstr . "\n";
     return;
  }

  $executeresult = "unknown" if ($executeresult == -1);

  print "SUCCESS.\n";

  # If this was a query, display the results.

  if ($sth->{NUM_OF_FIELDS}) {
    print "Columns: ";
    print join(', ', @{$sth->{NAME}}), "\n";
    $rowcount = $sth->dump_results();
  }

  print "Number of rows returned or modified: ",
        ($rowcount) ? $rowcount : $executeresult, "\n";
}
```

Let's go through this code and analyze what it does. It begins by bringing in the DBI library and the DBD for PostgreSQL. Then, it sets some defaults for the database name for the server, and a username if this would be used. After doing this, it connects to the database server. If the connection fails, it prints out an error message indicating the reason for the failure. Next, it defines a few variables, prints out a help message, and then enters a loop.

In this loop, the code continues reading from standard input until EOF is reached. For each line, the trailing carriage return character is stripped off. Then, any trailing white space is stripped off — this makes it easier to look for a semicolon at the end. After stripping off this white space, the program checks to see if the line ends with a semicolon. If so, the semicolon is stripped, the result is appended to the query string, and the runquery subroutine is called. After it returns, the query string is reset, the help is displayed again, and the loop restarts. If there was no trailing semicolon, the input is simply appended to the query string, followed by a space (for white space for separation from this line and the next).

After all the input is through, the program disconnects from the database server and exits. The printmessage subroutine is uninteresting; it simply displays a message. The runquery subroutine is the heart of the program. It handles most of the interaction with the database server.

It begins by taking a query string as a parameter and printing out a blank line to visually separate the results from the query. Then you come to this line:

```
    my $sth = $dbh->prepare($querystr);
```

Thus begins the query within the database engine. Depending on the database, the query may be checked for syntax now, or later. If there is a problem, an error value is returned, and the `unless` check following the call to `prepare` will print out the error and exit the subroutine. Otherwise, a statement handle is returned and stored in `$sth`. Whereas the database handle, `$dbh`, corresponds to all communication with a particular database, a statement handle corresponds to all interaction with one particular query of the database. From here on, only the statement handle will be used in this particular subroutine.

After preparing the statement handle, we execute it. This causes the query or request passed in to the function to be taken care of in the database itself. Again, there is a possibility of failure here. If the syntax is bad, some databases will abort at this point. If this happens, an error message is displayed and the subroutine returns.

Otherwise, if the request affected an unknown number of rows, this is noted. This could be the case, for instance, during a create table request. Regardless of the type of request, a message indicating a successful execution is displayed.

Next, the code needs to branch depending on what type of a query it was. In broad terms, there are two types of queries in SQL: select and nonselect queries. The former return data; the latter may make modifications but do not return any data from the database itself. If the query was a select one, there will be at least one field (or column) in the result set. Therefore, you can use `$sth->{NUM_OF_FIELDS}` to determine whether or not the query returned data. If it did, the code prints out a list of the columns, followed by the data itself. Otherwise, the code simply skips to displaying how many rows were affected by the request.

Using SQL

Now that we covered getting started with the DBI series of modules, the next step is to go through some of the basic requests you can make from your Perl scripts. These requests include creating new tables in the database, inserting data into tables, reading data from the database, deleting items and updating records.

Note that this section is not intended to be a thorough introduction to SQL. SQL is a very powerful and versatile language; it can be used to perform sophisticated data analysis and pull together data from many different sources. The following examples will go over some of the capabilities of SQL, but you should consult a good SQL reference or tutorial if you wish to learn the full scope of the language.

Note SQL is not really designed for interactive use as we are doing in this chapter; however, this can be a useful learning tool. SQL is designed such that you will write front ends to the database, tailored for your specific needs. These are the things that you will learn how to do in this section. I'll show you several things here, interjecting my comments between the items of information. Note also that SQL is case insensitive everywhere except inside string literals. Many users, however, prefer to give SQL keywords in all caps to distinguish them from surrounding text, and I use that convention here.

To help get a better handle on SQL itself, we'll use the ch23-1.pl example program provided previously. With this program, you enter in SQL commands directly, allowing you to concentrate on the SQL commands themselves and not worry about the underlying Perl code.

Creating a table

All data stored in a SQL database must be placed inside a table. SQL data is typed; that is, you must declare what kind of data will occur in each field ahead of time. The following table is created to have two fields, an integer field and a text field:

```
$ ./ch23-1.pl

Enter your query here.  After each query, enter a semicolon at the end of the
last line or on a line by itself.  When you're finished with the program,
press Ctrl+D.

CREATE TABLE mytable (
  number int,
  string text
);

SUCCESS.
Number of rows returned or modified: unknown
```

Now let's add some data. From here on, even though the program displays the help text, I'll omit it in the following section.

Inserting data

The following examples show how to insert new records into the database, in this case into the new table we just created.

```
INSERT INTO mytable VALUES (5, 'qwerty');

SUCCESS.
Number of rows returned or modified: 1

INSERT INTO mytable VALUES (5, 'Hello');

SUCCESS.
Number of rows returned or modified: 1

INSERT INTO mytable VALUES (10);

SUCCESS.
Number of rows returned or modified: 1

INSERT INTO mytable (string, number) VALUES ('Goodbye', 25);
```

```
SUCCESS.
Number of rows returned or modified: 1

INSERT INTO mytable VALUES (5, 'Hello');

SUCCESS.
Number of rows returned or modified: 1
```

These examples inserted five new records into the table. Note that the third query did not specify a string. This is permissible; values in the database can be empty (or NULL in SQL terms) unless this is specifically banned in the table definition. Before we fetch some of the data back, let's examine some things that could cause errors:

```
INSERT INTO mytable VALUES (5, Hello);


DBD::Pg::st execute failed: ERROR:  Attribute hello not found
Execute FAILED: ERROR:  Attribute hello not found

INSERT INTO someothertable VALUES (5, 'Hello');

DBD::Pg::st execute failed: ERROR:  someothertable: Table does not exist.
Execute FAILED: ERROR:  someothertable: Table does not exist.

INSERT INTO mytable VALUES ('Hello', 'Goodbye');

DBD::Pg::st execute failed: ERROR:  pg_atoi: error in "Hello": can't parse
"Hello"
Execute FAILED: ERROR:  pg_atoi: error in "Hello": can't parse "Hello"
```

The first query failed because the string was not quoted. The second failed because it tried to insert data into a table that had not previously been created. The third failed because it tried to insert a string into an integer field. Note that two error messages are printed for each problem: one generated by DBI and one generated by this code. You can disable the duplicate DBI error message by using $dbh->{PrintError} = 0.

Reading data

Now that there is some data in the database, let's read it back. Here are some queries to do just that. In the following examples, the SQL SELECT query allows you to retrieve data from the database.

```
SELECT * FROM mytable;

SUCCESS.
Columns: number, string
'5', 'qwerty'
'5', 'Hello'
'10', undef
'25', 'Goodbye'
```

```
'5', 'Hello'
5 rows
Number of rows returned or modified: 5
```

This is a basic query. The asterisk tells the database server to select all fields (also known as columns) from the table. These are returned in arbitrary order. Note that the entry that had a NULL string shows up as undef in the previous example.

The next example shows how to ask for only a particular column, instead of all of the columns, as shown here:

```
SELECT number FROM mytable;

SUCCESS.
Columns: number
'5'
'5'
'10'
'25'
'5'
5 rows
Number of rows returned or modified: 5

SELECT string, number from mytable;

SUCCESS.
Columns: string, number
'qwerty', '5'
'Hello', '5'
undef, '10'
'Goodbye', '25'
'Hello', '5'
5 rows
Number of rows returned or modified: 5
```

The previous two queries specifically request certain columns to be returned. The first requests only the number column be returned, and the second requests them both, but in a nonstandard order.

Now we can select certain columns, and re-arrange the order of the output. The next step is to select only those records that meet a certain criteria, such as the value in a particular column being larger than a certain amount. For example:

```
SELECT * FROM mytable WHERE number > 5;

SUCCESS.
Columns: number, string
'10', undef
'25', 'Goodbye'
2 rows
Number of rows returned or modified: 2
```

The previous query asks for both columns, but only those rows whose number value is greater than 5. In this table, two rows match that criterion, and they are returned:

You can use SQL to help sort the output as well, as shown in this example:

```
SELECT * FROM mytable ORDER BY number DESC;

SUCCESS.
Columns: number, string
'25', 'Goodbye'
'10', undef
'5', 'qwerty'
'5', 'Hello'
'5', 'Hello'
5 rows
Number of rows returned or modified: 5
```

This query returns all the data but requests that it be sorted in descending order by number. If you omit DESC, the results would be sorted in traditional ascending order.

You can go further and use SQL to calculate statistics on the data in the database, as shown in this example:

```
SELECT MAX(number), AVG(number), SUM(number) FROM mytable;

SUCCESS.
Columns: max, avg, sum
'25', '10', '50'
1 rows
Number of rows returned or modified: 1
```

Here you glimpse three basic statistical functions in SQL. The first returns the maximum value of the given column in the database; the second, the mean average; and the third, the sum of all values in that column. Notice that even though this operates on all five rows of the database, there is only one row of return information.

You can also get a count of the number of records:

```
SELECT COUNT(*) FROM mytable;

SUCCESS.
Columns: count
'5'
1 rows
Number of rows returned or modified: 1
```

Here, you see a way to find out how many rows are in the table; simply request a count of them. Again, only one row of information is returned.

You can combine the SQL count function with other criteria for a more complicated query. For example:

```
SELECT number, COUNT(*)
  FROM mytable
  GROUP BY number
  ORDER BY number;

SUCCESS.
Columns: number, count
'5', '3'
'10', '1'
'25', '1'
3 rows
Number of rows returned or modified: 3
```

Here is a more tricky example. This one uses grouping to restrict what is returned. What is happening here is that the results are grouped by number. Therefore, there is one output row for each *unique* value held in the column named *number* occurring in the input. Then, when the data is output, we apply the count and see that there are three rows in the input with a number of 5, and one each with a number of 10 and 25.

Updating tables

You can update the data stored in your tables after it has been placed there. To do this, you use the SQL update command. Here are some examples of this command:

```
UPDATE mytable SET string = 'Hi' WHERE number = 10;

SUCCESS.
Number of rows returned or modified: 1

UPDATE mytable SET string = 'Five' WHERE number = 5;

SUCCESS.
Number of rows returned or modified: 3
```

The first query fills in the missing text value. The second causes every row whose number value is 5 to have a string value of Five. Here are the results from these modifications:

```
select * from mytable;

SUCCESS.
Columns: number, string
'25', 'Goodbye'
'10', 'Hi'
'5', 'Five'
'5', 'Five'
'5', 'Five'
```

```
5 rows
Number of rows returned or modified: 5
```

You can see that the database carried out the actions you requested. Note that it is extremely important to remember the WHERE clause. If it is left off, every row in the table will be updated. For some databases, this could mean messing up millions of records of data! Here is an example of that:

```
UPDATE mytable SET string = 'Good Morning';

SUCCESS.
Number of rows returned or modified: 5
```

```
SELECT * FROM mytable;

SUCCESS.
Columns: number, string
'25', 'Good Morning'
'10', 'Good Morning'
'5', 'Good Morning'
'5', 'Good Morning'
'5', 'Good Morning'
5 rows
Number of rows returned or modified: 5
```

Deleting information

You can also remove rows of information from a table. To remove data, you'll use a syntax similar to that for the update command:

```
DELETE FROM mytable WHERE number = 5;

SUCCESS.
Number of rows returned or modified: 3
```

```
SELECT * FROM mytable;

SUCCESS.
Columns: number, string
'25', 'Good Morning'
'10', 'Good Morning'
2 rows
Number of rows returned or modified: 2
```

The database has thus removed three rows from the table, leaving only 2. Note again that you need to be sure to include the WHERE clause, or else every row in the table will be deleted!

The following example shows what happens when you delete everything:

```
DELETE FROM mytable;

SUCCESS.
Number of rows returned or modified: 2

SELECT * FROM mytable;

SUCCESS.
Columns: number, string

0 rows
Number of rows returned or modified: 0E0
```

The preceding command removed all rows from the table. The select query was successful but returned an empty result set. You can also completely remove a table. This will have the effect of deleting everything in it as well. For example:

```
DROP TABLE mytable;

SUCCESS.
Number of rows returned or modified: unknown

SELECT * FROM mytable;

DBD::Pg::st execute failed: ERROR:  mytable: Table does not exist.
Execute FAILED: ERROR:  mytable: Table does not exist.
```

Joining tables

One of the most powerful features of SQL, and one that makes it relational, lies in its capabilities to join together data from different tables. To present this information, you'll need to create two tables and add in some data for them. Here are the queries to issue. You can type these in to the same ch23-1.pl example program that you've been using thus far:

```
CREATE TABLE states (
  abbrev char(2) NOT NULL PRIMARY KEY,
  name text NOT NULL
);

INSERT INTO states VALUES ('AK', 'Alaska');
INSERT INTO states VALUES ('AL', 'Alabama');
INSERT INTO states VALUES ('KY', 'Kentucky');
INSERT INTO states VALUES ('KS', 'Kansas');
INSERT INTO states VALUES ('OK', 'Oklahoma');
INSERT INTO states VALUES ('TX', 'Texas');
INSERT INTO states VALUES ('NY', 'New York');
```

```
CREATE TABLE addresses (
  name text NOT NULL,
  address1 text NOT NULL,
  address2 text,
  city text NOT NULL,
  state char(2) NOT NULL,
  zip char(10) NOT NULL
);

INSERT INTO addresses VALUES (
  'Joe Brown',
  '1234 S. AnyStreet',
  'Apartment 12',
  'Oklahoma City',
  'OK',
  '12345-6789');

INSERT INTO addresses VALUES (
  'Jane Smith',
  '9876 W. Somewhere Street',
  NULL,
  'Buffalo',
  'NY',
  '98765');
```

There are several new concepts introduced here. The first is the NOT NULL specification. This means that, when data is being inserted into a table, the database will refuse to insert any request that leaves the given field empty. This specification is used to ensure data consistency. Another new concept is the PRIMARY KEY specification. When you specify this, two things happen. First, the database requires that all data entered must have a unique value for that field; no two rows in the table may have the same value there. Second, this specification enables certain optimizations within the query engine to make possible faster replies.

After you have completed the preceding items, your tables should look like this:

```
SELECT * FROM states;

SUCCESS.
Columns: abbrev, name
'AK', 'Alaska'
'AL', 'Alabama'
'KY', 'Kentucky'
'KS', 'Kansas'
'OK', 'Oklahoma'
'TX', 'Texas'
'NY', 'New York'
7 rows
Number of rows returned or modified: 7
```

```
SELECT * FROM addresses;

SUCCESS.
Columns: name, address1, address2, city, state, zip
'Joe Brown', '1234 S. AnyStreet', 'Apartment 12', 'Oklahoma City', 'OK',
'12345-6789'
'Jane Smith', '9876 W. Somewhere Street', undef, 'Buffalo', 'NY', '98765       '
2 rows
Number of rows returned or modified: 2
```

You can do a basic lookup on the states of residence of each person here. You might use a query like this:

```
SELECT name, state FROM addresses;

SUCCESS.
Columns: name, state
'Joe Brown', 'OK'
'Jane Smith', 'NY'
2 rows
Number of rows returned or modified: 2
```

But what if you want the full state name? Well, you conveniently have those (well, seven of them anyway) in another table. What you need to do is join the data from these two tables together. Here's how you might do that:

```
SELECT addresses.name, states.name
  FROM addresses, states
  WHERE addresses.state = states.abbrev;

SUCCESS.
Columns: name, name
'Joe Brown', 'Oklahoma'
'Jane Smith', 'New York'
2 rows
Number of rows returned or modified: 2
```

Great! You've just brought together data from two tables!

Before continuing, clean up these two tables:

```
DROP TABLE addresses;

SUCCESS.
Number of rows returned or modified: unknown
```

```
DROP TABLE states;

SUCCESS.
Number of rows returned or modified: unknown
```

When done, press Ctrl+D to exit the program.

Using Databases in Applications

In this section, I'll show you how to use Perl code to automate communication with a database. I'll start with a program that creates two tables and populates one of them. Then, I'll add an address book application, written in CGI, with a DBI back end to store the data.

DBI with the command line

Listing 23-2 presents a simple program that reads information in from the keyboard and inserts it into a database. This application could also be used to receive data piped in from a different program.

Note   Listing 23-2 is available online.

Listing 23-2: **Inserting information into a database**

```perl
#!/usr/bin/perl -w

use DBI;                # DBI library
use DBD::Pg;            # Postgres driver

my $DBUSER = $ENV{USER};
my $DBNAME = $DBUSER;

# Connect to the database.

my $dbh = DBI->connect("dbi:Pg:dbname=$DBNAME", "", "") or die
   "Couldn't connect to database: " . DBI::errstr;

$dbh->{PrintError} = 0;

CheckOrCreateTable("states",
                "CREATE TABLE states (
                abbrev char(2) NOT NULL PRIMARY KEY,
                fullname text NOT NULL)");
CheckOrCreateTable("addresses",
                "CREATE TABLE addresses (
                id varchar(40) NOT NULL PRIMARY KEY,
                name text NOT NULL,
                address1 text NOT NULL,
                address2 text,
                city varchar(30) NOT NULL,
                state char(2) NOT NULL,
                zip varchar(10) NOT NULL)");
```

```perl
my ($input, $abbrev, $full);

print "Enter states, one per line, with the abbreviation followed by\n";
print "the full name.  Press Ctrl+D when done.\n\n";

while ($input = <STDIN>) {
  chomp $input;

  my ($abbrev, $full) = $input =~ /^(\w\w)\s+(.+)$/;
  $abbrev = uc $abbrev;

  InsertState($abbrev, $full);
}

sub CheckOrCreateTable {
  my ($table, $querystr) = @_;

  if ($dbh->do("SELECT * FROM $table WHERE 1 = 0")) {
    print "Table $table already exists; not recreating.\n";
  } else {
    print "Creating table $table\n";
    $dbh->do($querystr) or die
      "Couldn't create table: " . $dbh->errstr;
  }
}

sub InsertState {
  my ($abbrev, $fullname) = @_;

  print "Inserting: $abbrev => $fullname\n";

  my $result = $dbh->do("INSERT INTO states (abbrev, fullname)
                         VALUES ('$abbrev', '$fullname')");

  unless ($result) {
    warn "Insert failed: " . $dbh->errstr;
  }
}
```

Listing 23-2 is a program that will do two simple things. First, it will create tables if necessary. Second, it will read data from the keyboard and insert it into a table.

When the program starts, it first connects to the database and turns off the error display. Then it checks for the existence of two tables and creates them if necessary. In the loop, it reads states and descriptions from the user. It makes sure that the abbreviation is listed in uppercase and inserts these values into the database.

The CheckOrCreateTable subroutine uses a new command: $dbh->do. This can be used as a shortcut for the normal prepare and execute sequence if you are not expecting any data to be returned. Then it runs a select that will never return any data (1 will never equal 0). If the statement succeeds, the table is already present and no additional action is necessary. Otherwise, the table is missing and it is created.

The InsertState subroutine simply displays a message and then sends an INSERT query to the database. This can help save you typing or enable you to pipe data into the program without having to know what the tables are or how to insert the data. Here is a sample run of the program:

```
$ ./ch23-2.pl
Creating table states
Creating table addresses
Enter states, one per line, with the abbreviation followed by
the full name.  Press Ctrl+D when done.

NY New York
Inserting: NY => New York
CA California
Inserting: CA => California
TX Texas
Inserting: TX => Texas
NV Nevada
Inserting: NV => Nevada
SD South Dakota
Inserting: SD => South Dakota
NC North Carolina
Inserting: NC => North Carolina
MD Maryland
Inserting: MD => Maryland
ME Maine
Inserting: ME => Maine
FL Florida
Inserting: FL => Florida
Ctrl+D
```

For every state you supplied, the program inserted a line in the database.

Note   Some database servers may cause this program to display diagnostic messages while it runs. For instance, some PostgreSQL servers may display messages about creating an implicit index. These messages are harmless and are for your information only; the program will detect if there was a problem with the database.

Try running the program again. You can add some more information. Also note that it will detect that the tables already exist and not try to recreate them:

```
$ ./ch23-2.pl
Table states already exists; not recreating.
Table addresses already exists; not recreating.
```

```
Enter states, one per line, with the abbreviation followed by
the full name.  Press Ctrl+D when done.

UT Utah
Inserting: UT => Utah
CA California
Inserting: CA => California
Insert failed: ERROR:  Cannot insert a duplicate key into a unique index
Ctrl+D
```

Notice that because the abbreviation for the state was declared a primary key, the database has prevented you from inserting a duplicate record for California. If you want, you can now examine the contents of the table with the query tool from earlier in this chapter.

Use the ch23-1.pl example program and enter in the following query:

```
SELECT * FROM states;

SUCCESS.
Columns: abbrev, fullname
'NY', 'New York'
'CA', 'California'
'TX', 'Texas'
'NV', 'Nevada'
'SD', 'South Dakota'
'NC', 'North Carolina'
'MD', 'Maryland'
'ME', 'Maine'
'FL', 'Florida'
'UT', 'Utah'
10 rows
Number of rows returned or modified: 10
```

If you want, you can go ahead and add entries for the remaining states, or you can just leave it at this. You'll need this table, with at least these 10 states, for the following examples.

DBI with CGI

One of the most popular uses of the DBI software is to store data for interactive Web sites. Because most SQL database servers have some built-in locking support, and this does not require locking the entire database, multiple processes can get along better. Additionally, the more powerful query capabilities and larger scalability of SQL databases over the DBM databases means that these are most often used when a large amount of data is in question. Here, I present a simple application: an address book. This address book contains no security; you might want to add on a separate table containing accounts and passwords and authenticate users that way. For now, though, we'll concentrate on the basics. Listing 23-3 shows the complete code for this application. I'll go through it in detail and demonstrate how it works. Before trying it out, you'll need to have created the two tables as specified previously.

Note   Listing 23-3 is available online.

Listing 23-3: **The address book application**

```perl
#!/usr/bin/perl -Tw

# Turn off output buffering.

$| = 1;

# Bring in the CGI library.

use CGI qw(:standard);

# Display errors if possible.

use CGI::Carp qw(fatalsToBrowser);

# Bring in databases and connect.

use DBI;
use DBD::Pg;

my $DBUSER = 'jgoerzen';
my $DBNAME = $DBUSER;

$dbh = DBI->connect("dbi:Pg:dbname=$DBNAME", $DBUSER, "") or die
  "Couldn't connect to database: " . DBI::errstr;
$dbh->{PrintError} = 0;          # Don't print errors.
$dbh->{RaiseError} = 1;          # Die on errors, and display to browser.

# Create a new CGI object.

my $q = new CGI;
my $NAME = $q->url(-relative => 1);

# Print the HTTP header.

print header;

# Select a default mode.

my $mode = "mode_" . ($q->param('mode') || 'start');

# Eliminate something invalid.
```

```perl
unless ($mode =~ /^mode_[a-zA-Z]+$/) {
  $mode = 'mode_error';
}

# Call the subroutine that handles that mode.

&$mode();

# End the HTML.

print end_html;
$dbh->disconnect;

### program exits here ###

sub mode_start {
  print start_html('Welcome to Address Book');

  # Display introductory text.
  print "Welcome to the address book!  With this application, you can\n";
  print "add entries to the address book and look up other entries.\n";
  print "There are currently <B>";

  # Find out the number of items in the database.
  # This is transformed to SELECT COUNT(*) FROM addresses
  print simplequeryval('COUNT (*)', 'addresses');

  print "</B> addresses in the database.\n<P>\n";
  print "Please select an action:";

  # Display the menu.

  print $q->startform(-method => 'POST');
  print $q->radio_group(-name => 'mode',
          -values => ['search', 'add', 'browse', 'modify'],
          -default => 'search',
          -linebreak => 1,
          -labels => {'search' => 'Search For Entries',
              'add' => 'Add a new entry',
              'browse' => 'Browse all entries',
              'modify' => 'Modify or delete an entry'}
          );
  print $q->submit('submit', 'Go');
  print $q->endform;
}

## This subroutine displays a list of all the entries in the database.

sub mode_browse {
  my $thisentry;
```

Continued

Listing 23-3 *(continued)*

```perl
  print start_html('Address Book: Browse');

  print "Here are all the entries in the address book.  You may\n";
  print "read them here and go back to the <A HREF=\"$NAME";
  print "\">main menu</A> when done.\n<P><HR>\n";

  # Generate the query and perpare it.

  my $sth = $dbh->prepare("SELECT id, name, address1, address2, city,
                           fullname, zip FROM addresses, states
                           WHERE addresses.state = states.abbrev
                           ORDER BY name");

  $sth->execute();

  # Fetch each row and display it.  Add a line after each one.
  while ($thisentry = $sth->fetchrow_arrayref) {
    print EntryHTML($thisentry, 1);
    print "<HR>\n";
  }

  # Close the statement handle.

  $sth->finish();

  # Add a link back to the main menu.

  print "<A HREF=\"$NAME\">Back to main menu</A>\n";
}

# This subroutine is responsible for adding information into the database.

sub mode_add {
  # Implement this a unique way.  Add some dummy information to the
  # database and then re-call this in terms of a modify!  This saves
  # coding effort, since essentially it's the same task anyway.

  my $id = GenerateID();

  $dbh->do("INSERT INTO addresses VALUES ('$id',
            'Put New Name Here',
            'Address line 1',
            NULL,
            'New City',
            'NY',
            '00000')");
```

```
  # Shove the id into the CGI object.

  $q->param(-name => 'id', -value => $id);

  # Now go over to modify.

  return mode_modify();
}

# Handle the modifications to data.  Need to have an id; if none given,
# ask for one.

sub mode_modify {
  my $id = $q->param('id');
  my $entry;

  print $q->start_html('Address Book: Modify');

  # If there wasn't an id passed along....

  unless ($id) {
    print "Please enter the id of the record you want to modify.  If you\n";
    print "do not know the id, you should use one of the options from\n";
    print "the <A HREF=\"$NAME\">main menu</A> to retrieve records and\n";
    print "click on modify from there.\n<P>\n";
    print $q->startform(-method => 'POST');
    print $q->textfield(-name => 'id',
            -size => 40,
            -maxlength => 40);
    print $q->hidden(-name => 'mode', -value => 'modify');
    print $q->submit('submit', 'Go');
    print $q->endform;
    return;
  }
  # Load it up from the database.  This time, use the 2-character
  # state abbreviation instead of the expanded state name.

  @entry = queryrow("SELECT * FROM addresses WHERE id = '$id'");

  print "Here is your chance to make changes.  If you prefer to cancel\n";
  print "the operation, just <A HREF=\"$NAME\">return to the main menu</A>.\n";
  print "<P><HR>\n";

  # Display the original record for reference.

  print "Original record, id <TT>$id</TT>:<P>\n";
  print EntryHTML(\@entry, 0);
  print "<HR>New value: <P>\n";

  # Display the form for the new record.
```

Continued

Listing 23-3 *(continued)*

```perl
  print $q->startform(-method => 'POST');
  print EntryHTML(\@entry, 0, 1);
  print $q->hidden(-name => 'mode', -value => 'modifySave', -override => 1);
  print $q->hidden(-name => 'id', -value => $id, -override => 1);
  print "<HR>";
  print $q->submit('submit', 'Change to above values');
  print "<BR>\n";
  print $q->submit('delete', 'Delete the above record');
  print $q->endform;
}


# This is called after somebody clicks a Submit button on the modify screen.
# Its responsibility is to issue either an update or a delete as appropriate.

sub mode_modifySave {
  print $q->start_html('Address Book: Saved Changes');
  my $id = $q->param('id');

  if ($q->param('delete')) {
    $dbh->do("DELETE FROM addresses WHERE id = '$id'");
    print "The requested record, with id of <TT>$id</TT>, has been\n";
    print "deleted.\n";
  } else {
    my $queryval = '';
    my $key;
    my $first = 1;

    # Generate the query.

    $queryval .= "UPDATE addresses set ";

    foreach $key ('name', 'address1', 'city', 'state', 'zip') {
      unless ($first) {
    $queryval .= ", ";
      }
      $first = 0;
      $queryval .= "\n $key = " . $dbh->quote($q->param($key));
    }

    if ($q->param('address2')) {
      $queryval .= ", \n address2 = " . $dbh->quote($q->param('address2'));
    } else {
      $queryval .= ", \n address2 = NULL";
    }

    $queryval .= "\n WHERE id = '$id'";
    $dbh->do($queryval);
    print "The requested change has been made.  The query used was:<P>\n";
    print "<PRE>\n";
```

```
    print $q->escapeHTML($queryval);
    print "</PRE>\n";
  }
  print "<HR>";
  print "Now go <A HREF=\"$NAME\">back to the main menu</A>.";
}

# This subroutine is used to implement a database search.

sub mode_search {
  print start_html("Address Book: Search");
  my $search = $q->param('search');

  unless ($search) {
    print "You can search through the database of addresses using this\n";
    print "screen.  Type your text below.  I'll search in all the fields\n";
    print "of the database and return any that contain a portion of the\n";
    print "text.  For states, you may use either the 2-letter abbreviation\n";
    print "or the full name.  These searches are case-sensitive.\n<P>\n";
    print "Search text:<BR>\n";
    print $q->startform;
    print $q->textfield(-name => 'search',
            -size => 40);
    print $q->hidden(-name => 'mode', -value => 'search', -override => 1);
    print $q->submit('submit', 'Search');
    print $q->endform;
    return;
  }

  print "<H1>Search Results</H1>\n";
  print "Here are the results for the search for: \n";

  print $q->escapeHTML($search), "\n<P><HR>\n";

  my $querystr = '';
  my $first = 1;
  my $key;
  my $thisentry;

  $querystr .= "SELECT id, name, address1, address2, city, fullname, zip\n";
  $querystr .= "FROM addresses, states\n";
  $querystr .= "WHERE addresses.state = states.abbrev AND (\n";
  foreach $key ('name', 'address1', 'address2', 'city',
        'state', 'fullname', 'zip') {
    unless ($first) {
      $querystr .= " OR\n";
    }
    $first = 0;
    $querystr .= "  $key LIKE " . $dbh->quote('%' . $search . '%') . " ";
  }

  $querystr .= "\n)\nORDER BY name";
```

Continued

Listing 23-3 *(continued)*

```perl
$sth = $dbh->prepare($querystr);
$sth->execute();
while ($thisentry = $sth->fetchrow_arrayref) {
  print EntryHTML($thisentry, 1);
  print "<HR>\n";
}

$sth->finish;


print "My query was:<BR>\n";
print "<PRE>\n";
print $q->escapeHTML($querystr);
print "</PRE>\n";
print "<HR>Now go back to the <A HREF=\"$NAME\">main menu</A>.";
}


sub mode_error {
  print start_html('Error');

  print "I'm sorry, there was an error.  Please use your browser's back\n";
  print "button and retry the operation.\n";
}

# This subroutine displays HTML of a given entry.  Only the first argument
# is required.  The arguments are:
#
# $entry, a reference to an array that DBI might return
#
# $editlink, set to true if there should be a link to the modify page
# for this entry.
#
# $textfields, set to true if the result should be text entry fields
# instead of normal text, such as might be used for modification.
#
# The return value is a string to send to the Web browser.

sub EntryHTML {
  my ($entry, $editlink, $textfields) = @_;
  my $retval = '';

  # Print out the start of the table.
  $retval = "<TABLE><TR><TD><B>Name</B></TD>\n";

  # Name
  $retval .= "<TD>";
  if ($textfields) {
    $retval .= $q->textfield(-name => 'name',
            -default => $entry->[1],
            -override => 1,
```

```
              -size => 40);
} else {
  $retval .= $entry->[1];
}

# If there's supposed to be an edit link, show it.
if ($editlink) {
  # Decrease font size.  Add a bracket.  Start the URL.
  $retval .= " <FONT SIZE=-1>[<A HREF=\"$NAME?mode=modify&id=";

  # Insert a URL-escaped version of the id.
  $retval .= $q->escape($entry->[0]);

  # Close it out.
  $retval .= "\">modify</A>]</FONT>";
}

# Print the rest.
$retval .= "</TD></TR>\n";
$retval .= "<TR><TD><B>Address</B></TD><TD>";

if ($textfields) {
  $retval .= $q->textfield(-name => 'address1',
           -default => $entry->[2],
             -override => 1,
             -size => 40);
} else {
  $retval .= $entry->[2];
}
if ($textfields) {
  $retval .= "<BR>\n";
  my $newval = '';

  if ($entry->[3]) {
    $newval = $entry->[3];
  }

  $retval .= $q->textfield(-name => 'address2',
               -default => $newval,
               -override => 1,
               -size => 40);
} elsif ($entry->[3]) {
  # If it's a two-line address, combine them with a <BR>.
  $retval .= "<BR>$entry->[3]";
}
$retval .= "</TD></TR>\n";
$retval .= "<TR><TD><B>City, State, Zip</B></TD><TD>";
if ($textfields) {
  $retval .= $q->textfield(-name => 'city',
               -default => $entry->[4],
               -override => 1,
               -size => 20);
```

Continued

Listing 23-3 *(continued)*

```perl
    $retval .= ", ";
    my @states = queryarr("SELECT abbrev FROM states ORDER BY abbrev");
    $retval .= $q->popup_menu('state',
                  \@states,
                  $entry->[5]);
    $retval .= " ";
    $retval .= $q->textfield(-name => 'zip',
                  -default => $entry->[6],
                  -override => 1,
                  -size => 10);
  } else {
    $retval .= "$entry->[4], $entry->[5] $entry->[6]";
  }
  $retval .= "</TD></TR></TABLE>\n";
  return $retval;
}


# This subroutine is used to generate a unique ID.  It does this by
# getting the current time and tacking the current process ID onto
# its end, which should be unique.  Note that many databases have a
# much better way of doing this built in.  PostgreSQL, for instance,
# has a sequence that you can use.  Others have a "serial" designation
# for fields.  If your database has that, you should use it, but beware
# that it is not completely portable.  I chose this because it is
# portable.  $$ is the pid of the current process.

sub GenerateID {
  return time() . ";$$";
}


###########################################################################
# Here are some database query functions.  They are around to
# make your life easier.  You can use them in your own programs, too;
# just copy them out of here.
###########################################################################

# simplequeryval... a wrapper around queryval

sub simplequeryval {
  my ($colret, $table, $collookfor, $colmatch) = @_;
  my $querystr;

  $querystr = "SELECT $colret FROM $table";
  if ($colmatch) {
    $querystr .= " WHERE $collookfor = $colmatch";
  }

  return queryval($querystr);
}
```

```perl
# Takes a query and returns the single value from the single column
# that the query resulted in.  Useful for things like getting COUNT(*).

sub queryval {
  my ($query) = @_;
  my @retval = queryarr($query);
  return $retval[0];
}

# Takes a query and returns an array of all values in the single
# column that the query returns.

sub queryarr {
  my ($query) = @_;

  return querycolarr(0, $query);
}

# Takes a query for a select and returns an array of
# all the values in the indicated column.

sub querycolarr {
  my ($column, $query) = @_;
  my @retval = ();

  my $sth = $dbh->prepare($query);
  unless ($sth) {
    return @retval;
  }

  unless ($sth->execute) {
    return @retval;
  }

  my $result = $sth->fetch;

  while (defined($result)) {
    push @retval, $result->[$column];
    $result = $sth->fetch;
  }

  $sth->finish;

  return @retval;
}

# queryrow takes an arbitrary query and returns the returned row.

sub queryrow {
  my ($query) = @_;
  my @retval = ();
```

Continued

Listing 23-3 *(continued)*

```
my $sth = $dbh->prepare($query);
$sth->execute;
@retval = $sth->fetchrow;

$sth->finish;
return @retval;
}
```

This program is quite a large one! It presents a more simplified CGI interface than the one in Chapter 22, but nevertheless, it is fairly large. I tried to add comments in the code to help you out, and we'll go over some issues here as well. Don't let the size overwhelm you; take it in small chunks, and you'll see how everything fits together.

Note that because most CGI programs run with the permissions of the Web server, it's not possible to auto-detect the database username by looking at the environment anymore. Therefore, before this will work for you, you'll need to change this line:

```
my $DBUSER = 'jgoerzen';
```

Just replace my username with yours and everything will work fine.

Initialization

This program in Listing 23-3 begins its life in a manner quite similar to many others that you've seen. It imports the CGI library. The next statement is interesting. It captures error-handling calls, such as `die` and `warn`, and instead of emitting an error to standard error (which would probably go into the server's error log), it emits the error to the user's browser.

After taking care of handling errors, the program imports the database libraries as before. There are a few other interesting things to note here. The `PrintError` option is turned off; there's no need to simply display an error message. However, `RaiseError` is turned on. This causes DBI to generate a fatal error (with `die`) whenever there is a problem. By turning this on, I no longer have to explicitly check for error conditions all over in my code, because with this CGI script, there's no need to be able to recover gracefully from such a condition.

A new CGI object is allocated, and it is interrogated to find out the name of the script. This is used for building up URLs later.

In the next sections, I discuss the major subroutines in the Listing 23-3 source file.

mode_start

When somebody starts the script, it enters this routine by default. The program displays some introductory information, explaining that this is indeed an address book. Then it wants to tell the user how many entries are in the book. To do this, it needs to get a count of the entries in the addresses table from the database. No problem! Thanks to a helper function, this is done inline without having the mess with statement handles right here.

After finishing the introductory text, a menu is displayed. Just to be different, it's made up of radio buttons and a Submit button. The user selects the operation to perform from the radio button and then clicks the Submit button.

mode_browse

The mode_browse function is the first function in the script that does some more deep-down work with the database. It begins by displaying some usual text. Then it proceeds to prepare a query. This query fetches the data from the addresses table and then joins that with the full state name from the states table. Finally, it orders the result by the name of the person.

The execute function is called, and then the results are returned. I use the fetchrow_arrayref here, just because it's a little bit faster. This isn't terribly performance-critical code, but I want to show you how it's done. For each record in the database, we get a reference to an array containing its fields. The fields in the array are given in the order they were requested in the select. This reference is passed on to EntryHTML for display. After that, a horizontal rule is printed to separate the records from each other. Finally, when all the rows have been retrieved, the statement handle is closed and the function finishes.

mode_add

When the user selects the option to add a new record, mode_add is invoked. Its job is to insert a new record into the database and let the user fill it out. But this code is sneaky about it. It inserts a new record into the database but then calls the modify function to let the user fill it out. This saves some recoding. So, the first thing to do is to nab a unique ID. For this, the GenerateID function is called. Next, a query consisting of an insert is executed. After the query is executed, the code shoves an ID parameter into the CGI object and then calls modify.

mode_modify

Like the other functions, mode_modify starts out by displaying some basic information. If no ID was passed in, it generates a form for the user to enter one. If an ID was received, the fun begins.

First, the program needs to retrieve the entry that the ID refers to. It does this by calling `queryrow`. It then displays the original record, and then a new record. Finally, it generates two Submit buttons: one to delete the record and one to save the changes. In either case, the `modifySave` function will be called next time to commit the changes to the database.

mode_modifySave

The `mode_modifySave` function is invoked after somebody works at the modify screen. If the user clicked the Delete button, the function goes to the database and deletes the requested data. On the other hand, if the user clicked on the Modify button, the function needs to issue an update query. It uses a loop to generate parts of the string for each key except for address2. This one is handled specially; the database value is set to `NULL` if the form field was empty.

Notice the usage of `$dbh->quote`. When you work with strings in SQL, you enclose them in single quotes. However, if you have a string with an embedded quote character, you have to escape the quote by doubling that character. You have to be careful to always watch out for quotes in the data so that no mistake could result from someone trying to use an apostrophe in the input, for example. If you were really concerned about security, you'd do the same with the `$id` variable, or else check it for valid characters ahead of time. You'll find that the quoting mechanism is used many times throughout the program in Listing 23-3 as well.

The query is changed if necessary, and to help you see what's going on, the final query is printed out to the Web browser. Finally, the program prints out a link to return to the main menu.

mode_search

The search function begins in a manner similar to the modify one. If no search term was specified yet, the function asks for one after displaying some help. If a search term has been specified, again a query is built up and send to the database. This query introduces a new operator: `LIKE`. When you use this instead of equals, it permits the use of wildcards. In this case, the percent sign is used, which means in SQL what the asterisk does in the UNIX shell. So, each field is searched using the percent signs to see if it contains the string anywhere.

As with the browse function, a simple loop processes the results from the query. After the loop finishes, the query is printed out for your benefit.

EntryHTML

The `EntryHTML` function is called by several others to generate an HTML rendering of the address of a given person. The function has several options; it can generate either a plain text rendering or a rendering that provides text fields for input. Much of the function is simply the selection between the various output options for displaying information and tables.

Query Functions

The Listing 23-3 program ends with a number of small query functions. These are utility functions designed to help you deal with requests for certain types of frequently used small groups of data. For instance, the `simplequeryval` function is provided to let you quickly receive a single value from a database, without having to go to the effort to prepare, execute, fetch, and finish with a statement handle. This can be quite a useful utility.

Examples

So that you can put together all the pieces, I want to show you two examples of the queries the program generates. Here is what the code generates when you make a modification:

```
UPDATE addresses set
 name = 'John Doe',
 address1 = '12345 S. Someone''s Ave.',
 city = 'Somewhere',
 state = 'SD',
 zip = '10101',
 address2 = 'Suite 9876'
 WHERE id = '939072323;2624'
```

Notice the quoting that occurred for `address1`; the apostrophe was doubled to prevent problems. When the data is read back later, it will appear normal. Here's an example of the query generated for a search:

```
SELECT id, name, address1, address2, city, fullname, zip
FROM addresses, states
WHERE addresses.state = states.abbrev AND (
  name LIKE '%Pierre%'  OR
  address1 LIKE '%Pierre%'  OR
  address2 LIKE '%Pierre%'  OR
  city LIKE '%Pierre%'  OR
  state LIKE '%Pierre%'  OR
  fullname LIKE '%Pierre%'  OR
  zip LIKE '%Pierre%'
)
ORDER BY name
```

Summary

In this chapter, you learned about communicating with SQL databases by using DBI. Specifically, you learned:

♦ DBI is a way to communicate with a SQL database in a mostly database-independent fashion.

✦ SQL is a powerful query language used by databases that communicate with DBI.

✦ Data in SQL is stored in tables and is organized into rows and columns.

✦ Entries can be empty unless NOT NULL is specified.

✦ Specifying PRIMARY KEY forces uniqueness for that particular column.

✦ DBI is useful in many different types of applications and can be used in both command-line and Web-based applications.

✦ It's important to remember to quote input for the server.

✦   ✦   ✦

Graphical Interfaces with X

GUIs with Perl/Tk

One of the most persistent trends over the past decade
is that of the graphical user interface (GUI) becoming
popular in the computing marketplace. There is a reason for
this. With a graphical interface, you can present information
and interact with the user in more ways than you can with
a text interface. This is because you can use the likes of
arbitrary pictures, different forms of input (mouse), and
multiple panes (windows) on the user's screen. By making
clever use of these features, such as realistic icons, intuitive
menus, and online help, you can make your program easier
to learn—and sometimes easier to use as well.

In this chapter, you will learn about GUI programming with
Perl/Tk. I'll start with an introduction to GUI programming,
which will help you decide whether or not a GUI is appropriate
for your application. After that, you'll learn about event-based
programming, which is a different way about learning about
keystrokes and mouse movements, and X clients. The next
three sections will take you on a tour of Perl/Tk, where you will
learn about different widgets in Perl/Tk and how to use them.
The chapter concludes with a look at geometry managers,
which are used to lay out widgets in your windows, special
concerns of Perl/Tk, and the SpecTcl interface design tool.

GUI Programming in Linux

In the introduction to this chapter, I mentioned a number of
benefits that you can derive from using a graphical interface.
However, along with all these benefits, there are also
downsides. GUI programming is much more complex than
programming for a plain-text interface. GUI programs require
more CPU power and carry a larger memory burden. They
require more bandwidth and so cannot be efficiently run

remotely except on fast links. Poorly designed GUI s can be more difficult to use than a corresponding text interface. Finally, GUI programs are generally hard to automate, especially the kind of data transfer that you are used to accomplishing with piping on the Linux command line.

In a nutshell, you need to evaluate whether a GUI is right for your program. A GUI can be especially useful if you are putting an interface on a program for people that need to have the least possible learning time, similarity with an existing sutie of GUI tools, and have little experience with a text interface. On the other hand, a GUI can be slower, larger, difficult to write, and hard to automate.

Basics of the X Window System

When you are writing a GUI under the Linux operating system, you are almost always writing a GUI that runs under the X Window System. If you are coming from a different GUI environment, such as Microsoft Windows, you will need to understand that although the X environment may look similar to Windows on the surface, underneath the system is quite different.

X is separated into two parts: the clients and the server. Generally, you have one X server running on each machine. The server is responsible for interacting directly with the hardware, displaying images on the monitor, reading input from a keyboard or mouse, and the like. This functionality is separate from the applications that run with X; the X server solely manages clients and server resources (such as the display). It does not provide any applications of its own.

Clients are the applications in the system. A client may be a word processor, an editor, a spreadsheet, a game, or any other program that you want to run in a graphical environment. There are also special clients that can run on your system. One such client is the window manager, which is responsible for managing the placement and decoration of the top-level windows on your system. A window manager can do things like create a title bar for windows, enable you to drag windows to new locations, minimize windows, and the like.

It's easy to get confused with the prevailing terminology. The X server is called a "server" because it manages access to shared resources, just like any other server on your system. In this case, the shared resources are your display, mouse, keyboard, and any other input devices that you might have. The different applications on your system need access to these things, and the server manages this access on behalf of the clients. From a technical perspective, the X server listens for connections on a predefined port just as other servers do, and clients connect to that port just as with other servers.

Location independence

Due to the separation of the client from the server in X, there are some fascinating possibilities that do not exist in other graphical environments. Chief among them is that it makes no difference to the X server whether or not a client is running on your own machine. To X, it is just as natural to have a client running on a machine down the hall but interacting with you on your own screen as it is to have the client running on your own machine. In fact, some users have clients running on a dozen different computers — perhaps spanning two or three continents — displaying on their X screens seamlessly integrated with applications running on the local machine. The clients, then, can connect over a LAN, over the Internet, or to the server running on the local machine.

Everything is dealt with in a location-independent basis. The "clipboard" in X, for instance, can hold data from any client and can be pasted into any client, regardless of location.

When you start up a client, it needs to know which server to connect to. This is generally specified by setting the DISPLAY environment variable. This variable is set for you by default when you start X; if you want to change it, you can do so. The X(1x) manpage contains information on the format of this variable as well as access control to prevent unwanted clients from connecting to your server.

Anatomy of a Client

When you are writing an application to run in the GUI X environment, you are writing an X client. You almost never need to modify the X server. It is bundled with the operating system and presumed already functional by the time any clients enter the picture.

Xlib

Like many things in Linux, X clients may have several layers of libraries. The lowest layer, known as Xlib, handles the actual communication between the client and the server. That is, Xlib is responsible for encoding requests to and decoding responses from the form suitable for transport across a network — or across the local machine. Xlib works on a very low level with the X protocol, providing an interface essentially to the protocol itself. Although it is technically possible to write an X client without using Xlib, few if any programmers do so today.

Widget sets

Because Xlib works on such a low level with the X protocol, most programmers (except widget set authors) prefer to use a widget set for their programs. This is because it is almost always easier and faster to think of the display in terms of buttons, menus, and pictures instead of manually painting the pixels and lines that form the buttons, manually displaying the menus and handling mouse input for them, and so forth. Many different widget sets are available from which a programmer may choose. Examples of widget sets include the Athena Widgets (Xaw), Tk, Gnome/GTK, Qt, wxWindows, and many others. In this chapter, I'll be using the Tk widget set, as implemented in Perl.

Each widget set has its own way of interacting with the programmer. Some may be tied to features found in specific languages; for instance, Qt is based on an object-oriented metaphor. Others may provide a more low-level approach, such as the Athena Widgets do. Not only that, but each widget set is responsible for rendering its own objects to the display. For instance, a scroll bar widget from the Athena Widget set looks and acts differently than one from the Tk widget set.

The Tk widget set is a modern, full-functioning widget set with sporting interface elements with 3D bevels. It borrows some look and feel from both UNIX and Windows environments, and it adds in its own unique ideas, to get a widget set that should feel quite natural to many people. Some of its own unique features include tear-off menus and tight integration with Perl.

Hierarchical windows

In Tk, a "window" is much more than you might be traditionally accustomed to considering a window. A window in Tk is everything from your application's window on the desktop to a button, a text entry box, a menu, or a group of similar items. Thus, windows in Tk are nested — arranged hierarchically. This corresponds to how items appear on-screen. For instance, a button might appear inside a configuration panel, which is inside a tabbed notebook, itself inside a top-level dialog box, which happens to be a child of the application's main window. The window hierarchy in Tk will reflect this ordering. When you are done with the dialog box, for instance, it is destroyed, and all the windows inside it are automatically destroyed as well.

Configuration

Because the nature of the programs in X is to use a hierarchy to the programs' advantage, configuration is hierarchical as well. This gives the user much more control over the applications than in Microsoft graphical environments. For instance, from the single X configuration system (X resources), one can configure not only the default background color of all windows on the system, but also the default color of one particular application — or even one particular dialog box in an application. You can go so far as to individually tweak each button in an application.

This is all thanks to the X resources system, which allows users to configure things at as high or as low a level as they like. You can configure the color of all buttons on the system, all buttons in an application, all buttons in a single dialog box, or one button in particular — just to pick an example.

In general, defaults can be set by an application or by the system administrator and selectively overridden by each individual user.

Event-Based Programming

With a traditional model, when you need to get input from the user, you prompt for it. You may display a menu of options, or some other similar interface. But the point is that in each case, you first display a menu or prompt, then read input from that menu or prompt only, and then act upon that input.

With a GUI, there are often dozens, or even hundreds, of possible options. The user may pop up a dialog box and then proceed to bring up a second dialog box. Each of these boxes may contain buttons, text fields, and the like. Simply displaying information and waiting for a response turns out not to be so simple in this case.

The answer to this is event-based programming. With this type of programming, you simply declare how things are to be drawn. Then, you indicate what is to be done when a certain event occurs. For instance, when the user clicks an OK button, you might want to call a subroutine to save the file. When the user clicks a Help button, you would want to bring up some online help.

With this model, after you initialize your program, your own code is finished executing; there is nothing for it to do until some sort of event occurs. When an event happens for which you were listening, the Tk system invokes the code that you had bound to that event. Frequently this code is a subroutine.

Having your own code invoked from somewhere else like this is termed a *callback*. The flow of control passes out of your own code until some particular event brings it back into your code. You handle the event and then control passes back to Tk again.

Thus, after initializing all your applications, you call the Tk `MainLoop` function. This function handles all the events for your program, makes necessary screen updates, and invokes callbacks as appropriate.

First Steps

For a first program, I'll show you how to pop up a simple window on the screen:

```
#!/usr/bin/perl -w

use Tk;

my $window = new MainWindow;
$window->title('Hi!');
$window->Label(-text => "Hello from Perl/Tk!")->pack;
$window->Button(-text => "Exit",
                -command => \&exitbutton)->pack;
MainLoop;

sub exitbutton {
  exit(0);
}
```

Note
To use this code, you will need the Perl::Tk library. Many distributions may include it on the CD or network site. If yours does not, you may find it at `http://www.perl.com/CPAN-local/modules/by-module/Tk/`. As of the date this text is written, the latest version there is named Tk800.015.tar.gz. Installation instructions accompany the distribution in the README file.

Going over the code, you can see that the script begins as any other Perl script does, with a call to the Perl interpreter. After that, the Tk routines are brought in by the `use` command. Next, the program creates a new top-level main window for the application. The title of this window is set and appears in the window manager. Then a Label widget is created. This widget gets placed in the main window because of how it is called: `$window->Label`. The text for the label is set using the normal syntax for Perl hashes. Finally, the label is packed. This means that it is actually set to appear on-screen by calling the Tk packer to fix its position. Unless you pack something with Tk, it won't actually appear.

After the label, a button is created. This time, it has specific text, just like the label. However, it also involves a callback. Note that you can simply pass a reference to a subroutine for the callback command. When the user clicks the Exit button, that subroutine will be called, which happens to cause the program to terminate.

Figure 24-1 shows how this program looks on-screen. Note that your screen may look different if you are using a different window manager (the below screenshot was made with Afterstep) or have different color preferences.

Figure 24-1: Perl/Tk Hello World

You can also create multiple top-level windows on the screen. Here's a modification to the program earlier in this chapter that does just that:

```perl
#!/usr/bin/perl -w

use Tk;
use strict;

my $window = new MainWindow();
$window->title('Hi!');
$window->Label(-text => "Hello from Perl/Tk!")->pack;
$window->Button(-text => "Exit",
                -command => \&exitsub)->pack;
MainLoop;

sub exitsub {
  my $w = $window->Toplevel();
  $w->title('Goodbye');
  $w->Label(-text => 'You are now leaving the demonstration program.')->pack;
  $w->Button(-text => "OK", -command => sub { $w->destroy;
                                             $window->destroy; })->pack;
}
```

This time, the first part of the program looks quite similar to the other program. However, notice the difference in the subroutine called when someone clicks the button.

This time, that subroutine creates a new top-level window. Thus, there will be two windows on-screen from this program when the Exit button is clicked. Some text is inserted by using a label, and a button is created. Notice that the callback for this button is not a call to a standard subroutine. Rather, it is a reference to an anonymous subroutine created in place! This anonymous subroutine destroys both windows. When all the windows are destroyed, the MainLoop returns, and the program exits. You don't have to explicitly call exit(0) in this case because the MainLoop automatically terminates when all the windows have been destroyed.

Object Attributes

Each object in your program has certain attributes, including color, the events that it is listening for, font information, and even the text or information that it is displaying. Listing 24-1 shows a program that enables you to manipulate those attributes.

Note   Listing 24-1 is available online.

Listing 24-1: **Sample program: a color picker**

```perl
#!/usr/bin/perl -w

use Tk;

# Create a hash to hold information about the three different color areas.

my %areas = ('red' => '', 'green' => '', 'blue' => '');

# Create the main window.

my $window = new MainWindow();

$window->title('Color Picker');     # Give it a title.

# Create the top label text.

$window->Label(-text => "You may select your colors here.")
       ->pack(-side => 'top');

# Create each area, pack it, and store it into the hash.

foreach my $name ('red', 'green', 'blue') {
  $areas->{$name} = ColorArea($name, $window->Frame);
  $areas->{$name}->{frame}->pack(-fill => 'x');
}

# Create the label for the bottom of the window.

my $colorlabel =
  $window->Label(-text => 'foo')->pack(-side => 'top', -fill => 'both');

# And update it.

UpdateColorLabel();

# Process events.

MainLoop;

# This is a subroutine to create an area in the window for each
# particular color.  Its arguments are a color name and a frame.
# The subroutine will create all its widgets inside that frame,
# and return a reference to a hash with information about the
# color.

sub ColorArea {
  my ($name, $frame) = @_;

  # Initialize the hash with some useful information.
  my $retval = {'frame' => $frame, 'value' => 128, name => $name};
```

```perl
    # Create a label with the color name.
    $frame->Label(-text => $name)->pack(-side => 'left');

    # Create a horizontal scroll bar.  When the bar is moved, call
    # the scrollit subroutine.
    my $s = $frame->Scrollbar(-orient => 'horiz',
                              -command => sub { scrollit($retval, @_) })
       ->pack(-side => 'left', -fill => 'x', -expand => 1);

    # Create an entry box.  It displays the variable, and will
    # automatically update it when modified.
    $retval->{entry} = $frame->Entry(-width => 3,
                                     -textvariable => \$retval->{value})
       ->pack(-side => 'right');

    # When the Return key is pressed, update everything based on the
    # keypress.
    $retval->{entry}->bind('<Return>', sub { setit($retval) } );

    # Save off the scrollbar into the hash.
    $retval->{scrollbar} = $s;

    # Update things now.
    setit($retval);

    return $retval;
}

# This subroutine is used to handle a scroll request.

sub scrollit {
  my ($hash, $cmd, $arg, $arg2) = @_;
  my $var = \$hash->{value};

  if ($cmd eq 'moveto') {         # Move to a specific location.
    $$var = $arg * 255;
  } elsif ($cmd eq 'scroll' && $arg2 eq 'units') {
    $$var += $arg;                # User clicked on arrow, move by 1.
  } elsif ($cmd eq 'scroll' && $arg2 eq 'pages') {
    $$var += 10 * $arg;          # User clicked on bar area, move by 10.
  }
  setit($hash);
}

# Set scrollbars and everything as appropriate.  Takes a hash as an
# argument, processes its value, and sets things up.

sub setit {
  my $hash = shift @_;
  my $value = \$hash->{value};
```

Continued

Listing 24-1 *(continued)*

```
# Do some sanity checks.  Strip off a fractional part, make sure
# between 0 and 255.

$$value = int $$value;
$$value = 255 if ($$value > 255);
$$value = 0 if ($$value < 0);

# Update the scroll bar.  Note the scrollbar needs its values in
# fractions.

$hash->{scrollbar}->set($$value / 255, $$value / 255);
UpdateColorLabel();
}

# Update the color label at the bottom of the screen.  Show the color
# string, suitable for use in HTML and X, and set the background
# to that color.

sub UpdateColorLabel {
  return unless ($areas->{red} &&
                 $areas->{green} &&
                 $areas->{blue});

  my $colorstring = sprintf('#%02x%02x%02x',
                            $areas->{red}->{value},
                            $areas->{green}->{value},
                            $areas->{blue}->{value});
  $colorlabel->configure(-background => $colorstring,
                         -text => $colorstring);
}
```

Before analyzing this code, please take a moment to run it and see what it does. You'll get a screen containing three scroll bars, three text entry boxes, and two labels. The top label has some information, and the bottom label changes as you move the scroll bars. You can also type a number between 0 and 255 into the text entry boxes, and after pressing Enter, the appropriate boxes on the screen will update (see Figure 24-2).

Now let's go over the code and see how it accomplishes this. The program starts by creating a window and giving it a title, as usual. It proceeds to create a label and pack it. It then executes a loop that creates entries in the areas hash for each of the three colors. Finally, it creates a label for the bottom of the window and updates it.

Figure 24-2: First color selection program

That is all of the main program. The subroutines, though, hold many of the secrets to this program. First, there is the `ColorArea` subroutine, which creates the label, scrollbar, and text entry box for each color. It begins by initializing a hash and inserting a label. It then creates a scroll bar, oriented horizontally. When the user interacts with this scroll bar, the `scrollit` subroutine is called. The scroll bar is packed, set to expand to fill the available area.

Then an entry box is created. Its width attribute is set to three characters. It operates upon the variable stored in `$retval->{value}`, to which it takes a reference. Whenever that value is modified, the entry box is automatically updated, and vice-versa.

After creation of the entry box, a binding for it is created. When the user presses Enter while the focus is in the entry box, the `setit` subroutine will be called. This will then update the scroll bars and color label.

Finally, the hash is touched up and `setit` is called to make sure that the area is properly displayed.

The `scrollit` subroutine is called from Tk whenever the scroll bar moves. It takes a command and one or two arguments. If the command is `moveto`, the argument is a fraction indicating where along the bar the item should be moved to. If the command is scroll, the item is adjusted by either 1 or 10 units, depending upon how the user clicked the bar. Finally, setit is called to ensure everything is up to date.

The setit subroutine does many important things. First, it ensures that the value being used is valid. Then, it calls the scrollbar's set method to update the position. It finishes by calling UpdateColorLabel to set up the label area at the bottom of the window.

UpdateColorLabel begins by ensuring that all three colors have been set up. Because it could be called before they are all ready, it should not do anything in those cases. If they are all set up, it generates a string. Then, it calls configure on the label to modify its attributes. These modifications do take effect immediately, so the color of the label, and the content of its text, are changed right away.

Each widget in Tk has many different attributes that can be set, either at creation time or later by using the configure call. The manpages for the widget, such as Tk::Label contain details. Also take a look at the Tk::options manpage.

You'll note that the program has a few flaws; for instance, the color items don't line up nicely and there is no Exit button. These will be fixed as you go along in this chapter.

Special Objects

Besides those that you have already dealt with, there are a number of additional objects that you might want to work with. I'll cover some of them here, and I'll modify the code for the existing program to use them.

Frames

A *frame* is an object that is simply designed to hold other objects. Its main purpose is to organize the packing of certain objects into subgroups, but it can also be used to visually set off one thing from the next. The example program used one frame for each color group. This allows the items inside the frame to be packed, and then the collection of items to be packed as one within the larger window. This behavior can simplify packing and eliminate some needs to use other packers.

Menus

Almost every GUI program will have a menu. Perl/Tk provides you with an extremely powerful menu interface. You can create menus just about anywhere, not just along the top bar as is common. Your menus can invoke commands, provide options, and include submenus.

Listing 24-2 shows a version of the existing software, with an addition of a menu bar and a few features to support it.

Note Listing 24-2 is available online.

Listing 24-2: Example with a menu bar

```perl
#!/usr/bin/perl -w

use Tk;

# Create a hash to hold information about the three different color areas.

my %areas = ('red' => '', 'green' => '', 'blue' => '');

my $dtextfg = '#000000';

# Create the main window.

my $window = new MainWindow();

$window->title('Color Picker');     # Give it a title.

# Call the subroutine to create the menus.

CreateMenus($window);

# Create the top label text.

$window->Label(-text => "You may select your colors here.")
        ->pack(-side => 'top');

# Create each area, pack it, and store it into the hash.

foreach my $name ('red', 'green', 'blue') {
  $areas->{$name} = ColorArea($name, $window->Frame);
  $areas->{$name}->{frame}->pack(-fill => 'x');
}

# Create the label for the bottom of the window.

my $colorlabel =
  $window->Label(-text => 'foo')->pack(-side => 'top', -fill => 'both');

# And update it.

UpdateColorLabel();
```

Continued

Listing 24-2 *(continued)*

```perl
# Process events.

MainLoop;

# This is a subroutine to create an area in the window for each
# particular color.  Its arguments are a color name and a frame.
# The subroutine will create all its widgets inside that frame,
# and return a reference to a hash with information about the
# color.

sub ColorArea {
  my ($name, $frame) = @_;

  # Initialize the hash with some useful information.
  my $retval = {'frame' => $frame, 'value' => 128, name => $name};

  # Create a label with the color name.
  $frame->Label(-text => $name)->pack(-side => 'left');

  # Create a horizontal scroll bar.  When the bar is moved, call
  # the scrollit subroutine.
  my $s = $frame->Scrollbar(-orient => 'horiz',
                            -command => sub { scrollit($retval, @_) })
    ->pack(-side => 'left', -fill => 'x', -expand => 1);

  # Create an entry box.  It displays the variable, and will
  # automatically update it when modified.
  $retval->{entry} = $frame->Entry(-width => 3,
                                   -textvariable => \$retval->{value})
    ->pack(-side => 'right');

  # When the Return key is pressed, update everything based on the
  # keypress.
  $retval->{entry}->bind('<Return>', sub { setit($retval) } );

  # Save off the scrollbar into the hash.
  $retval->{scrollbar} = $s;

  # Update things now.
  setit($retval);

  return $retval;
}

# This subroutine is used to handle a scroll request.

sub scrollit {
  my ($hash, $cmd, $arg, $arg2) = @_;
  my $var = \$hash->{value};
```

```perl
    if ($cmd eq 'moveto') {         # Move to a specific location.
      $$var = $arg * 255;
    } elsif ($cmd eq 'scroll' && $arg2 eq 'units') {
      $$var += $arg;                # User clicked on arrow, move by 1.
    } elsif ($cmd eq 'scroll' && $arg2 eq 'pages') {
      $$var += 10 * $arg;           # User clicked on bar area, move by 10.
    }
    setit($hash);
}

# Set scrollbars and everything as appropriate.  Takes a hash as an
# argument, processes its value, and sets things up.

sub setit {
  my $hash = shift @_;
  my $value = \$hash->{value};

  # Do some sanity checks.  Strip off a fractional part, make sure
  # between 0 and 255.

  $$value = int $$value;
  $$value = 255 if ($$value > 255);
  $$value = 0 if ($$value < 0);

  # Update the scroll bar.  Note the scrollbar needs its values in
  # fractions.

  $hash->{scrollbar}->set($$value / 255, $$value / 255);
  UpdateColorLabel();
}

# Update the color label at the bottom of the screen.  Show the color
# string, suitable for use in HTML and X, and set the background
# to that color.

sub UpdateColorLabel {
  return unless ($areas->{red} &&
                 $areas->{green} &&
                 $areas->{blue});

  my $colorstring = sprintf('#%02x%02x%02x',
                            $areas->{red}->{value},
                            $areas->{green}->{value},
                            $areas->{blue}->{value});
  my $fg = $dtextfg;

  if ($fg eq 'inverse') {
    $fg = sprintf('#%02x%02x%02x',
                  $areas->{red}->{value} ^ 0xFF,
                  $areas->{green}->{value} ^ 0xFF,
                  $areas->{blue}->{value} ^ 0xFF);
  }
```

Continued

Listing 24-2 *(continued)*

```perl
    $colorlabel->configure(-background => $colorstring,
                           -text => $colorstring,
                           -foreground => $fg);
}

sub CreateMenus {
  my $w = shift @_;

  my $f = $w->Frame(-relief => 'groove',
                    -borderwidth => 2)
          ->pack(-expand => 0, -fill => 'both');

  ##################################################
  # Program menu

  my $m = $f->Menubutton(text => 'Program',
                         -underline => 0)
    ->pack(side => 'left', padx => 2);

  $m->command(-label => 'Exit',
              -underline => 1,
              -command => sub { $w->destroy}
              );

  ##################################################
  # Options menu

  $m = $f->Menubutton(text => 'Options', -underline => 0)
         ->pack(side => 'left', -padx => 2);

  my $m2 = $m->cascade(-label => 'Demo Text Foreground', -underline => 1);
  $m2->radiobutton(-label => "Black",
                   -variable => \$dtextfg,
                   -value => '#000000',
                   -command => \&UpdateColorLabel);
  $m2->radiobutton(-label => "White",
                   -variable => \$dtextfg,
                   -value => '#FFFFFF',
                   -command => \&UpdateColorLabel);
  $m2->radiobutton(-label => "Inverse",
                   -variable => \$dtextfg,
                   -value => 'inverse',
                   -command => \&UpdateColorLabel);
}
```

One problem with the previous version of the code is that the text in the label box would become hard to read if the color being showed there was dark. This is because the text was black. However, one would have the same problem if the white color were selected; bright colors would have a problem. So, a menu is provided that offers a radio button selection of black, white, or inverse color text. Just to demonstrate cascading menus, and perhaps to leave some room for future expansion, this is a cascading menu beneath the Options menu.

To create the menu bar, you must first create a frame. This frame is set to occupy all available horizontal space such that it spans the entire top of the application. Note that you could just as easily make the menu vertical along the left or right side of the box, at the bottom of the box, or wherever you prefer. You can also make the Menubutton widgets as pop-ups from anywhere in your application. You are not required to use a set menu bar or location as with some other GUI environments. However, unless you have a special reason to deviate from the common approach, it's good to give your users what they expect. The so-called "principle of least surprise" often works in your favor with GUIs.

Note that the frame is given two attributes. The first sets the border (relief) to a groove, that visually sets the menu bar apart from the rest of the window. The second defines the width of this border.

Next, the menu buttons are defined with Menubutton widgets. These are the entry points into a menu hierarchy. Each top-level item in the menu bar is a menu button. The first is the Program menu. It contains a single command entry, which exits the program.

The second is the Options menu. Its single entry is a cascade, meaning a nested menu. Then, into the cascaded menu, the three radio buttons are added. Each specifies the text to show on-screen, the variable to modify, the value to store in that variable. Furthermore, they specify a command to run when that variable's contents are modified.

When you run the program, note the dashed lines in the menus. Click on one of those lines and a menu tears itself off, forming a separate window. Figures 24-3 and 24-4 illustrate this modified program. Figure 24-3 shows the start of the program. Figure 24-4 shows a torn-off menu.

Figure 24-3: Color selector with menu bar

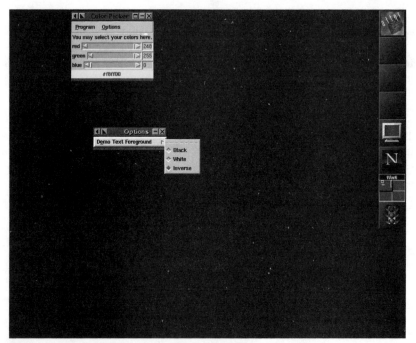

Figure 24-4: Torn-off menu bar for color selector

Text and canvas

These are two widgets that enable you to place other things inside. The text widget, for instance, is designed for presentation of text and enables you to place various items of text information, plus special capabilities like hotspots and other embedded widgets. It is frequently used to make things like a dialog box scrollable.

A canvas is similar in concept to a text widget but is designed to work with graphical objects such as lines, painting, and filling.

Geometry Managers

You may have noticed that some things in our sample program weren't exactly well lined up. For instance, it would be nicer to have all the scrollbars lined up and the same size. What we really need is a different way of arranging items in the window. The standard packer works fine for many things, but here, the grid geometry manager may work better.

Listing 24-3 shows is a version of the program that uses the grid geometry manager to place the items in the color area. Notice that the main window still uses the packer, but a frame within it uses the grid. You are free to use the frame to achieve such separation, which is indeed one of its most powerful uses.

Note   Listing 24-3 is available online.

Listing 24-3: **Sample with grid manager**

```perl
#!/usr/bin/perl -w

use Tk;

# Create a hash to hold information about the three different color areas.

my %areas = ('red' => '', 'green' => '', 'blue' => '');

my $dtextfg = '#000000';

# Create the main window.

my $window = new MainWindow();

$window->title('Color Picker');        # Give it a title.

# Call the subroutine to create the menus.
```

Continued

Listing 24-3 *(continued)*

```
CreateMenus($window);

# Create the top label text.

$window->Label(-text => "You may select your colors here.")
       ->pack(-side => 'top');

# Create each area, pack it, and store it into the hash.

my $colorframe = $window->Frame->pack(-fill => 'x');
my $row = 0;

foreach my $name ('red', 'green', 'blue') {
  $areas->{$name} = ColorArea($name, $colorframe, $row++);
}

# Create the label for the bottom of the window.

my $colorlabel =
  $window->Label(-text => 'foo')->pack(-side => 'top', -fill => 'both');

# And update it.

UpdateColorLabel();

# Process events.

MainLoop;

# This is a subroutine to create an area in the window for each
# particular color.  Its arguments are a color name and a frame.
# The subroutine will create all its widgets inside that frame,
# and return a reference to a hash with information about the
# color.

sub ColorArea {
  my ($name, $frame, $row) = @_;
  my $col = 0;

  # Initialize the hash with some useful information.
  my $retval = {'frame' => $frame, 'value' => 128, name => $name};

  $frame->gridColumnconfigure(1, -minsize => 300);

  # Create a label with the color name.
  $frame->Label(-text => $name)->grid(-row => $row,
                                      -col => $col++,
                                      -sticky => 'nesw');
```

```
# Create a horizontal scroll bar.  When the bar is moved, call
# the scrollit subroutine.
my $s = $frame->Scrollbar(-orient => 'horiz',
                          -command => sub { scrollit($retval, @_) })
   ->grid(-row => $row, -col => $col++, -sticky => 'nesw');

# Create an entry box.  It displays the variable, and will
# automatically update it when modified.
$retval->{entry} = $frame->Entry(-width => 3,
                             -textvariable => \$retval->{value})
   ->grid(-row => $row, -col => $col++, -sticky => 'nesw');

# When the Return key is pressed, update everything based on the
# keypress.
$retval->{entry}->bind('<Return>', sub { setit($retval) } );

# Save off the scrollbar into the hash.
$retval->{scrollbar} = $s;

# Update things now.
setit($retval);

return $retval;
}

# This subroutine is used to handle a scroll request.

sub scrollit {
  my ($hash, $cmd, $arg, $arg2) = @_;
  my $var = \$hash->{value};

  if ($cmd eq 'moveto') {              # Move to a specific location.
    $$var = $arg * 255;
  } elsif ($cmd eq 'scroll' && $arg2 eq 'units') {
    $$var += $arg;                     # User clicked on arrow, move by 1.
  } elsif ($cmd eq 'scroll' && $arg2 eq 'pages') {
    $$var += 10 * $arg;                # User clicked on bar area, move by 10.
  }
  setit($hash);
}

# Set scrollbars and everything as appropriate.  Takes a hash as an
# argument, processes its value, and sets things up.

sub setit {
  my $hash = shift @_;
  my $value = \$hash->{value};

  # Do some sanity checks.  Strip off a fractional part, make sure
  # between 0 and 255.
```

Continued

Listing 24-3 *(continued)*

```perl
$$value = int $$value;
$$value = 255 if ($$value > 255);
$$value = 0 if ($$value < 0);

# Update the scroll bar.  Note the scrollbar needs its values in
# fractions.

$hash->{scrollbar}->set($$value / 255, $$value / 255);
UpdateColorLabel();
}

# Update the color label at the bottom of the screen.  Show the color
# string, suitable for use in HTML and X, and set the background
# to that color.

sub UpdateColorLabel {
  return unless ($areas->{red} &&
                 $areas->{green} &&
                 $areas->{blue});

  my $colorstring = sprintf('#%02x%02x%02x',
                            $areas->{red}->{value},
                            $areas->{green}->{value},
                            $areas->{blue}->{value});
  my $fg = $dtextfg;

  if ($fg eq 'inverse') {
    $fg = sprintf('#%02x%02x%02x',
                  $areas->{red}->{value} ^ 0xFF,
                  $areas->{green}->{value} ^ 0xFF,
                  $areas->{blue}->{value} ^ 0xFF);
  }

  $colorlabel->configure(-background => $colorstring,
                         -text => $colorstring,
                         -foreground => $fg);
}

sub CreateMenus {
  my $w = shift @_;

  my $f = $w->Frame(-relief => 'groove',
                    -borderwidth => 2)
            ->pack(-expand => 0, -fill => 'both');
```

```
###################################################
# Program menu

my $m = $f->Menubutton(text => 'Program',
                       -underline => 0)
  ->pack(side => 'left', padx => 2);

$m->command(-label => 'Exit',
            -underline => 1,
            -command => sub { $w->destroy}
            );

###################################################
# Options menu

$m = $f->Menubutton(text => 'Options', -underline => 0)
      ->pack(side => 'left', -padx => 2);

my $m2 = $m->cascade(-label => 'Demo Text Foreground', -underline => 1);
$m2->radiobutton(-label => "Black",
                 -variable => \$dtextfg,
                 -value => '#000000',
                 -command => \&UpdateColorLabel);
$m2->radiobutton(-label => "White",
                 -variable => \$dtextfg,
                 -value => '#FFFFFF',
                 -command => \&UpdateColorLabel);
$m2->radiobutton(-label => "Inverse",
                 -variable => \$dtextfg,
                 -value => 'inverse',
                 -command => \&UpdateColorLabel);
}
```

When you run this code, you'll notice that things are aligned much better. In fact, the program finally starts to look nice and sharp. Figure 24-5 shows the program in action after the change to the grid geometry manager.

Special Concerns

Perl/Tk programs do have some unique concerns that do not necessarily affect non-GUI programs. One of them is that calling fork() from inside such a program can be somewhat tricky. After you fork, you need to be sure that only one process will continue on with the GUI interface. Both cannot, although it is possible for one to open a separate X connection. In general, if at all possible, you should fork before doing any interaction with Tk.

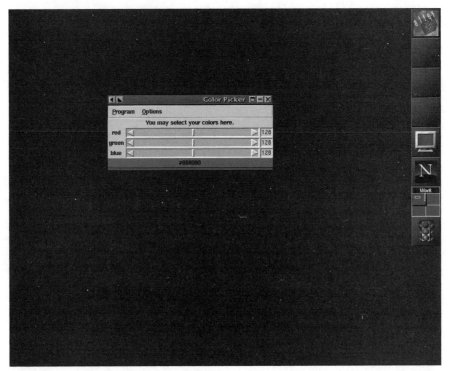

Figure 24-5: Sample with grid manager

Another concern lies with updating the interface. The only time that Tk can read input from the user or can update the on-screen elements is when it is in MainLoop. This has not posed any problems thus far. However, if you have a task that takes a long time, which can generally be defined as more than one tenth of a second, you need to ensure that this does not block Tk updates from taking place.

One way to do this is to explicitly call Tk's update subroutine, which is documented in the Tk::Widget(3pm) manpage. If you call this in the middle of your lengthy computation, you will allow all outstanding items to be processed.

Another option is to fork before initializing any Tk items. You can then set up a pipe or some other communication device between a process that does computation and one that handles the interface. This will probably be the best-performing option but will also be more complex to implement.

SpecTcl/SpecPerl

So far, interfaces to programs have been designed manually. There is also a program called SpecTcl that will enable you to lay out your interfaces from a graphical interface. This program does not necessarily ship with distributions; you can download it for free at http://www.scriptics.com/products/spectcl/.

When you invoke SpecTcl, you are first presented with a box asking about the language. Pick Perl. Then you get an empty screen as shown in Figure 24-6.

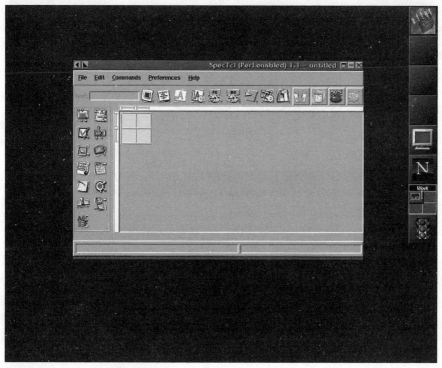

Figure 24-6: SpecTcl designer

After this, you simply drag items onto the grid. You can add your own columns or work with the ones there already. By simply dragging a few things onto the screen, you can create something that looks like Figure 24-7.

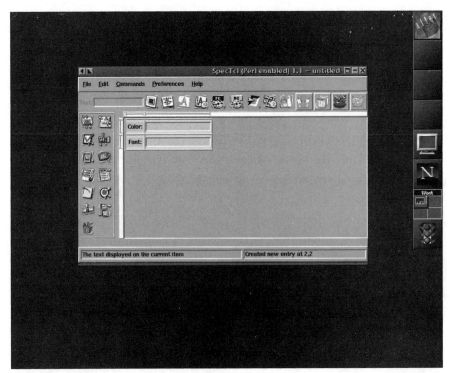

Figure 24-7: SpecTcl working on a program

Now, to generate the Perl code, select Build from the Commands menu. SpecTcl may ask you to save your interface; go ahead and do so. Now examine the Perl code. The result looks similar to Listing 24-4.

Listing 24-4: **Sample SpecTcl output**

```
# interface generated by SpecTcl (Perl enabled) version 1.1
# from /home/jgoerzen/t/SpecTcl1.1/bin/testinterface.ui
# For use with Tk400.202, using the gridbag geometry manager

sub testinterface_ui {
    my($root) = @_;

    # widget creation

    my($label_1) = $root->Label (
```

```perl
            -text => 'Color:',
    );
    my($entry_1) = $root->Entry (
    );
    my($label_2) = $root->Label (
            -text => 'Font:',
    );
    my($entry_2) = $root->Entry (
    );

    # Geometry management

    $label_1->grid(
        -in => $root,
        -column => '1',
        -row => '1'
    );
    $entry_1->grid(
        -in => $root,
        -column => '2',
        -row => '1'
    );
    $label_2->grid(
        -in => $root,
        -column => '1',
        -row => '2'
    );
    $entry_2->grid(
        -in => $root,
        -column => '2',
        -row => '2'
    );

    # Resize behavior management

    # container $root (rows)
    $root->gridRowconfigure(1, -weight  => 0, -minsize  => 30);
    $root->gridRowconfigure(2, -weight  => 0, -minsize  => 30);

    # container $root (columns)
    $root->gridColumnconfigure(1, -weight => 0, -minsize => 30);
    $root->gridColumnconfigure(2, -weight => 0, -minsize => 30);

    # additional interface code
    # end additional interface code

}
```

Notice that this code, although slightly more verbose and a bit less readable than the code generated before, is nonetheless quite readable and useful. You can build a good interface quickly using it.

Summary

In this chapter, you learned about writing graphical programs with Perl/Tk. Specifically, the following material was covered:

✦ Graphical user interfaces (GUIs) can be great tools to minimize learning curves and present things in new ways.

✦ However, GUIs are more complex to write and more resource-intensive to run.

✦ X has several layers for graphical programs, which may span multiple machines.

✦ Perl/Tk uses event-based programs, which deliver events to you instead of requiring you to specifically check for individual events.

✦ Objects in Perl/Tk are arranged hierarchically and have individual attributes.

✦ Frames can be used to organize some widgets separately from others.

✦ Several different geometry managers are available for your use.

✦ You can also use SpecTcl to create Perl/Tk dialog boxes and simple interfaces.

✦   ✦   ✦

Building GUIs with Gnome

One of the largest and most famous programming projects in recent years has been Gnome, the GNU Network Object Model Environment. *Gnome* is designed to create a complete environment: both a programming environment for developers and a consistent application environment for users. By providing a powerful, stable, and versatile environment, the idea is that programmers can develop applications quicker (because the system provides more functionality in its libraries) and users can have a less steep learning curve because all the Gnome applications will have similar interfaces. In addition to these features, Gnome supports drag-and-drop, inter-application communication, object embedding, session management, and many more features.

All of the Gnome features are based entirely on Free Software, as is Perl/Tk, which means that you can use it in your programs without having to worry about paying any license fees. For more details on Gnome, visit `http://www.gnome.org`.

Whereas Gnome has bindings for several different languages, including Perl, Gnome's primary language — and the one in which it is most mature — is C. Therefore, I'll use C as the programming language for Gnome in this chapter.

Gnome Components

Gnome is a framework for providing common services for applications relating to a GUI. These may not necessarily be strictly GUI items; for instance, there are configuration file parsers, command-line argument handlers, HTML parsers, and so on.

You'll find that many of the lower-level GUI interactions are done by using GTK, which is the toolkit library upon which Gnome is built. The purpose of GTK (the Gimp Toolkit) is roughly analogous to that of Tk in the Perl/Tk system discussed in Chapter 24: it creates windows, handles events, and so on.

GTK uses a library called the GDK (for the Drawing Kit) to handle the interactions with X. All these libraries, in turn, use glib for some basic features for portability.

The GTK/GDK libraries are based upon lower-level X libraries. To help you make sense of all of this, Gnome provides some scripts to help. Many Gnome applications elect to use GNU autoconf and automake; for details on those tools, see the info documentation for them on your system.

First Steps

Listing 25-1 shows a Gnome program that displays the same type of interface as the Tk program in Chapter 24, "GUIs with Perl/Tk." Because the build for Gnome applications can be tricky, I've included the following Makefile that you can use to build the programs in this chapter:

```
CC=gcc
CFLAGS := -Wall $(shell gnome-config --cflags gnomeui)
LINK := $(CC) $(shell gnome-config --libs gnomeui)

all: $(PROGRAM)
    @if [ "x$(PROGRAM)" = "x" ]; then \
        echo "To compile, use make PROGRAM=name" ;\
        echo "Where name is the executable; eg ch25-1" ;\
        /bin/false ;\
    fi

$(PROGRAM): $(PROGRAM).o
    $(LINK) -o $@ $<

$(PROGRAM).o: $(PROGRAM).c
    $(CC) $(CFLAGS) -c -o $@ $<

clean:
    -rm $(PROGRAM) $(PROGRAM).o
```

To use the Makefile in the preceding example to compile your code, you use make PROGRAM=ch25-1 for instance, to compile ch25-1.c into the ch25-1 executable.

Note   Listing 25-1 is available online.

Listing 25-1: **Simple Gnome example: ch25-1.c**

```c
#include <gnome.h>

void exitbutton(void);

int main(int argc, char *argv[]) {
  GtkWidget *window, *frame, *pack, *label, *button;

  gnome_init("ch25-1", "1.0", argc, argv);

  /* Create the window. */
  window = gnome_app_new("ch25-1", "Hi!");
  frame = gtk_frame_new(NULL);
  gnome_app_set_contents(GNOME_APP(window), frame);

  /* Create the widget packer. */

  pack = gtk_packer_new();
  gtk_container_add(GTK_CONTAINER(frame), pack);

  /* The main label. */

  label = gtk_label_new("Hello from Gnome!");
  gtk_packer_add_defaults(GTK_PACKER(pack), label, GTK_SIDE_TOP,
            GTK_ANCHOR_CENTER,
            0);

  /* The button. */

  button = gtk_button_new_with_label("Exit");
  gtk_signal_connect(GTK_OBJECT(button), "clicked",
            GTK_SIGNAL_FUNC(exitbutton), NULL);
  gtk_packer_add_defaults(GTK_PACKER(pack), button, GTK_SIDE_TOP,
            GTK_ANCHOR_CENTER, 0);

  gtk_widget_show_all(window);

  gtk_main();

  return 0;
}

void exitbutton(void) {
  gtk_main_quit();
}
```

Here's a look at how this application works. It's essentially the same as the first Perl/Tk program but because of Gnome, it all looks a bit more complex. You begin by initializing the application; the arguments to `gnome_init()` include an application name, a version, and the argument count and argument list passed in to `main()`.

Next, you create the main window (like MainWindow in Tk). You first call `gnome_app_new()`; again, the first parameter is the application name. The second parameter is the default window title. Inside the application, you need to create a contents frame, which the next two lines do.

Now, use the widget packer. I select the `packer` packer, which is essentially a port of the default packer from Tk. A new packer is created, and it is added as a sub-widget of the frame. Next, a label widget is created, and packed. Notice the similarity in the arguments to the packer to those for the one in Tk.

A button is created with an Exit label. After that, I'll install an event handler — confusingly named signal (which has nothing to do with Linux signals). This causes the Exit button function to be called when someone clicks that button, in a manner similar to the command binding in Tk. The button is connected, the widgets are displayed, and the main event loop is invoked.

Overall, the structure of this program is indeed quite similar to the Tk version, although Tk takes care of more of the details automatically (see Figure 25-1).

Figure 25-1: The sample Gnome application is running in the center of the screen.

As with X and Tk, Gnome apps have widgets that are in essence windows, although Gnome doesn't necessarily call them that. In the next section, I'll introduce a new top-level window.

> **Note** The examples in this chapter were written and tested with Gnome libraries version 1.0.54. Gnome can sometimes change rapidly; if your system does not have libraries of at least that version and you are experiencing trouble with any example, you probably need to update your Gnome system to a newer version.

Drawing Windows

In Perl/Tk, you saw how you can create new top-level windows with the widget library. You can extend this program two ways: first, so that you can create a new top-level window, and second, so that the program recognizes the window manager close event. Listing 25-2 shows the required code.

> **Note** Listing 25-2 is available online.

Listing 25-2: **Recognizing a close event: ch25-2.c**

```
#include <gnome.h>

void exitbutton(void);

int main(int argc, char *argv[]) {
  GtkWidget *window, *frame, *pack, *label, *button;

  gnome_init("ch25-1", "1.0", argc, argv);

  /* Create the window. */
  window = gnome_app_new("ch25-2", "Hi!");
  frame = gtk_frame_new(NULL);
  gnome_app_set_contents(GNOME_APP(window), frame);

  /* Create the widget packer. */

  pack = gtk_packer_new();
  gtk_container_add(GTK_CONTAINER(frame), pack);

  /* The main label. */

  label = gtk_label_new("Hello from Gnome!");
  gtk_packer_add_defaults(GTK_PACKER(pack), label, GTK_SIDE_TOP,
                          GTK_ANCHOR_CENTER,
                          0);
```

Continued

Listing 25-2: *(continued)*

```
  /* The button. */

  button = gtk_button_new_with_label("Exit");
  gtk_signal_connect(GTK_OBJECT(button), "clicked",
                     GTK_SIGNAL_FUNC(exitbutton), NULL);
  gtk_packer_add_defaults(GTK_PACKER(pack), button, GTK_SIDE_TOP,
                          GTK_ANCHOR_CENTER, 0);

  gtk_signal_connect(GTK_OBJECT(window), "delete_event",
                     GTK_SIGNAL_FUNC(exitbutton), NULL);

  gtk_widget_show_all(window);

  gtk_main();

  return 0;
}

void exitbutton(void) {
  static int displayed = 0;
  GtkWidget *appwindow, *top, *button, *blabel, *frame;

  if (displayed) return;      /* Don't display twice. */
    displayed++;

  appwindow = gnome_app_new("ch25-2", "Goodbye");
  frame = gtk_frame_new(NULL);
  gnome_app_set_contents(GNOME_APP(appwindow), frame);
  top = gtk_packer_new();
  gtk_container_add(GTK_CONTAINER(frame), top);

  /* Now the label. */

  gtk_packer_add_defaults(GTK_PACKER(top),
              gtk_label_new("You are now leaving the"
                            "demonstration program."),
                GTK_SIDE_TOP, GTK_ANCHOR_CENTER, 0);

  /* And the button.  Pack the label explicitly though. */

  gtk_packer_add_defaults(GTK_PACKER(top),
                          button = gtk_button_new(),
                          GTK_SIDE_TOP, GTK_ANCHOR_CENTER, 0);

  blabel = gtk_label_new("OK");
  gtk_container_add(GTK_CONTAINER(button), blabel);

  gtk_signal_connect(GTK_OBJECT(button), "clicked",
```

```
                         GTK_SIGNAL_FUNC(gtk_main_quit), NULL);
    gtk_signal_connect(GTK_OBJECT(appwindow), "delete_event",
                         GTK_SIGNAL_FUNC(gtk_main_quit), NULL);

    gtk_widget_show_all(appwindow);
}
```

The changes made to the code in Listing 25-2 include the handling of the
delete_event that occurs when someone clicks the Close button in the
window manager for the application. In the exitbutton() function, you see
a more concise method of packing some things; for instance, there is no
separate variable for the main label, more analogous to the Perl/Tk version (
see Figure 25-2).

Figure 25-2: You can see the two windows from ch25-2.c in this screenshot.

I'll move on to a version that implements the color picker. Because GTK already
comes with a color picker widget, that saves a lot of effort. In fact, its predefined
color picker is quite a bit nicer than the one that was built from scratch in the
sample Perl/Tk program. Listing 25-3 presents an example program that uses
the GTK color selector.

Note Listing 25-3 is available online.

Listing 25-3: **Example with GTK color selector, ch25-3.c**

```c
#include <gnome.h>

void exitbutton(void);

GnomeUIInfo FileMenu[] = {
  GNOMEUIINFO_MENU_EXIT_ITEM(exitbutton, NULL),
  GNOMEUIINFO_END
};

GnomeUIInfo MainMenu[] = {
  GNOMEUIINFO_MENU_FILE_TREE(FileMenu),
  GNOMEUIINFO_END
};


int main(int argc, char *argv[]) {
  GtkWidget *window, *frame;

  gnome_init("ch25-3", "1.0", argc, argv);

  /* Create the window. */
  window = gnome_app_new("ch25-1", "Hi!");
  gnome_app_create_menus_with_data(GNOME_APP(window), MainMenu, window);
  frame = gtk_frame_new(NULL);
  gnome_app_set_contents(GNOME_APP(window), frame);

  gtk_container_add(GTK_CONTAINER(frame), gtk_color_selection_new());


  gtk_widget_show_all(window);

  gtk_main();

  return 0;
}

void exitbutton(void) {
  static int displayed = 0;
  GtkWidget *appwindow, *top, *button, *blabel, *frame;

  if (displayed) return;    /* Don't display twice. */
  displayed++;

  appwindow = gnome_app_new("ch25-3", "Goodbye");
  frame = gtk_frame_new(NULL);
  gnome_app_set_contents(GNOME_APP(appwindow), frame);
```

```
       top = gtk_packer_new();
       gtk_container_add(GTK_CONTAINER(frame), top);

       /* Now the label. */

       gtk_packer_add_defaults(GTK_PACKER(top),
                               gtk_label_new("You are now leaving the"
                                             "demonstration program."),
                               GTK_SIDE_TOP, GTK_ANCHOR_CENTER, 0);

       /* And the button.  Pack the label explicitly though. */

       gtk_packer_add_defaults(GTK_PACKER(top),
                               button = gtk_button_new(),
                               GTK_SIDE_TOP, GTK_ANCHOR_CENTER, 0);

       blabel = gtk_label_new("OK");
       gtk_container_add(GTK_CONTAINER(button), blabel);

       gtk_signal_connect(GTK_OBJECT(button), "clicked",
                          GTK_SIGNAL_FUNC(gtk_main_quit), NULL);
       gtk_signal_connect(GTK_OBJECT(appwindow), "delete_event",
                          GTK_SIGNAL_FUNC(gtk_main_quit), NULL);

       gtk_widget_show_all(appwindow);
}
```

This program uses the GtkColorSelect() widget as well as a menu with some generic menu entries that GTK provides for use here. Figure 25-3 shows this code in action, with a tearoff of the File menu.

Miscellaneous Gnome Notes

Gnome is a large and rapidly evolving system consisting of tens of thousands of lines of source code. Its documentation is currently rather sparse; with Gnome, one of the best things you can do is learn by example from any of the hundreds of existing Gnome applications. Because the source code is available for so many Linux programs, you can look at the sources for these programs or for Gnome itself to see how it works.

The header files for Gnome and GTK also are useful for you to learn about Gnome's functions and the structure of its macros. Another resource is the (current prerelease) Glade interface designer, which is used to help you design the GUI for your program — which happens to be the part that Gnome is primarily involved in.

You can learn about Gnome and the current status of the various libraries, widgets, and code that are commonly used with it by looking at the Gnome homepage at http://www.gnome.org.

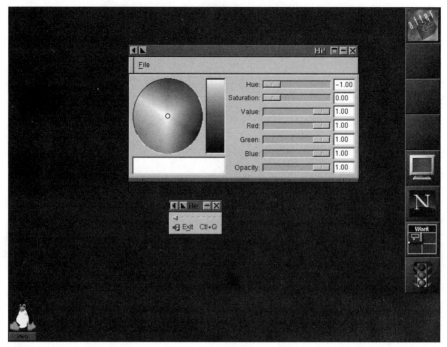

Figure 25-3: Here you can see the color selector as well as a torn-off menu.

Summary

In this chapter, I introduced you to Gnome. Specifically, I discussed:

✦ Gnome includes a widget set (GTK) and an object environment for your programs.

✦ GTK and Tk have many similarities because both are primarily designed for X.

✦ Because building Gnome programs is complex, programmers almost always use a Makefile or an autoconf system.

✦ Gnome uses widget packers as does Tk; the examples in this chapter used the Packer geometry manager.

✦ Gnome and GTK have many features ready for your use, such as color pickers and menu options.

✦ Gnome's documentation is sparse, but examining code and the information at the Gnome website is a good way to learn about the system.

✦   ✦   ✦

Putting It All Together

Archiving and Collaboration with CVS

You may sometimes find that there is a need to keep historical versions of your software around, or to coordinate development between multiple programmers. CVS (Concurrent Versions System) is designed to address both needs. In this chapter, you will learn the basics of CVS, how to configure CVS, daily usage of the software, managing tags and branches, using CVS on a network, and some special hints for CVS usage.

Introducing CVS

As software projects get larger, managing them can become more difficult. Teams of developers need to be coordinated, and each one might need to keep a personal copy of the files in a project for development work. Changes need to be synchronized so that one developer's work doesn't overwrite another's. When a release is imminent, the code may fork; some developers might be working on perfecting the release, and others on adding new features for the next release. However, eventually you might want to merge some changes from the release fork back into the development fork.

Another problem is with historical access. Sometimes, you might notice a bug that was introduced somewhere along the line, and you may need to go back weeks, months, or even years to find pristine code without the bug. This can often be difficult, involving painstaking and time-consuming restore off of magnetic tape backups. Sometimes it may be even impossible.

On top of all of this, add problems that can occur when developers work on their own machines and must somehow communicate changes over the network. Problems also can occur when users want to disconnect from the network for a time to work on code, and then commit changes when they return—for instance, to work on a laptop while on a trip. The changes may conflict with others, and nobody may ever know.

Enter *CVS*, the Concurrent Versions System. CVS is designed to address all these problems. The basic idea around CVS is that whenever a developer makes changes to the source, these changes should be checked in to the CVS repository. This repository holds the master copy of the code, and deltas (or diffs) representing historic information back to when the file was first created. The repository can be on a networked computer somewhere; it doesn't have to be local.

CVS enables you to keep your own development tree up-to-date with the repository. You do this by committing your changes to the repository and updating your own tree from the repository. If there is ever a conflict, CVS provides conflict resolution tools to help migrate changes in.

CVS also supports branches, enabling the code to be forked. Moreover, it also has support to merge these branches back together at a later date, again with conflict resolution tools. It has support to enable you to fetch a source tree suitable for product release with a single command, and to enable you to check out as much or as little of the code as you want.

With CVS, you can receive the current version of code, or any version committed in the entire history of the code. You can identify these versions on a file-by-file basis. You can retrieve diffs (a report summarizing the differences between two files) between any two versions of code, both on a file-by-file basis and on an aggregate entire-tree basis. In short, CVS is your friend!

Even if you are not working in a large development team, CVS has benefits. Although the conflict resolution probably will not benefit you if you are programming by yourself, the history features certainly can. If you want to make some experimental changes to the code, make a branch. If the changes don't work out, you can simply forget about the branch and go back to the main code—but the branch is still there for you to look at later to see exactly what went wrong. Or, if the changes work, you can merge the branch back into the main branch.

CVS stores all of this data in a compact, yet efficient, manner. It does not keep an entire copy of each version of the file. Rather, it simply records the changes that occurred between each version. This enables CVS to compute, and give you, any arbitrary version of the file—or to easily compare any two versions. It also saves tremendously on disk space.

To use CVS, you'll need a few pieces of software. First, you'll need RCS (Revision Control System), upon which CVS is based. Most distributions should come with this already; if yours does not, you can download it from `ftp.gnu.org` in the directory /pub/gnu; the filename will be something like rcs-5.7.tar.gz.

After you get RCS, you'll need CVS. Again, most Linux distributions should ship with it. If yours does not, you may download it yourself at `http://www.cyclic.com/`. Both RCS and CVS are licensed under the GNU General Public License.

If you intend to use the optional network transport, you may need some additional software. CVS can use rsh or its built-in server, cvs-pserver. However, something like ssh may be more secure, depending on your network and needs. This optional software is not required to get a basic CVS installation functional, but can be nice if you want to use CVS's network features.

The first thing that you have to do when you set up CVS is to establish a repository, which I'll cover in the next section. The repository holds the data from the CVS program itself, which consists of your files, their source code, and entire history. When you commit changes, the repository is updated, and when you check out code, it comes from the repository. CVS fetches the files for you and creates them in your directory where you can work with them privately. When you want to put your changes into the repository, you issue a commit request, which merges in your changes in.

Setting Up a Repository

Before you can use CVS, you must set up your repository. For now, I'll assume that you are the only one accessing it; I'll cover multiple users later.

Before you invoke CVS for the first time, you need to set up your environment. This means simply setting the `CVSROOT` variable. Assuming that you'll create a directory in your home directory named cvsroot, you can set the variable as follows:

```
$ export CVSROOT=$HOME/cvsroot
```

You'll probably want to add this to your .profile file such that it will be set automatically whenever you log in.

Tip   If you are using csh instead of sh or Bash, you can use `setenv CVSROOT=$HOME/cvsroot` instead of the `export` command above, and add it to your .cshrc instead of your .profile.

Next, create the directory:

```
$ mkdir cvsroot
```

You'll also want it to be protected from outside readers. You can accomplish this with the chmod command:

```
$ chmod 700 cvsroot
```

Now you must initialize the CVS repository. Do that with a quick CVS command:

```
$ cvs init
```

CVS calls an editor on a regular basis for you to enter logs and so on. If you don't have a default editor set, this probably will call either vi or ae. You can change the default by setting the EDITOR environment variable, as follows:

```
$ export EDITOR=emacs
```

As before, you might want to put this into your .profile file. That way, it is set automatically for future uses.

That's it! Your repository is now ready for use. Pretty easy!

Using CVS Daily

Now that you have created a repository, you're ready to use it. The first thing to do is to import a directory tree. This is done, naturally enough, with the cvs import command.

Suppose I have a directory with some various files. It doesn't matter what files, as long as they're something like source code. CVS can deal with almost any type of file, including binary files if so configured, but for now I'll focus on source files.

Here is my directory's contents. I copied a few examples of source code from earlier chapters in this book into the directory for example purposes:

```
$ ls -l
total 18
-rw-rw-r--  1 jgoerzen jgoerzen   637 Oct  5 10:22 ch10-1.c
-rw-rw-r--  1 jgoerzen jgoerzen  1141 Oct  5 10:22 ch10-2.c
-rw-rw-r--  1 jgoerzen jgoerzen   191 Oct  5 10:22 ch10-3.c
-rw-rw-r--  1 jgoerzen jgoerzen  1141 Oct  5 10:22 ch10-4.c
-rw-rw-r--  1 jgoerzen jgoerzen  3533 Oct  5 10:22 ch11-1.c
-rwxrwxr-x  1 jgoerzen jgoerzen  1276 Oct  5 10:22 ch11-2.pl
-rw-rw-r--  1 jgoerzen jgoerzen   639 Oct  5 10:22 ch11-3.c
-rw-rw-r--  1 jgoerzen jgoerzen   728 Oct  5 10:22 ch11-4.c
```

```
-rw-rw-r--   1 jgoerzen jgoerzen      318 Oct  5 10:22 ch12-1.c
-rw-rw-r--   1 jgoerzen jgoerzen      283 Oct  5 10:22 ch12-2.c
-rw-rw-r--   1 jgoerzen jgoerzen      464 Oct  5 10:22 ch12-3.c
-rw-rw-r--   1 jgoerzen jgoerzen     1013 Oct  5 10:22 ch12-4.c
```

Now it's time to import these into the CVS repository. The command is `cvs import` and it takes three arguments. The first is the path that the files should be placed under in the CVS repository. The second is a vendor tag, which can be used for branching the code at the point of import. The final is a release tag, which can be used to simply check out files at this version. For our purposes, these final options probably don't matter. Here's a command I'm using:

```
$ cvs import example ORIGINAL START
```

When you run that command, CVS brings up an editor for you to make a log entry. I made an entry simply saying **Initial import**. Save this file and then CVS will proceed.

```
N example/ch10-1.c
N example/ch10-2.c
N example/ch10-3.c
N example/ch10-4.c
N example/ch11-1.c
N example/ch11-2.pl
N example/ch11-3.c
N example/ch11-4.c
N example/ch12-1.c
N example/ch12-2.c
N example/ch12-3.c
N example/ch12-4.c

No conflicts created by this import
```

CVS informs you that all those files are new to the archive (N). Now you can check out the repository. Move the existing directory out of the way or change into some other path and run:

```
$ cvs checkout example
cvs checkout: Updating example
U example/ch10-1.c
U example/ch10-2.c
U example/ch10-3.c
U example/ch10-4.c
U example/ch11-1.c
U example/ch11-2.pl
U example/ch11-3.c
U example/ch11-4.c
U example/ch12-1.c
U example/ch12-2.c
U example/ch12-3.c
U example/ch12-4.c
```

CVS pulls the files down from the repository and populates your local directory with them. This is where you can now do your development work. First, type cd example to move into the example directory. Now, I'll step through the process as you modify a file. I'll make a small change to the ch12-4.c file to illustrate the process. I simply added a comment at the top of the file and saved the code. To make the change back into the repository, you simply run cvs commit. As before, it will ask you for a log entry. Save the log entry and exit your editor. You can then see something like this on your terminal:

```
$ cvs commit
cvs commit: Examining .
Checking in ch12-4.c;
/home/jgoerzen/cvsroot/example/ch12-4.c,v  <--  ch12-4.c
new revision: 1.2; previous revision: 1.1
done
```

CVS has checked in your changes to the repository. If you're curious, you can look at the logs for the file as follows:

```
$ cvs log ch12-4.c

RCS file: /home/jgoerzen/cvsroot/example/ch12-4.c,v
Working file: ch12-4.c
head: 1.2
branch:
locks: strict
access list:
symbolic names:
        START: 1.1.1.1
        ORIGINAL: 1.1.1
keyword substitution: kv
total revisions: 3;     selected revisions: 3
description:
----------------------------
revision 1.2
date: 1999/10/05 15:39:01;  author: jgoerzen;  state: Exp;  lines: +2 -0
Added a comment at the top  of the file.
----------------------------
revision 1.1
date: 1999/10/05 15:34:00;  author: jgoerzen;  state: Exp;
branches:  1.1.1;
Initial revision
----------------------------
revision 1.1.1.1
date: 1999/10/05 15:34:00;  author: jgoerzen;  state: Exp;  lines: +0 -0
Initial import.
=============================================================================
```

The output shows you the different versions, when they were created, who made changes, and what changed between them according to the developer. You can also compare the file in your current directory to any particular version in the repository. For instance, I could run this command:

```
$ cvs diff -r 1.1 -d -u ch12-4.c
Index: ch12-4.c
===================================================================
RCS file: /home/jgoerzen/cvsroot/example/ch12-4.c,v
retrieving revision 1.1
retrieving revision 1.2
diff -d -u -r1.1 -r1.2
--- ch12-4.c    1999/10/05 15:34:00    1.1
+++ ch12-4.c    1999/10/05 15:39:01    1.2
@@ -1,3 +1,5 @@
+/* This is the fourth program in Chapter 12. */
+
 #include <stdio.h>
 #include <unistd.h>
 #include <stdarg.h>
```

In this case, I asked CVS to compare the contents of the file ch12-4.c in the current directory to version 1.1 (-r 1.1) of the file in the repository. The result shows that I added two lines at the very top of the file, one with a comment, and one blank line. The -d -u are arguments to the diff program that CVS calls, which asks for a thorough comparison with the unified diff (a variant of a standard diff that is easier to read) output format.

Another thing that you can do is a cvs update operation. This brings in changes that others might have made such that your local directory is up-to-date with respect to the repository. Here's a sample invocation:

```
$ cvs update
cvs update: Updating .
U ch11-2.pl
```

This shows that the local directory had one file that was out-of-date (ch11-2.pl), and that this file was brought up-to-date. If there were conflicts—for instance, if you had modified the file and someone else had committed a change before you could—CVS will inform you of this and show you what is in conflict.

You also can add new files to your existing directory. For instance, if I want to add a file named demo.pl to this directory, first I need to copy it into my local directory. Then, I'd run this:

```
$ cvs add demo.pl
cvs add: scheduling file `demo.pl' for addition
cvs add: use 'cvs commit' to add this file permanently
```

```
$ cvs commit
cvs commit: Examining .
RCS file: /home/jgoerzen/cvsroot/example/demo.pl,v
done
Checking in demo.pl;
/home/jgoerzen/cvsroot/example/demo.pl,v  <--  demo.pl
initial revision: 1.1
done
```

If I later decide to delete this file, the procedure is similar. First, I delete the file from my own directory. Then, I use cvs remove to mark it as removed from the repository:

```
$ rm demo.pl
$ cvs remove demo.pl
cvs remove: scheduling `demo.pl' for removal
cvs remove: use 'cvs commit' to remove this file permanently
$ cvs commit
cvs commit: Examining .
Removing demo.pl;
/home/jgoerzen/cvsroot/example/demo.pl,v  <--  demo.pl
new revision: delete; previous revision: 1.1
done
```

Note You can still retrieve the historical versions of a file from the repository even after it has been removed; CVS never destroys historical information. If you want to rename a file, simply copy it to the new file name, add that file, remove the old one, and commit the changes.

Using Tags and Branches

As you may have noticed, each file in CVS has its own version number. This number is separate from any other files in the repository.

Sometimes, it is useful to refer to a certain version of the files in aggregate. For instance, you might want to refer to the state of the files with version 2.0 beta of a product that was released. If you know the precise date of that release, you can get the files that way, but there's an easier way—tags.

Tags

You can use tags to mark your files. They serve as a sort of checkpoint, enabling you to later refer to the state of files at that point by a single symbolic name. To assign a tag, simply use a command like this:

```
$ cvs tag RELEASE_2_0_BETA
cvs tag: Tagging .
T ch10-1.c
T ch10-2.c
```

```
T ch10-3.c
T ch10-4.c
T ch11-1.c
T ch11-2.pl
T ch11-3.c
T ch11-4.c
T ch12-1.c
T ch12-2.c
T ch12-3.c
T ch12-4.c
```

Later, if you ever want to retrieve the code as it was when your 2.0 beta release occurred, you can simply use `cvs checkout -r RELEASE_2_0_BETA`. Moreover, you can use this symbolic tag anywhere else you might use `-r` to specify a particular revision—with a `diff` or a `log` command, for instance.

You can view the tags for any particular file in the `cvs log` screen. For instance, after tagging my files, I can see this:

```
$ cvs log ch12-4.c

RCS file: /home/jgoerzen/cvsroot/example/ch12-4.c,v
Working file: ch12-4.c
head: 1.2
branch:
locks: strict
access list:
symbolic names:
        RELEASE_2_0_BETA: 1.2
        START: 1.1.1.1
        ORIGINAL: 1.1.1
keyword substitution: kv
total revisions: 3;      selected revisions: 3
description:
```

After this, the log screen continues to list the changes committed to this file. In the preceding sample output, you can see there are three tags—one created now and two created by `cvs import`.

Branches

Branches in CVS are a way for you to fork your code such that development can continue without touching the master tree. This has advantages, for instance, if you want to do an experimental rewrite of the code. Branches enable you to do this without modifying the main branch of code. This way, others can continue working on the existing code without any interference from a rewrite. Also, if the rewrite doesn't work out, the branch simply can be ignored and development can proceed as usual with the main branch.

To create a branch, you use the same tag command as earlier, but add a `-b` option to it, like so:

```
$ cvs tag -b DEVEL_BRANCH
cvs tag: Tagging .
T ch10-1.c
T ch10-2.c
T ch10-3.c
T ch10-4.c
T ch11-1.c
T ch11-2.pl
T ch11-3.c
T ch11-4.c
T ch12-1.c
T ch12-2.c
T ch12-3.c
T ch12-4.c
```

Now, you can check out code in this branch. Note that your existing directory will not be using this branch; the tag command effects only the repository:

```
$ cvs co -r DEVEL_BRANCH example
cvs checkout: Updating example
U example/ch10-1.c
U example/ch10-2.c
U example/ch10-3.c
U example/ch10-4.c
U example/ch11-1.c
U example/ch11-2.pl
U example/ch11-3.c
U example/ch11-4.c
U example/ch12-1.c
U example/ch12-2.c
U example/ch12-3.c
U example/ch12-4.c
```

Now that you have checked out the branch, you can make changes to it without affecting the main branch. In this example, I've modified a file, and I'll check in the changes as follows:

```
$ cvs commit
cvs commit: Examining .
Checking in ch12-4.c;
/home/jgoerzen/cvsroot/example/ch12-4.c,v  <--  ch12-4.c
new revision: 1.2.2.1; previous revision: 1.2
done
```

With CVS, every number in an odd position is a branch number and every number in an even position is a file version number. Therefore, in version 1.2, the first digit is a branch number (1), and the second is a file version number. By checking something in on the branch, it creates verison 1.2.2.1. That is, version 1 under the branch.

If you later want to merge the branch's changes back into the main tree, first check out the main branch (use `cvs checkout` with no options). Then use the `-j` option to merge in the changes:

```
$ cvs update -jDEVEL_BRANCH
cvs update: Updating .
RCS file: /home/jgoerzen/cvsroot/example/ch12-4.c,v
retrieving revision 1.2
retrieving revision 1.2.2.1
Merging differences between 1.2 and 1.2.2.1 into ch12-4.c
```

The update command retrieves the differences from the branch and adds them to the files in your current directory. Now, you need to commit the changes to the repository so that the branch's changes become effective in the main tree:

```
$ cvs commit
cvs commit: Examining .
Checking in ch12-4.c;
/home/jgoerzen/cvsroot/example/ch12-4.c,v  <--  ch12-4.c
new revision: 1.3; previous revision: 1.2
done
```

You've just reintegrated the branch onto the main development branch. Note, though, that the development can still continue separately on these two branches. At some later date, you may want to integrate them again.

Accessing the Network

Another feature of CVS is that it can enable remote access to the repository. This means that each developer can work on a separate machine, but they all can commit and fetch their code from a single central repository. CVS handles the network details completely and transparently; after it is configured, it behaves exactly as if the repository were local. You don't need to manually transfer files from one computer to another; CVS automatically takes care of whatever data transfers are necessary.

CVS can be set up in a number of different ways to allow network access. One method is to use a program such as rsh or ssh, or any other program that presents an rsh-like interface. The rsh option may be appropriate for small isolated lans, but because of the design of rsh, it can be a security hazard. Another option is an encrypting program such as ssh. This is advantageous because not only does it use a secure public key authentication system, but it also encrypts the data while in transit, meaning that it could be a good security win if the CVS server is on a remote machine somewhere that is accessed via the Internet.

Another option is to use CVS's built-in pserver. This has the advantage in that the people using it do not need to have standard Linux accounts on the CVS server. The disadvantage is that the pserver does not use a very robust security system and does not encrypt data.

I'll explain in this section how to use ssh for your networking as it generally proves to be the most secure option. If you opt to use rsh instead, the configuration is quite similar; the difference is that you must set up a .rhosts file on the server to permit connections from the client without having to provide a password.

Setting up the server

Before anyone can access the repository, you'll need to create a directory for it, as you did for the standalone installation you learned about earlier, and temporarily set your CVSROOT environment variable (on the server) to this directory.

You need to be a bit pickier about file permissions on the server. The recommended way to deal with this issue is to create a Linux group in /etc/group and place each person authorized to access the CVS repository into that group. Then, change the group on the directory and modify its permissions like so:

```
$ chgrp cvsgroup cvsroot
$ chmod 2770 cvsroot
```

The chmod command makes the directory group-readable and writable. It also sets the setgid bit in the directory itself, which means that any file placed into the directory has the same group as the directory itself, which can be used to help prevent problems later on.

Now, run cvs init on the server to set up the repository.

Generating ssh keys

I'll assume that your system administrator has already installed the ssh software on the client and the server. The first thing that you need to do is generate a public/private key pair. You do this by running ssh-keygen, like so:

```
$ ssh-keygen
Initializing random number generator...
Generating p:  .........................................++ (distance 1224)
Generating q:  ............++ (distance 202)
Computing the keys...
Testing the keys...
Key generation complete.
Enter file in which to save the key (/home/jgoerzen/.ssh/identity): Enter
Enter passphrase: Enter
Enter the same passphrase again: Enter
Your identification has been saved in /home/jgoerzen/.ssh/identity.
```

You'll be asked three questions: where to save the key, what passphrase to use, and a confirmation of the passphrase. Leave the answers to all of those blank and just press Enter. Then, you need to copy your ~/.ssh/identity.pub file over to the ~/.ssh/ authorized_keys file on the server. You can use a progam such as FTP to do this, or even scp. Make sure that the ~/.ssh directory exists on the server. You can then copy the file over with a command like this:

Caution Leaving the password blank will be OK if you are using this key only for the purposes of CVS. However, be aware that if, for any reason, your account on the client machine is cracked, an attacker may be able to get to your account on the server as well. CVS pserver uses a similar mechanism to avoid having to type in the password each time. If you prefer, you may set a password instead of leaving it blank; however, if you do, you may find CVS operations annoying since you will have to supply the password for each one.

```
$ scp ~/.ssh/identity.pub server:~/.ssh/authorized_keys
jgoerzen@server's password: Password
identity.pub              |              0 KB |   0.3 kB/s | ETA: 00:00:00 | 100%
```

You'll be prompted for your password for the server; enter it, and the file will be copied over. You can check to make sure that the procedure worked by running ssh *server*; you should be logged on to the server without requiring a password.

Your environment

Next, you need to set up your environment. This time, you'll need two environment variables. The form is like this:

```
export CVSROOT=":ext:user@server:/var/repository/path"
export CVS_RSH="ssh"
```

On the first line, replace user with your username; server with the name of the server, and /var/repository/path with the actual path to the repository on the server. After this is set (again, you'll probably want to place it into your .profile file), you are ready to use CVS! Interaction with the system is exactly the same as it would have been before, except this time, the repository is being automatically accessed via the network.

Tips and Tricks

Besides the basics that you've learned thus far in this chapter, there are some various tips and tricks that you can use with CVS to make things run just that much smoother. I'll go over several of them here; you should be able to use these tips with almost any project.

Keywords

One of the most unique features of CVS is that it can insert data into your text. It does this when you embed certain special keywords in your source. With these keywords, you automatically can have CVS put information such as file version directly into your source code. This way, when your code is used outside of CVS — on a printout, or maybe somebody has a copy of your product — you can quickly identify exactly which version of the code you are dealing with.

Table 26-1 shows a list of the available keywords.

Table 26-1 Embedded Keywords	
Keyword	**Meaning**
$Author$	Inserts the Linux username of the person that most recently updated the file.
$Date$	Inserts the date, in UTC (Coordinated Universal Time, sometimes also called GMT), of the most recent update to the file.
$Header$	Inserts the path to the file in the CVS repository, the version number of this file, the date in UTC of the last update, the Linux username of the person to make the most recent update, and the state of the file.
Id	The most commonly used form. It is the same as $Header$ but omits the full path to the file in the CVS repository, showing the filename only. Id is great because it gives you lots of information in a concise fashion.
$Name$	The name of the tag or branch under which this file was committed.
Log	Includes a log message from the most recent commit. This keyword can cause trouble in some situations, so it is best to avoid it.
$RCSfile$	The name of the file in the CVS repository.
$Revision$	The revision number of this file.
$Source$	The full path name of the file in the CVS repository.
$State$	The state of the current file.

Here is a short bit of sample code (notice that this code includes Id twice; once in the comment at the top and once in its body):

```
/* example.c
   $Id$
*/
```

```
#include <stdio.h>

int main(void) {
  printf("This is example.c $Id$\n");
  printf("Hello, world!\n");
}
```

After adding this code to the repository and committing the change, take another look at it. You'll see that CVS updated it automatically:

```
/* example.c
   $Id: example.c,v 1.1 1999/10/05 17:35:24 jgoerzen Exp $
*/

#include <stdio.h>

int main(void) {
  printf("This is example.c $Id: example.c,v 1.1 1999/10/05 17:35:24 jgoerzen
Exp $\n");
  printf("Hello, world!\n");
}
```

This program thus automatically prints out its version number each time it is run. With this mechanism, you can tell what version of a program somebody has even if they don't have the source! The output of this program, then, is:

```
This is example.c $Id: example.c,v 1.1 1999/10/05 17:35:24 jgoerzen Exp $
Hello, world!
```

In this case, you may prefer to use just $Revision$ or $Date$. That way, the end user doesn't have to sift through information that doesn't matter to anyone but your own developers, such as the last person to commit a change to the source.

Binary files

It is possible to track changes of binary files in CVS as well. However, special care needs to be taken. This is because CVS can do two things that could mess with binary files. First, it performs the keyword substitution as documented earlier. This is great for source files but could end up corrupting binary files. Second, CVS sometimes performs conversions for line endings when dealing with files, to help files work best in your environment. This, of course, can corrupt binaries.

To inhibit this behavior, CVS provides a special parameter, -kb. You *must* specify -kb when adding a binary file to the repository. When you do this, CVS no longer does anything that could, in any way, modify the contents of the file.

For instance, to add a copy of the `ls` binary to my reposotiry, I'd use this command:

```
$ cvs add -kb ls
```

After the initial add, you can deal with a file as you normally would with no special need to add `-kb`; CVS records that this is necessary and automatically uses it on your binary files after they have been added.

Using subdirectories

CVS has support for dealing with subdirectories in your code and repository. To add a new subdirectory beneath some existing code, simply use `mkdir` to create it locally, then use `cvs add` to add the directory. The directory will be added immediately and you can begin populating it with files.

The first parameter to the `cvs import` command can also be a directory tree. In this manner, you can import new code several levels deep in the repository.

Although it is not recommended, you can make directories manually in the repository by simply going to its directory and using `mkdir`. This can be a quick way to set up an infrastructure if you expect your reposotiry to be a large one.

The CVSROOT files

CVS provides some special configuration files that can customize various behaviors of CVS. To access these files, run this command:

```
$ cvs checkout CVSROOT
cvs checkout: Updating CVSROOT
U CVSROOT/checkoutlist
U CVSROOT/commitinfo
U CVSROOT/config
U CVSROOT/cvswrappers
U CVSROOT/editinfo
U CVSROOT/loginfo
U CVSROOT/modules
U CVSROOT/notify
U CVSROOT/rcsinfo
U CVSROOT/taginfo
U CVSROOT/verifymsg
```

You can find a detailed description of each of these files in the cvs(5) manpage. Most of these files are rarely used in CVS installations, but one that often can come in handy is `modules`, which I'll discuss here.

This file has many powerful options, but the basic purpose of the file is to make it easier to navigate files in large repositories. For instance, if you have a directory in your repository named projects/clients/acme/jet/engine, it is cumbersome for developers to have to use a command such as `cvs checkout projects/`

`clients/acme/jet/engine` to work on the code. It is even more annoying to have to change into several levels of directories to do so.

The modules file enables you to define names for these directories so that you can access them more easily. For instance, you might place the following line into your modules file:

```
jetengine              projects/clients/acme/jet/engine
```

This mechanism enables you to maintain your organization of the repository while at the same time making access to it convenient for your developers. Now, to access the code, one can simply run `cvs checkout jetengine` without having to specify the large path.

After you make a change to modules, or any other file in the `CVSROOT` area, you need to commit your changes. As soon as your changes are committed, they take effect.

Summary

In this chapter, you learned about the Concurrent Version System (CVS). Specifically, you learned:

✦ Problems can arise when multiple developers need to work on a single piece of code.

✦ The capability of accessing historic versions of your code can often be a valuable asset.

✦ CVS helps you manage access to your code.

✦ CVS archives every historical version of each file, which can be retrieved at any time.

✦ You need to create and initialize a repository and set an environment variable to set up CVS.

✦ You check out a copy of the files from the repository, work on them in a local directory, and then commit the changes back when working with CVS.

✦ You can create branches in CVS with `cvs tag -b`, which allow development to be forked.

✦ CVS works over the network with tools such as rsh, ssh, or CVS's own server. Of these, ssh is recommended because it is the most secure.

✦ You need to take special care when dealing with binary files in CVS.

✦ CVS can work with subdirectories, which can be added with `cvs add` or `cvcs import`.

✦   ✦   ✦

Understanding Security and Code

◆   ◆   ◆   ◆

In This Chapter

The importance of
good code

Linux security
overview

Security guidelines

◆   ◆   ◆   ◆

Many types of programs need to be secure. Network servers, setuid applications, e-commerce tools, and many other categories of software are security-critical. In this chapter, you will learn why this topic is such an important one. Then, you will be introduced to the big picture of the Linux security mechanisms. Finally, guidelines for writing secure code will be presented.

The Importance of Good Code

In our modern lives, the importance of computers in our lives can be daunting. Microchips in digital alarm clocks wake us up in the morning. Water for drinking or showers is brought to us by a system of pipelines, managed by computers. Electricity is sent via a computer-managed grid system. Cars regulate fuel injection by computer. Computers can be found all over in a modern workplace, on every desk in some locations. The nation's banks, securities exchange systems, and t rade systems are all computerized. Distribution of food is controlled by computers. Airplanes are designed with the assistance of computers, and some can not fly without the onboard computer. Emergency systems, such as 911 systems in many areas, rely on computers to provide vital services. Even hospitals use computers in a lot of equipment.

With such a staggering reliance on computers, one thing should be clear: bugs in code could cost a company millions of dollars and could even result in loss of life. Even if your code is not being used for life-saving systems such as 911 service, still, having bad code—for instance, allowing a security breach—can cost your company millions of dollars in damages, lost sales, and downtime. Companies large and small have been bitten by software bugs, which have indeed caused millions of dollars in losses for a single glitch.

Writing bug-free code is only half the battle, however. Writing maintainable code is important as well. If code is hard to follow, others that need to work with it may have difficulty following your code. Furthermore, with large projects, you can find yourself having trouble following your own code, especially if you haven't worked with parts of it for some time.

Linux Security Overview

Thus far, you have read about the various components of the Linux security system, but they have not been presented all together as a big picture. Here, all the pieces of the puzzle are put together for you so you can see how they work.

The security system contains two parts: authentication and access control. The former is responsible for ensuring that a user requesting access to the system is really the user with the account, and the latter is responsible for controlling which resources each account has access to, and what sort of access is permitted.

The cornerstone of both systems is the user account system. Each user that will need specific access to a Linux machine is given an account on that machine. This account contains a username and password for authentication. Each user also belongs to one or more groups, which are discussed in the next section, "Authentication."

Authentication

When a user first attempts to access the machine, whether this access is by sitting at the console, logging in via telnet, or accessing files via FTP, the user must first log in—that is, authenticate the account to the system. This is done by providing the username and password. If both are correct, the system grants the user access to the system.

This data is defined in the /etc/passwd file, and possibly the /etc/shadow file. These files contain the username, a numeric uid for the account, an encrypted password, a default group, and various other bits of information such as a real name and home directory.

Your program can, and indeed must, access these files through calls such as `getpwnam()`, `getpwuid()`, `getgrnam()`, and the like.

Note   Systems such as NIS (also known as yp) and Kerberos can mean that authentication information is not stored in /etc/passwd. This is one reason that it is important to always use the library calls rather than manipulating the file directly.

If a user is properly authenticated, access is granted and the group list is set. The group list indicates which groups a given account is a member of. This information becomes important when dealing with group permissions. Each group can have a list of members, which can be numerous. You can grant certain access to members of that group in aggregate form by simply granting group access to that particular group. For instance, if you have a team of Web site designers, you can make them all members of a certain group, cause the files they create to become part of that group, and set the file permissions such that anyone in that group can modify them. Thus, each user can still use an individual account and yet be able to work on all the files for the department.

Access control

At this point, access control takes over. The system needs to define which resources each account has access to, and what sort of access is permitted. For instance, on most systems, access to home directories should be restricted to one's own home directory; users should not be able to modify files in the home directories of other users on the system. As another example, somebody should not be able to read e-mail sent to another user; you should only be able to read your own e-mail.

Therefore, there is a permissions system in Linux that governs these types of issues. Because many of the system's functions are accessed through the file system, a logical place to start is to place permissions information in the file system data itself.

File System Permissions

Each inode on your file system contains three pieces of information relating to access control: the uid of the user that owns the file, the gid of the group that owns the file, and the file's access permissions. Note that when I say "file," I refer to any entry in the file system, which can include devices, FIFOs, and directories.

Cross-Reference   For more details on the inode system, see Chapter 11, "Files, Directories, and Devices."

The uid refers to the numeric uid of the account that owns the file. The person using this account should have full control over the file, being able to change its permissions, modify it, read from it, and so on.

The gid refers to the group id of the group that owns the file. The exact permissions for the group are defined by the access permissions. Note that, although members of the designated group can be granted modify, read, and execute access, they cannot be granted permission to modify the file's own security settings.

The final piece of security data in the inode is the access control data. This defines what sort of access is permitted for each of three categories: the owner of the file, users in the designated group, and everyone else. For more details, see the chmod(2) and chmod(3) manpages.

Process Permissions

Each process on the system has some security data that is brought with it. The most prominent of these are the uid and gid of the process. When you first log into the system, your first process (typically a shell) is set to those permissions. Any other processes that you start (except for the setuid or setgid programs, described later in this chapter) have the same uid and gid. This uid and gid information is then compared to the requirements in the file system to determine whether or not any particular access request should be allowed. Strictly speaking, with most situations, process permissions do not themselves regulate access to resources but rather are used together with other permissions mechanisms to work with access.

There are some exceptions to that rule, however. For instance, you cannot sent a KILL signal to a process that you do not own — that is, with a uid different than the one in your own process. Furthermore, the root user (uid 0) is allowed to do many things that ordinary users can't; that is, processes with a uid of 0 have these extra permissions.

As a special additional note to this system, there is the setuid/setgid system. This is somewhat of a hybrid between the file system and the process permission system and is used to give processes different uid or gid values than they would normally be entitled to. This mechanism is a complex one, with many details to concern yourself with.

Cross-Reference For information on setuid and setgid programs, see Chapter 12, "Processes in Linux."

Security Guidelines

Among all the concerns surrounding writing good code, security necessarily comes in at the top. Any program that deals with anyone or anything that is not completely trusted to always do exactly as told or behave exactly as expected must be prepared to deal with these things. Security problems can come from people actively trying to penetrate your security, or from things as simple as someone providing unexpected input to a program or running the wrong command. Security issues can also arise from receiving unexpected input from other programs, or encountering unexpected interaction issues with other systems.

Consider, for instance, a company selling goods on the Internet. This company will have a Web site, maintain customer information, and probably have customer credit card information on hand as well. If the security of this system is broken, thousands of people could suffer from credit card fraud. The company with the security breach could suffer a serious public relations nightmare.

Even if you do not do business on the Internet, you can be vulnerable simply by virtue of having an Internet connection; people might still find a way to penetrate your systems. Worse, too much access to systems can mean that people — even with legitimate access — can cause trouble, either accidentally or purposely.

Security principles

When either writing your own code in a security-conscious environment, or when maintaining systems in such a setting, there are several guidelines to keep in mind. Following these guidelines can help to reduce the potential for security breaches.

Grant As Little Access As Possible

One principle is that your programs should not only grant as little access as possible, but they should also require as little access as possible. By using the security mechanisms built into the Linux operating system, you can stop many security problems dead in their tracks.

Let's consider one quick example. On many Linux systems, incoming mail is stored in the /var/spool/mail directory, which has a file for the inbox of each user on the system. In certain situations, when working with mail, a mail reader may need to create an account in that directory.

How would you go about allowing that? Well, one option is to make the directory world-writable, enabling anyone to create whatever files desired in the directory. This is a bad idea; somebody may be able to create a file corresponding to the mailbox of a user that has not yet received any mail, and thus forge an e-mail. Or, a user could simply store data there until the file system is full, preventing any new mail from entering the system. So granting less access would be a good idea.

To do that, you need to use either setuid or setgid, because only certain programs should have access to that area. Your first thought might be to make mail readers setuid to root. This, however, is not a good idea. If a mail reader has a security problem, then the entire system can become compromised.

A better idea would be to make the directory group-writable and then make mail readers setgid to that particular group. This way, even if a security flaw is discovered in a mail reader somewhere down the line, the damage will be limited to only the files that the particular group has access to.

Networks Are Insecure

With the rise of the Internet and LAN systems, finding a computer that is not networked in some fashion is becoming increasingly difficult. With this networking comes a new class of security problems.

A prime concern is that data traveling across a network is not encrypted. This means that any traffic on your local Ethernet can be intercepted and read by others with computers on the same segment, without your knowledge. Furthermore, traffic going across the Internet can be intercepted at computers at either end of the communication, or at numerous routers in between. Additionally, it is sometimes possible for an attacker to insert data into the stream; for instance, one might add a phantom `rm -rf ~` command to a telnet session.

A second class of problems arises when it is necessary to allow or deny access to a particular service according to the machine from which the request comes. This is often used to allow, for instance, only users in certain departments or on an internal network to access resources, to control which computers are trusted to NFS-mount directories, and the like.

However, verifying that a given computer really is the machine it claims to be can be difficult. It is trivial to unplug an Ethernet link from a server and hook it up to a laptop configured with the same IP address; one might be able to gain root access to NFS mounts or intercept passwords from clients attempting to connect to server services. For Ethernet, you might try to thwart such an attempt by relying on certain MAC addresses; however, many Ethernet cards today can be configured with arbitrary MAC addresses.

One solution to these problems that you might consider is encryption and public-key authentication, which will be discussed later in this chapter.

Beware of Timing Issues

Sometimes, programs expect that things will occur in a certain amount of time. For instance, many programs expect DNS queries to typically finish within a matter of seconds, and they generally do. Programs may expect a response within a certain amount of time from another process. They may even expect a certain delay from another process or from the user. Finally, they may expect that two programs of the same type will never be run concurrently.

All of these are general programming problems, but they apply to security as well. Consider, for instance, the action of editing some system configuration file — say, /etc/passwd. If you have several administrators working on a single Linux box, there is a possibility that two or more of them will want to edit the file at the same time. Doing so can be disastrous; text editors typically used to edit these files do not have any kind of synchronization built in to prevent problems. Furthermore, even just editing the file with a text editor can be dangerous; users can change information with tools such as `passwd` and `chfn`, and you can overwrite their changes by manually editing the file if they are unlucky enough to make the change while you have the file open.

The solution to a situation like this is file locking, which you can access on Linux with either `flock()` or `fcntl()`. When you use file locking, you can indicate to other processes that you are busy with the file and that they should not access the file until you are done. In this particular case, Linux provides tools such as `vipw` and `vigr` for editing these files, with file locking in place. The other tools mentioned earlier in this chapter use file locking as well, so there is a safe way to edit your configuration files.

 For more details on file locking, please see Chapter 14, "Introducing the Linux I/O System."

Denial-of-Service (DoS) Attacks

One type of security issue is the denial-of-service (DoS) attack. This attack does not result in a direct compromise of data but rather makes this data unavailable to users, typically by crashing a machine or server process. Even though no (or little) data is lost or stolen with this kind of attack, it can still be devastating.

A DoS attack can occur in many different ways. A bug in an operating system or program might make it vulnerable to this type of attack, but not to a security breach. An attacker can simply flood a network connection with useless data, rendering it essentially inoperable. Many requests could be made to a particular type of server, causing the load on the machine to skyrocket. Or requests could be very large, eating up available memory or disk space on the server and eventually causing it to crash.

Two types of attacks are mentioned here: program bugs causing crashes, and resource starvation. Resource starvation occurs when the server is prevented from having access to the resources it needs, and thus is unable to deliver appropriate results to the client.

You need to take steps to avoid both types of problems. Of particular note at this point is the resource starvation issue. You need to make sure, especially when using dynamic memory in C or a language such as Perl that uses it implicitly, that you do not simply read an unlimited amount of data from a network or client. If you do, you can read so much data that you eat up all available memory on the system, which can cause both your program and even the entire system to crash.

Trust As Little As Possible

This is a big one that can almost be thought of as encompassing all the other rules. As an example, we talked about buffer overflow attacks in Chapter 8. These security holes almost always arise because programmers automatically assume — or trust — that the input data will be less than a certain size. You should not implicitly trust input data like that.

Another example lies with CGI programs, as discussed in Chapter 22, "CGI Programming." Sometimes, the user provides a filename for the script. This file may then be displayed back to the user. Because CGI scripts generally run with special permissions (those of the Web server), they can be especially vulnerable to attack. Consider, for instance, a CGI script that does not check on the data input. It may expect the user to give a filename such as foobar.txt. What if the user instead requests /etc/passwd? Well, if you don't check the input data, your program will be dishing out copies of the passwd file to anyone on the Internet! You might try to always append a certain path to the input; for instance, foobar.txt becomes /var/lib/cgi-data/foobar.txt. Well, all someone has to do is request the file ../../../etc/passwd, and once again, they get a copy of the passwd file. So you see, you must not trust that the user will not specify a different directory; you need to validate the input before using it.

Still another example has affected the products from several of the world's largest computer companies. Several of their operating systems have made assumptions about the data arriving from the network: that the packets will be well-formed and valid, for instance. Crackers, though, managed to generate packets that were invalid. However, the operating system did not check for validity and happily processed the packet. The result: it was possible to crash any machine with an Internet connection running the bad code from anywhere on the Internet, by anyone. Trusting incoming packets to be well-formed was a serious mistake in this situation.

Common problems

In addition to the preceding general principles, there are some common problems to be aware of. Some of these are not tied to any specific operating system; others occur specifically in Linux or UNIX settings.

Race Conditions

A *race condition* is one of the most common problems in software. Even worse, it is one of the most difficult to track down (it often appears to cause random problems) and can still lead to serious security problems.

A race condition is a particular type of timing issue. It occurs when multiple processes need to work with a single set of data or files, and the result depends on which process finishes first. Recall that in a multitasking system such as Linux, you are never guaranteed that no other process is also running while yours is, and thus you must keep in mind that files can be manipulated, even between two lines of source in your program.

One example of a race condition is actually the problem with editing configuration files mentioned previously. Another prominent problem in Linux is the /tmp race.

Many programs scripts store temporary files in /tmp. This has been a quick way to store data for short periods of time. However, a serious race condition is involved with this or any other world-writable directory.

Because anyone can place files, directories, and symlinks in /tmp, there can be a problem. Consider, for instance, if a random user on the system knows that the administrator frequently runs a program that creates a file in /tmp. This random user notices the files are all the same, or of a similar pattern. So, the user goes into /tmp and creates a symlink, named as a temporary file, to /etc/passwd. The next time the administrator runs the tool, the contents of /etc/passwd are overwritten by temporary file output, meaning that nobody can log into accounts!

This attack is not limited to attacking the root user. It can be directed at any user on the system that uses programs or scripts that create files in a world-writable directory.

Let's look at some possible ways to prevent the problem. You might think of checking for the existence of a file or link before creating one. This does not prevent the problem; it just makes it a bit more difficult to exploit. Remember that, due to multitasking, an attacker can create a file in the directory between the time you check for its existence and the time you try to open it!

Therefore, you need to look at other solutions. One of the easiest is to create a temporary directory inside the current user's home directory. This will bypass the issue altogether, because a user's home directory should not be world-writable. You can place whatever files you want in there; just be sure to clean them up when your program exits, or you'll have a lot of upset users.

Another option is to create a directory in /tmp and place files in there. Take care to specify the permissions for the directory when creating it, and to check that it was successfully created.

Buffer Overflows in C

Buffer overflows typically happen when more data than expected is given to a program, thus overflowing the memory previously allocated for space. A skilled cracker can exploit the problem to crash the system, or worse, to breach system security.

You can beat the problem several ways. First, you can use dynamic memory, which can shrink or grow in proportion to the data read in — but watch out for resource starvation, described later. Another option is to carefully limit the size of all data when using statically allocated memory. Both of these options, along with more details on the problem, are described in Chapter 8, "Memory Management."

Metacharacters in the Shell

Many programs are either written in a shell scripting language itself or call shell programs or scripts, passing along input data as command line arguments. However, there can be a problem. For instance, if you pass along arbitrary input, an attacker could play a trick such as embedding a semicolon in the input. After the semicolon, an arbitrary command — perhaps an `rm` command to remove files, or a command to display password files — could be run. This is bad news for you, because it effectively gives even a remote user of your programs such as CGI scripts full control as if local.

Note that the semicolon is not the only potentially harmful character; there are several others, including leading dashes (which can cause the following data to be interpreted as command line options), embedded newline characters, and several more. The best way to prevent this attack is to accept only a limited range of characters: generally, alphanumeric data, the period, and underscore.

Writing secure code

Now that you've learned about a number of the security problems that you might face as a programmer, let's explore some pointers to help you write secure code. Some of these have broader implications than just security issues, but all can have a significant impact on your program's security.

Check Return Values

Failing to check return values is one of the most common mistakes, and it has implications outside the security realm as well. Many functions, particularly those that do input, output, or memory manipulation, return a result code indicating the success or failure of an operation. This result code is often ignored, but you fail to check it at your own peril.

The most basic situation is this: when an operation fails, the program or user that requested the operation should not think that it succeeded. This means that an appropriate error code must be returned or error message displayed, depending on the situation. As an example, consider a program that copies files. This program will need to check to ensure that each read was executed successfully. Furthermore, each write will need to be checked as well to make sure that the disk is not full, preventing the copy. Moreover, the close of the output file will need to be checked too — sometimes, writing is delayed until that point, and you need to check that result to be safe.

Sometimes, something worse can happen. Consider a program that creates a directory and then changes into it. If this program doesn't check the return values from either of those calls, if the create directory operation fails, it will end up manipulating files in the wrong area. This can be particularly disastrous if the program wants to clean up after itself with a command such as `rm *`!

A security breach or DoS attack can even result. Consider a program that uses `fopen()` to open a file, but does not check that the open succeeded. The first time the program tries to write to the file, it will crash with a segmentation violation due to a bad pointer. All an attacker has to do is coerce a failure in the `fopen()` call, and the server goes down.

Dynamically Allocated Memory Helps

Many buffer overflow attacks can be thwarted by writing your program using dynamically allocated memory.

Note In Perl, all strings implicitly shrink and grow; they are implemented dynamically internally, but you don't need to worry about the details. Therefore, Perl code is generally considered immune to buffer overflow attacks.

This is a great way to enable your program to read and process data of arbitrary size. Using statically allocated memory means that you must constantly worry about sizes, whereas dynamically allocated memory can be allocated with the proper size automatically.

However, consider the caveats. You can make a resource starvation attack easier, in both C and Perl, if you read in data of unlimited length and allocate memory for it. Also, for C programmers, lots of use of dynamic memory can lead to memory leaks unless you are careful. Frequent memory leaks can also turn into a resource starvation issue. Most would agree that running out of memory is not as bad as having a full-fledged security compromise (which could let an attacker crash your box anyway), but still it is something to be aware of. Refer to Chapter 8, "Memory Management," for more details.

Exercise Extreme Caution with setuid or setgid

This is perhaps the most dangerous situation you can be placed in. You are essentially granting users additional privileges while they run your program. You need to be particularly careful to observe warnings about race conditions and buffer overflows in this situation. Not only that, but you also need to be aware of your program's interactions with others. You need to consider whether you will be able to delete more files than normal, what user ID any programs that your programs execute will run under, what effect libraries will have on your program, and all the other concerns pointed out in this chapter.

You can try to help out the situation by dropping special privileges as soon as possible; that is, revert to the permissions of the user than invoked the program. Then, you can switch back to special permissions later if you need to. Also, you may want to permanently get rid of the special permissions once you're done with them.

Many people justifiably prefer to avoid setuid or setgid programs whenever possible; this is good advice. See if there are other alternatives available; could you use a domain socket or FIFO to communicate between privileged and unprivileged parts of code? If so, that may be a preferable way to go.

Use File Locking

You have already seen examples of the problems caused by race conditions and synchronization issues. A great way to avoid these problems is to make frequent use of file locking. This way, you can prevent a situation in which two programs might be manipulating a single piece of data at one time — a situation that can lead to data corruption without even requiring a cracker trying to cause it!

Use Encryption

When you need to transmit data over the network that should not be intercepted, you ought to use encryption. One popular way to do that is to use SSL; on Linux, the SSLeay library (available at `http://www.ssleay.org/ssleay`) is commonly used to do this. By using encryption, you can thwart would-be snoopers, giving them no useful data.

Furthermore, encryption makes it extremely difficult, or even impossible, for an attacker to insert unwanted data into a connection. Thus, by encrypting your network traffic, you obtain many advantages.

The disadvantage of this is that encryption can use CPU time, and for a heavily loaded server, this usage could add up. However, in many cases, this downside is negligible and will never be noticed. Another potential disadvantage is that laws regarding encryption can be tricky; for instance, US law prohibits export of some encryption technologies, and some other countries ban the usage of them altogether.

Use Public-Key Authentication

Another feature of the SSL system is its support for public-key authentication. By using these features, you can ensure that the remote machine really is the one that it claims to be. There is no need to rely on inherently unreliable indicators such as IP address or MAC address; if the remote machine is able to present the proper credentials, access can be granted; otherwise, access can be denied. This type of system can also be used to authenticate individual users of programs, as is done by systems such as ssh (see `http://www.openssh.org/`).

Track Security Forums

Keeping up to date with security issues can be key to preventing them. When you hear about problems in other people's code, or a new problem (such as the /tmp race issue), you can examine your own code for the problems and hopefully release a fix before anyone else even realizes you were vulnerable.

One of the most widely known and most respected security forums in the UNIX/ Linux community is the Bugtraq mailing list. This is an open discussion list with subscribers numbering in the tens of thousands, including some of the world's most prominent Internet, UNIX, and Linux security experts. You can find various introductory information in the Forums area of `http://www.securityfocus.com/` and detailed information at `http://www.securityfocus.com/forums/bugtraq/ faq.html`.

Some good newsgroups to watch include `comp.os.security` and `comp.security.unix`, as well as groups in `comp.os.linux.*`.

Also, track the releases from your own distribution. Check your distribution's home page for information, or take a look at `http://www.linuxlinks.com/Security/` for links to many good Linux-related security sites.

Summary

In this chapter, you learned about the importance of security to your code, some security concepts, and how to apply these to your own software. Specifically, the following was covered:

✦ Good code is a worthwhile long-term goal.

✦ The Linux security model consists of two parts: authentication and access control.

✦ Your code should be written such that as little access is granted (or requested) as possible.

✦ Networks are fundamentally insecure; they can permit snooping, have trouble verifying that a computer is the one it claims to be, and be vulnerable to data insertion attacks.

✦ You can address these problems with encryption and public key authentication.

✦ Timing issues, such as race conditions, can pose a serious, but difficult to track down, security risk.

✦ Denial-of-service (DoS) attacks can exploit bugs or use resource starvation in order to crash or impair your servers.

✦ Misplaced trust in insecure systems or users can create problems for your code.

✦ Buffer overflows are a common and serious security risk for some types of C programs. Using dynamically allocated memory can help with these problems.

✦ File locking can be used to reduce concurrency (timing) problems.

✦ The setuid and setgid features can be dangerous and should be avoided if possible.

✦   ✦   ✦

Optimizing Performance

Y ou'd be hard-pressed to find a programmer that does not want to make programs run faster, regardless of platform. Linux programmers are no exception; some take an almost fanatical approach to the job of optimizing their code for performance. Many of the example programs you've seen in this book are of the *run once* variety; there isn't a need to worry about performance because the impact of even a severe performance problem probably can be measured only in milliseconds at worst. However, if your program is parsing ten million log entries, or must handle 200 website hits per second, tables quickly turn. Something that wastes 5 milliseconds with a single execution ends up wasting 13 hours of CPU time when it is run 10 million times. This is no figure to scoff at, certainly. Even if we assume only 20 website hits per second, a value not too unheard-of in today's world, that 5 millisecond performance problem can end up wasting 2 hours of CPU time each day. You literally can be talking about the difference between code that is capable of keeping up with the demands put up to it and code that cannot.

As hardware becomes faster, cheaper, and more plentiful, some argue that performance optimization is less critical — particularly people that try to enforce deadlines on software development. Not so. Even today's most advanced hardware, combined with the latest in compiler optimization technology cannot come even close to the performance benefits that can be attained by fixing some small problems — or even going with an entirely different and much faster design.

In this chapter, I'll discuss some things that can cause serious performance problems, how to choose an appropriate design for some various software from a performance standpoint, what calls are expensive and what calls are relatively quick, and how to replace some expensive calls with some quicker ones.

Principles for Faster Code

There are several ideas that you can apply to your programs to make them perform better. These ideas are not a magic solution for every performance problem, but if you keep them in mind while writing and revising your code, you will usually end up with better and faster programs.

Three measurements

When we talk about performance, there are several different things to consider. One is the absolute amount of time it takes the software to complete a given task. For instance, even if a webserver keeps up perfectly well with client requests, there can be a 15-second delay before the server begins to send pages to the client each time. In such a situation, the server is failing to perform adequately in terms of the amount of absolute time it requires to get things done. Its CPU utilization and I/O usage may be minimal, but somewhere it's still failing.

Another consideration is the amount of CPU time that a program requires. This is a measure of the time that the computer's processor spends executing code on your program's behalf. Note that this is often less, usually significantly so, than the program's run time. Many programs tend to spend most of their time waiting for something to happen—input to arrive, output to be written to disk, and so on. While it is waiting, the CPU can be servicing other requests, and so the program is not using CPU time. However, some programs, particularly those performing analysis or complex calculations, may be primarily CPU-bound programs. For these, a savings in the amount of CPU time required may result in a substantial savings in absolute time. It is important to note that the run time of a piece of code may be microseconds or all the way up to months. However, this time has no effect on other processes on the system. On the other hand, if your program uses a lot of CPU time, this can slow down all the processes on the system. This effect is even worse if your program tends to run multiple copies of at once.

One can further separate the CPU time into system and user time. The system time is the amount of CPU time used on your behalf by the kernel. This could accrue by calling functions such as open() and fork(). The user time is the amount of CPU time used by your program. This might be used by arithmetic, string manipulation, and so on.

A third consideration for performance is the time spent doing I/O. Traditionally, this has been one of the slowest parts of many programs, and remains so today. However, it's difficult to get an accurate measure of this value. This is because caching and asynchronous updates enable modern operating systems such as Linux, to defer some I/O operations to a time when the system is less busy and the their impact poses less of a performance penalty on the running processes. Some programs, such as network servers, spend most of their lives handling I/O; ot spend comparitively little time with I/O tasks. Therefore, optimization of I/O can be critical with some projects and completely unimportant with others.

Loops

One of the most frequent causes of problems with performance occurs inside loops. Loops magnify the effects of otherwise minor performance problems because the code may be executed anywhere from dozens to millions of times inside the loop. Therefore, there is a big payoff for optimization of code that is executed inside a loop.

One of the simplest and yet most effective things you can do is move code outside the loop that doesn't need to be executed every time through the loop. For instance, recall this code from Chapter 6:

```c
#include <stdio.h>

int main(void) {
  int counter;
  int ending;
  int temp;
  int five;
  for (counter = 0; counter < 2 * 100000000 * 9 / 18 + 5131;
       counter += (5 - 3) / 2) {
    temp = counter / 15302;
    ending = counter;
    five = 5;
  }
  printf("five = %d; ending = %d\n", five, ending);
  return 0;
}
```

Several things here could be moved outside the loop. For one, the variable five is never changed; you could set it before or after the loop. The ending condition of the loop is calculated every time through. A faster approach would be to store that value in a variable and simply compare counter to that variable each time through. Not only that, but the increment value is also computed each time through the loop. This, too, could be calculated beforehand.

The ending variable could be calculated only once, after the loop is through, by simply looking at the value of counter at that point. Finally, the assignment to the variable five is dead code; nothing except the final printf() ever uses that variable, so that assignment could be removed entirely if you would just print the number 5.

In Perl, I frequently see programmers use code such as the following:

```
while ($string = <BIGFILE>) {
  chomp $string;
  # some processing here, perhaps
  print "Input: $string\n";
}
```

Several things are wrong here. If you're going to print out a newline after $string anyway, why bother stripping it off in the first place? Second, to make things faster, you should avoid interpolation when practical. So, a faster version may be like this:

```
while ($string = <BIGFILE) {
  # some processing here, perhaps
  print "Input: ", $string;
}
```

Of course, whether or not you really need to be concerned about this depends on the kind of usage your program will get. Many programmers use code similar to the first example in programs that are designed for interactive use and may read only three lines from the user. There's no real harm there. However, if the code is going to be running millions of times, you can run into some difficulties.

Another thing you can do is use the /o option with regular expressions in Perl that occur inside a loop. This means that Perl will compile the regular expression only once, instead of every time it is used. This can result in a substantial speed improvement. The only downside is that if you build your regular expression pattern by using variables or interpolation, Perl will not notice if it changed while you are in the loop, and it will continue using the original value. Still, you'll find that few regular expressions change while inside a loop, so this is a tip that can frequently be a performance booster.

Help the optimizer

Modern compilers such as gcc have optimizers that can aggressively optimize the code that they generate. However, they can do only so much. There are things that you can do to help the optimizers with their task.

One thing you can do is use the const keyword for any variable that is not supposed to change throughout its lifetime. Not only is this a valuable safeguard for you, but it also enables the compiler to make assumptions about the variable that may speed up code involving it.

If you have a small function that is called frequently, you can declare it inline. This means that the compiler will insert the actual code for the function in the caller if possible, rather than inserting a jump to the function's address as might normally be used. By doing this, the control flow of the program is not interrupted, enabling modern pipelining CPUs to predict future instructions to execute more effectively. Furthermore, it can mean a few less instructions to execute because of the lack of overhead for pushing information on to the stack, making the actual call, handling the return value, and so on.

Avoid floating-point numbers

Floating-point data types, such as `float` and `double` take more time to calculate than do their integer counterparts. Therefore, unless you really need the extra attributes of floating-point numbers, you should try to avoid them. This is especially true on the i386 architecture, where the floating-point unit is rather slow, and some machines in that architecture line have no floating-point units at all.

A common usage for floating-point numbers is dealing with dollar values. Programmers often reason that because there's a decimal sign in the input, there must be a decimal sign in the computer storage of that input as well. Not true! Some clever programmers use integers to store these values. They simply might multiply the dollar values by 100 and then add the cents value after that. To go back to a human representation, the reverse operation is done—the cents are subtracted and the number is divided by 100.

Sometimes, floating-point numbers cannot be avoided. But when they can, it's a good idea to do so.

Recode time-critcal code blocks

If you have the expertise to do so, another route you can take is to rewrite sections of your code that are causing delays in a more low-level language. For instance, a Perl programmer might rewrite part of a program's core logic in C to speed performance by leveraging a compiled and preoptimized language. Similarly, a C program might use assembler to do the same thing.

This is not always an option, and in the case of assembler coding, can be a serious detriment to the portability and future usability of the code. However, manually writing algorithms in assembler is the ultimate control you can have over how the CPU executes your algorithm and gives you the opportunity to write the most efficient algorithms possible.

Increase block size

Many operations are done on blocks of data. Some of the most common are reading and writing of binary data. One easy way that you can speed up your programs is to increase the buffer size in your program. This enables you to transfer more data at once. By doing so, you decrease the frequency with which you must call one of the I/O functions, which is very good as these calls can be time-consuming.

Expensive versus Inexpensive Operations

Often, I might refer to a given operation as expensive. Relatively speaking, this means that it requires a lot of time to complete, a lot of I/O activity, or a lot of some other type of resource. When you optimize your code, you want to get rid of the expensive operations and replace them with the inexpensive ones. Linux gives you a lot of flexibility; there are often multiple ways to accomplish something. Sometimes it's simple to decide which method to use. Other times, whether a given operation is more or less expensive than another may depend on exactly how it is being used in your code.

System calls

System calls in general are fairly expensive operations. These include anything that requires a switch into kernel mode. This category is large and essentially includes everything in section 2 of the manpages and some things in section 3 as well.

Therefore, it's a good idea to minimize usage of system calls where possible. Several of the following topics relate to that, but even for those not explicitly mentioned, be aware of the performance implications.

fork

The fork() call is often necessary and indeed quite useful. By itself, forking is not slow, but if you use it frequently, it can add up. Consider, for instance, a web server that might fork for each new connect. If it's getting hit dozens of times per second, this can really add up to a lot of forking going on. This is one reason that single-process web servers such as Boa, that use select() for multiplexing, can outperform multi-process servers.

Apache takes an interesting approach to the problem. It forks a number of server processes when it first starts. These processes continue running, and do not exit. When connection requests come in, they are sent to one of the processes. If it's out of processes, a new one will be forked, but it will not exit after it has serviced its request; it will wait for more requests.

exec

Another system call that is quite often used is exec. This one is almost always used immediately after a fork, so the above information applies here as well. This call can be quite expensive, as the new program will have to do initialization such as loading libraries and so on.

system

This call is essentially a `fork`, `exec`, and `wait` all rolled into one. However, it's somewhat worse than that because it invokes a shell to run the specified command. Invoking a shell is very expensive; its initialization may consist of several million instructions as it loads various profiles and initialization scripts. Therefore, frequently using `sytem` is a bad idea.

I once saw a network server that ran code like this very frequently:

```
system("ls /etc");
```

This is an incredible waste of resources. The program has to fork and execute the shell. The shell must initialize, and then the shell forks and executes `ls`. Although this may be acceptable for a quick program that runs only occasionally, it is certainly sub-optimal for a network server.

A far better option is to use `opendir()` and `readdir()` to read the directory yourself. This requires only a little bit more code on your part but will execute far faster. Keep in mind that this is what `ls` is doing anyway.

Compiler Optimizations

After you have done what you can to optimize your own code, the compiler can be helpful with optimizations as well. As you already saw in Chapter 6, "Welcome to gcc," these can have a significant impact on the performance of your code.

Most programmers prefer to develop code with optimizations turned off because they can interfere with the debugging process. When the program is prepared for release, usually it is compiled with optimizations of level -O2 or -O3.

The optimizer on modern compilers can sometimes help out with some mistakes that you might make. For instance, in some programs, it can detect that there are things calculated inside a loop that could be calculated outside the loop for speed benefits.

Not only that, but the optimizers often can simplify arithmetic expressions. For instance, the arithmetic done in these programs involves a lot of constants. The compiler can evaluate as much as possible at compile time to reduce the impact of it at execution time.

The compiler also can do many optimizations on the generated assembly code. These optimizations are enabled by -O2, although a few might only be enabled by -O3. Exactly what these optimizations do depends on your platform. For instance, Linux on the 64-bit Alpha would have significantly different optimizations than Linux on a Pentium machine.

Using gprof

One tool that you can use to analyze your program's execution is the GNU profiler, gprof. This program shows you where your program is spending most of its time, how frequently various parts of your code are executed, and where your program is spending most of its time.

Listing 28-1 shows a sample program that I'll use for the profiling.

Note   This program specifically is designed to be slow. If it takes too long on your system, you can modify `getmaxval()` to return something smaller.

Note   Listing 28-1 is available online.

Listing 28-1: **Example for profiling**

```
#include <stdio.h>
#include <stdlib.h>
#include <time.h>

int getmaxval(void);
int getincrement(void);
void dosomething(int *data);

int main(void) {
  int counter;
  int data = 1;

  srand(time(NULL));

  for (counter = 0; counter < getmaxval(); counter += getincrement()) {
    dosomething(&data);
  }
  printf("Data = %d, counter = %d\n", data, counter);
  return 0;
}

int getmaxval(void) {
  int bignumber = 1000000;
  return bignumber * 1500 / 2 + 1500 * 5 - 2100 / 2 * 10 / 2;
}

int getincrement(void) {
  int randval = rand();

  return randval / 15000000  - 1000 / 12 / 5 / 2;

}
```

```
void dosomething(int *data) {
  int randval = rand();
  data += rand() * 9105 / 100000;
}
```

To be capable of using this with the profiler, you need to compile with a special command-line option. Here's a way to compile:

```
$ gcc  -a -g -pg -o ch28-1 ch28-1.c
```

The -pg option enables the basic profiling support in gcc. The -a option enables a more detailed (annotated) output.

Now run the program as normal:

```
$ ./ch28-1
Data = 1, counter = 750002258
```

Note that your program will run somewhat slower when profiling is enabled because it is spending time collecting data as well as running normally. The profiling support in the program creates a file named gmon.out in your current directory. This file is later used by gprof to analyze your code, and contains information derived from analyzing your program while it runs.

Now run gprof to get the output. This will be voluminous, so it's a good idea to redirect it to a file so you can use less or a similar file viewer, or print it out:

```
$ gprof ch28-1 gmon.out > profile.txt
```

Listing 28-2 shows the output from gprof from profiling this program. I'll include the output here, and then I'll analyze it and come to some conclusions about the program.

Note   Listing 28-2 is available online.

Listing 28-2: **Sample gprof output**

```
Flat profile:

Each sample counts as 0.01 seconds.
  %   cumulative   self              self     total
 time   seconds   seconds    calls  ps/call  ps/call  name
 38.82      3.89      3.89 11883133 327354.75 327354.75  dosomething
```

Continued

Listing 28-2 *(continued)*

```
27.35     6.63    2.74 11883133 230578.92 230578.92  getincrement
18.46     8.48    1.85 11883134 155682.84 155682.84  getmaxval
15.37    10.02    1.54                                main
```

```
%         the percentage of the total running time of the
time      program used by this function.

cumulative a running sum of the number of seconds accounted
 seconds   for by this function and those listed above it.

 self     the number of seconds accounted for by this
seconds   function alone.  This is the major sort for this
          listing.

calls     the number of times this function was invoked, if
          this function is profiled, else blank.

 self     the average number of milliseconds spent in this
ms/call   function per call, if this function is profiled,
          else blank.

 total    the average number of milliseconds spent in this
ms/call   function and its descendents per call, if this
          function is profiled, else blank.

name      the name of the function.  This is the minor sort
          for this listing. The index shows the location of
          the function in the gprof listing. If the index is
          in parentheses it shows where it would appear in
          the gprof listing if it were to be printed.
             Call graph (explanation follows)
```

```
granularity: each sample hit covers 4 byte(s) for 0.10% of 10.02 seconds

index % time    self  children    called     name
                                                  <spontaneous>
[1]    100.0    1.54    8.48                   main [1]
                3.89    0.00 11883133/11883133     dosomething [2]
                2.74    0.00 11883133/11883133     getincrement [3]
                1.85    0.00 11883134/11883134     getmaxval [4]
-----------------------------------------------
                3.89    0.00 11883133/11883133     main [1]
[2]     38.8    3.89    0.00 11883133         dosomething [2]
-----------------------------------------------
                2.74    0.00 11883133/11883133     main [1]
[3]     27.3    2.74    0.00 11883133         getincrement [3]
-----------------------------------------------
                1.85    0.00 11883134/11883134     main [1]
[4]     18.5    1.85    0.00 11883134         getmaxval [4]
-----------------------------------------------
```

This table describes the call tree of the program, and was sorted by the total amount of time spent in each function and its children.

Each entry in this table consists of several lines. The line with the index number at the left hand margin lists the current function. The lines above it list the functions that called this function, and the lines below it list the functions this one called. This line lists:

index   A unique number given to each element of the table.
         Index numbers are sorted numerically.
         The index number is printed next to every function name so
         it is easier to look up where the function in the table.

% time   This is the percentage of the 'total' time that was spent
         in this function and its children. Note that due to
         different viewpoints, functions excluded by options, etc,
         these numbers will NOT add up to 100%.

self   This is the total amount of time spent in this function.

children This is the total amount of time propagated into this
         function by its children.

called   This is the number of times the function was called.
         If the function called itself recursively, the number
         only includes nonrecursive calls, and is followed by
         a '+' and the number of recursive calls.

name   The name of the current function. The index number is
         printed after it. If the function is a member of a
         cycle, the cycle number is printed between the
         function's name and the index number.

For the function's parents, the fields have the following meanings:

self   This is the amount of time that was propagated directly
         from the function into this parent.

children This is the amount of time that was propagated from
         the function's children into this parent.

called   This is the number of times this parent called the
         function '/' the total number of times the function
         was called. Recursive calls to the function are not
         included in the number after the '/'.

name   This is the name of the parent. The parent's index
         number is printed after it. If the parent is a
         member of a cycle, the cycle number is printed between
         the name and the index number.

Continued

Listing 28-2 *(continued)*

```
If the parents of the function cannot be determined, the word
'<spontaneous>' is printed in the `name' field, and all the other
fields are blank.

For the function's children, the fields have the following meanings:

    self      This is the amount of time that was propagated directly
              from the child into the function.

    children  This is the amount of time that was propagated from the
              child's children to the function.

    called    This is the number of times the function called
              this child '/' the total number of times the child
              was called.  Recursive calls by the child are not
              listed in the number after the '/'.

    name      This is the name of the child.  The child's index
              number is printed after it.  If the child is a
              member of a cycle, the cycle number is printed
              between the name and the index number.

If there are any cycles (circles) in the call graph, there is an
entry for the cycle as a whole.  This entry shows who called the
cycle (as parents) and the members of the cycle (as children.)
The '+' recursive calls entry shows the number of function calls that
were internal to the cycle, and the calls entry for each member shows,
for that member, how many times it was called from other members of
the cycle.


Index by function name

    [2] dosomething          [4] getmaxval
    [3] getincrement         [1] main
```

I'll analyze the results. The information is split up into two separate sections: the flat profile and the call graph.

The flat profile shows how much time was spent in each function. From the information presented, you can see that the dosomething( ) function was the most time-consuming, using almost 40 percent of the time of the program. Following that are the remaining functions in the program. You can also see that each of these three functions was called nearly 12 million times.

Next you see the call graph. The purpose of this is to show you how much time was spent in each function and any function that it calls. The call graph is separated into sections, one for each function in your program. The specific function being described in each function is denoted by the bracketed number on the left (for example, [1]). Above this number line, you see a summary of the functions that called this one. For instance, here is one such summary:

```
index % time    self  children    called     name
                                             <spontaneous>
[1]     100.0    1.54    8.48                main [1]
                 3.89    0.00 11883133/11883133    dosomething [2]
                 2.74    0.00 11883133/11883133    getincrement [3]
                 1.85    0.00 11883134/11883134    getmaxval [4]
```

For each line, the values include the amount of time spent in the primary function when it was called by the given function. In the second through fourth entries in the call graph (you see the first one above), you can see that they were all called from main. After the primary line, you can see a summary of each function it called, along with an indication of how much time was spent in those functions when called from the primary one for each section.

If this report does not provide fine enough granularity for you, you can instruct gprof to operate in line-by-line mode, where the basic unit of analysis is the source code line instead of the function. This is invoked with -1. In the following example, I also turned on -b, which causes gprof to omit the explanatory text from its result:

```
$ gprof -b -l ch28-1 gmon.out > profile2.txt
```

Listing 28-3 shows the profile that results from this command.

 Note   Listing 28-3 is available online.

Listing 28-3: **Gprof example with line granularity**

```
Flat profile:

Each sample counts as 0.01 seconds.
  %   cumulative   self              self     total
 time   seconds   seconds    calls  ps/call  ps/call  name
25.50     2.56      2.56                              dosomething (ch28-1.c:36)
10.38     3.60      1.04                              getincrement (ch28-1.c:28)
 9.68     4.57      0.97                              getincrement (ch28-1.c:30)
 9.58     5.53      0.96                              getmaxval (ch28-1.c:24)
 9.33     6.46      0.94                              dosomething (ch28-1.c:35)
 7.83     7.25      0.79                              main (ch28-1.c:15)
 5.69     7.82      0.57 11883133 47967.15 47967.15  getincrement (ch28-1.c:27)
```

Continued

Listing 28-3 *(continued)*

```
5.49      8.37    0.55 11883134 46284.09 46284.09  getmaxval (ch28-1.c:22)
3.89      8.76    0.39                              main (ch28-1.c:16)
3.39      9.10    0.34                              main (ch28-1.c:15)
2.40      9.34    0.24                              getmaxval (ch28-1.c:23)
2.30      9.56    0.23 11883133 19355.17 19355.17  dosomething (ch28-1.c:34)
1.70      9.73    0.17                              dosomething (ch28-1.c:37)
1.60      9.89    0.16                              getincrement (ch28-1.c:32)
1.00      9.99    0.10                              getmaxval (ch28-1.c:25)
0.25     10.02    0.03                              main (ch28-1.c:18)

                   Call graph


granularity: each sample hit covers 4 byte(s) for 0.10% of 10.02 seconds

index % time    self  children    called     name
                0.57      0.00 11883133/11883133     main (ch28-1.c:15) [2]
[9]      5.7    0.57      0.00 11883133         getincrement (ch28-1.c:27) [9]
-----------------------------------------------
                0.55      0.00 11883134/11883134     main (ch28-1.c:15) [7]
[10]     5.5    0.55      0.00 11883134         getmaxval (ch28-1.c:22) [10]
-----------------------------------------------
                0.23      0.00 11883133/11883133     main (ch28-1.c:16) [8]
[12]     2.3    0.23      0.00 11883133         dosomething (ch28-1.c:34) [12]
-----------------------------------------------


Index by function name

  [12] dosomething (ch28-1.c:34) [4] getincrement (ch28-1.c:30) [7] main
(ch28-1.c:15)
   [6] dosomething (ch28-1.c:35) [14] getincrement (ch28-1.c:32) [8] main
(ch28-1.c:16)
   [1] dosomething (ch28-1.c:36) [10] getmaxval (ch28-1.c:22) [2] main
(ch28-1.c:15)
  [13] dosomething (ch28-1.c:37) [11] getmaxval (ch28-1.c:23) [16] main
(ch28-1.c:18)
   [9] getincrement (ch28-1.c:27) [5] getmaxval (ch28-1.c:24)
   [3] getincrement (ch28-1.c:28) [15] getmaxval (ch28-1.c:25)
```

From this report, you can find that fully one quarter of the program's execution time was spent on line 36 of the code, inside the dosomething() function. This is not terribly surprising, as this line of code gets information from the random-numbr generator (a fairly expensive operation) and then performs arithmetic on it.

A second in line is line 28, another call to `rand( )`, followed by line 30, which does a lot of math in that result. Coming in close on the heels of those are lines 24, which again do some calculations, and 35 — another call to `rand( )`.

Another report that is available is the annotated source listing. Here's a way to get output from it:

```
$ gprof -x -l -A ch28-1 gmon.out > profile3.txt
```

The `-A` option requests annotated mode; `-l` requests line-by-line mode, and `-x` requests that the program annotate as many lines as possible. Listing 28-4 shows the output from this command.

Note   Listing 28-4 is available online.

Listing 28-4: Output from gprof –A –l -x

```
*** File /home/jgoerzen/t/ch28-1.c:
                #include <stdio.h>
                #include <stdlib.h>
                #include <time.h>

                int getmaxval(void);
                int getincrement(void);
                void dosomething(int *data);

    ##### -> int main(void) {
                  int counter;
    ##### ->    int data = 1;

    ##### ->    srand(time(NULL));

    ##### ->    for (counter = 0; counter < getmaxval(); counter +=
getincrement()) {
    ##### ->       dosomething(&data);
                  }
    ##### ->    printf("Data = %d, counter = %d\n", data, counter);
    ##### ->    return 0;
    ##### -> }

    11883134 -> int getmaxval(void) {
    11883134 ->    int bignumber = 1000000;
    11883134 ->    return bignumber * 1500 / 2 + 1500 * 5 - 2100 / 2 * 10 / 2;
    11883134 -> }

    11883133 -> int getincrement(void) {
    11883133 ->    int randval = rand();
```

Continued

Listing 28-4 *(continued)*

```
11883133 ->    return randval / 15000000  - 1000 / 12 / 5 / 2;

11883133 -> }

11883133 -> void dosomething(int *data) {
11883133 ->    int randval = rand();
11883133 ->    data += rand() * 9105 / 100000;
11883133 -> }
```

```
Top 10 Lines:

    Line      Count

      22    11883134
      27    11883133
      34    11883133

Execution Summary:

      20    Executable lines in this file
      20    Lines executed
  100.00    Percent of the file executed

 35649400    Total number of line executions
1782470.00    Average executions per line
```

The idea is that you can see, for each line of code, exactly how many times it is executed. This program executes all the functions on a fairly constant basis, so they are each executed approximately the same number of times, as gprof shows you.

The profiler is telling us here that the calls to rand() and the lengthy arithmetic were the most processor intensive. Because they were all occuring inside a loop, this is not surprising. If these can be eliminated, or at least reduced, then the speed of the program should be improved significantly. As an example, perhaps it would be sufficient to calculate a random number once before entering the loop, and then use it where required. Also note that line 35 (int randval = rand()) is a senseless call to rand(); that value is never used. Not only that, but also these arithmetic operations could be simplified beforehand rather than doing so each time through the loop.

After you have made changes to your code, you will want to re-test the program to ensure that the changes really did improve performance. If not, then perhaps the change you made was not any faster, or even a bit slower. Also, when comparing profiling output from gprof before and after making changes, keep in mind that if you replace, for instance, one line of code with ten new lines, you need to compare those ten lines all together to the one original line.

Summary

In this chapter, you learned about optimizing your code for speed. Specifically, you learned:

✦ Performance optimization becomes increasingly important when a given piece of code is executed more frequently.

✦ You can differentiate between elapsed time, CPU time, and I/O time when analyzing the performance of your programs.

✦ Loops are a primary cause of problems, as they tend to magnify the problems of any code running inside them.

✦ You can boost performance by helping the optimizer, taking care to use keywords such as `const` when possible.

✦ System calls are notoriously expensive and their use should be minimized.

✦ You can use gprof, the GNU profiler, to find out which sections of your code are causing the largest delays.

✦   ✦   ✦

Glossary

advisory locking A type of locking that requires each participating program to be aware of the need for locking and participate in the locking mechanism. Advisory locking is the standard way of implementing locking in Linux. *See also* locking.

append mode A mode of writing to files in which the operating system *atomically* seeks the end of the file and performs the write for each actual attempt to write data to the file. This mode is generally invoked when the file is opened with `fopen()` or `open()`. *See also* atomic operation.

assembler A program that translates low-level commands that correspond to CPU instructions into binary machine language. Often invoked by a compiler.

asynchronous I/O A type of I/O in which the requested operation may or may not be done before a call returns. Asynchronous I/O allows your program to continue processing data and lets the operating system fulfill the requests in the background whenever it is most convenient. Asynchronous I/O is also known in some situations as non-blocking I/O.

atomic operation An operation that is guaranteed to complete its task fully before being interrupted by another similar operation or returning.

blocking I/O A characteristic of an operation that causes the execution of the program to be put on hold until a certain event occurs. For instance, the `read()` call will, by default, block until it has data to return to the process.

Bourne shell The traditional default shell on UNIX systems. On Linux systems, Bash is the typical implementation of it.

Bash (the Bourne-again shell) An enhanced version of the Bourne shell that adds many new features and some features from tcsh and ksh.

bounds checking A feature of a compiler or a language. It generates an error if boundaries for types are exceeded. For instance, if you have an array with 5 elements and you try to read element 10, this would trigger an error if bounds-checking is used. C and C++ do not generally have this feature.

buffer Any area used for temporary storage of data while or before it can be processed. In C, a buffer might also refer to any character array (string).

buffer overrun The condition in which more data is placed into a buffer than the size of the buffer allows. This is typically a problem for C or C++ programs, and often results from reading in too much data or copying too much data into a buffer.

cc The canonical name for the C compiler on a UNIX system. On Linux, this refers to the gcc compiler.

CGI The Common Gateway Interface, a system of passing data to and from a program or script. CGI programs are used to read input from and generate on-the-fly pages for Web sites.

chgrp The name of both a system call and a shell command that is used to change the group owner of a file or directory in Linux.

chown The name of both a system call and a shell command used to change the owner of a file or directory in Linux.

compiler A program that is used to transform input in a high-level language to assembler code or machine code. In Linux, a typical use is to transform C, C++, Pascal, or Fortran code to Assembler code. The standard C compiler is gcc, and the C++ compiler is g++.

cpp The C Pre-Processor, part of the C compiler package.

cross-compiler A compiler that runs on one architecture, but generates assembly or machine code for another architecture.

CVS The Concurrent Versions System, an application designed to help programmers track changes between versions, manage branches in code, and archive previous work. See Chapter 26 for details on CVS.

DBI The Perl Database Interface, a standardized library for communicating with various SQL servers.

deadlock A condition that occurs when two or more processes are each waiting on the others to release a given resource. This is a potential problem with locking or other methods used to avoid race conditions.

debugger A program that assists you with finding known or potential bugs in your code.

dereference (a pointer) Accessing the memory pointed to by a pointer instead of the pointer itself. In C and C++, the dereference operator is *.

device special file A specific type of special file that corresponds to a hardware device. Device special files come in two versions: block devices and character devices. Block devices are used to interface with devices that handle data by the block, such as hard drives, tape drives, CD-ROM devices, scanners, and the like. Character devices are used to interface with peripherals that handle data one character at a time, such as terminals, printers, serial ports, and mice.

dynamic library A library that is designed to be loaded at run time instead of at link time.

dynamic linker The program that takes care of resolving dynamic library dependencies at run time. On Linux systems, the dynamic linker is ld.so.

dump A shorthand version of core dump. This is also the name of a backup program.

dynamically allocated memory This is memory that is explicitly allocated and freed by a program. In C, this allocation is typically performed with `malloc()` and the memory is later deallocated with `free()`. Unlike statically allocated memory, the size of the memory block to be allocated does not have to be known at compile time, but the memory must be managed manually.

ELF The Executable and Linking Format, a way of storing data in executables and handling dynamically linked libraries.

end-of-file This is the condition that occurs when the position within a file is at the end. Also could refer to the error code returned by I/O functions when a program attempts to read past the end of a file. In terms of non-file I/O, it can also mean that there is no more data to read (which is the case if the other end of a socket closed the connection, for instance).

EOF Acronym for end-of-file.

exclusive lock With respect to file locking with a function such as `flock()`, indicates a type of locking in which only a single process may have a lock on a file at any given time. See the discussion under shared lock for details.

FIFO (First In, First Out) A named pipe. That is, a pipe with a name in the file system.

file locking A particular type of locking applied to files on the system, commonly implemented as advisory locking.

gcc The GNU C Compiler, the standard C compiler in Linux.

g++ The GNU C++ compiler, the standard C++ compiler in Linux.

gas The GNU Assembler.

gdb The GNU Debugger, a powerful debugger available for your use.

GECOS field The part of the system's account database (often in /etc/passwd) that contains the real name of a particular user. Today, the GECOS field may also contain information such as office number, telephone numbers, and the like. The acronym's meaning is no longer relevant, but refers to the General Electric Comprehensive Operating System that early UNIX versions sometimes needed to interface with.

gid The numeric group id of a particular group. This is often, but not always, defined in /etc/group and used for security in places such as the file system and processes. *See also* uid.

globbing Using shell wildcards (such as the asterisk, question mark, brackets, and so on) to select a group of files or directories.

gprof The GNU profiler, used to analyze the performance of your programs.

GUI A Graphical User Interface. On Linux, a GUI is typically implemented using X.

hard link A type of link that is implemented by having two or more directory entries point to the same inode (and thus the same data) on-disk. *See also* symbolic link, link.

home directory The place reserved for each user on the system to store his or her own files. Each user's default home directory is specified in the system's accounts database, typically /etc/passwd.

ident A protocol defined in RFC 1413 to be used to identify the owner of the process on the remote end of a TCP/IP socket connection. The ident protocol is not guaranteed to be correct, and as such, should be treated as advisory information only in many situations.

inode A data structure holding data corresponding to the physical storage of a file's data. Much of the inode's information can be retrieved by calling stat.

IPC Inter-Process Communication, theoretically covering any method of communication between processes including network communication. However, it is generally used to refer specifically to what is known as System V IPC—that is, shared memory, semaphores, and (deprecated) message queues.

IP Internet Protocol, the base of other protocols such as TCP and UDP.

ld The standard linker for Linux.

library A collection of functions and symbols, typically related to a specific purpose. Libraries may be either static or dynamic.

link With respect to file systems, a link refers to either of two methods (symbolic link and hard link) of making a single piece of data accessible by two or more filenames in the file system. With respect to program compilation, it indicates the action of combining multiple object files together to generate a final executable or of loading dynamic libraries into memory at runtime. *See also* symbolic link, hard link, linker.

linker A program that links together various object files, libraries, and initialization code to generate a final executable. *See also* dynamic linker.

locking A method of ensuring that only one process will have access to a given resource at a time, or that multiple processes share the resource in ways such that they do not conflict with each other. In Linux, this usually refers to advisory file system locking, meaning that it is a way of ensuring that participating processes do not step on each others toes when accessing files.

lvalue Any entity (such as a variable) to which a value can be assigned. In languages such as C, the value must occur in the left side of the equals sign. Perl, for instance, has lvalues such as scalars, arrays, and hashes. The lvalues in C include types such as characters, doubles, integers, and other data types. *See also* rvalue.

make A rule-based tool to build projects automatically.

Makefile A file holding the rules for make.

manpage Short for *manual page;* refers to the online documentation for a particular function call, program, or command. For details on manpages and accessing them, please see Chapter 1.

memory leak The condition resulting when memory is allocated but never freed.

minibuffer In Emacs and XEmacs, the small buffer at the bottom of the screen. The minibuffer is used to answer prompts, such as what file to load, or to type M-x commands.

multiplexing Generically, any method of using a single communication channel for handling multiple separate pieces of data. In Linux programming, this generally refers to a single-process TCP/IP server. Such a process will handle multiple clients all in a single process, and use a call such as `select()` or `poll()` to manage them.

nesting Using one object to contain other objects of the same type. Or, more generally, any situation in which you might find an object or operator inside the scope of another of the same type. As an example, you might have nested arrays in Perl or nested conditionals in Bash.

non-blocking I/O The opposite of blocking I/O, and a synonym of asynchronous I/O.

object file A file holding compiled binary code that has not yet been linked. On Linux, these files have a .o extension.

OOP Object-Oriented Programming, a method of programming in which encapsulation and abstraction are key elements of design.

optimizer An algorithm that is applied to generate more efficient or smaller output code. Many compilers and interpreters have optimizers. In C, the gcc compiler has an optimizer that may be controlled with -O.

Perl An interpreted programming language known for its strong data-processing capabilities. Depending upon whom you ask, Perl stands for either the Practical Extraction and Report Language or the Pathologically Eclectic Rubbish Lister.

pipe A unidirectional communication device that uses a set of two file descriptors. Typically used to communicate between two processes on a local machine.

pointer A special type of variable in C or C++ that holds the address of another variable. The variable pointed to is usually the one that the program is actually interested in, but may have to use pointers to access it.

port With TCP/IP programming, a unique identifier for the endpoint of a communications channel on a machine. The port is used by the kernel on the receiving end of communication to determine to which process the data should be sent. Server processes typically use a well-known pre-arranged port number; clients generally have a random number assigned by the operating system.

process A given instance of a program executing on a system. Processes are generally isolated from each other save for a few select methods of communication.

profiler A software analysis tool designed to help you spot performance-critical or slow portions of your code.

pseudo-terminal A virtual terminal used to simulate a real one in order to allow a process to intercept or manipulate the data between the real terminal and the processes running with it.

race condition The situation in which two or more processes may attempt to access a single resource at once, the result of which may be loss of data or unpredictable results, depending on which process wins the race and gets its execution time slice first. This typically is a problem with file system access, and file locking is a typical remedy. Another case might be shared memory, with which semaphores are often used.

recursion An algorithm implemented in terms of itself. For instance, a recursive function might call itself to process data in finer detail. An example might be a function that traverses a directory tree, calling itself for each subdirectory encountered.

recursive make Using recursion in a Makefile to build components of a program. Usually used to build components residing in subdirectories.

regular expression (regexp) A pattern designed to be applied to data to determine whether or not it matches, or to pick out pieces of data.

reliable protocol A protocol that guarantees that all data sent is delivered intact, without changes, and in the order sent. In other words, if the data gets through at all (if there are no network failures preventing it), the data is guaranteed to be correct.

rvalue Any entity in a language that generates a value that can be assigned to a variable. In a language such as C, when using the = operator, an rvalue must occur on the right side of it. *See also* lvalue.

script A short program written in an interpreted language such as Bash or Perl.

segfault Shorthand for segmentation fault. *See also* segmentation violation.

segmentation fault Another name for segmentation violation.

segmentation violation A fatal error that occurs when a program tries to access memory that it is not permitted to access. In virtually all cases, this error occurs when the program in question has a bug relating to pointers. It may be caused by any number of things. A few possibilities are accessing an array past its end, dereferencing a null pointer, attempting to access memory that has been freed, attempting to access memory not yet allocated, attempting to write to pages that are read-only, attempting to free memory that has not been previously allocated, and many other possibilities. Note that some of these actions do not guarantee a segmentation violation error; this is just one possible outcome. A segmentation violation is accompanied by the delivery of signal 13 to the offending process.

semaphore A method of IPC used to synchronize access to arbitrary resources. Semaphores are typically used to provide locking for shared memory transactions.

serialization The process of converting an in-memory data structure into flat data that can be stored on disk or transmitted across the network. The goal of serialization is to create a representation of the data structure that can be later used to recreate the original.

setgid property Indicates that, in contrast to standard practice, a given program takes on group permissions different from those of the person running it. *See also* setuid property.

setgid bit The actual bit in the file system permissions area that indicates that a program is to be treated as setgid. The group of the file indicates the group that it is to be set to.

setgid() call A call used to change permissions in an already-running program.

setuid property Indicates that, in contrast to standard practice, a given program takes on user permissions different from those of the person running it. A program is said to be setuid only if the setuid bit is set for it. This mechanism is usually used to give the program more permissions that it would normally have, and should be treated with extreme care.

setuid bit The actual bit in the file system permissions area that indicates that a program is to be treated as setuid. The user of the file indicates the user that it is to be set to.

setuid() call A call used to change user permissions in an already running program.

shared lock With respect to file locking with a function such as `flock()`, indicates that more than one process may hold a shared lock at any given time. See also exclusive lock. Shared locks are frequently used for reading from files, and exclusive locks for writing. This way, many processes can read at once, but if writes occur, only the writing process may hold a lock.

shared memory A method of IPC that allows multiple processes to write to a single block of memory.

shell A command interpreter used to provide a command-line interface to the system. Shells are also used to run shell scripts, or collections of shell commands in a single file.

signal A message sent to a process, either by the operating system or another process, indicating that a certain event has occurred.

signal handler A function registered by a process to handle a certain signal or set of signals.

sliding window An algorithm used in communication channels requiring acknowledgment of successful receipt of data. A sliding window allows the transmitter to send data before acknowledgments of the previous packet are received, but places a limit on how far ahead of the acknowledgments the transmission may be. This type of algorithm improves speed without sacrificing reliability. For details, see Chapter 18.

socket One end of a bidirectional network communication connection. On Linux, sockets act as file descriptors for the purpose of many I/O system calls.

special file Any entry in the file system that does not correspond to a standard file on disk. These entries could be things such as devices (see device special file), FIFOs, symbolic links, or perhaps even directories.

spinlock A condition resulting from a bug in a program in which the program is spinning, or in an infinite loop.

SQL Structured Query Language, a language used for manipulating databases running under a variety of servers.

stack In general, and LIFO (Last In, First Out) data structure. More specifically, a stack is used to hold information about function calls. In C and C++, a frame is added to the stack for each call to a function. The frame holds the caller (used when returning from the function), local variables, and perhaps other state information. The compiler automatically frees the frame when it is no longer needed. A debugger such as gdb will allow you to inspect the contents of the stack for a running program.

stat call A system call used to find out information about a particular entry (file, directory, anything with an inode) in the file system. Given a filename, the call provides information such as size, creation date, modification date, inode number, permissions, and more.

statically allocated memory Memory that is allocated and deallocated automatically by the C or C++ compiler. Normally, this memory is used as global variables or as local variables in functions. *See also* dynamically allocated memory.

symbolic link A "soft" link in the file system, implemented as a special file that points to another. *See also* hard link, link.

symlink Shorthand for symbolic link.

TCP Transmission Control Protocol, a reliable protocol used for bidirectional communication on the Internet. TCP is based upon IP.

terminal 1. A device used to display textual data. This could be your own console, an xterm, or some other device. 2. A device entry in the /dev directory corresponding to a communication channel to a real or virtual terminal.

/tmp race A specific instance of a race condition that occurs when programs attempt to create or write to files in /tmp without taking security issues into account.

UDP User Datagram Protocol, an unreliable protocol used for sending small messages across a network. UDP is based upon IP.

uid A numeric value used to identify a particular user (mnemonic: user id). Each account on the system has a unique uid, which is often (but not always) specified in /etc/passwd. The uid is used by the security mechanisms in Linux in places such as the file system and processes.

umask A bitmask specifying the default permissions for a newly-created file. The value of the umask is specified with the standard octal notation as used with calls like chown() and chgrp(). However, this mask has an inverted sense; that is, it indicates what permissions *not* to give files.

unlink In simple terms, a request to delete a file or a special file from the file system. More precisely, unlink() deletes one of the hard links to a given inode, and will only delete the actual data on-disk if the link being deleted is the last one for that data on the file system.

X Also known as X11 or the X Window System; X is a protocol used for exchanging information used to present a graphical user interface.

Index

my2cents.idgbooks.com

Register This Book — And Win!

Visit **http://my2cents.idgbooks.com** to register this book and we'll automatically enter you in our fantastic monthly prize giveaway. It's also your opportunity to give us feedback: let us know what you thought of this book and how you would like to see other topics covered.

Discover IDG Books Online!

The IDG Books Online Web site is your online resource for tackling technology — at home and at the office. Frequently updated, the IDG Books Online Web site features exclusive software, insider information, online books, and live events!

10 Productive & Career-Enhancing Things You Can Do at www.idgbooks.com

- Nab source code for your own programming projects.

- Download software.

- Read Web exclusives: special articles and book excerpts by IDG Books Worldwide authors.

- Take advantage of resources to help you advance your career as a Novell or Microsoft professional.

- Buy IDG Books Worldwide titles or find a convenient bookstore that carries them.

- Register your book and win a prize.

- Chat live online with authors.

- Sign up for regular e-mail updates about our latest books.

- Suggest a book you'd like to read or write.

- Give us your 2¢ about our books and about our Web site.

You say you're not on the Web yet? It's easy to get started with IDG Books' *Discover the Internet,* available at local retailers everywhere.